Community Music at the Boundaries

Lee Willingham, editor

Community Music at the Boundaries

WILFRID LAURIER
UNIVERSITY PRESS

Wilfrid Laurier University Press acknowledges the support of the Canada Council for the Arts for our publishing program. We acknowledge the financial support of the Government of Canada through the Canada Book Fund for our publishing activities. This work was supported by the Research Support Fund.

 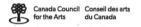 

Library and Archives Canada Cataloguing in Publication

Title: Community music at the boundaries / Lee Willingham, editor.

Names: Willingham, Lee, editor.

Description: Includes bibliographical references and index.

Identifiers: Canadiana (print) 20200298550 | Canadiana (ebook) 20200298623 | ISBN 9781771124577 (softcover) | ISBN 9781771124584 (EPUB) | ISBN 9781771124591 (PDF)

Subjects: LCSH: Community music—History and criticism. | LCSH: Music—Social aspects.

Classification: LCC ML3916 .C734 2021 | DDC 780—dc23

Cover design by Martyn Schmoll. Text design by Angela Booth Malleau.

This book is printed on FSC®-certified paper. It contains recycled materials, and other controlled sources, is processed chlorine free, and is manufactured using biogas energy.

Printed in Canada

CONTENTS

LIST OF FIGURES AND TABLES

TERRITORIAL ACKNOWLEDGMENT

FOR MANY THOUSANDS OF YEARS, Indigenous peoples in Canada have been making and sharing music as part of their daily traditions, community-building, healing, and celebrations. On behalf of the contributors to this volume, we, the editorial team, acknowledge that it is our privilege to live and work on the traditional territories of the Haudenosaunee, Anishinaabe, and Neutral peoples, who continue to live in community and continue to provide wisdom and songs that richly enhance our lives.[1]

---

1 On 25 October 1784, Sir Frederick Haldimand, the governor of Quebec, signed a decree that granted a tract of land to the Haudenosaunee (Iroquois), also known as the Six Nations, in compensation for their alliance with British forces during the American Revolution (1775–83). As settlers, we live in the Haldimand Tract lands alongside the Grand River in Southern Ontario.

FOREWORD
On the Scholarship of Boundary Walking
Roger Mantie

JUST AS TASTES AND STYLES in music change over time, so do trends in the academy. After many decades during which the social sciences and humanities attempted to emulate the study of the natural sciences, the late twentieth century was characterized by intellectual currents known by names such as "the interpretive turn," "the textual turn," "the narrative turn," and so forth. Influenced in part by post-structuralist thought and by resistance to the positivist research paradigm, scholars began placing greater emphasis on language's power to shape our realities. This "turn" toward language helped challenge and undermine, among other things, many of the assumptions that had sustained the privileged white male universal subject of the Enlightenment. Unfortunately, after decades of "moral" victories at the hands of eloquent theorists and philosophers, many of those who belonged to "subjugated" groups found themselves no better off than before. Marx's trenchant criticism would seem to have been overlooked: "Philosophers have hitherto only interpreted the world in various ways; the point is to change it."

Although not necessarily as widespread as the turn toward language in the late twentieth century, the early twenty-first century has witnessed the rise of "the practice turn" and the emergence of "new materialists" and "post-humanists." Rather than solely emphasizing language, the new materialists, post-humanists, and practice theorists place greater emphasis on "things" and on what people *do*. These scholars still work mainly discursively rather than by marching in the streets, but their focus on practices tends to place a stronger spotlight on material realities. This may not fully address Marx's concern, of course, but in fairness to the philosophers (and other academics), thoughtful examination *is* a form of action. Where would we be today without the critiques of Marx, Nietzsche, and Freud?

For practice theorists, practice includes things both said and done. Hence, how we talk about activity is indissociable from the actions themselves. As Michel Foucault has argued, disciplines *discipline* by claiming as natural and self-evident the knowledge they create and use to fortify their positionality. Disciplinary institutions, such as the university music school, define and exclude, thereby ensuring their privileged position and status. That is, their "practice" (as words and deeds) tends to position music in a way that, for example, brings into existence the very idea that Western European art music represents the pinnacle of cultural achievement. Boundary-securing (what Foucault would call a "dividing practice"), such as requiring Western notation fluency as proof of musicianship and musicality, serves to protect and exclude.

The contributors to this book bring to our attention a particular kind of activity: practices in music arising in response to the boundaries, both symbolic and physical, that have historically marginalized the voices, both literal and metaphorical, of those not fully embraced or even recognized by institutionalized music learning and teaching. Since the 1980s, but especially coming to the fore in the early twenty-first century, these practices have coalesced under the umbrella term "community music." As is hopefully clear from the diversity of activities discussed in this volume, community music isn't just one thing. Community music is many things – which is why it is so important to talk about and try to make sense of it.

Books such as this are important because they help bring into existence a "counter-narrative" to the hegemony of the Western European art music canon and all that it represents. It is not that the university music school and its traditional practices are bad or wrong, but rather that they do not represent the full range of musical experiences. Formal "music education" with its "democratization of culture" agenda has an unfortunate legacy of exclusion, despite occasional overtures to the contrary. Music, Christopher Small reminds us, is too important to be left to the musicians. Or perhaps better still, music is too important to be left to those who define themselves according to overly narrow definitions of the word "musician."

The pages that follow shed light on the multiplicity of ways that music can be facilitated with various populations in a range of settings. Chapters on aging amateur musicians, community youth orchestras, people living with dementia, refugee trauma experience and PTSD, music's presence in health care, children with disabilities, children in challenging circumstances, and the "socioeconomically disadvantaged" all speak to ways community musicians seek to enrich lives through music participation – not in the salvationist sense (or based on ridiculously excessive claims, as if music can cure cancer), but in the sense that the universal proclivity toward music can be leveraged to improve quality of life. One sees a similar ethic in chapters that describe ways that music serves as a bridging or mediating mechanism, such as in Jo, Veblen, and Potter's study of Korean elders in Canada, for whom music serves to "re-create memories" of their homeland; in Laurila's examination of a singing partnership between an Indigenous women and girls' drum circle and a male police chorus; and in the four chapters documenting the various ways music is being used in prisons and other correctional facilities.

This glowing endorsement of community music activities risks painting an undernuanced picture, however. It is not all wine and roses. Community music is decidedly "Western" in its knowledge and assumptions about the world, something that does not always translate easily to non-Western contexts, such as when working with First Peoples. Brydie-Leigh Bartleet's chapter helps remind us that community music interventions, regardless of their well-meaning intent, risk becoming yet another "colonizing endeavour" rather than a pathway to positive self-determination if one is not properly attuned to epistemological differences. Even when operating firmly in a Western context, community music is not a cure-all for the perennial problem of cultural tradition and change. As Southcott and de Bruin illustrate with their case study of Melbourne's Banda Italiana Musicale Vincenzo Bellini, generational change often results in tensions between "heritage and modernity," an intractable problem that community music cannot simply facilitate away.

Community Music at the Boundaries is an appropriate title for many reasons. To take but one example: this book is a product of a time coincident with the American presidency of Donald Trump, which has, among many other things, focused attention on borders, boundaries, and walls. And while it is tempting to adopt an air of moral superiority toward "Make America Great Again" populist xenophobia, community musicians should be mindful of the cold reality that the ideal of inclusion can only exist in the presence of exclusion. "Community" has no conceptual meaning in the absence of boundaries (which is why, I believe, Lee Higgins has repeatedly emphasized the root word "hostile" in his conceptualization of hospitality). This is to say that our world cannot exist without borders and boundaries; they are what makes social life intelligible. The real power of community music, then, lies not in the fiction of trying to eliminate boundaries (or pretending they don't exist), but in embracing the challenge of "walking" them. (Disability studies haunts us with the impossibility of writing the previous sentence, for example.)

Community Music at the Boundaries is also apt as an homage to, and perhaps reassessment of, Lee Higgins's (2006) PhD dissertation, "Boundary-Walkers: Contexts and Concepts of Community Music," the principal focus of which was "institutionalized music activity" (p. 32). Higgins proudly brandished the flag of the outsider, proclaiming how community music "affirms and embraces the margins" (p. 275). "Formal" music learning and teaching continues to provide a convenient foil for community music. One is left wondering, however, if community music now needs to think less in terms of margins and more in terms of liminality and thresholds (or perhaps Gloria Anzaldúa's Borderlands). Having established a solid academic disciplinary base and ensconced itself in higher education – having gone "from the margins to the mainstream," as it were – community music may have to reckon with no longer being the outsider looking in, but instead, being something of the mestiza: not quite insider, not quite outsider. In short, a boundary-walker.

To reiterate, practices include things said and done. Hence, this volume participates in the construction of this thing known as community music. While some practitioners may lament the codification and standardization that is the price of admission to the academy, believing this saps community music of its vitality and betrays its activist origins, I would counter that institutionalization is entirely consistent with community music's rich legacy of boundary-walking and represents a new form of activism. Our success today may lie less with "circumnavigat[ing] the margins" than in being "tolerant within the play of differences" and being confident in our "contribution to the human activity of musicking" (Higgins, 2006, p. 275). As we move forward, we need to be mindful of how our language helps to construct our realities. This should not prevent us from speaking, however. We need to raise our voices as we walk the boundaries, narrating and celebrating musical activity that includes, bridges, heals, and invigorates. In his opening keynote at the 2017 "Walking the Boundaries" conference in Waterloo, Ontario, Glen Carruthers declared, "Community music has the capacity to change the world." I would argue that it already has, and hope this volume will help ensure it continues to do so.

ACKNOWLEDGMENTS

ANY PROJECT OF THIS SCOPE owes much to many, too many to name properly. The following must be acknowledged, however. My colleagues and dean at Laurier's Faculty of Music are influencing hundreds of community musicians and future facilitators and continue to inspire, challenge, and affirm. Thank you, Dr. Glen Carruthers, Dr. Deanna Yerichuk, and Dr. Gerard Yun. To esteemed scholars and friends, Dr. Lee Higgins and Dr. Roger Mantie, whose wisdom and expertise I constantly rely upon, I offer my deep thanks. To community music graduate students who helped edit and shape this volume, Rebecca McKay, Fiona Evison, Niki Kazemzadeh, and Nathan Stretch, we are forever grateful for your invaluable contribution. Thank you, Joshua Manuel, for your meticulous care in putting the final manuscript together. Your careful "touch" is on virtually every page. Finally, to the Social Sciences and Humanities Research Council, Canada (SSHRC), whose funding supported the creation of this book project, thank you.

Cover artwork is by Andy Macpherson, activist, artist, musician, educator. The spiral depicts people and their life journey with music situated on a sixteen-piece quilt on which various dimensions of community music are stitched together in unity.

INTRODUCTION

Lee Willingham

BOUNDARY WALKING, or "beating the bounds" as it was known during Anglo Saxon times in England was a ceremony where young and old, often led by religious leaders, would walk around the edge of a precinct or parish. Most often taking place on a high holiday (such as Ascension Day), an aim of this pre-map ritual was to become familiar with the dividing lines, or bounds, that delineated district territories. The elders, accompanied by youth, would ensure that the jurisdiction was clearly laid out for both the protection of the community and to maintain respect and order with neighbours so that the knowledge of the perimeter would be passed down to succeeding generations.[1]

This volume, *Community Music at the Boundaries*, sets out to deepen the reader's understanding of how participatory music making is carried out to the benefit of the musician and the wider community, with a specific emphasis on those populations that have been deemed marginalized, vulnerable, or in many cases underserved. Much in the same manner that the boundary walkers of old passed along the knowledge of their own community lines, the authors of these chapters provide insight into the values and practices of our discipline, exploring the people, places, contexts, and indeed, the music making itself.

Focusing on the boundaries, edges and margins of various settings is an intriguing idea for community musicians, as the 32 contributors to this book of essays attest. An international community music conference brought together scholars and practitioners from around the world to Wilfrid Laurier University in Waterloo, Ontario, Canada, the first of its kind in North America. As the participants grappled with the role that music plays in the lives of marginalized

---

1 Beating the Bounds Definition, Oxford Learners Dictionary, https://wshc.org .uk/blog/item/beating-the-bounds-a-parish-tradition.html.

sectors and explored ways that music is able to connect and bridge diverse populations, the idea of this book was born. Partially funded by the Social Sciences and Humanities Research Council of Canada (SSHRC), this volume represents the broader views of scholar-researchers and practitioners who are living and working in settings where music and people intersect, resulting in a wide array of experiences and outcomes.

Early on, community music defined itself by inclusionary principles. The "welcome" was at the forefront. All are invited to join in the music making, and in many instances this would be considered a radical welcome, an invitation of accessibility and safety – come one, come all! The hospitable posture that community music holds carries with it complexities. Who can make music? Where? Why would people want to do this? To what benefit? Where are the boundaries of inclusion and what are the rules? These are questions that have no bumper sticker answers; they are boldly addressed in this book. The range of expertise and experience revealed through these author contributions are grounded in the validity of familiarity and authenticity of discernment as challenging situations are tackled – the type of circumstances, or similar, in which the readers may very well find themselves on occasion.

The invitation to contribute to this volume yielded a unique set of offerings. Experienced authors who research and write regularly for scholarly publications are here, and the reader might well admire their polished and powerful skills of conveying ideas and hypothesizing new concepts, evident in these pages. In turn, the experienced practitioner-facilitator who works with people regularly in experiencing music making has an important voice. The descriptive narrative of their discoveries and sage advice offer the reader exemplars of practice, ways of implementing theory and demonstrations of foundational principles in action. It is also noted that several contributors are writing in their second or third language, and they are to be thanked and commended for overcoming the challenge of writing in our often-awkward scholarly English! The unevenness of style and syntax is part of this book's life in the boundaries, a truly unique compository of ideas, strategies and discoveries.

The broad span of section topics organize chapters in groupings with similar themes. These themes emerged unsolicited and unprompted. Clearly, areas of health and wellness, incarcerated settings, reforming education and ensemble playing, and cultural identity including Indigeneity are top of mind as areas where community music has place and import. It is a heartening reassurance that music making and humans continue to be inseparable, whether in well-supported and friendly situations, or in settings of oppression and danger.

One means of measuring the worth of a project is to note who is not present, who did not step forward to contribute. Who is not here. This volume cannot claim to be comprehensive in scope. There are omissions, to be sure. Sadly, there is not a section on racial justice and music. Themes in areas of gender identity and the LGBTQ2+ communities and their place in the practice of participatory music making are absent. There is not a section on ecological justice. Authors did not bring to the reader ideas on systemic poverty or on socio-political and/or religious oppression. Those who felt compelled to contribute were those who had knowledge of and personal experience in community music as an emerging area of study and practice, primarily those who have been educated from a Western perspective, building on Euro-centric privilege and assumptions. This is by no means a criticism of the authors or their works in this book. It is, however, a timely observation about who it is that steps across the boundaries into the circle. As community music has been a voice of activism, influencing its sister disciplines of music education, music therapy and various aspects of performance, it continues to evolve in scope and relevance. But for now, the absence of these identified areas of social justice and human wellbeing are a beacon of invitation for further work. This begs the question: what is community music's responsibility in these missing areas?

This collection is a start, an initial stab at focusing attention on the boundaries and music's role there. These pages contain a wealth of resources, case studies, stories, and above all, challenges. The reader is encouraged to choose those chapters that interest and inform work that is close and immediate. The reader is urged to think critically on these topics and specific examples describing music's work at the boundaries. And above all, the reader is invited to examine their own practice in the light of the 32 perspectives offered here.

PART I

COMMUNITY MUSIC

Walking the Boundaries of Contexts and Borders

THIS INTRODUCTORY SECTION frames contexts for community music in a variety of boundary settings. Yerichuk and Krar interrogate the ideas of community, inclusion, and the boundaries that are inevitably formed when communities emerge. Turner investigates the language used in disadvantaged contexts, challenging conventional discourse as unrepresentative of culturally democratic processes found in community music practice. Castellano describes a program for urban homeless families in New York City where an inclusive, community centered curriculum used music as the medium for social cohesion, enjoyment, expression, and collaboration while Camlin identifies "gaps" within both resources for the arts and preparation for practice in the field. Carruthers tracks the journey of community music as an emerging discipline, finding place in institutions (a different sort of boundary) of higher learning alongside traditional conservatoire environments.

CHAPTER 1

The Problem of Community
What Does It Really Mean to Be Inclusive?

Deanna Yerichuk and Justis Krar

HOW, YOU MAY ASK, could community be a problem? If anything, community should be seen as a *response* to problems. Many community music scholars have understood community as something much more than an actual group of people bounded by geography or likeness or shared activities, emphasizing community as a kind of antidote to social problems. Some scholars have understood the *community* of community music in terms of creating feelings of belonging, particularly for people who did not feel connected to a social group or society (Chadwick, 2011; Garrett, 2010; Goodrich, 2013; Howell, 2013; Rinde & Schei, 2017). Other community music scholars have viewed community as a form of active participation or open access in music-making (Kennedy, 2009; Rønningen, 2017; van der Merwe, 2017), which is also often framed as a kind of response to the elitism of Western Art Music (Boon, 2015) or as an antidote to the passive consumption of commercial culture (Garofolo, 2011; Smith, 2013). The community of community music is mostly framed as a solution to problems and almost always as something entirely good: "whatever the word 'community' may mean, it is good 'to have a community,' 'to be in a community.' ... Company or society can be bad; but not the community. Community, we feel, is always a good thing" (Calhoun & Bauman, 2013, p. 1). How then, you ask again, can this "warmly persuasive word" (Williams, 2014, p. 76) possibly pose a problem?

Yet community does pose a problem for community music, because it is based on a fundamental contradiction. On the one hand, community points to an inclusive ideal in which boundaries are erased and everyone is welcome. Yet on the other hand, actual communities are formed by *creating* boundaries within which particular groups of people come together and feel a sense of belonging, while other people do not belong. In other words, communities are formed not just by people belonging together – what we might think of as processes of inclusion – but also by how other people can't, don't, or choose not to belong –what we could think of as processes of exclusion. The problem of community is in fact a problem of inclusion. Community cannot be created without boundaries that bring some people in while leaving some people out.

While any community anywhere is formed through this tension of including some people while excluding others, this contradiction is especially important to name and grapple with in community music, frequently defined as an "active intervention" (Higgins, 2012, p. 4) in which a facilitator, positioned in the centre, welcomes participants into a music community. Indeed, Higgins defines community as an "act of hospitality" (p. 133) in which the community musician creates the welcome, or sets the terms to include participants. Yet the musical and social choices made by the facilitator around access, structures, and process all establish ways of engaging that will encourage some to feel a sense of belonging while others will not.

Scholars have pointed to inclusivity as a core principle of community music (Higgins & Willingham, 2017), usually based on the widely held idea that everyone has a right to make music (Veblen & Olsson, 2002), an idea that we, the authors, also embrace. Over the past five years, there has been a noticeable scholarly uptake of the terms "inclusion" and "inclusivity" in relation to community music, yet there has been strikingly little analysis of what those terms mean or how inclusivity could or should be enacted in community music settings. We are equally troubled by the terms inclusion and inclusivity when they are understood as a *fait accompli* rather than an active continuing effort. Scholarly conversations around questions of inclusivity have been deepening recently, exemplified in the recent research project *Excellence, Inclusion, and Intervention in Music* (Royal College of Music, 2019) led by Jennie Henley (Royal College of Music) and Lee Higgins (York St. John University). In this chapter we build on the growing focus on inclusivity. We aim to move past a superficial understanding of inclusion, seemingly defined simply by the absence of exclusion – that is, by an open-door policy – and instead argue that musically inclusive strategies need to be matched with socially inclusive strategies, as well as analysis of the relationship between facilitator and participants. If inclusivity is indeed a core principle in community music, we argue for an active process of "doing inclusivity," which requires active and continual work in creating the best possible participatory music experiences for the specific participants in the specific context. This chapter begins with a critical analysis of the concept of "hospitality" as used in community music literature in order to grapple with the facilitator's role is setting conditions for participation. We then draw from the literature on inclusive education to argue for inclusivity rather than inclusion as the term for inclusive practice. Finally, we offer a provisional approach to inclusivity in community music, drawing from our research on inclusion/inclusivity in community music scholarship.

Ultimately, we believe that inclusive practice is both a critical practice and an ethical one. Unless they ask questions about who is in the position to be welcoming and hospitable, and who is on the "outside" to be welcomed in, community musicians risk engaging in the very kinds of exclusionary practices that many of us are seeking to avoid in our efforts to be inclusive. In this chapter, we build on calls to ask critical questions of who is leading what kinds of music for whom (Bartleet & Higgins, 2018; Lines, 2018; Yerichuk, 2014) – ethical questions that must be taken up whenever claims of inclusion are being made. As Lawthom and Whelan succinctly state, "people are counted in or out of settings with potentially serious consequences" (2012, p. 11). The point here is not to remove all conditions, as impossible a task as removing boundaries. The point, rather, is to recognize the power the facilitator has as the host, and to encourage facilitators to grapple with this paradox of being the host who simultaneously opens up and defends boundaries in fostering community through music.

How Hospitality Is Inclusive and Exclusive

In his frequently cited book *Community Music: In Theory and In Practice*, Lee Higgins defines community as "an act of hospitality" (2012, p. 133), drawing from Derrida's concept of hospitality (Derrida, 2000). Hospitality, argues Higgins, asks the community musician to offer participants an unconditional welcome – a welcome that serves as the foundation for community music: "people, participation, places, equality of opportunity, and diversity" (p. 133). Hospitality has been taken up by numerous scholars in the field of community music (e.g.,, Balsnes, 2016; Hill, 2016; Howell, 2013; Sattler, 2013; Snow, 2013; van der Merwe, 2017), and this is for good reason, in that the concept speaks to a music activity that usually requires no auditions, skills, or experience to participate. The facilitator – the "hospitable" host – welcomes participants – the "guests" – into the music-making without expectations of music skill or experience. However, the use of the term hospitality to define community music establishes the space as belonging to the facilitator, which sets up a particular power dynamic that tends to go unnoticed by most community music scholarship. The facilitator–host establishes the terms for engagement.

Even adopting the stance of unconditional welcome is a decision the facilitator – host makes as the owner of the space, for isn't the host the person in charge – the authoritative owner – who can welcome guests, or not? Hospitality sets up a specific dynamic that tends to locate the facilitator at the centre while positioning participants on the outside to be welcomed in.

Furthermore, what is often overlooked by scholars who use the term hospitality is Derrida's point that the word "hospitality" has contradictory meanings: both "host" (friendly and welcoming) and "stranger" (dangerous and not welcome). The root of the word "hospitality," Higgins notes, is also the root for "hostile" (p. 138). While Higgins provides some analysis of this paradoxical notion of hospitality, few other scholars have recognized this uncomfortable line that facilitators must walk – that is, they must remain open and welcoming even while defending the boundaries against people who will not engage according to the conditions the facilitator has set. David Lines (2018) provides the most detailed reflection to date on this dual nature, arguing that Derrida's concept of hospitality as employed by Higgins was intended to underscore "the importance of the relational aspect of the community music act [that] involves a negotiation of power between that which controls the self and others and the possibility of opening to difference and the unknown element of the other" (Lines, 2018, p. 391). Facilitators may aspire to provide an unconditional welcome, but they are also setting conditions to participation in ways that often stay hidden. Simply removing auditions or skill requirements does not remove all conditions. In a facilitator-oriented intervention model, the community musician determines the kind of music activity, the processes, and the roles, sets the tone for the workshop, and guides the group toward outcomes. Some approaches to community music are more collaborative so that participants and facilitator can together determine the repertoire or processes or even outcomes, but if the facilitator is cast as the host who is hospitable, these collaborations are always "allowed" by the facilitator rather than driven by the participants. The host, as argued by philosopher Gerasimos Kakoliris (2015), is sovereign – the master of the domain. Consequently, the facilitator–host always welcomes and defends at the same time. There is no unconditional welcome, because, as Kakoliris points out, Derrida's concept of hospitality cannot actually separate the hostile from the hospitable:

> Since there is no hospitality without time restrictions (it is not possible to come to your place as a visitor and stay there forever), or without numerical restrictions (if you invite me to your place, I cannot bring all my relatives and friends), the host exercises his or her sovereignty by selecting, filtering, choosing his or her guests or visitors – by deciding

who to offer the right of hospitality to, and also by fixing the period over which they can stay. (pp. 148–149)

Community music activities are always bound by time, and while some activities may well welcome as many people as possible, there are usually expectations for participation that restrict how people may participate, such as assuming that participants will pay attention, or be respectful of others, or participate in the same kind of music-making. These kinds of restrictions are normal and in fact necessary for a collective music-making activity to succeed, something that Lee Higgins (2012; 2020) has continuously emphasized in his concept of hospitality. Indeed, Higgins points out that facilitators have a responsibility to ensure the safety and well-being of participants through restrictions:

> [I]f I did not discriminate between whom I did and whom I did not welcome into the workshop space, it would denote that I would have renounced all claims to be a responsible music facilitator. It might also mean that I would have opened myself to whatever is violently opposed to me without reservation. Unconditional hospitality is not to be desired beyond what can be known or realized. (2012, p. 140)

Removing all boundaries is not only impossible task but also undesirable, for the facilitator must make decisions that protect the well-being of participants. As Higgins argues, a responsible music facilitator *has* to make exclusions. Thus the task when cultivating an inclusive community music practice is not to remove all conditions, however strong the impulse to provide an unconditional welcome. Rather, it is to recognize the power the facilitator has as the host; it is also to encourage facilitators to grapple with this paradox of being the host who simultaneously welcomes and defends by removing some borders to be more inclusive while erecting other borders to exclude in ways that honour the safety and well-being of participants.

Moving from Passive Inclusion to Active Inclusivity

The act of hospitality is fundamentally a commitment to inclusive practice; it reflects an ethical stance on the part of the community musician that emphasizes care and concern for participants (Lines, 2018). However, facilitators need to think carefully about themselves, their participants, and the kinds of musical and social structures and processes required to include people in meaningful ways. What exactly, then, is meant by inclusive practice, and why do we use the term "inclusivity" rather than "inclusion"? Our analysis of community music literature (Yerichuk & Krar, 2019) found no discernible difference between these words – it seems that community music scholars used them interchangeably. However, scholars in inclusive education have defined inclusion and inclusivity in ways that inform the development of our notion of inclusive practice.

The idea of inclusion first emerged in the 1970s in the field of special needs education, or education focusing on children diagnosed with developmental disabilities (Berlach & Chambers, 2011). Initially, inclusion meant incorporating children with special needs into mainstream classrooms. However, since the 1970s, the field of inclusive education has made significant distinctions between the terms "inclusion" and "inclusivity." Forlin (2004) argues that inclusion refers to integrating children with special needs into classrooms, whereas inclusivity focuses on active teaching processes that provide optimal learning for all students (p. 196). Berlach and Chambers (2011) similarly define inclusivity in a classroom context as "embrac[ing] the challenge of providing the best possible learning environment for *all* children" (p. 530, italics theirs). They in fact frame the distinction between inclusion and inclusivity with an eye to power relations – the relationship between dominant and non-dominant groups:

> Inclusivity is thus defined in terms of non-dominant group *participation*, whereas inclusion is seen as having more to do with non-dominant group *incorporation*. Concomitantly, inclusive practice is defined as a mindset or a worldview that permits inclusivity to be realised. (Berlach & Chambers, 2011, pp. 530–531, italics ours)

Inclusivity is an active process of encouraging full participation, whereas inclusion is simply incorporating non-dominant groups into an environment without thinking about structures and processes that might impede participation once in the room.

While these scholars focus on children with disabilities actively participating in school classrooms, we see an important parallel to community music. Drawing from the distinction made in inclusive education, we see inclusivity as active whereas inclusion is passive. Inclusivity is an ongoing practice, whereas inclusion is simply a completed checklist. While inclusion opens the doors to "everyone," inclusivity struggles with questions of access, structures, unequal social conditions, and structures and processes of music-making to strive toward creating an equitable space. We intentionally use the word inclusivity in this chapter to focus on the active and ongoing process of "doing inclusivity" rather than on a passive inclusion, which Rønningen (2017) describes in part as "not simply a matter of granting access, but about reaching out to those not attending" (p. 36). To this we add the active and continual challenge of creating the best possible participatory music experience for diverse participants.

Inclusivity is an *ongoing practice* that engages continuously in musical and social strategies to shift boundaries to increase participation from groups the music activity is intended to serve. This working definition requires some explanation. First, by arguing that inclusivity is an ongoing practice, we are arguing that inclusion is not simply done or not done but requires sustained effort, not just in how a music activity is set up but throughout musical and social processes. As a part of the ongoing practice, facilitators need to think carefully and critically about their own positionalities and their relationship(s) to participants. Another key component of our argument is the idea of shifting boundaries: here we call attention to the stubborn fact that boundaries always exist around a community. We cannot really remove boundaries, but we can shift terms of participation so that the music activity is accessible to the particular people the activity is meant to serve.

Related to shifting boundaries, the final idea embedded in our central argument is that context matters. Social and musically inclusive practices are context-specific. There is not a checklist of items to be applied to all community music projects everywhere. There are times when exclusions are necessary, such as when holding auditions for a choir with a particular musical and political goal, or when restricting access to women of colour to create a safe space to make music away from dominant male and white spaces. The point of inclusive practice is not to ensure that all community music activities are wide open for "all" people to participate; the point is rather to analyze the specific context of place, people, and purpose to determine the specific musical and social strategies that might encourage full participation of specific groups of people. One final caution: inclusive music practices are in our experiences an ongoing struggle. Strategies will backfire or create other problems. Some barriers will emerge that weren't clear from the beginning. New problems and opportunities will emerge. We encourage an attitude of openness and a willingness to experiment and change.

Doing Inclusivity in Community Music: A Socio-Musical Approach

Given the difficult position of the facilitator as host of the community that both welcomes participants and upholds conditions to participate, we offer here a preliminary approach for inclusive practice in community music, drawing from the findings of our research on how CM scholars have defined and operationalized inclusivity, as well as specific approaches to inclusive practices (Yerichuk & Krar, 2019). The following approach also draws from the nine domains of community music (Schippers, 2018; Schippers & Bartleet, 2013); the twelve continuum transmission frameworks developed by Huib Schippers (2010, p. 124); and the ethical questions of what, when, why, how, who, and where posed by David Lines (2018). We have also been deeply inspired by the work of Lise Vaugeois (2009), whose scholarship on social justice as a practice informs our stance of inclusivity as a practice.

We want to emphasize that this approach is provisional, serving as a starting point for developing inclusive practice. The following is not a refined tool and certainly is not intended to act as a yardstick by which to measure whether inclusivity has been achieved. Indeed, our focus on inclusivity as a practice insists on a continuous process. As we described at the beginning of this chapter, inclusivity is an ideal to strive toward within the messy reality of communities formed through exclusions and inclusions. Our approach to inclusive community music practice has the following four considerations:

1. *Identifying the purpose.* The purpose of the community music activity is the driving force behind all questions about inclusivity. The purpose is informed by the *people* involved (both facilitator and participants), as well as the *place*, meaning the specific social, cultural, geographical, and local contexts (see Schippers, 2018). No individual or group can implement inclusive practices effectively without first articulating the purpose of the music activity, and that purpose can only be articulated in relation to the places and people involved.

2. *Identifying leadership and control.* Closely related to purpose and equally critical is addressing the question of who controls the music activities. Who decides what kinds of music will be used, what processes and what structures? Is decision-making located in one facilitator, or is it collective among all participants, or is it somewhere in between? If there is a facilitator separate from the participants, who is that facilitator, not only in terms of musical experience but also in terms of positionality (race, gender, class, sexuality, ability/disability, etc.)? Similarly, who are the participants? Finally, and perhaps most importantly, what is the relationship between facilitator and participants, given the social location of each?

3. *Musically inclusive structures and processes.* Once questions of purpose and control have been considered, specific strategies for inclusive community music can be considered. Musically inclusive structures begin with access – for example, are auditions or previous musical experience required? Musical inclusivity should also consider how music is shared or learned to determine the most appropriate techniques that encourage participation by the targeted groups of people.

4. *Socially inclusive structures and processes.* Socially inclusive structures first recognize that some people face greater barriers to participation than others. For example, working parents, newcomers, people with disabilities, and people affected by homelessness each experience different kinds of circumstances that could be mitigated by where, when, and how music-making happens. Furthermore, music activities could incorporate socially inclusive processes that engender belonging among participants, such as ridesharing, sharing musical expertise, and cultivating leadership among participants.

We offer these four considerations collectively as a tentative approach to thinking through inclusivity in relation to the purpose and goals of the music activity and the needs and opportunities inherent in the community ties engaging in music-making.

Identifying the Purpose

Purpose answers the fundamental question of why this music in this place with these participants in this moment. The purpose of the community music initiative in the specific context will determine the kinds of considerations that need to be made to include the people the initiative intends to serve. For example, some community music initiatives serve a specific group that shares a common identity, be it ethnocultural (Chadwick, 2011; Johnson, 2012; Joseph, 2014; Li & Southcott, 2012), socio-cultural (such as LGBTQ2+) (Bird, 2017; Snow, 2013), or shared musical-cultural (Joseph, 2014; Snell, 2014). Community music initiatives that seek to build shared identities within marginalized communities demonstrate the ways in which specific kinds of exclusions within music-making may in fact contribute to a more inclusive society. For people marginalized on the basis of ethnicity, sexual orientation, gender, or other oppressions, exclusions are faced on a constant and daily basis. The musical spaces dedicated to people who share similar forms of marginalization/oppression carve out space for people to share experiences and build collective identity. In these cases, excluding dominant groups may in fact provide more space for voices that have been marginalized economically, politically, and/or socially. Determining the purpose of the activity shapes what the inclusive practice will look like. The question of purpose, however, cannot be fully answered without strongly considering the people involved and the context of place.

People. By "people involved," we refer to the participants and facilitator, if indeed there is a distinction to be made. That is to say, we recognize that there are many community-based music practices around the globe that are not framed as an active intervention and so do not have a facilitator *per se*, but might be better understood as "music of a community" or "communal music-making" (Higgins, 2012, p. 3), or what Schippers (2018) has more recently termed "community music as an organic phenomenon" (p. 24). However, for our purposes, we will focus specifically on community music activities that do have a facilitator to think carefully through the relationship between facilitator and participants.

Inclusivity cannot be addressed in any meaningful way without first examining who the facilitator is, who the participants are, and what the relationship between them is. Facilitators need to locate themselves not only in terms of musical experience compared to participants, but also in terms of race, class, gender, cultural background, geographic location, and the particular socio-musical context of the group. A particularly important question to consider is whether the facilitator is an insider or an outsider to the group. Several scholars note the importance of an insider status in particular contexts, such as newcomers (Balsnes, 2016), youth (Balandina, 2010) and reaching out to distinct cultural communities (Daria, 2018). Facilitators who are outsiders to the participants with whom they work need to think carefully about their relationship to their participants. Does the facilitator understand the kinds of values, interests, needs, and challenges those participants generally experience? Are there dynamics at play related to gender, ability/disability, race, ethnicity? What kinds of musical experiences do the participants bring with them? Instead of assuming that the participants have no musical experience, facilitators might ask a more open-ended question: what kinds of musical and social experiences do the participants have and want? Overall, relationship-building is key if facilitators are to honour the participants and adapt according to the group and the individuals of that group.

Place. People are deeply rooted to place, understood not just in terms of geographic location but also in terms of identity and particular local histories and contexts (Schippers, 2018). A community music activity and the structures and processes of that activity can only be inclusive when they are responsive to the specific place. For example, regarding a developmental community arts program in South Africa, Oehrle (2010) describes the specific socio-economic, cultural, and historical context that informs the specific challenges the project faces, such as the AIDS crisis and, before that, decades of Apartheid rule that created unequal educational systems (p. 382). People's abilities to participate in that arts project were affected by these specific contexts and conditions of their place and space. In another example, this one provided by Goodrich (2013), an orchestra wanted to give out tickets to people living in homeless shelters to attend their concert but found that few were able to attend because the shelter closed before the performance ended (p. 53). The specific context of place matters when setting the purpose and then when creating inclusive strategies.

A final word on the purpose of the music activity: it is quite possible that "inclusivity" is not in fact the correct frame. Community music initiatives that focus on social justice may refuse to reinforce the centre/margin relationship created by the active intervention model, aiming instead to use music to challenge or change systems that create marginalization in the first place. Lise Vaugeois (2009) defines social justice as "the work of undoing structures that produce raced and gendered [and other intersecting] oppressions and systemic poverty as well as the work of challenging discourses that rationalize these structures" (p. 3). When inclusion assumes a privileged centre (the facilitator) that welcomes the marginalized (participants), then inclusion/inclusivity doesn't ever really address the system that creates a centre and a margin – it may in fact simply reinforce this relationship. This critique of inclusivity warrants more careful and thorough treatment. For now, we stay within the frame of inclusivity to consider how certain critical questions might shift the boundaries of inclusivity to consider the relationship between facilitator and participants more deeply and, next, how decisions get made within the group.

Identifying Leadership, Control, and Autonomy

Questions of leadership and control are tightly linked to purpose in developing inclusive community music practice. The fundamental question is who decides what kinds of music, where, how, and for whom? The question of *who decides* is a deeply critical one that asks community musicians to consider the relationships within the community music initiative and how power informs those relationships. Some community music models have decision-making processes that are centralized with the facilitator, and some are more collectively held among the participants; there are also a multitude of collaborations that fall somewhere in between. In our analysis of community music scholarship, we found very few articles suggesting that ownership of the musical process should in fact belong to the people engaging in the music, the exception being Bartleet (2009), who contributed to a large-scale research study of community music in Australia that aimed to discover the music-making activities happening in communities. Bartleet's work indicates there are community music models in which the participants, or the community, determines the music rather than the facilitator.

At the other end of the spectrum are community music activities in which a facilitator takes on a strong leadership role and exercises substantial control over the music activity. This is not to suggest that it is bad for the facilitator to occupy the centre but rather that it is dangerous for the facilitator not to

notice their position. It often happens that choral conductors or band directors exhibit a more centralized leadership role, which may make sense in the
context of those particular music activities. However, some community music
scholarship has highlighted ensemble models that have found ways for participants to take on leadership roles to develop social and musical policies and
processes (Yerichuk, 2015).

In describing community music projects that were not ensemble-based,
Howell (2013) and Phelan (2008) each described the facilitator role as more
that of a convenor gathering a group of people to create without direct guidance. In these examples, participants have significant control over what kinds of
music are to be used as well as the processes. Howell even describes how participants could opt in or out of the music-making at any time – a particularly
important focus on self-agency in her context of working with refugee children.

Some community music projects share decision-making between facilitator and participants by encouraging participants to provide feedback or collaborate in designing the musical process. We saw this collaborative approach
in various contexts in community music scholarship, including community
musicians working with children (Boon, 2015), youth (Balandina, 2010), families (Niland, 2017), and newcomers (Balsnes, 2016). There were a few ways in
which participants were able to garner increased roles in decision-making, from
contributing repertoire suggestions and leading music-making (Balsnes, 2016),
to collective creation processes (Boon, 2015), to more formally organized
structures for overseeing aspects of the social operations of the music-making
(Garrett, 2010; Yerichuk, 2015). Collaborative decision-making also nurtures
collective responsibility to the musical community by decentralizing control
of the music activity from the facilitator to participants.

In summary, does the context require strong, centralized leadership from
the facilitator? Are there ways to encourage the musical and social contributions of participants so that they can contribute meaningfully, or even lead?
Based on the literature we analyzed, these critical questions about the relationship between facilitator and participants arose most frequently in articles in
which differences between facilitator and participants were most obvious, such
as facilitators without disabilities working with people with disabilities (Boon,
2015; Carpenter, 2015), and non–minority-identified facilitators working with
people from minority cultures, such as newcomers (Balandina, 2010; Balsnes,
2016). In this respect, a clear outsider status may help facilitators more easily
recognize the differences that need to be addressed, but we caution that all
facilitators need to think carefully about who is attending the music activity,
and – perhaps more importantly – who is not attending. We will return to this
point later in the chapter when we consider social barriers to participation.

Strategies For Musical Inclusivity

Once purpose and leadership/control have been considered, the process of inclusive practice begins. In our analysis of community music scholarship, we noted a trend in the literature of inclusivity understood primarily as musical access. That is, concerns about inclusivity tended to focus more on removing auditions and/or creating a welcoming atmosphere so that participants with less music experience felt encouraged to participate. While we believe that inclusivity needs to grapple not only with musical barriers but also with social barriers to participation, we begin here by considering musically inclusive strategies first, for these tend to be clear, concrete, and relatively easy to implement. The following ideas are organized according to (1) access, (2), content, and (3) process. We emphasize that the following is not intended as a checklist to be completed, but rather as a series of factors to consider in relation to the purpose, people, and place of the community music activity.

Access. Perhaps the most common barrier to accessing musical activities are auditions, which exclude people from participating in music activities who may not have the skills, knowledge, or "talent" required by auditioned music groups. Clearly, if the goal of the musical activity is to enable anyone to participate, the gatekeeping function of auditions runs counter to inclusive music-making, especially participatory music-making. In contemporary (Western) modernity, where music-making is often perceived as an activity only for professionally trained musicians, participatory music is predicated on removing the gate that might deny access to music-making. Many community music initiatives aim to be musically inclusive by welcoming participants regardless of musical skill or experience (Balsnes, 2016; Garofolo, 2011; Garrett, 2010). In some cases, participants may not need to read music (Bird, 2017; Carpenter, 2015); in other cases, there is more of a psychological barrier – that is, people are afraid they are not skilled or talented at music-making (Kennedy, 2009). Access may also mean that the facilitator needs to adopt a friendly and non-judgmental attitude to create a musically inclusive space.

Process. One consequence of policies that welcome participants regardless of skill or experience is that multiple entry points to music-making must be provided. Often this is seen in purely musical terms – someone with basic skills can participate at their level, and as their musicianship advances so too does the nature of their participation. For example, Garofolo (2011) describes a marching band festival in the United States in which beginners joined in with experienced musicians by playing whatever notes they knew. Allowing participants to find their own way within the group allows them to participate from where they are musically, such as through dance or unpitched percussion (van der Merwe, 2017), or by participating in non-musical roles, such as making tea (Hassan, 2017). Note, however, that social relations shape participants' musical comfort. For example, in a study on South Africa's Field Band Foundation, van der Merwe (2017, p. 124) found that female members often felt more comfortable dancing rather than learning an instrument. In thinking through how to be musically inclusive, it is important to think about the ways that gender, race, class, sexual orientation, and physical ability can shape how people perceive their own or others' skills and capabilities.

Consider the structure of music-making and whether participants have flexibility in attending or in how they participate. For example, whether participants can attend sporadically may be more important for more vulnerable communities, such as refugees (Howell, 2013), newcomers (Balsnes, 2016), and people affected by homelessness (Goodrich, 2013). Yet even some community choirs, such as the Gettin' Higher Choir in Canada researched by Kennedy (2009, p. 189), and the ReVoice Choir in England researched by Hassan (2017), were structured with open memberships in which participants could come and go.

Facilitation strategies may also be considered. Ensuring that all participants feel included might require flexibility in allowing participants to choose how they engage. Balsnes (2016) noted that rehearsal start and end times were often fluid, that participants could choose the number of rehearsals to attend, and that dress codes were kept very simple. Howell described an ensemble in which the participants worked with one another to determine how they would participate, choosing what instruments they wanted to play and simply jumping in on the songs that were being played (Howell, 2013, p. 70). We note, however, that these strategies to remain open and inclusive serve some people better than others. Balsnes, for example, found that the open processes meant that the songs stayed relatively simple, which resulted in some Norwegian-born choristers leaving the group because they found little musical growth or challenge over time. We see this as an example of how exclusions are always a part of inclusive work and why keeping the purpose in mind is critical. The newcomer choir that Balsnes describes was intended to provide a welcoming space for newcomers, so the processes were designed to suit the particular needs of this community.

Content. Inclusivity focuses on the kinds of music being made. Here again, the kinds of music should be guided by the overall purpose and context of the music activity. Some inclusive strategies may use repertoire that empowers participants' voices – for example, by choosing music that is familiar to the participants (Balandina, 2010; Balsnes, 2016), and/or by creating new compositions based on participants' stories (Balsnes, 2016). Another strategy might be to mandate culturally diverse repertoire that is not necessarily representative of the participants themselves but would introduce participants to a broad range of sounds, languages, and cultures (Yerichuk, 2015). Yet another strategy might focus on improvisatory processes for music creation (Boon, 2015; Mastnak & Neuwirthová, 2017; Snake-Beings, 2017). Boon (2015), for example, described a process of dance creation with students of different physical abilities: "we would undertake the creative process together by emphasizing openness to unpredictable musical outcomes and the collaborative invention of new music and choreography" (p. 156).

Focusing on repertoire also means focusing on techniques of music transmission. For community music activities using sheet music – among the articles we studied, this most frequently meant community choirs – singers often had the choice either to follow the sheet music or to learn the material through lyrics sheets, rote learning, or audio recordings (Balsnes, 2016, p. 184; Carpenter, 2015, pp. 204–5).

Musical inclusivity really is about opening up ways to value the musical contributions of participants. The techniques described here are concrete and relatively easy to implement, depending on the particular context of music-making. Strategies such as removing auditions, creating multiple pathways to participation, developing inclusive processes, and diversifying the repertoire all contribute to a richer experience for more participants. However, music inclusivity is only part of building an inclusive community music practice. Inclusive music spaces must also attend to social barriers.

Strategies for Social Inclusivity

Social inclusivity in community music is much more challenging to address and continuously develop than musical inclusivity. That being said, several examples in community music scholarship offer some guidelines for thinking through socially inclusive strategies.

Recognizing social conditions. Inclusive community music practices require recognition of the social conditions the participants experienced that create barriers in the first place. This means in part recognizing the kinds of oppression people experience that structure the ways they can or will participate in any given music activity. The specific social, cultural, physical, financial, and psychosocial contexts create very particular conditions regarding who can and cannot participate in activities. This is especially important for community musicians looking to engage in participatory music-making as a form of social justice, as it requires a shift in focus from individuals who experience marginalization toward the systems that marginalize people in the first place. What McFerran and Rickson (2014) suggest about music therapists is also true for community musicians – therapists/facilitators need to be "constantly attentive to the system," which "involves critically considering how the musical experiences mirror and are impacted by the surrounding systems" (p. 83). This shift toward thinking about the conditions that marginalize groups of people is perhaps clearest in community music scholarship that focuses on working with people with disabilities. The social model of disability described by Niland (2017) argues that "disability does not exist solely within individuals but arises from social attitudes, environments and policies that create barriers to participation that may impact on identity, self-esteem and sense of belonging for people who experience disability" (p. 276). Similarly, Boon (2015) demonstrated within her musical activity how it is the *environment*, not bodies, that creates disability issues:

> For a woman using a wheelchair, it is not her body or the wheelchair, but the stairs that disable her. The barriers of inaccessible architecture, historically shaped attitudinal barriers to disabled people, and the resulting institutional discrimination are now the disabling factors, not the individual body of a person. Within these terms, disability becomes a social and environmental issue, not a medical one. The social model of disability helped me construct barrier-free music workshops. (pp. 154–155)

Both authors reframe inclusive strategies to consider how barriers are created in the first place, and both of them position participants as capable rather than as lacking – it is the conditions that require fixing, not the participants. This shift in thinking may then open up different approaches to working with people with disabilities, for example, in which strategies are less about accommodations and more about creative exploration according to abilities. Boon, for example, describes how she and her participants began to explore wheelchairs as part of the dance and as a facet of self-discovery. Her work demonstrates how cultivating an analysis of the social conditions that create barriers may open up multiple ways of identifying; it also addresses barriers to participation while offering innovative artistic exploration and creation.

Reducing barriers to participation. Financial barriers are perhaps the easiest to identify and mitigate. Sometimes community music activities are offered at little or no cost (Goodrich, 2013; Kennedy, 2009; Rønningen, 2017), or subsidies are provided to low-income participants (Yerichuk, 2015). In one example, those subsidies were provided in part through a model where participants who could afford it paid more to support members who couldn't (Bird,

2017). Childcare might also address a hidden financial cost for some parents (Yerichuk, 2015).

Time commitments may prevent some more vulnerable groups from participating (Barnes, 2013; Oehrle, 2010), particularly if there is a demand for a sustained, regular time commitment. Availability in these cases is often related to household income, in that family members may need to work multiple jobs and/or irregular hours. Ongoing commitment to participation could dissuade "families who may have financial and time impediments" (Barnes, 2013, p. 27). Regarding a Norwegian choir, Balsnes (2016) notes that refugees were more likely to attend if there were reduced expectations of regular attendance, but also that rehearsals were timed to begin once a language class finished to facilitate participation from newcomers already in the building to learn Norwegian (p. 183).

Reducing physical barriers is clearly critical to an inclusive music-making experience. "Physical environments may be inaccessible for mobility or sensory reasons, or the [music] programme may have normative expectations of children's behaviour and performance," argues Niland (2017); this "presents a barrier to the rights of children to engage in their musical cultures" (p. 275). Certainly, a commitment to community music activities in fully accessible spaces (Yerichuk, 2015) is a critical first step in including people with mixed abilities, and the examples above around reframing disabilities may contribute to socially inclusive music-making.

For some people with physical disabilities and for people without access to vehicles or adequate public transit, transportation may pose another barrier. Strategies to address transportation might focus on building networks among participants, such as developing a text message process for people needing or offering rides (Balsnes, 2016) or coordinating ride shares between disabled participants and participants who can drive (Carpenter, 2015). Another possibility is to locate music-making closer to those who face transportation challenges (Barnes, 2013). Taking music to the community might go far to ensure that "the places where musicing happens are accessible to the communities that they need to serve" (van der Merwe, 2017, p. 124).

Another kind of barrier is related to psychosocial safety, which requires thinking about music-making as a psychologically safe space from a social perspective. In musical terms, safety might mean helping people overcome their fear of being judged for sounding bad; by contrast, social safety is about recognizing that certain groups of people have been marginalized in ways that threaten their personal security (an example being women fleeing from violence). Goodrich (2013) described a situation in which an orchestra gave tickets to women who had experienced violence, but few attended, because they feared they might compromise their locations by being seen. This example demonstrates that creating a safe space is literally about ensuring that participants do not compromise their physical safety. But creating a safe space may also be about psychological or emotional safety. This aspect is particularly important for facilitators who do not share the same vulnerabilities as the participants with whom they work. Boeskov highlights how a project for Palestinian refugees needed to recognize that participants might have "feelings of sorrow, sadness, ambivalence or even anger" and that "such [community music] practices come with a heavy ethical responsibility of dealing with these feelings in appropriate ways" (Boeskov, 2017, p. 96). While this approach might seem more aligned with therapeutic settings, we are not suggesting that community music activities need to be therapeutic in focus, or that facilitators need to be therapists. Instead, we are suggesting that recognizing the various vulnerabilities of participants is essential for facilitators who work with people experiencing marginalization if full participation is to be ensured.

Fostering social inclusivity among participants. Many of the above steps tend to rest on the facilitator to implement. However, for community music activities that decentralize control in favour of more collaborative or collective music-making communities, there is increased opportunity for collective efforts toward socially inclusive community music practices. Perhaps a key area of focus is the nurturing of social relationships among participants, such as by creating opportunities for social interaction outside of music-making, particularly in sharing food (Hassan, 2017; Balsnes, 2016). Relations among participants are vital to the group's social bonds. Participants within a musical community can become a "support network" who "look out for each other, teach each other, manage each other" (Chadwick, 2011, p. 156). The support that participants offer one another can extend beyond the music-making space, promoting a social wellness in the participants' daily lives and fostering an inclusivity that reaches beyond the particular music activity.

This increased participation may lead to people seeing themselves as a resource within the group, be it through musical participation, or social activities (such as preparing food) (Balsnes, 2016; Hassan, 2017), or suggesting repertoire and leading music-making (Balsnes, 2016), or establishing formally organized structures to oversee aspects of the social operations of the music-making (Garrett, 2010; Yerichuk, 2015). Socially inclusive strategies may lead toward more collaborative models of community music, which may strengthen socially and musically inclusive practices as individuals begin to look out for their own and one another's needs and capabilities.

Conclusion

Clearly, inclusivity is not simply a checklist of items. It requires thoughtful, critical, ongoing reflection on purpose, place, and people – including the facilitator, not just the participants –to develop inclusive structures and processes from both musical and social perspectives. We are not arguing that community music should be more inclusive or that facilitators should end all exclusions. Instead, we are calling for an inclusive practice that moves beyond technicist approaches to reflection (e.g., "How did I do with my facilitation this time?," and "How can I do better next time?") and passive approaches to inclusion (e.g., open-door policies), toward reflection that is firmly grounded in critique. The four considerations we have described in this chapter – (1) purpose, (2) leadership and control, (3) musically inclusive strategies, and (4) socially inclusive strategies – are intended to offer the field of community music a preliminary approach that may deepen how scholars consider inclusivity. We hope this is the beginning of a conversation that has much more to explore, including the use or adaptation of critical frameworks developed in other fields. Anti-oppression, anti-racist, and feminist frameworks, and (more recently) intersectional analytical frameworks, offer robust ways for scholars and practitioners in community music to think deeply and critically about how music activities relate to social justice work, as well as the ways in which community music may be at risk of reproducing the systems that have marginalized people in the first place.

We want to emphasize again that this framework is intended as a starting point rather than a refined tool or a measurement of whether inclusivity has been achieved. As we noted at the beginning of this chapter, inclusivity is an ideal to strive toward within the messy reality of communities formed through exclusions and inclusions. What kinds of inclusivity, what kinds of strategies, and indeed whether inclusivity is the right frame at all, all depend on the specific purpose, place, and people. Communities are formed in the particular and local, and formed because *some* people find a sense of belonging.

Whether community is an ideal (a positive feeling of belonging) or a physically located group of people, or takes some other form, the community can only be fully inclusive as an imagined ideal. In reality, communities exclude in order to include. Simply saying that no one is turned away does not eliminate boundaries around the community. Social and musical choices establish ways of engaging that will make some feel a sense of belonging even while pushing other people away. There is no escape from exclusions. The work of inclusivity is impossible work, but it is in the act of engaging in this impossible work that change becomes possible. This conundrum faced by inclusive community music can be neither avoided nor solved, just constantly and joyously tackled.

CHAPTER 2

Words of Choice

Challenging a Discourse of Disadvantage and Social Change in Community Music

Kathleen Turner

Introduction

As a practice that is primarily concerned with inclusion, diversity, and equality of access, community music work is frequently offered as a direct response to problems of socio-economic disadvantage. We seek space for creative decision-making and express a desire to empower others, and many of us working in this area view our community music practice as a tool for tangible social change. In an unequal world, community music is offered as one possible bridge to ensure that people, regardless of their circumstances, can access opportunities to participate in the cultural life of our society. Furthermore, the skills and confidence we build together within the music workshop can have an impact on the broader community. However, as I shall explore in this chapter, the language associated with socio-economic disadvantage can directly contradict the welcoming ethos of community music and has the potential to create unseen boundaries between the facilitator and community members. In this chapter, I offer my experience of learning as a community musician and researcher working in two Irish DEIS primary schools, where the language of disadvantage frequently undermined or failed to reflect the richness of our musical community. In contrast, the descriptive language offered by the community itself was rich, evocative, and powerful. Community members (both children and staff) described themselves as skilled, valued and valuable, exceeding expectations, and influential. As a consequence, I began to problematize my understanding of the term "social change," seeking to unpack what changes were occurring, questioning who was changing and how that change was articulated. This chapter is offered as an invitation for community musicians to develop and critique how we use language to document our community music projects, so as to ensure that communities are characterized by words of choice rather than by a limited and limiting discourse of disadvantage.

The Discourse of Disadvantage

As a community musician, I view our work as an "expression of cultural democracy" (Higgins 2012, p. 7). The freedom to make musical decisions can have a positive impact on our personal development and well-being in a multitude of ways, as has been documented by a number of social, education, and community music researchers (Campbell, 1998; Greene, 2000; Higgins & Campbell, 2010; Caldwell & Vaughan, 2011; Higgins, 2012; Veblen et al, 2013; Hallam et al., 2014; Flynn & Johnston, 2016). The transformative potential of this creative decision-making motivates my work as a facilitator. However, I am troubled when this same decision-making power fails to extend to the language used to describe our musical communities. For example, when applying for funding for programs to address disadvantage, how often are our communities characterized primarily by needs rather than abilities? How often are we called upon in documentation to emphasize the social benefits of our music-making, rather than explore the skills and artistic identities of the communities concerned?

Kathryn Deane explains that in successful community music, "equality is central and the music making itself somehow tells the tale of the community that's making it" (Deane in Harrison & Mullen, 2013, p. 41). In this music-making space, communities speak for themselves. Fundamental principles of CM identified by Higgins and Willingham (2017), such as empathy, kindness, wholeness, and respect for diverse perspectives, are reflective of communities that are complex, multifaceted, and rich in experience and emotional resources, regardless of their socio-economic circumstances. However, the language frequently used to describe communities that experience socio-economic disadvantage can be limited and limiting in scope. This has been demonstrated well in the Irish context by Maurice Devlin in his report, "Inequality and the Stereotyping of Young People," commissioned by the Equality Authority of Ireland. Devlin provides a valuable overview of the main concerns regarding the experiences of Irish youth (Devlin, 2006). Besides undertaking secondary research, Devlin facilitated focus groups with young people. The participants in these were from a range of ethnic, religious, geographical, and socio-economic backgrounds (Devlin, 2006, p. 9). In his report, he summarizes his findings and presents them in a local as well as an international context. He also relates his findings to the Irish media's presentations of young people.

Devlin frames his discussion within an understanding of the term "stereotype" as a generalized notion that is fixed and shallow and therefore damaging (Devlin, 2006, p. 11). He cautions against even positive blanket statements regarding social groups, viewing them as "a simplification of a complex social reality" and as often "patronising in tone and disempowering in effect" (Devlin, 2006, p. 11). I refer to Devlin because he highlights to good effect the importance of language and meaning, arguing that language itself has an impact on identity formation even while often failing, because of its limitations, to include the wealth and depth of experience when referring to any "one group" (Devlin, 2006).

Devlin in the course of his work offers four key objectives that emerge from it: (1) the redistribution of resources to ensure equality of access, (2) equal representation in decision-making, (3) relationships founded on respect, and (4) recognition of all identities (Devlin, 2006, p. 16). These objectives serve as the basis for a more positive outlook for Irish youth and could arguably be partly met by engaging in community music activity. Consider some of the key attributes of a community musician identified by Lee Higgins in *Community Music: In Theory and In Practice*:

Community musicians ...

+ seek to enable accessible music making opportunities for members of the community;
+ put emphasis on the variety and diversity of musics that reflect and enrich the cultural life of the community, the locality, and of the individual participants;
+ are particularly aware of the need to include disenfranchised and disadvantaged individuals or groups;
+ recognize the value and use of music to foster intercultural acceptance and understanding (Higgins 2012, p. 5).

With these in mind, community music can be used to undermine the negative stereotyping of people who are disadvantaged by advocating greater access to cultural and artistic resources, and by facilitating an environment where people's opinions are sought and valued and diverse perspectives and identities are accepted. However, this must be extended beyond the music-making and into the documentation and communication of work. The diversity of group perspectives must be reflected not only in sessions and workshops, performances, musical events, and recordings, but also in evaluations, funding proposals, and reports, as well as, crucially, in our academic research. Is the personal agency of every group member fairly reflected if the primary descriptors used are terms such as *at risk, vulnerable, poor, disadvantaged, disenfranchised,* or *hard to reach?* As I acknowledged in previous work, this language had a direct impact on how I worked, including how I subtly fixed my own identity as a facilitator (the *seeker* of social change) as well as that of group members (the *subjects* of social change) (Turner, 2016). When I began to question this discourse, I woke up to how my community was changing *me.* As a result, my appreciation of our community was deepened and my understanding of my role as a community musician was greatly broadened.

A Changing Perspective on Social Change

> [O]ur roles as change agents need to be considered with great intentionality and sincerity; we have to be open to change; we have to tell others about our experiences and perspectives; we have to listen to the interpretation of other witnesses; and finally, we have to explore multiple meanings of equity and care and act to promote our understandings of these concepts. (Sparkes in Ellis and Bochner, 2002, p. 222)

Early in my career, I characterized my work primarily as a tool for social change. I still consider community music to hold great transformative potential and look to the work of colleagues such as Julie Tiernan, Thomas Johnston, Phil Mullen, Dave Camlin, and Grainne McHale as examples among myriad best practices. However, my *relationship* with the term "social change" has shifted significantly.

As a doctoral student at the Irish World Academy of Music and Dance, University of Limerick, I engaged in arts practice research using the tools of auto-ethnography and narrative inquiry. In this research process, I was encouraged to turn the lens of inquiry onto myself and challenged to reassess my identity as a community musician. This opened doors to a deeper level of reflexive practice: that which Elliott (2005) refers to as "a heightened awareness of the self, acting in the social world" (p. 153). Kim Etherington describes reflexivity as

> an ability to notice our responses to the world around us, other people and events, and to use that knowledge to inform our actions, communications and understandings. To be reflexive we need to *aware* of our personal responses and to be able to make choices and how to use them.

We also need to be aware of the personal, social and cultural contexts in which we live and work and to understand how these impact on the ways we interpret our world. (Etherington 2004, p. 19)

Note the inclusive nature of Etherington's language; *our* responses, *our* actions, *our* contexts, *our* impacts, *our* interpretations. If community musicians seek to instigate social change, then we must also be willing to unpack *what* changes occur and question *who* is changing and *how* that change is articulated. When we tell the story of our musical communities and the changes they result in, we must also turn a "self-critical eye onto one's own authority as interpreter and author" (Alvesson & Sköldberg, 1999). If we seek social change, do we include ourselves as open to being changed?

When I asked these questions of my own practice, I had the opportunity to reshape my views on the purpose and character of my musical community. Rather than a group or area characterized by need or vulnerability, group members described a community that is *skilled, valued* and *valuable, exceeding expectations,* and *influential.* These themes (and the connecting points between them) were gleaned from perspectives offered by teachers and children following a concert that we had prepared together. The lessons learned from that experience are shared here in narrative form and illustrate lessons that I aim to carry forward into my practice as a community musician.

I do not claim that the themes outlined here passively emerged. Rather, they are offered as evidence of themes that repeatedly resonated with me during the interviews and focus groups I conducted. I am offering a representation of my process of "meaning making through the shaping or ordering of experience ... understanding one's own or others' actions ... organizing events and objects into a meaningful whole ... connecting and seeing the consequences of actions and events over time" (Chase, 2011, p. 421). Evidence of these themes is presented through a storied framework of my interviews with a school principal, Jacinta, and a teacher, Ann. I use lengthy examples of interactions and begin to connect these to conversations that emerged in my focus groups with the children. I will begin to draw lines of connection, asking how their responses might inform, challenge, or enrich the stories we tell one another about our musical community, the stories I tell myself and others about my role within our musician community, and the wider program's role within the city. These themes are what begin to form the foundation of "the story-teller's reality" (Etherington, 2004, p. 112).

A Community Music Narrative

In our musical community, I meet with children aged four to twelve on a weekly basis. We work together to sing, write songs, and rehearse in the after-school choir, and many of the children also take part in an after-school orchestra. Every year we hold a gala concert to celebrate and showcase all our new work. However, this year we organized a special concert to feature in my research, a project the children referred to as my "four-year homework." For this concert, the children helped design the concert space and chose their favourite songs from our repertoire and their favourite orchestra tunes. While I acted as the facilitator of the event, the children invited the audience to ask questions about their musical experiences. I aimed for a space where the children would feel entitled to speak for themselves, choosing their own language to describe their experiences of music-making and their identities within our musical community, free from any preconceived assumptions about personal/social benefit or "problem-solving."

A Skilled Community

The weeks immediately after our concert *are* extremely busy in the school calendar, packed full of pre-summer tests and the infinitely more pleasant school tours. While I managed to meet the children in the few days that followed the concert, it is two weeks before I have the opportunity to meet properly with the principal, Jacinta. When we do finally sit down in her office, I am delighted to see that she appears to feel as positive about the concert experience as I do. After a brief overview of the purpose of the interview and a discussion about her involvement in our music program, her respect for the children and their creative skills is the first thing she spoke of.

> Jacinta: [I]t was a mighty experience. Because first of all, children were all there. They were all very accomplished individuals. I thought they were all very confident, they were competent, they were comfortable. They had all the language they needed. They knew how things were going to run. They were familiar with the whole procedure. I was blown away by their comments, their vocabulary, their language, their ease of communication, their confidence.

Jacinta's response reminds me of my own at our annual gala performances. Each year I'm so immersed in the weekly workshops and rehearsals that I don't notice time passing and progress being made. The performances finally allow me to step back, take stock, and acknowledge just how capable our children really are. Jacinta feels that this was also echoed in the parents' experience of the concert.

> **Jacinta:** Because their children are succeeding. Their children are performing, their children have confidence, they're learning songs and singing. And they want to be part of that. It's trickled down through, so it trickles and trickles and trickles everywhere and it touches everyone and I just thought this had definitely worked.

When I meet with the teacher, Ann, later that same day, she also remarks on the children's artistic ability and their confidence in articulating their thoughts. She particularly noticed how the children responded to being the hosts of the concert, answering questions and occupying the role of host and expert.

> **Kathleen:** Can you maybe describe how you felt at that performance – what was your experience of it?
>
> **Ann:** Lots of things I suppose. Initially it would have been pride just to see the children. To see how proud they were of themselves. How proud they were to have so many of their parents and relations there. To see how confident they were. The idea they were the musicians. They had seen the musicians visit here and now they were actually the visiting musicians. They really took it on board.
>
> **Kathleen:** If there were particular words that you could use to describe the children at the performance, what would they be?
>
> **Ann:** Enthusiastic, proud, confident, just enjoying themselves. Relaxed. They didn't feel like they were on show like they were being wheeled out to be you know ... to be put on show. 'Twas very much about them. 'Twas their performance. And yeah ... they were able to be themselves.

A Community That Exceeds Expectations

For the senior members of the children's orchestra, it was important that the audience be aware of how much work had gone into the acquisition of the musical skills. Twelve-year-olds Amelia, Angelina, Rebecca, Jeff, and Gillian spoke about this at length.

> **Kathleen:** What does it feel like generally to perform in front of people? Because you've done a lot of that recently.
>
> **Amelia:** It's great.
>
> **Kathleen:** What's great about it?

Amelia: All the people watching us and we were so great together.

Angelina: All the parents I'd say were definitely proud of us.

Gillian: All my family and all were saying they were proud of me. And they didn't even watch it, they just knew I was going to be great.

Kathleen: How does that feel when they were saying that kind of thing to you?

Gillian: Great.

Jeff: Feels like you've accomplished something.

Rebecca: Feels like they're gonna get you a treat for it! [Laughter]

Amelia: We all love a treat.

Kathleen: Gillian?

Gillian: When you're practising and then you go to a concert, like ... in the sessions it's so boring because they're just shouting out notes and you're trying to get it right. But then at the concert it feels like it all paid off.

Kathleen: All the hard work?

Jeff: Yeah.

Gillian: Like some people even come on Thursdays to practise over and over again if they don't get it.

Angelina: Like ...'cos if people go to choir like Cara, you know the way she goes to choir and orchestra and the cello, that means the only day she has off is Monday.

Kathleen: It's a huge amount of dedication.

Angelina: On Tuesday and Wednesday she does orchestra and then on Thursday she does the cello and then on Friday she has to do the choir.

For this group of young musicians, part of the pleasure of the concert came from observing the reaction of the adults in the audience.

Kathleen: How did that performance feel for you guys? Gillian?

Gillian: Felt like an amazing experience because all the audience were giving themselves into it while we were singing and playing. And they were all listening. And you could tell by their faces and they were all smiling and dancing.

Kathleen: What do you think you saw in their faces?

Gillian: Like you thought you saw amazement like 'cos they probably thought we were going to sing something easy but the way that we sang probably gave them a shock.

Kathleen: What do you think shocked them – anybody?

Rebecca: The way that ... they way that we did with our bows and the way the singers could do harmonies.

Kathleen: So you could do more than people thought you could?

Rebecca: Yeah.

Kathleen: And what do you think they felt when they saw what you could actually do?

Rebecca: Amazed.

Angelina: Proud, like if they were related to anyone doing it.

Kathleen: Absolutely. Am .... Anybody else want to talk about what they remembered last week in that concert?

Angelina: It made me feel like I was an adult. Because everyone was asking us questions and everything.

Kathleen: How did that feel?

Angelina: It felt really weird. Because usually we'd be asking other people questions and this time they were asking us questions. It was like the opposite way around ... It was fun!

Julie and Shannon from fifth class also focus on the sensation of having the space to listen and be listened to during the concert. Many of the audience were adults the children knew as visiting artists and musicians who had come to perform in their school.

Kathleen: How did you feel at yesterday's concert?

Shannon: I felt happy because I liked when people were answering our questions and I felt like we were the musicians instead of them.

Julie: I felt good because it was nice to see how the musicians that we listened to feel when we're asking them questions.

Kathleen: How did that feel?

Julie: Good.

Kathleen: Yeah? What was good about it?

Julie: It felt like we were like real musicians. And that we really were singers.

Shannon: Because we got to hear everyone else and they got to hear us.

Angelina's group compared the perspective of the audience to their own expectations as junior singers in the annual gala concert. They repeatedly referred to a sense that they were surpassing the expectations of the adults in the audience, just as the junior singers (aged five to seven) had succeeded to a level beyond what they had anticipated.

Angelina: It might make people feel ... if you go there and like if you don't really expect that much, if you expect it to be like a small concert especially like with the juniors because they were like ... they were singing really well and all of them doing the actions but you sort of expected all of them to be like my little brother just sitting there and looking around.

Kathleen: ... So the juniors, they passed your expectations then?

Amelia: Yeah.

Angelina: They were really good. That's probably like how adults feel about us. The way we're saying that the juniors were actually really good for their age. Adults are probably thinking that as well about us.

Jeff: Yeah, they wouldn't expect much.

Kathleen: ... What do you mean by that, that they wouldn't expect much?

Jeff: Like the thing that ... since we're just kids they didn't think that we would do as much as normal adult musicians. But they probably got a big surprise when all the juniors went up.

Amelia: I think we even beat the adults playing the violin. We were better than them.

Jeff described the concert as having a "bigger" feeling, even though it was shorter than the annual gala performances. He had difficulty elaborating on this, but Angelina and Gillian attributed this sensation to the atmosphere created by adults asking them questions.

Angelina: It was smaller and bigger at the same time.

Kathleen: What do you mean by that, Angelina? Smaller and bigger?

Angelina: Because it was smaller inside, it was like a small room and it was a short enough concert. But then like it was bigger because everyone was asking us questions.

Gillian: Like giving their all. Like all the singers were giving their all.

Angelina: So like it felt like a better concert. Like bigger.

Other groups also referred to a sense of excitement and pride for being recognized by the audience. Ten-year-old Maggie placed particular value in this:

Kathleen: ... What did it feel like for you yesterday, being in the concert? Let's go around the circle ... Maggie?

Maggie: I felt really excited. Because at the concert I loved the compliments I got and I loved answering the questions because it made me feel really good in myself.

Kathleen:	Fantastic. What kind of compliments did you get?
Maggie:	Like, some people were saying thank you and some called me a model for the school and things like that.
Kathleen:	A model for the school, that's a really lovely thing.
Maggie:	And a good speaker.

We go around the circle to give everyone a chance to respond. Maggie's friends limit their responses to brief answers – they're not quite as keen to elaborate but they tell me they felt "joyful, 'cause the music was good," "brave, even though I thought I was going to be all shy," "proud," and "happy." When we reach David for his turn to respond, he is waiting with enthusiasm.

| Kathleen: | David, you're dying to tell me – how did you feel? |
| David: | I felt happy to be in choir because I got loads of compliments, I was singing my heart out. [laughter] |

A Valuable and Valued Community

I bring my attention back to Jacinta's memories of the concert. She highlights the importance of pride or, more specifically, a sense of being valued and having skills that are of value.

| Kathleen: | What words would you use to describe the children themselves at the performance – were there any particular words that would leap to mind for you? |
| Jacinta: | Lots of them. I mean first of all there's no performance anxiety. They have built up this self-esteem ... This is how we perform, this is what we do, this is the way we present ourselves, we are valuable, we are valued, let's show people, let's enjoy it. So it's joy ... just accomplishment. Our children don't perform in front of people [if] they're embarrassed, they've no confidence. So that's not there anymore. They want to get up. They want to show off. They want to tell people what they've done and what they've learnt. They're just so comfortable within their own skins I think. Comfortable with the whole concept. They know the music language. They understand what you're asking them. And they know how to respond. They're not shy. What else could I say ... It's just the comfort around music. Which I wouldn't have had as a child. And it's a challenge that they rise to and they achieve and I think it's just they're valued. They feel valued. |

Ann also refers to a sense of value, and makes explicit connections between value, respect, and a keen sense of unity within the school during the children's involvement in the program.

> **Ann:** [I]t certainly had a kind of a unifying effect on the school. I think even just having the sound of music in the school is just fantastic. We've seen the change in the children ... and they feel they can have ownership of it. During any of the sessions, the respect the children feel, that's important in our school. To be respected is a buzzword here. But it's more than that. It's something that we really believe in and they got that out of the classes as well. Everybody's opinion was respected and it was expected of you to respect other peoples' opinion.

There are many aspects of "value" that both Ann and Jacinta attribute to the concert and to the program overall. These include growing self-esteem, pride, respect for self and others, children's ownership of creative work, and their emotional release within a safe space. Elements of this discussion were echoed in my discussion with the eleven-year-olds, Emma, Lizzie, Geoff, Bob, Orla, and Cara, all of whom are members of the school orchestra and/or choir. Cara is also a member of the cello ensemble and was referred to in Angelina's group as particularly involved in the program, attending rehearsals four afternoons per week for orchestra, choir, and cello.

> **Kathleen:** I want to ask you what is it like to make up a song or to play your instrument – can anybody describe to me how does that feel?
>
> **Cara:** Special.
>
> **Kathleen:** What's special about it?
>
> **Cara:** Because you're putting all yourself into what you're doing.
>
> **Kathleen:** If you were to describe that to someone who didn't know what you meant and when you say *putting your whole self into it*, what does that mean?
>
> **Cara:** Like, you put all your emotions into the songs and the music that you make. So, it makes it special.
>
> **Orla:** It's fun. You get to express yourself into the songs and stuff.
>
> **Kathleen:** When you say we express ourselves what do you mean?
>
> **Orla:** Like all our emotions and stuff.
>
> **Kathleen:** What does that feel like to put your emotions into the music?
>
> **Bob:** Good, because you get to explain it. What do I do with something fun.
>
> **Geoffrey:** Like if you can hear different songs and you can tell why, what you feel ...

In this particular group, all the members had younger siblings who were also part of the program. During our discussion, they described the respect they received as musicians from adults but also from their younger siblings. We discussed the possibility that they were inspiring their younger brothers and sisters.

Kathleen: What do you think that other people feel when they see you performing or playing or practising or singing – what do you think other people feel? Do you have any ideas?

Cara: D'you know if it was your parents now like, if it was your parents like they would be all crying because they'd see you up on stage. They'd be tears of joy. But other people, then they might be interested or happy or something like that.

Orla: My brother was at the concert, it was his first time seeing me playing the cello.

Kathleen: And what was that like?

Orla: It felt weird for me. But then like for him, like, he said like, that when he gets older he wants to do it.

Kathleen: Really and how old is he now?

Orla: Eight.

Kathleen: Fantastic. So, you're inspiring your wee brother.

Orla: Yeah.

Kathleen: What does that feel like? Hands up who has younger siblings who've seen you play? All of you have younger siblings who've seen you play. So, what do you think … what do you think, does that have an effect on them?

Emma: Yeah, because they can learn from their older brothers or sisters.

Orla: Because if we make mistakes, they know not to do that.

Emma: So, they learn from us.

Orla: Yeah, they learn from us and then we kinda learn from them as well.

Kathleen: How do you learn from them?

Orla: … when we watch them on the stage and all and they're more like up enjoying it and we're just like standing there singing so we could start doing stuff like them.

Kathleen: Yeah 'cos they really go for it don't they.

Orla: Yeah.

Cara: That's because they're younger like and they don't really take notice ... we're all looking at the camera like ... just trying to act normal! [Laughter]

Kathleen: There's something to be said for that isn't there about the way that younger kids can just go for it and they don't worry about what anyone else thinks.

Orla: They've more imagination like than other people do.

Kathleen: Yeah ... it's tricky to hold on to that isn't it?

In this extract, I felt that the respect they had for their younger siblings as fellow artists was evident. I recognized the self-consciousness they described in older musicians – or, as Cara said, the desire to "act normal" – and appreciated the contrast they drew between this and their younger siblings, who were able to demonstrate more freedom or "imagination" on stage.

An Influential Community

As the previous extract demonstrates, the members of our program were aware they were influencing one another – an example of peer-to-peer learning. However, I was also interested in the influence of the musical community beyond the school. The program does, after all, aim to play a role in the social regeneration of our city. With that in mind, I asked both staff and students about their understanding of regeneration as a process and of our role in that. In my conversations with Jacinta and Ann, I asked them about the effect or "reach" of the project, both within the school and beyond in the wider community. From both women's responses, it seemed that the real heart of the project was inside the school walls. For Jacinta in particular, this is connected to the school anthem, which was composed by a group of fourth-class children in 2014. In this extract, she begins by speaking about the whole program but eventually narrows her focus to the anthem itself.

Jacinta: [F]or these small children to take it on. And learn it. I think it has improved listening skills. I think [it] has improved discipline in the school. There is no doubt about it. It's improved confidence – I can see it at assembly. We're trying to help these children to become more competent ... not in performing, just in expressing themselves. So that has come through. There is a joy in the children learning the songs. There is a joy in them performing the songs. They get joy from the reaction of adults. Things like our school anthem, that's embedded the ethos of the school in a song written by the children. So that's important. We're going to keep that forever – that'll be sung forever. Their children will

be singing it. It's up all over the school. So, there's history starting you
know. And then the songs the children wrote themselves. I mean ... I'm
completely overawed by what those children have produced. I didn't
think it was in them. I didn't think they could do it and I'm ... I have
to say I'm ... I don't know what word I'd use for it. I'm humbled.

A point in this part of our conversation has echoes of my discussion with
Cara and her friends: Jacinta speaks about students learning from one another
and attributes this (like Ann) to a sense of unity and connectedness. She opens
this topic by referring to our gala performances, not just the concert experience.

Jacinta: There's always a big bang at the end. And the children need that and
they love it ... It polishes them off and it polishes off the end of term
and the end of the year. And it just gives unity to the children in the
school.

Kathleen: In what sense unity?

Jacinta: Because a choir in itself is a gathering of children. They all have an
interest. So, there is children in sixth class now that know children in
second class. You know, children in fourth know children in second
and first class. So, it's brought this group ethos there together. And
they want to perform and they want to be together and they want to
sing.

This moment brought back to mind a brief point that Angelina made
about supporting fellow members of the orchestra. She described the sense of
satisfaction it gave her.

Angelina: You know like when you're doing the concert, you know the person ...
beside you is doing really well, sometimes it makes you feel like really
happy. 'Cos then you know that you were practising with them and
they were really good. I don't know how to explain it ...

Kathleen: So, you've helped them?

Angelina: Yeah. 'Cos like sometimes if someone misses a day and someone needs
to go over into a corner and teach them the notes and teach them
their bows and everything ... and then when they're good at a concert
it makes you feel really happy. Because you sort of like taught them
some of it ...

Gillian: So, imagine how the teachers actually feel.

At this point, Angelina's classmates interject to explain that she frequently
helps other members of the orchestra.

Amelia: 'Cos Angelina's like the person who knows. The head of second violin and she helps people, don't you?

Kathleen: So, you're like the leader of second violin?

Amelia: The oldest.

Kathleen: That is really cool. That's brilliant.

Angelina: I could be in first violin. They said last summer holidays I could go in the first violin or be the leader of second violins.

Kathleen: So, you chose to be a leader?

Gillian: Yeah. She could have come into first violins with me but that would have been a bad choice. [Laughter]

Jeff: Yeah that would have been! [Laughter]

In the midst of this conversation, I realize how much I have missed in the development of the children in the orchestra. This young musician is actively seeking out opportunities to educate and support her fellow orchestra members. She turned down the chance to be in first violin with her friends to do so. Angelina has become an influential member of our musical community.

If so much richness is happening within our school walls, surely that must feed back out into the community. My hope, and indeed our intention as a program, has always been to contribute to social change. I raise the key question with Ann, Jacinta, and the children I speak to – what is their understanding of "regeneration," and what, if any, effect is the program having on our city? The answers challenge my expectations significantly. Ann voices her frustration with the labelling that is implicit in "regeneration."

Ann: [T]o me a school is a school is a school. And this is our school. You know ... My expectation is just the fact that any child or any group of children could come out and produce something like this. Because I suppose there is a strong kind of very rich tradition of singing in this area. And so, I'm never surprised to hear the beautiful singing. Because you know, the parents and the grandparents, there would be a lot of them that would be beautiful singers too.

Ann is quite specific about the differences she has observed in the school community that she attributes to the program. However, when I ask whether these changes have extended outside the school, she is not convinced. Ann specifically refers to her concerns regarding labels, compartmentalizing, and making assumptions according to geographical areas, which she associates with disadvantage.

Kathleen: [W]e were talking about the school there. Do you think it's had any particular effect on the wider community and on our city as a whole? Maybe not.

Ann: I would hope it has but I don't know. I suppose there is a problem always to compartmentalize, people from the outside compartmentalizing.

Kathleen: When you say the outside what do you mean?

Ann: So, we're a DEIS school and we would have had people who knew when the violins were going on ... It doesn't follow through with them sending their children here. And that has nothing to do with the school or the children, it's just there are other things at work that influence people.

Kathleen: What do you think those are?

Ann: It's hard to know. For some people maybe it's to do with breaking away and not being seen to belong to this label.

Kathleen: What label?

Ann: Disadvantaged label ... I mean you'll often hear people say *oh you've a certain address you won't get a job* or that kind of thing. I suppose maybe it's true in some cases. But then I don't know how much of it actually is real and how much of it is just a perception.

Ann explains that while local parents are supportive of the school, it does not always mean they will send their children to it. She attributes this to the problem of the "disadvantage" label.

Ann: I suppose for them they just see it as a way with breaking links ... Breaking links and maybe getting on better in life. I mean they're doing it for the right reason in that they're doing it for their children. But it's a hard one to ... I mean we battle with that ourselves promoting the school and whatever ... But it's hard to ... get inside the minds of people and see why they're ... how to change it. It is difficult.

Kathleen: Do you think that community music and what we're doing ... could that have a role to play in that, in changing that perception?

Ann: It could ... I suppose it's just a very complex question ... I suppose really it's about, at the end of the day, people standing up and being proud of where they come from. And I suppose if you were to follow that line of thought you'd say, well yes, it should follow through. But I think maybe too I suppose the problem with our area, it has become very fragmented.

While our program was set up with the intention of contributing to social regeneration, Ann sees our greatest strength to be our separation from the word itself and the labels she associates with it.

> **Ann:** I have to say the way everything is done through the program has always been very respectful of the children. It should never be a case where the children are brought up and put on a stage *ah look they're from a regeneration area* ... It should never be about where they're coming from ... They should be taken as children. Children are children and they shouldn't be used to make ... other people feel good. And that isn't happening, which is fantastic ... Our children are no different to children anywhere else. And they should be treated like that, the same as our parents ... I mean, social regeneration can happen in any area. It doesn't have to be a disadvantaged ... because an area is old, because an area needs literally to be rejuvenated. So, it shouldn't be really about economic ... it should be about just breathing life back into a community. Because there's great people in the community and I suppose if they're respected, well then, they'd hopefully come on board as well. But it is ... I suppose something that we all need to watch.

Ann highlights the danger that labelling and misperception could have posed to the life of the program, and this has only been prevented by ensuring mutual respect throughout.

> **Ann:** When labels are used there's a danger that people get pigeon-holed into certain things.

When I raise the same topic of our influence in the city and on regeneration in my focus groups with the children, several refer to the joy that music offers, not only to them as choir and orchestra members but to the audiences they meet and perform for. For them, this is a form of influence. As eight-year-old Tara says, "we make music for the city and make people joyful and happy." However, many of the children refer to the limitations of our program. Maggie, who loves singing, is particularly skeptical about our influence outside the school gates: "If I'm being realistic, honestly it wouldn't really change the whole city. Might make them happy if they came to listen. But you can't change anyone with your music. They can only change themselves." Several group members seem to think that the limitations exist because we only work with two schools – why aren't we open to every child?

> **Bob:** We're not encouraging kids enough to play. So, like, give them one chance to play it and then they might like it.

This desire to extend the remit of our program was expressed repeatedly; James said, "If you give out flyers and people saw them, we might get people to join the choir." David said, "If I could, I'd get a singing class going." As I recall these conversations with the children, I see how willing they are to reach out to other children and invite them in. The musical community they describe is inclusive, hospitable, and actively seeking to connect, regardless of geography or socio-economic framework. I sense that they have a much more useful understanding of "social change" than the definition I have been carrying into my work.

Through these conversations with Ann, Jacinta and the children from orchestra and choir, my understanding of our program has broadened. I begin to see our music-making through multiple lenses; my perspective is altered by the interactions presented here and by many others that are too numerous to make it to the page. There is no singular story of our program. Nevertheless, I would like Jacinta to have the final word on the subject.

> **Jacinta:** Singing the anthem of the school – that brings everyone together. I think that's very important. Gets our message out there.
>
> **Kathleen:** What message do you think that is?
>
> **Jacinta:** *Here we are.* Here we are, this is us, this is what we do. This is how we perform. This is what has come out of us, it's valuable and it's valued. Here we are.

Change-Maker Identity: The Community Musician as Agent *and* Recipient

Dave Camlin proposes that it is essential for us to question our practice and ourselves: "You make sense of your practice by talking about it and getting other people's perspectives on it – challenging your assumptions when necessary in order to develop" (Higgins and Willingham, 2017, p. 134). During my work I encountered numerous stories of how music-making had impacted positively on community members. Nevertheless, I also heard (and listened to) stories that contradicted this message of social change. In particular, ten-year-old Maggie's words continue to ring in my ears:

> If I'm being realistic, honestly it wouldn't really change the whole city. Might make them happy if they came to listen. But you can't change anyone with your music. They can only change themselves.

Maggie made this statement when asked about the potential influence of our program on the wider city. However, she also expressed joy in her experience as a singer and told me that she had been described as a "model for the school," a title she took great pride in.

Maggie's responses are a powerful demonstration of the nuanced conversation required in our use of the term "social change." Maggie is not saying that change is not *possible*: she is saying that we can only change ourselves. This has powerful implications for our understanding of the community musician as an agent of social change. First, it requires that if we approach the community music workshop by asking our community members to be open, we must also be open to change occurring within ourselves, not only seeking the benefits of music-making for others but actively recognizing that those benefits are mutual and collective. This requires us to be vulnerable as facilitators, to be actively aware and reflexive, and to be willing to explore and acknowledge the multiple selves that make up our identity. We must ask what we carry into the workshop with us – our values, experiences, troubles, and triumphs.

The second implication for community practice involves a reconsideration of the term "social change." In seeking this, we set out on the journey of music-making with the implicit belief that change is not only possible but likely. This term is hinged on hope; it is, therefore, inherently beautiful. But it is dangerous if left unchallenged. The danger is not in the words, but rather in whom we consider to be included in the *process* of social change. If community musicians are exclusively the instigators, then we paint ourselves as the heroes of the story. We give ourselves too much credit and our community members too little. However, if we include ourselves in this process, then as Maggie says, we too can be transformed. By keeping this in mind, we can continue to use the term but in doing so add a deeper reflexive layer to our community music practice.

As a community musician and community music researcher I have the luxury of choosing words to describe my practice. I select the words that define me – I choose how I characterize my role to the outside world and to you, the reader. While I once understood my role as an agent of social change, I now see the community musician as someone who encourages imagination, celebrates personal and collective expression, supports aspiration, champions achievement, embodies and facilitates creativity, hopes for kindness, asks for value, and engenders pride. I do this for myself as well as for others, because our music-making has changed *me*. This richer definition was not available to me until I asked my community members – children and teachers who influenced my practice, informed my understanding, and taught me to be more empathetic, more alert to kindness, and more awake to moments of personal change within as well as without.

CHAPTER 3

Collaborative Musical Experiences with Urban Families Experiencing Homelessness in the United States

Lindsey G. Castellano

"YOU COULD STAY HERE with me forever," a five-year-old boy exclaimed as he ran up to me after class. His older sister had a look of concern as she asked, "Do I have to leave?" This was the sixth out of eight ninety-minute classes in our after-school music program at a resource centre for families experiencing homelessness in New York City. I looked over at my co-facilitator, Clayton, who was learning dance moves from a mother and her three daughters, and I noticed the line of parents and children waiting for our attention.

One of the participants who had been patiently waiting to speak to me was twelve-year-old Maria. She quietly asked to share a song she had recently written – a notable event, for this student was typically reserved and cautious about sharing or engaging with the group or facilitators. The lyrics spoke of her inner struggle with the love she had for her father and the confusion about his abusive behaviour that had led her and her mother to seek refuge at a homeless shelter. When Maria had finished singing, her mother came over to talk to me. She told me about the aspirations she once had to be a professional dancer, the pain of having one of her sons in jail, the fear she felt about being located by Maria's father, and the distress of living in a shelter. Maria's mother also expressed her hope for a safe and successful future for her daughter, her gratitude for the resource centre and our program, and her admiration for her daughter's ability to create something beautiful out of the darkness they had endured. She was telling me about Maria's interest in music and how she would sing to music videos on YouTube when a staff member from the resource center let us know they had to close the facility for the evening; our music class had ended two hours earlier.

Another day after class, the mother of a thirteen-year-old boy, who was always animated and engaged in class, told me she had never seen her son focus on an activity for more than ten minutes before his experience in this program. As the family resource centre was closing on one of our last days of class, the mom of a twelve-year-old called from the door that it was time to go, the staff needed to close the centre. The teen handed me a note she had stayed late to write; it read, "I really enjoyed learning new things including the violin with you ... I would like to resign [sic] up for as many years as possible. If I ever get to be famous and rich I will always remember you."

The eagerness of the family members to contribute to and extend the class activities reaffirmed that I had been right to take on a two-hour weekly commute to an underserved and dangerous part of the city; when the program started, the resource centre had cautioned us to not walk alone to the subway, for there several staff members had been assaulted on their way home.

The program had thirty participants from six families who were experiencing or had experienced homelessness and domestic abuse. I had initially planned to facilitate after-school music classes with a colleague for primary school children. The end result was an intergenerational experience in which entire families participated and wholeheartedly engaged. A community was thereby created and fostered that produced an unexpected and significant experience for the participants, myself included.

Related Literature

A 2018 national estimate of homelessness by the US Department of Housing and Urban Development found that 17 out of 10,000 people in the United States experienced homelessness (2018). The report estimated that 33 percent of the people experiencing homelessness are a parent living with at least one child. The US Department of Education reported that 1 in every 30 children in the US public school system experienced homelessness (cited in Bassuk, DeCandia, Beach, & Berman, 2014).

Individuals experiencing homelessness often endure multiple, interrelated issues such as an absence of basic resources, neglectful family situations, mental illnesses, and substantial losses, including of community, family, friends, pets, possessions, routines, privacy, and security (Bassuk & Friedman, 2005; Pluck et al., 2011; Somerville, 2013; Kim et al., 2018). These interconnected issues may prevent psychological development, inhibit self-sufficiency (Arnett, 2000, 2004 as cited in Kim et al., 2018) and trigger or intensify prior traumas (Bassuk & Friedman, 2005).

Trauma may be defined as a distressing or disturbing experience (Cox, 2013). It can result from a number of experiences, including – but far from limited to – neglect, domestic or community violence, and physical or emotional abuse (Faed, Murphy, & Nolledo, 2017). In addition to the trauma of homelessness, individuals experiencing homelessness may be victims of abuse, which increases the likelihood that they will develop trauma-related symptoms and post-traumatic stress disorder (PTSD) (Kim et al., 2018).

The ability to soothe oneself is compromised in people who have experienced trauma and developed PTSD (Van der Kolk, 2002, p. 386). Van der Kolk (2002) suggested that PTSD victims have similar characteristics to infants in that they lack the ability to self-regulate their emotions. Given the inherent communicative nature of music and the soothing results music has between mothers and children (Custodero, 2002), music is well-suited to assist in regulating emotions for people with PTSD (Van der Kolk, 2002). Post-traumatic stress does not occur in all people who have witnessed a traumatic event, although other symptoms may develop and persist such as depression, anxiety, and disassociation (Hall, 2012, p. 7).

A 2010 report by the US Interagency Council on Homelessness reported that over 80 percent of homeless mothers with children had experienced domestic abuse (McCoy-Roth, Mackintosh, and Murphey, 2012). McCoy and colleagues (2012) noted that these children were more likely to have emotional and behavioural problems. Morewitz (2016) reported that homeless youth experience daily stress from food insecurity, school issues such as conduct problems or conduct disorders, antisocial behaviours, and negative peer interactions.

Multiple studies support music as a beneficial endeavour for people who are dealing with the stress from a traumatic event (Knight & Rickard, 2001; Khalfa et al., 2003; Lee, Chung, Chan, & Chan, 2005; Osborne, 2009; Yehuda, 2011; Hall, 2012; Kim, 2014). Osborne (2009) indicated that musical intervention has the power to heal victims of trauma. Music increases mental and physical health by reducing the neurological and physiological elements of stress (Nilsson, 2008; Yehuda, 2011). Music also influences psychological well-being through the positive effects it has on emotions, engagement, relationships, and meaning (Croom, 2015); it can also stimulate self-regulation (Saarikallio, 2011).

The effects and benefits that music has on moods have been widely studied (Sloboda, Lamont, & Greasley, 2009; Kawase & Ogawa, 2018), and its use in influencing emotional states can be traced back to the ancient Greeks (Garrido & Davidson, 2013). Music is multifaceted and well-suited for communication, for it is inherently human (Custodero, 2002; Osborne, 2009). It allows people to engage on a fundamental preverbal level and enables connections (Kim, 2014). Social connections are especially significant for individuals who have experienced trauma (Charuvastra & Cloitre, 2008). A 2007 study found that homeless young adults reported an association of increased social connectedness with a decrease of trauma-related risks (Haden, Scarpa, Jones, & Ollendick, 2007, as cited by Kim et al., 2018).

Social connectedness increases feelings of self-esteem, decreases a sense of isolation, and assists in recovery from trauma (Nooner et al., 2012 as cited by Kim et al., 2018). Osborne (2009) observed immediate benefits from musical interventions with children who had witnessed the brutalization of war. He reported that individuals who were despondent at the beginning of the musical session left laughing and dancing, while initially hyperactive participants left calmed and focused (Osborne, 2009, p. 333). Carr and colleagues (2012) used music to treat symptoms of trauma, which led to increased socialization of subjects, lowered anxiety, and enhanced self-esteem. Carr and colleagues (2012) also indicated the value of interacting with people who share similar experiences.

Music may engage people in a safe and enjoyable context, assisting in the relation of a healthy self-image and social identity (Carr et al., 2012). In addition to or as part of music's healing effects, music allows for various responses such as distraction, action, or reflection (Custodero, 2006). Current literature on the relationship between music and community further supports music as a beneficial and positive experience for participants (Osborne, 2009; Yehuda, 2011; Carr et al., 2012; Hall, 2012; Kraus et al., 2014; Higgins & Willingham, 2017).

Method

Background. Weekly ninety-minute after-school classes were held for eight weeks at a resource centre for families who at the time were experiencing or had recently experienced homelessness in New York City. The resource centre notified the families they worked with about the program and invited them to participate. Due to staff and space constraints, the centre limited participation to thirty people; they conveyed disappointment in doing so after more families than we were able to accommodate expressed interest in this musical opportunity. Parents and caregivers expressed a desire to participate with their children, and as a result, thirty individuals of all ages participated, bringing diverse perspectives, backgrounds, and learning styles. The youngest participants were three-week-old triplets, who attended class with their mother and two older siblings; the eldest member was the grandparent of one of the children.

The participants' interests and engagement guided the musical curriculum. Each class consisted of an all-ages musical portion to encourage community-building through group musical and movement activities. These opening and closing group activities encouraged the inclusion and engagement of the wide range of ages and learning styles of the participants. As an activity during the first class, we wrote a welcome song that incorporated the ideas of the participants: "We will dance, we will play, we will sing today, 'cause we all learn from each other each and every day." The simplicity of the lyrics and melody allowed us to create variations of the welcome song with different musical gestures, genres, and styles. Each week we would sing the welcome song and then we would repeat it with invited ideas and variations from the participants; a few of the variations included rapping the song, singing it in Spanish, and adding dance moves.

In addition to group singing and movement activities, the program had small group instrumental instruction. The resource centre expressed a desire to have the program participants develop instrumental skills, which the children and parents were excited about. They were able to recruit donors, which allowed us to purchase eight violins, eight ukuleles, a keyboard, and a variety of percussion instruments within an $800 budget.

The first thirty minutes of class focused on group activities that welcomed the participants and encouraged them to join in as they felt comfortable. The small group activities divided the program participants according to age and incorporated my musical knowledge as a violinist and my colleague's musical skill on the ukulele. The two small groups alternated between twenty minutes of violin and twenty minutes of ukulele. The keyboard and percussion instruments were used in community-building activities before and after the small group instrumental instruction.

The weekly small violin group played in the hallway of the resource centre while the ukuleles sat in a circle in our normal meeting room, which was just large enough to fit everyone and the instruments. The centre was on the third floor of an old building, which housed offices with the exception of a room that housed supplies for the families and allowed enough room for us to gather and move in the space with the families. Each week we set up a tiled carpet that created a warm and inviting place for activities. It had been donated by a local carpet store.

The resource centre provided snacks for the family members before and after our music classes. Two social workers, who were familiar with all of the participants, supervised the space and assisted with set-up. They occasionally participated in the musical activities and provided support as needed.

At the end of the program, the resource centre bussed the families to Teachers College, Columbia University, to perform on a Saturday afternoon. It was about a sixty-minute bus ride, but the participants specifically expressed an interest in seeing the university. The performance was similar to our weekly classes, with community-building activities shaped by the participants' interests, ideas, and play. The performance also consisted of individual works the participants had prepared outside of class. During the musical activities the children and caregivers were individually interviewed by one of three music educators from Teachers College. Out of the thirty participants, eighteen were present at the performance and were interviewed. The interviews were recorded with the written and verbal consent of the parents and guardians.

Meeting the families' basic safety needs, so that they felt secure and encouraged to engage, was central to our program. Maslow (1943) proposed a theory of human motivation with interrelated, hierarchical needs as depicted in Figure 3.1. Although structured, the hierarchy is adaptable, for a higher-tier need may arise before lower ones are met (Maslow, 1943).

As the participants' basic needs of safety were met in the context of our community music program, we strove to strengthen an inner sense of self and community through shared musical experiences. The children's and parent's psychological need to feel a sense of belonging and accomplishment was addressed as they made friendships and created music. Reflecting Maslow's (1943) hierarchy, as the participants' basic and psychological needs were fulfilled, the focus could change to self-fulfillment needs; this correlated with our finding that the participants' musical and self-identities were enriched as they participated in collaborative musical activities throughout the program.

Research method. Qualitative data were collected through semi-structured interviews, field notes, and a document review from an in-class drawing activity. All of the participants were informed about the intent to evaluate their experiences in the program, and legal guardians signed consent forms to participate. Open-ended interview questions provided rich qualitative data that allowed for in-depth consideration of the implications of the program. Interviews were conducted with the parents and children as well as the director of the not-for-profit resource centre and my co-facilitator to consider various perspectives on the collaborative endeavour. The interviewed children ranged in age from five to thirteen. Two academic specialists were also interviewed to further explore the experiences of educators who had worked extensively with underserved communities that had endured trauma.

The parents and caregivers who participated in the program were asked open-ended questions about their musical background, the musical culture of their family, and their experience in the program. They were invited to comment on their experiences in the program and asked what they noticed about their children during music classes and why they were interested in participating. They were also asked to recall a special memory from the program: *Why did you participate in this program? Why did you continue to participate? Can you tell me about a special memory from class? What did you notice about your child(ren) during class? Do you think they liked it? How do you know? What did your child(ren) learn? Is there anything else you would like to share about your musical experiences? Is there anything else you would like to share?*

The children were asked about their favourite activity from the program, what they learned, and anything they would like to share about their experience: *What was your favourite activity we did? Why was it your favourite? What did you notice about your mom or dad during music class? Do you think they liked it? How do you know? What did you learn? Is there anything else you would like to share about your musical experiences? Is there anything else you would like to share?*

To augment the semi-structured interviews, data were collected from a document review of an in-class musical drawing activity. The participants were asked to draw a self-portrait of their musical selves at the beginning and end of the program. We were interested in comparing the drawings to see if the participants' perception of their musical selves changed over the course of the program. At the concluding interviews, each participant was presented with his or her musical self-portrait and asked to share insight or comment on the illustrations.

A semi-structured interview protocol was developed accordingly for the director of the not-for-profit resource centre and my co-facilitator. Evaluating the experiences of an administrative member of each of the collaborating organizations provided various viewpoints and more reliable data. The themes addressed in these two interviews were: Ease of Integration, Organizational Issues, Curriculum Impact, Community and Family Impact, Suggestions and Additional Feedback. Examples of questions included: *How do you feel Music For Everyone fit in with the resource centre's vision? How do you feel about the implementation and structure of the program? What do you think could be improved? What aspects of the program did you enjoy? Is there a particularly moving memory that stands out to you from the program? How, if at all, has this program influenced you? What, if any, changes have you noticed in the children and parents? Is there anything else you would like to share?*

The interviewed academic specialists were Dr. Helen Verdeli, Professor of Psychology and Education at Teachers College, Columbia University, and Dr. Nigel Osborne, former Reid Professor of Music at the University of Edinburgh. Dr. Verdeli has been trained as a clinical psychologist and has worked with

Global Mental Health providing psychiatric care for people internationally, focusing on Syrian refugees in Lebanon as well as communities in low- and middle-income countries such as Haiti, India, and the nations of sub-Saharan Africa. Dr. Nigel Osborne has worked extensively with individuals who have experienced the devastations of war. His musical interventions have taken him to severely war-torn nations such as Bosnia, Syria, and Lebanon. His therapeutic musical interventions have expanded into a full education program addressing health, social care, shelter, nutrition, and economic development in Syria and Lebanon.

The interview protocol for Dr. Verdeli and Dr. Osborne addressed their backgrounds, scholarly interests, and pedagogical approaches, as well as the evolution of their methods and suggestions for working with underserved communities. Questions included: *How do educators who work with people living in life-threatening circumstances create spaces for learning? How, if at all, have your scholarly interests changed or developed? What are the perceived characteristics of an effective pedagogy for individuals enduring daily stresses?*

Conceptual Framework

To further understand the program in terms of a shared musical experience and how this collaborative endeavour might influence the participants' identities, Bronfenbrenner's (1979) ecological model for human development was used as the basis for the study's conceptual framework. This model was simplified and adapted to examine the relationships the participants encountered between

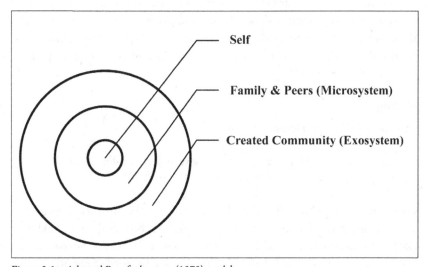

Figure 3.1   Adapted Bronfenbrenner (1979) model

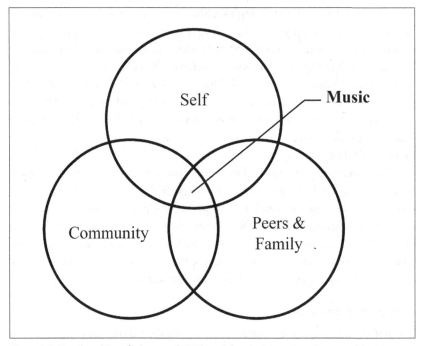

Figure 3.2 Developed Bronfenbrenner (1979) model to depict music at the core of the intersecting relationships within the context of the community music program.

self, family and peers (microsystem), and the created community (exosystem) in the context of our community music program. See Figure 3.1.

In the context of our created community, music was used to build and foster relationships with one's self, family and peers, and the community. The Bronfenbrenner structure was further developed to display the interconnected relationships, with music at the core, in the context of the community music program. See Figure 3.2.

Findings

Parents and Children Document Review

> Children's drawings are unique and can give us precise information about the young artist. (Farokhi & Hashemi, 2011, p. 2220)

Out of the musical-self drawings, I have chosen a few for this chapter that are representative of a range of responses. Mäkelä, Nithikul, and Heikkinen (2014) discuss the validity of drawings for research. The scientific community has recently acknowledged their value, specifically because of the access they provide to the creator's conscious and unconscious mind. A child's mind can be reflected in his or her drawings (Thomas & Silk, 1990, as cited in Farokhi & Hashemi, 2011). Children who are being evaluated can find making drawings more enjoyable than answering questions, as cited by Lewis and Greene (1983) in Farokhi and Hashemi (2011).

Farokhi and Hashemi (2011) explored children's social, emotional, physical, and intellectual development by observing and analyzing their drawings; they found that perceptions of self, others, and the environment can influence conceptual representation in a drawing. In the interviews, we showed each participant his or her drawings and asked them to tell us about their self-portraits. Through the initial comparison of the participants' drawings from the first and last sessions, we explored the possible influence of the collaborative musical endeavour on the participants' individual and social identities.

Given how powerful drawings can be as an evaluative tool (Mäkelä, Nithikul, & Heikkinen, 2014; Deguara, 2019), we compared the self-portraits from the first and last sessions side by side along with participants' comments on their drawings from their presentation of them in-class and again during the interview. As a structure for analyzing the self-portraits, we considered the two-level analysis, denotation and connotation, as explored in Deguara (2019).

Deguara (2019) describes drawing as a complex process in which thinking and meaning-making can be derived through an analysis of the visual representation containing two levels of interpretation: the surface level, and symbolic message or what Barthes (1977) as cited in Deguara (2019) refers to as the denotation and connotation levels. We analyzed the self-portraits for the direct meaning of what they represent as well as the hidden or unconscious meaning they may also convey. In addition, analyzing the drawings relied significantly on the children's verbal explanations of them on the day they drew them and again when they were presented side by side in the interviews. This was similar to the approach taken by Picard and Gauthier (2012), which relied on verbal clarification by the drawing's creator in their study of the development of expressive drawing abilities of children and adolescents.

The first document review focused on thirteen-year-old Talia's musical-self drawings. Her initial drawing was a self-portrait in which she surrounded herself with music notes. In Talia's depiction of her musical self-portrait from the final class, she drew a blooming flower and wrote, "Music is Life" (see Figure 3.3). There was a noticeable shift from a literal self-portrait to a metaphorical, expressive drawing. Talia explained in the interview that as she gained skills with the violin and ukulele, saw her parents and siblings participate in music, and looked forward to participating and creating in the program each week

Figure 3.3 Self-portrait document review: Thirteen-year-old Talia's musical-self drawing from the first and last day of the program.

with her family and new friends, music became more than an enjoyable hobby; it became a positive life force.

Deandra, the mother of five children in the class as well as an active participant, drew a picture of herself the first day with a microphone, keyboard, footprints, and two eighth notes (see Figure 3.4). In the interview, when she saw her musical self-portrait, she told us the following about her first drawing: "This is me ... I love to sing, I love the piano, and I love to dance."

In a similar shift as in Talia's example, Deandra's drawings moved from a literal self-portrait to a metaphorical depiction of her musical-self:

> The keyboard is still there. The musical notes are even more now. These lines are kind of like the hospital, these lines are the heartbeat. This is our heartbeat rhythm. And everything that's in my heart is always pertaining to music no matter what it is that I do, or what I'm going through. It also reflects the family moods and everything. So, sometimes we might be an F minor, or a D major, or whatever it may be.

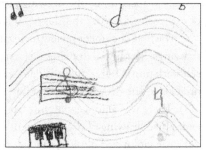

Figure 3.4 Self-portrait document review: Mother of five Deandra's musical-self drawing from the first and last day of the program.

Figure 3.5 Self-portrait document review: Six-year-old Jason's musical-self drawing from the first and last day of the program.

This comparison may suggest that as she shared musical experiences with our community and her family, her musical identity reached outside of herself to incorporate her family and the lifeline that music had been for them. Deandra went on to say: "It's about what you feel in your heart. We're all born with a [musical] beat whether we known it or not, it's your heart and your mom's heart."

A notable finding from the document review of the musical-self drawing activity was made when we compared six-year-old Jason's drawings from the first and last day of classes. In reference to his first drawing, Jason said: "This is me playing the trumpet." In his illustration from the final class, he explained: "This is me and my friends, making music." The change in Jason's illustrations of his musical-self suggested that our shared musical space influenced his identity (see Figure 3.5). Referencing the Bronfenbrenner model from Figure 3.2, it seems that Jason's sense of musical-self had been influenced by his microsystem of peers and family members. He developed friendships with his peers as shared musical experiences with the created community and his family members, and he depicted this in his musical drawing, clarifying it further in his explanation.

An additional finding from the drawing activity came through the comparison of Jason's first drawing with his younger brother, Ray's, first self-portrait (see Figure 3.6a). Ray's drawing looks similar to Jason's: he places himself in the middle of the page with instruments in his hands. Ray said, "That's me playing maracas," as he explained his picture and talked about how he liked the drums and trumpet.

Also notable is that Ray's self-portrait from the last day resembles his father's drawing (see Figure 3.5b). Ray's father drew himself surrounded by speakers, and his five-year-old son, Ray, drew his musical-self in the likeness of his father's illustration. Ray commented on his self-portrait from the last day of

Figure 3.5.1 Self-portrait document review: Six-year-old Jason's musical self-drawing from the first day of class (left) and his five-year-old brother, Ray's self-portrait (right).

class: "That's me playing speakers. There is trumpets coming from the speakers." We showed him his father's drawing, and he said: "Same thing. He's playing speakers too." The similarity in the drawings indicates how strongly Ray's family members influence his self-identity and suggests the significant influence of the microsystem from the developed Bronfenbrenner model (Figure 3.2).

Ray's father, Jim, commented on his musical self-portrait from the first day:

> That's me recording my raps. I write lyrics." When he saw his drawing from the final class during the interview, he said: "This is kinda similar, but we have a new music system now that involves the whole family. (Figure 3.6)

Fig. 3.5.2 Self-portrait document review: Five-year-old Ray's musical-self drawing from the last day of class (left) and father's musical-self drawing (right).

Figure 3.6 Self-portrait document review: Jim, Ray's father, musical-self from the first and last day of the program.

Jim's explanation of the drawings suggested a change in his musical identity: it had shifted to incorporate his family members; as he explained in his interview, the picture metaphorically involved his family. Also noted was the difference between the stance he drew for himself in the two drawings: in the first, he showed his back, with a vague hint of a neutral facial expression; and the second, he was standing open-armed with a smile on his face. As a facilitator and observer of the program, I noticed how Jim's confidence grew as he participated in the program as well as his eagerness to help others during activities. This finding was supported by his daughter's response during her interview to the question, *What did you notice about your mom or dad during music class? Do you think they liked it? How do you know?*:

> My dad learned to cooperate better with others and my mom learned to …
> I don't really know. She's always been happy with other people. I guess
> she just embraces other things more … They smiled a lot. There was a
> lot of smiling.

Tammy, a twelve-year-old in the program, drew herself "singing a whole bunch of words." Regarding her self-portrait from the final class, she explained:

> So this is me, and I'm listening to the speaker, but it's on the radio. These
> are stars, because like last night, I was up just listening to music. Some-
> times I fall asleep with headphones on my ears. (Figure 3.7)

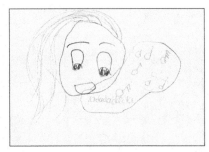 

Figure. 3.7 Self-portrait document review: Twelve-year-old Tammy's musical-self drawing from the first and last day of the program.

Tammy's interview provided more insight about her connection with music outside of class:

> I'm just used to listening to music, like when I used to live with my grandmother, she had the radio, like we'd always put it on, and just listen to music.

An eleven-year-old in the program, Annie, explained her drawing: "This piece of artwork is me singing *Chick-a-boom-boom*. And did you know that I made a smiley face?" Her drawing from the final class labelled the instruments she had drawn: "That was a drum with sticks and that was the trumpet" (Figure 3.8).

Annie pointed out in her interview: "You saw the back of it, right?" On the back of her drawing from the final class, she had written with colourful words:

Figure 3.8 Self-portrait document review: Eleven-year-old Annie's musical-self drawing from the first and last day of the program.

Figure 3.8.1 Self-portrait document review: The back of Annie's musical-self drawing from the last day and her sister, Talia's self-portrait from the last day of the program.

"Music is my life." It is notable that her sister, Talia's, drawing (see Figure 3.3) was a self-portrait that said: "Music is Life." Annie explained: "It says music is my life. Because I like listening to reggae, hip-hop, umm what's it called ... I forgot ... R&B!" These similarities support the significance of the relationship between self and the microsystem of family and peers developed through collaborative musical experiences in the context of the created community.

Interviews

The collected data from the interviews supported the finding that the program had been a positive experience for the eighteen interviewed participants. This reinforced my observations and experience as a facilitator as well as the data from the interviews with my co-facilitator and the director of the resource centre. Common words appeared throughout all the interviews: *community, need, want, understand,* and *love.* The themes that emerged from this coded data included Relationships, Identity, Benefits, and Need.

Parents and children. In response to the interview question, *What did your children enjoy about this program?,* a parent replied: "I think it's basically the interaction for them. The interaction with the different people. That's what I've heard them say and that's what I've witnessed." A common theme from the parents' and children's interviews was the importance of developed relationships and a sense of belonging. The parents felt that the sense of belonging they received from participating in the program was significant. Quotes like "Coming here, it was like welcoming a person to your home ... made you feel like you were part of something" and "I feel more safe, comfortable, [I feel] welcomed" made it clear that this was just as meaningful an experience for the parents as it was for their children.

One parent commented on the final performance at Teachers College:

I've never been inside of a city college before. Never. Ever. So, just this experience alone, this is my first time, so you see me in here just taking pictures and, I never seen this kind of stuff before. So the experience for me, my kids, [is significant].

A twelve-year-old from another family also mentioned her excitement about Teachers College:

I want to do the best I can in school. I really want to go to Columbia. When I found out the teachers in Music For Everyone go to Columbia, I was very excited. One day I would like to be there. I have a lot of goals and try my hardest to make my dreams come true.

The program was beneficial and provided an outlet for the families that reached beyond the class. A father of six children explained his experience in the interview:

A lot of people hear [that we are homeless] and think so negative about it. This experience for me, my kids, we can have stuff to talk about other than: "Did you hear them gun shots last night?"

The interviewed children in our program also expressed meaningful moments they had experienced. A twelve-year-old student recalled a memory from the program in her interview:

[There] was this one day where I was just in a bad mood, and then I came [to music class] … and we just started smiling, and then my whole day got better after that. Everybody just leaves happy.

Another student told the interviewer about how she enjoyed actively engaging in music and explained her desire to make friends:

Music is fun and makes me happy. When I sing for my family and teachers I see it makes them happy too. I think I may be able to make a lot of friends through music.

All of the children and parents were able to recount at least one specific or favourite memory from the program. The described recollections varied from solo class performances to leading group activities. The memories all indicated a sense of accomplishment and feeling of belonging.

Facilitator and administrator. The data received from these two interviews supported the positive effect the program had on the participants. The director of the resource centre recalled her observation of the children and parents:

> It was really, really fun to see the smiling faces, and these kids who are just experiencing such joy, and having such a great time playing music, and being around friends, and making new friends, and seeing the connection, not in all cases, but in some cases, being able to see the bonds that were being strengthened between mother and child, and father and child. It was really interesting to see, in some cases, a few of the parents were [initially] withdrawn, and they seemed like they were bringing their kids to enjoy this class, and ... you guys made a lot of effort to really engage them, and pull them in, and to make them feel like they [were] part of the learning experience, and not just passively dropping off their kids to some activity.

The director noted that the program integrated the varying styles and approaches of music educators and social workers:

> I think that is one of the unique pieces of the program that we were bringing together [music] teachers and social workers, working along, side by side, maximizing on the two different approaches, and trying to synthesize [them].

Both the director and my co-facilitator, Clayton, felt that a collaborative approach with open communication was important for the program to work effectively.

The director noted an overwhelming desire that the homeless families had for social resources and opportunities. The resource centre had initially wanted to limit the class to twenty participants. Then families who had heard about the program showed up at class, and the director increased the class size to thirty. She also noted that they did not do any outreach for the community programs as their clients immediately expressed an interest when the opportunity was mentioned in their meetings with the social workers. The director expressed a desire to accommodate all of the interested families, which would have entailed implementing daily classes.

Clayton too felt that the program had been a positive and desirable experience that increased the participants' interest in learning and making music:

> I believe the participants are hungry to learn more, try new instruments, and participate in further music making ... Being in a positive learning

environment is exactly that – positive. I was reminded of the power of community and family.

The director described the importance the program had for the parents, who were able to focus on their children and the music instead of the daily stress and trauma they were enduring. She explained her experience of the community music program's significance for the participants:

> Kids were saying, "I look forward to this day. This is the day that I look forward to most." A lot of [parents] said, "I wish there were more programs like this. I wish you guys could do this more than one day a week." I think people like coming because they felt a sense of belonging and they felt the sense of community. If you consider the things that homeless families have experienced, just creating that opportunity for families to build relationships with one another, to learn about the experiences of others that validates their own experiences and makes them feel less isolated, because they know they're not the only ones who experience this.

Issues were also identified in the program with regard to space and resource limitations. Although the group activities were well-received by the created community, the small-group instruction was restricted by age differences, the mix of learning styles, and the ratio of students to facilitators. The resource centre expressed its desire to have instrumental instruction, and the participants were eager to learn an instrument. However, there were only twelve instruments – six ukuleles and six violins – to distribute among the thirty participants during small-group instrumental instruction, for which we divided the class in half. The parents helped as teaching assistants during this part of the class because of the limited number of instruments; the parents did take time to play with the instruments before and after class.

In addition to the limited number of instruments, there was a wide range of students. The youngest child who participated in the small-group instrumental was four years old, and the oldest was fifteen. In an interview with him that my colleague conducted, he talked about the time constraints resulting from the ratio of participants to facilitators: "I often felt myself drifting toward the younger students in class just because they needed a lot of attention." The older students expressed a desire to learn additional skills on the instruments and were frustrated by the time the younger students consumed.

Academic specialists. The qualitative data collected from the interviews with the two professors supported community music's ability to help people endure life's challenges. Dr. Osborne noted the beneficial elements that music offered traumatized people when he observed a change in the children's attention, joy, concentration, self-esteem, and physical presentation. He also reported that parents said their children were sleeping better. He found that by engaging people in enjoyable and challenging activities, he was able to provide relief for traumatized individuals:

> We were creating situations that would take the children's attention away from what they were suffering. What was strange was when we started doing this kind of distraction work, how powerful it was, and we realized that something else was happening; the experience of the music was having a greater effect than simply distracting from the horror of what was around them.

Music was not the primary resource Dr. Verdeli utilized in her work, but she employed it as an intervention if it was relevant and traditional to the community in which she was working. Dr. Verdeli noted the importance of music for traumatized communities,

> People need to feel that there is a continuity with their previous life and music gives that sense. Continuity, that not everything is gone. There are memories, there's a common community, shared heritage. Community building is very important to people; it regulates mood, it provides a way for people to express themselves, it gives them a voice.

In circumstances where individuals may not have security, music may serve as a constant in their lives.

Some fundamental and inherent aspects of music may provide engaging and inclusive opportunities. Dr. Osborne explained how music both connects and communicates:

> In our evolution as human beings before we learned how to speak we had musical communication. It is an essential way of communicating deep human knowledge, motivation, and state of mind and body.

He also discussed the galvanizing social energy of music that he observed: one person's attitude could have a multiplying effect on the group.

Both professors discussed the benefits of incorporating a community's practices and traditions, which guided their pedagogical approaches. Observation of cultures, social idioms of distress, and working with local experts can assist in developing a meaningful intervention. Dr. Verdeli iterated: "We know our treatments, but they know their communities."

Similarly, Dr. Osborne described an approach driven by the needs and interests of the participants:

> I work in a very different way to what I would do in a mainstream school, university, or music college. It's all aural, nothing written down; it's a different pedagogy. The children learn what music can do by doing it.

Much as had resource centre director in her discussion of the homeless families' eagerness for opportunities, Dr. Verdeli described the problem of access for underserved communities. Dr. Osborne voiced the importance of offering coping mechanisms and providing opportunities for traumatized individuals. Working with communities that have endured trauma requires sensitivity to their situation as well as understanding: "You get trust with a traumatized person ... so you must be very careful to use that trust well."

Field notes. A notable event I recorded in my field notes involved Jason, a seven-year-old with autism, who rarely communicated verbally or interacted with anyone, and sat among various percussion instruments scattered on the rug. He was playing with a toy car when I placed a drum near him and tapped softly on it. Jason paused from running the car along the lines of the carpet and softly tapped back on the drum. I copied his rhythmic gestures and he began to smile. He started to sing, "If you're happy and you know it ...," completing the phrase on the drum. Jason continued to build rhythmic gestures into the song while I repeated his rhythms. I looked up to see his teary-eyed father watching as his son enthusiastically engaged in music-making. Kim (2014) described a similar breakthrough as she experienced a bond with a previously non-reactive student using a musical intervention involving imitation (p. 267).

Another notable event involved one of our younger members, Isaac, who was six and had been diagnosed with autism and was non-verbal. We were learning about dynamics and playing together as a group. Our musical activity invited the participants to take turns conducting the group, who had percussion instruments. Isaac sat on his mom's lap and with her support conducted the group. Isaac's face lit up with a smile as he led everyone in playing loud and soft. He looked especially thrilled to have the group stop playing when he gave a gesture to stop and then begin playing again when he gave cue to start. His mom later shared what a special moment she felt that was for her son, who had never experienced a leadership role before.

A thirteen-year-old girl had been assaulted outside the shelter where she was staying and had to relocate and enrol in a new school, where she found it difficult to develop new friendships. When I met her, she was quiet, reserved, and hesitant to participate, and told me she did not have any friends. Over the course of the eight-week program, I observed her as she began to show initiative, expand and extend her musical activities, develop friendships, volunteer to share, and assist her peers. At the performance, she sang a song she had written and performed a dance she had choreographed with several friends she had made in the program. She demonstrated confidence in herself and developed friendships through collaborative musical experiences.

Discussion

The collected qualitative data indicated that the program was a positive and significant experience for the participants, even with the limitations of time, space, and assistance. To incorporate the emerging themes from the analyzed data and explore the outcomes of shared musical experiences for homeless families, the study's conceptual framework was further developed. The collected data indicated that the participants' identities (self, social, and musical) were influenced by the fostered relationships of the community music program. Given that identity is fluid (Moore, 2016; Alvesson, Ashcraft, & Thomas, 2008), the intersecting circles depicted in Figure 3.9 will likely change, as circles are removed and additional ones are welcomed. For the purpose of this study, the focus was on self, social, and musical identities, with the participant at the centre of these intersecting identities.

Understanding the needs and interests of the participants was central to our program. The participants' need for attention was evident and was discussed in the interviews with the director of the resource centre and my co-facilitator. In addition, the two academic specialists discussed the need for opportunities that underserved communities have. I too witnessed this need for attention and opportunities, as students and parents frequently stayed after

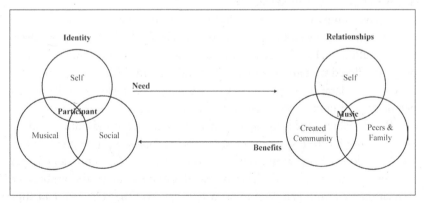

Figure 3.9 Conceptual framework: The individual within the context of the community music program.

our goodbye song to share stories, music, achievements, and disappointments and to express their appreciation. The time before and after our music classes created social opportunities and strengthened our created community. This finding is supported by related literature that indicates the significance of social connectedness (Carr et al., 2012; Kim et al., 2018).

In an interview, one of the mothers from the program mentioned the time we spent together after class:

> It was awesome we learned dance moves and that was special that we shared our music and dances. When Clayton got up and danced that was the most magical experience I have ever seen. I've never seen someone take such an interest in the moves and sounds we use and incorporate into everything we're doing, even our welcome song ... I noticed the kids really crave the individual attention of Lindsey and Clayton.

A twelve-year-old also commented on the attention Clayton and I provided during and after class:

> They keep it balanced and everyone is treated the same, everyone has fun, and they also ask questions like, "Did you have fun today?" and when we close out, we sing this beautiful song and everybody just leaves happy.

To discover the needs of a community, listening and observing are essential. This was discussed in the interviews with both professors and supported by related literature (Custodero, 2006). Working with people from underserved communities also requires sensitivity to their situation. In addition, Dr. Osborne expressed the delicacy and significance of relationships with individuals who have experienced trauma.

In community music, the musical instruction is not as important as the personal and social well-being of the participants (Veblen, Messenger, Silverman, & Elliott, 2013). The sense of belonging through our community music program offered the participants stability and security. This was supported by the collected data; as one parent stated: "Coming here, it was like welcoming a person to your home ... made you feel like you were part of something."

Relationships are deeply significant in our lives. Social and cultural experiences account for the majority of occurrences in people's lives (Bronfenbrenner, 1979). St. John (2010) reminds us that relationships are also fundamental in creating a community: "At the heart of teaching and learning is the importance of relationships and quality of interactions" (p. 93). The collected data supported the importance of relationships that were developed in the program through shared musical experiences; the related literature (Higgins, 2012; St.

John, 2010; Veblen, Messenger, Silverman, & Elliott, 2013; Kim et al., 2018) found the same.

The musical-self drawing activity explored the relationship between identity and community music. Students were asked to "draw your musical-self." The document review of musical self-drawings indicated that the participants' identities had been influenced in the context of the program.

Jason's drawing addressed how he viewed his musical-self. This shifted from an individual to a collaborative perspective: his first drawing was a portrait of him playing the trumpet; his musical self-drawing eight weeks later depicted him playing music with friends. Talia's musical identity was enriched as her illustration evolved from a self-portrait to an abstract image, one that expressed a fostered and significant relationship with music: Music is life. Ray's rendering of his brother and his father's musical self-portraits support how significant relationships are for one's self-identity.

The father's musical self-drawings from the first and final classes did not depict an obvious change in identity. However, it seems that his overall self-esteem had been positively influenced by the community music program. I saw this in his growing enthusiasm for facilitating musical activities and for assisting other participants. His amplified engagement and participation over the eight weeks may suggest that his self and social identities were enriched as his self-esteem and sense of belonging increased in the context of our community music setting. As an adult, the father had had more time over his life to build and form his own musical identity; this program may have been an opportunity to share that identity with his son and build that relationship.

At the conclusion of the program, I met with the director, participating social workers, and the CEO of the not-for-profit resource centre to discuss the program's future. Though he was provided with the collected data and findings that the inclusive and intergenerational shared musical experiences had been a highly positive experience for the participants, the CEO felt that our community music program should be performance-based and that the focus should shift from using music as a medium for enjoyment, expression, and collaboration, to increasing the grades of the primary school students. He asked: "If not to improve grades … why music?"

Conclusions

A lot of people hear [that we are homeless] and think so negative about it. This experience for me, my kids, we can have stuff to talk about other than: "Did you hear them gun shots last night?"
—Program Parent

Underserved communities have a significant need for opportunities to connect. Community music programs provide these opportunities to connect and foster a sense of belonging. In addition, the positive effects from building relationships in the context of community music programs may form or strengthen the participants' identities.

When implementing a community music program, observation of and sensitivity to a community's needs and interests is important to creating an effective learning space and meaningful experiences for the participants. Individuals who experience homelessness often endure multiple, interconnected issues, including trauma from abuse or neglect in addition to the hardships of their unstable living conditions.

Trauma may be defined as a distressing or disturbing experience. It can result from any number of different events and can have a multitude of effects on individuals. Mild stress from everyday life, hardships arising from socioeconomic status, homelessness, and the brutalizing aftermath of war are all situations in which trauma may be experienced with various degrees of severity.

The collected qualitative data from this study supported community music as a beneficial and significant experience for urban families who had experienced homelessness and were victims of domestic abuse. The findings suggest that community music has an inherently therapeutic element and that it enables participants to experience relief from trauma. The findings also indicated that the participants' self, social, and musical identities had been enriched by their participation in the shared musical experiences of our community music program.

The beneficial neurological, emotional, and physiological effects of music have been widely studied (Sloboda, Lamont, & Greasley, 2009; Carr et al., 2012; Croom, 2015). These beneficial elements of music may extend beyond community music sessions into the everyday lives of the participants and factor into their identities. Collaborative musical experiences can be profoundly significant in the lives of children and adults who have experienced homelessness or other trauma; in a world of unsafe and unstable living conditions, music may provide a sense of security and consistency. The outcome of this collaborative initiative was meaningful in that it provided a structure for participants to enrich their sense of self, build relationships, and identify with the created community. This was particularly significant as our created community was a social group outside of the label homeless, which can be obtrusive and limiting. Music presented an opportunity for creative expression through shared experiences and participation. This had a positive and potentially lasting impact.

Suggestions for Further Study

Given that the CEO's interest was in the development of a methodology that would result in the improvement of the children's grades in school, it could be beneficial to further explore the impact that community music may have in other areas of participants' lives. Numerous studies link the improvement of performance in school to active engagement in music-making (Rauscher, 1997; Schellenberg, 2004 and 2006; Wetter, Koerner, & Schwaninger, 2009). Buckner, Bassuk, and Weinreb (2001) conducted a study with children who had experienced homelessness or were from low-income households between the ages of six and seventeen. The findings reported that homeless and housed children scored similarly in terms of achievement in school. Further research is suggested to investigate the relationship between community music programs and performance in school for children who have experienced homelessness.

Several studies suggest that engaging in a learning environment with participants of various ages is beneficial to all participants (Bowers, 1998; Alfano, 2008; Higgins & Willingham, 2017). The varying ages among the participating families may have played a beneficial role in our program. Further research is suggested to investigate this benefit. In addition, the present study supported the benefits of university/community partnerships (Bushouse, 2005; Harkins, 2014), given the inherent need for opportunities to connect in underserved communities and the need for university students to gain experience.

Acknowledgment

Thank you to my co-facilitator and researcher, Clayton Dahm, for his time, talent, and invaluable contributions to the creation and implementation of our program and this study. Thank you to Dr. Lori Custodero and Dr. Harold Abeles for their guidance and support in the program and evaluation. My sincere gratitude to the families from this program who shared their time, talent, and trust with us.

CHAPTER 4

Mind the Gap!

Dave Camlin

Background

IN THIS SECTION, I outline the terms of my inquiry, including the current disparity in access to public funding for arts and culture in the United Kingdom, the changing value of music in light of the ongoing disruptions to the field of cultural production, and the need for new approaches to addressing these issues, especially when it comes to how we train musicians to develop a professional practice within such ongoing complexity.

The Gap between the Haves and the Have-Nots

To better understand the complex interrelationship between musician identity and the field of cultural production, I frame my argument around two distinct but related conceptual "gaps" that require bridging: first, the unequal distribution of public funds for cultural participation; and second, the "gap" between study and practice in the arts. While at first glance these may seem like separate concerns, I hope to demonstrate that they are intimately connected.

The first "gap" is the one that exists between the haves and the have-nots in terms of political access to the means of cultural production and reproduction. Two competing views of culture have evolved over time in relation to cultural participation: on the one hand, an approach referred to as the "democratization of culture"; and on the other, the idea of Cultural Democracy, "when people have the substantive social freedom to make versions of culture" (Wilson, Gross, & Bull, 2017, p. 3). From the perspective of Cultural Democracy,

> [t]he picture of cultural creativity emerging through our research strongly challenges the underlying logic of the prevailing approach to UK cultural

policy – what its critics call the "deficit model." Within this paradigm, dominant for the past 70 years that the UK has had an arts council, the leading ambition has been to widen access to a particular cultural
offering that is publicly funded and thereby identified as the good stuff.
(Wilson et al., 2017, p. 6)

Despite decades of investment in the arts in the UK on the basis that "participation in arts activities brings social benefits [which are] integral to the act
of participation" (Matarasso, 1997), public funding of the arts has not found
its way into all layers of society, but rather has remained principally within a
minority elite. The Warwick Commission's findings that "the wealthiest, better
educated and least ethnically diverse 8 percent of the population accounted for
at least 28 percent of live attendance to theatre, 44 percent of attendances to
live music, and 28 percent of visual arts attendances" (Neelands et al., 2015)
are alarming, not just because of the inequality of access to publicly funded arts
and culture they illustrate, but also because of the failure of the "deficit model"
of culture to have done much about it.

Hysteresis

This maintenance of privilege has gone on despite other significant changes in
the field of cultural production in relation to the value of music, which have
produced conditions that we might view as a complex and unfolding "hysteresis"
(Camlin, 2016a, p. 7). Hysteresis is defined as:

the structural lag between opportunities and the dispositions to grasp
them which is the cause of missed opportunities and, in particular, of the
frequently observed incapacity to think historical crises in categories of
perception and thought other than those of the past. (Bourdieu, 1977,
p. 83)

Also referred to as "the disruption between habitus and field and the consequences of this over time" (Hardy, 2008a), the term "hysteresis" contains the
idea that the field – of music, in this instance – has been disrupted and has
not yet stabilized (Camlin, 2016a). Constant innovations in information technology – digital distribution driving down sales of recorded music since 2000,
and more recent developments in VR (virtual reality) and AR (augmented
reality) technology that have changed the experience of live performance, for
example – mean that musicians can no longer be certain of how they will make
a living over the course of their career. Paradoxically, the same technological
developments that seem to have democratized the means of musical production
and consumption (cheap music apps, free online instruction, near-zero cost
of streaming music, and so forth), and the attendant rise of the "prosumer"

(Matarasso, 2010), threaten the livelihoods of those who are attempting to make a living out of their musical creativity.

Changing Value of Music

As a consequence of these complex disruptions to the field of music, its value has become unstable, and this has profound implications, for musicians in particular, and especially for those just emerging as practitioners.

Social value of music. The first of these disruptions has come about as a result of changes in understanding of the social value of arts and culture in the late 1990s – referred to above – in response to the idea that arts participation can generate social "goods" (Matarasso, 1997). This has led cultural discourse away from more self-perpetuating arguments about "art for art's sake" and toward a more instrumentalized discourse regarding music's "extrinsic" value to people and society. Within some policy frameworks, there is a recognition that reducing an understanding of music's power to this simple dichotomy is not helping to articulate its value terribly well. We therefore need to "break down the divide between the intrinsic and the instrumental camps" (Crossick & Kaszynska, 2016, p. 5). Despite this recognition, the arguments still rage.

Economic value of music. The second of these disruptions concerns the radical and ongoing shifts in the ways that people have accessed and used music since the advent of the internet, and how these changing patterns of consumption have disrupted music's economic value (Anderson, 2009). One consequence of the disruption to the economic model is more consumer choice, which puts added pressure on the "deficit model" as people choose to access culture on their own terms. The dominance of the "aesthetic" model of music (Elliott, Silverman, & Bowman, 2016) coincided neatly with the scarcity model of musical distribution, which may well have helped strengthen the paradigm of the economic value of "aesthetic" forms. However, as consumer choice has increased, and the "zero marginal cost" (Mason, 2016; Rifkin, 2015) of distribution of musical goods has become more widespread, the relative economic value of those goods has waned, to the point that music is expected to be "free in all senses of the word" (Price, 2013). This decoupling of the aesthetic model of music from its economic value raises important questions about the use of public funds to support forms of cultural production that predominantly benefit a minority elite. It is these significant changes in the field of music that have required changes in the "habitus" (Bourdieu, 1977) of its practitioners.

New Philosophies

In response, a range of new and broadly progressive philosophies surrounding music and cultural participation are emerging, including the emergence of community music (CM) as an academic discipline (Higgins, 2012; Higgins & Bartleet, 2017; Higgins & Willingham, 2017; Veblen, Elliott, Messenger, & Silverman, 2013), socially engaged art or SEA (Helguera, 2011; Kester, 2005; Roche, 2006), artistic citizenship (Elliott, Silverman, & Bowman, 2016), everyday creativity (Hunter, Micklem, & 64 Million Artists, 2016), and a resurgence of the Cultural Democracy movement (Wilson, Gross, & Bull, 2017). Alongside these new – or revitalized – philosophies we also find new ideas about the kinds of dispositions musicians/artists need to possess (Bennett & Burnard, 2016) in order to establish themselves in this complex and contested emerging field of cultural production. My own research has focused on what might be learned from institutionalized responses to the disruptions to the field (Camlin, 2015b; 2016b) and the ways in which musicians' dispositions are changing in response (Camlin, 2015a; 2016d; 2016a; 2017).

The Gap between Study and Professional Practice

The implications of all of these complex disruptions to the field of music for emergent musicians is profound and highlight a further "gap" in the way they are able to prepare for a professional career. This second "gap" – between study and professional practice in music – has always concerned music educators; how music education prepares its students to "inhabit" the professional field of music is understandably of primary concern. However, the dramatic changes in the composition of the field of music – especially since the advent of free digital distribution of music – have disrupted practice to such a degree that the "habitus" or "cultural personality" (Söderman, Burnard, & Hofvander-Trulsson, 2015) of music practitioners, that is, the way they "inhabit" the field of music, has had to change in order for them to sustain a successful practice.

Case Study: Sage Gateshead

To explore these implications for emerging music practitioners, I wish to draw the reader's attention to a case study of a UK music institution that has historically been concerned with both "gaps" –that is, with developing a socially engaged program of music participation while simultaneously training musicians to be practitioners within such a program. Against the complex backdrop of policies and philosophies described above, Sage Gateshead (Sage Gateshead, n.d.) emerged in the early twenty-first century as a regional music centre for the northeast of England. Employing its first staff in 2000 and opening the doors of its Norman Foster–designed iconic building in December 2005, it rode the policy wave of the social impact of arts and culture to achieve a position of national significance as a cultural institution. The organization has always articulated its artistic program as *equally* performance and participation, emphasizing the aesthetic dimension of music's power in its hosting of Royal Northern Sinfonia as its resident orchestra, alongside an ambitious learning and participation (L&P) program.

The evolution of the L&P program highlighted the need for a workforce of musicians of sufficient size and with the appropriate knowledge, skills, experience, and corresponding value base to deliver the organization's ambitions around music participation. This "gap" in the existing workforce provided the rationale for an equally ambitious musician training program, which started around 2003 with an innovative eighteen-month traineeship. By 2010, this had further inspired the establishment of two undergraduate music programs, including the UK's first BA (Hons) Community Music program alongside an established BMus (Hons) Jazz, Popular, and Commercial Music program, which was relocated to Sage Gateshead from a local FE college.

There is a certain paradox in seeing the "institution" as a site for social and cultural change. Cultural institutions might be considered some of the best examples of the "deficit model" of culture, often reinforcing the dominant paradigm that "high art" is more deserving of state support than the emergent heterodoxies outlined above. More specifically, recent reports bring into serious question the "impact of major cultural buildings" like Sage Gateshead on urban regeneration, owing to the fact that "the regeneration of places is usually accompanied by gentrification, the rise of the "experience economy," and the disruption and exclusion of communities as those who live there and produce there are forced out by rising property prices (Crossick & Kaszynska, 2016, p. 8).

In the current climate, there is therefore a certain measure of skepticism that ought to be applied to any claim about the efficacy of institutional approaches to broadening access to public funds for arts and culture. It is this uncertainty that qualifies any of the benefits I shall be going on to describe about this particular approach. Nevertheless, cultural institutions represent more dominant positions within the field of arts and culture, benefiting as they do from higher levels of financial support from governments. The rationale for this study is that institutional approaches to the thorny issues surrounding cultural access and participation can provide useful and valid insights into how the field of arts and culture is responding generally to the disruptions it currently faces.

The scope of this study is centred around the community of music practitioners that has emerged from within Sage Gateshead as a result of its musician training programs. The community members include established musicians – performers, teachers, producers – alongside trainees, students, and alumni of both undergraduate programs and its traineeship and advanced traineeship. The purpose of the study is to build up more detailed knowledge of the attributes – skills, values, attitudes – of those musicians who have benefited from Sage Gateshead's musician training programs and to understand how these attributes might be changing over time in response to the cultural shifts described above. In particular, it is to understand how musicians' attitudes toward the social value of music – through teaching, facilitation, community music, health musicking (Stige, 2012), and so on – might be changing over time in response to the waning of music's economic value (i.e., collapsed sales of recordings, performance fees, and so no).

Method

The study was conducted as progressive cycles of "action research" (McNiff, 2013) over three years (2015–18), with elements of participatory action research (PAR) (Chevalier & Buckles, 2013) informing research design. Undergraduate students in Sage Gateshead undergraduate music programs – that is, musicians "emerging" into professional practice – co-designed an online survey as the basis for interviewing more experienced musicians within the broader regional community of practice. This survey was administered in a number of ways, depending on circumstances:

+ As a Google form that respondents completed on their own time.
+ As the basis for a structured interview between the undergraduate student and the respondent.
+ As the basis for a semi-structured interview between the undergraduate student and the respondent.

There is therefore an inevitable lack of consistency in the way that data were collected. However, the rationale for this flexible approach to data collection was that it made it possible to capture the more experienced musicians' views in as ecologically valid a way as possible. Having selected their subjects, students were invited to consider what would be the best way for them to collect the data, and these approaches varied considerably. Some respondents were happy to undertake the online questionnaire on their own time, while others preferred to have a more informal chat about their practice with the student, using the survey questions as prompts.

"Purposive sampling" (Plowright, 2010, p. 42) was used as the basis for data collection. Through discussion with lecturers, undergraduate students identified other musicians who had influenced their own development, and these individuals received personal invitations to participate. Justification for this approach lies in the different ways in which practitioners inhabit the field:

> Where a smaller scale project is envisaged, then data about the most significant individuals and institutions in the social space are the most useful, because these field participants occupy the most dominant field positions, and therefore also occupy positions within the field of power, where they are able to determine the value of field-specific capitals. Here, the data collected are not a statistical sample, but should be a particular subset of individuals selected because of their powerful influence on the field. (Hardy, 2008b, p. 240)

The ways in which those individuals perceived to be occupying a strong position within the field inhabit that position – that is, their practices, behaviours, attitudes, and values – is useful situated knowledge for "newcomers" to the field about its "old-timers" (Lave & Wenger, 1991), for it helps them reflect on their own position and develop ways of strengthening it. Therefore, besides asking for basic demographic information, we invited respondents to reflect in their own words on their career ("What do you do?") and how they have come to be where they are in their career ("How did you get to be where you are now?"). Through the subjective narrative accounts that emerged, we hoped to be able to build an understanding of the professional lives of more established musicians from the perspective not just of their "professional capital career creativities" (Bennett & Burnard, 2016, p. 124) that is, "field-specific strategies, which take on a new significance or career advantage" (p. 124), such as their musical/pedagogic skills, but also their "human capital career creativities," as identified and defined in the following terms:

1. Community-building creativity, which represents professional networks and communities of practice.

2. Inspiration-forming creativity, which includes role models, inspirational figures and supporters.

3. Career-positioning creativity, which represents the creation of capacity through interest, recognition, new markets (including market "engagement"), and professional learning.

4. Bestowed gift-giving creativity, which refers to capital that is "given away" in forms such as mentorship and pro bono work. (Bennett & Burnard, 2016, p. 126)

Supplementary questions were asked of respondents about their professional networks; their own inspiration; their qualifications, dispositions, skills, and values; and their attitudes toward professional learning and working without financial reward. We also invited respondents to reflect on the relative weighting of different aspects of their portfolio (e.g., performance, teaching, composition, and production) in terms of time spent on each activity and proportion of income arising from each activity.

Emergent Themes

At the time of writing, thirty-three musicians had completed the survey. Twenty-five of them (76 percent of responses) spent at least five days a week on their music work. Effectively, then, the majority of respondents were full-time musicians. The remaining eight respondents spent no fewer than three days per week on music-related activities.

Professional capital career creativities. A range of musical skills were identified as contributing to respondents' positions of strength within the field of music, especially "aural perception, a good knowledge of music theory," and "the idiosyncrasies of stylistic playin'," alongside "significant confidence on an instrument" or "being very good at the particular musical activities that I do." Domain-specific skills were mentioned – that is, skills of technical production on a voice, instrument, or mixing desk. Sight reading, good rhythmic skills, and "the ability to write and arrange music to suit your group" were also highlighted. Musical flexibility emerged as a core creativity. This included:

+ experience playing with many people, being in many different musical situations with people more experienced than yourself;
+ flexibility in approach to suit the needs of the people you work with; and
+ being able to work with a variety of settings, genres, and ages.

A critical understanding of the context of practice was emphasized, including a "comprehensive knowledge of relevant research, sound pedagogical/teaching methods and skills," and the practical skills of "navigating new software and online platforms."

Many respondents talked of the intrinsic rewards of international touring or "writing charts that occasionally I get to hear played by great musicians." Those respondents whose portfolios included music production spoke highly of the satisfaction gained from having "contributed to great programs at the world's leading broadcaster," or "hearing recordings I've worked really hard on, on national radio, TV, etc. It makes it all worthwhile."

Human capital career creativities. Responses to questions about human capital career creativities drew a range of responses, which, when taken together, appear to indicate significant shifts in musician identity, which in turn facilitate the development of authentic socially engaged practices in service of more marginalized members of society.

Respondents highlighted the importance of pro-social professional dispositions such as "being reliable, always on time and prepared," alongside the importance of an "easy-going friendly nature" and an "ability to demonstrate kindness and compassion," as well as to "enthuse and engage." An "understanding of human behaviour" and the interpersonal skills of working with a "wide variety of people and personalities" were balanced with the need to foster one's own "creativity, self-care, resilience, determination, discipline (to practice / learn repertoire)."

Career-positioning creativity. All of the musicians who responded to the survey worked across more than one sub-field of music, highlighting the importance of "portfolio" working as a way of maintaining a stable position in an unstable environment. In other words, they spread their time across a number of music-related activities. Respondents' time was divided among numerous

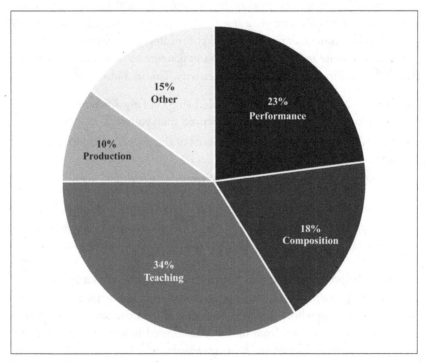

Figure 4.1 Time Spent on Musical Activities

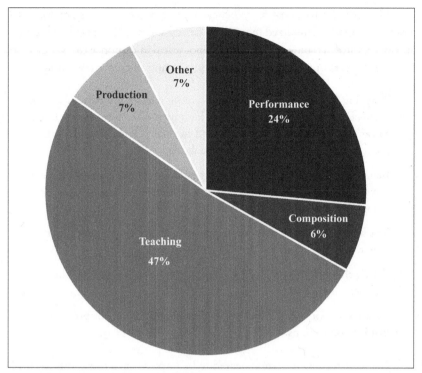

Figure 4.2 Income Derived from Musical Activities

activities as shown in Figure 4.1, while the income derived from these activities broke down in the proportions show in Figure 4.2.

Some respondents ($n = 29$) were willing to share information about their earnings. In relation to the UK average annual income (around £26,000 per annum), 5 respondents (17 percent of the sample) earned "about the average," with 8 (28 percent) earning more than that, and 16 (55 percent) earning less than or significantly less than the national average annual income.

For these musicians, perhaps the clearest point to note is the centrality of teaching, understood here as a broad range of pedagogical activities in formal, non-formal, and informal settings – within their portfolios. Collectively, these account for the most time spent on musical activities besides being their main source of income. Furthermore, while the relationship between time spent on different musical activities and income derived from those activities is roughly equal most of the time, for teaching it is significantly higher (47 percent of income for 34 percent of activity), suggesting that for these musicians, teaching is an effective means of stabilizing income across a broad portfolio of professional work.

However, for the most part, the teaching aspects of people's portfolios are not merely instrumentalized means to financial stability. The teaching is clearly its own reward, as some of these comments reveal in response to the question, "Which aspects of your current career do you find the most rewarding?":

> Teaching is ultimately the most rewarding part of my current career, particularly the 1-1 instrumental tuition / mentoring where you are able to get alongside students and respond to their particular needs at that point in their personal and professional development.

> Being able to introduce music to many different people in many different ways. Seeing the response, growth and enjoyment that people get from doing music.

> Teaching and leading sessions, supporting others to get more joy from music.

> Seeing children enjoy making music and their enthusiasm when they see me enter their school.

> Creating art with people, finding insight and meaning, seeing progression, making connections.

Many of the values that appeared to be important to this group of musicians seemed to derive from their teaching responsibilities. In addition to more universal dispositions about flexibility, patience, openness, fun, a positive mindset, and a "determination to succeed in a competitive and difficult industry," respondents talked with some passion about the values that underpinned their educational work:

+ An egalitarian approach and view that music is for everyone rather than for the "talented" few, along with a strong belief in the sociological and personal benefits of making music.

+ To understand the role music has played in people's lives in a broader historical context, rather than a purely modern perspective. To believe that everyone has something musically interesting to offer regardless of how far into the musical journey they are. To support people taking chances, creating new things and staying true to a meaningful underpinning of their music.

+ It's important that participants shape and have a say in the way they learn.

+ Compassion, opportunity for all, diversity (of approach, understanding, perspective, expectations, cultures, material, contexts) ... beauty / aesthetic enjoyment, valuing relationship, social consciousness, meaning making, humility, bravery.

These responses reveal a significant shift in attitudes toward teaching as well as the role artists have to play in facilitating cultural participation. Historically, teaching may have been seen by artists as a "negation" of professional identity (Bennett, 2012; Camlin, 2016c, p. 45), yet these musicians clearly derive a high degree of personal artistic fulfillment through their teaching work. Being able to view educational/participatory work as integral to an artistic identity clearly helps them think outside the traditional constraints of "performance" and "teaching" as discrete fields.

Challenges of portfolio working. Some respondents recognized the challenges of balancing these different aspects of their professional identity:

> Initially community music work was very rewarding – seeing young people embrace the music, bond as a group, and flourish as musicians. At a certain point I stopped enjoying the teaching – I was using all my energy to enable other people's creativity but not stimulating my own. I formed my current company to enable me to work with other professionals creating new work in a variety of contexts, hardly any of which now involve community music.

Another respondent said:

> There isn't enough money in teaching for me to support myself without doing it full-time. There are not enough opportunities in music performance full-time, and the few there are often require creative compromise. Balancing both teaching and performing is quite unreliable, but is the only way to ensure that my life as a musician encompasses the aspects of music I find to be important.

The respondents spoke of the inherent challenges of professional life at the highest levels of practice – for example, "sight reading sessions, orchestral recordings, depping for the first time on a new show in the West End" – as well as the challenges of balancing the various aspects of a portfolio career while "keeping my approach fresh." This highlighted the often precarious nature of this kind of professional life:

Because I am self-employed obviously the infrequent work and pay plus the alternative work patterns make life a challenge.

Managing the different demands upon my time (professional and personal).

The constant hustle to get projects off the ground, raise money, find time for R&D and think two steps ahead.

The most challenging part of my career has historically been the uncertainty of ongoing work twinned with the strange hours that one has to lead as a musician.

The bureaucratic/economic elements of teaching and playing in bands.

The short-term contracts and low pay.

Carving out enough routine time to keep on top of things like emails and invoicing.

One respondent noted that because "work is sporadic, and income difficult to predict, it's too easy to take on too much work." This sentiment was echoed by another: "I'm often rushing from one session to another (and trying to fit around my family life) so some days can get quite full on." The challenges of balancing professional responsibilities with a healthy personal/family life was a common theme:

Working as a musician can be very lonely. Despite the fact I work with people, I don't always feel like I have colleagues due to the nature of the work. There is a lot of travelling involved and I work very erratic hours.

Balancing parenthood with gigging and rehearsing schedules, work expectations.

Being a freelancer with no regular jobs and 3 kids!

It makes home life different and a challenge with relationships and roots.

For some respondents, there were inherent frustrations about the systems they were required to work within, including "frustration with political agendas overwriting academic research when it comes to curriculum or organizational priorities," as well as "financial pressures and lack of access to progress with academic study / access to training / restraints on time."

Community-building creativity. Thirty-one of thirty-three respondents (94 percent) felt that the various professional networks they were part of were either "important" or "very important" to their career. These included online networks based around music (e.g., forums and project websites as well as Facebook groups relating to specialist areas of interest). Professional associations were another important means to feel part of a wider community, with respondents citing PRS, GEMA, Musicians Union, and Sound Sense as valuable professional networks. One respondent elaborated:

> Through work with Musical Futures I developed an incredibly strong and influential network of academics, musicians, teachers, and hub leaders on twitter who have allowed me to get advice and many work opportunities.

More significant, however, were the more informal networks of musicians that respondents encountered as active members of a wider "community of practice" – a community that included current band members, other artists on the local music "scene," "colleagues who I worked with at Sage Gateshead who are now freelance," and "key significant teachers [who] have become long term friends and colleagues," as well as networks of local musicians developed out of "connections made at university whilst studying." As one respondent noted,

> informal networks get created through usually playing with others in function bands, jazz combos. You could be the best player in the world but if you're not out playing it's of little use. Even my production work stems from knowing these players.

These informal networks may coalesce around musical styles, instrument-specific connections, or cross-disciplinary engagements such as theatre work. Respondents also mentioned "international connections with those I've created projects with," as well as "artists I meet at festivals and gigs."

Inspiration-forming creativity. As well as the diverse range of individual famous musicians, teachers, composers, artists, songs, and genres cited as inspiration, respondents identified significant family members and other members of their "community of practice" – at all levels of proficiency – as providing inspiration (e.g., "my colleagues and people I work with, band mates; people around me, participants; the children, families & teachers I work with"). One respondent commented,

> I am inspired by musicians (and non-musicians) who dedicate themselves to doing their "own thing" and being true to themselves, whether it's a high level of proficiency in a given genre or simply giving it everything whilst only knowing 2 chords!

This recognition of the inspirational potential of "everyday creativity" (Hunter, Micklem, & 64 Million Artists, 2016) represents a much more culturally democratic view of inspiration than might be found in a more traditional mindset of the "aesthetic" value of music, and is further indication of the democratic values that underpin more emancipatory artistic practices.

Bestowed gift-giving creativity. On the question of working without financial reward, respondents had much to say, highlighting the complex and highly situated nature of "pro bono" work. All respondents acknowledged the need to work for free – and sometimes the value of it – while also highlighting the sensitive and complex nature of these kinds of decisions. One respondent summed this up by acknowledging, "it's complex for different people for different reasons, I'm happy to work without financial payment at times." Leaving aside charitable causes, reasons given for doing "pro bono" work usually included "some kind of commensurate return":

If I feel it is progressing my skill level.

When it is viewed as a donation, as it is worth money.

When the performance is an unconstrained expression of my own relationship with music.

When I believe that the music is my contribution to the ongoing story of human music making.

Repertoire sharing / training.

As an incentive to continue the work / project in a paid capacity.

As an opportunity to "assess" the client and see what will work best.

To build up contacts or a reputation.

Artistically / creatively fulfilling.

Working with great people.

Supporting family members.

The careful balance of "reciprocity" in "pro bono", transactions was clearly explained by one respondent who was "very happy to [work for free], provided it is received by someone who understands the offer. Some people will take your blood if you let them, so I choose who I give my time to for free carefully."

Some respondents noted that their attitude toward working for free changed as they became more established, and especially as they started their own families:

> I think you have to start out this way to let people know you can deliver what they want. However, it's also important to value your ability and have the courage to progress into paid work. It's not easy to decide when this happens but it definitely has to. Once you're into the realm of charging people for your time, it's probably not wise to go back. Especially if word travels that people are getting freebies and angering your paying clients.

> Having kids means I really need to prioritise my time so I don't really play in bands for free (or very little reward) any more unless for example it's a festival the whole family want to go to.

Many respondents spoke favourably about giving their time for free in mentoring situations, perhaps because of their involvement in a community of practice where they had once been on the receiving end of others' time and attention:

> Things like mentoring and networking are particularly valid if it is a two-way process and you are getting out as well as putting in.

> Happy to mentor students/emerging practitioners pro bono in some circumstances & provide free "tasters" to build new work opportunities but would expect to be paid in other contexts.

> In terms of mentoring – this I don't view as work. It is a learning experience for both the mentor and the mentee and adds to both's CV. Bringing money in may taint the relationship. I currently mentor a couple of younger, less experienced people in the industry and I do it because I enjoy being a part of their career and learn a lot from mentoring them myself.

This willingness to work for free under some circumstances recognizes the complexities of the ways in which "cultural capital (and increasingly social capital) takes precedence as the medium for expression of field interests" (Grenfell, 2012, p. 156), and may also indicate a willingness to engage in the "gift" economy (Hyde, 2012) as a viable alternative to financial transactions. As music has been the first field in the arts to experience such profound disruption to its economic value (Anderson, 2009, p. 32), these changes in practitioner dispositions toward a reconstituted field – where the relative values of different kinds of capital are in flux – are significant. They provide valuable insight into how the values and attitudes of music practitioners are changing in response to changes in the field, in turn providing useful insights into how the field of music itself may evolve.

Discussion

In this section, I discuss the ramifications of the closure of Sage Gateshead's higher education (HE) music programs as they relate to the changing mindsets of musicians to encompass more socially engaged practices and attitudes, and the importance of "vigilance" in how we might proceed to a more democratic and socially engaged musical future.

Program closure. The undergraduate programs at Sage Gateshead became a casualty of the unfolding hysteresis in the field of music when the decision was made in 2017 to close them. Despite their regional importance and their evident success as a means of musician training, the collaborative business model with University of Sunderland was judged to be underperforming against the collective expectations of both institutions to make a significant financial profit from them, and their subsequent closure became a business decision owing to low recruitment in an increasingly competitive market. Though it was ostensibly a short-term tactic to improve financial performance, a more critical analysis might also view their closure as a "turn"" toward a more conservative institutional approach to musician training generally, representing a reinforcement of a more orthodox understanding of music and its historical traditions, and perhaps even a conservative backlash against the need for more progressive solutions to the inequalities of cultural participation. As this disappointing decision reveals, bridging the gaps in cultural participation through progressive approaches to musician training is therefore not something we should take for granted. During the ongoing hysteresis in music, we might reasonably expect similar casualties. The pressures on HE music departments is intense, and their ongoing existence more precarious, especially in the light of the sinking of the music curriculum further down the educational supply chain (Jeffreys, 2018; Romer, n.d.).

As a consequence, capturing the knowledge that is developed through more socially engaged programs, in order to influence future developments in musician training, is likely to prove a complex and challenging task, given their precarity. In the case of the Sage Gateshead programs, their closure also closes the window of opportunity for a more longitudinal study of evolving regional musician "habitus" over time. However, the insights realized through more than a decade of institutionalized "situated learning" in music at HE are still valuable, as they offer a glimpse of the attitudinal shifts required of musicians in response to the rediscovered value of music as a holistic practice, not just a performance art. It is to the importance of these attitudinal shifts that I now turn.

Musical futures. The uncertain world of the future calls on us to develop a more sophisticated understanding of the value of music. Perhaps the only thing we can be certain of about our future is that it is much less certain than at any time in the last seventy years, and mutuality, trust, and cooperation – the very qualities and values that are engendered through musical participation (Tarr, Launay, & Dunbar, 2014) – are going to become increasingly important values to guide our citizenship. A combination of factors means that the world of 2050 will be a radically different one than the one we currently experience (Camlin, 2016a; OECD, n.d.; United Nations, 2015). The projected 30 percent increase in global population by 2050, attendant falls in potential support ratio (PSR) and fertility rates, aging populations facing increasing dementia rates, the impact of global warming, mass migration, the decline of global economic growth rates, rises in global earning inequality, the computerization of employment, increases in depression rates (OECD, n.d.; United Nations, 2015) – all of these factors point to an increasingly uncertain future for us as a species. As competition for increasingly scarce global resources intensifies, we can expect the mobilization of "divisive and conflicting identities" (Appiah, 2016) to intensify as well, leading to an increasingly fragile situation. We might see the recent political upheavals in Western liberal democracy – the rise of populist leaders, the current political turmoil in France, Spain, the UK, and elsewhere – as evidence that these more partisan identities along racial, religious, class, and territorial lines are becoming mobilized in the competition for what appear to be increasingly scarce resources.

What it will mean to be a musician in such an uncertain future is beyond anyone's comprehension. However, if music is to make any kind of valuable contribution toward mediating the demographic, economic, and environmental challenges facing us over the next thirty years, the only thing we can be certain of is that our old ways of thinking about and "doing" music will not be sufficient. These societal challenges call on us to broaden our understanding of music's power from the primacy of its economic value to a more socially engaged and holistic understanding of how it might condition and mediate everyday experience. Changing attitudes toward music and its value to people and society is not something that will happen overnight, especially within communities of musicians, who perhaps have the most to lose from such a reconstitution. For some of the respondents in the current study, for example, their teaching work may come across more as a pragmatic approach to stabilizing their income in a precarious situation, rather than as something "socially engaged" – as motivated by the *economic* value of teaching rather than anything more culturally democratic.

However, I also feel that the responses of musicians to the questions in the survey give us some cause for hope, representing as they do a cultural shift in understanding the value of teaching as part of a professional portfolio. They also represent a shift in mindset, one that is occurring as a result of the dialogue, disagreement, and reflection that goes on naturally within a "community of practice" in response to changes in the field which constitutes it. It is within these emergent communities of more socially engaged practice that the reconstituted value of music – as a holistic practice, not just a performance art – will be (and is now being) realized. Socially engaged musicians – agents working in solidarity with the socially marginalized – are the most influential voices in this discourse because they represent values furthest from the "old" way of thinking of music's value (i.e., in primarily economic terms). Hence, participation in the kinds of "communities of practice" described in this chapter, like the activities they produce, "engender a kind of egalitarian consensus building" (Turino, 2016), thus promoting more humanistic values. Membership in this kind of community of practice provides a valuable space for the community's members to experience "values and practices diametrically opposed to a capitalist ethos" (Turino, 2016); in this way, it provides them with a way to exist in a more socially just way with one another. It is at least partly for this reason that I think this kind of approach has value and should be promoted.

Vigilance. We should not assume that the evolution of the field of music into a more holistic and socially engaged practice will occur naturally, without critical interrogation of many of the assumptions that underpin such practice by its practitioners, audiences, and participants. Current research suggests that the policy of funding cultural institutions to deliver more democratic means of access to publicly funded arts and culture "has reached a dead end" (Wilson, Gross, & Bull, 2017, p. 19). If we accept that our best efforts to broaden cultural participation over the last twenty years have largely failed (Neelands et al., 2015), we must also accept that we need to do something differently about it in the future. In this instance, doing something differently entails being more critical of the assumptions that have underpinned past efforts at broadening access. In order to develop a critical appreciation, not just of the practices we seek to understand, but also of how our own social existence may "condition" our responses to those practices, we need to be more "vigilant" in our understanding, by which I mean more critical of our assumptions, approaches, and positions of privilege. It is possible to see such interrogation emerging within the various utterances captured in this study, as practitioners negotiate a variety of different musical identities as producers, teachers, and performers, but there is also clearly some way to go.

First degree vigilance. The "art for art's sake" position is perhaps a good example of what Bourdieu, Chamboredon, and Passeron (1991) term "first degree monitoring," or "waiting for the expected or even alertness to the unexpected" (Grenfell, 2012). This is an essentially uncritical stance, which might be characterized as, "we know that art is good for us, and therefore if we create more great art that more people have access to, the world will be a better place." The basic premise of the argument – "art is good for us" or more specifically, "the art that is good for me is good for everyone" – is not up for discussion, and to challenge it is to be heretical. Perhaps the reason why some flagship cultural projects collect no baseline data or longitudinal studies of their impact is that to do so would be to implicitly critique the foundations of deeply held beliefs about what art is and what it does. This position is intellectually lazy and needs challenging whenever we encounter it, especially in our own work.

Second degree vigilance. Second degree vigilance – or "spelling out one's methods and adopting the methodic vigilance that is essential for the methodical application of methods" (Grenfell, 2012) – begins to recognize the complexity of social situations and the corresponding need to question methods of investigation that appear simply to reinforce pre-existing beliefs and assumptions. Many attempts at broadening cultural access flounder because they become locked in the discourse of the "democratisation of culture" and how predefined ideas about culture may be made more accessible. The UK government's recent White Paper on culture is perhaps a good example, for it suggests that the purpose of cultural policy is to "increase participation in culture, especially among those who are currently excluded from the opportunities that culture has to offer" (DCMS, 2016).

This kind of approach represents the hegemonic privileging of a "rational community" (Biesta, 2006) of culture – that is, a community that already exists and has been canonized through the act of "distinction" (Bourdieu, 1979), and whose purpose is not only to reproduce itself but also to broaden the consensus around what distinguishes it from other forms of cultural expression. Extending the boundaries of who can be included in this kind of cultural community seems like a democratic ideal, because of the access it provides to dominant forms of cultural expression, but it raises some important challenges. Acknowledging the complexity of cultural participation (i.e., rather than the easily understood mantra of "great art for everyone"), recognizing that certain types of art might be "good" – in a variety of ways – for certain people, under certain conditions, is simply not as easily understood; it doesn't make for a simple sound bite. The reality of cultural participation is more complex than it at first appears, and acknowledging that complexity makes it less straight-forward to comprehend.

Moreover, as the Warwick Report shows, the "deficit model" of culture doesn't really work in terms of doing the thing it says it wants to do, which is, provide greater access to cultural participation for those excluded from the "rational community" of culture. The "8 percent" figure quoted earlier should really give us pause for thought. If access to cultural participation has not been democratized over the past two decades, despite our best efforts, we really need to be doing something differently, and this change has to start with how we train cultural practitioners.

Third degree vigilance. It is only when we recognize that much of the discourse about cultural participation is formed and framed *within* the "rational com-munity" of culture that we can begin to understand why so many people are excluded from it. What Biesta terms the "other" community – that is, those excluded from the "rational community" of culture – is in fact the majority of the population. While the rational community of culture is formed by con-sensus over what qualifies as "Great Art," the only thing that unites this "other," excluded community is the fact that it doesn't share the commonalities of the "rational community." Alphonso Lingis refers to this community as "the com-munity of those who have nothing in common" (Biesta, 2006, p. 64; Lingis, 1994). Understanding this "other" community – outside of the experience of the elite consumers of publicly funded art and culture – means breaking free of the constraints of the "rational community" and critically analyzing the social conditions that underpin the participation – or rather, the apparent non-participation – of the constituents of this 'other' one:

> Only with third-degree monitoring does distinctively epistemologi-cal inquiry appear; and this alone can break free from the "absolute of method." The polemical action of scientific reason cannot be given its full force unless the "psychoanalysis of the scientific mind" is taken further by an analysis of the social conditions in which sociological works are produced. (Bourdieu et al., 1991, p. 3)

Crucially, the place of encounter between the "rational community" and the "community of those who have nothing in common" is not an institutional one. The place of genuinely human encounter is where we meet one another as unique, singular individuals, not as representatives of some wider community.

In short, the sharp end of cultural inclusion is the encounter between a more socially engaged artist and a less culturally engaged individual, and it is the relationship they form that transforms cultural experience, not just participation in the art form. Each party needs to be willing to encounter the other, and it therefore falls to the practitioner to prepare for such an encounter by questioning and challenging his or her own assumptions about cultural participation, in order to "meet" the "other" with as few cultural expectations as possible. These questions and challenges about assumed cultural value can all be explored through participation in a "community of practice," highlighting the need for the kinds of programs discussed in this chapter.

Acknowledging the validity of the experience of individuals from outside the "rational community" disrupts the "deficit model" of culture by emphasizing the different ways in which culture can be enacted or participated in, while preserving the value of cultural expression as a universal human "right." Such an acknowledgment leads to what Bakhtin termed a "plurality of independent and unmerged voices and consciousnesses, a genuine polyphony of fully valid voices" (Bakhtin, 1984, p. 6). Besides strengthening existing practice, the "community of practice" model of musician training outlined herein supports the emergence of such heterodoxical positions; the individual testimonies of respondents indicate that even within such a small sample of practitioners, the sheer diversity of their practices is perhaps what unites them.

Conclusion

Despite our best efforts, the gap in access to subsidized means of cultural participation between the haves and the have-nots still exists. In fact, it's growing. The idea that we can rely on cultural institutions to lead on implementing a more democratic form of cultural access is not borne out by the evidence, and this places a severe limitation on the emergent findings of this study. Bridging the gap between the 8 percent of the UK population who consume 44 percent of attendances at live music events (Neelands, University of Warwick, and Hargreaves, 2015) and the rest of the population may be something that institutions are not best-placed to accomplish.

This particular study reveals that the real site for changes in cultural participation may lie at a more individual level than institutions may be naturally disposed to inhabit. As institutions represent the most distinguished forms of capital of the "rational community" of culture, developing more democratic forms of cultural engagement will requires them to "break" (Bourdieu et al., 1991) from their own world view to encourage the dissensual voices of the "community of those who have nothing in common" (Lingis, 1994) to contribute to cultural discourse and policy. Either that, or such development has to take place outside of the institution altogether. As Etienne Wenger suggests:

> Institutionalization must be in the service of practice. Practice is where policies, procedures, authority relations, and other institutional structures become effective. Institutionalization in itself cannot make anything happen. Communities of practice are the locus of "real work." Their practices are where the formal rests on the informal, where the visible counts on the invisible, where the official meets the everyday. Designing processes and policies is important, but in the end it is practice that produces results, not the processes and policies. The challenge is to support rather than displace the knowledgeability of practice. With a lack of institutionalization there may not be enough material to hold the organization together. Conversely, excessive institutionalization stalls the organization insofar as the practices end up serving the institutional apparatus, rather than the other way around. (Wenger, 1999, p. 243)

It is in the practices and approaches of individual artists or groups of artists operating with social and ethical intent – existing either within or outside of cultural institutions – that the sparks of cultural democracy are to be found. The democratic nature of locally based artist-led "communities of practice" that seek to re-create themselves by democratizing the means of cultural production in order to broaden cultural participation does support the call within the cultural democracy movement to resist seeing the institution as the natural site of a more emancipatory form of cultural production, and instead recognize the socially engaged artist as a more likely alternative.

The implications of this are considerable. How can the way cultural participation is funded and supported be restructured to privilege the practices of individual artists and groups of artists operating within ethical and technical constraints, rather than more institutionalized forms of cultural practice, which may be hamstrung by neoliberal ideology about consumption and economic value?

These are not just questions for funders and artists; they are also questions for institutions. Do cultural institutions still have a role to play in broadening cultural participation? Or have they demonstrated through their lack of "vigilance" in the use of public funds that their natural inclination is merely to re-create the cultural norms that qualify their dominant position in the field and reinforce inequitable access to public funds which support cultural participation? In short, are institutions best placed to be the agents that bring about such shifts in the means of cultural production and reproduction? Or is it time for a shift in cultural policy, to provide more opportunities for individual artists and groups of artists to bring about the changes in access to cultural participation that are needed to enable every citizen to lead a creative and fulfilling life?

The questions for the higher education sector are equally important. At what point do HE institutions need to confront the possibility that their cultural training programs are significant contributors to the unequal distribution of cultural participation, helping reinforce particular forms of cultural participation that perpetuate the inequalities of access they have aspired to overcome? And what would more emancipatory forms of artist training in HE look like?

While there are many similar programs to the ones developed at Sage Gateshead springing up around the world, there are lessons from at least the last twenty years that we still need to learn. If the current turn toward participatory practice emerges as a form of capital that musicians can use to strengthen their position in the field, it is perhaps inevitable that it is the habitus of already dominant players in the field that will adjust first, in order to occupy stronger field positions. After all, "it is the people who are richest in economic capital, cultural capital and social capital who are the first to head for new positions" (Bourdieu, 1996, p. 262). Ironically, there is therefore a risk that more privileged forms of participatory practice will come to dominate, to the exclusion of more culturally democratic forms.

Unless we are "vigilant" in the Bachelardian sense of critically analyzing the social conditions that underpin cultural participation, there is always a risk that institutionalized development of forms of cultural knowledge capital will reinforce and perpetuate the inequalities in cultural access and participation that our cultural and educational institutions say they have been working to overcome. To that end, it behoves us not simply to "mind the gap," but to be mindful *of* the gap — to be more "vigilant" of how it is constituted, and how our own practices might inadvertently reinforce it — if we are to bring about a more culturally democratic society. Finding new ways of "giving voice" to perspectives outside of the "rational community" of culture — for example, by supporting the emergence of more socially engaged communities of musical practice as described herein — continues to be an important way to bridge gaps in cultural participation.

CHAPTER 5

The Borders Are Open

Community Music in Higher Education

Glen Carruthers

BY WAY OF BACKGROUND, we founded the Laurier Center for Music in the Community in 2008, introduced the graduate program in 2013, and then just last year introduced the undergraduate program in community music. So we really have been exploring the area of community music as an institution for quite some time now.

When I initially proposed a title for this chapter – "The Borders Are Open: Community Music in Institutional Settings" – I committed to addressing the place of music in educational institutions. It is typical of my myopic view of the world that when I think of an institutional setting I think of a university. What other institutions could there possibly be in the universe other than universities? Of course, after I thought about this a little bit, I realized the title is entirely misleading. I *am* going to talk about music in universities. But universities are institutions and it is interesting to consider that others in this book offer perspectives on different institutional settings, such as correctional and health care facilities.

There is in institutions a kind of fluidity of intent and purpose. We set out to do one thing and end up doing another. We think we're doing one thing and are, in fact, doing another. Also, between institutional settings, such as universities and correctional facilities, there is a lot of subtle overlap. I am sure some students feel incarcerated here at Laurier! Fair enough. We also know that much deep learning takes place in incarcerated settings, and in that regard, there are some wonderful programs in which Laurier is involved. One is called Walls to Bridges and explores the kind of deep learning that occurs when prison populations learn alongside the non-incarcerated population. But when I thought about institutions and what they set out to do and what they really do, I decided that the fluidity is very positive. By their nature, institutions are about order. They propagate order. In some cases, this order is explicit. Certainly in correctional facilities you have walls, you have barbed wire, guards, and so forth. Universities are much more subtle than that and, in some ways, perhaps more insidious. The kinds of boundaries that are a part of who we are in the universities are not always easily perceived. One needs to think about these things.

We have in music schools obvious disciplinary boundaries. Students will take theory for an hour and have ten minutes off and then take music history for an hour and have ten minutes off and then take something else. We have stylistic boundaries, of course. Some universities concentrate on popular music, others on jazz, and others on classical music. There are also boundaries in terms of student populations, and this is something about which I have written before (2005; 2012). We have a process whereby prospective students are put through a kind of sieve and we say to some applicants, "Yes, you can come and be part of our institution," and to others, "No, you can't be part of our institution." Once the students are in the system, we have a tendency to replace the sieve with a funnel and stream some students into music theory, some students into music therapy, some students into community music, and so forth.

There are also boundaries of intent and purpose. This is something we talk about all the time these days. When I started in the university system a very long time ago, it seemed that what we were doing was self-evident. We rarely had to talk about it because it was self-evident. We were learning about music. But now there is such emphasis on the part of government, parents, and students themselves on employability, training for careers, and the like, that all of a sudden much of what we thought was self-evident is no longer self-evident. That raises a big question. What is the purpose of a music school within a university? If we acknowledge that a university is an institution set apart from our society, in some respects the music school is a kind of microcosm set apart from the university.

So, we have a kind of cloistered atmosphere within the institution, which is very good for some students and not so good for others. The danger is that any time we have boundaries, any time we have borders, we have insiders and we have outsiders. Insiders will generally feel a kind of comfort, they'll feel a sense of trust, because they're part of the group. Those on the outside experience a kind of discomfort and a kind of distrust. And so, one of the things that I ask as the dean, and that I think about a lot, is how do we break down these borders that are (in a sense) intrinsic to our institutions? I suppose one can also ask, "Why is that even important?"

Someone that I read quite a bit, Marshall McLuhan, is I believe a great, great thinker who was much misunderstood (as are many great, great thinkers) in his own time. In the years since his death in 1980, there has been considerable scholarship across multiple disciplines focusing on Marshall McLuhan. Here is a quote from McLuhan that is packed with layers. People "on frontiers, whether of time or space, abandon their previous identities. Neighborhood gives identity, frontiers snatch it away" (1970, p. 44). When you think about what he's saying here it's ironic, because neighbourhood is generally something we consider to be a good thing. An identity is something we consider to be a good thing. But McLuhan is saying that if we want to move forward, we have to challenge our suppositions about identity. We have to challenge our suppositions about who we are, to leave the comfort of our neighbourhood and move beyond it. I have very few regrets in my life, but I often tell my students, "You know what, if I could do this all over again, the only thing I would do differently is that I would have stepped outside my comfort zone a little more often when I was younger." It gets harder to do as time goes on. And so, I think stepping outside our institutional comfort zone is necessary, and it's simply symptomatic of a kind of stepping outside our comfort zones generally that is a process in which we all need to engage. Sometimes this will occur naturally, but often it needs to be cultivated purposefully.

The Facebook community is a very good example of the kind of comfort I'm talking about. We "friend" our friends and then we see what our friends think. And if you have friends like I do, they're in large part friends because they think the way I do. So, you come to have a kind of comfort, a sense of trust, about the world around you. If my friends had determined the outcome of the American election it would have been a very different outcome than what actually happened. If you looked at my Facebook feed you would think it inconceivable that Donald Trump won the election. So there must be a hell of a lot of people whose Facebook feeds don't look like mine. And I think that it's dangerous for us not to be aware of that difference. We need to step beyond the confines we establish for ourselves, explore what is out there, so that we're not blindsided like so many of us were by the results of the American election.

César Aira, one of Argentina's great writers, wrote a wonderful book called *Ghosts*. In that book he describes the Umbutu, which is a pygmy tribe of central Africa. They're a nomadic tribe. They move around and they build huts:

> The huts are isotopic shells in which an opening can be made anywhere. The Umbutu make just one opening, a door facing the neighbors they like best. Say the lady of the house is cross with her neighbor for some reason or other, no problem. They block off the door, and they open up another

one facing the neighbour on the other side. The researchers who have observed this system, failed to draw the logical conclusion. The house of a truly sociable Umbutu would be all doors and so not a house at all. Conversely, a finished and complete construction presupposes hostility. (Aira, 2008, p. 59)

When I read – you might do the same thing I do – I write things down that are of interest to me and I keep a record of them. I read *Ghosts* many years ago, but clearly this description of the Umbutu struck a responsive chord and it came back to me in preparation for this talk. I believe that universities, and institutions like universities, especially music schools, are historically based on hostility. They presuppose hostility. They presuppose otherness. They presuppose there are people who belong and people who do not belong. That hostility is at the core of our public institutions and of our universities in particular, and this is something that needs to be challenged. Why does it need to be challenged? Well, it's obviously the right thing to do. Any organization of an institution that has, as its foundation, hostility, needs to mitigate that hostility. Certainly, a publicly funded institution like a university in Canada cannot afford, in any sense, to encourage a sense of otherness on the part of students and people outside the institution. Universities depend on students and on public support for sustenance.

The mitigation of this inherent hostility is crucial to the survival to our university music programs. In the province of Ontario, applications to post-secondary music programs have declined dramatically over the past several years – by 33.8 percent between 2012 and 2015. Applications to mathematics programs have grown in the same proportion as applications to music have declined.

Table 5.1 Applications to university music programs in Ontario (Ontario Universities Application Centre, 2012–2015).

Ontario Applications by Program	2012–13	2013–14	2014–15	2015–16	Total
Music	−6.4	−6.1	−13.9	−7.4	−33.8
Engineering	+10.6	+13.8	+5.7	+4.5	+34.6
Arts	−1.7	−7.0	−7.1	+0.4	−15.4
Science	+7.2	+2.0	+2.0	+3.4	+14.6
Mathematics	+13.5	+6.6	+3.2	+10.5	+33.8
Agriculture	+13.5	+0.7	+13.2	+6.1	+33.5

I've taken elementary logic so I know how this works. The only logical conclusion is that all of the people who would have studied music a few years ago are now studying mathematics! Seriously, there is a message here. There's a message for people like me, who have responsibility for an institution or for a unit within a larger public institution.

"So, what's the problem?," is the question I ask. "Is it music? Is it something about music?" Well, we all know the answer to that. Absolutely, it's not music writ large. An extraordinary example from the Canadian context is the final tour of the Canadian band The Tragically Hip. This was a presentational event in one sense and participatory in another. The front man, Gord Downie, had been diagnosed with an inoperable brain tumour. The band, including Downie, responded by making a final tour across Canada. The final concert of that tour was broadcast. People gathered in squares all across Canada, in Waterloo Town Square here, to watch that final performance. The reason I bring this up is that the audience this performance reached in real time was 11.7 million. That's the number of people that watched that telecast – one third of the population of Canada. By contrast, 6.6 million enlightened Canadians voted for Justin Trudeau. So, in our most recent national election, 6.6 million people elected the prime minister, but 11.7 million people watched The Tragically Hip. Again, elementary logic tells us Gord Downie should be prime minister!

So, music is not the problem. I don't think people are the problem. Some of my best friends are musicians. They're lovely people. The cost? University costs money, there's no question about it, but there's no correlation between cost and the decline in applications to music. Applications are up dramatically in other disciplines. It's not the facilities – there have been some terrific new music buildings and performing arts facilities constructed recently. It's not music, it's not people, it's not costs, and it's not facilities. It has to be the curriculum. Curriculum at most Canadian universities reflects the hostility that I referred to earlier and that's the root of the problem faced by music programs today.

The following figure shows two examples chosen at random from the first-year music curriculum in Canadian universities. The research was done by friends of mine and is reproduced here with permission. They looked at music programs in Canada, looked at the core programs, and discovered what you see here. Performance elements – either ensemble or private study – take up a large proportion of the curriculum. Music theory and musicology (mainly music history) are the other major components. You see that the proportions vary slightly, but once you have music theory, and music history, and studio instruction, and ensembles, there's little to no room for anything else.

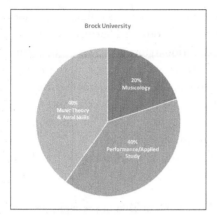
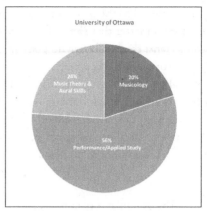

Figure 5.1 University music programs in Canada, proportion of core program devoted to musicology, theory & aural skills, performance/applied study. Comparison of Brock University and University of Ottawa. (Walker, Hennessy, Ingraham, Lewis, & Hammond, 2014).

In fact, what our programs comprise is largely talking about music that has been written by other people or learning to interpret music that has been written by other people. The curriculum is, in that sense, text-based – either musical scores or prose texts about music. When you walk down the halls here in the music building and you see the students weighted down with full backpacks, they probably have a banana and a laptop but the rest of it is books. It's extraordinary how text-driven our thinking within universities is about all things musical.

Those who know Marshall McLuhan know that I am circling back now to his work. McLuhan wrote a book called *The Gutenberg Galaxy: The Making of Typographic Man* in 1962. McLuhan, if you don't know his work, is very, very hard to read. *The Gutenberg Galaxy* is his most approachable book in many respects. Like many of you, I buy many of my books used, and in the copy that I bought of *The Gutenberg Galaxy*, I noticed only recently that someone has written inside the front cover, in large capital letters, the word "ESOTERIC." This is a good summary of McLuhan's work, although not necessarily of this particular book. The premise in *The Gutenberg Galaxy* is that we have become dependent on print media, and McLuhan believes that print media are suspect. They're limiting, they're restrictive, and they create regional cultures. He believes that electronic media are *delimiting* and create a global culture.

This raises the question, is there a parallel in the study of music? Has our reliance on notation within universities, for example, created a regional culture? If we take regional to mean narrow, as distinct from global, then I would say yes. In terms of admission to music programs, one of the primary determinants is and always has been the ability to read music. Those who read music fluently are admitted to the program and those who don't read music fluently are not. It doesn't matter that some of those people who don't read fluently are brilliant musicians; they will have no place in a traditional post-secondary music program (of the sort described in Figure 5.1). There will be no place for those individuals. It's the first step in discriminating one application from another. Beyond that, however, in McLuhan's terms, the meaning – in this case, notation – has, to a large extent, subsumed the message, which is music. Our attention has become focused on the visual extension of an aural medium.

Here's a quote that talks about the relationship between the eye and the ear:

> The dominant organ of sensory and social orientation in pre-alphabet societies was the ear – "hearing was believing." The phonetic alphabet forced the magic world of the *ear* to yield to the neutral world of the *eye*. Man was given an eye for an ear. (McLuhan & Fiore, 1967, p. 44)

McLuhan's message is a very interesting one: that the process of translating one medium into another can be a perilous one. This is the thesis of an article by Barton McLean from about twenty-five years ago. McLean's position is that music notation has the same limitations as print media or the phonetic alphabet. McLuhan and McLean agree on this.

McLean posits something that we all know to be true, which is, that a primary characteristic of humans is to be observed in their extension systems. There are a lot of examples. The most obvious – it's a cliché to talk about this one but it's such an obvious and helpful example – is food. We need food in order to survive, but we make an art of food. One only needs to go to a fine restaurant to know what an art food can be. Music begins with the premise that we need sounds to communicate and then we make of those sounds, art. So far so good – that's all fine and wonderful. It's the next step that is perilous. In order to share recipes, we write them down. In order to share music, we write it down. Then we act as our own intermediary or engage someone else as an intermediary – a chef, a professional musician – to translate text into an edible or audible form. Ironically, what was edible or audible to begin with has been translated into text and subsequently reconstituted. I think that universities and music programs have, to a large extent, put imaginative music-making at the disposal of comparatively few students. The composers and the improvisers, certainly. But many other music students in universities are focused on translating one medium into another. We're translating sound into notation and then we're translating it back – the outcome is twice removed from the original creative impulse.

Let's add yet another dimension to this discussion. I'm going to turn to the realm of literature, ironically, to talk about the limitations at best, or the perversity at worst, of the written word, of using written words or text to describe something that is not inherently text-driven. Here is something from Andreï Makine, the great author from Siberia, who sought political asylum in France and continues to write in France. He writes, "And I had already had my European education. I had already tasted the terrible Western temptation of the word.'What is not said does not exist!' this tempting voice whispered to me" (Makine, 1999, p. 183). And then from Penelope Fitzgerald, who, coincidentally, also uses lowercase letters for the title of her book *the blue flower*. " [B]ut she knew also that her uncle, like most men, believed that what had not been put into words, and indeed into written words, was not of great importance" (Fitzgerald, 1995, p. 142). The takeaway is that we in the West tend to become seduced by words. We become focused on what people are telling us, and not motivated or guided by our instincts, be they musical or otherwise.

There's more to this than meets the eye, to confuse the metaphor even further! Let's turn to Aldous Huxley's book about masturbating nuns, *The Devils of Loudun*. This is the book on which Penderecki bases his opera of the same title.

> "In the beginning was the word." So far as human history is concerned, the statement is perfectly true. Language is the instrument of man's progress out of animality, and language is the cause of man's deviation from animal innocence and animal conformity ... into madness and diabolism. Words are at once indispensable and fatal. (Huxley, 2009, p. 300)

I acknowledge that McLuhan may not believe that in the beginning was the word, but that's not the point. The point is that in the same way that text is not neutral or innocuous, neither is our reliance on text neutral or innocuous.

The notion that if something can't be described, it doesn't exist, is perilously close to a way of thinking that I've been introduced to over the last eight years or so – since coming to this university. That is, if you can't monetize something, it has no value. This focus on monetization and this reliance on texts is like a magician's use of misdirection. It focuses our attention away from what really matters. Let me give an example from the Canadian Association of Fine Arts Deans, of which I'm a board member. We turned our attention as an organization to curriculum a couple of years ago. It's very rare that you get a group of deans together talking about curriculum – budgets, human resources, policy, and so forth usually carry the day. The session was called, somewhat awkwardly and clearly written by a committee, "Curriculum Review and Redesign and

Opportunities of Alternative Streams of Revenue Generation for Creative Arts Programs." You will see that the notion of curriculum becomes tied up with the notion of budget, which of course is in turn tied up with enrolment. All of a sudden, we are diverted from what we set out to concern ourselves with and we are now concerned with attracting students to our program by making the programs as attractive as we can. This is based on a misguided theory given voice in Dickeson's (2010) book, *Prioritizing Academic Programs and Services: Reallocated Resources to Achieve Strategic Balance.* This book is the *Mein Kampf* of the academic world. It reads like a joke, it is so over the top, but it's not a joke. It's serious and is being taken seriously by bureaucrats and functionaries everywhere. The upshot is that an academic program that fails to generate revenue should be redesigned so that it does generate revenue. Curriculum is, in this way, monetized. Another example of the same phenomenon is the extent to which the economy drives our thinking about the arts. I'll give an example of that. I never rant on Facebook. Two things I don't do on Facebook: post pictures of kittens, and rant. My wife posts pictures of kittens, and neither of us rants, except once. I can't even remember what drove me to write the following, but it was 22 April 2013:

> OK – time to vent. Put this in the pet peeve category. I'm constantly being forwarded studies, invited to functions, asked to submit information, etc. etc. concerning the economic impact of the arts. I swore I'd boycott all this nonsense years ago, but people are so excited by the economic impact of the arts, I feel downright anti-social for not getting pumped about it. I mean, really – who cares? Some people get rich off the arts, others scrape by because of the arts, restaurants do a good business, people stay in hotels, and so forth, but this is hardly the point. Why don't we talk about the arts? Who decided it was the money that mattered? Not the artists, that's for sure.

My point is that when describing something or monetizing something becomes an end in itself, we are, in fact, missing the point. I have one more example. I was asked to stand in for the business dean at a function a couple of years ago. This was an "Aha" moment for me. There was a rich man talking about how, at the beginning of his career, he borrowed a lot of money from his friends – clearly, he had friends unlike my own friends when I was in my twenties, but that's beside the point. I'm making up numbers but let's say he borrowed $200,000. He invested it, and then, within a couple of years, he had several million dollars. At this point in the story, the room burst into applause. I am not exaggerating when I say I was the only person sitting there waiting for the punchline. I mean, "I made millions of dollars which I then did something helpful with." But no, the punchline was that this individual had made a lot of money – end of story. I remember thinking at the time that this was a very interesting example of people becoming obsessed with human constructs. Money has no real meaning other than the meaning that we ascribe to it.

This raises the question, "So what's the point?" That's what I would have asked the rich man in the same way that I suppose someone could ask me, "What's the point? Why do we study music in an institutional context? Why is this so important? Why have I devoted my career to it?" Well, my first response would be that the aesthetic value of music is reason enough to devote a lifetime to its creation, study, and dissemination. I know that there will be people in this room that disagree with that viewpoint, but that's my viewpoint. Aesthetic value is reason enough. But that doesn't mean we should abdicate responsibility for sharing it. That would be like saying, "Food is a wonderful thing, but we have no responsibility to share it." Of course, sharing what we value is what makes us rich, not necessarily in monetary terms, but in other more important ways.

If we agree that music is valuable, that it has social importance, that it has aesthetic value, then it is incumbent upon us to find ways to share it. Sharing is the premise of what our prime minister's father, who was also our prime minister, called a "just society" – a society that places value on social relevance, social justice, on the betterment of society. We can only do that, I believe, if we liberate the study of music from its symbolic extensions. Only then can we refocus on what truly matters, which is the music itself and the social and personal uses to which we apply it. Community music programs, with their emphasis on social responsibility and not on the resolution of Italian sixth chords, emancipate music from its symbolic extensions.

I want to turn by way of conclusion to Percy Grainger. He's in many ways like Marshall McLuhan. Grainger was misunderstood in his own time, and we now recognize that he was a thinker far ahead of his time. He was in many ways a community musician. He in fact wrote an article called "Community Music" in 1930, long before that term was widely used to describe participatory music-making. Ten years ago I wrote that:

> For Grainger, the social dimension of any musical interaction was not the by-product of an aesthetic demand. Rather, the aesthetic and social dimensions were so closely correlated that one without the other was anathema to him. If music did not generate community capital, then it was not art with the capacity to change the world, but entertainment that affirms the status quo. (Carruthers, forthcoming)

What community music is *not*, is entertainment that affirms the status quo. Community music has the capacity to change the world. If music is the means to a social end, then music teaching and learning needs to be repurposed with that goal in mind, in the home, in the community, and perhaps most importantly in our schools and our universities.

Grainger wrote a remarkable letter to Olin Downes in 1942. He had this to say:

> I feel that if we are going to go on spending as much time (for instance, in the schools) as we do on music, that at least a considerable part of the music should fit us to face the complicated facts & problems of modern life (cosmopolitanism, racial questions, aviation, chemistry, engineering & how other human forces & natural forces act & counteract) ... If music is not going to play its part in making mankind more loving, compassionate, understanding, thoughtful, restrained, scientific & concentrated I don't know why we are giving so much time to it. (Balough, 1982, p. 94)

I believe, like Grainger, that curriculum should be designed to prepare students to enhance the quality of life in our civil society and to advance and protect the enduring values of peace, respect for difference, and care for the vulnerable. Music can indeed, as Grainger says, help us become more loving, more compassionate, more understanding, more thoughtful. That is certainly the role of community music, and that is certainly the role of community music in higher education.

(Editor's note: This chapter is edited from a keynote address given at a conference at Wilfrid Laurier University, Waterloo, Ontario, in May 2017. The conference theme was "Walking the Boundaries: Bridging the Gaps in Community Music.")

PART II

COMMUNITY MUSIC
*Walking the Boundaries of Education, Ensembles,
and Changing Paradigms*

THE TEN CHAPTERS in this section delve into the practices of facilitation in specifically defined music-making contexts. Mullen provides a framework for music practice in challenging situations; Parker-Cook examines gender inequities in high school music education; and D'Alexander demonstrates the value of orchestral music engagement in developing social identity with youth in underserved areas in the United States. Coffman and Dabback provide perspective on ways older adults make music in structured community-based ensembles, and (Annie) Mitchell's research study identifies best practices in conducting, musical direction, and performance in community music orchestras in New South Wales, Australia. Rowan introduces strategies of empathy, mindfulness, and deep listening in building community musicianship with older populations, while Coppi and van der Sandt, situated in northern Italy, argue that community music principles are applicable to music education in a variety of ways, including intergenerational, formal, and non-formal contexts. Technology as a means of learning, imagining, and meaning-making is the focus of Greher's chapter, highlighting the flexibility that community music practices offer learners who may find themselves outside of traditional music education pathways. The final two chapters are somewhat autobiographical in style: Marsella narrates his role as director of a neighbourhood community school, the Regent Park School of Music; and Moser recounts his journey as a community music composer and facilitator.

CHAPTER 6

Do, Review, Improve

Establishing a Framework for Quality Delivery within the Community Music Sector

Phil Mullen

Introduction

THIS CHAPTER IS ABOUT the development of a quality framework for community music practice with children in challenging circumstances (CCC). This framework is called Do, Review, Improve (Youth Music, 2014, revised 2017) and was produced by the National Foundation for Youth Music (commonly known as Youth Music) in England.

Youth Music

Since its foundation in 1999, the National Foundation of Youth Music has been disbursing approximately 10 million pounds a year to music projects with young people in England. Over this time, Youth Music has funded more than 3,000 projects working with children and young people aged birth to twenty-five.

Over the past decade, these projects have increasingly been with children in challenging circumstances. While some work happens in school settings, the majority is in non-formal settings such as youth centres or hospitals, and the musical approach is consistently non-formal. Projects operate in all regions of England with children and young people up to the age of twenty-five.

Youth Music's stated goal is to create a musically inclusive England. In addition to funding music programs for children and young people, Youth Music has generated a number of evaluation and research studies, which often focus on the development and achievements of those considered to be experiencing challenging circumstances. It has also supported initiatives such as training and workforce development, as well as organizations that work strategically towards musical inclusion.

Community Music in England

Community music in England has a well-documented history (Higgins, 2012; Higham & McKay, 2011). Over the past fifty years, community music has grown from the efforts of a few isolated individuals trying to map out new ground in music participation to a nationally established profession with activities in every English county. Community music has been a visible part of music provision in England over at least the last decade and has become an increasingly important part of music education in its broader sense.

In 2005, the Music Manifesto identified three categories of music learning in England:

- *Formal*: what takes place in statutory provision or with statutory funding in schools, colleges, and music services.
- *Non-formal*: what takes place outside formal education provision, but can include out-of-hours' work in schools, supervised by adult professionals.
- *Informal*: what happens when young people organize and lead themselves without adult supervision. (Music Manifesto, 2005)

Deane and Mullen (2018, p. 78) argue that community music practice is part of non-formal provision, although the work now often takes place within school hours, particularly within special schools. They also state that

> [a]n attempt has been made since 2012 to join up these systems of provision while preserving their distinctiveness. Each county or large metropolitan borough has a "Music Education Hub" (Department of Education, 2011), a partnership organization of the range of music education providers charged to provide specific activities and outputs for children and young people. (Deane & Mullen, 2018, p. 178)

The Drive toward Inclusion in English Music Provision

In the United Kingdom, as in many countries, there has been an increased drive toward educational inclusion over the past three decades; however, the country is still not fully educationally inclusive. The British government ratified the UN Convention on the Rights of the Child in 1991, and the UK was one of ninety-two countries that endorsed the Salamanca Statement in 1994

(UNESCO, 1994). However, in 2008 the UN Committee on the rights of the child was critical of the levels of inequality that still existed:

> The Committee notes with appreciation the numerous efforts of the State party in the sphere of education, in order to guarantee the objectives set out in the Convention. However, it is concerned that significant inequalities persist with regard to school achievement of children living with their parents in economic hardship.
>
> Several groups of children have problems being enrolled in school or continuing or re-entering education, either in regular schools or alternative educational facilities, and cannot fully enjoy their right to education, notably children with disabilities, children of Travellers, Roma children, asylum-seeking children, dropouts and non-attendees for different reasons (sickness, family obligations etc.), and teenage mothers. (United Nations, 2008)

Whether because of sensitivity to this criticism or not, the English national plan for music education (DfE, 2011) was explicit in promoting "equality of opportunity for all pupils, regardless of race; gender; where they live; their levels of musical talent; parental income; whether they have special educational needs or disabilities; and whether they are looked after children" (DfE, 2011, p. 9).

The plan went further in that it identified the fact that many groups of children faced barriers to music learning and was clear about who those groups of children were:

> Children's personal circumstances can inhibit the type of engagement they have with music education. For example, barriers prevent some pupils with special educational needs or disabilities from making music ... Similarly hubs will need to consider how children who are looked after; those who are Gypsy, Roma or Travellers; those who are carers; those not in education, employment or training (NEET); or those who are educated from home can have access to music education. (DfE, 2011, pp. 17–18)

While the goals of the national plan in relation to inclusion and equality of opportunity are quite clear, the organizations given the main responsibility for the plan's implementation – the newly formed music hubs – were mostly dominated by local "music services." These organizations had not previously been tasked with ensuring appropriate inclusion for all. Practical wisdom suggests that while some hubs and music services have thrived with regard to inclusion, others have continued to struggle. A 2017 report identifies that while students with special education needs make up 14.4 percent of the school population, they make up only 2.81 percent of the pupils in music hub choirs and ensembles (Fautley & Whittaker, 2017). At the time this chapter was written, seven years after the new plan was published and hubs were set up, musical inclusion in England was still very patchy and depended very much on the culture of the local organizations rather than on the agenda set by the national plan. Matt Griffiths of Youth Music identifies some of the barriers to hubs working more inclusively:

> These barriers can include hub lead partners focusing too narrowly on instrumental tuition of a limited duration, the large bias towards orchestral instruments and repertoire, and not being between 7 and 11-years-old. They might also include having a disability, not being in school, being unable to clearly describe your musical goals and ambitions, or those not being regarded as "proper" music. (Griffiths, 2014)

Youth Music and the organizations it funds can be said to be leading the drive toward inclusion, and their quality framework, Do, Review, Improve, is an attempt to lay down markers as to what is inclusive pedagogy and what makes good inclusive practice.

Children in Challenging Circumstances (CCC)

"Children in challenging circumstances" is the term favoured by the charity Youth Music for work with children who might otherwise be called vulnerable, marginalized, or at risk of exclusion. A number of typologies of challenging circumstance have been developed (Lonie, 2010; Ward, 2012). One such typology (Mullen, 2011) groups children in challenging circumstances by the strategies that are found to work best with them:

- *Young people with a challenge that is a permanent life condition, such as a disability, impairment, or condition such as Asperger's syndrome.* With these young people, it is vital to adapt instruments, material, curricula and the environment to fit their needs, abilities and interests. Technology and App culture have helped change the musical landscape for a number of these children in England.
- *Young people with a challenge that is related to where they live.* This can include challenges such as rural isolation or living in areas of social and economic deprivation. Community music organizations may find challenges in bringing the young people together and in raising their aspirations.

- *Young people with a challenge in their current life circumstances.* This includes those who bully or are being bullied, those who live in state or foster care, refugees, and others. Deep trauma is often an issue and community musicians need to employ emotional intelligence. (Goleman, 1998)

- *Young people with behavioural, emotional, and social difficulties (BESD – now renamed SEMH – social, emotional and mental health).* Of all the groups mentioned, these young people are least likely to do well academically (Taylor, 2012). Work with this group is intense and specialized, requiring workers with high levels of empathy (adapted from Mullen, 2011).

For all these groups, practice wisdom suggests that it is not enough to work on musical development alone. Attention must be given to the whole person and to their personal and social selves.

Musical, Personal, and Social Outcomes

Youth Music, in its 2015–16 Impact Report (Youth Music, 2016), argues that young people in challenging circumstances face barriers to personal and social development and that access to appropriate musically inclusive programs can improve not only musical but also personal and social outcomes for them. There is significant evidence to support this claim.

Hallam (2015) cites multiple studies evidencing children's personal and social development as a by-product of music education programs. Saunders and Welch (2012) show how soft or transferrable skills, such as "self-confidence, team working, the ability to focus or concentrate, listening, working to guidelines, relating to others, forming positive work relations, and making friends can be developed through non-formal approaches" (p. 8). Dillon (2010) cites the following personal and social outcomes for children in state care (looked after children) after they have been part of non-formal community music programs:

- Improved negotiation skills and co-operative working developed through group work;
- Learning to trust peers by relying on and supporting others in the course of the project;
- Developing both a capacity to express themselves and a stronger sense of self-awareness through music-making, particularly by writing lyrics;
- Increased levels of self-discipline and a sense of responsibility for their actions;

- A sense of achievement attained through developing new music-making skills, the production of high-quality musical outputs and performing;
- A positive sense of belonging and shared identity with other young people in care, which supported their understanding of the context in which they were living;
- Making friends through a positive activity;
- Developing positive relationships with adults (music leaders and carers) who modelled constructive ways of both working with others and dealing with conflict, and who live a life engaging in a positive activity such as music-making;
- Having the opportunity to have fun and "escape" their problems through a positive activity;
- Cutting across all of the outcomes was increased confidence, both on a personal and a skill-based level;
- Increased self-esteem and sense of self-efficacy. (Dillon, 2010, p. 4)

Deane, Hunter, and Mullen, in a review of Youth Music's national youth music-mentoring program, found the following effects on the young people involved:

1. Engagement – music as a "hook," to get young people into the program

2. Trust – the shared interest of music-making, the credibility of the mentor as a respected musician

3. Transferable skills – communication skills, giving and receiving criticism, increased confidence, developing resilience

4. Success – doing something well and getting praise for it, stepping out into the professional world

5. A safe place – developing a community with peers and adults

6. Social pedagogy – room for a more equal relationship between mentor and mentee

7. Telling the tale (expressing yourself) – most directly with rap lyrics, but seen in music generally

8. Therapeutic aid – music not as therapy, but as therapeutic

9. Creative cooperation – not only in group projects but also creating music with the help of a mentor

10. Personal reflection – on life challenges, understanding of self, and the art they do. (Deane, Hunter, & Mullen, 2011, p. 12)

The evidential conclusion that non-formal community music-working can make significant changes not only in musical but also in personal and social outcomes for many participants has several implications. First, if involvement in community music practice is enabling positive transformation in the lives of children in challenging circumstances, those who are frequently among the most vulnerable in society (and it does), then this is to the public good:

> Rather than explicitly tackling the conditions of material poverty, physical illness, or disability often experienced by young people facing additional challenges, the music project serves as a way of raising consciousness and expressive ability, facilitating a deeper understanding amongst the young people of their own abilities and providing opportunities to communicate and connect with other people. (Lonie, 2013, p. 10)

Community music practice of this type, if cost-effective, is something that is worth government support as one pathway toward a more inclusive society. It is important to identify precisely those factors within the practice that have the beneficial effects on children and young people. Once these are known, they should be disseminated widely in the community music field, if not beyond, so that the work can consistently achieve these outcomes.

Underpinning Theory

While a number of theories of personal and social change may have relevance for community music practice, including flow theory (Csikszentmihalyi, 1990), identity theory (Marcia, 1993), and attachment theory (Bowlby, 1969), one that has been seen to have quite immediate applications to inclusive practice is self-determination theory (Deci & Ryan, 2000a). Deci and Ryan have focused their work on the reasons why people do things – their intrinsic motivations. Deci and Ryan have identified that when people are not steered by physical drives or extrinsic factors such as financial insecurity or close family members in need, they have three needs: to feel competent, to feel autonomous, and to have feelings of relatedness to others. They argue that these needs are crucial for psychological well-being and that not meeting these needs can lead to diminished well-being. According to Deane and colleagues, inclusive music approaches can address these three intrinsic needs through:

+ their commitment to mutual goal setting and realisation; and a commitment to positive feedback – both of which can develop a sense of individual and collective competency
+ their focus on group building and honouring the individual's contribution to the group, thus developing a strong sense of relatedness
+ shared ownership coupled with the importance of individual and group creativity, which together encourage a sense of autonomy. (Deane, Holford, Hunter, & Mullen, 2015, p. 41)

Most of the points made above can be easily mapped onto the Do, Review, Improve framework. In other words, the framework can be used as a tool to directly promote children's and young people's self-determination and by extension their psychological well-being.

Quality in Inclusion

Working with children in challenging circumstances is a complex endeavour (Deane, Holford, Hunter, & Mullen, 2015). For example, the work may take place outside the quite structured environment of schools in environments not really suited to music provision. In these environments, the workshop leaders have to be very flexible to work within the constraints of the space. Also, in the case of groups such as children in state care (called looked-after children in England), there may be a number of different professionals who have to approve the children's involvement in the music program in the first place. These professionals may not understand or value the work of community musicians, and this can become a barrier to engagement (Chambers, 2013). The different factors that make up these children's challenging circumstances can also play a strong role in making it complicated and difficult for them to engage. Mark Bick lists eight barriers to working successfully with CCC, including disengagement, low resilience, and low self-esteem. He reminds us that:

> [w]here low confidence is combined with a powerful desire to engage with music, then the slightest critical comment or even the possibility of success can trigger strong negative emotional reactions. We need to be willing to ride any resultant emotional "storms," give the student space and assure them that we are willing to persist. (Bick, 2013, p. 58)

Many community musicians and organizations have found ways to overcome barriers to engagement and work well with CCC. The musicians may work intuitively, responding very much to what goes on in the moment. Sometimes they may not be able to clearly articulate what they are doing but there is an observable expertise, a way of knowing and doing:

Quality in musical encounters with children in challenging circumstances isn't just something that happens. It is structured into the work. Musicians – knowing that they need to work reflexively, to change plans and go with the flow – set up "skeletal" structures to enable the work to achieve high quality outcomes. These skeletal structures are often only known to the musicians themselves and are often understood intuitively rather than articulated. A lot of the time they don't even know they are structuring the work at all. The work tends to have a "loose/tight" structure – tight in areas like respect for self, others and instruments, to ensure that moods and activities don't overspill into destructive energy, while remaining loose enough to allow for experimentation, interaction and emotional expression. (Deane, Holford, Hunter, & Mullen, 2015, 2015, p. 88)

By developing and honing their work over what is now decades of experience, community music organizations and individuals have evolved a common practice that is recognizable and effective. Saunders and Welch (2012, p. 37) observed a limited number of community music workshop sessions in detail. They found "striking" similarities across different community music organizations and different community musicians.

In a 2015 report for Youth Music, Deane and colleagues recognized that certain approaches are effective in engaging and deepening the engagement of CCC. They listed the following factors that build for quality in working with CCC:

+ An environment conducive to group working
+ The engagement of the participants
+ Shared ownership
+ What the participant brings: developing their own voice
+ Peer-working and independent learning
+ The importance of creativity
+ Non-musical qualities of the musician: flexibility, reflexivity, attending and responding
+ Diagnostic working – reading the individual and the group (Deane, Holford, Hunter, & Mullen, p. 84)

In their recommendations to Youth Music, they stated that

a clear, unequivocal (yet still flexible) pedagogy for musical inclusion work needs to be developed. This needs to be broad enough to be universally adoptable across the whole range of non-formal music education. The development needs to build on work to date (including quality frameworks such as Youth Music's Do, Review, Improve) and ensure a range of voices are listened to. (Deane, Holford, Hunter, & Mullen, 2015, p. 133)

The 2017 update of Do, Review, Improve is not a national pedagogy for the non-formal sector, but it does lay down markers as to what that pedagogy could and should focus on.

Do, Review, Improve

The framework, which was updated in November 2017, now consists of two sections: organizational responsibilities criteria and session criteria.

The organizational responsibilities criteria section has four subsections, each with a number of statements that establish what quality *is* in this context. Those subsections are:

1. Health and safety of all

2. Contracting and support for music leaders

3. Young people's pastoral and progression needs

4. Planning and evaluation

This is all about what happens beyond the workshop session and is essentially the responsibility of project managers.

The session criteria section also has four subsections:

1. Young people centred

2. Music leader practice

3. Session content

4. Environment

This section is obviously about the session and is mostly, but not completely, the responsibility of the music leader. For example, one exception to this is on environment and states, "There is a suitable ratio of young people to music leaders (and other project staff where required)" (Youth Music, 2017). This ratio may well need to be negotiated in advance between the project manager and the host organization.

Organizational Responsibilities

This section of the framework is new, with nothing similar to the 2014 original. The first part of it, *Health and safety for all*, is fairly straightforward – it ensures that organizations have appropriate policies in place.

The section on contracting and support for music leaders includes several interesting statements. C1 states: "Contracts include time for structured reflection and evaluation activities with key staff or volunteers involved in planning and delivery" (Youth Music, 2017). This statement amounts to a commitment from the major funder in the community music field to support (by implication *financially* support) structured reflective practice by the workers. While practice wisdom suggests that community musicians have reflected on their work informally for some time, this criterion now aligns with the 2015 recommendation from Deane and colleagues:

> Reflective practice is a central feature of inclusive working. It needs to be systematic, with reflections documented and carried through into actions. Greater use of collective reflective practice in organisations would provide a firmer basis for quality practice and workforce development. (Deane, Holford, Hunter, & Mullen, 2015, p. 134)

Perhaps an even more significant point in the framework is C4: "Organisations support the emotional wellbeing of staff with regular catchup/supervision sessions" (Youth Music, 2017).

Here is recognition that working with CCC can be challenging for the workers themselves and that dealing with very vulnerable children can uncover vulnerabilities among the workers that might not be so pronounced in a mainstream environment. While not stipulating the need for the level of non-executive supervision that might be expected within fields such as psychotherapy, it is an important recognition by a funder that the work is emotionally complex.

In the section on young people's pastoral and progression needs, statement PP2 posits: "When participants are referred by another organization, information is requested to inform planning and communication (for example about musical ability and experience, pastoral needs, special educational needs and/or disabilities)" (Youth Music, 2017).

Practice wisdom suggests that the lack of pre-knowledge about participants has been to date a significant issue for community music workers throughout England. Also, their counterparts in the somewhat more formal music services often suffer from the same problem. Working with, for example, students with autism within a larger group, peripatetic teachers sometimes only discover that their students have autism when they display a negative reaction to volume levels or a sudden change within the session. Youth Music has taken a step forward for quality in inclusive working by recognizing the issue of pre-knowledge and embedding it in a national framework for good practice.

The final statement in the framework's first section on Organizational Responsibilities that we will focus on here is PE1 in the subsection on planning and evaluation: "PE1 Programmes are planned to ensure that duration of contact time and frequency of engagement are sufficient to achieve the intended outcomes" (Youth Music, 2017). This statement binds the work to an outcomes-focussed approach, requiring the community music organization to resource each project in terms of time allowance in such a way that it ensures the outcomes are achieved. This, of course, is common sense. Who would resource a project with less than what is necessary to achieve the goal, or promote wastage of public money by giving more resources in person-hours than are needed? The statement is asking all organizations that embrace the framework to hold themselves accountable in terms of achieving the goals they have stated in their funding applications, and, perhaps more importantly, to agree to take it on themselves to analyze what exactly is needed to achieve those goals. This is significant when we remember that many of the promised outcomes, to be achieved through a musical encounter, are personal and social ones. By their nature these are difficult to quantify, and it is often difficult to pinpoint precisely how they will be achieved. Furthermore, these outcomes are, more often than not, to be achieved with those children and young people most personally vulnerable and most socially excluded in our society. This points to a confidence in the sector and in the methods adopted by the sector to continuously replicate the types of evidence-based outcomes mentioned earlier in the chapter.

The second part of Do, Review, Improve, based around the session, makes the importance of a young-person-centred approach very clear by devoting a whole subsection to this way of working. Perhaps the statement that lays out Youth Music's point of view most clearly is Y3: "The young people's musical, personal, and social development are monitored, and achievements are celebrated and valued. Young people are supported by music leaders to set their own goals and targets" (Youth Music, 2017). This makes it explicit that it is not just the music development that is at the heart of the work. It also places the locus of evaluation (Rogers & Koch, 1959) firmly within the young people themselves.

This empowerment of the young person goes further in the subsection on session content in statement S2: "Ownership of session content is shared between the music leader and young people. Participants contribute to decision-making and have the opportunity to take on leadership roles where appropriate" (Youth Music, 2017). The concept of shared ownership does not disempower the community musician / music leader. It simply emphasizes a non-didactic approach to the community music workshop that has been part of both community music and some music education work for decades (Mullen, 2002; 2008; Higgins, 2012). The Canadian music education innovator Murray Schafer stated:

> It is my very strong feeling that in the future we might expect to experience a withering of the teacher's role as an authority-figure and focal point in the class. In truly creative work of any kind there are no known answers and there is no examinable information as such. After providing some initial questions (not answers), the teacher places himself in the hands of the class and together they work through problems. (Schafer, 1975, pp. 25–26)

In the same book, Schafer emphasized the importance of understanding the role group played by dynamics in musical encounters (Schafer, 1975, p. 26). This is also included within the framework in S4: "Activities are designed and delivered in a manner that is accessible to all and tailored to each individual whenever possible, taking account of their starting points and aspirations. Group dynamics and pace of learning have been considered" (Youth Music, 2017).

Young People with Special Educational Needs and Disabilities (SEND)

Drake Music, a national organization that uses music technology with people with disabilities, was asked by Youth Music to interpret the original 2014 framework in relation to people with special educational needs and disabilities. They picked a number of the statements and have given exemplars that certainly have applications beyond working with SEND participants and perhaps beyond CCC working altogether. Some of their examples, such as the first one below, help open up new ideas about what it can mean to interact musically and why challenging commonly held perceptions of the leader's role in a music session can be a valuable and creative experience (Mullen, 2008; Schafer, 1975):

> Criteria—Y1 Music-making reflects the young people's interests, with recognition of their existing musical identities.
>
> "Many disabled young people have less opportunity to make choices and be 'in charge' than their non-disabled peers. Access to music-making can increase these opportunities."
>
> *Example: A music leader initiates a "call and response" music activity with a musician with learning disabilities. Each time, the music leader and support*

worker wait for the participant to begin playing before they respond. The young musician can enjoy the power of keeping the others waiting in silent suspense. (Youth Music / Drake Music, 2017)

The second example given here certainly applies to both disabled and non-disabled young musicians and could be seen as essential learning for all visiting music educators:

Criteria—E2 Consideration has been given to the physical space, with available resources being best used to make it accessible and appropriate for the target group.

"Many spaces provided for music-making are less than ideal; but for many young disabled musicians, getting the environment right can limit distractions and make a crucial difference to them engaging with the experience."

Example: A music leader is given the school hall to use for music-making sessions involving young musicians with Autistic Spectrum Conditions (ASC). The hall is large with boomy acoustics and features strip lighting which quietly hums. In addition, other classes use the hall as a cut-through to other rooms and kitchen staff prepare lunch in the adjoining room. Some of the young musicians become distracted by these unintended disruptions and after a few weeks of trying to make it work, the music leader requests a new space with natural light and/or standing lamps, improved sound-proofing, and in a quieter part of the school site. (Youth Music / Drake Music, 2017)

It could be argued that the specialized outlook that Drake brings to this framework can, in some ways, help broaden understandings for all music educators around musical inclusion, around working with people with disabilities, and around the breadth of thinking that one needs to bring to the educational and creative environment.

Uses of the Framework

Youth Music asks all the organizations it funds to use the framework (Youth Music, 2017), and in May 2017 it toured England giving training on the framework to more than 150 organizations. It does not want this framework to be seen as onerous, however, and insists that "you don't need to score yourself or rank yourself against others" (Youth Music, 2017).

Instead the framework can be used as a tool to promote structured reflection, to think about both the principles and the methods of the work and how they connect. Do, Review, Improve is a tool for "planning, peer observation or self-reflection" (Youth Music, 2017). It can certainly be used by organizations not linked to Youth Music. In addition, it could be used as part of training programs, to stimulate discussion, and indeed as a source of ideas when designing training programs.

Case Study – Exchanging Notes

The author interviewed Victoria Kinsella, senior researcher at Birmingham City University and a researcher into Youth Music's "Exchanging Notes" program, about the use of the framework as part of this program. The Exchanging Notes program brought together out-of-school music organizations with schools over a four-year period with the aim of exploring how music intervention can impact young people's musical and educational outcomes. As part of the project, each music organization and its partner school had to work together to plan sessions, deliver them together if possible, and develop partnership working. As part of the funding agreement, they also had to use the quality framework.

Researchers visited each school three times per year, using the quality framework to make notes throughout the session. They then used these notes to engage in reflective conversations with the music leader and schoolteacher. The most interesting thing for Victoria about the quality framework was the different ways it was used across the projects – there were no set criteria from Youth Music about how it should be used.

Victoria felt that a very successful use of the framework was where both partners went through it all in detail at the start of the year as a way to think about the long-term goals of what they were doing. This was potentially something new for the music organizations, for many of them were used to short-term projects with performance outcomes; this new approach required them to think about long-term aspects of planning and what they would mean for young people's outcomes longitudinally. From this, some projects focused on one or two aspects of the framework each week as a way to focus teaching and learning. Because there are so many criteria, it is a bit difficult to focus on all aspects of the quality framework all of the time. This approach provided very clear objectives for reflection and also served as a tool for planning sessions.

Projects that did not have time for reflection focused more on the *doing* of learning; for example, the focus of the sessions was on developing pieces for performance, often in ways that had previously been done with other groups. Without reflecting on what they were doing, it was very difficult to critique the teaching and learning that was going on within the sessions and to evaluate progress.

The use of the quality framework in the program highlighted the need for reflection within the sessions. This can be difficult, but when designing a project as a partnership, you need to also design time for reflection after a session to inform the next one, and longitudinally to evaluate long-term progression.

The quality framework also started to break down some of the differences in language between formal and non-formal music education, although this did not come about very quickly. Schoolteachers are quite defined by assessment and performativity school measures, and music leaders have a different fundamental approach; therefore, it took a long time for both to understand the other's ethos. The quality framework enabled those types of discussions to begin and perspectives to be shared in quite a safe manner.

In terms of the different sections of the framework, what was quite useful was the section on young-person-centredness. When conversations were focused on this, the young people remained at the heart of the sessions and everything else flowed from that. Centring the discussion around young-person-centredness resulted in a trusting space where both teachers and music leaders could develop more critical thinking over time. The criteria for success changed and became more young-person-centred.

For Victoria, a key turning point for one project was when she was observing a session and the team had the quality framework on the wall in the classroom. This session wasn't quite working. During a break, the teacher and the music leader discussed the quality framework and made adaptations to the session that helped it work better. This was an example of the teacher, the music leader, and reflection coming together in practice.

Some projects did not fully engage with the quality framework. On some occasions there was probably a lack of understanding of the benefits of using it, and sometimes no one took a lead with utilizing it. In projects that were successful, the teacher and the music leader were both on board with the framework. Victoria thinks that in longitudinal projects there has to be time for reflection – time to think, sit down, plan, and critique. Otherwise, there is a layer of critique and development that is just not there in the project.

While it is not known whether the schools will continue to use the framework after the project (if the community music organizations continue to be funded by Youth Music, it will be part of their contractual obligation), Victoria regards the framework as a really useful reflective tool that is particularly helpful for projects that bring schools together with out-of-schools providers (V. Kinsella, personal communication, 2018).

Discussion

Do, Review, Improve is a short framework produced by one funding organization for practical application by its grant holders. While all grant holders are asked to use it, they are not made to do so in a proscriptive way; it is up to each organization to find what way works best for them. It can be argued that the framework is more than something for just these organizations. In an English context, the only previous national document that sought to really examine what community music practice should be was the Music Educator's Code of Practice. Do, Review, Improve is more detailed and more specific in terms of practice. It also has its roots in, and aligns closely with, a number of research and evaluation projects commissioned by Youth Music over the years to look specifically at music with CCC. It has also benefited from two consultation processes, one in 2014 and one in 2017, that involved people from all parts of the field – practitioners, support workers and academics. So it has good credentials.

It is not an exhaustively comprehensive document. For example, more could have been said about making an environment emotionally safe (Everitt, 1997), and the section on health and safety lacks detail. That said, the statements on sessions themselves are a clear exposition of how principles and values of inclusion can play out in practice. They unequivocally favour empowerment and shared ownership as an important tool for musical, personal, and social development, leaving no doubt as to the generality, and to an extent the specifics, of a transformative pedagogic approach. The emphasis here is on youth voice and agency (Lonie, 2013), and the framework identifies the core difference between so-called formal and non-formal pedagogical approaches in terms of engagement, involvement, and change. It does not say much about the music itself, nor does it deal with how to troubleshoot potential behavioural issues within the session, but other than these areas, it covers in broad strokes most of what practice wisdom would suggest are the main concerns likely to arise within sessions with CCC. On this basis, it can be seen as somewhat comprehensive.

It has proven its use as a planning tool, as an instrument for provoking deep reflection and critical thinking, and as a means to bring together and promote understanding between music providers with different ways of working and different vocabularies around how they work. In particular, it focuses providers on the young-person-centred nature of community music delivery.

In terms of reach, it will certainly reach most of the workers involved with Youth Music's grant-holding organizations. There are nearly 200 of these organizations in England. How far beyond this it will reach over time is hard to say. It was discussed as part of the Asia Pacific Community Music Network's gathering in Auckland in November 2017, and no doubt this chapter will raise awareness of the framework internationally. No quality framework designed for a single country is likely to be seen as a usable global resource for community musicians and organizations. Contexts are different, and the understanding of the term community music differs from country to country (Veblen, 2002;

Tiernan, 2009, p. 10). Consequently, Do, Review, Improve cannot be taken out of context and used for the same purposes in another country. However, if community musicians are seeking principles and practices of a music pedagogy that has liberated itself from the formal concerns of pre-set curricula and standardized assessment, then the framework may be a very useful starting point. Notably, the framework acknowledges that there can be quality in non-formal music education in relation to transformation of the self and surrounding society, and that this quality can be both identified and applied when working with CCC. Furthermore, the framework foregrounds the importance of the locus of evaluation being within the participant, giving them the tools to construct their own identity, rather than accepting an often negative identity conferred on them by others (Marcia, 1993). If the principles within the framework are adapted appropriately to local context, they may well point the way to a future education that is humane, collaborative, and empowering for the most vulnerable members of society.

CHAPTER 7

A Music Educator's Journey toward Addressing Gender Barriers in Music Education

(A Non-Researcher's Research and What Happened Next)

Elizabeth Parker-Cook

Introduction

THIS IS NOT GOING to be the type of academic research you are used to reading. Let me just say this, right at the beginning: I am not an experienced researcher. I don't have a slew of articles published or a lot of excellent peer-reviewed research completed. I am sure this will immediately become apparent. So, even though there is research presented in this chapter, it isn't really about that. This is a story about how my own research changed my teaching practice. Are you still reading? Oh good! Well, it all started as a question: "Where are all the girls in my guitar classes?" It was not as if the girls in my class were less talented or less interested in music than the boys, but every year I had only a handful of female-identifying students in my guitar classes. As an educator, this puzzled me. I have always been interested in gender issues and after years of observing gender dynamics in my classrooms, I decided to pursue a Master of Community Music degree in hopes of finding some answers.

Why not a Master of Education, you ask? Well, when I read about community music, and its values of inclusivity, collaborative music-making, and using music to create change, it seemed the perfect place for me (Bartleet & Higgins, 2018). I had real-world experience in education and had worked in both very traditional and highly non-traditional settings. What was missing, I felt, were perspectives from outside traditional education. I felt – and still feel – that community musicians and school educators had a lot in common, but especially the ability to create a cohesive community with a diverse group of individuals through the arts. I was doing my job, teaching my students the right skills, and what I wanted to do was take it a step further and build a community.

I decided that the first step in changing my practice was to do some research into gender issues. I read many interesting studies about gender issues related to music in schools and gender issues in the music industry. However, this research will focus on gender issues related to the music industry, as this is the information that most changed my practice. After an extraordinarily long time, and much, much reading, here are the highlights.

First, A Few Important Definitions

Gender is a social construct, that is, a series of learned behaviours reinforced by society (Hayes, 2010). Often one's gender identification falls outside the established "norms" of male and female, so that people identify themselves as gender-fluid, non-gendered, transgender, or other gender identities (Hayes, 2010). Perhaps one of the limitations of this study is that students are seen as solely male or female, so that much of the nuance of gender identification is missing. Though students expressed an understanding of gender as a continuum during the interviews, as well as an impressive degree of gender sensitivity, they did not express to me that they felt themselves to be anything other than male or female.

I like to use the European Institute for Gender Equality's definition of *gender roles*, which says that gender roles are behavioural and social norms expected from males or females (n.d.). Study participants had a strong understanding of this concept and of the stereotypes surrounding the idea of gender roles and music.

Finally, this point is one of my own invention, so you know it is the best one. In the research I used the phrase "unfriendly lyrics." My intention in using this term was so that students in the study would identify lyrics they found offensive, but I also wanted them to identify *how* the lyrics offended them. I felt that if I asked them about misogynist or sexist lyrics, I would be leading them when I wanted them instead to make their own conclusions and judgments. Should have I come up with a better term? Probably, but if not, it is too late now.

So, on to the Research Highlights!

In my experience, students often develop their ideas and images about music from their exposure to the music industry through media such as videos and reality shows. They receive messages in many ways, the most obvious of which is through song lyrics. I have no wish to judge or implicate any particular genre of music, but when I was doing my research, I found that literature related to song lyrics was most often associated with genres such as rap and heavy metal. Johnathan Gruzelier states that heavy metal lyrics treat women as sex objects as part of a quest for male social bonding (Gruzelier, 2007). Rap music has been studied for misogynist lyrics and for using women as objects in videos (Kolawole, 1995).

Another gender difference in the music industry has to do with the branding and marketing of people as musicians. Kristin J. Lieb's 2013 book *Gender, Branding, and the Modern Music Industry* provides a wealth of information about this topic. Person brands operate differently than product brands, and female pop stars are typically short-term brands whose success is based mainly on their youth and sexuality (Green, 1997). According to Lieb, male artists may decide to play up other parts of themselves, but female artists largely play up sexuality and beauty and downplay their musical talent (Lieb, 2013).

However, female musicians are not the only ones who face challenges in marketing. Solo male pop musicians are picked by labels based on their facial beauty and muscularity (Hawkins, 2007). Hawkins attributes this to the 1980s marketing emphasis on appearance, which caused society to care more about their appearance (Hawkins, 2007). Gradually, the male *look* became as important as the sound of their music (Hawkins, 2007).

The part I found both most interesting and most infuriating was that women were often represented in musical settings as consumers of music rather than as producers, while men were portrayed as authentic makers of music (Leonard, 2007). For example, in music videos women are frequently used as adornment or decoration for the male instrumentalists. According to Jhally and Kilbourne (2010), women learn to see themselves as objects, sometimes under the guise of empowerment, which creates a dangerous pattern for young women who receive the message that only their looks matter (Lieb, 2013). Many of the sources discussed how female musicians are represented by their clothing. Lieb says that artists being marketed as "temptresses" begin to wear more tight-fitting clothing that exposes more of their body (Lieb, 2013). In today's competitive music industry, dressing more provocatively can gain a female musician an edge in sales. Consumers are so used to this that often only performers who are extremely scandalous stand out, according to Caputi's (2003) concept of "everyday pornography," which states that pornography has become so mainstream that people no longer recognize it (Lieb, 2013). This theory says that the way women are represented normalizes a culture of violence against women (Lieb, 2013). Many study participants, both male and female, remarked on the sexualization or objectification of women in the music they heard on a daily basis.

Besides reading about gender issues in the music industry, I focused on music and youth. I found inspiration in several studies. First, according to Green (1997), younger students are less likely to be involved in subcultures because they lack the resources and maturity, which means they rely on mainstream presentations of music as culture. Second, according to Lesley J. Pruitt, even though half the world's population is under the age of twenty-four, youth still view themselves as outsiders to society (Pruitt, 2014). They are usually portrayed in a negative light in the media (Pruitt, 2014). As such, sometimes young people feel as if they are being excluded from discussion, or they have difficulty communicating due to cultural differences or lack of education. Musical communication offers a chance to communicate in a way that is not tied to intelligence and that leaves everyone feeling part of the dialogue (Pruitt, 2014). Music can play a powerful role in altering identity at an individual or group level; it can also lead to a more peaceful understanding of self, develop self-esteem, and help in healing (Pruitt, 2014). For girls this can be especially empowering, if, as Pruitt says, girls have more of a tendency to self-censor in public (2014).

I find the topic of gender related to music endlessly fascinating, and as a result, I read many more sources than what you find in the reference section. If you have done research on this topic, you are probably yelling at this book in frustration. I know there are many, many interesting and relevant studies and that many have been completed since I conducted my research in 2015. However, since that time I have had a son and twin girls, so I have not had the free time to peruse said studies. You should read them, though, if you have the time.

Then I Attempted Some Research

Armed with my newfound background knowledge, I decided to gain some insight into my students' perspectives. First, I should explain a few things. Confidentiality of the students in this study was very important to me. In my original research, I gave them code numbers instead of names, but in this article, I have used fake names, as I feel that codes would be too impersonal. When the students are mentioned, I do not use their real names or provide any identifying information or information about their school. However, to give you some context, I can tell you that the research site was a school in a suburban city in Ontario with a student population of more than 1,400. The students at the school came from a variety of ethnic backgrounds. An effort was made to use maximum variation sampling by identifying students who had had a wide variety of musical experiences with the guitar both inside and outside the school.

The study data were collected through interviews with 14 students: 7 who identified as female and 7 who identified as male. The interviews were individual, in person, and recorded using an audio recorder. Students were largely asked the same set of questions, with some variations (you can read these in the appendix.) The interviews took place over a two-month period, and most of them lasted around 20 minutes, with the longest lasting around 50. The students were from grades ten to twelve and had a range of guitar experiences, from five months up to seven years, with a variety of levels of proficiency and dedication. Five male and six female participants had taken at least one guitar course at the school; courses were offered in grades ten, eleven, and twelve, and all but one male had previously taken at least one music class in high school. Now that this is out of the way, you should probably know what sort of information I was seeking in these interviews. My intention had been to ask a wide variety of questions about music in their lives to gain a sense of how the students in the sample viewed music in their lives, at school and in the media. The main research question was: What is the effect of gender on the musical lives of teenage guitar players? I also sought to answer:

1. What stereotypes exist about guitar playing and gender roles? Are there stereotypes surrounding musical genres in terms of gender roles?

2. How do teenagers believe both genders are represented in the media? How does this fit with what they see at school or in their lives?

3. How is playing the guitar emotionally and socially different for girls and boys?

A longer list of questions is included at the end of this article as an appendix.

As you can imagine, the interviews generated a great deal of data. There was far too much for me to discuss all of it here. So I will focus on the points of data that changed my practice, and those were largely about how these students saw music in the media.

Today's music educators understand that their students come to their classrooms bringing their own musical experiences and perceptions about music. Students come to my classroom having been bombarded with a variety of musical messages. I believe that part of my job is to help students begin to navigate the musical discourse and, if possible, add their voices to the conversation. To do this, I needed to understand what they perceived to be true about the music industry, and not what I perceived of their perceptions. After clearing the hurdle of not one, but two ethics committees to talk to my own students, I felt ready to start my journey once again. No, I felt more than ready. I, the noble educator, was boldly seeking knowledge, and this knowledge would change the world! Then my first interview yielded this statement from a girl I will call "Sameena":

> I don't know what a school or teacher could do. I feel like it's mostly in the hands of the media. I feel like media plays such a huge role in how people ... think, what they're supposed to do. It all comes from like the media.

Ah, well then. Maybe I would not be doing any world-changing after all. At least, I was right about the importance of the media in their lives. I began to focus on students' views and perceptions of the music industry and musicians in the media. Study participants were asked how male and female music artists were portrayed in the media. All participants felt that both male and female artists were sexualized in the media or made to be sex symbols, with each participating gender more likely to see this in their own gender.

In general, the participants felt that women in the music industry were more often seen as singers. Participants also felt that even when a female artist played an instrument, this ability was downplayed in favour of their singing, as stated in the examples below:

> Well, it's funny. I can't think of any female guitarist in the media, which is exactly what I think we're getting at here. Because, uh, you see a lot of female singers and they have male guitarists backing them up. In terms of Taylor Swift, she just does the singing. She writes all her own songs, but she just does the singing. So, uh, she's massively popular now because of her voice, not because of her guitar ability. But I'm 100% sure she can play guitar. I've seen her play guitar before. So there's not like a focus on a female guitar player. There's more like, yeah she can play guitar, but it's not the focus of her ability. – "George"

The female participants in the study also felt that women faced more pressure to look flawless than male artists. Beauty and an ideal body shape were considered to be a very important factor in the success of a female artist:

> I find that when you're watching behind the scenes stuff, guys they'll maybe dust a little bit of powder on and it's like, good to go. Or maybe they'll try to like throw some fake dirt on there, make him look a little tougher. But then with girls it's like: no, no, no, you have to be flawless, to quote Beyoncé. And just get 'em all ready and pretty and sparkly. – "Nina"

> Well I guess we have that ideal in body shape, perfect face, hair, whatever like that and because these singers aren't just singers. They're supposed to be like role models and idols. People don't see the thicker girls and

the girls who are too skinny as idols. They want that perfect ... perfect girl. – "Fatima"

I feel like a lot of pressure is put on female artists because it's like no matter how talented they are, a lot of weight is put on how they look as to how popular they'll be. – "Melinda"

According to the study participants, the importance of image was a problem for many male artists as well, not just for female artists. Participants felt that males in the music industry were more likely to be sexualized if they were singers, frontmen, or guitarists:

I see a lot of like sort of slick male guitarists. In the sense that like, that male singer-songwriter is like really cool. He's something you look up to. Man, it's really cool that's he's playing and singing by himself and writing all those songs. I see a lot of male guitarists. I don't really listen to Ed Sheeran, but from what I gather he has that sort of image. Like you sort of look at him and he's a little bit of a strange looking dude. He's not terribly attractive but then he sits down with a guitar and starts singing and you're like, "man that's incredible." He's sort of elevated to a new level, almost and I think that's the media perception of male guitarists. You single them out, they're much slicker. Like you don't see that kind of focus on a male drummer. Or a male bass player. It's just the male guitarist. – "George"

Could this perception be enough to silence or discourage those who do not feel that they fit the ideal image? I cannot say with any authority, because my group was so small, but I can say that many of the female participants in this survey listed insecurity as a reason they did not join or start a band, and more female than male participants stated that they practised alone or only played guitar in private. The importance of image in the media is clearly being felt and internalized by these teenagers, providing a boundary to their participation and success in music classrooms.

Students receive many messages about image through music, but that is not the only source of messages in music. Lyrics provide the most accessible and most obvious gender messages to students. Students were asked if they could identify unfriendly lyrics they had heard in genres of music or in specific songs, if possible. The aim of this question was to see how much students listened to and internalized the messages in the lyrics of their favourite songs. Most study participants could think of songs and genres of music with unfriendly lyrics toward women without much thought or prompting; rap, hip hop, and metal were the most commonly identified sources of unfriendly lyrics. (Again, I am in no way trying to blame these genres for perpetuating any type of negative gender message, so please do not send me hate emails. I am just telling you what the students told me.)

Participants felt that the lyrics identified were unfriendly because of they expressed misogyny, objectification, aggression, and the sexualization of women. The statements below indicate their understanding of the objectification and dehumanization of women in particular:

> There are songs that portray women as like an object. And like kind of a possession and how to get it or how they want it. Or how like they treat it too. And how they treat it like as an object. Or her as an object. – "Hope"

Study participants often mentioned derogatory or gender-specific swearing in music, as in the excerpt below:

Tamika: Well, there's a lot of profanity and they're always calling women "B" and Hos and whores. It's like, really? That's more the mainstream rap. Like they're on MTV and go on tours and stuff. That's where you usually see it.

Researcher: Do you find female rap artists any better with the language?

Tamika: No.

Researcher: Why do you think that is? They're women, why wouldn't they use better language about women?

Tamika: Because they're trying to keep up with the men.

In this excerpt, Tamika raises an important point: women are often forced to participate in musical cultures of misogyny or risk losing fame or income (Kolawole, 1995).

Some participants also identified lyrics or genres of music that they viewed as unfriendly toward men, but this was not as common. Pop songs and break-up songs were the most commonly identified as unfriendly, largely because they made all men seem the same, portrayed them in a negative light (cheaters, jerks, losers, etc.), or promoted unrealistic expectations for men's behaviour toward women (for example, that men should be overly romantic or that they should follow women's direction in a relationship). Some participants' views of this are below:

> Well, recently there's been a lot of pop songs about like heartbreak and everything. They kind of bash some guys in there, too. Certain lyrics, they'll talk about guys being heartbreakers or losers or whatever. – "Melinda"

Yeah, especially the singers that write from experience and have bad experience with guys. And if they were to put it into one of their songs, it's like
giving that one guy ... their look on that one guy to all guys. – "Sameena"

Most of the comments about unfriendly lyrics toward men came from female
participants; most of the males did not mention any unfriendly lyrics toward
males. While both points of view are valid, the lyrics deemed unfriendly toward
females were much more aggressive or violent than those deemed unfriendly
toward men.

Personally, I found this sad, but not nearly as sad as the fact that only two
of the fourteen participants stated that they avoided music with unfriendly
lyrics. Most said they heard and noticed these messages, and one stated that she
usually ignored them but thought differently about the artist afterwards. This
type of wilful ignorance surrounding the lyrics in our music suggests, I think,
why artists continue to be successful with lyrics that demean and objectify. I
wondered why students would hear these lyrics, be offended or angered, and
then choose to ignore them. Could it be that they did not possess the musical
knowledge and skills to do anything else in response to them? And did it have
to be that way?

So, What Happened Next?

As my research came to an end, I began to imagine what I, as a music educator, could do with all this information. I had been given a wonderful and rare
opportunity to sit with my students and discuss their opinions about music,
without any other students, schoolwork, or time constraints getting in our
way. This was all well and good, but unless I actually did something with this
information, then it was really just a thought exercise. Alright, I did not change
the world. However, it did change my practice, and that changed my world,
just a little.

Remember at the beginning of the chapter, when I said that the article was
not really about the research? (You should, because everyone knows that to
skim a large chapter like this one, you have to read the beginning and the end.)
Anyway, I told you this and then proceeded to tell you all about the research.
Well, all of that was about giving you context for this next part. (Unless you
skipped it, due to the skimming trick mentioned above. No hard feelings if
that is the case.)

I came to two important realizations:

1. It was important to me that my students be able to critically consider
   the music they interacted with in their lives. I wanted to give them the

vocabulary (both verbal and musical) to discuss and respond to the music in their lives instead of feeling forced into just living with it; and,

2. I felt it was important that students be given the skills to respond to this music by being able to create their own music. I wanted them to be able to add their thoughts and views to the musical discourse, rather than feeling that they were stuck in the role of passive consumer.

I mean, how strange is it that students see their relationship with music as so important yet so one-sided? How strange to teach students that they can participate in music-making in class or on their own but not in the real world. There are many reasons why the young women in my study said they felt they could not start a band, despite their interest in doing so. But what if one of those reasons was that they didn't have the tools to do this on their own? I wanted to give them the tools to use their own musical voice. (Figuratively. Students are super loud, so they've got the literal voice covered.) Did the students come to any such realization? Who knows?! I would have had to go through two more ethics committees to find out, so I did not ask.

I decided to take the next few years and focus on teaching students to develop composition and song-writing skills in my classes. With practice, students can begin to use these skills to express their opinions, thoughts, and feelings musically. They do not have to passively accept the messages they see and hear in the media. I also decided that I needed to create projects that challenged my students to think critically about the music industry. If I could teach students to question, think about, and address media messages, they would hopefully feel more comfortable using their voices (and instruments) to create their own music. I decided that these two things had to work together and that doing one without the other would not create the inclusivity I sought. I saw these gender issues as a kind of barrier in my classes that prevented some female-identified students from continuing in the program and publicly participating in music, and I wanted to help break this down. However important it is to break down gender barriers that prevent students from participating in musical activities, it is not just a matter of education. After the research, I came to realize that this was a matter of student wellness. Half of the fourteen participants mentioned using guitar or music to cope with death, depression, bullying, or stress. This was mentioned nearly equally by male and female participants:

> Unfortunately, I've been having a lot of issues this past year, just like mentally. It's been like a real strain, and just learning guitar and being able to escape and playing music that I really, really, really love has absolutely helped me cope with what's around me. – "George"

I know when I lost my horse it was so hard for me. It was one of the hardest things I've ever been through because I just love that horse more than life. And it's like, I had no idea what to do, so I'd get home, lock myself in my room, and listen to music. The only thing that could make me remotely better. – "Melinda"

Well, just recently, last year, I've lost five family members. And last month I lost my best friend – she died in a car accident. But playing guitar, I get to zone out and feel better. At the beginning of January I was really depressed but as soon as guitar started I got to zone in, clear my mind and everything and everything's for the better. – "Hope"

I think that most of the school music educators I know, like any musical community leaders, seek to provide an environment where students' wellness is a priority. The tough part about this in practice is that even though our primary music communities are located in our school, our students bring musical influences and experiences from a variety of places. As a result, music educators cannot afford to ignore our student's music if we hope to create the kind of community where our students can thrive. This is a small study, done by an amateur academic, and as such, I make no claims that my conclusions apply to anyone else in other educational situations. However, I will tell you what happened to me in my classroom, with my students.

First, I decided that all my grade nine classes would do two composition assignments. One within the first six weeks of class, and one in the last two months. I aimed to show the students that everyone could write music, whether we used instrumental composition or song writing. I focused on building the confidence and basic skills needed to be able to communicate musically. I wanted to normalize the idea of writing music. I decided that I would also have all grade nine music students tell me about important musical experiences in their lives using a podcast project. I also implemented critical thinking assignments in all grades in order to allow students to point out problems they saw in the music industry and actively respond to these perceived issues. I never allow them simply to point out a problem without taking some type of small action. For example, I choose different issues inherent in society (and therefore music) and ask students to identify a problem, provide evidence of it, and then take an action to respond to it. Students may point out misogynistic lyrics, provide examples from artists, and then write a parody or reimagining of those songs to address their perceived issues.

I want to be clear, before going further. I have always taught composition in my classes, for it is part of the Ontario curriculum. However, since my research,

I have not simply taught it – I have made musical literacy a focus of my courses. I think it has improved the participation of all students in my music classes; in addition to that, my music programs have grown, the gender balance has greatly improved, and I feel as if I am giving the students skills they can use to improve their wellness in their daily lives. I cannot provide any evidence of this beyond my own perceptions, because I have moved schools and have no wish to spend any more time with ethics committees when I have so many young children. You will just have to take my word for it. Or don't, that's fine, too. The important thing is that I feel I am better serving the students who enter my classroom and feel that my work is more relevant to their lives. Like I said, this was not the kind of research you are used to reading.

Concluding Thoughts

So, to summarize: I did a small research study to learn about the perceptions of my students related to gender issues in music. I found out that while they saw many issues with sexism, gender inequality, misogyny, and gender roles, especially in the media, they essentially ignored these issues. I decided that the best way for me to combat this was to take a twofold approach in my teaching: focus on developing stronger critical thinking skills related to music and media literacy, and focus on teaching my students about song writing, in order to give them a voice in the musical discourse. I contend that both of these things are needed together in order to create a more gender-equitable music classroom. I changed my practice in an attempt to reduce the gender barriers that many students face in music class, and I have continued to do so because my students have told me it has improved their wellness.

I told you earlier that this chapter is not really about the research, and even though I went on and on about my research after that, I really meant it. If there is anything to take from my experience for music educators, I hope it is this: find a barrier that is preventing your students from making music, and do something to lessen or break down that barrier. It could be gender in the music industry or racism or classism or anything else that concerns you as an educator and that affects your students. Learn all you can about it from as many people as possible. Then decide on what you can do with this knowledge that will change your practice. It may be insignificant to everyone else, but in your musical community it can be massive. All you have to do is figure out where to start.

Appendix: List of Interview Questions

Interviews were semi-structured, and the order of questions sometimes varied. Additional questions may have been asked to clarify or pursue topics that were raised by participants.

1. How would you define gender roles?
   a) How do you see gender roles in your life?
   b) Give an example of a time where you felt people were being treated differently because of their gender.
   c) How often do you notice gender differences in your life?

2. How did you begin playing guitar? What made you want to play this instrument? How did you learn to play?
   a) Do you think playing guitar is different for boys and girls? Why? Can you give an example of a time you noticed this?
   b) How do girls and boys learn guitar differently?

3. What does playing guitar mean to you?
   a) How do other people react when they find out you play guitar? Give an example.
   b) Tell me about how playing music makes you feel.
   c) Have you ever experienced resistance by parents, friends or other people to you playing guitar? If so, explain.
   d) Do you ever feel that you are limited in your choice of songs or styles of music because of your gender? Give an example of this.

4. What stereotypes have you encountered about guitar players?
   a) Tell me about a time you felt these stereotypes were true.
   b) Give an example of a time when you felt these stereotypes were untrue or unfair.

5. Do you think there are types of music that are for girls?
   a) Are there types of music for boys?

6. Tell me about a time you experienced or observed someone who didn't meet the gender norms in their taste in music.
   a) Tell me about what you think normal behaviour would be for a male guitarist.
   b) Give an example of something that would be strange for a male guitarist to do.
   c) Tell me what you think normal behaviour would be for a female guitarist.
   d) Give an example of something that would be strange for a female guitarist to do.

7. How are male guitarists portrayed in the media?
   a) How are female guitarists portrayed in the media?
   b) Does this media portrayal seem accurate to you, based on your experience with guitarists?
   c) Do you see more guitarists of one gender? Why do you think this is?

8. What kinds of lyrics have you heard which relate to gender?
   a) Do certain types of music have lyrics that bash one gender? Give an example of a song.
   b) How do songs by men talk about women?
   c) How do songs by women talk about men?
   d) How do songs by men talk about men?
   e) How do songs by women talk about women?
   f) Do you feel that there are any types of music that are hostile towards men or women? Give an example.

9. Who do you think is more likely to play guitar, boys or girls?
   a) Who do you think is more likely to join a band – boys or girls? Why do you think this is?
   b) In your experience as a teenager, do male and female guitarists play in groups of mixed genders often or do they stick to their own gender? Explain.
   c) Give an example of how playing guitar might be different for boys and girls.
   d) What do teenagers think of boys who play guitar?
   e) What do teenagers think of girls who play guitar?

10. What emotions does playing guitar make you feel?
    a) Give an example of a time when playing guitar helped you get through a hard time or made you feel better.
    b) Give an example of a time when playing the guitar made you feel upset or angry.

11. In school, which music classes have a reputation of being for boys?
    a) Which music classes have a reputation of being for girls?
    b) How would a boy in a "girls" class or a girl in a "boys" class be seen or treated by others?
    c) What do you think schools could do to make classes comfortable for both genders?
    d) How do you think schools could help to make guitar more gender equitable?
    e) How does the gender of the teacher make a difference? How so?

CHAPTER 8

Music-Making Opportunities for Children from Underserved Populations

Impact and Transformations through Community Youth Orchestras

Christine D'Alexander

I remember one night after rehearsal when I got dropped off at home after rehearsal and was carrying my viola on my back. There were police helicopters flying above our house and they were really low close to the houses. Cops were asking my mom if she saw the guy they were looking for and I remember being scared for her and my brother. Something bad happened again in the neighbourhood ... there were police cars everywhere with lights flashing and a lot of noise. I didn't know what was going on, and I wanted to just go back to orchestra and forget it all. When I'm there I can sometimes forget about some of the stuff that happens around my neighbourhood and I feel like a different person ... less stressed and just normal. – Jesus, age ten

YOUNG PEOPLE HAVE IMPORTANT ideas and opinions regarding how to make their schools, neighbourhoods, and communities-at-large better places. As in young Jesus's story above, children feel emotional turmoil just as raw as what adults experience. It is important to inquire – through what modes of music-making and community-building can we help children, teens, and young adults become resilient, reflective agents of positive social change? As community musicians, practitioners, teachers, and researchers, we must look for ways to prepare our youth to develop a deep engagement with our communities and become tomorrow's leaders. Inspirational learning communities are essential for children, so that they will learn to listen to one another, work together to identify challenges and solve problems, and acknowledge and respect diverse points of view. Through community music-making in a youth orchestra setting, children can transform their musical and social identities through empathetic practices and meaningful collaborations.

Introduction

Community music-making has been integral to the artistic and cultural fabric of the United States since before the country was founded. Built on the premise that everyone has the "right and inherent ability to create and participate in music" (Higgins & Willingham, 2017, p. 11), community music reflects diversity, culture, and social practices among people bound together by the intrinsic joy for music-making. Musical activity in community music-based contexts can promote self-expression and communication skills, and encourage unity as a means of cultural education, "which, in turn fosters tolerance and mutual respect" (Leglar & Smith, 2010, p. 344).

Recent studies have begun investigating the links between music and brain development, literacy, and cognition among children (Ilari, Keller, Damasio, & Habibi, 2016; Steele, 2017; Hallam, 2010), but few to date have addressed the possible social, cultural, and emotional benefits of music education for children (Rickard et al., 2013). In recent years, scholars and researchers have begun turning their attention to the musical, social, and cultural contexts that may enable or hinder children's musical development and identities (D'Alexander, 2015; Ilari, Keller, Damasio, & Habibi, 2016). However, little research has been done to date concerning musical and social skills development among children from diverse social, ethnic, and cultural groups – particularly in terms of skills and identity development through participation in community-based programs. Given the scarcity of research on young people's development of musical and social skills, particularly in underserved, at-risk communities, it is vital to acknowledge, explore, understand the musical and social practices children experience through community-based youth orchestra programs in relation to the development of children's musical and self-identities.

Community Orchestras in the United States

In the United States, community orchestra models are typically shaped by the needs and interests of a particular community; they aim to provide life-long musical learning. Most community orchestras, including youth orchestras, involve collective music-making and the sharing of experiences during and outside of rehearsals and performances. These community ensembles can provide engaging social and musical experiences for the players, thus fostering relationships as well as identity formation. They are communities of practice (Wenger, 1998), as well as performance, and as such provide a vital context for learning and communication.

There are reports from the 1730s of concert activities in Boston, Massachusetts, and Charleston, South Carolina, spreading beyond their church-based beginnings into more secular venues (Leglar & Smith, 2010). The town of Lititz, Pennsylvania, six miles from Lancaster, had a community orchestra as early as 1765. That orchestra supplemented church services with instruments such as strings, flutes, and French horns. In the early nineteenth century, many community music activities were established that thrive to this day. In 1809, the Boston Phil-Harmonic Society was founded. By 1842, the Philharmonic Symphony Society – the oldest orchestra in continuous existence in the United States – was benefiting from a thriving community music scene.

Musicians in community orchestras can be of almost any age. They may hail from a variety of professions and educational backgrounds. These orchestras enrich and energize their members as well as their communities. Participation in a community orchestra is a viable form of active music-making (Shansky, 2010). Community orchestras and ensembles provide cohesion for community members and players as well as an environment "in which people whose paths would never cross in the ordinary way can find common group in their shared interest in music" (Leglar & Smith, 2010, p. 352).

The Community Youth Orchestra Model

Community youth orchestras offer children of all ages the experience of participating in a large, multitalented, and demographically diverse group. These ensembles expose young people to a wide range of repertoire and opportunities. They also serve as gateways for young musicians to become future supporters of community orchestras.

In the United States, the first community youth orchestra was founded in 1924 in Portland, Oregon. The Portland Junior Symphony Association, later renamed the Portland Youth Philharmonic Association, trained young musicians in the 1920s, with a focus on high standards and sharing music with the community. It performed a concert in Salem, Oregon, the very year it was founded (www.portlandyouthphil.org).

Community youth orchestras have expanded greatly over the past fifteen years in the United States (Apsler, 2009). According to the League of American Orchestras (www.americanorchestras.org), in 2016, there were more than 500 youth orchestras, found in all fifty states and the District of Columbia. These ensembles offer young musicians various approaches to learning music through participation. They help children reach collective goals and provide a venue for them to express themselves through performance. Community youth orchestras also serve as spaces for collaborative learning, musical exploration, and personal and social growth. They instil confidence and offer a multitude of learning experiences (Higgins, 2012). These orchestras typically prepare children for scheduled performances while engaging local community members and families in musical experiences. They typically rehearse between one and five days per week, depending on the orchestral program.

Oftentimes, these ensemble traits include performances in community centres, outdoor venues for the invited public to attend, major concert halls, schools, or churches. Youth orchestras of an advanced calibre may take part in collaborations with professional orchestras, soloists, and other professional artists and competition winners from their own communities; they can also commission new music for their ensembles (Lane, 2016). The community orchestras provide musical and social value for their musicians and audience members and for the community-at-large. They also have enormous intrinsic value: their members carry a sense of joy and love for the music, share friendships, and work together to foster pride through shared music-making.

Children in community youth ensembles participate for a variety of reasons. Scherber (2014) investigated what drew young people to participate in ensembles and found that they did so for both musical and social reasons. They wanted to develop and improve their musical skills, learn new music, experience diverse musical opportunities, have fun, spend time with friends, and form new relationships. King (2014) found that orchestra activities provided social (i.e., besides musical) benefits, including teamwork opportunities. Young people also developed self-esteem and found relief from daily stressors. Given all these benefits, it is no wonder these ensembles are gaining popularity with young people.

Rise of Community Youth Orchestras in Underserved Areas

The last decade has seen a steady increase in the number of community youth orchestras in underserved areas in the United States. These ensembles vary in size, curriculum, age and skill level, and degree of formal or informal learning. El Sistema–inspired programs are becoming increasingly popular, with more 287 programs in fifty-five countries in 2018 (www.sistemaglobal.org). A number of barriers may prevent children from underserved areas for gaining access to music education. These barriers include lack of music education opportunities in the school day, lack of community music ensembles geared to young musicians in their neighbourhoods, difficulties with transportation (i.e., lack of a vehicle or public transit challenges), time constraints due to work schedules and childcare, and financial constraints related to instrument rentals, transportation, and childcare. Children and families who find themselves at a disadvantage, including migrant populations and at-risk youth in low-income communities, often thrive when they join community youth orchestras.

These ensembles, whether they are inspired by El Sistema or not, provide accessible music education and performance opportunities, as well as social opportunities for children from a variety of socio-economic environments. Because the rehearsals usually take place after school and/or on weekends, they have an especially strong impact on at-risk youth. Rehearsal spaces offer safe havens for children to develop productive relationships with family and peers (Steele, 2017). They also bridge boundaries between socio-economic statuses, ethnic backgrounds, age groups, and skill levels.

Latino Children in the United States

Over the past two decades, Latinos have become the largest, fastest-growing population in the United States. They are also the youngest ethnic group in the country (Kelly-McHale & Abril, 2015; Casellas & Ibarra, 2012; US Census Bureau, 2013). At present, they constitute 17 percent of the US population; projections are that by 2050, they will comprise 25 percent (Hungerford-Kresser & Amaro-Jiménez, 2012). The number of Latino children has risen dramatically, so that Latino students are now the majority student population in two of the largest American states – California and Texas. Latino youth are a vibrantly diverse and culturally rich cohort. Families and communities play a significant role in many cultural experiences and identities to which Latino children are exposed. Cultural preferences and personal tastes develop from exposure to a variety of experiences (Jeynes, 2003; Williams, 2013).

As a matter of equity and social justice, it is imperative that teachers, including music teachers, attend to the needs of Latino students both at school and in their communities. Culturally responsive teaching approaches are necessary in order to reach diverse groups of students. It is important that teachers and mentors "not only acknowledge and understand diverse cultures represented ... but ... act upon their understanding through all interactions with students and their families" (Kelly-McHale & Abril, 2015, p. 160). Culturally responsive teaching must extend beyond acknowledging various outward experiences of culture such as foods, traditional music, and clothing, and delve deeper into Latinos' cultural practices and values. (The same is true, of course, for all ethnic groups.) It is important for teachers to experience and embrace new communities through immersion, learn about different cultural traditions, and recognize and combat their own biases and preconceptions.

Description of Site

Mountain Ridge is part of a majority Spanish-speaking, low-income, at-risk community in Los Angeles, California. It is a vibrant community full of culture and tradition. Unfortunately, the neighbourhood surrounding the Mountain

Ridge orchestra program suffers from high crime rates, drug use, and frequent police activity. Driving through the neighbourhood during the day, one looks up at a sea of palm trees dancing in the ocean breeze against a blue sky and smells the savoury aromas of home cooking wafting from the small, often dilapidated houses lining each block. It is common to see children whizzing by on sidewalks with their scooters and skateboards, and men or women ringing small bells on their carts, selling fruit or ice cream for neighbours to enjoy.

During after-school hours, Mountain Ridge becomes a hub for music-making. An El Sistema-inspired youth orchestra program, Mountain Ridge holds rehearsals during after-school hours and on Saturday mornings. Eighty students between seven and fifteen, most of them Latino, are enrolled in various music classes or rehearsals. The program includes small and large ensembles, choral and chamber music, and music theory. Most children in the ensemble receive between eight and eleven hours of instruction per week, depending on their age and ensemble. The children all seem to know one another from the social activities that take place during programs, or from extra-curricular activities offered by the orchestra, such as community potlucks and picnics and free concert performance field trips throughout Los Angeles. When not in music classes, the children of Mountain Ridge can be found outside playing tag and hand-clapping games, recruiting other peers for impromptu soccer matches, or eating snacks by the outdoor picnic tables. The children are kind to one another and eager to have their teachers join in their games or gossip sessions.

During rehearsals, one can expect to be greeted by parents and siblings. Folding chairs line the perimeter of the main rehearsal space, and there is a very communal feel to the area. Younger brothers and sisters run around and play in close proximity to their parents while orchestra rehearsals carry on just a few feet away. English and Spanish are mingle in overheard conversations among parents and family members, though older adults speak mainly Spanish to one another. Teachers and teaching artists move in and out of orchestra sections, answering questions, guiding students to make music, or playing along with them as smiles are traded back and forth during practice sessions. Rehearsals always seem to be light in nature, and the conductor and teaching artists consistently use positive language when working with the young musicians. Dialogues and discussions are common between the conductor's podium and the children seated nearby, and the conductor often involves the parents and family members in conversations as well.

The teaching staff genuinely enjoy being there and working with their young protégés, and it is common for parents and staff to chat after rehearsals and exchange hugs and pleasantries as families part ways to go home.

Vignettes

Jesus, 10, viola. Jesus, a timid ten-year-old boy, joined Mountain Ridge and began playing the viola at the age of eight. Short for his age, he would often forget his instrument at home, apologetically confessing to his youth orchestra mentors and teachers that it had been chaotic in his house before school, and he and his mom forgot to grab it before being picked up by the bus. An undocumented immigrant from Guatemala, Jesus gravitated to the viola almost immediately, expressing that he loved the warm sound it made and preferred it to the violin's E string. Over the course of the first six months of participation, his teachers and mentors often observed a withdrawn, quiet child who at times would whisper underlying threats to stand partners in the section – a clear sign that something was emotionally challenging him. Children who bully others are often being bullied themselves, and it was later learned that Jesus endured endless harassment at school from classmates and peers, particularly during recess. Cruel names – "loser," "dork" – and an array of expletives were hurled at him throughout his days at school, and it was disheartening and painful to see how these torments took hold of his innocence and persona during orchestra rehearsals. One day during our conversations, Jesus opened up about his shifts in identity between school and Mountain Ridge:

> It's hard when I'm at school because the kids are mean and ruin my day. So by the time I get to orchestra, I'm angry and just want to go home and be alone. There's no one I can really hang out with at home, my brother is six and my mom is busy working and taking care of him. I guess by the time I leave rehearsal I'm better, usually ... Sometimes I still am angry about school when I leave but the people here are way nicer and always want to help me ... I'm more happy here and like it way better. I want to try and be better and am starting to make friends here, which I like, but I don't want to go back to school. My little brother is curious about music since I play it now. He will join the orchestra next year when he turns seven. He wants to play the viola. So, I can help him with that and we can be in music class together.

Over the next several months of orchestra programming, Jesus slowly began opening up to peers and teachers. In addition to confiding in his teachers and orchestra friends about the bullying at school, it was also learned that he felt an immense amount of stress about being an undocumented child, though felt being in music was helping him bond with other students with the same interests. During the course of participation, he began to demonstrate leadership qualities in the viola section, and he began sitting next to students with less experience and helping them with note reading, posture, and support. It was observed that once he began to take ownership of these roles, Jesus began to feel more comfortable in this environment and with his musical routines and social circles.

Mia, 12, cello. I heard the vivacious Mia, a chatty, high-energy twelve-year-old cello player, sprinting down the hallway as her sneaker soles rubbed again the linoleum floor and came to a screeching halt just before turning into the doorway to chat with me. "I heard you sprinting down the hall," I slyly remarked. "Uh … I wasn't sprinting!" she insisted, her dark brown eyes wide and bright and a mischievous smile on her face that secretly made me smile. Always the outspoken one with something to say, Mia had been playing the cello for three years, having fallen in love with it since the first day of music lessons at Mountain Ridge. Born in Los Angeles, she is the quintessential extrovert, constantly surrounding herself with friends and chatting up any teacher, parent, or peer in immediate ear's length. Usually rotating between first and second stand in cello sectionals and rehearsals, Mia would endlessly try to converse with the orchestra conductor and teachers, whether it was before or after rehearsals or during moments of pause when the group needed to work on a section. I imagined she would forget there were eighty other students in the rehearsals as she became consumed with the music and social conversations around her. A self-described tomboy, she was forging her own style, with Converse shoes, different-coloured shoelaces, and vintage T-shirts displaying photos of The Smiths, Depeche Mode, and Led Zeppelin. She would come to rehearsals proudly announcing she cut her own bangs, which was apparent. Mia's individualistic qualities and exuded confidence were beautiful to observe, especially as most twelve-year-olds are only beginning to discover their own identities, individualism, and place in the world. Mia was a natural-born leader. She already identified as a musician, and dreamed of becoming a professional cellist when she "grows up":

> Playing my cello inspires me to be a better person and try harder to reach my goals. It takes a lot of practice but I think I'm getting better and that makes me happy and want to keep moving forward on my instrument. The music we play here is more challenging and fun than in school and a lot of times I'm bored in those rehearsals. Most of my friends are in this orchestra and we hang out a lot of times on weekends, and our parents take turns letting us have sleepovers and going to each other's houses … which is cool because some of my friends live kind of far away and I don't see them until orchestra so we are like a family that gets together at the end of the days and on weekends, and our parents are friends now, too.

Mia aspired to attend a specialized arts high school in Los Angeles and would wake up early before the school day to practise her cello. Her mother mentioned that she would call up mentors and older students and receive informal cello lessons through FaceTime and Skype. One of the most determined, persistent children I have ever come across, she clearly had the intrinsic drive to set and reach her own goals. The joy and enthusiasm she had for music and for her social life was contagious. Mia always created an uplifting mood for the people surrounding her in her own little musical community within the Mountain Ridge orchestra.

Jason, 12, violin. Born in East Los Angeles, Jason began learning the violin on his own when he was eight years old. He had a natural talent for music and quite a developed ear from a young age. During one of our first encounters at Mountain Ridge, he nonchalantly walked up to me while playing the opening bars of the Mendelssohn Violin Concerto, Op. 64. His violin scroll was tilted down toward the floor as he slid into every one of the opening shifts; even so, I was deeply impressed that he had already learned the first eight bars of the concerto by ear and through YouTube videos. He was passionate about music and proudly disclosed that he also played the recorder and was enrolled in mariachi groups in Los Angeles, thanks to his grandfather, who also played the violin. Jason had a younger sister, also a violin player in the orchestra, and I was surprised how well they got along. Members of the orchestra looked up to Jason. He was kind to everyone, was a musical role model for others in the section, and genuinely enjoyed being surrounded by friends in the orchestra. He did not have many friends in his social circle at school, admitting that he had low self-esteem due to his small frame and skinny body. However, his orchestra friends viewed him differently, and he felt most "at home" when with that peer group. Children older than Jason would watch him play, for he volunteered to play for whoever would listen to him. His knowledge of notable violinists was impressive – he had researched most of them through internet videos. He and I had many conversations about the violin greats: we chatted about Itzhak Perlman, Gil Shaham, and Hilary Hahn (and her Instagram account dedicated to her violin case). He was obsessed with Lindsey Stirling and every song she had released. It was easy to sense his innate love for music and the comfort that he found being part of this orchestral community. He felt that he already knew how to hold the bow perfectly and that he was a wiz up and down the fingerboard, so he was often reluctant to accept the technical guidance offered by his teachers. During his years learning violin without a formal teacher, he had developed a number of bad habits with regard to posture and technique, and his teachers tirelessly worked with him to try and correct everything. Slowly, he was making progress, and he was praised for finally allowing others to constructively critique and assist in his playing. Jason thrived in this environment, gaining self-esteem and social skills he had lacked before he began participating:

> [In orchestra] I want to learn new things I didn't know before ... like vibrato and more shifting. I just learned how to shift and I'm getting good at it. I watch how Lindsey Stirling plays a lot and I'll put on her songs and play the violin part along with her. I'm seeing her concert next month and going to her book signing. Some of the other kids here said they wanted to go too, so maybe we'll go together. She's my favourite violin player and I'll play her songs for my family and at family parties when I have my violin.

Jason always enjoyed performing for others, often volunteering to play a solo piece he was working on at Mountain Ridge to whomever would listen to him. He performed solos during informal talent shows led by the Mountain Ridge staff, led the violin section throughout much of the concert season, and was hoping to learn how to play the cello in the future, in addition to progressing on the violin. Demonstrating undeniable talent and drive to become a better violinist, Jason was offered free violin lessons from a violin player in a local professional symphony orchestra and was getting ready to transfer to an arts magnet school for the remainder of his school years. Mountain Ridge has had a powerful impact on his musical identify formation. He has a sense of ownership of his violin, his family and community, and his place in the orchestra.

Misty, 9, violin. Misty, a bubbly nine-year-old, had been playing her instrument for just over one year. She always had a wide grin on her face and had an infectious giggle that made everyone smile. The Mountain Ridge teaching artists always knew when she was around, because of her laugh and her obvious lack of personal space. Misty's older sister was also a violinist in the orchestra, though the two of them hardly spoke in rehearsals. Almost daily, Misty would hound her teachers, asking when she could move from a half-size violin to a three-quarter-size. "Miss, when can I get the bigger one?," became a routine part of the conversation four to five days a week. The pint-size firecracker of the violin section, she was close to her family and enjoyed singing songs and drumming on any object she could get her hands on:

> Music is present everywhere in my house ... like when my mom is cooking, I make a beat to it ... like how she cooks. I think I want to play drums and violin but my parents said I can only play one and they want me to play

violin so that's fine. But we always have music playing at home, in the car. I like to listen to relaxing music at night but then we listen to different music when we are cleaning or cooking. I like different kinds and my family listens to classical music too because we play it in orchestra sometimes.

One of the youngest students in the orchestra, Misty spent much of her off-instrument time with three other girls of the same age. She chatted about the trials and tribulations of fourth grade to friends and teachers, often attended tutoring sessions offered by Mountain Ridge, and enjoyed coming to orchestra early to read a book while sitting under a table on a beanbag chair. As a nine-year-old, Misty was just getting started on her path as a musician, but her curiosity toward musical learning, paired with her enthusiasm and confident excitement from sitting with older friends in rehearsals, struck me as unique – I had not seen anything like it before. She had a bold, strong presence, full of sassiness and humour. Older students took Misty under their wing, treating her like a little sister; her adult teachers and mentors proudly witnessed her musical growth with the instrument. Her identity continued to take shape through social and musical interactions with her peers and older counterparts.

Summary and Approaches

Often, we find ourselves teaching the way we were taught, and it can be difficult to break that cycle. However, it is possible to advance musicianship in students while increasing their social capital and empowerment. Providing positive, goal-oriented, mindful feedback and constructive criticism and sharing ideas through active discussions and dialogues can result in deeper levels of engagement and self-confidence. It can also strengthen student effort, expression, energy, interpretation, and ownership. Providing helpful, honest opinions through music-making builds empathy and self-worth in children and adults as well as in the collective (Higgins & Willingham, 2017; Bartel & Cameron, 2004). Furthermore, positive feedback and active dialogue can motivate and empower youth to acquire self-confidence, empowerment, and problem solving and decision-making skills, while developing their musical artistry.

Allowing children agency, or choice in what they do and control, may increase their engagement in a musical setting, their eagerness to participate, and their enjoyment of learning (Green, 2002; Lindley, 2013). For example, facilitating dialogue between students, teachers, and conductors regarding repertoire or song selections can provide students with a sense of purpose and voice. Of course, all pieces proposed to students should have a sensible place in the program. However, opening up this conversation to students, and allowing them a place in the discussion, allows them to experience collaboration among their peers and teachers, read and understand the nuances of musical scores, and share desires and goals pertaining to their orchestra and rehearsals. This allows them to feel a sense of ownership of and pride in their ensemble.

Also, reaching students through social, off-instrument activities and conversations can help them connect to one another and to the community. In a musical environment such as collective rehearsal time, the young musicians listen to one another and model practices and behaviours, and come to rely on one another rather than on the conductor, teacher, or mentor (Govias, 2013) – particularly when they experience "interdependence at an extremely tangible level, and appreciate their collective strength and capacities when working in concert" (p. 39). Through this communication, children can begin to understand the importance of interdependence and musical communication as well as the need for community.

Choice-based instruction can extend beyond repertoire selection. Relinquishing part of the control in a classroom or ensemble space can allow social learning to take place among students. Youth can be allowed to democratically determine their own musical and social activities, establish their own objectives and benchmarks, decide on positive incentives for the ensemble, and explore ideas for future rehearsals. Providing meaningful experiences and contexts for students relevant to the events in their lives and their feelings about them can have positive effects on their musical and social identities; it can also bring them closer together, as an ensemble as well as with their families and their community.

Also essential to the youth orchestra model is the importance of working with each individual child, meeting them "where they are" in regard to their musical *and* social starting points. When teaching or mentoring, one must be mindful to educate the whole child. This means attending to their cognitive, social, emotional, and physical development (Kochhar-Bryant & Heishman, 2010). Incorporating the whole child into one's teaching and refraining from catering solely to a child's musical progress can significantly strengthen relationships with students and their families. In most community youth orchestras, especially in El Sistema-inspired ensembles, children typically attend rehearsals and programming during after-school and evening hours and/or on weekends. Children often bring to rehearsals a variety of new social and emotional experiences they encountered the previous week. These experiences can be positive or negative, can relate to school, their home life, or their community, and can challenge them to communicate and process emotions in a healthy way.

The community youth orchestra model can empower youth by taking both musical and non-musical approaches. Musical and social mentors can provide support in a variety of ways. Some ideas for this follow:

+ Off-instrument time in small groups. This allows students time to interact, problem-solve, and work together and can be facilitated through group score study, role playing, and team-building activities.

+ Bonding activities focused on leadership, responsibility, and empathy. This can include facilitated or non-facilitated talking circles, community service opportunities, and student-led ensembles or rehearsals.

+ Tiered mentorship. This can involve young adults in mentorship activities with the orchestra players. They would mentor the young musicians while simultaneously receiving professional development training in child development, teaching, and holistic class management.

Implications and Pathways to Implementation

Establishing, nurturing, and growing a thriving community youth orchestra requires many hands. The saying "It takes a village" rings true for community music; indeed, it defines community music, for many people must work together for it to meet its goals. All community youth orchestras vary in terms of their mission and philosophy, teaching and learning approaches, rigour in terms of rehearsal schedule and skill, choice of repertoire, and community involvement (Ilari, Keller, Damasio, & Habibi, 2016). But at the most fundamental level, every such orchestra provides (or should provide) equitable musical access and enjoyment for children, nurture musical curiosity, and create better citizens and lifelong learners.

Engagement with both the orchestra and the community is critical. Reach out to those in the community who may already be advocating music education, community music, and orchestra learning. Perhaps these people are professional or community orchestra board trustees, professional musicians, local education policy-makers, or members of professional music ensembles such as symphony orchestras. Strive to engage in partnerships with local schools and arts organizations, and be responsive to local, state, and national arts standards.

Work with local school districts and honour, learn from, and engage with school music teachers. Music teachers often excel at creating community within their programs due to the strong culture of performance, teamwork, and large-ensemble work (Stringham, 2016). Perhaps the local school orchestra would like to do a side-by-side performance with your community youth orchestra or share a concert program. Working with school districts is a fantastic way to help with recruitment and retention, and in turn, school orchestras may see a benefit – children playing in both school and community groups will most likely excel at music more quickly, strengthening both ensembles and paving the way for new leadership roles among your ensembles. Also, engage in dialogue pertaining to the challenges and opportunities facing local schools. It is very possible your orchestra can help in a number of ways.

Most importantly, know your community and its constituents. Visit local libraries, restaurants and grocery stores, schools, churches, businesses, and social services, and meet and chat with community members. The more one understands the community and the people it serves, the stronger a bond can be established between the community orchestra and that community. Celebrate the diversity and vibrancy of the community and its people, and share the joys of music with them.

Involve families and community members in your community youth orchestra. Whether your program is El Sistema-inspired and runs multiple times a week, or runs for only a few hours on weekends, utilizing volunteers and mentors will strengthen the community's bonds with the orchestra; it will also alleviate many of the tasks and duties required to keep all parts of the orchestra moving. For example, establish a parent network and hold monthly or quarterly meetings after a rehearsal. This is a wonderful time to update families on vision, goals, and progress. Newsletters are another easy way to feel closer to families and the community, especially when it is difficult to meet them face-to-face. Newsletters should always be translated into whatever language(s) are dominant in the community. The newsletter might feature short biographies of teachers, pictures of students and short interviews with them, programming updates, and practice tips.

Concluding Thoughts

I have had the privilege and honour to teach and work in underserved communities for nearly ten years. Never had I imagined the profound impact it would have on my life and future work. Community music, to me, embodies collaboration and sharing of ideas and practices no matter what age, empowering the whole self, and creating and experiencing joy through meaningful interactions with others.

CHAPTER 9

Time to Face the Music?

Possibilities for Community Music with Older Adults

Don D. Coffman and William M. Dabback

It was a magical moment. The outpouring of genuine appreciation for the band's performance was something the director had rarely, if ever, experienced to that degree. Each piece had its share of small flaws, yet the concert had received a standing ovation that lasted long enough for a couple of curtain calls. Afterwards, one player asked, with an expression of utter amazement, "Did they like us because we're good or because we're old?" (Coffman & Levy, 1997, p. 17)

Old age ain't no place for sissies.
– Bette Davis

GOOD OR OLD? Praiseworthy or pitiable? Does this player's question reflect some experience with ageism, the prejudice and discrimination that older adults may encounter? The idea that older adults can learn to play instruments in late life may surprise those who perhaps unconsciously hold some ageist prejudices. What motivates these adults? What challenges them? What success do they have? What do they gain in return? How do they approach their aging? Like this?

Almost everyone fears growing older. We know that the body reaches its maximum physical maturity between the ages of nineteen and twenty-six and then gradually begins to deteriorate, which affects the senses, the cardio-vascular and neuromuscular systems, the brain, and internal organs. Primary mental abilities (e.g., number and word fluency, vocabulary, inductive reasoning, spatial orientation) have been observed to decline with age, usually affecting performance in daily life after age sixty, and more noticeably after the mid-seventies (Schaie, 1996). Older adults require more time to encode and select information, sustain attention, and divide attention between tasks (Cavanaugh,

1997). Reaction time typically slows after age sixty-five (Bee, 1996). These physical changes associated with aging can be challenging, yet negotiating role and identity changes due to retirement, illness, loss of a spouse, and other adjustments in professional and personal circumstances may present the most significant boundaries adults must address in their later years. Is it any wonder that statements like this have appeared?

> *All diseases run into one – old age.*
> – Ralph Waldo Emerson

Yet, many writers assert that growing old is not simply deterioration. Margaret Morganroth Gullette, for one, has countered these negative perspectives with books such *Declining to Decline: Cultural Combat and the Politics of the Midlife* (1997) and *Agewise: Fighting the New Ageism in America* (2011). She and others before her have argued against long-standing assumptions about the elderly and unfavourable behaviours toward them. For instance, when we assume that the old have little productivity left to offer, we marginalize them. This attitude may partly explain why the idea of educating the old is relatively new (e.g., the first issue of *Educational Gerontology* dates to 1976).

Community musicians who wish to work with older adults and who wish to be aware of possible ageist biases ought to understand older adults' needs. A pioneer in adult education (McClusky, 1974) noted four learning needs: coping needs (e.g., physical well-being, economic self-sufficiency); contributive needs (meaningful participation in society); influence needs (being agents for social change); and expressive needs (participating in activities for their own sake and not necessarily to achieve a goal).

Cohen (2000) championed a focus on expressive needs – or as he put it, the creative spirit in everyone. For Cohen, this creative spirit (1) strengthens our morale in later life, (2) contributes to physical health as we age, (3) enriches relationships, and (4) is our greatest legacy (p. 11). In short, Cohen contended that nurturing creativity addresses other needs as well. He went further to present adult development as phases of human potential: (1) midlife re-evaluation (40s to 60s), (2) liberation (60s to 70s), (3) summing up (70s and older), and (4) encore (80s and older). These phases could be characterized negatively (e.g., midlife crisis, empty-nest, retirement), but viewed as phases of potential, Cohen's message of "If not now, when?" is one of hope and resonates with this notable assertion:

> *Aging is not lost youth but a new stage of opportunity and strength.*
> – Betty Friedan

This chapter focuses on older adults who make music in structured ensembles – an approach that can differ from other forms of community music, such as workshops. We rely on two sets of parameters to situate these ensembles within the framework of community music. The first set delineates three perspectives for viewing community music:

> [W]e propose three broad perspectives of community music: (1) community music as the "music of a community," (2) community music as "communal music-making," and (3) community music as an active intervention between a music leader or leaders and participants. While it is possible for a given musical group or event to display more than one of these perspectives simultaneously, we believe that clarifying the differences between the perspectives permits a better understanding of the multiple occurrences of community music-making around the world. (Coffman & Higgins, 2012, p. 845)

The second set specifies a definition for a community music ensemble:

> An instrumental or vocal group typically comprised of volunteer amateur or semi-professional musicians. Derived from the Latin *communitas* and Old French *comunité*, modern senses of the word *community* include (1) a group of people viewed collectively due to proximity, common interests or characteristics and (2) the quality of relationships in a group, such as shared goals, values, identities, participatory decision making, and mutual support. In combination with the French *ensemble* (from the Latin *insimul*, at the same time), the term community music ensemble connotes a group of musicians, a locale, a unity of purpose, and concerted action or ethos. (Coffman, 2013, p. 366)

Extracting the relevant elements of these parameters leads to our focus on localized musical groups of older adults who have gathered due to their shared interests in communal music-making. Directors of these groups are not likely to refer to themselves as community musicians or view their leadership efforts as interventions, yet their efforts to empower the performers in their groups embrace the facilitating roles adopted by many who identify themselves as community musicians.

New Horizons Bands

Grow old along with me! The best is yet to be.
— Robert Browning

Our experience is with bands that are part of the New Horizons International Music Association (NHIMA). NHIMA traces its roots to 1991 in Rochester, New York, when about sixty adults responded to a newspaper invitation from Eastman professor Roy Ernst to learn to play a musical instrument (Ernst & Emmons, 1992). Since then, the movement has grown into an international organization comprising more than 200 programs in the United States, Canada, Australia, and Europe. NHIMA is an affiliation of autonomous musical organizations; it shares a newsletter and a website (http://www.newhorizons music.org) and has national institutes (i.e., "band camps" – gatherings of players for a few days of intensive music-making). Most groups rehearse once or twice a week in senior centres, music stores, schools, or churches and are led by retired school ensemble directors or by university music professors.

Unlike many community music bands, NHIMA bands do not limit membership to proficient players; groups do not have auditions. Another distinction is that the programs often offer a single large concert band plus an array of small chamber groups and sometimes individualized instruction for players, thus providing first-time access to instrumental music for novices and a re-entry point for more experienced players. Dr. Ernst's beliefs permeate the organization, which has touched the lives of thousands of participants:

> When I started the first New Horizons band in 1991, my philosophy was that anyone can learn to play music at a level that will bring a sense of accomplishment and the ability to perform in a group. Thousands of New Horizons musicians have proven that to be true, many starting in their late retirement years with no musical background at all.
>
> Another aspect of my philosophy for New Horizons is that the style of instruction must be completely supportive and free of competition and intimidation. New Horizons directors feel liberated and find new enjoyment in teaching when they don't have to give grades, take groups to competitive festivals and have participants compete for seating in a section. My motto is, "Your best is good enough."
>
> The goal of New Horizons groups is to create an entry point to group music-making for adult beginners and a comfortable re-entry point for adults who played music in school and would like to resume after long years of building careers and raising children. (http://newhorizonsmusic .org/dr-roy-ernst)

The NHIMA philosophy emphasizes accessibility and safety, which are hall-marks of community music practice:

> A New Horizons Music program should be inclusive rather than exclu-sive. Every person has musical potential that can be developed to a level that will be personally rewarding. Many adults have been made to feel unmusical, often by parents or music teachers. It is common at New Horizons informational meetings to hear people say things like "My par-ents said, 'No one in this family has musical talent, so you're not going to start music classes.'" Or, "My music teacher said, 'Move your lips, but don't make any sound.'" Those scars last a lifetime, and the people who carry such memories will need assurance. (http://newhorizonsmusic .org/concept-and-philosophy)

Because these groups operate somewhat like school bands, some commu-nity musicians may not view them as examples of community music activity, particularly in the intervention sense. These groups can be viewed as exam-ples of non-formal teaching and learning: they offer systematic and deliber-ate instruction, yet they exist outside of formal teaching institutions. To the degree that their directors operate from learner-centred perspectives teaching and learning, allowing participants some degree of self-direction, the groups begin to display more of the spirit of community music aspirations when they "encourage and empower participants to become agents for extending and developing music in their community" (Higgins, 2012, p. 86).

NHIMA participants' gender and experience vary with age (see Tables 1 and 2), but the typical NHIMA participant is about sixty-seven years old, equally likely to be male or female, Caucasian, married, a former player, holder of a college degree, and relatively wealthy (Carucci, 2012; Coffman, 2008; Jutras, 2011). In the middle range of ages (65–74 years), the proportion of males to females is about even, while below that range, females outnumber males, and above that range, males outnumber females (Coffman, 2008). Some research indicates that novices are twice as likely to be women than men (Coff-man, 2008; Coffman & Schilf, 1998).

Research suggests that NHIMA contexts benefit older adults with regard to structure, motivation, close community, and opportunities for personal growth and identity revision. NHIMA involvement can confirm participants' perceptions of themselves as healthy, vibrant adults engaged in activities about which they feel passionate. Supporting the counter-narratives of authors like Gullette (1997; 2011) that push against stereotypes of older adults as frail,

Table 9.1 NHIMA Participants. Figures are percentages, except for mean age.

	Coffman (2008) $n = 1,652$	Jutras (2011) $n = 1,283$	Carucci (2012) $n = 1,170$
Mean age (range)	67.31 (23–93)	66.5 (17–93)	67.9 (40–93)
Male–female proportion	46–54	50–50	50–50
Prior experience (yes)	71	79	73
Have college degree	69	75	–
Marital Status			
Married/partnered	76		79
Widowed	11		10
Divorced	7		6
Single, never married	3		5
Separated	1		–
Income Level			
< US$50,000	30		
US. $50,000-$100,000	40		
>US $100,000	30		
Race/ethnicity			
Caucasian	97.6		
Asian	0.8		
African-American	0.8		

Note: Data for this table compiled from Coffman (2008).

disengaged, and intellectually disinterested, NHIMA participants seek challenge and stimulation through musical activity. Members cite musical and social engagement as the most important aspects of participation (Coffman, 2008; Coffman & Adamek, 1999; Rohwer, 2012), and they report a wide range of benefits associated with those types of engagement.

In one of the more recent large-scale surveys of NHIMA participants, Jutras (2011) identified four categories of benefits: musical skill and knowledge development, social benefits, personal development, and health effects. These findings align with the results of other studies (Coffman & Adamek, 1999; Coffman, 2008) and are closely related to motivations for participation.

Table 9.2 NHIMA Participants, age by gender (%)

Age	Females	Males	Total
>85	12	34	46
75–84	112	193	305
65–74	326	332	658
55–64	281	135	416
45–54	91	22	113
35–44	23	3	26
<35	10	3	13
Total	855	722	1,577

Note: Data for this table compiled from Coffman (2008).

It seems clear in extant research that people join New Horizons groups primarily to make music with other people. Coffman and Adamek (1999), Coffman (2008), Carucci (2012), and Rohwer (2012) all write that active music-making draws people to programs. The desire for social engagement is almost equally as strong a motivator (Coffman, 2008; Coffman & Adamek, 1999; Rohwer, 2012; Tsugawa, 2009). Kruse (2009) and Dabback (2009) both write of the importance to participants of group dynamics and a sense of community. Dabback cites feelings of belonging and support as facilitating social interactions and a consequent passion for participation. Knowing who participants are and who they would like to be provides insight for instruction and a broader view of music participation in older age.

Theories for Guiding New Horizons Bands

You are never too old to set another goal or to dream a new dream.
– C.S. Lewis

The practice of guiding others can be anything from authoritarian (teacher-centred and learner-dependent) to autonomous (learner-centred and self-governing). Three words – *pedagogy, andragogy,* and *heutagogy* – have been used to distinguish points along a continuum. *Pedagogy* (literally, child-leading) is the most familiar term when instructional practices are being discussed, irrespective of student age. Teachers decide what is taught (or learned) and presume that learners lack the means to learn on their own. This authoritarian perspective has dominated educational practice for centuries, and it is no surprise that community musicians have often distanced themselves from school music practices of teacher control, detailed instructional sequences (curricula), and specific goals and assessments. Referring to community music strategies as pedagogies seems inappropriate. Community musicians strive to relinquish control so that participants in their workshops and projects can direct their own experiences, even when the participants are children.

The less familiar term *andragogy* (literally, man-leading) was proposed to signify adult learning and adults' capacities for self-direction. Advocates like Malcolm Knowles (Knowles, Holton, & Swanson, 2012) asserted that children depend on authority figures for their learning, while adults are more self-directed and independent. This dichotomization between the child learner and the adult learner is, to some degree, oversimplified, because exceptions can be found: children can self-direct their learning, and adults can require leading. Knowles and his associates (2012) proposed six core adult learning principles that are relevant for a variety of contexts and goals, including New Horizons ensembles:

1. *Need to know.* Participation in New Horizons bands is voluntary, so adults come with reasons to learn. Novices want to gain proficiency, while skilled players seek exposure to new repertoires and improvement of their performing skills. Some wish to learn how to play with others in a group.

2. *Self-concept.* Participants display varying levels of self-directedness. Less proficient players rely heavily on guidance from instructors and other members. More proficient players can show high levels of independence, forming their own small groups, acquiring their own music, and scheduling their own rehearsals and performances.

3. *Role of experience.* Participants bring decades of life experiences and they can know quite a lot about music from listening to it, even if they have not played an instrument. They also know how to work cooperatively in groups.

4. *Readiness to learn.* Some players are hesitant, unsure about what they can do or whether they will enjoy the experience. Others are eager to rekindle the pleasures they experienced making music years ago. The bands' culture of acceptance helps players find roles in the ensemble that suit them.

5. *Orientation to learning.* Participants often can identify how they prefer to learn. They are problem-solvers and find creative ways to find answers or facilitate their own learning.

6. *Motivation.* Intrinsic motivation is high, because participants join to make music with others. Concerts can motivate them to prepare more intensely for group rehearsals, but the satisfaction of playing their instruments and enjoying the camaraderie sustains their involvement.

Even though the andragogical perspective has dominated adult education discourse, a growing dissatisfaction has resulted in the more recent advocacy for *heutagogy* (literally, self-leading) – a term crafted and promoted to highlight a conceptual progression in explaining adult learning, because

> [a]ny examination of learning experiences and curricula designed around andragogical principles certainly demonstrated the capacity for linking into the adult experience and recognised the advantages of self-directed learning. However, curricula were still very much teacher-centric with little opportunity for any real involvement at a micro or even macro level by the learner. (Hase & Kenyon, 2007, p. 112)

Hase and Kenyon (2001) made a fine-grained distinction between the self-*directed* learning of Knowles's andragogy and the self-*determined* learning of heutagogy. This amounts to a shift toward maximizing learner choice and minimizing leader control. Learners are encouraged to reflect, to learn how to learn through their own efforts, and to focus on developing their capabilities rather than simply gaining knowledge:

> Learning is an integrative experience where a change in behavior, knowledge, or understanding is incorporated into the person's existing repertoire of behavior and schema (values, attitudes, and beliefs). For example, it is possible to acquire a set of competencies that one can repeat in familiar or known circumstances. However, if learning has taken place, competencies can also be repeated and even adapted in unfamiliar, unanticipated situations. (Hase & Kenyon, 2007, p. 112)

The heutagogical ideal of self-determined learning can be observed in NHIMA programs, even ones that rely substantially on designated leaders. Many programs have seen members form their own small groups, such as polka bands or Dixieland bands or chamber ensembles. The groups rehearse on their own, acquire their own music, and schedule their own performances. They are self-directed, self-determined, and collaborative. Group members' enthusiasm, dedication, and resourcefulness can demonstrate aspects of heutagogy. Some groups may have a more experienced player assuming a leading role; other groups have members of similar abilities. In either instance, members can be empowered agents, capable of solving their own musical challenges.

Understanding New Horizons Band Members' Possible Selves

The great thing about getting older is that you don't lose all the other ages you've been.
– Madeleine L'Engle

As older adults, NHIMA members have crossed several boundaries while moving through life transitions. Most are close to or past the end of their professional careers. They have raised their children and perhaps welcomed grandchildren and great-grandchildren. Some have experienced the loss of a spouse. Many participants have identified these milestones as opportunities to seek new experiences and growth, and researchers have identified these tipping points as further motivation for joining NHIMA groups (Coffman, 2008; Dabback, 2006; Tsugawa, 2009). Participation helps members construct meaning and make sense of their lives as senior adults and musicians, often with a focus on the journey rather than a need for high achievement or affirmation (Tsugawa, 2009). In this way, competence is linked not only to learning but also to identity through engagement with and responsiveness to others as they seek the good of a group larger than themselves (Dabback, 2006).

Self-concepts extend both backward and forward in personal time frames. They guide actions toward goals through constant anticipation and future orientation, but these realities, rather than being concretized, are in constant flux. Markus and Nurius (1986) conceptualize self-concepts as possible selves, which "are linked to the dynamic properties of the self-concept – to motivation, to distortion, and to change, both momentary and enduring" (p. 954). Possible selves represent the timeline of personal self-conception and provide a conceptual link between cognition, motivation, and action. They serve two integral functions regarding individuals' behavioural choices: they provide information to make judgments regarding action, and they serve as motivational influences to achieve goals and avoid negative outcomes. Some possible selves reflect ideas of what individuals would like to become, while others represent what they are afraid of becoming. These manifest in action to achieve desired selves or in the avoidance of feared possible selves. As incentives for future actions (pursuit or avoidance), they provide context for evaluation and interpretation for self-conceptions, including criteria for evaluating outcomes.

Each person has a repertoire of possible selves that provides links between self-conception and motivation. Collections can include "the good selves (the ones we remember fondly), the bad selves (the ones we would just as soon forget), the hoped-for selves, the feared selves, the not-me selves, the ideal selves, the ought selves" (Markus & Nurius, 1986, p. 957). Theory suggests that those with a balance of possible selves are the most motivated to achieve (or avoid) the manifestation of those selves. Through this lens, agency can be viewed as an ability to develop and maintain a balance of distinct possible selves. Conversely, a lack of agency may be related to well-defined negative possible selves reflecting fears and insecurities in the absence of strategies or concepts of how to escape them (Markus & Nurius, 1986). Ibarra (1999) proposed that the more vivid possible selves seem to an individual, the more motivation they provide to change and move toward (or away from) their realization. People incorporate positive and negative potentials into their identity schemas only when they are strongly elaborated with specific plans for achieving hoped-for selves or, conversely, avoiding feared selves (Freer & Bennett, 2012).

Although to date no researchers have specifically utilized a possible-selves framework in investigations with NHIMA populations, the theory can provide insight into participants as they navigate the various boundaries of later life. People join groups because they are pursuing something they desire. The large majority of participants are returning to music engagement after many years away. As they reclaim their musical identities, they are reclaiming lost possible selves. Others are experimenting with new possible selves as they engage with this type of music activity for the first time or challenge previous musical identities, such as the way that some women choose instruments denied to them earlier in life because of their gender (Dabback, 2008a; Tsugawa, 2009). They build conceptions of who they would like to become by choosing to enter the activity and engaging with others who also seek new experiences. A low attrition rate reflects members' decisions that participation is worth the time and effort. With his simple yet influential motto, "Your best is good enough," Roy Ernst set a different tone and parameters for participation from many other non-formal music experiences. Everyone is welcome and everyone may participate at whatever level and degree of engagement they wish. NHIMA groups offer participants freedom at an institutional level to explore who they want to be as musicians while also providing structure and instructional assistance to guide members on their journeys.

Well-Being

Research suggests that people involved in New Horizons programs experience quality-of-life improvements (Coffman & Adamek 1999; Rohwer & Coffman, 2006; Tsugawa, 2009). Could some of these effects relate to the presence and influence of possible selves? Studies with older adults suggest that this may offer a viable future path for NHIMA research. Dark-Freudeman and West (2016) used an underlying framework related to thoughts of decline that come with aging:

Our most important selves – combined with the self-regulatory beliefs we have about what we can or cannot do to achieve them – affect our expectations, our behaviors, and ultimately our well-being. Believing that we have the ability to attain our most important hopes and avoid our most dreaded fears, especially when faced with declines that may threaten our ability to do so, may be central to maintaining positive psychological functioning or well-being, especially in late life. (Dark-Freudeman & West, 2016, p. 140)

In their study, these researchers concluded that developing and maintaining domain-specific self-efficacy related to possible selves may be essential to mental health and development in later life.

Bolkan, Hooker, and Coehlo (2015) found that the presence of health-related possible selves was significantly associated with fewer depressive symptoms. The researchers pointed to a similar data trend regarding social relations but did not identify as strong a relationship, possibly because few participants reported any feared possible selves relating to those relationships. In a study by Ko, Mejía, and Hooker (2014), those with social possible selves, and specifically those with both hoped-for and feared possible selves, made higher overall daily goal progress. The authors concluded that balanced possible selves provide stronger motivation than either hoped-for or feared possible selves on their own. Similarly, Hoppmann, Gerstorf, Smith, and Klumb (2007) found that engaging in activities consistent with one's possible selves increased positive effect on that day and decreased the risk of long-term mortality.

Creech and colleagues (2014) used data from three case studies to explore whether older people reclaim or create possible positive musical selves when actively engaging in music activities with others and whether the generation of these positive possible selves relates to increased self-reported well-being. Aligned with other authors, they found that possible selves influence decisions regarding what is worth time and energy while remaining fluid and accessible in response to life transitions. Participants structured their time around commitments and skills development necessary to build and support musical identities as conceptualized in possible selves, which were shaped in part through observation of role models and through experimentation. The desire to improve and gain experiences and skills provided underlying motivation.

Similar to Murray (2017), Douglas (2011), Dabback (2006), and Creech and colleagues (2014) identified three factors in well-being in relation to musical engagement: purpose, autonomy, and social affirmation. People found purpose through structure in routines and in musical activity as a medium to develop skills and work toward personally defined goals. Autonomy emerged from the freedom to explore possible selves and the opportunity for expression, which also resulted in a sense of control in both musical and extra-musical contexts. Significant others provided social affirmation of people's conceptions as musicians; meaningful performances and a sense of giving back to communities contributed to a sense of validation.

Social Affirmation

Possible selves form largely through social comparison as people engage with significant others (Markus & Nurius, 1986). Ibarra (1999) identified the importance of others in the formation of possible selves, including observation of role models, experimentation with provisional selves, and the evaluation of new conceptions compared to both internal and external standards. Freer and Bennett (2012) confirmed that aspirational role models and peers serve as important models for developing images of future selves in important contexts. Rossiter (2007) explored the roles that teachers and mentors can take on in motivating learners to build self-conceptions of who they would like to be or who they would like to avoid becoming. Interactions, discussions, observations of practice, and space to experiment allow learners to try out various identities and refine their possible self-concepts.

The role of significant others in affirming New Horizons participants' conceptions of themselves as musicians and engaged older adults has been well-documented (Dabback, 2006; Rohwer, 2013). Spouses and children support members' activities, and it's common to hear people say of their children, "I went to all of their concerts, and now it's their turn to do the same for me!" But, perhaps, more importantly for the development of possible selves, players and singers find role models within their groups that Ibarra (1999) identifies as integral to the adaptive process. Some models are musical (e.g., section leaders); others are inspirational and perhaps aspirational (e.g., nonagenarians who remain dedicated well into their ninth decade of life). The communities themselves provide support for experimentation. Some people dedicate hours every day to practice and preparation, while others perhaps only engage in practice once a week at rehearsal, yet all are still welcome. Instruction obviously varies from group to group, yet most directors embrace the openness of the New Horizons ideal and, as Rossiter (2007) writes, facilitate interactions and spaces to experiment that allow learners to try out various identities and refine their possible self-concepts. Engaging in the practices of musicians (practice, rehearsal, concerts) also supports the development of self-conceptions (Dabback, 2008b). In some cases, activities such as performing at nursing homes for elderly people who evidence decline provide opportunities for comparison (Dabback, 2006) and the development of feared possible selves to be avoided.

Health

A conversation with a group of NHIMA participants often turns to discussion of health and the benefits to it of program participation. There has been little research to capture or measure actual physical and mental changes that occur through participation. One of the only studies of this type (Rohwer, 2009) found no statistically measured changes in breathing before and after rehearsals. Yet participants consistently self-report positive health outcomes. Rohwer and Coffman (2006) reported that 26 percent of their participants perceived improved mental capacity and breathing after joining a New Horizons band. Of Coffman's (2008) study population, 68.2 percent reported some effect on health, largely in emotional well-being but also in physical and cognitive effects. Likewise, Jutras (2011) specifically cited concentration, mental health, and memory as valued outcomes of engagement.

Perras, Strachan, and Fortier (2015) found positive associations between possible selves focused on physical activity and physical activity identity as they sought to understand why some retirees engaged in increased physical activity while some did not. In a second study, Perras, Strachan, and Fortier (2016) found that exercise/physical activity identity can mediate the relationship between physical activity possible selves and physical activity. The researchers suggested that interventions that focused on the development of physical activity possible selves could offer a way to strengthen exercise identity and in turn encourage identity-consistent behaviours. In a similar study, Hsu, Lu, and Lin (2014) found a positive relationship between physical self-concept and participation in moderate physical activity. In addition, possible selves meditated the link between older adults' physical self-concept and psychological well-being.

Personal Development

New Horizons musicians point to personal development and satisfaction in learning as important aspects of participation. Learning and relearning musical skills (Coffman, 2008; Griffith, 2006) and self-improvement (Coffman, 2008) complement the desire for musical and social engagement. As stated previously, several authors have used the constructs drawn from self-determination theory (Ryan & Deci, 2008) in research and have reported on various ways the psychological needs of competence, autonomy, and relatedness are satisfied through participation (Dabback, 2006; Douglas, 2011; Murray, 2017).

Older adults consistently report fewer and more specific possible selves than younger cohorts, and they tend to focus on the continuation of current activities and relationships (King & Hicks, 2007). Yet Smith and Freund (2002) state that adults continue to focus on personal growth and fulfillment throughout their lifespan. In their study, 206 participants aged 70 to 103 evidenced a desire to achieve or re-experience something in their hoped-for selves. Avoidance was the most common theme in feared selves.

Final Thoughts

Anyone who stops learning is old, whether at twenty or eighty. Anyone who keeps learning stays young.
– Henry Ford

Possible selves provide guidance for people to decide what is worth their time and effort and what activities to discontinue. This future orientation continues to serve as an effective motivational system into older age. Goals that are relevant to identity underlie future-oriented identity conceptions. Individuals construct their personal development through later life by pursuing these goals. In this way, possible selves can be understood to represent the underlying motivation to engage in self-improvement, maintenance of abilities, and the minimization of losses through self-regulatory processes. According to Frazier, Johnson, Gonzalez, and Kafka (2002), the malleability of possible selves is vital for older adults as they experience age-related social and health changes. Those selves allow for reinterpretation of past and current experiences and consequent meaning-making. In other words, older adults' personal definitions of aging can be understood and even changed to preserve well-being through knowledge of their self-images of their futures.

The benefits of NHIMA participation are largely self-reported through surveys and interviews rather than scientifically measured, yet how many of those perceptions can possibly be traced to members' possible selves? Do participants see themselves as working toward hoped-for selves through music participation and therefore perceive gains they are making in their physical, social, personal development, and emotional realms? These areas seem to directly connect to McClusky's (1974) four learning needs (coping, contributive, influence, expressive) and their relation to creativity (Cohen, 2000). If possible selves can be understood as representing the underlying motivation to engage in self-improvement, maintenance of abilities, and the minimization of losses through self-regulatory processes (Frazier, Johnson, Gonzalez, & Kafka, 2002), then NHIMA participation potentially reflects processes of reframing possible selves in which members engage to maintain well-being and satisfy their needs.

What seems clear is that NHIMA engagement provides space, opportunity, and support for the development and maintenance of possible selves. As in

Creech and colleagues (2014), organizations provide time structure, role models, room to experiment, activities that support identities, goals, opportunities for personal development and skill development, means of expression, and a community that affirms the value of musical engagement in support of possible selves. Members observe others in vibrant musical activity, and supported by peers and instructors, they freely experiment with who they would like to become. They also have opportunities to develop balance through feared selves, perhaps in comparing themselves to older adults in the nursing homes that so many NHIMA groups visit or in other similar contexts. Through this lens, "Your best is good enough" assumes much greater meaning than a simple open invitation to play. It is an invitation to *become* through music – to strive toward possible selves that provide direction, meaning, and motivation in later life.

CHAPTER 10

And the Melody Lingers On

Building Social Capital through Community Music Participation

Annie Mitchell

Introduction

IN THE NORTHERN RIVERS region of northeastern New South Wales, Australia, two leading community music organizations are the Clarence Valley Orchestra and Chorus (CVOC), based in Grafton and founded in 2014, and the Lismore Symphony Orchestra (LSO), founded in 2003 with the mission to bring classical music to Northern Rivers audiences. Over the past three years, I have conducted a research project that aims to identify best practices in conducting, musical direction, and performance in community music and to investigate the impacts of community music participation on musicians' performance and teaching practices. This project emerged from my tenure as a double bassist in each orchestra, four years with CVOC and thirteen with the LSO. The research uses both orchestras as case studies, interviewing each orchestra's conductor, surveying the musicians, and triangulating this information with my participant observation as a musician/researcher. I collected a wealth of musical data, but some of the richest information came from the boundaries of this research. Participants were eager to share stories of how community music improved their health and well-being, how participation in community orchestras facilitated social inclusion of musicians and of audiences, and how these musical activities provided opportunities for lifelong learning and access to culture. These benefits were also apparent for the audiences: increased cultural access and social networking is particularly valuable for people in rural communities and for isolated and vulnerable groups such as the elderly. The activities of each orchestra connect diverse groups around the region: the orchestra musicians but also the audiences, who include young families, music students, professional musicians, the elderly, and community service groups. The CVOC supports young musicians and has launched a highly effective program of philanthropy and social benevolence for the Clarence Valley community. This chapter investigates how these two orchestras have contributed to building social capital in their local communities.

Theoretical Background and Literature Review

Social capital is defined as "the network of social connections that exist between people, and their shared values and norms of behaviour, which enable and encourage mutually advantageous social cooperation" (Collins English Dictionary). The Organisation for Economic Co-operation and Development (OECD, 2007, p. 102) extends this definition of social capital to include "networks together with social norms, values and understandings that facilitate co-operation within or among groups." Social capital is characterized by reciprocity (Abbott & Freeth, 2008), trust (Paldam, 2000; Abbott & Freeth, 2008) and cooperation (Paldam, 2000); services and outcomes are intended to mutually benefit the group or community rather than individuals. Such capital is evidence that a society is functioning harmoniously and effectively. Elements of social capital include social and civic engagement, mutual trust and community (Hyyppä & Mäki, 2003, p. 770; Stolle, 1998), participation in voluntary associations (Hyyppä & Mäki, 2003, p. 770; Putnam, 2000) and in hobby groups, and/or religious involvement (Stolle, 1998).

Lin (2001, p. 6), who defines social capital as "investment in social relations with expected returns," credits the success of social capital to four factors: increased flow of information, social ties and their influence, the social credentials of leaders and participants, and reinforcement of identity and recognition of individuals and members of groups. Social capital theory has been used to explain improved performance of diverse groups (Evans & Carson, 2005), the value derived from strategic alliances (Koka & Prescott, 2002), and the evolution of communities (Dale & Onyx, 2005).

From the literature emerge three forms of social capital: bonding, bridging, and linking. Bonding social capital connects people through a sense of shared identity and common beliefs, which together reinforce existing relationships and the group as a whole (OECD, 2007, p. 103; Wilks, 2011, p. 291). Bridging social capital is more outward-looking, stretching "beyond a shared sense of identity" (OECD, 2007, p. 103) by engaging more diverse groups and creating new social connections between previously unassociated people (Wilks, 2011,

p. 281). Linking social capital facilitates interactions between "people or groups further up or down the social ladder" (OECD, 2007, p. 103).

An increase in social capital fosters positive community outcomes such as increased community spirit and empowerment (Hyyppä & Mäki, 2003, p. 777), more socially inclusive and cohesive communities, affirmative group identity and affiliation, positive human relations, effective networking, civic and economic capacity-building, and the development of local leadership (Davies, 2011). Benefits to individuals that are attributed to participation in social-capital-building activities include improved health and well-being, stronger friendship ties, longer lifespans (Putnam, 1993), mutual attachment, and greater reciprocity. Putnam (2000, p. 116) identifies the arts as bridging and linking agents, in that cultural events bring diverse groups together in ways that transcend social barriers. Bourdieu's (1984) perspective is less positive; he highlights the divisive potential of the arts, including music, and the possibility that they will foster elitism. A further issue is the importance of civic activity (as distinct from social activity) for addressing social issues and enhancing social outcomes, for example, through rural restructuring and revitalization, mental health programs, public housing, active citizenship, social inclusion, and cultural diversity (VicHealth, 2004).

In Australia, many remote communities are economically, culturally, and socially marginalized and declining; they lack access to culture, hold fewer community events, offer fewer educational choices, and face more economic insecurity and hardship (relative to urban communities). Regional communities are often underserviced, and their populations are more likely to be disadvantaged and vulnerable. Issues in rural Australia identified by Duffy and colleagues (2007) in Duffy and Waitt (2011, p. 45) include dying country towns, difficulty finding and keeping jobs, and youth exodus to cities in search of jobs and to relieve their boredom. These problems are exacerbated by lower income levels, reduced social health in rural communities, declining standards of living, lack of access to goods and services, social isolation, poor health, substance abuse, and suicide (Cocklin & Alston, 2003; Dunphy, 2009; VicHealth, 2001, in Duffy & Waitt, 2011). The negative effects of unemployment, violence, low socio-economic status, poverty, and technological change on mental health, worsened by inadequate support and care networks and economic and educational opportunities, have been highlighted by the World Health Organization (2001).

The Clarence Valley surrounding Grafton and the Lismore region 130 kilometres farther north both exhibit to some degree the social characteristics outlined above. Grafton has around 18,700 people; Lismore in home to 27,569 according to the 2016 census (Australian Bureau of Statistics, 2016). These regions are home to significant populations of marginalized and vulnerable communities and groups. They have high populations of tertiary students and are home to many elderly and retired people, many who are ill and/or disabled. Both have a high proportion of low-income, government-supported, and charity recipients. Many people in both places are employed or self-supporting, fit and active, yet they align with the boundary groups identified by Willingham & Carruthers (2018) as people "who have not found themselves able to fully participate in musical communities." To the good, these two regional communities are also home to many people who attend or participate in cultural and musical events. In both regions, one finds a strong sense of local identity and belonging, a wealth of creative practice and practitioners, a large "alternative" lifestyle counterculture, and a large cohort of "tree-changers"[1] and "sea-changers"[2] who have been drawn to the area by its natural beauty and relaxed lifestyle and out of a sense of environmental ethics. Balanced with this diversity is a long community history of farming, agriculture, and forestry, as well as community support networks. Many families have lived in these places for generations. The diversity of these regions is evident in two of their defining symbols. Since the 1973 Nimbin Aquarius Festival, the Lismore area has become known as the Rainbow Region, a "meeting place of countercultures and for the articulation of social and environmental ideals that challenge mainstream practice" (Ward & van Vuuren, 2013, p. 63). Grafton's Jacaranda Festival, launched in 1934, was the first Australian folk festival and is Australia's oldest floral festival (Grafton Jacaranda Festival, 2017). Also defining these regions is the presence of Southern Cross University's main campus at Lismore, which serves both. Many of the students there are "first-in-their-family" students or from challenging socio-economic backgrounds.

A prominent theme in the literature is the benefit to community wellbeing of citizen participation in the arts:

> There has long been an appreciation among community artists, art workers and volunteers of the social impacts of engaging in the arts. These benefits extend beyond individuals considered disadvantaged or "at-risk" to the overall health and wellbeing of societies and communities, particularly

---

1 Tree-changers – people who have moved from the city to the country in pursuit of a more relaxed lifestyle.
2 Sea-changers – people who have moved from the city to the coast in pursuit of a more relaxed lifestyle.

as they struggle to deal with economic, social and environmental crises (McHenry, 2009, p. 61).

Festivals provide opportunities to build social capital through network-ing, capacity-building, and the development of entrepreneurial ability and local leadership (Davies, 2011). They also provide opportunities for building communities in which there is a collective sense of belonging, integration and cohesion, fellowship, and celebration (Gibson & Stewart, 2009; Duffy & Waitt, 2011, p. 47). The importance of festivals to community belonging, identity, history, and sense of place is articulated by Lyndon Terracini, festival director as well as artistic director of Opera Australia, (2007, pp. 11–12). He states that festivals

> should be about fundamentally understanding what resonates within the people who live there, left there, or died there; and about translating those deep local associations for benefits of a much wider audience ... Where big ideas take root, where inspirational individuals and artists who believe passionately in their cultural and artistic responsibilities can plant seeds that will grow and nourish the minds of a broader community.

Putnam (2000, p. 116) identifies volunteerism and philanthropy as key measures of social capital. Major themes of this chapter are the contribution of two community orchestras to the social capital of the NSW Northern Rivers region, the importance and outcomes of volunteerism and philanthropy result-ing from each orchestra's mission and performances, their impact on the social health and well-being of their community and members, and their creation of belonging and identity through community engagement.

Methodology

This chapter grew out of a research project titled "Conducting, Musical Direc-tion, and Performance in Community Music Ensembles and Their Influence on Pedagogy," which aimed to identify best practices in conducting, musical direction, and performance in community music and investigate the impacts of community music participation on musicians' performance and teaching practices. Three regional community orchestras were studied, using multiple qualitative methods. Data collection involved five semi-structured interviews with the conductors and musical directors of each ensemble, thirty-eight ques-tionnaires with orchestra musicians (response rate of 45 percent), participant observation by the author as researcher and double bassist with each orchestra, and press reports and audience feedback. The data underwent thematic analysis, categorized by themes of best and worst conducting and ensemble practices, leadership styles, skills and attributes of musical directors and effective ensemble musicians, and the influence of community music performance on pedagogy and individual musical development.

From the boundaries of this research emerged some of its richest information: participants' stories of the benefits of community music for health and well-being; the social inclusion of musicians and audiences; and lifelong learning and cultural accessibility, particularly for rural communities and isolated groups such as the elderly. Further research was conducted into the Clarence Valley Orchestra and Chorus (CVOC) and the Lismore Symphony Orchestra (LSO); their engagement with the surrounding community; and their contribution to the well-being and quality of life of orchestral members and followers. Case studies of the activities of these two orchestras exemplify bridging the gap: the philanthropy of the CVOC in addressing social welfare, disadvantage, and educational access; both orchestras breaking boundaries between country and city by engaging urban guest conductors and musicians; and the LSO's linking of academia and community through the orchestra's partnership with Southern Cross University (SCU).

Presentation of Data

Over its brief four-year existence, CVOC's performance programs, musical activities, and ethos have contributed significantly to building social capital and providing cultural access in the Clarence Valley by bringing musicians together, reinforcing community belonging and identity, bridging isolation, and contributing to philanthropy, civic initiatives, and music education. CVOC has around forty musicians and a choir of a similar size. It performs two concert series each year: an ANZAC (Australian and New Zealand Army Corps) Centenary Commemoration Concert in April, and a Proms concert in October – a highlight of Grafton's week-long Jacaranda Festival.

Musical benefits. The orchestra members who participated in this research reported that engagement in community music improved their musical performances, refined their ensemble skills, and provided them with more opportunities to play music. These creative activities, underpinned by musical appreciation and a mutual love of music-making, bonded musicians in a shared journey of lifelong learning. The benefits of community music performance were many: the participants learned new and more challenging repertoire; gained greater confidence and overcame their performance anxiety; improved their technique; learned how to sight-read and how to interpret scores; and developed a better musical "ear." The musicians stated that their musical experience and knowledge grew through concert performances. "It gives me a purpose to play my instrument each week and keeps me playing at a more professional level. It keeps me practising, makes me play with more discipline, and increases opportunities to play with other professional musicians." The performance and ensemble skills practised by orchestra members can be modelled and taught to music students. "I can advise students who play in school ensembles [on] the attributes required to be a valued member of a group." Such attributes are not relevant just to music; they are also life skills, transferrable to many aspects of life and work.

Health and well-being. The musicians reported significant benefits to their personal health and well-being from community music engagement. These ranged from general feelings of belonging, friendship, mutual support, and "aging gracefully" to the positive effects of community music engagement in dealing with life-threatening illnesses and overcoming grief and the death of loved ones. These testimonies tend to support Putnam's (2000) claims that joining an organization halves an individual's chance of dying within the next year.

Identity, self-worth, and social inclusion. Similarly, the musicians confirmed that participation in these orchestras enhanced their sense of identity, self-worth, and social inclusion. The camaraderie and teamwork involved in being part of a group, with common goals and artistic and civic objectives, increased members' ability to relate to people, their personal enjoyment and fulfillment, and their confidence to undertake other roles and projects. One orchestra respondent extended the benefits of this network to include audiences, which he described as a vehicle of belonging to humanity through an intergenerational transcendent vessel: "a group of former strangers with a new-found boundary-crossing, bridge-building, game-changing consensus view of what the opportunities and problems in life might actually be; wherein they might find, not necessarily the answer to life's big questions, but the ability to ask better ones."

Affirmative aging, access, and outreach. Older members of the CVOC reported that their community musical engagement had contributed to their affirmative aging. Many members of the choir commented that it kept them motivated in life and in performance, remarking what a fantastic bunch of people the orchestra were to perform with. CVOC performances provided cultural access for many elderly audience members, with free bus transport provided for some concerts to enable attendance by those who had been marginalized by disability, poor health, or lack of a car. People would have had to travel miles from a country town at great expense to hear anything similar:

CVOC performances create a place where the elderly retired can come along and feel part of an exciting show which is something different from the norm in Grafton. The concerts are quite entertaining ... Programming is something for every one's tastes and not too much of the same thing. This suits Grafton's older audience and it benefits them immensely through an uplifting experience. [As well as classical,] an orchestra of our size and quality is now playing anything from Latin to swing to a rock style, all within the same program, keeping it interesting and uplifting for the audience. I've been told so many times from audience members "I've been to all of them" and "it's great for Grafton – I hope you're not going anywhere!" (CVOC Conductor, personal communication, 2017)

This ethos of social outreach is further exemplified by CVOC's ANZAC Commemoration concert tour in April 2018 to the smaller towns of Inverell and Tenterfield. Tenterfield, population 4,000 (Australian Bureau of Statistics, 2016), is 215 kilometres northwest of Grafton. Inverell, population 16,500 (Australian Bureau of Statistics, 2016), is 230 kilometres west of Grafton. Neither town has an orchestra, and both are much deeper into the state's remote interior, so they lack their own cultural services.

Contribution to community. The CVOC's contribution to the community is widely recognized by the people of Clarence Valley as well as by the local MP, Chris Gulaptis, who read out an official letter of congratulations in the New South Wales State Parliament after the 2015 Proms concert: "More than 70 local musicians performed flawlessly to a packed house of 1,000 people." Again, after the 2017 Proms concert, his press release reported "how fantastic is it for a town to have their own orchestra and a great one at that!" The CVOC conductor concurred: "Having a musical group performing at their best entertaining the general community, will attract 'the followers,' not only as somewhere to go and hear great music, but also to enhance their well-being towards classical and contemporary music culture." He also noted that community audiences were able to hear international artists perform with a local orchestra in a regional town, without having to pay city prices – a valid economic consideration for most audience members from a small country town.

The CVOC conductor writes compositions for his musicians, and for the choir. He does this in ways that align with the individual skill levels of the members, which range from Grade 3 AMEB (Australian Music Examinations Board) to Grade 8 standard and up. This learning environment provides excellent opportunities for younger musicians to play alongside professionals and "learn the ropes" of what it takes to perform to a good standard. The arrangements usually make the orchestra sound much better, for they are written in ways that facilitate a cohesive outcome.

Place, history and identity. The importance of festivals in reinforcing a sense of place, history, and identity has been discussed in the literature. CVOC's "An Afternoon at the Proms" concerts are a highlight of Grafton's annual Jacaranda Festival. This festival, founded in 1934 (Grafton Jacaranda Festival, 2017) is Australia's longest-running floral festival, celebrating the beauty, life, and community of Grafton at a time when its abundant jacaranda trees are in bloom. The ANZAC concerts raise a hat to the many servicemen and women from the Clarence Valley who served in the First and Second World Wars, as well as the Korean and Vietnam wars. This reinforces the sense of history and civic service of the region's people. Australia's treatment of its armed forces personnel when they returned from the Korean War (1950–1953) and the Vietnam War (1955–1975) is a highly sensitive issue. Recognition of their service and sacrifice is especially welcomed today, for these "forgotten veterans" generally were not afforded appropriate honours or recognition and were made to feel ashamed, to their profound distress.

> You came here as the sons of Anzac, you left as the fathers of our professional army ... I do regret the fact that we haven't paid, in my view, sufficient honour and attention to the men who are here today and the many other men who are still alive and fought in the Korean War. (Julia Gillard, Australian Prime Minister, 2011, speaking in Kapyong, South Korea, marking the 60th anniversary of the Battle for Kapyong.)

In paying belated homage to Australian Vietnam War veterans, Prime Minister Gillard's speech commemorating Vietnam Veterans Day (19 August 2011) stated: "This was Australia's longest war, yet we treated the returning veterans with shame. And so, we remember" (Julia Gillard, The Weekend Australian, 2011). The venue for CVOC concerts is Grafton's historic Saraton Theatre, a 950-seat theatre built and owned by Greek immigrants, the Notaros family. The Saraton Theatre has been integral to Grafton's community life since its erection in 1926; for more than ninety years it has provided a venue for important civic gatherings as well as concerts.

Philanthropy. Throughout its four years of existence, the CVOC has contributed significantly to the social and economic welfare of marginalized and disadvantaged groups in the Clarence Valley, building social capital through a proactive ethos of philanthropy, outreach, and educational access. The CVOC is a not-for-profit community organization and all members are volunteers, yet it has been able to donate more than $42,000 from its concert proceeds to local charities and services. These donations include $22,650 to the Clarence Valley Returned and Services League (RSL) Sub-Branches, Grafton Legacy, and DefenceCare to support returned servicemen and women, their families, and needy personnel. Another $8,600 has been donated to Grafton Rotary Midday Charities and Social Futures Grafton, a community organization that links people with disabilities, their families, and their carers to their communities and promotes regional fairness and inclusion, in addition to providing housing for the homeless. Other donations include $2,500 to Grafton's Salvation Army Band for new hymn books and music stands and $2,500 to the Grafton Ambulance Station for medical equipment.

Music education. CVOC's philanthropy extends to music education. It offers yearly scholarships of $1,200 to CVOC music students studying at an Australian university or music institution. Scholarships have been presented to four promising CVOC students, who have commenced study at the University of Queensland, Flinders University, the James Morrison Jazz Academy (JMJA), and the Australian Institute of Music (AIM). In small regional centres, the biggest disadvantages are lack of critical mass for groups and lack of appropriate music to play (genre and difficulty). One orchestra member observed: "In this town there are little to no job opportunities for young, intelligent 17 to 30-year-olds, so any budding musos leave town. Better social and job prospects for 17 to 30-year-olds would do wonders to the increase in musicians here." Money is also an issue in the Clarence Valley: very few schoolchildren can afford to pay to perform in music ensembles outside school. CVOC is free of charge to perform in.

The scholarships encourage younger players to join CVOC as juniors, stay in the ensemble to gain experience under a conductor, where they can play in a large ensemble with supportive audiences, then apply for a scholarship at the end of their tenure with CVOC before going to university. Students often return to the ensemble after higher education, honing the skills they have learned and returning to the community experience, because they enjoyed it so much the first time around; in this way, they enrich the cultural and musical capital of the ensemble.

Headlining international artists. Programming an international artist is a highly successful strategy for linking a local ensemble and regional audience with the broader musical world. The guest artist for CVOC's 2017 An Afternoon at the Proms concert was pianist David Helfgott, whose life and career were portrayed in the Academy Award-winning movie *Shine*. Playing with an internationally acclaimed pianist was a highly challenging and motivating experience for the orchestra. The concert was sold out and greeted with great enthusiasm and applause by the audience, who demonstrated a collective sense of engagement in this powerful musical experience, plus ownership and pride in having such a talented and famous resident in the region. The CVOC conductor attested to the impact of this concert on the musicians and the community:

> It would not be often that some of the CVOC players would ever get to play with a pianist of world renown. It was a great experience for all to see what can be achieved when an ensemble works together for the final outcome of bringing great music to the Clarence Valley. This can only enhance the orchestra's camaraderie by making community music at its best, creating memories of a lifetime that we can all reflect back on in the future. (CVOC Conductor, personal communication, 2017)

Lismore Symphony Orchestra: Benefits to music performance and teaching. The LSO is now in its fifteenth year. It has around forty musicians, with additional players recruited for larger symphonic works. A combined regional choir of between 75 and 150 singers joins the LSO for major choral concerts. The LSO performs two concert series each year, in June and December. At times, extra concerts are scheduled featuring guest artists or guest conductors.

Orchestra members reported that participating in the LSO had contributed greatly to their musical performance and music teaching. The LSO's repertoire is above the comfort zone of many members, so concert preparation requires diligent practice, which results in greater confidence, marked improvement in performance, and an appreciation of diverse styles of music. The ensemble skills thereby learned are a vital part of musical education. The players improve their time-keeping skills; they also learn how to adhere to form and contribute to timbral balance and blend. In particular, this orchestral training helps solo musicians fit into group musical performances. A concert pianist stated: "Coming from a solo performer background, it [playing with LSO] has sharpened my awareness of working within the requirements of the orchestra as determined by the composer and the conductor." Ensemble playing develops personal skills that are highly applicable to other areas of career and life, such as greater self-discipline and the ability to take direction and cooperate constructively with all types of people. Music teachers who perform in the LSO reported that this experience increased their confidence when it came to running and conducting school ensembles and managing performance challenges such as correction and recovery during a live performance. It also helped them model the playing of challenging new repertoire. One participant reported that through community music performance she "has been given responsibilities beyond which she thought she was capable." Another performer, who teaches in a different discipline, attested to the transferability of skills learned through group work: "It helps me have high expectations with compassion, knowing what can be achieved as a group – the power of many." All of this provides regular opportunities for lifelong learning for musicians and music teachers, who gain teaching, performance, and (for some) conducting skills by networking with other musicians.

Partnership with Southern Cross University. Since 2016, the LSO has partnered with Southern Cross University (SCU), an arrangement of mutual benefit: LSO has a free rehearsal and performance venue in the university's concert hall, and SCU's community engagement and cultural profile is enhanced. This partnership has considerably broadened the learning experience of SCU music students, most of whom possess a contemporary music background. Proficient university music students are invited to perform in the orchestra, and sound production students gain work experience as audio and lighting engineers; others assist with stage management or marketing, or they act as ushers. Student immersion in this artistic culture and involvement in the environment of a regularly performing orchestra provides opportunities for their own professional experience, exposes students to classical music and musicians, and develops their knowledge of classical repertoire and performance practices. I integrate the study of the LSO concert repertoire, performance practices and classical musicology into relevant SCU music education subjects for pre-service teachers studying to become secondary music teachers.

The LSO/SCU partnership builds social capital by bridging gaps between disparate groups such as classical and contemporary musicians. This engagement links social capital that provides access to professional cultural events with community-engaged educational experiences for SCU students who would otherwise have little opportunity to attend classical concerts. One graduating SCU music student attested to the enrichment that LSO concerts provided: "Annie's passion and enthusiasm for Western art music was infectious. Instead of attending my formal graduation ceremony, I spent my cap-and-gown-hire-money on tickets for myself, partner, and children to Lismore Symphony Orchestra's latest concert at SCU, where Annie played double bass" (Graduate, 2016). Low-income, elderly, and marginalized members of the Lismore regional community can attend these concerts at little cost, as SCU is served by buses and public transport.

Guest international conductors. Through a programming initiative similar to that of CVOC, the LSO participates in concerts that feature headline guest artists or conductors. In 2016, Australian conductor Richard Gill was engaged to conduct Handel's *Messiah*, to be performed by the LSO and a 150-voice combined regional choir. Bringing in an internationally renowned conductor who specializes in orchestral, choral, and operatic works to lead a regional community orchestra and choir greatly invigorated and challenged these ensembles. Within a short but highly intense rehearsal time, the quality of performance, attention to musical detail, interpretative subtlety, and artistic nuance of both orchestra and choir were immediately, and greatly, improved. Linking regional practice with global expertise provides unique opportunities to educate performers and broaden the musical appreciation of local audiences. The concert was sold out and greatly acclaimed by the audience and the press. This initiative continued in 2018 with a scheduled performance of Mozart's *Requiem*.

Summary and Conclusion

The musical outcomes of this research project revealed that community music participation increases knowledge of repertoire, competence in playing diverse musical styles, and ensemble expertise, besides developing transferrable lifelong learning skills including leadership, teamwork, collaboration, and communication. Community music participation can enhance traditional music education practices by modelling good conducting, musical direction, performance, and ensemble practices to students; by providing mentoring to young musicians in community ensembles; and by teaching best-practice strategies to pre-service music teachers. These results, which exemplify bonding social capital, are drivers of curriculum change, informing university music education curricula and pedagogy on several levels.

Important pedagogical findings emerged from this research. Community music engagement offers diverse opportunities to support learning. Research participants' stories revealed the benefits of community music, which included social inclusion for both musicians and audiences, lifelong learning, and enhanced cultural access, particularly for rural and isolated communities. Two examples were featured: the philanthropy of the CVOC, which improved educational access, and that of the LSO, which broke boundaries between country and city by engaging urban guest conductors and musicians. These activities provided valuable learning opportunities for music students and also, significantly, for participating music teachers and professional musicians. Each of these orchestras has established and nurtured a community of practice in its region, providing lifelong learning opportunities for their members and extending their pedagogy into local schools and the community. The skills people thereby develop are easily transferred to workplaces and aligned community groups.

The benefits of community music engagement were repeatedly acknowledged by the participants in this research. Bridging social capital is built by the positive contributions of community music performance to participants' well-being, health, self-esteem, and affirmative aging. These benefits have permeated the regional community through audiences' active participation and attendance at CVOC and LSO concerts, their reported sense of belonging and identification with these communities of practice, their pride in the artistic achievements of these ensembles, and their collective sense of ownership in the cultural life of their community.

The civic benefits of the work of CVOC and the LSO are excellent examples of building social capital. The altruism and social ethos of two ensembles, whose mission is to bring professional musical entertainment to their communities through the voluntary musical practice of hundreds of committed musicians, has greatly increased cultural enrichment, audience engagement, and access to arts in regional New South Wales, not only in the Clarence Valley and Lismore but also more remote areas. Marginalized, isolated, and disadvantaged groups and individuals benefit from linking social capital; the benevolence and charity of these orchestras has enriched the cultural life of each community and improved the lives of needy individuals.

CHAPTER 11

Mindfulness and Empathetic Considerations for Music Ensemble Directing

Brent Rowan

Definitions

Empathy. The action of understanding, being aware of, being sensitive to, and vicariously experiencing the feelings, thoughts, and experience of another of either the past or present without having the feelings, thoughts, and experience fully communicated in an objectively explicit manner; also: the capacity for this (Merriam-Webster, 2017).

Mindfulness. The practice of maintaining a nonjudgmental state of heightened or complete awareness of one's thoughts, emotions, or experiences on a moment-to-moment basis; also: such a state of awareness (Merriam-Webster, 2017).

Music Ensemble. For the purpose of this chapter, a music ensemble refers to a traditional wind band that meets on a weekly basis working toward public performances and semi-formal concerts.

Introduction

AS A DIRECTOR (facilitator/conductor/leader) of a musical ensemble, when performance is part of the process, it can be a challenge to listen to the group and understand how to approach learning the music. This chapter explores how I use the concept of mindfulness when directing musical ensembles. I am not using the term mindfulness in the way that Kabat-Zinn (1995) does, that is, as a mindfulness meditation. I think of mindfulness as a way of actively being aware in the moment of everything that is happening in the space the musical ensemble occupies. Anodea Judith (2004) writes that "[m]indfulness means paying attention ... [It] takes our entire awareness into the present moment, enabling full experience ... a state of observation" (p. 425). Essential tools for the director are deep listening, patience, respect, trust, authenticity, and humour. Awareness of the group's needs, wants, and abilities is fundamental for developing cohesion within the group and trust between the director and the group. An empathetic director who understands this can make more informed rehearsal choices in order to achieve the musical goal. Peter Block (2009) explains that the role of a leader is to "listen and pay attention ... [C]onvening leaders create and manage the social space within which citizens get deeply engaged ... [L]istening may be the single most powerful action the leader can take" (p. 89).

Janice Marturano (2014) defines being mindful as "you are present for your life and your experience just as it is ... for exactly what is here, as it unfolds, meeting each moment with equanimity" (p. 8). A director who has a strong sense of self-awareness, listens to their body, is aware of their emotions, and understands the impact they have moment to moment is being mindful. A mindfulness approach is something often overlooked by the traditional conductor. I often say to my groups that I am trying to work myself out of a job. If they really know how to listen to one another, the music will flow and a "conductor" will be unnecessary. However, good leadership that instils confidence in the group can result in a more meaningful experience. It is not just about waving your arms and giving some musical advice. Norman Lebrecht (1991) writes that "[t]he physical act of conduction can be easily learned; the intangible, spiritual side has to come from somewhere within" (p. 8). A director who is aware of their own thoughts, emotions, skills, knowledge, and actions has the necessary assets for an empathetic approach to music-making.

The concept of mindfulness and empathy is not new to music directing. Richard Wagner "spouted theories about energy and intelligence in conductors" (Lebrecht, 1991, p. 12), and his understudy Hans Guido Freiherr Von Bülow in the mid-1800s was known for letting his energy and life influence flow in his conducting style. Unfortunately, he passed on the abuse he received from his own father as well as his musical father, Wagner. This style of conducting influenced other conductors, who became somewhat demanding and abusive, the opposite of mindful and empathetic. Fortunately, in the same era the esteemed conductor Arthur Nikisch "was the archetypal conductor ... He does not seem to conduct ... rather to exercise a mysterious spell ... 'I can only conduct if I feel the music in my heart,' said Nikisch" (Lebrecht, 1991, pp. 30–31). This is a clear example of mindfulness – knowing yourself and being in touch with your emotions. I am told countless stories of the piano teacher who used a ruler on the back of the hand when mistakes were made and the band director who yelled and screamed as a way to motivate his players. My own experiences with piano lessons and bands, growing up, were quite contrasting. My piano teacher was one of the most caring and compassionate teachers I ever had, while my first community jazz band director chose the yelling and screaming approach most of the time. My piano teacher would show interest in how I was doing and engage in conversation, helping strengthen our human connection. In contrast, the jazz band director would throw his watch at the drummer and say, "Get a sense of time!" Two movies come to mind to illustrate these contrasting experiences: *Mr. Holland's Opus* (1995), "[a]n inspiring drama about a music teacher who over a 30-year period turns a job into a soul-satisfying vocation, thanks to his patience, passion, and kindness" (Brussat); and *Whiplash* (2014), in which "[a] young and talented drummer attending a prestigious music academy finds himself under the wing of the most respected professor at the school; one who does not hold back on abuse towards his students."

Susan Smalley and Diana Winston write: "A classic definition of mindfulness often includes the words non-judgmental, open, accepting, and curious to describe the attitude you can cultivate when in this state" (Boyce, 2011, p. 15). For me this sounds like one of the most important principles of community music. I feel that a director who practises mindfulness and empathy can provide a more meaningful musical experience for an ensemble. For the past twenty years I have directed a wide variety of community music ensembles, including traditional concert bands, youth jazz ensembles, and adult learning bands in the New Horizons Band program. This chapter reflects on and summarizes my observations from inside those community music ensembles. I have arranged those observations under the following key terms: listening, patience, memory, trust, authenticity, humour and awareness.

Teaching Philosophy

My approach to teaching involves deep listening. An awareness of students' needs, knowledge, abilities, desires, motivations, and emotional well-being can greatly assist with the learning process. I listen to what students say and observe how they look (including their facial expressions, body language, and emotional expressions) in order to arrive at the most efficient methods to present information. I feel that if a student does not understand a concept, either I have not presented it clearly enough or the environment has not been welcoming and supportive enough to engage the student in learning. I prefer to establish clear goals and learning outcomes but to allow my instinctual improvisation ability to guide the learning process. My emotional expression demonstrates my passion for music, and sharing my knowledge is important to me. I seek to provide students with the knowledge and skills they need to grow as human

Figure 11.1   Music ensemble. Photo by Bob Johnson

beings; I see myself as a bridge for them to cross into richer and more meaningful life experiences.

Listening

Listening is one of the most important skills. It provides clues for appropriate
actions and allows the experience of the moment to have the greatest impact on
the participant. Sound therapist and deep listening practitioner Gary Diggins
(2016) suggests that "[b]y means of silent body language, facial features, interruption, correction, suggestive questions, or energetic reactions, it is possible for
a listener to subliminally steer or influence a speaker's narrative ... The circle we
create of sharing must be free of impatience, free of demand, and certainly free
of judgement." How the director listens can greatly influence the participants'
experience. Be mindful of how and what you present, for perception influences
the outcome. Wearing the musical emotion of the music for the group to see
can help them understand what the music is trying to say. Gary also notes: "As
listeners, we also have to be constantly aware of the semantic context from
which something is being communicated." What is the member saying when
they ask a question? We listen with our ears to the words, but a deep listening
practice listens beyond the words and develops an understanding of what the
speaker needs to express.

Patience

Working with groups of people from variety of backgrounds and with different levels of ability can present certain challenges. Developing group focus so that communication channels can flow is fundamental. In an interview, Phil Mullen mentioned laying down ground rules, having clear boundaries, and continuing to remind the group of expected rehearsal behaviour (personal communication, January 2016). Unfocused rehearsals get out of control, leading to difficult communication as well as frustration for members who are trying to listen. Patience is important. Give the group time to acquire expected behaviours, give them time to talk when appropriate, say what you need to say in a variety of ways, speak clearly, and repeat yourself. The next step is waiting for the music and concepts to be acquired. Sometimes the players will understand what is required but will need more practical application. Pete Moser notes "what creates a positive learning environment ... non-judgemental leadership, laughter to free the spirit and loosen inhibitions, patience, well explained boundaries, listening" (McKay & Moser, 2005, p. 15). An impatient director stops and lectures over and over about the desired concept instead of just letting the players play it out! Patience can be thought of as awareness in empathy. When asked what her most valuable skill as a facilitator is, Phoene Cave says, "patience, patience, patience and empathy, empathy, empathy aided by confidence and a passion and knowledge for what you are doing" (Higgins & Willingham, 2017, p. 115).

Respect and Connect: Memory

One of the easiest ways to demonstrate empathy is to remember what participants say. Use a previous comment as material to reinforce a point you need to make or to lighten up a situation needing some humour. Perhaps a member tells you something about themselves that gives you a way to connect the concept for them. Remembering what you have said and the experiences of the group is an important skill. A director who can recall conversations and musical experiences with members can help make connections and either show opportunities for growth or demonstrate that learning has occurred. Pointing out these connections can help build respect. Most people like to learn but sometimes forget when they are learning! A member once said to me that "I am teaching them without them knowing I am teaching them." I believe he was saying that we were having so much fun in rehearsal we did not notice how much information was being processed.

Demonstrating that you are a knowledgeable and conscientious human builds respect. Conductors like Arthur Nikisch and Hans Leipzig demonstrated this: "[I]f ever ... late to a rehearsal ... [he] would fish into his pocket for a few gold coins and present them as an act of contrition to the musicians' pension fund ... Players regarded him as one of their own and welcomed him to their backstage poker games ... [W]hen a horn-player complained that his part was unplayable, [he] grabbed the instrument and blew it perfectly. There is no better way to earn respect from an orchestra" (Lebrecht, 1991, pp. 33–34).

Trust

"Trust ... People need to know that you understand and care for them, that you have experience and that if they trust you they are safe" (McKay & Moser, 2005, p. 6). A director who understands the community can help connect people to that community. Being able to reference local current events and being in touch with individuals helps the group feel that the director is connected to them and their community. This does not mean you need to have a break from rehearsal and discuss politics, but being and showing you are aware and not living inside a music bubble does remind members that you are a normal human being and part of their community.

Demonstrate a knowledge of the material and admit what you do not know, but follow up with research and learning yourself so that you are also growing as a result of your interaction with the group. It is not just about you spouting information at them! Katherine Zeserson notes: "You need to establish yourself as a trustworthy person. People need to feel that you know what you're doing, and that you are committed to their flourishment, so they will be happy to follow your lead" (McKay & Moser, 2005, p. 129). From the definition of mindfulness comes the idea of not passing judgment. Members who trust that they will not be judged for taking a risk can only feel this way in a safe space. From a 2015 study titled "Talk, Listen, and Understand: The Impact of a Jazz Improvisation Experience on an Amateur Adult Musicians Mind, Body and Spirit," I noted: "Mentioned numerous times throughout this study was the idea of a safe place to play wrong notes (i.e. creating a non-judgmental atmosphere). It is important to let the members try something and not feel judged" (Rowan, 2017).

Authenticity

Know and be comfortable with yourself and be that genuine person. People have a deeper experience when information is delivered from the heart. Steve Lewis note: "I am convinced that the deeper your work comes from inside you the more likely it is to impact on others. So, find out who you are" (McKay & Moser, 2005, p. 37). Self-awareness as a leader and accepting who you are allows you to be more grounded. A flighty group leader lacks the focus needed to provide a sense of accomplishment. "Don't hide your ignorance, keep musical secrets, or withhold the key to the technique till the end of the workshop; it is disempowering" (McKay & Moser, 2005, p. 137). Show you are human and that you can make human connections. As Patricia Shehan Campbell notes: "the genuine interest and excitement that exudes from a fine musician as s/he sings it, plays it, dances/moves it are the qualities that motivate effective music-making with the students" (Higgins & Willingham, 2017, p. 18). Be your authentic self, know your craft, show your emotions, know who you are and do not be afraid to show it!

Humour

Perhaps the most important element when working with a community group, humour is a common thread or theme through each essential tool. "Smiles: It's a fact that the voice opens when you laugh. The sound of laughter relaxes the body, breaks the ice, makes friends" (McKay & Moser, 2005, p. 16). A mindful director with an understanding of empathy can use laughter to allow the mind, body, and spirit to open up so we can build trust, respect, show emotions, and feel safe. Douglas James Stevenson (2004) writes that "creativity and laughter at least highly overlap, if not highly correlate ... Where there is humor there is always creativity." Laughter does not segregate, or show favourites across religion, culture, race, sex, or demographics, when used with a positive, light-hearted intention.

Awareness

While I was researching director considerations, I found that the term awareness appeared frequently. Awareness is a part of everything:

+ Knowledge: What do they know, what do you know, what are they getting?
+ Trust: Have you gained any, and can it be strengthened?
+ Respect: Is it flowing both ways?
+ Patience: How much time do you allow for concepts to sink in?
+ Listening: Are you hearing the music, emotional, physical, and energetic reactions?
+ Visuals: What actions and reactions do you notice?

The following quotes provide excellent advice when it comes to awareness:

+ "Watch out for eye contact, body language and the amount of fidgeting" (McKay & Moser, 2005, p. 17).

+ "Remember all the time you are working things are going simultaneously at three different levels: individual, interpersonal and group" (McKay & Moser, 2005, p. 19).

+ "Give music to whoever is there. You are part of a continuous stream called lineage, and it is a living lineage" (Boyce, 2011, p. 111).

+ "You need to be alert to the student's wide range of signals and cues" (Higgins & Willingham, 2017, p. 29).

+ "The most important voice in the room is their voice, not mine ... Try to listen for that unspoken dialogue that's going on" (Higgins & Willingham, 2017, p. 70).

+ "It is not about you. Pay attention constantly: keep looking around the room, check body posture, facial expression. Notice people's fears and their pride, so you can include both their skills and their doubts" (McKay & Moser, 2005, p. 129).

Summary

Recognition of the moment without judgment is essential for mindful practice and an empathetic approach to music ensemble directing. As Andy Karr and Michael Wood say, "Labeling things 'beautiful' and 'ugly' masks what they really look like, when you pick and choose in this way, all you really see are the masks, which are your own mental fabrications. Living artistically means appreciating things just as they are, in an intimate, unbiased way" (Boyce, 2011, p. 102). It is about the journey and growth of the participants. The product is important, for it provides a sense of accomplishment, completeness, and acknowledgment of the consistent hard work put in, but the process is what deeply develops the individual or allows for growth, ensemble, and community. Jon Kabat-Zinn states: "It sounds almost un-American just to settle for what is, but that is a misunderstanding of the potential for living in the present moment, it's not a matter of settling. It's a matter of recognizing that, in some sense, it never gets any better than this" (Boyce, 2011, p. 61)

I include a list of do's and do not's that have been a critical component of my own leadership development.

Table 11.1

Director do's	Director do not's
• Smile, be happy	• Belittle, demean, speak harshly
• Enjoy what you do	• Single out one person in a negative way
• Show emotions	• Judge
• Admit your mistakes	• Undermine participants
• Listen	• Make it all about you
• Care	• Carry the responsibility of the members' outcomes
• Remember	• Choose music that is uninspiring

CHAPTER 12

Musica per tutti – Community Music as Meaningful, Emancipatory, and Affirming Alternatives to Formal Music Education in Italy

Antonella Coppi and Johann van der Sandt

Introduction

IN THIS CHAPTER, we look at community music and community-based musical activities, more specifically the manifestation of El Sistema in Italy (El Sistema delle Orchestre e dei Cori Giovanili ed Infantile in Italia) – its relevance and possible applications in the more traditional field of music education. We explore complementary perceptions and thinking about music education spaces and contexts and also offer a take on music education, viewed through alternative lenses, with particular reference to community music practices.

Music education in the twenty-first century has much to consider in order to stay relevant and meaningful and to ensure that it addresses the needs of the contemporary child in a changing global environment. Are community music practices meaningful, emancipatory, and affirming enough to serve as possible alternatives to the traditional ways of music education? To answer to this question, we will examine the global community music phenomenon through the lens of alternative pedagogies such as transformative pedagogy; lifelong, life-wide, life-deep learning; placed-based education; and authentic learning.

An common scenario is that children are not accepted into the government's music school system, either because not enough teachers are available or because the child is labelled insufficiently talented. We argue that other credible music-making activities can serve either as a supplement or as an alternative to formal music education opportunities, an example being El Sistema delle Orchestre e dei Cori Giovanili ed Infantile in Italia,[1] an organization that strives to bring high-quality music education to underrepresented communities. The organization (El Sistema) is showing a rapid growth across Italy at a time when the arts are receiving less and less funding at state and provincial levels. Its openness to a multitude of teaching styles offers its students access to different learning experiences. El Sistema can thus be seen as a community music activity that can play a significant role in promoting active music-making, particularly for people who do not have access to standard formal educational opportunities or who choose not to partake in them (Koopman, 2007, p.151).

Music Education: A Bridge to Connect People and Culture

Maintaining a proper diet, pursuing relaxation techniques, and making time for physical recreation are all essential for a healthy lifestyle – and so is music (Kreutz, 2008, p. 4). Music should always be part of school systems, and all students should have exposure to it. Music allows people of any age or culture to think creatively, express themselves freely, and develop self-esteem; all of these are important for a successful life. In an article questioning the validity of music as a universal language, Campbell (1997) examines different views of music and its uses from the perspectives of diversity (culture-specific distinctions) and universality (homogeneous properties). Campbell concludes that music can be viewed as a valuable universal language (1997).

The benefits of music education for children, not only in Italy but everywhere in the world, are widely recognized. Research into cognition conducted in the United States stresses the fact that music creates pathways in children's brains and enriches their sensory environment.

According to SIEM (Società Italiana di educazione musicale – Italian Society for Music Education), a partner of ISME, music also contributes to children's "school readiness." It prepares them in the following areas: language, literacy, inclusion, well-being, and life skills.

Music is also one of the most important modes of communication available to children. It helps them develop their cognitive abilities and to settle into and become part of their cultural and social environment.

Music has a positive effect on children's behaviour, which improves significantly when they are exposed to it. It is essential to involve children in music because they become better at self-control in school and at home, besides having more positive interaction with peers. According to Hallam (2010), children's behaviours in terms of cooperation, collaboration, and group efforts improve when they are exposed to music, primarily when it involves rhythmic

---

1 http://www.federculture.it/2013/02/sistema-delle-orchestre-e-cori-giovanili

activities. Exposure to music fosters self-expression and creativity in young children and encourages them to engage in playful experimentation.

The Italian school system includes music education from an early age – children in preschool as well as primary and middle school receive on average two hours of musical instruction every week. But after that, free public music education closes its doors, which means that secondary school students do not have formal access to music education. Some high schools specialize in music, but access to them is limited: only a fixed number of students can enrol, and the entrance exams are rather strict. After the age of fourteen, Italian children's only options for music education are in informal and not-formal environments. Italy is currently in an economic recession, and public schools – and private schools as well – are losing a significant portion of their funding. This is forcing school districts to make serious choices about program funding. A loss in funding often translates into less money for elective courses in music.

In an article about the writings of Fedele D'Amico, La Face (2017) highlights D'Amico's view that music education in Italy is the Cinderella of school subjects: it is taught poorly when it is taught at all. La Face writes that whatever the curriculum documents say, Italian music education since the 1970s has lapsed into a sort of naive educational spontaneism, completely divorced not only from historical models but also from culture as such. The learning/teaching process has been progressively eroded in the name of "common competence" (p. 65).

Bridging Music Education and Community Music

Research has shown that the power of musical engagement is strong enough to improve academic achievement and contribute to the social and mental well-being of individuals. A detailed report on music's impact on children's and young people's intellectual, social, and personal development states that music engagement helps develop literacy, self-esteem, creativity, social and personal development, and health and well-being (Hallam, 2010). José Antonio Abreu, the founder of El Sistema, has said that "music has to be recognized as an agent of social development in the highest sense because it transmits the highest values – solidarity, harmony, mutual compassion." Music has been credited with the ability to "unite an entire community and express sublime feelings" (Tunstall, 2012, p. 35). Music is a distinctive aspect of being human and can act as a bridge to connect people to culture, the arts, and the humanities (Elliott, Silverman, & Bowman, 2016). Music can be a vehicle for transformative educational experiences. Research has shown that music education creates a favourable climate for social inclusion.

Educational authorities worldwide encourage frameworks for interdisciplinary teaching and seek to develop engaged populations and communities of practice in a safe, positive, and nurturing environment (Abril & Gault, 2016). The growing numbers of immigrant children arriving in Italy require research and support, aimed at guaranteeing their right to be protected, educated, and housed, all in a safe legal and social context, in accordance with UN's *Convention on the Rights of the Child* (UNICEF, 1989), as subscribed to by the Italian government in 1991.

Article 27 of the UN *Convention on the Rights of the Child* states:

> States Parties recognize the right of every child to a standard of living adequate for the child's physical, mental, spiritual, moral and social development. The parent(s) or others responsible for the child have the primary responsibility to secure, within their abilities and financial capacities, the conditions of living necessary for the child's development. (UNICEF, 1989).

There is evidence that engagement in musical activities has an impact on social inclusion (sense of self and of being socially integrated). Lindgren, Bergman, and Sæther (2016) examined children's music programs in Gothenburg and Malmö to see whether they fostered individual and social development as well as intercultural social inclusion. They found that there are different ways of constructing social inclusion through music. Viewed from an integrative sociological perspective on music education, the children were positioned primarily as representatives of the musical community rather than as independent agents in control of the music and their learning (Lindgren, Bergman, & Sæther, 2016, p.65). This was a rich environment for enhancing social inclusion.

Combating social exclusion and promoting social inclusion are common concerns all over the world (Schippers, 2009). In the European Union, a multitude of government organizations and agencies view the arts in general, and music in particular, as key to solving social problems. In May 2011, the European Music Council (EMC) invited active parties from the field of music education to discuss how to implement UNESCO's *Seoul Agenda: Goals for the Development of Arts Education* (UNESCO, 2010). The seminar's main task was to explore how that agenda could be adapted to music education in Europe.

The Bonn Declaration reflects common focal points for the development of music education in Europe. It acknowledges the principle of subsidiarity and calls upon political decision-makers at the local, regional, national, and European levels to define standard policies for promoting music education in Europe and to put those policies into practice. Of great importance is the

Bonn Declaration's reflection on music's power to confront social and cultural challenges, as well its inherent ability to serve as a vehicle for social integration and social inclusion (Dudt, 2012, p. 133). The declaration includes some suggested actions that yet have to be adhered to, to reach the goal of music education for all children.

> Music is a powerful tool for the inclusion of people that are excluded for whatever reason (gender, age, socially, economically, culturally, etc.), and it may serve as a tool for building bridges and for meeting the social and cultural challenges. Intercultural and socio-cultural training (including personal development and group work) should be integrated into the training of all musicians and Music Education practitioners at all levels. Likewise, workers from other disciplines should receive training in music in order to facilitate cross-over between sectors. They must be exposed to music to understand its value entirely. Music Education institutions in the formal sector and organizations offering non-formal Music Education should offer more activities which are aimed at addressing and resolving social and cultural challenges. (EMC, 2012, p. 4)

The Seoul Agenda reflects the conviction

> that arts education has an important role to play in the constructive transformation of educational systems that are struggling to meet the needs of learners in a rapidly changing world characterized by remarkable advances in technology on the one hand and intractable social and cultural injustices on the other. Issues ... included ... were peace, cultural diversity and intercultural understanding as well as the need for a creative and adaptive workforce in the context of post-industrial economies ... Arts education can make a direct contribution to resolving the social and cultural challenges facing the world today. (UNESCO, 2010, *Introduction*)

The three goals of the Seoul Agenda are closely linked and cover essential aspects of arts education. The Bonn Declaration reflects the arguments of the Seoul Agenda and offers interpretations of the three goals, placing its emphasis on music education in Europe. In Table 12.1 are some important and closely related goals of the Seoul Agenda embraced in the Bonn Declaration.

The Bonn Declaration, which concludes with a set of recommendations for decision-makers, is an essential political document that has helped Europe's music education sector achieve the objectives laid down in the Seoul Agenda, paving the way for recognition of the value of music education in the twenty-first century in Europe.

Table 12.1   Seoul Agenda goals embraced in the Bonn Declaration (EMC, 2012)

Access to music education	Constitutes the first goal of the Bonn Declaration, which raises questions such as: Who is offering music activities? Are these music activities available to all those wishing to take part in them, and if not, then why? The document emphasizes the right of all citizens to a music education and states that any obstacles encountered by those wanting to participate must be addressed.
High-quality music education – prerequisites	Discusses whether those providing music education have received the necessary training for the jobs they are performing. Any shortfalls should be overcome through collaborations between formal, non-formal, and informal music education providers, with responsibility for the adequate training lying with both the educational institutions preparing the practitioners and their later employers.
Social and cultural challenges	The music education sector is addressed in the third goal of the Bonn Declaration. It is agreed that there is more to music than its artistic value, and music education has proved itself to be an instrument for overcoming inequalities in society. This must be recognized by those active in the field of music education; however, those seeking to use music education for such means should be adequately informed and have received the relevant training.

Il Sistema is regarded as high-quality music education with distinct features that enable it to foster social and cultural changes, according to the above-mentioned objectives set out in the Seoul Agenda.

For most readers of this text, a discussion why to include music education in the school curriculum would be redundant. Let us simply quote Hoffer (2017): "Just as an education in mathematics consists of much more than learning how to add and subtract, and an education in science means more than observing the patterns in the weather, an education in music involves much more than a little singing or superficial listening. Young people need to be taught reading, science, math, and history, and they also need to be taught music" (p. 5).

It is our hope that policy-makers will soon start to realize the value of the Seoul Agenda and the Bonn Declaration, given that in a recent study, "Exploring the Global Decline of Music Education," published four years after the Seoul Agenda and the Bonn Declaration, music educators concurred that music education was in decline throughout the world (Aróstegui, 2016, p.96). One reason for this is suggested by Graham Welch of the University of London, a respected music educator, who referred to the overall "lack of understanding shown by policy makers regarding the lifelong impact of Music Education on children and young people" (quoted in Sussman, 2014).

The vacuum that has developed as a result of the disconnect between the "decline of Music Education in schools and the importance music has in popular youth culture and in creativity within the new knowledge economy" (Aróstegui 2016, p. 1) provides an opportunity for community music scholars to advocate community music interventions as a supplement and complement to traditional music education offerings.

Opportunities to engage with music have expanded in Italy, as evidenced by the growth in Il Sistema–inspired programs, from five in 2007 to the current sixty-five. Various other settings offer musical experiences that together constitute an expanding landscape of what can be called informal music education – for example, Mus-e Italia.[2] In its earlier iterations, community music "often positioned itself outside mainstream Music Education – this was part of its radical agenda" (McKay & Higham, 2011 p. 7). Early writings on community music stated that one its identified purposes was "to replace the education system with an educational community" (Small, 1996, p. 221). Community music's negotiated shift in identity and in "its pedagogic practices in the context of *non-formal* and *informal* education and *music-making*" is evident in recent research. The position of community music as an influential concept "within the system of Music Education now seems more secure and less critical" (McKay & Higham, 2011, p. 7).

When examining community music – in particular, when looking at the tensions that often arise when hard boundaries are drawn between (formal) music education and community music. For many, "Community music is simply a way of 'dressing' music teaching-and-learning in different clothes" (Silverman, 2005, p. 2).

In Italy, and more specifically in South Tyrol, where both authors of this chapter are working, the connections between Music Education and community are many. School ensembles provide entertainment for many organizations throughout the year, adult choirs, "Musikkapellen," and semi-professional musical theatre productions, to mention only a few. Given that the list of musical activities and offerings is impressively long, surely some form of music education must exist outside the school walls.

Elitism is another source of tension that often splits music education from community music. Silverman (2005) writes that "Music Education has been too narrowly defined and exclusive, and that school music serves, primarily,

---

2   https://www.mus-e.it/

an elite" (p. 4). Elitism in music education is seen as a "qualitative difference between music learning that cultivates a participatory culture and one that maintains a 'singular vision' or fixed agenda" (O'Neill, 2012, p.173). In contrast to formal music education, community music cultivates a participatory culture and regards all participants as having a natural potential for making music. "No matter how good our intentions, there is something fundamentally limiting about viewing music learners in terms of their musical performance problems (or lack thereof) instead of their potential" (O'Neill, 2012, p. 176). Music education "that adheres to traditional (dominant) discourses and [evades] historical, political, and contextual constructs" leads to disconnected students, thus depriving them of the optimal educational potential of music (Brown & Volgsten, 2005, p.5).

Formal (i.e., elitist) music education "potentially subverts, marginalizes, represses, and even destroys the common music of ordinary people and de-values it in, or excludes it from, general education" (Jorgensen, 2008, p. 33). Interesting examples of this can be found in many previously colonized countries where European missionaries sought to musically educate Indigenous peoples by teaching them European Christian hymns, instead of using the inherent power of the music of their own communities. This resulted in music used for education being labelled as "elite" and music heard in social settings being labelled as "common."

Il Sistema Italia perfectly meets the criteria for communal music-making. It provides a means to express cultural democracy and foster cultural, human, experiential, social, and spiritual capital. The result is a more fully rounded holistic education for individuals.

Community Music as an Agent for Different Styles of Music Learning

O'Neill (2012) urges music educators to view music learners as individuals in the process of *becoming* ""a person or learner is not a state of *being* but is always in the process of *becoming*. Whereas the idea of *being* a music learner suggests a bounded and static entity, with a nature that is prescribed, determined, or unchangeable, *becoming* a music learner is infused with notions of unfolding, openness, and dynamic potential" (p. 164). This opens the way to a transformation in perspective: community music settings provide a more "inclusive, differentiating, permeable, critically reflective, and integrative experience" (p. 164).

Music educators, as well as community musicians, are encouraged to explore new pedagogical and curriculum initiatives involving many alternative pedagogical approaches to adjust the lens through which we view music education or the music experiences offered to learners (p. 164). Il Sistema Italy is one possible music education intervention.

Community Music and Situated Learning

In reading Bronfenbrenner's book *Making Human Beings Human: Bioecological Perspectives on Human Development*, one acquires an understanding of the complex interactions and interconnections between multiple learning contexts. Bronfenbrenner's emphasis on the instability and unpredictability of learning environments shows that it is vital that we prepare "learners with knowledge and strategies to deal with a complex world" (O'Neill, 2012, p. 171). Community music activities and projects are rooted in the local, in the participant's "own" place or immediate environment, where they constitute a form of social co-participation. These activities do not rely primarily on cognitive processes and conceptual structures; rather, they emphasize social engagement as a proper context for learning to take place. "A critical pedagogy of place for music, then, might be grounded in consideration of socio-musical places" (Regelski & Gates, 2009, p. 178). One can also think about community music interventions in terms of a "community of practice," as advocated by Lave and Wenger (1998). "The idea that learning involves a deepening process of participation in a community of practice has gained significant ground in recent years" (Smith, 2003, p. 1).

Both models – community music and communities of practice – strongly emphasize a sense of belonging to a social entity. This belonging to a community of practice, a community music project, can be seen as a social affiliation for the individual and can serve to "inform, challenge, broaden, and transform our conceptualizations and representations of what music learning means in our everyday lives" (O'Neill, 2012, p.167).

"Situated learning" as an instructional approach is essentially "a matter of creating meaning from the real activities of daily living and where learning occurs relative to the teaching environment," so that "students are more inclined to learn by actively participating in the learning experience" (Lave & Wenger, 1998). Field trips where students participate in unfamiliar environments can be seen as an example of situated learning. El Sistema and Il Sistema Italy offer situated learning environments in which the participants' music experience is part of their daily or weekly activities and they learn by doing and by cooperating:

> Contemporary views of learning increasingly consider life to be one long learning journey: in every activity in which we engage, we are learning and improving in our practice. Learning from this perspective is truly life-long in that it occurs over time, and life-deep in that it is shaped by an individual's various religious, social and moral values. It is also life-wide in the sense that an individual's experiences occur across many settings (King, Kersh, Potter, & Pitts, 2015, p. i).

Lifelong and life-wide learning processes are efforts "towards recognizing and connecting students' learning across formal and informal contexts." These learning processes represent opportunities for learning and education to cope with "the changing requirements contemporary knowledge societies pose" (Erstad & Sefton-Green, 2013, p. 1). "As a ubiquitous presence in society – albeit a somewhat more marginalized one in formal education – music indeed can be "life-wide, life-long and life-deep'" (King, Kersh, Potter, & Pitts, 2015, 14). Life-wide learning is a very inclusive concept of learning and development that involves a breadth of experiences, guides, and locations. Since "music is a universal feature of human society and an important part of our collective celebrations and statements of beliefs, values, and issues," it is seen as an integral part of human growth and development (Barrett & Westerlund, 2017, p. 75). Music, and participation in community music activities, is seen as a "phenomenon of Communicative Musicality." Life-long and life-wide learning results as "music lays down the foundations of human connectedness, identity work, and language" (Barrett & Westerlund, 2017, p. 75).

Life-wide learning involves steering the individual's interests, which have intrinsic value. An example is provided by El Sistema delle Orchestre e dei Cori Giovanili ed Infantile in Italia. The participants gave a performance outside a formal educational environment, in an informal (non-educational) setting.[3] This helped the participants enhance their self-awareness, encouraging them to value this experience as an opportunity for learning and development.

Learning cannot become lifelong and life-wide without being life-deep (Bélanger, 2015). Life-deep learning "embraces religious, moral, ethical, and social values that guide what people believe, how they act, and how they judge themselves and others" (Banks, 2012). Communal music-making activities, characterized by active participatory music-making by all participants, provides a possible platform for life-deep learning, for it situates learning in an activity, instead of it being received passively (Scott, 2006, p. 17). Il Sistema is a participatory experience in which individuals are actively involved in the musicking process. "El Sistema has fostered a remarkable renewal of interest in the transformative potential of music and the power of Music Education. Importantly, this movement has highlighted the principle that access to participatory music is a universal right" (Creech, González-Moreno, Lorenzino, and Waitman, 2016, p. 36).

---

3 In C. Small (2011), Musicking. Small outlines a theory of the term "musicking," a verb that encompasses all musical activity. This term is now widely used and accepted.

Community Music and Intergenerational Learning

Community music activities also provide the opportunity for intergenerational learning, as "intergenerational practice aims to bring people together in purposeful, mutually beneficial activities which promote greater understanding and respect between generations and contribute to building more cohesive communities" (Vanderbeck & Worth, 2015, p. 33). Created events for communal singing provide opportunities to promote dialogue, collaborative learning through participatory doing, and mutual understanding. Intergenerational music engagements "become places to share expertise and knowledge without the barriers of age, class, race, gender, and education" (O'Neill, 2012, p. 173).

Intergenerational engagement offers the following benefits to society, individuals, and communities. One can see that community music activities perfectly match the criteria for an environment where intergenerational music engagement can flourish:

- Intergenerational engagement unites segregated generations and builds better understanding between them.
- It encourages active citizenship and social participation.
- It encourages cross-generational work.
- It exchanges of tacit and explicit knowledge among generations.
- It challenges social problems cross-generationally.
- It supports lifelong and life-wide Learning.
- It maintains and builds human and social capital simultaneously (Fischer & Kugemann, 2008, p. 6).

Although research data about the scope of intergenerational learning in El Sistema and Il Sistema are not available, we could add our voice to Creech, González-Moreno, Lorenzino, and Waitman (2016) that such "inspired programs, in seeking to address salient social development goals, could broaden their scope and focus, to include intergenerational groups in music-making. This could be a distinctive and powerful feature of programs that have at their heart the aim of social development" (p. 84).

Community Music Activities as Authentic Learning

Authentic learning is a type of learning that "engages all the senses allowing students to create a meaningful, useful, shared outcome" (Revington, n.d.). Community music activities have the potential "provide the learner with opportunities to connect directly with the real world." Scholars agree that the promotion of music in schools is vital in the current educational climate, but they also call for opportunities for music outside of school. The "frequent calls for 'real-life,' 'authentic' experiences in education in which students gain 'deep understanding' of essential learning'" (Southcott, 2006, p.1) serve as openings for the community musician to promote community music projects. There is a functional similarity between authentic learning environments and community music activities, in which performances are part of "essential learning and authentic experience" (Southcott, 2006, p. 1). Performance is essential to communal music activities, for it helps develop positive music identities (MacDonald, 2013, p. 9).

Through performance, participants in community music activities learn about "stage etiquette, audience etiquette, stage set-up, how to deal with performance anxiety, how they personally react to being on stage, [how to] recover from mistakes, listening skills, how to perform under pressure, and [how to] perform with others" (Mann, n.d.).

Il Sistema programs are characterized by the presence of certain core authentic learning opportunities. They offer participants collaborative opportunities to be part of a real product (an authentic, acoustic music creation) to be shared with the community, ensuring a personalized growth experience for the individual participants. Creech, González-Moreno, Lorenzino, and Waitman (2016) emphasize that El Sistema–inspired programs provide participants with frequent opportunities to immerse themselves in an ensemble experience. In this way, "children gradually accumulate authentic experiences of participating in the creation of beauty and sharing this with others" (p. 44).

Community Music and Transformative Learning

Transformative learning includes the idea of people changing how they interpret their experiences and interactions with the world (Cranton, 2002, p. 64). From a music educational perspective, Cranton is pointing to *transformative* learning as allowing for the possibility of change "that moves us beyond merely solving problems and providing adequate opportunities for learners to acquire the basic skills and knowledge necessary for music learning" (O'Neill, 2012, p. 164).

Transformative music engagement focuses on the idea that "all music learners in all contexts of development have strengths and competencies" – yet another principle of community music theory. Music educators need to move away from "viewing music learners from within a deficit versus talent/expertise framework" (O'Neill, 2012, p.166). All human beings "are genetically endowed to be musical creatures in the same sense that we are designed to be linguistic" (Hodges, 2000). By tapping the inherent musicality of the participants, community music facilitators can empower learners to embark on a transformative journey – empowerment being a prerequisite for transformation (Cranton, 2016).

The diversity of community music interventions makes them a form of music engagement that is dynamic, transformational, and multidimensional. This type of music engagement "operates on many independent levels (personal, sociocultural, systemic)" (O'Neill, 2012, p. 165). Motivation empowers participants to "own" the music activity, thus increasing their meaningful participation; in this way, the participants (learners) gain "a sense of relevance, purpose, and fulfilment" (O'Neill, 2012, p. 165). "The type[s] of activities that stimulate real involvement give pupils something to do, not something to learn; and the doing is of such a nature as to demand thinking or the intentional noting of connections; learning results naturally" (Dewey, 2011). Community music activities offer all participants the opportunity to take ownership of the musical product by developing their musical skills and knowledge and sharing in "participatory cultures that work toward common endeavors while creating highly supportive and generative learning environments" (O'Neill, 2012, p. 166). This is real transformative music engagement in action.

For music education to act as a transforming agent, it has to "go beyond considerations of musical syntax, aesthetics, and performance. It needs to relate to the realities of individuals and communities in which it engages. It must not only establish its value in cognitive and emotional connections alone, but also search for social and thus, personal, transformation" (Schmidt, 2005, p.9). According to Creech, González-Moreno, Lorenzino, and Waitman,

> there is considerable evidence of the transformative impact of El Sistema and Sistema–inspired programs at an individual level, with many reports of enhanced self-esteem, raised aspirations, personal development, and improved psychological well-being. There are also hopeful indicators that support the view that El Sistema and Sistema–inspired programs are having a positive and transformative impact upon communities. (2016, p. 131)

According to Coppi (2017), Il Sistema Italia displays important characteristics of transformative music engagements in which participants take ownership of the musical product by developing their musical skills and knowledge (p. 213).

The Value of Music Experiences for Children in the El Sistema Program, Italy

Music is a language, and it can become a common language (Hallam, 2010). Music education enables children to communicate through that language. As demographic changes increase the diversity in classrooms, in schools, and in all other educational contexts, new ways must be found to bring learners together in activities that break down barriers (Higgins & Willingham, 2017). Children can participate in music experiences at a variety of levels of engagement. Music can enrich their lives, promote cultural awareness, make schools better places to learn, and promote pride of accomplishment (Elliott, Silverman, & Bowman, 2016). Music education helps children achieve personal and collective growth by creating social bonds, promoting responsibility, raising achievement levels, and helping them learn self-discipline as well as tolerance for differences. It also offers constructive entertainment.

According to Campbell and Scott-Kassner (2013) as quoted in Mathis (n.d.), a child's self-esteem

> improves when the child has a better sense of self. This better sense of self can be directly related to music when the children see themselves as competent. Emotional development also increases through music in the following ways: children begin to have empathy for other cultures through musical practice and are easily motivated and inspired by music; children involved in music also cope better with anxiety and more often remain relaxed and stress-free.

Music belongs to all children, and children's involvement in musical activities has steadily positive effects on children's cognitive and emotional behaviour (Orman, 2002). A music teacher can do so much for a student in a variety of ways, and each teacher should embrace this. No student should be "weeded out" or told he or she does not belong in a music classroom: all students deserve the opportunity to grow and develop by participating in musical activities. According to Abril and Gault (2016), music educators need to understand the children's abilities as well as areas of deficit in order to develop effective strategies to support students' success.

The Italian National Guidelines for Curricula for Early Childhood and Primary School (Indicazioni Nazionale per il curricolo delle scuole dell'infanzia e del primo ciclo di istruzione)[4] recommends that music educators consult with fellow educators to build a repertoire of strategies for including all students. These recommendations are in line with those suggested by Coates (2012):

+ To achieve successful inclusive music education, educators should develop creative approaches, maintain high expectations for their students, and utilize such principles to create effective learning

---

4 http://www.indicazioninazionali.it/wp-content/uploads/2018/08/Indicazioni_Annali_Definitivo.pdf

opportunities for all students, providing multiple means of representation;

+ utilizing a variety of visual, auditory, and kinesthetic formats for presenting information, providing also multiple means of expression,

+ creating a variety of options for students to demonstrate knowledge and understanding and providing multiple means of engagement, and,

+ developing a variety of motivating, challenging, and age/developmentally appropriate music experiences to enhance learning.

El Sistema–Inspired Program in Italy

El Sistema–inspired programs have produced unexpected transformations in many countries, especially in countries with disadvantaged communities. Coppi (2017) reported in *Community Music. Nuovi orientamenti pedagogici* (Community Music: New Pedagogical Approaches) on various El Sistema–inspired programs worldwide, comparing these to Italian programs (El Sistema) and highlighting their shared pedagogical principles. She also compared these programs to those found in Italian formal, informal, and non-formal educational environments.

Coppi (2017) endeavoured in her book to

+ make Italian people aware of the work of El Sistema scholars and its pedagogical potential;

+ contribute the music educational and pedagogical theory in Italy;

+ offer an analytical mapping and screening of the state of active projects until June 2017, including organizational and didactic information;

+ start an Italian national educational debate, especially regarding the role of music as an instrument for social change, multicultural integration, and inclusion;

+ find new paths for future research into the relationship between music education and social inclusion.

According to Coppi's research, many teachers reported hugely increased levels of concentration, discipline, motivation, and attendance. Today El Sistema is a tested model around the world. A variety of programs have applied it, for besides creating great musicians, it can dramatically change the life trajectories of hundreds of thousands of disadvantaged children.

El Sistema, notwithstanding its noble mission, is not without controversy. An article in the *New York Times* reported that Venezuelan president Hugo Chávez's embrace of the El Sistema had angered some of his supporters and had been "seized on by Chávez opponents, provoking rare criticism of two of Venezuela's most celebrated and popular figures: the movement's revered founder, José Antonio Abreu, and its most famous product, the conductor Gustavo Dudamel" (Wakin, 2012). El Sistema has also been strongly criticized by Geoffrey Baker (2015), who stated that the social aspect of *El Sistema*, which is widely hailed as lifting disadvantaged youths out of slums, has not always been Abreu's primary concern. According to Baker, Abreu's main focus has always been on the show element of the music and that his model is far from democratic. It is clear that Baker thinks little of Abreu, whom he describes as a divisive figure, respected by those who support El Sistema but loathed by "non-believers."

Luigi Mazzocchi, a Venezuelan now living in the United States, where he has developed a successful career as an orchestra violinist, concurs with Baker. He describes the model as "excellence in musical performance seriously compromised by a culture of fear and authoritarianism, a narrow view of Music Education, and a lack of accountability and transparency" (Scripp, 2015, p. 2). Mazzocchi adds that despite his gratitude for the musical training he received in El Sistema, "the system nonetheless needs to reform its working conditions, leadership model, and culture in order to ensure its positive social impact and better serve as a model for Music Education in the future" (Scripp, 2015, p. 1). Shieh (2015) contends that El Sistema's methods are a mystery even to its followers. "One of its sharpest critics has gone so far as to call it 'voodoo' (Toronyi-Lalic, 2012), and in a notable response, one of its strongest advocates has declared, '*Sistema* may be voodoo, but it works' (Govias, 2012, para. 5)" (p. 568). But notwithstanding the criticisms made of Abreu and El Sistema, the system has been lauded in many publications (Allan, 2010; Arvelo, 2005; Tunstall, 2012; Baker, 2014; Cline, 2012; Creech & Long, 2012; Donald, Stathopoulos, & Lorenzino, 2012; Govias, 2010; Majno, 2012; Majno & Fabris, 2012; Bates, 2014; Booth, 2011; Burns & Bewick, 2012). We add our voice to that of Creech, González-Moreno, Lorenzino, and Waitman (2016), who conducted a systematic literature review and found that El Sistema has far-reaching implications and benefits in the following areas: personal development, psychological well-being, social skills, membership in protective social networks, and significant and cumulative gains in academic and musical achievement.

It seems that the positive outweighs the negative. The Italian El Sistema scholar Maria Majno heeded the plea of Claudio Abbado to help launch the program in Italy and around the world. El Sistema-inspired programs have been successful in Australia and in many parts of Africa. In a study conducted on an El Sistema-inspired program in South Africa, Devroop (2012) reported generally increased levels of self-esteem, optimism, happiness, and perseverance in children after they participated in an instrumental music program. There were also increases in the subjects' optimism and happiness. There were moderate to moderately strong positive relationships between participation in instrumental music and self-esteem, optimism, happiness, and perseverance (Devroop, 2012). This El Sistema-inspired program struggled to introduce the resources of music, against those who viewed the program as irrelevant to the community.

Sistema Europe, founded in 2012, is a network open to all European El Sistema and El Sistema-inspired organizations as well as to individuals who aspire to carry out activities true to its principles. Through that network, members can learn about, develop, and share Sistema practices, plan joint projects, attend performances and training events, seek mutual advice and guidance, and tap funding opportunities.[5]

In 2010, thanks to Claudio Abbado – an enthusiastic supporter of the Venezuelan project since 1999 – El Sistema was established in Italy, where it was named El Sistema delle Orchestre e dei Cori giovanili e Infantili in Italia.[6] At present, there are more than sixty-five nuclei in Italy's El Sistema National Program. The Italian Sistema delle Orchestre e dei Cori Giovanili e Infantili serves as an example for other Italian organizations endeavouring to start similar musical programs. Maria Majno, vice-president of Sistema Europe, asserts that today, in Italy, the project is rapidly taking shape by implementing a national structure with official ties to the original model (a bilateral agreement that was signed in February 2011). In parallel, a network of regional initiatives is developing, with marked features with the local characteristics that are a distinguishing trait of the country's eclectic style. According to the very diverse regional contexts, the focus may be directed to widespread in-school training (e.g., the Alto Adige/South Tyrol region), to the involvement of children as ambassadors of peace (Pequeñas Huellas in Piedmont), to a full-fledged, established music school renewing its course (Fiesole in Tuscany), to expanding youth ensembles (Emilia-Romagna), to pilot projects for the disadvantaged (the southern regions and some immigration-laden communities), or to productions aiming for higher artistic results, as in the previously mentioned pyramid of increasingly proficient ensembles, with exposure that rewards musical excellence (2012).

Between 2010 and 2018, the Italian network of regional initiatives grew from fifteen to sixty-five nuclei. In Italy, as well as in Venezuela, most of the activities involve what are called nuclei. Most of these nuclei are children's

---

5 http://www.sistemaeurope.org
6 http://www.federculture.it/2013/02/sistema-delle-orchestre-e-cori-giovanili

orchestras, but there are also special educational projects for children with disabilities, in particular for children with hearing disabilities. One of these, Coro Manos Blancas, comprises two groups of children: a singing group, and a group that moves in choreographed hand movements (wearing white gloves – *manos blancas*), thereby experiencing the music in their own unique way.

Italian nuclei share the following characteristics:

1. They acknowledge the power of music and how it can change children's lives (the emphasis being on with children who lack family support and children with a background of a drug, internet, and other substance abuse issues).

2. They focus on teaching methods (including how to encourage peer teaching, how to get a short-term result, and how to monitor individual progress).

3. They constantly develop ways to work with diverse groups of children (e.g., of different age groups, and of different family backgrounds or religious beliefs – how to communicate, and how to support dialogue, tolerance, understanding, and acceptance of difference).

4. The focus on how to set up a nucleus (structure, working methods, fundraising, dealing with parents, community involvement).

5. They develop conducting skills, following the specific El Sistema methodology but adapting it to the reality of the diversity of the children in groups.

6. They work with local talent: Italian music teachers are at the core of the system.

7. They focus on quality repertoire, including classical music, Italian folklore, and music from other countries (incorporating music from the birth countries of the children in the group).

8. They encourage participation and collaboration with international pedagogues and artists (master classes, performing camps, composing with and for the children, etc.).

Italian Sistema programs share many goals with other international programs, in that they aim at

+ fighting educational poverty with music;
+ teaching children to succeed in a collaborative environment at the highest level;

- building children's confidence and self-worth; and
- encouraging children to recognize that they are part of a larger entity.

El Sistema delle Orchestre e dei Cori Giovanili ed Infantile in Italia seeks to foster tolerance, dialogue, and togetherness throughout communities. By teaching music to young children from diverse social, economic, and cultural backgrounds, the program aims to educate and inspire the children, to support them to work toward a promising future embracing harmony and dignity for all.

Some Reflections on El Sistema, Italy

When working toward an inclusive educational environment, embrace diversity and acknowledge differences so as to weave a tapestry of unique individuals, one in which the participants' heritage and unique abilities are recognized or respected.

The presence of the "other" in school, juat as in society, has the potential to generate conflict, thereby undermining not only the group but also the individual, especially when children or teenagers are involved. Coppi (2017) writes that teachers involved in music programs should take care to respect and appreciate the personality of each child, their history, their roots, and their culture. El Sistema and community music share values in this regard: El Sistema programs, when they succeed as community music interventions, can serve as a bridge between integration and inclusion – both processes are highly advocated by Italian political and social advocates. Feelings of uneasiness and concern about the education of new generations can be sensed in formal and non-formal Italian groups. There is a shared need to build children with strong personalities who will oppose violence and bullying and embrace positive societal values. El Sistema pedagogic nuclei are concerned with the principle of empowerment (nurturing an environment conducive to the development of personal knowledge, skills, and competences). The group as a whole, as well as the individuals in the group, are motivated to set goals and are then helped to develop and formulate appropriate strategies to achieve them using existing resources (Coppi, 2017). This supports the idea of taking effective action to achieve goals and controlling how actions influence events.

Coppi's data analysis (2017) indicates that the Italian system (El Sistema) is strongly oriented toward the founding principles of El Sistema. Emphasis is placed on establishing valuable connections, as well as an environment of inclusion between the institution and the individual, between the school and teachers, and between teachers and pupils and their parents, in order to bring about positive change to the participants' social context, making it more attractive, open, democratic, free, and legitimate. This is linked to the accumulation of cognitive skills.

El Sistema Italy has shown a surprising predisposition toward the capability approach. That approach, as developed by Amartya Sen, Martha Nussbaum, and others, "is a broad normative framework for the evaluation and assessment of individual well-being and social arrangements, the design of policies, and proposals about social change in society" (Robeyns, 2005). Coppi's data (2017) indicate that Italian El Sistema programs resonate strongly with El Sistema programs worldwide in that they focus on the moral significance of the individuals' capacity to achieve the best possible quality of life. The capability approach, in a musical context, has the potential to reinforce an individual's dignity because it is the nature of musical activities to prioritize the human factor. That approach, transferred from an economic context to a (musical) educational one, suggests that the person must be able to express his or her range of competences – thus affirming the principle of individual (and individualized) capacity. The development of the person's persona facilitates his or her own needs (Nussbaum, 2001, p. 34). A person's capacity to live a good life is defined in terms of valuable "beings and doings," such as being in good health and having loving relationships with others (Wells, 2013). It is greatly encouraging that data are available that point to the multidimensional characteristics of the El Sistema programs, mainly working towards the normative goal of capability expansion – that is, the expansion of the individual's capacity to make valued, informed, and responsible choices in other spheres of life.

Coppi (2017) has shown in her research results that the theoretical foundations of El Sistema Italy are very much in line with those of Sistema Europe in terms of their focus on multiculturalism, as well as their choice of repertoire and mixture of performing groups. Out of the more than seventy nuclei investigated, 78 percent made positive use of varied repertoire with multicultural accents and a creative mix of different performing groups – all indicators that inclusion and diversity were being promoted. Of the nuclei investigated, around 58 percent were strongly inclined toward complimentary educational strategies such as inclusion and use of the educational philosophies and methods of Kodály, Suzuki, Orff, Jacques Dalcroze, and the teachers' own approaches. These strategies led to relational intervention and a constructive milieu of prevention and recovery in working with children (from the early childhood right through adolescence to youth), with particular emphasis on children of migrant backgrounds.

Coppi's research was recognized in June 2017 by Federculture (Italy's national association of public and private bodies, institutions, and companies in the field of cultural policy and activities), as well as by the Comitato Nazionale Orchestre e Cori giovanili ed infantili in Italia (National Committee for youth and children's choirs and orchestras in Italy). It serves as an essential source of reflection and stimulus for significant discussions as to the use of music education in contexts and settings outside the formal educational environment.

El Sistema delle Orchestre e dei Cori Giovanili ed Infantile in Italia strives to bring high-quality music education to underrepresented communities. Its mission has spread across the country at a time when the arts are being defunded at the state and national levels. Its openness to a multitude of teaching styles offers its students access to different learning types.

Coppi (2017) has identified challenges, such as the need to address the lack of pedagogical unity in some El Sistema programs as well as the need to foster cooperation among different role players. El Sistema programs apply the principles of music-making to social change and to building bridges in a multicultural setting. They connect people across cultures, continents, and religious beliefs, using music to bridge those chasms. Around the world, today's approach to education shows itself to have a dangerously strong commitment to a culture of competition and authority. El Sistema programs employ teaching artists (i.e., professional performing musicians) to "lead the way to a new world of pedagogies of transformation and sustainability, diversity and inclusivity" (Coppi, 2017). In this way, music as a practical tool for dialogue among peoples promotes and enhances solutions to social and economic challenges. Coppi's observations about El Sistema programs resonate strongly with that of Dr. Yeou-Cheng Ma, Assistant Professor of Clinical Pediatrics at the Albert Einstein College of Medicine and Executive Director of Children Orchestras Project, that the power of music is immeasurable and filled with endless possibilities (Manegold, 1994).

Coppi (2017) concludes that El Sistema Italy develops children's identities simultaneously with their musical skills. Both aim to provide an ideal environment for growing up in an emotionally and socially sound and dignified manner.

Conclusion

El Sistema–inspired programs in Italy are constructive community music interventions offering integrative opportunities for listening, improvising, musical invention, and performing. They offer an environment in which different types of learning can occur. With a focus on individual identity, participation, social context, equality of opportunity, diversity, and inclusion, El Sistema can be a valuable alternative or supplement, not necessarily a substitute, but an enriching addition to formal music education offerings, especially for children of high school age who lack formal access to music education. An essential part of making music is singing and playing. All children need to be equipped with the essential human skill of making music – *musica per tutti* – for this ensures their connectedness to being human, and to nature, and allows nature to help shape decisions that benefit people and the ecosystems on which we depend. El Sistema provides an infrastructure that offers music activities to all individuals, whatever their background.

CHAPTER 13

Music Technology as an Intuitive and Inclusive Pathway to Musical Thinking, Learning, and Doing

Gena Greher

Introduction

IN AN ERA IN WHICH access to diverse musical styles, genres, and practices can be had at the mere click of a smartphone app, the gap is widening between formal, school-based music education practice and the multiple ways that our students actually create, perform, and understand music on their own, outside of school and the Western European Art Music tradition. Since the very beginning of music education in public schools, music students in the United States have been steeped in the culture of the Western music canon. This manifests itself mostly within large, ensemble-based school music teaching practices, almost to the exclusion of most other forms of musical engagement.

Music literacy, or what is presumed to constitute music literacy, is an issue that can drive a wedge between music educators with regard to the more formal school-based approaches to teaching music and the informal and non-formal ways in which our students may participate in music-making on their own. In this chapter, *informal* learning refers to an ad hoc approach with little or no outside intervention and goal setting, whereas *non-formal* refers to a slightly more goal-oriented approach, with adult facilitators and mentors setting broad overarching goals but allowing students to set their own personally meaningful goals (Brennan, Monroy-Hernandez, & Resnick, 2010; Peppler, 2017; Resnick, 2017; Resnick & Rosenbaum, 2013). As Rodriguez (2012) points out regarding the teaching of popular music in school, the question of who is musically literate generally favours the person with notational skills, as opposed to the person whose musicianship developed through aural means. Many researchers believe that we can reach a much broader range of students' creative and expressive interests and needs by acknowledging the value of an aurally based form of music literacy (Allsup, 2016; Green, 2002; Hess, 2014; Kratus, 2007; Mantie, 2008; Rodriguez, 2012; Williams, 2011). The focus on notation-based music literacy, combined with a lack of sequential instrumental feeder programs in many US communities, can often lead to few or no options for students to participate in school-based music classes as they mature out of elementary schools into secondary schools. As a result, for most middle and high school students, school-based music becomes less relevant, and consequently participation in music-making within the confines of school begins to wane (Williams 2015; Williams, 2011). Yet, paradoxically for adolescents, their musical interests outside of school are quite strong and play a strong role in their identity and peer group formation (Crozier, 1997; Csikszentmihalyi & Larson, 1984; North & Hargreaves, 1999).

In addition to all this, there are few pathways in music education for the many students we come into contact with who have behavioural, cognitive, and physical challenges. On the surface, this would preclude their being able to participate in many of the more traditional modes of music-making. These students may get to take classes to learn *about* music without the benefits of ever *making* or *creating* music. Imagine for a moment a school-based sports program where the students listen to a coach or other knowledgeable adult talk about team sports like football, baseball, basketball, soccer, or any other sport that may be of interest to students. These experts might possibly show some videos of the games, and perhaps the students might get to attend a game or two. Then imagine that they never actually get to participate in any of the sports to explore their interests or experience the energy, athleticism, and camaraderie of being part of the action. On the surface, this approach to teaching sports, or more to the point, teaching *about* sports, seems stark and counter-intuitive. Yet for many students in middle school and beyond, if they are not predisposed to large-ensemble musical traditions, or they have learning, behavioural, language, or physical challenges, their school music experiences will be fairly similar to this hypothetical sports program. These students may not have an opportunity to participate in music-making in any meaningful, expressive, collaborative, or creative manner.

Non-classical and non-Western music practices that might take place in community settings, on the other hand, will often focus on participatory experiences, where there's an emphasis on local music traditions as well as more popular genres of music that involve informal and non-formal aural exploratory approaches to music-making, rather than a skills- and notation-based pedagogy.

Turino (2008) believes that participatory music-making in informal settings has a unique value because of the social engagement that occurs through these experiences. With the vast array of inexpensive digital music technology tools currently available for musical exploration, collaboration, and creating, music technology can be a route for many students into developing their own musical intuitions. This chapter will explore two technology partnerships developed between our university and one of our partner schools to engage at-risk and non-traditional music learners in creative music-making and musical thinking through an interdisciplinary STEM focus.

These projects took place either as part of an after-school offering or during an enrichment block designed to allow at-risk students a chance to investigate an area of personal interest. Since the proposed music projects were voluntary for these middle school students and outside the purview of the school's typical class structures and curricular benchmarks, we considered this to be closer in function and spirit to community outreach. The challenges in engaging students in these environments are explored with regard to how we might prod the culture of music education in general toward the ethos and inclusivity of community music practices. What do we gain and what do we need to give up in our quest for flexibility and inclusivity as we shift our role from that of all-knowing teacher to more of a facilitator?

Who Gets to Be a Musician: Toward a Culture of Inclusivity

For those of us who believe that active music-making and music creation are experiences that all students should have, how might we traverse the disconnect between traditional music education practice and the multiple ways our students understand and participate in music outside of school? Music technology encompasses multiple modalities as entry points for students to explore musical ideas without prior knowledge of traditional music notation or music theory. As such, music technology can present many more possibilities for at-risk and non-traditional music learners to connect with their inner musical selves as well as provide alternative opportunities for community-building. Creating a community through shared music making can quite often be a by-product of school music classes, though it may not necessarily be an explicit goal. It is however that very sense of community that can often help many marginalized students connect with one another and the larger school culture through their mutual musical interests (Greher, Hillier, Dougherty, & Poto, 2010; Hillier, Greher, Poto, & Dougherty, 2012; Hillier, et al., 2015).

Ironically, it's the socialization aspect and sense of community that was fostered by their music teachers through their various school music experiences that many of our music education students cite most often as a reason they find music education so appealing. For many of our students, teaching sequentially through a notation-based approach to learning music is the only form of music instruction they have ever experienced. Understanding how to get people to make music without knowing all of the theoretical pieces is a major challenge to their thinking. So it is not too surprising for music education students, who are enculturated into the ensemble- and skills-based traditions of the field, to find that they face a steep learning curve when approaching the teaching of music outside the traditional large-ensemble paradigm, let alone reach a comfort level working with challenging populations and/or teaching with technology (Greher, 2017).

Ideally, expressivity, accessibility, and the right to create should be the foundation for all music programs. Yet there are often few context-specific experiences for music education students to work with diverse populations to gain an understanding of effective teaching strategies for working with them (Darrow, 2003; Hammel, 2001; Hourigan, 2009). Lack of preparation often leads to tensions and ambivalence among music education students toward teaching non-traditional music learners. There are even fewer opportunities for music education students to gain experience in learning when, how, and why to employ technology, and which type of technology will facilitate rather than hinder one's pedagogical goals (Bauer & Dammers, 2016; Dorfman & Dammers, 2015; Gall, 2013). Unless they see music technology successfully integrated into a classroom, it may be difficult for students to imagine a more holistic and inclusive vision of what music education could be, and as a result the perception that music technology is a less valid form of music making will persist.

A Community of Musicking in After-School Programs and Enrichment Blocks

The music technology outreach projects we have developed for middle school students at our university are aimed at building upon the social nature of adolescents, which often seems not to be prioritized in more formal educational settings. We focus on music technology as a means of capitalizing on the opportunities for sonic explorations with little to no formal knowledge as well as supporting the development of twenty-first-century skills through interdisciplinary, project-based, collaborative learning. There are tensions and challenges to be sure for both our music education students and the professors and teachers they assist, for they often struggle to find the right balance between their overall project goals and learning to follow the leads and interests of their students.

One of the projects discussed in this chapter resulted from the creator of a new technology, the Makey Makey Invention Kit (see https://makeymakey .com), who at the time was conducting research for his dissertation. The technology's creator was looking to discover what happens when you allow students to tinker and generate ideas based on their interests and intuitions (Resnick & Rosenbaum, 2013; Rosenbaum, 2015). The principal of this school was eager to have this project, the Makey Makey Invention Lab, be one of the offerings in his newly created enrichment block due to both its interdisciplinary STEM emphasis and the inherent appeal the music-making would have for the students. This project was more exploratory in nature from the outset and challenged the expectations of many of the university students who would be helping to assist – and in some cases lead – an additional session. Similar to Bamberger's work (Bamberger, 1999; Bamberger & Hernandez, 1999–2000), it was designed to build on the musical intuitions of the students through aurally based musical activities.

The other project is an after-school project that grew out of an NSF-funded grant that was the idea of one of my computer science colleagues. I had worked on two previous NSF grants with him that resulted in a book and the creation of an interdisciplinary general education class in computing and music. While I was unable to participate in this particular grant, I did connect him with one of my music colleagues for this project and introduced him to the principal and music teacher of the participating school. I also served as an informal adviser and recommended several music education students as teaching assistants (TA). The goal of this project was to teach coding and musical notation in a school-based after-school program in conjunction with the school's music teacher. As is evidenced by the very specific researcher-initiated goals inherent in this project, there was at the outset less focus on student interests than was the case in the enrichment block project. Each project's goals and objectives played a key role in how the projects unfolded with respect to the push and pull between formal and non-formal teaching approaches, and how to facilitate student-interest-driven learning and engagement, as well as what the university participants learned from these experiences.

Engaging Students in Their Own Learning: The Makey Makey Invention Lab

The Makey Makey Invention Kit, created by two doctoral students at MIT's Media Lab, was intended to allow students to tinker with and explore the possibilities of electrical conductivity and circuitry (Resnick & Rosenbaum, 2013). Due to one of the creators' own involvement in music, he was particularly interested in exploring the device's potential for music-making and creation. The kit is a small and relatively inexpensive device that mimics the functions of a game controller. All you need to do is connect it to a USB port in any computer for it to function as a keyboard controller; there is no need to install additional software. By attaching alligator clips from the Makey Makey to any material that conducts electricity, students can complete an electrical circuit and trigger sounds or other actions from the computer. In the case of our school-based enrichment block, the goal was to have students create musical instruments of their own design, create original compositions, and/or explore musical improvisation.

At the introductory assembly where we introduced a series of music class opportunities for this enrichment block, the students witnessed the Makey Makey device turn a group of students into a "human synthesizer." This was achieved by having one person hold the alligator clip attached to the device's ground while the other students were holding alligator clips attached to a programmed note or sound to complete the circuit. When the person holding the ground touched a person's hand holding one of the alligator clips, the sound would play. This was an instant hit, and two sections needed to be set up. The MIT doctoral student led one section as part of his research; two of our university graduate TAs led the additional section.

Before implementation of our ten-week project at the school, the researcher held a Makey Makey workshop for a group of our university students and local teachers. For the first part of the workshop we created groups of three or four participants and let them loose on the Makey Makey devices, including a table loaded with conductive and non-conductive materials, to see what they discovered. Except for providing them with the brief human synthesizer demo and asking a few questions regarding how they thought this worked, we gave them little to no direction. We just let them explore the materials and see what they discovered and created before going on to a more formal discussion and debrief and showing some videos of other people's projects. One of the participants, who would eventually be one of the TAs for the second section of the enrichment block, wrote that

> I found the lack of demonstration an interesting way to go about the introduction of this new technological tool. Without a proper introduction on how the Makey-Makey works, the class was at a loss at what to do with it. I don't think this was a fault in how the tech was introduced, but a prime example of how the individuals in our class have been taught traditionally; without personal input or experimentation.

In another post, this same participant wrote:

> It has the potential to change the students' views of the world into a
> more open idea of what has the possibility of being an instrument. And
> it gives the direction of the classroom into the hands of the students in a
> new way. It also has the potential to drive students away from music and
> in a more technical direction. But, if used in a thoughtful manner, the
> Makey-Makey could be a very useful teaching tool in the music educator's
> classroom.

One of the teachers in this workshop felt that in order to introduce this
to her middle school students,- she would need to provide step-by-step directions. In fact, when we did introduce this to middle school students, we did
it exactly as we did for the adult workshop, not with step-by-step directions,
and the students exhibited no hesitation with regard to getting their hands on
the materials and exploring.

Between the two sections, the one run by the doctoral student and the
one run by our graduate students, the class with the doctoral student at the
helm has come the closest to the kind of facilitation and non-formal learning
approaches one associates with community music practices. This isn't to say
there weren't glitches throughout both sections of the project, mostly due to
scheduling and room assignments. On any given week it was anyone's guess as
to where this class was meeting, which would not be the case during a regularly
scheduled school day class. However, while our students did a fantastic job and
learned a great deal from these middle school students regarding leading with
students' interests in mind, in a discussion after the end-of-project showcase,
the graduate students who ran the alternate section discussed how they were
focused more on teaching *about* the science connection and the musical concepts rather than on letting the students *explore* and *discover*.

What set the environment of the doctoral student's class apart from
attempts by our university grad students was that his overarching goal in
designing the Makey Makey and in running the class was to "empower creativity for beginners" (Rosenbaum, 2015, p. 16) and not necessarily to teach *about*
science or music. He was looking for the students to tinker and make things,
whether it was creating instruments or compositions or someplace in between.
The device was designed to provide them with immediate aural feedback. In
other words, the students explored, connected things, saw and heard what
they were doing immediately, and then reflected on and revised their designs
and compositions based on their instincts, along with feedback (perhaps) from
their peers and/or adults. His only agenda item from week to week was his

willingness to be flexible and let the students lead with their own ideas. Paramount for this particular series of classes was allowing the students to design projects that were personally meaningful to them (Rosenbaum, 2015). This approach yielded a great deal of experimentation and eventually the uncovering of the science and music concepts they were intuiting. Students were mostly using household conductive materials, though one group that caught his attention was intent on creating their own human synthesizer. They used skin-to-skin contact rather their conductive materials. In addition, they had figured out on their own a rather complex configuration where one student was able to switch back and forth between two different pitch classes in perfect rhythm, while the student acting as the ground created a rhythmic pattern involving all three of the other members of the group.

Even under the doctoral student's tutelage, where the students did uncover and explore several musical concepts, the university TAs had difficulty reconciling musical exploration versus the teaching of musical concepts as their goal. This comment from one of the TA's who assisted him highlights the tension in his thinking with regard to what he believed was important versus what the doctoral student's actual goal was. According to this TA:

> I think the experience challenged student's perceptions of what a music class could be and what one could do with technology ... At the end of it all, I think students ended the class with a sense of accomplishment having had the opportunity to showcase their instrument inventions... On the other hand, I do not feel we were able to accomplish teaching musical concepts so much as we were able to cultivate student interest in musical possibilities.

The TA at this point missed the importance of cultivating interest in music as a first step toward learning and understanding. However, this TA also made note of the day a student brought in a motorized Lego piece, wondering if it could work with the Makey Makey. Even the Makey Makey's creator wasn't sure if it would work, so he let the student explore some possibilities on his own. As the TA wrote in his reflection:

> No one knew if the Makey Makey would be able to trigger the Lego motor or not. It turned out that it did and this led to a new discovery for the student and the ways in which a Makey Makey could be used. This new discovery sent the student's mind into new directions about what he could create which led to his motorized drum type creation.

As this TA then noted, "If the student had not been free to explore the Makey Makey and its possibilities without restriction he never would have made the discoveries he did." At this point it's important to remember that these students were at-risk students who needed remediation in many areas of study. Yet as one of the TAs in the alternate section noted, many of these students who were labelled "adjustment" students by the school's administration were extremely creative and receptive to this more exploratory approach to teaching and learning. As she additionally reflected, "this made me think that those general classrooms could use more of the experiential techniques that were used in the Makey Makey Invention Lab."

At the ice cream and sharing showcase at the project's conclusion, it was evident that the students in both sections had created unique and inventive instruments and were quite proud of their accomplishments. Yet the graduate TAs who led their own section felt that the projects in the doctoral student's section were more inventive, and perhaps they could have done less "teaching about" the Makey Makey than they did to allow for more imaginative ideas. They attributed that to their own lack of a specific vision for how they wanted to run the project along with a lack of clear communication between them. The doctoral student's vision, while flexible and focused on letting the students set the learning goals, was clearly communicated to his students and TAs. What might appear to be a free-for-all exploration, in reality is also supporting students' willingness to learn how to work as teams, discover new uses of the technology at hand, and use basic electronic circuitry to have fun, play games, and make music. As one of the TAs in the second section noted, "if fellow teachers do not have a cohesive vision outside the classroom, inside the classroom can become convoluted and the lesson goals are subject to change polarity from week to week."

Music and Coding: Teaching a Computer to Sing (TACTS)

As stated previously, the goal of this particular project was to work on computer literacy skills with middle school students through their interests in music. The project would meet twice a week with each session involving singing, which was led by their music teacher during the first part of the class, and then learning to code the songs they had learned through several computer programs, such as Scratch and Pencil Code, led by the university professors during the second half. In addition to learning to code, there was the goal of teaching these students traditional music notation. The two lead researchers on this project, a computer science professor and a music professor, were not K–12 teachers. In addition to all the variables affecting any research project, there was a steep learning curve for them with regard to working with fifth and sixth grade inner-city students, with a majority of these students being considered at-risk by the administration; this added another layer of challenge. As stated in a journal article (Heines, Walzer, Crawford, & Al-Rekabi, 2018), one of the realities of this project is they knew there would be difficulty keeping students engaged in this project, since it didn't begin until after the students had already spent seven hours in school and all they really wanted to do was play.

During these sessions, the school music teacher would lead the first half of class, during which students learned songs through singing. They would have an informal discussion circle to talk about their interests, and sometimes they would listen to recordings of their singing during the previous session and comment on how they thought it sounded. The music teacher, even during her regular music classes during the school day, allows for a good mix of direct instruction, hands-on exploration, and discovery, tinged with the element of humour and surprise needed to keep a diverse group of middle school students engaged in making music. So it was not difficult for this highly skilled teacher to intentionally transition to a more informal approach during this part of the class to help the students make the transition from a "school mindset," as well as allow them to have agency in their own learning. A great deal of relaxed, light-hearted humour permeated these discussions. When there was an issue learning a new song, she elicited ideas from the students regarding identifying the problem and asking them to suggest ideas for improving their performance. For the most part the students, including the boys, were singing and learning and reflecting even though most of the songs had been chosen by the teachers. In keeping with a less formal learning environment, there was a social aspect to the way the class was conducted, which went a long way with regard to student engagement and classroom management issues during this part of the class session. There were definitely teacher goals in play, but the students had input into how the outcomes played out.

In each session there was a snack break, and then the coding half of the class would begin. In the class I observed during the end of year 1, the second part of the class was very teacher-directed, with little of the lightness and informality of the first half and little or no group discussion or input. A university professor would lay out the agenda, some new information might be taught, and the students would set to work.

Conversations with the researchers and music education TAs and my own observation revealed some misalignment of the goals and teaching approach with the learning context. As the researchers reported, the initial model for the class was that it be more of a "laboratory class," which was how they conducted their college classes (Heines, Walzer, Crawford, & Al-Rekabi, 2018). In contrast to the school music teachers, who led the first half of the sessions, the college professors usually set the agenda without input from the students. This, and the time of day, was another factor in lagging student motivation. Students walked in after the break, grabbed computers, individually went to their tables, and began working; this was in stark contrast to the sense of community that had been fostered during the first half of class. Through their own personal observations, interactions with the students, and feedback from their assessment team, the researchers recognized that they needed to change their approach in order to improve student engagement. So toward the end of the first year and moving into the second year they adopted more of a "computer clubhouse" model, where students worked in pairs or one-on-one, with a professor or university TA more as mentor/facilitator (Rusk, Resnick, & Cooke, 2009). With more of a "clubhouse" mindset and with the help of several additional music education TAs, the researchers were able to focus on building relationships with the individual students and to show more flexibility as to how this part of the class was run. As one of the music professors observed: "Over time, I have learned that my role as an instructor takes on many perspectives including a facilitator, co-creator, careful listener, and guide."

Overall, both the music education TAs and the professors they were assisting learned some valuable lessons in this community setting regarding flexibility. There was definitely an ah-ha moment with respect to the importance of letting students play and explore their individual interests. As they reported, the university researchers eventually learned that they needed to give up the idea of total control of the lesson and "go with the flow" (Heines, Walzer, Crawford, & Al-Rekabi, 2018). After the researchers switched their teaching approach so that it felt less like a school classroom, the music education TAs saw first-hand the changes in the students' attitude and engagement once they got to know the students and their interests. They also helped model the more informal facilitator role for the university professors, so as is the case in many community music settings, everyone was learning from one another. As one of the researchers observed:

> A few of the TAs implicitly understood how to speak to the children in a coded language of shared lived experience. Some of that language focused on being a girl, being a minority, and being a creative person. Although I could appreciate their connections, I could never speak in quite the same way with the kids. Thus, our TAs provided a tremendous level of personalized support and connection with the participants, and with the facilitators.

The school music teacher believed that "the students were able to see themselves as musicians and computer scientists because the TAs were an example to them of what they could be in just a few years." Most importantly, the researchers learned how vital it was to set goals that would challenge and engage their students and how to scaffold exploratory experiences. As the music teacher discussed:

> Where I can't go back in [sic] time and "fix" past projects, I can take the things I've learned and use the knowledge to make future projects better – to refine and refocus. I am going to be the project facilitator for a coding after-school program ... This project focuses on coding, sisterhood, and community service. I am looking forward to being a facilitator on this project where the students lead the way and dictate the goals of the project, and I just help them meet their goals.

With the Makey Makey group taking more of an explore-and-discover approach as their research goal, in contrast to the highly specific coding goals of the TACTS research group, the amount of student agency was greater from the outset. However, over the longer time frame of their grant, the TACTS researchers were able to adjust and adapt their approach so that it was less formal and more learner centred. As the researchers and the teacher noted, some students made progress throughout their participation in the project. The music teacher noted:

> The combination of music with computer science was an interesting blend. Some students came in with a deeper knowledge of one subject area over [sic] the other. It was exciting to see students build their knowledge. One student, in particular, has continued [sic] learning the computer language C++. Other students have increased their knowledge in music, and have become leaders for the other students in the music room, helping other students learn to read music. Several students wished the program didn't end, and are anxious for more after school opportunities.

These technology experiences provide an important window onto what is needed to help our music education students overcome their professional blind spots and to create music-making experiences for people with a minimum of formal music knowledge that will allow anyone to participate. To provide this type of learning opportunity for all of our music education students, we created a new pedagogy class focusing on informal participatory music-making practices for both school and community settings. It includes a service-learning component to allow our students to put into practice the concepts of informal learning with participants who have a diversity of musical interests and abilities. The clubhouse approach permeates how this class is run, and includes observing and assisting at several of our local area music clubhouse sites. These clubhouse sites strongly emphasize developing musical thinking through technology, and they have full complements of music technology workstations in addition to guitars, drums, and keyboards. Our students also work in other community settings such as senior centres and organizations devoted to working with special needs students; they also organize pop-up drum circles on campus.

As suggested by Higgins and Bartleet (2012), the community music approach favours flexibility within the learning process. It values students' social well-being and growth in addition to striving for musical excellence and understanding. This was confirmed by one of the researchers, who stated: "What is clear to me is that being sensitive to sociocultural factors and advancing informal learning practices have much to offer students of all kinds." In these types of settings, we strive to help our music education students realize the importance of letting their students know that their ideas matter. These hands-on experiences provide our music education students with opportunities to safely navigate the tensions inherent when shifting one's practice from a focus on teacher-directed instruction toward one of student-centred learning, which is often a difficult transition to make. As Higgins (2012) might suggest, we are laying the groundwork for our future music educators to promote a more *welcoming* culture of *hospitality* toward those students who would otherwise have been excluded from participating in music.

CHAPTER 14

Dreaming Big with the Regent Park School of Music

Richard Marsella

IN DECEMBER 2009, I received a call from out of nowhere: "Would you be interested in running a music school?" At that time, I had been running events on Parliament Hill in Ottawa for two years and was seeking to head home to the Greater Toronto Area. "You'll need to be more specific," I replied to my friend, who was recommending me for the job. I was not keen to run a for-profit music school. But when I learned it was the Regent Park School of Music, which had been seeking new leadership for six months, I was intrigued. For years, I had known about their work in the community, and their model, which offered youth from Regent Park heavily subsidized music lessons. Three interviews later, I found myself excited to come home to what remains a perfect fit: Executive Director of the Regent Park School.

Early Years

Both of my degrees are from the University of Toronto in music education. While finishing my Master's, I had started up a not-for-profit initiative called Music Roots Seminars Inc., which delivered an annual event in my hometown of Brampton, Ontario, where we marched with homemade musical instruments and 700 grade four children in an event called the Parade of Noises. Many of my ideas in music education, from noise in the classroom to constructive anarchy, were born here. This experience helped me develop early administrative chops – grant writing, forming a board of directors, strategic planning, working collaboratively with several partners, and leading a team through a truly unique experience – all the while making the weird feel normal.

I led Music Roots Seminars Inc. for five years, which was highly fulfilling and impactful, for I was helping young children see and hear music from a different perspective. Although the work was loosely linked to the grade four arts curriculum, it certainly celebrated the less travelled path in music education. When I was interviewed for my position with the Regent Park School of Music, I drew on much of this experience. I would like to think I was brought on by the board of directors to help chart a path of expansion, which included some of these alternative methods in music education.

In early 2010, I began my journey leading the Regent Park School of Music. When I started, we were running programs in Regent Park, with nominal satellite work in the Jane and Finch neighbourhood. At that time, we were reaching about 250 kids between the ages of three and eighteen with mostly traditional programming, classically based in the instruments you'd expect to see: piano, guitar, violin, voice, choir. Royal Conservatory of Music exam prep was a pillar of the school – we were sophisticating young children from Regent Park and Jane and Finch with violins. No offence against that approach, which remains an option for our young students to pursue, but in our first strategic planning sessions, I recall presenting different options to our board of directors, who embraced every discussion with a refreshing acceptance that inspires me to this day.

Founded in 1999 by a group of spirited professionals who wanted to see young kids from Regent Park engage with after-school music, the Regent Park School of Music began with around seventy kids studying music in a church basement. The school's mission has always been to provide access to a quality music education for kids who would not otherwise have it – to help them find their voices and break the cycle of poverty subsequently. The Regent Park School of Music is half about music education, the other half about social work.

My first task was to draft and execute a strategic plan. Good design is everything. I'd seen many examples of strategic plans becoming mere exercises. I loved the suggestion from my board of directors that I not only lead the plan's development so as to build in ownership of the concepts presented, but also be responsible for implementing it. This would avoid the cut-and-run scenario seen all too often with strategic plans, when consultants have no real skin in the game.

I began with a series of round tables, including with current students, graduate students, parents, faculty, the board of directors, and founding members of the organization. It took several hours and several important meetings to get merely a glimpse into the rich history of this organization. I remain a firm believer that one cannot attempt to set a course of action or new direction for any team without first looking back and listening to those you're collaborating with. One early learning was how surprised I was by how open our board was to some of the ideas I was proposing in the strategic plan – that we break free of the Royal Conservatory model and try to etch out a new curriculum, helping our students find their voices, on their terms, using not only classical music but also composition, experimentation, and *other* musics, to name just a few ideas. I found some closed-mindedness among certain faculty members, but never once did they present an either/or scenario. To this day, we honour where we came from, and I acknowledge that for some students, the classical path is the best prescription for engagement.

The first strategic plan set a path not only for curricular diversification but also to expand our student reach from 300 to 3,000 by 2015. We planned to launch a new satellite location in Parkdale, and also to expand our work in the Jane and Finch corridor. Our Regent Park location at that time was in an old row house the organization owned at 534 Queen Street East. The moment I began, there were meetings to explore moving into a brand-new space, in the Daniels Spectrum, an arts and culture centre to be built in the heart of the newly revitalized Regent Park, which at that time was just beginning a fifteen-year revitalization plan, the largest of its kind in North America, led by the developers, The Daniels Corporation. Our move into the Daniels Spectrum was a pivotal decision for us as an organization. Our new tenant neighbours would include ArtHeart, the Regent Park Film Festival, Pathways to Education, and Native Earth Performing Arts. Suddenly our student body was connected to a much larger community in Regent Park.

It really has taken a village of influential people to help steer the Regent Park School of Music to a successful place. The story is that when the school fell on difficult financial straits in 2002, well before my time, a few early supporters pooled together enough money to purchase the row house on Queen Street, putting the school on more solid footing. At that time, when the school had to make the decision to temporarily shut down, to get its books in order, we saw a groundswell of support, from faculty volunteering their time for a brief period, in order to not let down the kids we were serving. Many years later, those graduate students still reminisce about that gesture, saying how important it made them feel. That's partly the business we're in: to make our students feel super-heroic. Since then, I have kept that story in mind, managing a budget of now over $1 million, which we monitor closely to ensure our model will be sustainable for years to come. We currently reach more than 1,000 students and offer close to 1,400 student experiences, and we never want to shut the doors down to the rich relationships we're fostering in our after-school programs.

Our attitude is that once we commit to a child, we will carry them, from no matter what age they start with us (some as early as three years old), through to graduation, at eighteen years of age.

Case Studies

So many stories have been written in the hallways of our school. Here are just a few that have stuck with me over the years:

Nikita is hearing impaired, and early educators in her life told her to stay away from music. Since she began her journey with the Regent Park School of Music, we've encouraged the opposite, as her love of music runs deep. She is rising above, taking everything from flute to steel pan and theory. She's fallen in love with music, and we want to feed this love to whatever end she's interested in taking it. Our mantra with a student like Nikita has been to celebrate with her, to not treat her hearing as an impairment at all, and to celebrate the joy of music from her unique perspective. Nikita immediately becomes a super-hero, not somebody with a deficiency.

Brad McGoey is a faculty member. His short time with us, two years, was so impactful. Although some faculty members have been with the school since its inception in 1999 (at present there are more than eighty-five of them), Brad made such a big impact, truly taking the tenets of the school and embodying them with every lesson. Brad began as a volunteer, and because the mandate of the school resonated with him, he was a valued member of our faculty by the time he left. He has promised, when back in the Toronto area, to return to the school family whenever he can.

Guadalupe, who graduated from the school shortly after I began and then joined our front desk staff. She eventually became our full-time administrative coordinator, while graduating from the University of Toronto with a degree in criminology. She now works as a legal assistant with one of the top firms in the country, Ernst & Young. We're all very proud of Guadalupe's development – at how she grew alongside the school in such a meaningful way. Her family was displaced by the Regent Park revitalization, and she began at Regent Park School of Music at such a young age, helping the neighbourhood grow, adding her vibrant leadership to the mix.

Chris Hatley is a past member of the school's board of directors. He was on my hiring committee, and ever since that fateful first interview, he's been one of my key advisers, supporting every difficult decision, helping facilitate the first strategic planning sessions, and still mentoring me since stepping down from more than a decade's worth of volunteerism on our board. Chris has been one of those champions in my life, and I am so glad to have connected with him.

Malcolm is a current student, in grade twelve, who has some developmental challenges and is currently thinking about studying music (percussion) post-secondary. A team of us has rallied behind him, from two long-time board members who pick him up from high school and drive him to his lessons at the school, to our administrative team, who are meeting with his high school guidance councillor and his sister to discuss how we can help him realize his dream of post-secondary music studies.

We have other amazing stories, from Thompson, to Cecilia, to Stacy and Charlotte, of students who have followed similar paths. Although the point of our school is not to send students to Carnegie Hall, or study music post-secondary, when it happens, it is profoundly rewarding.

New Directions

Since I began in 2010, I've technically been running two organizations, the Regent Park School of Music and the Regent Park School of Music Foundation. The foundation was set up in 2003 when the row house was purchased, as a way to protect the school's assets and provide some risk protection for it. In 2014, the boards of directors of the school and the foundation agreed that it would be wise for the foundation to invest in fundraising. The foundation, like, say, the Sick Kids' Foundation, would fundraise exclusively on behalf of the school. This decision, to invest significantly in a fundraising professional, Jane O'Hare, to lead the Regent Park School of Music Foundation, has proven to be another very wise decision – and an abnormal one, for such a small organization – because it helps us punch as hard as we can in the sector, remain influential, and dream big. It has also allowed us to collaborate on the budget each year, with the school owning most of the expenses and the foundation most of the revenues. We also share responsibility for devising the strategic direction of both organizations. Thus, our 2015 to 2018 strategic plan was conceived of much differently than our approach in 2010: the executive directors of both organizations work together, along with a committee comprised of members from both boards.

This second strategic plan that I was involved in drafting focused more on the student experience and the impact of our programs, and less on the *number* of students. For in 2015, we never reached our initial goal of 3,000 students, and throughout the process, our board of directors knew that the goal did not really matter. We had set a path to grow, and when the school grew to 1,000 students (it has recently hovered between 1,000 and 1,300), we realized that it's more about growing smartly, offering a more comprehensive and rich experience for the family of students we're currently reaching, than about simply growing for its own sake. In the back of my mind, though I know I'll fail trying, the goal is to be able to know the name of each student we work with. Call it idealistic, and naive, but I like what that secret goal represents for me, the human touch. Time and time again, it's so important to instil this sense of caring in our students.

With our 2015–18 strategic plan, we established new pillars for the school that would allow us to strengthen its mandate. Although we remain faithful to our core programs in Regent Park and Jane and Finch, we thought it import-ant to invest in curriculum development, students with special needs, First Nations programming, and youth who have had brushes with the law. Each of these new pillars has bloomed into very meaningful work in the sector. We're now excited to expand on them – for example, the University of Toronto has begun to research our work with students who are in detention. As well, we have gained support from our provincial Ministry of Child and Youth Services to develop this important work, and we hope to share it with other cities in the province. We're also working closely with Toronto First Nations School, reaching every student at that school and expanding into their high school program. Our work at Jane and Finch was recently awarded the largest gift in the history of our school, which has linked us with York University to research various aspects of our programming at Jane and Finch; that work will inform our future programming decisions. The importance of quality research in the sector will without a doubt help us make calculated decisions down the line, connect with new supporters, and expand some of the ideas we're exploring to quite possibly beyond the City of Toronto.

Since the Regent Park School of Music Foundation made its decision to reorganize itself and bring on a small fundraising team, the two organizations have effectively doubled their total budgets, from around $500,000 collectively, to currently more than $1 million. For example, our annual fundraiser event, when I started in 2010, was always involved a lot of heavy lifting to ensure that 200 staunch supporters attended. It still raises one fifth of our annual budget in one evening, and although it remains a large effort, it's shared, and our com-mittee has grown to more than twenty influential people, well supported by our foundation. Overall, it's a much more refined process when it comes to fundraising and generating interest in our cause. I'm now better poised to do what I'm meant to be doing, which is help the school reach its fullest potential.

This collaboration between the Regent Park School of Music and the Regent Park School of Music Foundation took time to ferment. In 2014, when Jane was first hired, we had to sort out our new relationship, such as how does one organization manage all of the tax receipts when both organizations receive donations? Now we've hit our stride, working together to leverage major gifts for the school, collaborating on the direction of both organizations so that we travel together, and helping refine our program delivery. This has allowed me and my team to focus more on the crux of our mandate, which is connecting with youth in need and ensuring that our programs are being delivered as effectively as possible. I have now realized, especially with this bolstering of our model and with the foundation playing such a strong role, that financial stability can bring forward true change. Such is the case with our current York University partnership, where a retired physics professor and entrepreneur has connected us in a game-changing way.

There's always room to grow, whether it involves communications between our office and our more than eighty faculty, or parent engagement, or volunteer management. Not a day goes by that I'm not thankful, feeling comfortable enough to make a daily difference, yet justifiably anxious about the responsibility of improving the lives of the 1,000 youth we engage with on a weekly basis. It runs all of the emotions, in any given week!

Failures and Learnings

From all of my managerial learnings over the years, you get to the stage where the challenges you face are similar to past ones. Even so, the odd one surprises you and reminds you of how unique this work is. You build confidence in your work while always remembering that it has repercussions. I've seen decisions we've made in community music save the lives of the students we're serving.

It's a great pleasure to watch colleagues at the Regent Park School of Music office grow, stick with the mission for several years, and make a huge impact in the process. I love to share the load, and our organization is the culmination of hundreds of voices working together in harmony. I love it when somebody latches on to what we do, and the next thing we know, our organization's path has changed forever. If every interaction, every word is taken so seriously, then it becomes more than fun to watch your impact grow as part of the greater good: there you have it, I just solved the meaning of life with that last sentence.

Over the past eight years, I've learned a lot about myself as a manager, as well as how to run a community music school. Some of my strengths include the ability to meet with stakeholders from various disciplines and backgrounds, sell them on the importance of our work, explore ways to logically collaborate, and work toward doing just that, bringing healthy collaborations to life, all with our students' success in the foreground. Some of my self-diagnosed weaknesses as a manager have included: trying to please everybody, always. This flaw has sometimes affected my decisions, both short- and long-term. Over the years, especially when we were about to move to the Daniels Spectrum, I had to lean at times on our board of directors, out of fear (for the first time in my life) of burning out. I have worked on improving my time management skills, trying to perform as best as possible, always wanting to bring my best game to this very important work. This is not a role that one should simply dial in – the kids deserve better. I recall our board meeting with me and offering some ideas on how to improve my work, from keeping Fridays meeting-free, to the meeting structures with my team, to simply making the most of it.

When I started, I inherited a staff and faculty of around fifty. It's always tough being the new person on a team and trying to align different philosophies. After my prior job in Ottawa, where I worked on several high-stakes events on Parliament Hill, with the Prime Minister's Office and several other important stakeholders, hammering out compromises and ensuring that everybody was smiling by the end, I was sure I was well poised to work with Regent Park School of Music.

Through the awkward art of human resources – a term I've never really come to grips with – I've learned a lot about myself as a leader, and as a human. I appreciate the team approach to a project as rich as the Regent Park School of Music, where every participant is helping lead the enterprise. That being said, I think it's important to sometimes say no, always with a good reason and with compassion. For a long time I found myself at the end of each year having rarely said no to any idea that crossed my desk! It's taken me a while to understand the importance of taking on *less*, so that what you do take on means *more* in terms of student experience and impact. Sometimes it *is* wisest to say no to an idea, but to do so without fostering a spirit of no instead giving every decision its fair consideration. One mustn't be afraid to disappoint. I think the whole team appreciate this much more in the long run, as we all begin to trust one another's judgment in a special way. The word *trust* is key to building a dream team. Unless we are trusted by all the stakeholders we work with – from school principals, to parents, to students – nothing will prosper. Last year, we said yes to more than sixty-five events. In hindsight, reviewing with our team, we established that about fifteen of them did not have the experience of our students in the foreground. So now we're trying harder to commit to fewer events – about fifty a year – and to focus on making them more meaningful for our students.

The former Toronto police chief Bill Blair has roots in Regent Park, so he was more than sympathetic to and supportive of our work. We met several times – he even connected our team with his gangs and guns unit to help us better understand the gang model, our true competition in this line of work. We compared music education with that model and found that both bring a very real sense of belonging, learning, ability to grow, expression, and hierarchy. Our police partners in Regent Park and Jane and Finch remain serious allies in our efforts to keep children on a positive life trajectory. I'll never forget Bill Blair telling me that when a child is eleven years old, and loses a family member to gang violence, if he's not already immersed in a better life by then, he'll probably succumb to the less constructive options available, including revenge and joining a gang, and the cycle will continue. The more I see gang violence prevail, the more I want to go on the offensive, placing donated pianos in public spaces, for example, like with our Pianimators program at Westview Collegiate. But when you look at it, with the 1,000 students we're currently engaged with, and with our program continuing to grow, it's imperative to work harder at keeping the students right in our midst engaged and loving the experience. This is part of the long-term solution; so is sharing as much knowledge as we can with similar organizations and schools battling the same competitor.

I've never considered myself a leader of anybody. Perhaps it's my disrespect of authority, or my rejection of responsibility. I have enough trouble dressing myself in the morning or even acting *normal* ... but I've truly enjoyed my journey thus far, connecting with some awesome people from so many unique walks of life. I've surrounded myself with great people, and my mentors have helped plug the gaps in my approach.

Never once has our board of directors taken me to task for my approach. They've been nothing but supportive and complimentary, besides offering refined expertise in accounting, management, different areas of the law, and so on. Their advice has always been more than prudent, as well as useful for keeping our school on the right path. I've since developed and executed two strategic plans with the school, each of them effective at bringing forward change in the sector, one child at a time. Our board has been instrumental in helping me negotiate the lease at the Daniels Spectrum, developing a policy manual for staff and students, crafting regulations for accessibility, and more. Every single week brings a new set of challenges, some long-term, some requiring immediate attention. As my role with school matures, so does the relationship with the board. Some of its members have been with the organization longer than me, and we prioritize governance, an important factor in attracting the right board members to our cause. Some board members look for legacy projects as their tenure wanes; others always seem to be a phone call away, adding their special talent to the mix. For example, we recently added a retired clinical psychologist to our board, who is committed to helping our faculty build their confidence on that side of the equation, ensuring that a comfortable and successful work environment is achieved. Our students face very real challenges, from mental health to poverty, so it takes a well-thought-out program to provide the scaffolding they require to level the playing field. In strengthening our professional development, we're ensuring that our faculty and students are set up to succeed together.

Partnerships

A lot of my success (and failure) so far at the Regent Park School of Music boils down to humans. Some of it is related to space, bricks and mortar, infrastructure. But most of it comes down to humans, and trust. I try to leave no stone unturned when it comes to collaborative opportunities. The Reggio Emilia model has always resonated with me, whether it means working with local firefighters to organize a parade, or with an inventor who has builds weird musical instruments. A community music school, at its core, must come together. You don't have to have musical chops to make a difference in community music. Your ability to crunch numbers and predict trends can be significant to us.

We've experienced great and not-so-great partnerships over the years. The ones that have thrived deserve much reflection, to help inform areas for future growth. A great partnership should help each stakeholder grow to something larger, something unimaginable prior to the collaboration. We've experienced this on many occasions with partners like the Musical Stage Company, the Canadian Music Centre, the Sarah McLachlan School of Music, and key donors who have helped us dream big and supported those dreams financially. Some artistic supporters have continued over the years to grow alongside us. Roger Waters collaborated with our kids on three different tours, and Broken Social Scene, Jully Black, Jackie Richardson, and Jim Cuddy and his son Devin have all enjoyed multiple collaborative chapters in their lives with our students. This is special, and you know it's genuine when they return for more.

Conclusion

I was recently asked to share a vision for community music with an anonymous donor who wanted to help us share a national model. If that were to happen, I'd certainly take many of the great learnings shared in this chapter, to help others interested in fostering their own models in their respective communities save time, and hopefully apply some of my learnings to their work where applicable.

The sector is on the brink of something big. Several universities now embrace its importance, seeing the potential for employment and strengthened community health. If we can continue to develop course work (in social work, psychology, and music education) to equip future workers in community music with the right tools, we'll be much better off. These days, between music therapy, music education, community music, and music and health, we seem to be well-siloed, though all of us are moving toward the same end, which is to strengthen ties between humans via music.

Time, patience, and my growth over the years. Here's a lesson for all in similar positions: sometimes you've got to let it ferment. The work gets more difficult over time. Every year at graduation, the sadness of saying goodbye to long-time students grows. The bonds are deeper. I suppose the roots of that first organization (Music Roots) I launched in 2002 are continuing to set with my work at Regent Park School of Music. I remember recently mentioning, to the executive director of a similar community music school in Toronto, how difficult it is to continue each year. He's been at it for more than twenty years, and he agrees – longer you do it, the deeper the roots latch, and the harder it is at graduation time every year.

As I approach my first decade at the Regent Park School of Music, with the school poised to soon turn twenty as an organization, it's important to reflect on the impact we've had collectively. I feel so proud to have given almost a decade of my life to this important cause, and feel inspired to continue searching, refining, connecting, and dreaming big.

CHAPTER 15

Creative Community Composition

Pete Moser

I Am a Composer – How Did That Come About?

I WAS BORN IN 1957 in north London into a liberal artistic family, and music surrounded me from the start! Some of my first memories are of playing and listening to the piano. My father was a refugee who had escaped Nazi Germany in 1936 with his brother and parents and had learned cello and piano as a child and played chamber music with his family in their house in Berlin. His love of music never diminished, and though he was a statistician and educator by profession, music – playing it and listening to it – was at centre of his life. I grew up with music at home and at school and made many visits to the opera. Classical music of the Western canon was my life until my early teens, when, of course, the popular music of the late 1960s and early 1970s invaded my psyche. I started playing guitar and jazz piano and singing – writing songs and tunes and forming bands with friends. This was the music of the Beatles, Crosby, Stills, Nash and Young, Steve Miller, Bert Jansch, Pink Floyd, Led Zeppelin, Stevie Wonder, and Deep Purple. My understanding of chords started to develop without any theory, simply with a feel for what worked, and I learned how to sing in harmony while busking with friends on the Underground. Leaving sixth form college, I set out for an overland trip to India in search of Buddha, hitching though Iran and Afghanistan and spending months in Nepal before coming home knowing that music was to be my life.

So began a period of study. I was committed to learning how music worked. What did different composers do to create their pieces, where did their ideas come from, and how did they inspire structures? I studied at Southampton University with some great lecturers and a composer in residence – Eric

Graebner – who helped a little cohort of creatives develop their ideas. Fascinated by Bach, Dufay, Beethoven, Wagner, Mozart, Steve Reich, and Webern, I sight-read through everything I could get hold of, analyzed many scores in a formal way, and finally wrote a dissertation that compared music through the ages. I remember now that the key to this research was that everything started from the first idea – that a composition grew from its first phrase. Simple as that! Over the following ten years I was lucky to be able to experiment with my own music, working in theatre and writing songs, scores for musicals, accompaniments for dances, choral arrangements, and music for film. It was a glorious time, during which a third element to my musical palette developed: a passion for and fascination with music from around the world – Chile, Brazil, Tanzania, Japan, France, Scotland, India, South Africa, and Spain. I worked with great world musicians from the UK and also travelled – sometimes on serious research trips, other times to work and play. By the time I was in my early thirties my musical language and experience was maturing, and at the centre was a fascination with creating large pieces that used popular music and that had classical structures, along with an interest in curious ensembles and orchestras and an ability to write quickly and with confidence.

I Am a Composer with a Conscience – How Did That Come About?

The postwar years in the UK were the time of the welfare state and of a new equality for all. My mother was a labour councillor in Holborn, with a Swiss father and a mother who was a Christian Scientist. She studied at the London School of Economics (LSE) during and after the war and was in a cohort of people who believed in a socialist future. Then she met my father, who had a liberal Jewish background, and their partnership strengthened in the 1950s and 1960s in tandem with their belief in internationalism and in education for all. Her passion for helping people and troubled children developed during her years as a psychiatric social worker at Hammersmith Hospital in a special unit devoted to families. I remember the liberal sixties and parties at our house that drew a heady mix of political and cultural figures. By then my father had moved on from a professorship at LSE to lead on government statistics in the civil service. He founded *Social Trends*, a publication that tried to make social statistics interesting and useful to a wider public, and on a number of occasions he stood up to prime ministers about releasing figures at the correct time.

I responded to this in my own way, involving myself in campaigns to free the Soledad brothers and Angela Davis, as well as writing and publishing an underground political paper at my school that required a great deal of research – on one occasion I even went to the South African embassy to interview someone about apartheid. Travelling to the East gave me an entirely new social and political world view, one I have nurtured to this day. I regularly read about the key issues in the countries I travel to. Over the past five years in particular, I have been touched by the issues facing the Indigenous peoples of Canada, Australia, and New Zealand. Before then, I had been particularly fascinated by how culture and politics work together in the countries of South America. I made three trips to Cuba (1986, 1990, 2007), an extended working visit to Chile, and four visits to work in the Brazilian Amazon.

In the development of my political agenda, the final ingredient was the theatre company Welfare State International. WSI was a celebratory arts organization that had grown out of the 1960s with slogans such as "Engineers of the Imagination," "Pathological Optimists," "Guardians of the Unpredictable," and "Civic Magicians." Throughout the 1970s and 1980s, WSI became increasingly driven by the community arts agenda and values. I encountered three mentors there, all of whom believed in social justice. John Fox, the founder and director of WSI, was a writer and visual artist whose work was always responsive to place and often very challenging to the status quo. Boris Howarth, a poet and musician, was a co-director of WSI. The two of them developed huge festivals for which WSI became famous. They also conducted intimate private ceremonies – weddings, namings, and funerals – in which the arts and music served as essential components. The third of my influences was the late, great Adrian Mitchell, a political poet who had performed at Albert Hall with Allen Ginsberg in the 1960s and whose poems cut to the truth with a rock'n'roll anger. We became great friends, and I toured with him over many years, writing many full shows and song cycles as well as individual songs for special occasions.

And So, I Became a Composer in the Community

Throughout the 1980s, we of the WSI would arrive in a town and, in the process of making a new piece of celebratory theatre, start to build local partnerships and gather people together to form a band or a choir. The small-scale community arts fascinated me. A project in the submarine town of Barrow-in-Furness in 1983 was the start of this passion for and fascination with music, people, and cultural politics. *King Real and the Hoodlums* was a community film project with a script by Adrian; it was a rewrite of *King Lear* set in a nuclear wasteland. I wrote songs, connected with local soloists and musicians, formed a street band, and set up a recording studio in an old mill down by the water. After a few years of touring, in 1987 I settled in Barrow for a three-year music residency that truly changed my life – I was now a community musician. And at the centre of my practice was, and is, a passion for creative composition, political context, and engagement with people. This passion became a life mission as I moved across the bay to work in the seaside resort of Morecambe, where over twenty-five years I have developed a charity that delivers a community music program that reflects my values and has allowed me to develop my skills and interests as a composer in the community.

In the following brief case studies, I hope to show how research drives social content, musical style, and performance (in its widest sense, including gigs, tours, recordings, films, and publications).

Morecambe Streets

Starting point. To connect with people from different parts of the community by talking about things in their lives that they had particular feelings about and using this as the creative impetus.

Research. Where are the groups within the community who would welcome us and what is the right approach in each situation?

My role. To produce the project by finding the groups and the artists, develop the methodology for creative engagement, and then be a "maker in the moment" carrying out conversations that are both socially investigative and creatively inspired.

Musical style. Melody was the driving force and was the first musical element. The songs aimed to reflect the passions and interests of each individual. They ranged from rock'n'roll to blues, folk to pop, classical to country, rap to nursery rhyme, and much more.

Output. The project ran for two years. We performed live shows in community centres, pubs, and schools, published a beautiful multi-textured book, recorded a CD, and made a reading desk that toured libraries with folders of 450 songs and a CD player with a selection of the fifty "best."

(There is more information about this project and two other key Morecambe projects – Flights of Passage and The Long Walk – in my chapter on sense of place in *The Oxford Handbook of Community Music*.)

Street Symphony

Starting point. To fuse classical form with popular instrumentation and musical styles and take performers and audiences on a creative journey.

Research. How many bands can we find that will be able to learn by ear, read music, improvise, and represent the diversity of the community?

My role. To produce the project by finding the right performance context and the bands, to compose and arrange the four movements, to rehearse separately with each band, and then to conduct the main rehearsals and the show.

Musical style. A four-movement "classical" symphony form with a sonata-form first movement, followed by a slow theme and variations, a "samba-bhangra-samba," and a final rondo featuring each band in the interludes. The musical content included folk song, tango, Phrygian jazz, pop song, and Latin grooves.

Output. an hour-long show at a festival with up to 100 players from street bands, creative jazz orchestras, and brass bands.

Travellers' Tales

Starting point. A Lancashire festival commission to create a project engaging a section of the community that doesn't generally connect with cultural offerings.

Research. We decided to work with the Gypsy, Romany, and Traveller community and had to find the right gatekeepers who would help us. These included local authority officers who worked with the GRT community, schools where there were high numbers of GRT young people, and a musician from the local traveller community and his mother. After a series of conversations, we started listening to relevant traditional music and reading whatever we could find that would help us understand how to approach the project.

My role. To produce the project, responding to commissions and finding groups and artists, writing songs with people, arranging music, and performing and recording the songs.

Musical style. We wrote a set of eight songs, all in popular musical genres that had been chosen by the individuals or groups we were working with. These reflected the styles of music generally favoured by the community, from country to rockabilly, soul to folk, pop to rap.

Output. We performed the set of songs in a designed environment at the festival, at three schools, and then at our venue in Morecambe. They were recorded and shared with the participants.

Sing the Docks – A Huge Piece That Focused a City

Starting point. A commission to develop a singing project in a neglected part of the city, over three years, as part of the Preston Guild – a citywide celebration held every twenty years. This included the composition of a new Guild Anthem.

Research. Who would come and sing, what should our suite of songs be about (social history and geography of the Docks), what do people think of the place where they live, and where were the local musicians who could become involved?

My role. Overall producer (in every aspect), songwriter and workshop facilitator, choir conductor and performer.

Musical style. The new Anthem was in a classical choral style, whereas the suite of songs were in a folk style appropriate for the local context.

Output. By the third year of the project we had more than 350 adult singers as well as 60 schoolchildren. We performed the complete Sing the Docks suite at the Festival both outdoors at Preston Docks and indoors as part of the Guild weekend. The Anthem was sung at key civic moments throughout the whole year of festivities.

Frontierland

Starting point. To create an event to celebrate twenty years of our charity, More Music, bringing together many of the elements of our community to perform together.

Research. What was an appropriate form for the event, who would we include, where could we perform, and who was the audience?

My role. To work with a group of emerging practitioners to devise and create the event, to rehearse elements, and to collectively compose and then conduct the main second act.

Musical style. The show included elements of everything More Music produced, from rock and rap to jazz and choral, from UK folk to Chinese traditional tunes and more. The first act was in four separate spaces, each featuring a particular group and style of music. In the second act everyone came together to play a through-composed piece conceived with a very simple graphic score and showcasing a group of excellent professional musicians who work or have worked with More Music.

Output. Two nights of extraordinary music-making!

Each of these projects has taken me down the line in terms of risk – both social and creative – and the dividends have been enormous. An interesting idea or a commission starts a process of development, and oftentimes an end performance has to be achieved before the music has been written or the community engaged. The resulting adrenalin rush pushes for new engagement, creates new songs in moments, invents new forms and structures, and in the end makes change happen. The shows and the personal connections inspire us as musicians to carry on doing the work we love, inspire the community participants to be creative and to connect with others in new ways, and hopefully inspire our peers and funders to take risks, to walk the line, in the understanding that the outcomes from creative community composition will be worth all the investment and time.

References

The following websites hold information that I believe is important or that has inspired me:

Gulbenkian Foundation. A brilliant report about the civic responsibilities of arts organizations. It includes a very clever set of metaphors that help to define our role. http://civicroleartsinquiry.gulbenkian.org.uk/resources/rethinking -relationships-phase-one-of-the-inquiry-into-the-civic-role-of-arts-organisa tions

INSPIRE MUSIC. A compilation of well-analyzed case studies developed as a Paul Hamlyn Foundation project. http://www.inspire-music.org

Musical Futures. A website about the work that community musicians deliver in schools. It has had an international impact. https://www.musical futures.org

Sing Up. The website of a national singing program that developed from the Music Manifesto research (2004–7) and the State of Play conference in London (January 2007). https://www.singup.org

Youth Music Network. Youth Music has been a significant source of funds for those who work with young people in England. This website gathers its research and learning in a constantly evolving process. https://network.youth music.org.uk

Restless Art. A blog by writer and thinker François Matarasso. https:// arestlessart.com

PART III

COMMUNITY MUSIC
Seeking Relationships with Indigenous Communities

COMMUNITY MUSIC'S FOUNDATIONAL principles have influenced the process of building relationships between Indigenous and settler peoples. Bartleet reconceptualizes the interventionist concept of community music and examines the possibilities for finding spaces of intercultural sharing. Laurila builds on the idea of using song as a means to bridge cultural divides and develop "ethical space." Marais's outstanding work with Indigenous youth in Northern Ontario (Canada) is illustrated in the image of the Sacred Canoe, a research project that has been a catalyst for building self-esteem and creative expression among vulnerable youth populations in remote Indigenous communities.

CHAPTER 16

Community Music at the Cultural Interface

What the Experiences of Working alongside First Peoples
Can Bring to Our Understandings of Community Music

Brydie-Leigh Bartleet

Introduction: Community Music at the Cultural Interface

AS THE FIELD OF community music has become increasingly international-
ized, insights from many different cultural contexts have both expanded and
challenged commonly accepted approaches, priorities, and ideas around what
constitutes "community music." While the term and concept of community
music as an intervention has its roots in the UK counterculture era of the late
1960s and 1970s (Higgins, 2012), it has since grown to take on different meanings in a wide variety of cultural contexts around the world. As the field has
developed and grown internationally, other forms of communal music-making
have contributed toward broader international conceptualizations of the field
(Bartleet, 2017; Bartleet & Higgins, 2018). As such, the term "community
music" can now be articulated in a variety of ways, reflecting myriad cultural
contexts and musical situations (Higgins & Willingham, 2017; Bartleet &
Schippers, 2013; Veblen, 2013). Of course, since time immemorial, music has
been made by and with communities in order to express local identities, traditions, values, beliefs, aspirations, and social interactions (see Tomlinson, 2015).
However, as communities and their circumstances have changed over time,
sometimes the need has arisen for what might be termed active *interventions*
to establish or restore lost or compromised music practices within community
settings (Schippers, 2018). Other times, musical interventions have been used
to establish or restore peace or a sense of well-being in social, cultural, and
political situations where dysfunction, conflict, or natural disaster has caused

damage or to provide a safe space for people to meet and make music together. In many parts of the world it is these interventions that have commonly become referred to as "community music."

For our international field of community music practitioners and scholars this ever-increasing cultural diversification has not been without its challenges and tensions, particularly in regard to understanding and articulating what community music *is* and *does*. In the context of the field's largest international network, the International Society for Music Education's (ISME) Community Music Activity (CMA) Commission, we have commonly made sense of this changing field by deferring to the field's UK roots and the interventionist perspective as a "lens" for viewing this diversity of practices. Rather problematically, this means the interventionist approach continues to be seen as the prevailing norm in the context of all this diversity, and anything that doesn't fall within that category is seen as Other. As a colleague of mine recently suggested, it is almost as if we have now two approaches: the "interventionist" on one hand, and what he calls the "Indigenous" on the other. I suspect his choice of the word "Indigenous" might be due to the fact that a substantial amount of this work has been described through the lenses of ethnomusicology and entails cultural practices and rituals that are deeply grounded in and Indigenous to particular cultural communities. However, rather problematically, positioning these two different perspectives like this also gives rise to what could be described as a "clash of cultures," a "cultural mismatch" or even "cultural dissonance" within the field of community music.

Rather than viewing all of these perspectives as irreconcilably divergent, I see this space as full of possibilities for intercultural sharing and a reconceptualizing of our field. Australian Indigenous scholar Martin Nakata (2007) calls on us to act on these tensions that arise from the "interfaces" between cultures and to embrace the new insights that can emerge from those spaces. What Nakata argues is that without a struggle, without these tensions, only the voice of a single dominant culture is heard. If we begin to conceptualize the intercultural and international developments of community musicians in terms of Nakata's cultural interface, then we can move on from the somewhat oppositional ways of thinking about what is and is not community music, according the dominant "interventionist" model. The practices and ideas that emerge from this might not neatly fit into one domain or the other or in support of one or the other, but from this complex space many sets of interrelated understandings can emerge (Nakata, 2007, p. 200). This also allows us to take comfort in our sense of discomfort and to realize that any tensions we might be feeling as community musicians, or indeed more broadly in our field, are a sign of health and growth. My sense is that there are important implications for us in Nakata's cultural interface, as well as clues for how we can reconceptualize future agendas for the field of community music.

This line of thinking prompts us to critically reflect on the democratic values we espouse as a field and re-examine the concept of musical intervention. For instance, in parts of the world where colonization has caused and continues to cause devastating damage, oppression, and large-scale systemic inequities, this notion of an "intervention" is a deeply loaded concept that requires careful consideration. In Australia, the term "intervention" is associated with a highly controversial and problematic political package of changes to welfare provision, law enforcement, land tenure, and other measures in 2007 to address allegations of child sexual abuse and neglect in Northern Territory Aboriginal communities (AHRC, 2007). Many might argue that in this case of recolonization, in these tragic circumstances, musical interventions are indeed needed more than ever, but in such circumstances, community music facilitators are challenged to ask themselves, on whose terms this musical activity is happening, whether those terms are appropriate to the cultural context in which they are operating, and whether the intervention is acting as another colonizing endeavour or promoting a more positive sense of self-determination for the participants. Such considerations are prompting community music facilitators to take a reflexive view of their own cultural legacy in their music-making as they work from and alongside different cultural world views (see Ashley & Lines, 2016). My sense is that if we are truly committed to walking the boundaries, bridging the gaps, and fostering the conditions needed for cultural reconciliation and healing, it is time for some deep and hard conversations about how we navigate the complex cultural politics of this community work.

In this chapter, I hope to open up some of these conversations, and share in a personal way some of the lessons I have learned from grappling with these issues and working across cultures as a community musician and researcher alongside Indigenous artists and Elders in Australia for many years. In doing so, I hope to prompt further considerations of how we can be more effective cross-cultural community musicians.

Situating Myself as a Community Musician

Before proceeding any further it is necessary to acknowledge the cultural politics that are evoked by the nature of my personal background and subjectivities. I am a non-Indigenous woman, and the critical perspectives I bring to bear in this chapter are reflective of my subjectivities and experiences. I am a first-generation migrant who grew up between cultures in South Africa and Australia, and a person who spent her formative years living through the height and demise of apartheid. You could say I am a settler twice over. As such, I am mindful of how this leads me to engage in what Mackinlay and Barney (2014) have called "a dangerous act of representation, one where the potential silently lies for us to continue to use our White race, power, and privilege in theoretical, epistemological, and pedagogical ways as part of the ongoing colonial project" (p. 59). The risk that I run here is that the very politics and power dynamics I seek to critique in this chapter can become reinscribed through my writing of it. With this in mind, in the words that follow, I try to be open and critical about my own subjectivities, acknowledging the role that my background plays in my work as a community musician, educator, and researcher and ultimately the fact that my voice here is not the voice of an Indigenous person. Likewise, the position I write from and critique here is that of a privileged white woman. It is a settler's perspective.

That said, the words of a senior Indigenous colleague of mine, Professor Adrian Miller, a proud Jirrbal man, always remind me that cultural reconciliation is everyone's responsibility. As he once said in a meeting on reconciliation, it is about unity and respect between Indigenous and non-Indigenous peoples, and we all have a role to play. These words do not eliminate the complex cultural politics I have just outlined, but they do remind me about the importance of *all* of us having this conversation. These words also resonate with the powerful lesson in the lyrics of my favourite song by Indigenous musician Kev Carmody and non-Indigenous musician Paul Kelly, "From Little Things Big Things Grow." This has become a kind of anthem for reconciliation in Australia, and a powerful reminder of what can grow from taking a small but brave step.

Setting the Context

To put my introductory words into a concrete community and educational context, I'd like to begin with a story. The story of the most beautiful and memorable moment in my intercultural community music work to date, and a story that has two parts.

> We'd taken a group of students up to Tennant Creek, Warumungu country, as we'd done since 2009. We've travelled some 2,500 km's from our home to work alongside our Indigenous and non-Indigenous collaborators all week in the lead up to the annual Desert Harmony Festival. Tonight is our chance to perform together. The lead up to this moment has been magic. Our students have had many workshops and song sharing session[s] in the music centre and under the trees, exchanging knowledge and ideas about their family, their land, and [their] language. The intercultural sharing that has happened has been priceless. To me this exchange has been the very epitome of what I believe community music

can, and should be. Led by Indigenous musicians, working in relationship with one another, espousing all the community music values of participation, inclusion, love, care, and respect for difference. As we stood and performed that night under the lit-up eucalypt[us] trees, on the sacred ground of the Nyinkka [lizard] to a crowd of 100's of local Aboriginal people it felt electric. This felt like what reconciliation could be. And music was the powerful medium for it. By the end of the performance we were on an absolute high after three rowdy encores.

Now we get to the point in the story that I have usually shared. After the performance ends, we all gathered for a group shot. The ecstasy of that night was written on our faces for all to see. I shouted out to my husband and collaborator Gavin who has been in the audience with our 2-year old twin girls in their pram to join us. I wanted him in the photo. I wanted to acknowledge the relationships and ties that bind us as a family to these people and this place, but he doesn't come up and stays where he is in the shadows. When I went up to him and chided him for not coming, I noticed his ashen face. He talked to me in whispered sharp phrases, and said we needed to get the girls out of there. There had just been a violent altercation between a man and a woman. He had hit her to the ground. Hard. It happened right before Gavin's and the girls' eyes, as well as all the local kids. It had been hidden by the night time shadows. Sadly, this is an all too common occurrence where we work. I choose to speak of it now, because it throws into stark reality, the harsh and deeply complex social, cultural and political environment I have just described, and the complexities I face as a community musician seeking to find ways to respond. It jolts us out of what can sometimes become a rather romanticized community music tale of this work together, that can all too easily overlook the daily reality of this place, its complex cultural politics, what colonization has done, and continues to do, and music's co-existence with it.

In Tennant Creek, domestic violence statistics are among the highest in Australia, homelessness is 30 percent higher than the national average, rates of kidney disease are the highest in the world, and Indigenous people are disadvantaged on every social indicator. This is the result of a colonial legacy of massacres, genocide, stolen land, and repeated government policies that have been squarely aimed at eliminating Indigenous people and their cultures and denying them the sovereignty, dignity, and human rights that are justly theirs. Countless people continue to suffer the intergenerational trauma of one of the most potent weapons of colonial violence used on Indigenous people, the removal of their children (Mackinlay & Barney, 2010). It was only in 2008 that our then prime minister Kevin Rudd formally apologized to these Stolen Generations (Australian Government, 2008).

But this darkness is mixed with such light, such joy, and such strength. Indigenous people in Australia have engaged in communal song, dance, art, and music-making in deeply interconnected ways for more than 60,000 years. They were engaging in community music-making long before British colonizers landed on Australia's shores, and they have used it as a powerful form of resistance ever since. This enduring musical and cultural strength and sense of community connectivity continues to hold so much wisdom, and insights about what community can and should be. This is precisely the kind of situation many would say is ripe for community music interventions. Indeed, there is a long history of community arts and music programs (run by both Indigenous and non-Indigenous facilitators) that attempt to join the dots between pressing social needs and this enduring cultural strength, and to connect cultures through shared music-making. But in such circumstances, community music facilitators have been seriously challenged to ask themselves on whose terms this musical activity is happening, whether those terms are appropriate to the cultural context in which they are operating, and whether the intervention is acting as another colonizing endeavour or promoting a more positive sense of self-determination for the participants, as well as cultural reconciliation. As my colleague Te Oti Rakena (2018) has reminded us, from a Māori perspective, in such circumstances local engagement, ownership, and self-determination are seriously needed for real engagement and change to actually occur.

But how, you might ask, do you work toward that? How can community musicians get in behind this strength that is already there? How can they contribute to the momentum and further build up this resistance and strength? How do you move forward given all this complexity? Should you even move forward at all? To begin to answer these questions, I'd like to turn to three interrelated and multifaceted concepts that have informed and been deeply embedded in my intercultural work. These are concepts that have been shared and modelled by the Indigenous musicians and Elders we've worked with over the years (see Bartleet et al., 2015; Bartleet et al., 2016). I've chosen these three because they all speak to the question of how community musicians can respond and how they can think critically about their ways of knowing, being, and doing (see Martin & Mirraboopa, 2003). These concepts revolve around three Rs: relationships, responsiveness, and reflexivity.

Three Rs for Engaging in Intercultural Community Music Practices

1. Relationships. This intercultural community music work begins and ends with relationships. It survives and thrives due to relationships, and without these the music-making would cease very quickly (see Mackinlay, 2008). But building these relationships takes time, repeated visits, and ongoing work, which has meant that I've certainly had to take a step back as a facilitator and rip up any agenda, workshop plans, or preconceived ideas of what we could do together. I have been challenged to stop, slow down, sit down, and make space for this most necessary dimension of our work. This way of relating to one another, musically and relationally, has unfolded dynamically in social spaces that have been deeply informed by Indigenous perspectives (see Bartleet et al., 2014).

This has meant moving away from Western ways of conceptualizing what relationships might be and moving beyond "just talking" toward new ways of relating and collaborating. It has involved engaging with Indigenous conceptualizations of hospitality and welcome. This is poignantly illustrated by our collaborators giving us what are called "skin names," which have in essence "adopted" us into the kinship system. These skin names facilitate greater connection and teach us about not only our relationships toward one another, but also the culturally appropriate behaviour that accompanies these relationships. Stemming from these relational ways of working is the related concept of reciprocal exchange. As one of my Aboriginal research collaborators, Sandy O'Sullivan (2016), a proud Warudjuri woman, has argued, reciprocity is a complex way of seeding knowledge and understandings, trust and engagement. It is not merely just "give and take" musically speaking. Reciprocity is expressed as a relational connection that is informed by personal, social, and environmental contexts.

So much of this could be missed if one was to bombastically intervene in a situation like this as a community musician. So much of this could be missed if one didn't take the time to slow down, sit down, and listen. So much of this could be missed if people went in thinking they would run a musical intervention to bring a new approach too such a complex and difficult situation (as has happened many times in the past). So much can be learned if one "makes space" (to evoke a reconciliation concept from Canada; see Steinman, 2011) for what is there already to emerge, or more pointedly to re-emerge. And the learnings that emerge are far greater than any "cultural competency" course might teach.

2. *Responsiveness.* The concept of "making space" relates to my second R: responsiveness. Working in this intercultural way has involved a conscious effort to make space for Indigenous ways of knowing, being and doing, and making space to meet our Indigenous collaborators on their own cultural terms. Of particular relevance to us as community musicians is the concept "dadirri," or deep listening. Dadirri is commonly referred to as the Aboriginal gift, and Miriam Rose Ungunmerr (1988), a proud Ngan'gityemerri woman, has written eloquently on this. She says the principles and functions of dadirri are a knowledge and consideration of community and the diversity and unique nature that each individual brings to a community. Dadirri provides a way of relating and acting within community; it means non-intrusive observation, or quiet watching and deep listening and *hearing with more than the ears*. And having learned from this kind of deep listening, then enacting a plan to act in a way that is informed by this learning (see Atkinson, 2002, pp. 16–18). The following story illustrates this concept. Some of the reflections included in this story are drawn from the journals of my collaborators (names removed for anonymity):

> The arts organization we work with up in Tennant Creek were approached by Elders from a community in the Barkly Region to see if they could make a documentary with music and story about their traditional homelands. Through this project, families were reunited on their traditional country for the first time in well over 40 years. They had been forcibly removed.
>
> After a long period of negotiations and permissions, they had finally arrived. They were so excited that everyone temporarily forgot about the project and the filming! Onlookers could see that real healing was happening in this place. Everyone noticed how the country came alive under the feet of the people who were intimately tied to it as they walked on their country, their home. Colours were brighter, birds sang louder, the desert was soft on people's spirits and hearts and sang to them at night.
>
> Lesley Thompson – one of our long-standing collaborators – sat by the significant waterhole and played his signature country tune about that country, Walapanba. He later told me he found water all over the red dirt the next morning signalling to him his song had awoken the rainbow serpent. The desert lights shone at night for the people to see. The women told stories about those spirits, about what it meant for them to be there. Everyone said that wherever their footprints went, the spirits came to visit.

It was only sometime later that I started to begin to understand what this meant. I'd noticed Lesley would often just walk away after a jam and sit down outside and stare into space. I couldn't work out why. Then one day, I decided to follow him. He told me to look up. The sky was filled with birds. I'd never thought anything of these birds, until he told me those birds were the spirits, and they were watching what we were doing. They were curious to see who was playing music there.

What he taught me was that there was learning that was happening just by being there. It was unspoken, it was felt. It was learning from the country that you felt in your body, heart, and spirit. It said, you've got to slow down. You've got to connect and be responsive. It's only then that you can think about making music. This is how we can come to know each other, and ourselves. From these little things, big things grow.

There are many lessons in this story for us as community musicians about how to be responsive in this kind of context, about how to be present, quietly aware, watch, and engage in a deep listening where we hear with more than our ears.

3. *Reflexivity.* This deep way of responding to the world leads me to ask how as community music facilitators we harness the power and potential of these ways of knowing, being, and doing *without* sliding dangerously into some kind of cultural appropriation of these concepts and world views. To answer this, I'd now like to turn to my third R: reflexivity.

For me as a non-Indigenous community music facilitator, engaging in this kind of intercultural work has meant continually and reflexively critiquing my cultural biases and assumptions, and ultimately the systematic privilege that I benefit from as a non-Indigenous person. This concept of privilege has taken me some time to understand and unpack. Basically, to have privilege is to have an advantage that is completely out of your control (Goodman, 2011). Many a time this has meant metaphorically sitting on the side of the desert road and unpacking Peggy McIntosh's (2004) famous invisible knapsack of white privilege. In these reflexive moments, I can unpack all twenty-one of her privileges. To give just a few examples:

I can if I wish arrange to be in the company of people of my race most of the time.

I can avoid spending time with people whom I was trained to mistrust and who have learned to mistrust my kind or me.

If I should need to move, I can be pretty sure of renting or purchasing housing in an area which I can afford and in which I would want to live.

I can be pretty sure that my neighbors in such a location will be neutral or pleasant to me.

I can go shopping alone most of the time, pretty well assured that I will not be followed or harassed.

I can turn on the television or open to the front page of the paper and see people of my race widely represented.

When I am told about our national heritage or about "civilization," I am shown that people of my color made it what it is. I can be sure that my children will be given curricular materials that testify to the existence of their race. (McIntosh, 2004, p. 31).

Of course, there are many different dimensions of privilege (whether these relate to socio-economic privilege, gender privilege, heterosexual privilege, or able-bodied privilege), and the intersectionality of these is complex to navigate. This can lead to ambiguities, contradictions, and double binds (see also Kowal, 2015) for us as community musicians navigating this cultural terrain. However, my sense is that these are significant and important questions that we as community musicians need to ask ourselves if we genuinely want to engage across cultures and be allies for change. For me, it has led me to constantly question how I can reconcile my white privilege with being a community music facilitator who champions freedom, equality, and democracy. This line of thinking has always led to a similar place for me. It is a place called *colonial guilt* (see Selby, 2004). It is here that I often find myself caught in a vortex of shame. Guilt over my privilege and what I have, shame over what has been done to my collaborators, and shame over the fact that if I am not careful, if I am not reflexive, I too could be enacting yet another colonizing endeavour without even knowing it. Then that guilt turns to anger as I look around and see so many of my colleagues, friends, and some family members complicit in all of this, and oblivious to their own privilege and how they continue to benefit from it. It resonates with the meme commonly shared on social media: "Privilege is when you think something is not a problem because it's not a problem to you personally" (David Gaider).

Yet when we ask ourselves these sorts of reflexive questions and begin to *understand* how privilege can sometimes silently manifest itself in the nooks and crannies of community music settings, and in particular can become magnified in such intercultural settings, this becomes a powerful antidote to the immobilization of the guilt I have just described. It can lead to an unlearning of privilege, and this process strongly resonates with the ideals and values we hold dear in our field of community music. It can lead to a sense of liberation for all, and to an answer to the question of how as community musicians we can respond. This resonates with the well-known quote from Lilla Watson, the Indigenous, Murri visual artist, activist, and academic: "If you have come here to help me, you are wasting your time. But if you have come because your liberation is bound up with mine, then let us work together."

Conclusion

My sense is that as the field of community music continues to expand into diverse cultural contexts, it can play a key role in bridging cultures and fostering the conditions needed for cultural reconciliation and healing. However, as I have argued in this chapter, my sense is that there are some hard questions we need to ask ourselves if we are truly committed to working in and across cultures. There are some major considerations we need to reflect upon to ensure that our work does not act as yet another colonizing endeavour, but rather promotes a positive sense of self-determination for those involved. There is a pressing need for community music to make space for Indigenous ways of knowing, being, and doing to come to the fore, and to prioritize important concepts and practices such as "relationships," "responsiveness," and "reflexivity" in this work. The result won't necessarily be that community music takes away the darkness of the violent colonial history that continues to pervade our world, but that it can help us find a path. This sometimes requires courage, belief, and a willingness to take a step forward. A willingness to invest time, over time, to build and deepen *relationships* in reciprocal ways that can lead us to a much greater awareness and *responsiveness* to the world around us, and a *reflexive* view of ourselves and where we stand in it. From these little things, big things can grow.

CHAPTER 17

Song as the Catalyst That Promotes Envisioning Ethical Spaces

Kelly Laurila

WHAT!! YOU'RE SINGING with the police!? Why would you want to do that? These are the exclamations and questions that I and the other Indigenous women and girls in our drum circle get when we sing with a police chorus. It is precisely because of these remarks that the women have chosen to partner with them. History in Canada would suggest that the kinds of relationships that exist between Indigenous peoples and the police are primarily negative and violent. To fathom a singing partnership defies how Indigenous and Settler peoples, and more specifically, how Indigenous women and the police, have conceived of each other in the past, as well as how they see each other in the present. With the reconciliation process under way in Canada, some Indigenous and Settler peoples are seeking and creating ways to contribute to better relationships among each other. In my search of the literature, I have not been able to find any sustained singing partnership between Indigenous peoples and the police in Canada, until now. In this chapter, I will share with you my doctoral research interest of how song brought the Indigenous women and girls and police chorus men together and set us on a journey of encountering each other in a way not previously known or understood.

The Call to Action from the Truth and Reconciliation Commission (TRC) of Canada

My research interest was prompted by the Truth and Reconciliation process that is under way in Canada and the Call to Action by former Aboriginal Justice Murray Sinclair (TRC, 2012). He has asked Canadians what they will do to contribute to reconciliation between Indigenous and Settler peoples. A public apology was made in 2008 to the Indigenous peoples by the then-prime minister, Stephen Harper (Aboriginal Affairs and Northern Development Canada, 2008). The federal government publicly acknowledged the traumatic impact (i.e., spiritual, emotional, mental, and physical) of government policies on Indigenous children who were forced to attend residential schools, as well as the legacy of those policies for subsequent generations (TRC, 2012). A time of public truth-telling enabled by the TRC has brought forward more than 6,000 witnesses, most of them survivors of those schools, who are sharing their tragic stories of abuse. This sharing has established the undeniable truth that they were brutalized; it is also helping them heal (TRC, 2015).

This sharing is prompting some Canadians to learn about and question the colonial underpinnings of Canadian society and how it has imposed systemic injustice on Indigenous peoples (Barker, 2010; Regan, 2010). This truth-sharing is also prompting some Indigenous peoples to wonder how to move forward, and to ask themselves whether reconciliation is even possible at a time when injustices are ongoing (Alfred, 2014; Simpson, 2011; Manuel & Derrickson, 2015). In among these apprehensions and questions there are many stories and projects that involve Indigenous and Settler peoples coming together for the purpose of building greater understanding and developing respectful relationships (e.g., Canada Council for the Arts, 2016; Davis & Shpuniarsky, 2010; Decter & Isaac, 2015; Dupuis & Ferguson, 2016; Reconciliation Canada, 2015).

A core premise of the TRC process in Canada is that Indigenous and Settler peoples need to build better relationships (TRC, 2015). Once they have done that, they will be able to work together to address the social, political, economic, and environmental injustices that continue to divide them. The need for better relationships and to address injustices was emphatically stated twenty-one years ago in the comprehensive report of the Royal Commission on Aboriginal Peoples (RCAP, 1996). Justice doesn't just happen. It is the result of building relationships in ways that promote understanding, communication, and mutual resolution of injustices.

Who I Am in the Context of the TRC and My Research Interest

Reconciliation is very personal to me, and so is my research. This is as it should be from an Indigenous research perspective (e.g., Absolon, 2011; Wilson, 2008) and from other qualitative research theoretical perspectives (e.g. Myerhof & Ruby, 1982; Probst & Berenson, 2014). As a woman of Indigenous Sáami and Settler Irish heritages, a long-time song carrier with a local, urban Indigenous women's and girls' drum circle, and a collaborator with Settler choirs, I am interested in learning how song can contribute to reconciliation.

Having Indigenous roots has motivated me to see the injustices that Canada's Indigenous peoples have experienced. I can relate to some things, such as growing up with little connection to my Sáami culture because my grandfather had left his ancestral land in northern Finland, where certain cultural aspects had been stolen from him by government policies and acts of assimilation. For the past twenty-seven years I have found kinship with the Anishinaabe peoples in southern Ontario, who have invited me into their cultural ceremonies and teachings. So I am both the colonizer and the colonized. I was born in Canada and am Indigenous, but I am also European and a Settler on this land. I acknowledge that what I know resides somewhere between Indigenous and Western knowledges.

Connecting the personal with my research on reconciliation, Gale Cyr once asked me what my intention was regarding reconciliation (personal communications, 17 May 2015, 6 June 2015). I have asked myself this too. I think about my identity and my own journey toward reconciling all that I am. I want to find peace and acceptance among the contradictions I harbour as a Indigenous Sáami and Irish settler. I am aware that Indigenous peoples in Canada have suffered more than five centuries of oppression, racism, and injustices. I wish for peace and better relations between Indigenous and Settler peoples, but I have learned that this cannot happen without justice (TRC, 2015). I have come to realize that reconciling my identity with my ancestral roots is part of the greater reconciliation process that is happening in Canada. I am reminded of the words of now Senator Murray Sinclair at a public gathering in 2016: "Know where you have been, because that will tell you where you are going. Know where you are going, because you will then know why you are here. When you know why you are here, then you will know who you are." These words speak to the individual and personal reconciliation one needs to carry out to be in better relationships with Indigenous peoples (i.e., knowing the history in Canada will guide a better future) and the responsibility each person has to create justice with Indigenous peoples.

The Present: The Space Between Indigenous Peoples and the Police

An ideological chasm has developed between Indigenous and Settler peoples. But it is *colonial* ideology that has created the epistemic and systemic violence that sustains both sides' misunderstandings, assumptions, and stereotypes. That colonial ideology has led to social, economic, political, and environmental injustices, the lasting tragedy of the residential schools, and the racism and discrimination faced by Indigenous peoples to this day (Kelm, 1998;

Kirmayer, Simpson, & Cargo, 2003; Manuel & Derrickson, 2015; Milloy, 1999; RCAP, 1996; Sutherland, Maar, & Fréel, 2013; TRC, 2015; Weber-Pillwax et al., 2012).

A specific tool of harmful power over Indigenous peoples is the justice system (Amnesty International Canada, 2009; Blackstock, 2016; Cao, 2014; Chan & Chunn, 2014; Christmas, 2012; Edwards, 2001; Monchalin, 2016; Native Women's Association, 2017; Tasker, 2016; TRC, 2015). The justice system is where treaty settlements are being stalled, disputed, and denied (Manuel & Derrickson, 2015). It is there, too, that the police arrest Indigenous peoples at unjustly high rates and that Indigenous men and women are incarcerated at rates that are wildly disproportionate to their population size (Cao, 2014; Chan & Chunn, 2014; Comack, 2012; Monchalin, 2016). It is there that many violent interactions play out during land occupations and protests (e.g. Belanger, 2014; Christmas, 2012; Edwards, 2001). And, finally, it is there that so little is done to investigate the shockingly high numbers of murdered and missing Indigenous women and girls (Amnesty International Canada, 2009; Native Women's Association, 2017; Monchalin, 2016; Tasker, 2016). How did these injustices and violent relationships between Indigenous peoples and the police come to be this way? A look at the past can help us understand the present.

The Past: The Space Between Indigenous and Settler Peoples

From before European contact to the present, Indigenous peoples have had their own intimate epistemological understandings of their environment. These have given rise to geographic, political, economic, and social structures specific to their communities (Belanger, 2014; Dickason & McNab, 2009; Helin, 2006). When Europeans began to appear in new territories such as what is now known as Canada, they brought with them an ideology different from those of the Indigenous peoples they encountered (Frideres, 2011; Wright, 2003). Europeans justified their colonization project through the legal Doctrine of Discovery, whereby they could claim new lands for the European monarch that they deemed to be vacant (i.e., *terra nullius*) (Manuel & Derrickson, 2015; TRC, 2015; Wright, 2003). They believed it their inherent right to claim the lands they came upon; they saw no need to acknowledge that those lands were already inhabited by Indigenous peoples.

Early contacts between Indigenous and Settler peoples were somewhat amicable, perhaps because the Indigenous peoples were essential to the survival of the early colonists with regard to food sources, hunting, trade, and military alliances, and as guides. In exchange for their assistance, Indigenous peoples received some benefits. They were provided with metal, firearms, and other materials and foodstuffs (Belanger, 2014; Frideres, 2011). Early treaty agreements between Indigenous and Settler peoples emphasized the importance of maintaining peaceful relations as they crossed each other's territories and traded goods. One such agreement was the well-known 1643 treaty called the Two Row Wampum, in which it was agreed that each nation (i.e., Indigenous Haudenosaunee and European Dutch peoples) would respect the other in independent and peaceful coexistence (Tehanetorens, 1993).

Indigenous scholars (e.g., Amagoalik, 2012; King, 2013; Alfred, 2014) note that the time of peace and friendship was relatively short, compared to the long history of broken treaties, aggressive missionary activities, the compelled transfer of Indigenous peoples to unfamiliar and often unproductive reserve lands, efforts to assimilate Indigenous peoples through various legislative acts such as the Indian Act, and the forced attendance of Indigenous children at residential schools. Indigenous peoples were cast aside when they were no longer needed. Thomas King (2013) would say that they became an inconvenience to Settler society and the nation's progress. According to King (2013), Settler peoples never expected Indians to survive civilization; they expected that natural law would result in their dying out.

The Past: The Space between Indigenous Peoples and the Police and Military

A Google search for "pictures of Indigenous stand-offs" provides telling information about the kinds of relationships that have existed between Indigenous peoples and the police and military. A photograph of a stare-down at a stand-off is all too common. The two sides are not far from each other, sometimes standing only inches apart; but they are a chasm away from knowing who the other really is and why the impasse happened. Many conflicts have arisen out of clashes of ideology and perspectives. Just two examples are the Oka Crisis of 1990 in Quebec (Belanger, 2014; Obomsawin & Koenig, 1993) and the Ipperwash Crisis of 1995 in Ontario (Edwards, 2001; Kawaja, Sereny, & Tierney, 2006; Reed et al., 2011). Both these incidents were the result of Settler peoples exercising their power when confronted with different perceptions and assumptions about land rights. These incidents were the culmination of broken promises and disregard for Indigenous peoples' traditional relationships with the land. These disputes also exposed the immense chasm that has existed between Indigenous and Settler peoples for generations as a result of destructive government policies, violent confrontations, and military control, as well as the many unresolved justice issues affecting Indigenous peoples. Knowing the kind of violent past that has largely defined relationships between Indigenous and Settler peoples – in particular, between Indigenous peoples and the police and military – a question arises: What kind of relationship can there be into the future?

The Future: Conceiving an Ethical Space

I am intrigued by the concept of "bridging." The metaphor of a bridge implies that the bridge is extended through a space so as to connect two sides (here, Indigenous peoples and Settler peoples). But, to relate this to my project, what interests me is the space *on* the bridge and what it gets filled with. For my doctoral research, I began thinking about the space between Indigenous peoples and the police. I saw a space filled with historical and present-day racism, discrimination, and ignorance that has resulted in misunderstandings, assumptions, stereotypes, and mutual violence. In this space I saw an undercurrent that continues to impact how Indigenous peoples and the police continue to know and relate to each other.

I have encountered various terms in the literature that seem to describe the "space" of a bridge: the space-in-between (Ventres, 2016); making space (Bartleet, Carfoot, & Murn, 2016); mutual space (Blair, 2016); and ethical space (Ermine, 2007; Poole, 1972). The concept that resonates most with me is *ethical* space, as conceived by Roger Poole (1972) and later adapted by Cree educator Willie Ermine (2007). Poole (1972) developed a philosophy regarding the subjective nature of knowledge, and he recognized that one's truth (or subjectivity) is shaped by one's world view. He discussed there being moments when one becomes aware of one's own subjectivity and realizes that others might, therefore, have their own subjectivity (or truth). In that moment there is a space between the intentions of one and those of the other. It could be considered an ethical place, one in which unspoken intentions confront each other and the entities decide how to engage with each other.

Ermine (2007) connected this philosophy of ethical space to the conceived space of what *could* be between Indigenous and Settler peoples if they attempted to enter it from a place of not knowing and wanting to learn and understand each other. He talked about the opposing entities (e.g., Indigenous and Settler peoples) being aware of the existence of the Other but the space between not yet being explored. This space is not empty; it contains what is not said or acknowledged. Ermine (2007) stated that while Indigenous and Settler peoples are well aware of each other, it is this unstated acknowledgment of each other's presence that constitutes many of the deeper thoughts, interests, and assumptions that influence the relationships between them.

Ermine (2007) suggested that ethical choice in this space can be made to comprehend these deeper knowings. In choosing to move into this space, the entities can also choose *how* to engage with each other. They can make a moral choice to learn about each other, about the other's history, and about what has led to the divisions that are creating the harms and hurts. Through this process of engagement and dialogue, both may come to realize that their understandings and experiences may be different from the other's.

Applications of the Concept of Ethical Space

Discourses on ethical space and its applications are sparse in the literature. The noteworthy discussions are limited to Indigenous law and Canadian legal systems (Ermine, 2007), Indigenous research (Brant Castellano, 2015; Ermine, 2007; Longboat, 2008), education (Kapyrka & Dockstator, 2012; Longboat, 2011; Styres, Zinga, Bennett & Bomberry, 2010), media (Bryce, 2014), and reconciliation (Absolon, 2016). Consistent across this literature is the perspective that a space can consciously be created for shared Indigenous and Western knowledges, in such a way that each can complement the other but without being integrated into the other.

Although not specifically pertaining to discourses on ethical space, I have found other conceived notions of what might be considered implied ethical space. In academia, for example, Nerida Blair (2016) discussed the contested space that Indigenous scholars work and live in and the need for a mutual space where the knowledges of Indigenous and Settler Australians can coexist. In the arts, Elizabeth Mackinlay (2016) discussed how stories can make room for paying attention to the little differences and the effects these differences have on what she refers to as decoloniality (i.e., decolonization of colonial knowledge practices). In another example, it was found that through a partnership between music students from Griffith University and the Indigenous Torres Strait Islanders in Australia (Bartleet, 2012; Bartleet, Bennett, Power, & Sunderland, 2014) in order to complete certain assigned tasks such as writing lyrics and recording songs, efforts were needed to build relationships and share tasks. When the students became part of the project, rather than just observers, a *space* was created for new relationships between the Indigenous peoples and the university students. An interesting finding here was that some of the university students developed new insights about themselves and how they had previously conceived Indigenous peoples.

In the community music literature, I found notions of an ethical space through such terms as *magic moments, bridge between worlds, no man's land, building bridges through song, song as a space to bear witness,* and *creating dialogue within music.* Mercédès Pavlicevic (2012) used the term magic moments (p. 197) to describe those precious moments when participants in a singing group experienced a shared meaning and/or experience that created a feeling of belonging. Over time, as participants continued singing together, magic moments were experienced, and there seemed to be a threshold for change into something new. Pavlicevic considered magic moments key to transformative work in music. Song has been perceived as a bridge that connects. For example, a music production conducted by Emily Burridge (2006), of British heritage, called "Bridge Between Worlds," involved a full orchestra along with the Indigenous peoples of the Marimbu Xavante reservation communities in Brazil. Emily visited one of the communities on a number of occasions and worked with the people to compose a recording of various Indigenous songs. From the recordings, she positioned the songs within Western symphony music; this created a presence of two different world views in and of song.

This next finding speaks to a space that offers a glimmer of hope for a different kind of being in the world, be it ever so fleeting. During the First World War, in 1914, on the Western Front, a spontaneous Christmas Eve truce broke out in the no man's land between the enemy trenches (Bajekal, 2014). This brief truce began with soldiers starting to sing Christmas carols. In some places, German soldiers climbed out of the trenches, calling out, "Merry Christmas" in English. Others held up signs reading, "You not shoot, we not shoot." Thousands of British, Belgian, and French soldiers put down their rifles and came out of the trenches to mingle and sing with the German enemy. The troops exchanged gifts of cigarettes, food, buttons, and hats. The space in between became, for a time, a place of peace and singing together.

In another example, Caroline Bithell (2014) used the words "building bridges through song" (p. 217) to describe the founding of a music festival in 1947 called the Llangollen International Musical Eisteddfod. This festival was designed to bring communities together in the small town of Llangollen in North Wales after the trauma of the Second World War. It was believed that music and dance could be a "vehicle" (p. 218) to promote peace and cooperation.

In 2008 in Australia, Indigenous and Settler people gathered to form a collaboration called Musicians Without Borders. Their purpose was to bear witness through song to the traumas experienced by the "Stolen Generation" (Barney & Mackinlay, 2010). Here, music provided a space to acknowledge and express understanding of the trauma of residential schools. Beverley Diamond (2016) has discussed how some Indigenous singers are using their performances to open a dialogue about the atrocities their peoples have experienced. For example, Indigenous performers such as Susan Aglukark (an Inuk singer/songwriter), A Tribe Called Red (an Aboriginal group that digitizes Pow Wow music), and Digging Roots (an Aboriginal husband and wife who play mostly reggae music) combine different strands of world music, while opening a dialogue with their audiences. This, Beverley tells us, disrupts musical expectations as well as stereotypes of Indigenous people.

Song Enabled an Ethical Space of Engagement between the Indigenous Women's and Girls' Drum Circle and the Men of the Police Chorus

When I began my doctoral research, I had no idea that my perspective on the singing partnership with the police chorus would change dramatically. My focus had first been on the impact that the police chorus and Indigenous drum circle singing together would have on the audience. But while I was conducting a comprehensive search of the literature, a particular reading shifted my gaze toward what was happening within and between the men of the police chorus and the women and girls of the drum circle. I say "within" because I became aware of the conversations the police chorus members were having among themselves, and well as the questions they were asking and the books, newspaper articles, and news items they were sharing. Meanwhile, I was having conversations with the women and girls about how they were starting to see the police chorus men and even the police as a whole in new ways. In a review of the literature on music and conflict transformation, Bergh and Sloboda (2010) discussed the tendency of performers and organizers to feel more optimistic than their audiences about music's power to transform conflict situations. The authors stated that this may have to do with the performers spending more time together than the audience members. I wonder if this difference in perception comes about through the performers' personal engagement and the resulting desire to make a difference. A truism may be relevant here: "perception is reality." Whether it's true or not doesn't matter – the perception held by the individuals is what is true. I observed that our drum circle and the police chorus were not only talking to each other but were also starting to connect and care about each other. So I started to focus more on what was shifting between us that enabled us to talk to each other and less on what kept us apart. I then wondered whether these interactions could serve as a space for meaningful change beyond the partnership. Could it lead to changes in the relations between Indigenous women and the police?

What I have just written might make it seem as if I have forgotten about the audience – those who came to see the drum circle and police chorus perform together. In response, I would point to Bergh and Sloboda's (2010) finding that performers have an elevated sense of the impact of their singing performance. That was what happened here, and this perception is what motivated us to "hang in there" – we believed we are making a difference with the audience. That perception also motivated us to welcome the audience into our beliefs and intentions. We hope to educate them and to reveal a tangible means to change how we saw each other.

Six years ago, it was meant to be that I met a member of a Police Male Chorus. I say "meant to be," for I believe our Creator provides the ultimate direction for one's life; so, this was not by chance. I was walking one day past a display booth at a local college when the words "police chorus" caught my eye. Before I could turn away, believing that I had nothing in common with the police except animosity, I was drawn to those words and to the man at the booth. Not knowing what to say, I ridiculously said, "So you sing?" We both laughed at the obviousness of that statement, but those words and the laugh were, I believe, what created a space for us to talk further. I asked him what the police chorus's mission was, and he said it was to reach out to the community through song and to build better relationships between police and communities. I shared the outreach that our drum circle was doing and mentioned that we were also trying to build better relationships and understanding between Indigenous and Settler peoples. I shared my experiences of Indigenous people and how some individuals were struggling to cope with the trauma of the residential schools. He, in turn, shared his experiences with Indigenous people in trouble with the law and spoke of his empathy for the traumas many of them had experienced. This meeting was definitely meant to be! As our conversation continued, I asked him if there was a chance that our drum circle and the police chorus could perform together. The answer was yes, and our first singing event, "Bridging Communities through Song," took place on 13 February 2013.

The collaboration between the police chorus and the drum circle hinged greatly on trust – and, at times, lack of trust. Mistrust on both sides prompted doubts and absences and delays in meetings to plan the first concert. It took more than a year for us just to get comfortable with our drum circle being in the same room as the police chorus. After all, these were *police*, and their uniforms were a visual reminder of the harm that had been done to so many Indigenous people for so long. I am not sure that all of us in our drum circle, Mino Ode Kwewak N'gamowak (Good-Hearted Women Singers), believed that trust was possible. In fact, it was more likely that we didn't expect trust to happen. How can Indigenous women and girls trust the police after all the past and (sometimes) present violence between them? Despite these doubts, our drum circle wanted very much to stay with this partnership to see where it would go. We hoped it would lead to discussions with police services about the need for policing policies and practices to change.

Trust factored into a dramatic change in the relationship between the drum circle and the police chorus. Four years into our singing partnership, our two groups gathered together for a rehearsal before our third annual Bridging Communities through Song concert. After the rehearsal, I told the chairman of the chorus that our drum circle was going to go upstairs to sing a few songs because we had lost three people to suicide that week. We thought we were alone in that part of the church. While we were singing with our drums, the church deacon ran up to us, made a racist remark, and demanded we vacate the church. For our safety, I told the women and girls to quickly gather their bundles and leave. When I arrived home, I emailed the chairman of the chorus to advise him of what happened and that we would not be returning to this church. Instead, we would just do the concert without further rehearsals and to hope for the best.

Well, the outcome of this incident was that, unknown to me, forces rallied in support of the Indigenous women's drum circle. The Police Chorus found an Indigenous-friendly Mennonite Church where we could rehearse together. When our drum circle came to the doors of the Mennonite Church, the pastor was standing there waiting for us! His first words were, "Welcome, please come in." I cried then, and it brings tears to my eyes now as I write this. Those words were exactly what we needed to hear. I am reminded of a song I have heard, "God Welcomes All (strangers and friends)" (Bell, 2008, p. 40, cited in Kanata Centre for Worship and Global Song, 2016). I want to believe that God/Creator indeed welcomes all and that the actions of one church are an anomaly to the bridging I see happening with other churches in our community.

Not only did the Police Chorus change church venues so that we could have another joint rehearsal together, but they also told us that they could not remain with a church (for their own weekly rehearsals) that continued to hurt and oppress Indigenous people. I am still reeling from the incredible impact their decision has had on me and our drum circle. That they stood alongside us (not in front, and not over) shows that they *meant* their words – their actions came from within them. As the women were packing up after that particular rehearsal, the police chorus began to sing a song, "You'll Never Walk Alone" (Rodgers & Hammerstein, 1945). That song was for *us*!! In that moment (I would say ethical space), song became a bridge to connect their hearts to ours. Song spoke to us when no words would suffice! We were no longer just singing partners; we were human beings relating to one another on a heart level. The women and girls began to see that the police chorus members were not just saying what they thought we wanted to hear; their actions told us they were standing with us.

I have seen and felt the men's efforts to help the women and girls feel safe and welcome in their presence. While at this point in my research it is just my impression, I believe that the men are becoming aware of the efforts they need to make to support the Indigenous women and girls (i.e., that they are aware of the past and present violence between police and Indigenous peoples and the lack of trust that has resulted). I have witnessed the efforts the men have made to talk to the women and girls and seek an understanding of their histories and identities. I realize that the chorus members have had to take a political stance because of their partnership with us. Leaving the church where they had already paid a year's rent on their space was a political act. It was also political when I asked the chairman of the police chorus if they would sing with us at a residential school for a commemorative event in the fall of 2016. The event was an opening ceremony to remember the traumas experienced by the survivors of the Mohawk Institute Residential School in Brantford, Ontario. It is striking that the police were coming to a residential school by invitation rather than to show their power and authority. Showing up in their uniforms and risking how the Indigenous people might react to their presence was political, yet the police chorus accepted the invitation and the risk that came with it.

Before the decision was made to invite the police chorus and drum circle to perform at the residential school, I felt an ethical obligation to talk with selected Indigenous teachers and Elders to hear how they would feel about a police chorus being present at the site of a residential school. I found support in their words. They recognized that some people would be upset by a police presence, but they also thought it could be the beginning of something new – a new way for us to see each other. I thought about how singing together could be a way of disrupting how Indigenous people and the police know each other. As it turned out, a disruption happened at the sacred fire later in the evening. I was standing by the fire when an older Indigenous woman came walking up to me. She had a stern look on her face. "I did not want those men here," she told me. "When I saw their uniforms, I was going to leave." But then her face softened and she teared up. "But, when I saw you looking at each other while you were singing, I felt hope." This woman hugged me and then left. It was song that had brought the police chorus men and Indigenous drum circle women and girls to the residential school, and it was song that enabled this woman to see something different between the police and Indigenous people.

There was another time that the police chorus took a political stand in support of our drum circle. This one related to the Sisters in Spirit vigil that is held in various cities across Canada every 4 October to commemorate the missing and murdered Indigenous women and girls. Because of systemic racism and violence, Indigenous women are four to six times more likely than other women in our society to die as a result of violence, and their deaths are more likely to be underinvestigated by police services (Native Women's Association of Canada, 2017). In the fall of 2016, I asked the chairman of the police chorus if they would sing with our drum circle for this an annual vigil, recognizing that what I was asking was political and that the police chorus would again be risking public ridicule. I also ventured to ask if there could be a representative from the local police services to speak about what they are doing regarding giving due diligence to the investigations of any missing and murdered Indigenous women and girls in our region. Having been in partnership with the police chorus now for four years, I felt that we were at a place where I could risk asking more of them about justice for Indigenous peoples. The chairman agreed to both of my requests, and we sang together at the vigil. Two deputy chiefs from police services spoke at this event and publicly acknowledged their support of the singing partnership. Importantly, they also conveyed that they were aware of the violent history between police services and Indigenous people and the need to do better. Not all who were present liked the police being present at this vigil, but not all disliked it either. In fact, some people came up to us Indigenous women and asked questions about why the police were singing with us. Asking questions is a great start to dialogue and understanding.

I have noticed that a lot of the conversations among the women and girls in the drum circle have been about their past experiences of mistrusting the police and how, because of their more recent exposure, perhaps they *can* be trusted at times. When I stand back from these conversations, I notice that the police chorus members themselves are going through their own experiences of trust. I believe they must have trusted us at least a little to take some of the risks they did for us. Perhaps they trusted in the greater good that their actions would demonstrate support of the women and girls, or maybe it was trust that the women and girls would stand with them in these tenuous political and public singing partnerships. My research hasn't yet answered this question for me.

Concluding Remarks: Engagement of the Ethical Space Between and Within

The Indigenous women and girls in our drum circle believe that engagement with the police is necessary if we ever hope to understand each other and bring about equitable and respectful policing policies and practices. The current way is not working.

As we engage with each other for the annual Bridging Communities through Song concert, for periodic additional singing events, at our planning meetings, and at our feasts together, we are creating conversations in the space between us. We are asking each other questions and sharing stories and information about ourselves and our histories. Relationships are developing between us as we get to know each other, and meanwhile, within ourselves, we are re-evaluating our previous attitudes toward each other. I believe that this process can do much to create a new critical consciousness, which in turn can lead to social change and, in our case, to changed relations between Indigenous people and the police.

Somewhere along the way, both the women and girls in the drum circle and the men in the police chorus made a conscious decision to do more than just sing together; they would also *engage* with each other. This engagement required a commitment from each one of us. We could have just been singing partners, but as we began to understand each another, a recognition developed that something greater than ourselves could come out of this.

Ethical space requires a commitment to engage. Engagement involves nurturing the relationship in mutual and respectful ways, from the earliest stages to years down the road. This is what is needed for there to be reconciliation between Indigenous and Settler peoples and, in particular, between Indigenous people and the police. I know that there are some who will choose not to learn; who will remain ignorant of the history of Indigenous people in Canada and of the racism and oppression that continue to impact Indigenous people's lives. Perhaps one day they will join with the many Settler people who are already seriously taking action to learn and to build better relationships with Indigenous people. In the meantime, our Indigenous drum circle is moving forward and revelling in the friendships and support we have found in our partnership with the Waterloo Regional Police Chorus, whom we can now call our allies. As I close this chapter, I am reminded of Brydie-Leigh Bartleet's words that song can change the world (2016). I believed this!! Now I know this! Song allowed space for the change that is happening between the police chorus and drum circle. I am also happy to report that conversations have extended beyond the police chorus and are now taking place with the local police services, including the police chief. It all started with song.

CHAPTER 18

The Sacred Canoe
The Search for Truth and Reconciliation through Cultural Partnership

Glenn Marais

My Journey into the North

FIRST NATIONS PEOPLE have a beautiful culture amid a history that is as black as the night on a fly-in reserve, hundreds of miles from what we call civilization. My perspective on this cultural ideology is altered every time I travel up north and realize that what has been deemed savage in the past has more dignity and grace than the civilization that has been imposed and enforced by centuries of colonialism and governmental policies of isolation and discrimination. We ask First Nations people to share their magnificent culture at ceremonies and to sell and gift their art and culture on the global stage as representative of a Canada that is viewed as a multicultural jewel, yet the truth is that the diamond has been encrusted with coal by the dark shadow of history. This is the bitter truth of a history that robbed Indigenous people of generations of paternal love and traditional education through the residential school system, leaving its children in a spiritual and cultural orphanage, raised by parents who had themselves been raised without love. It is a cyclical nightmare of abuse and genocidal action that continued with the sixties scoop and continues today with the missing Indigenous women and high percentage of incarceration among indigenous people. Today's generation of First Nations youth now grow up amid the rampages of their parent's tortured souls whose pain has been manifested in drug abuse, loveless homes, and empty hearts. We ask them to carry on living in this quagmire we have created and offer few lasting or meaningful attempts to help.

First Nations people must contend with boil-water advisories, far from adequate housing, band corruption whereby a nepotistic hierarchy awards the best jobs to a select few, and bleak employment opportunities in isolated communities hundreds of miles from modern conveniences and opportunities. These facts and statistics are usually reported in the back pages if at all, occasionally bursting forth when a tragedy or disaster occurs as in Attawapiskat in 2013, when the Red Cross declared the community to be under a state of emergency. The public response was shock and outrage at the conditions described in this community within Canadian borders. First Nations people are Canadian people who have been denied the basic tenets and rights of citizenship by virtue of their birth heritage and who have to contend with a historical legacy that has subjected these proud people to the cruelty and oppression of a self-righteous colonialist society for far too many years. But the changes never come. The promises remain unfulfilled, treaties continue to be broken, and the stereotypes remain.

Many First Nations students must attend high school in Thunder Bay, away from their families, and are subject to all manner of challenges: racism, and ostracizing and stereotyping by a xenophobic community, in addition to the loneliness and isolation that all lead to a rise in drug abuse, teen pregnancy, and most alarmingly a suicide rate that is becoming a national epidemic. Fear and uncertainty await outside the reserve: they may feel a heightened sense of sanctuary inside the reserve, but perhaps it is the same security that a long-term prisoner would feel. There may be safety in the knowledge of your own existence within comfortable borders, but locked in and without freedom your soul gets weighted down. First Nations youth can only fly so far on Icarus's wings without getting too close to the sun and falling without mercy back to the hollow cage of the reserve. Family, culture, and the land are your home, and it must be hard and almost terrifying to imagine leaving these things behind to try and find a future at a high school in a large city.

The report of the Truth and Reconciliation Commission sets out a mandated declaration of a way forward, a way for Canada to once again walk beside First Nations people akin to the spirit of the Two Row Wampum that decreed a partnership between First Nations and settlers without either interfering in the other's culture. The Sacred Canoe was developed from my work in the Far North and my desire to be a proponent of effective and strategic development through the arts to help facilitate change and growth in our relationships with First Nations people.

Music Is the Pathway

I use music as a conduit to connect with young people on reserves and to help bridge cultures and levels of understanding in our relationships. Music is a deep and important part of First Nations ceremonies that were banned on reserves and in residential schools. It has been a long, slow battle to resurrect this vital component of First Nations tradition. Thankfully it is back, resonating and growing swiftly from Pow Wow to Pow Wow, mother to daughter, father to son, elder to youth, in a resurgence of culture that is literally resurrecting Indigenous people from the ruins of residential schooling and the inherent trauma it inflicted on generation after generation. Indigenous people's deep understanding of and connections to the natural world, to family, and to the balance of life are reflected in their music, which has an ancient sound. Taken to the basic forms of drum and chant, the rhythms of the hand drum and the cadence of the vocals pulsate and swing in harmony like water, air, earth, and fire. The power of the massive Pow Wow drum, surrounded by musicians lost in a trance of rhythm and voice, seems to shake the very earth itself. Above this transcendent beat comes the ancient cry of the Elders, the voice of the universe. A voice that trembles, rises, and falls in a powerful cadence and melodic dissonance that climbs up the back of your spine and through your head and nimbly caresses your soul, reminding you of what it is like to feel pure raw emotion – to feel eminently alive. The sound of the ancients, the cry of an infant, the whisper of the Elder, all reside in the glorious chants that swirl and spin around the drum. The songs that tell stories, that celebrate life and death, wisdom, loved ones come and gone, all reign in a glorious tribulation of life through music. I consider myself fortunate to be able to bear witness to the cultural renaissance that is beginning to spread among First Nations people.

The Concept of the Sacred Canoe

It is in this philosophy perhaps that we can open the door to true healing and a new Canada; that we look at First Nations as our friends and family first and ask ourselves if we would allow this to happen to our own family and not do everything in our power and might to improve their lives and return the light of hope and belief to our First Nations people. Truth and Reconciliation asks us to reach out in many different ways through calls to action. I believe in this principle and have seen the positive effect on the lives of young people in the Far North.

The idea for the Sacred Canoe came from my work in the North and my research during my Masters in Community Music graduate program at Wilfrid Laurier University, where I formulated this conceptual and ideological presentation. The outline was a play or presentation that reflected on the original exploration of Canada by canoe of our First Nations people in partnership with the early settlers and traders and that presented the concept of a new path forward in a spiritual or sacred partnership for returning to the spirit of the Two Road Wampum and of two cultures working in parallel and not interfering with each other's cultural infrastructure and social paradigms. Our First Nations people shared their knowledge of the waterways and their canoe-building techniques and designs with European explorers and traders. The canoe opened all of Canada geographically to exploration, trade, and development. The Sacred Canoe seeks to reopen Canada in the spirit of the Two Row Wampum from the Iroquois culture, whose members believed that two cultures could work side by side without interfering with each other. It was in this spirit that this project was created – it set out to send a message about truth and reconciliation and the path forward by creating projects that would answer one or more of the ninety-four calls to action presented in the Truth and Reconciliation Report. In the original draft of the production, two canoes were going to be set up on stage, running parallel to each other, with a Pow Wow drum between them. One canoe was to represent the historical path, and the other one the Sacred Canoe representing the path forward, and both were going to be used as percussion instruments, with drummers striking the bodies of the canoe in sync with the Pow Wow drum. The staging concept and project development changed and evolved with its natural growth in partners and creativity. The flexibility and patience of everyone involved was inherent to the project's success.

The Path Forward

The path forward was extremely challenging, with many logistical, planning, and staging dilemmas. Having two performances within the parameters of a high school schedule was difficult enough, but staging the production in two different locations on the same day and adding a comprehensive gallery show to it in a municipal performance space raised that challenge to a whole different level.

The more than 150 pieces of art had been created as part of a collaborative partnership with a teacher, Dave Donner, and his students from Webequie's Simon Jacob Memorial School. We requested photos from the community and students at Sacred Heart and each selected one to reproduce, using etching on Plexiglas with ink pressings of the etchings. In addition, students created their own First Nations–style paintings, guided by the teachings of Elder Todd Jamieson. Each picture had to be framed and hung and transported to the gallery; in addition, four large art panels, created by a former art teacher, had to be transported and installed.

Figure 18.1 The Sacred Canoe, Sacred Heart Catholic High School
Art Department, 2017, Acrylic painting on canoe.

One overarching purpose of this entire production was to develop and implement ideas from all partners, never holding a fixed point of reference for any one aspect of it. All ideas were embraced and utilized when possible, and we all kept an open mind to changes in play structure and staging. During my search for donated canoes to be painted, I received a message through Facebook from a friend who had a canoe from the 1960s – a wooden, seventeen-foot canoe that was a family heirloom. When I went to pick it up, my first impression was that it was too big; however, we had committed to using it, and the family were ecstatic at the potential of their canoe to enjoy a "new life." When we brought the canoe to the school, the Head of Art, Dawn Ellis-Mobbs, was astonished at the size of it, and we decided we should return it. Here is when the alchemy began. The students saw nothing but potential in the epic size of the canoe and its fantastic capacity to become a piece of art. Thoroughly persuaded by their passion and determination, we moved it inside. In looking back at that critical moment, I realize that being open to possibility and respecting student voices was vital to the project. The donated canoe they had enthusiastically and resolutely endorsed became the centrepiece of the project and came to symbolize the potential of what we were trying to achieve. The canoe became a shining icon and a personified ideal of what Truth and Reconciliation could look like. The finished canoe required two stands – a vertical one for the high school performance and a horizontal one for the gallery – and each was custom-designed and created by local artisans.

There were many moments during the development of the Sacred Canoe that I would stop in and look at the painting of it for motivation and inspiration. Elder Todd Jamieson, who worked hand-in-hand with the art students, smudged the canoe at every visit and at the beginning of each show, and by the time it reached the gallery, all of us were sure it had attained a spirituality of its own and the power to inspire and heal.

Leading Authentic Voices

Mohawk Educator Suzie Miller

In my research, I learned about the wampum belt and how it was used in negotiating treaties and trade agreements between the Haudenosaunee people and early settlers. Through a mutual acquaintance, I was able to contact Suzie Miller, a Mohawk woman, and educator from the Grand Erie district. I planned for her to come and speak to the students and staff at Sacred Heart about her personal journey, the history of her people, the Haudenosaunee, and the historical significance of the Wampum belt. She taught us that the belts were like history books: in the oral tradition of First Nations peoples, stories weren't written down. The reference to the Haudenosaunee as the original First Nations came from the story of the Peacemaker, who rode in a stone canoe and travelled the great rivers, where he met Hiawatha and gave the message of peace to be carried to the people. This was the origin of the five-nation confederacy created among the Mohawk, Onondaga, Cayuga, Oneida, and Seneca Nations. This grew into the Six Nations Confederacy when they welcomed in the Tuscarora Nation from Virginia. She shared her knowledge of the Iroquois Confederacy and its system of governance, which was matriarchal and accorded the women in the nation with the highest respect. The women selected the chiefs, sat in advisory positions during council debates, and determined when the hunt would take place. The Wampum belts all had different meanings and were used to commemorate and record agreements. She shared examples of the silver covenant chain and how it connects two people together; the dish with one spoon, which is an agreement between tribes to always share the bounty of harvest; and the perpetual tree, which shows the growth and continuation of life from generation to generation.

There is another Wampum belt, named the Two Row Wampum, that documents the original agreement between the first settlers and the Haudenosaunee. It was in this spirit of partnership and equality that Canada's trade agreements and treaties with First Nations people were formed. Wampum belts were woven to recognize each agreement and treaty, using quahog shells of purple and white. The two purple rows signified the ship and all the ways of first the Dutch, then the French, and finally the English. The other purple row represents the canoe and all the ways of the Haudenosaunee. The message of the belt was to travel down the river of life as brothers and sisters, with respect and without interference.

This played an important part in the Sacred Canoe, as early exploration and trade were conducted in the spirit of partnership, with Europeans relying on First Nations' knowledge of the waterways and canoe-building technology to expand their trade. In exchange, the settlers offered goods brought over to Canada. This was the beginning of a long and prosperous time in Canada's pre-Confederation growth.

Suzie's personal story was deeply compelling. She spoke of being unaware of her heritage due to her grandmother being ashamed to reveal their identity and passing that shame on to her mother who passed it on to her. She felt lost and uncertain of who she was until her mother revealed that she was a First Nations woman, and a member of the Six Nations Confederacy, the Haudenosaunee people. Her grandfather went to a residential school, the Mohawk Institute in Brantford, in 1833, and she understood why they wouldn't want to acknowledge their heritage, based on her knowledge of the schools and the treatment given to First Nations people in the past. She has dedicated her life to educating First Nations people on their heritage and culture, and it has given her a sense of place and peace with herself and a deep, resilient pride in her culture.

Ojibwa Drummer and Cultural Educator, Jacob Charles

Jacob Charles is a gentle giant. He stands 6'8" tall and is a friendly, charismatic educator of First Nations music and culture. He is an Ojibwa man on a mission to heal and educate through knowledge of cultural practices, music, and the example of his life. He built a traditional lodge on land he owns on Georgina Island after receiving a vision in which he stood before a lodge with hundreds of birds in the sky above it. He believes that the vision was calling to him to build this lodge for his people. He runs a cultural centre that offers tours on the island, sharing his people's culture and love of music; he also tends a farm, where he teaches youth how to farm and raise livestock. He plans to raise buffalo on his land one day. He brings educators and Elders to the island, at his own expense, to teach his people about natural healing and herbology, and he works very hard at inspiring and educating people from all different cultures. Like David Bouchard and Suzie Miller, Jacob's grasp of his culture's importance and of his true calling came late in his life. He had a troubled youth, getting into drugs and alcohol abuse, finally seeking and receiving healing at a native treatment centre, where traditional ceremonies and music were practised. Ceremonies weren't welcome on the reserve of Georgina Island, and it has taken a lot of effort to bring them back and convince others of their importance in this community and in others across Canada.

Jacob's sessions with the students were very informative, engaging, and honest. He shared the painful aspects of his history, including not being allowed to speak their language and not being able to leave the reserve in groups of more than three, for any more than that was considered a war party. He told us how bannock, which has become a native staple, was actually a ration, from the days when hunting wasn't allowed on reserve. He also shared the beauty and spirituality of his culture, speaking about his connection to the land and cultural practices that ultimately saved his life. When Jacob drums and teaches, he practises smudging, and he brought samples of each herb, explaining their significance: sage for purification, sweetgrass representing kindness, spruce for healing. But the most sacred herb is tobacco, which is given as a gift in ceremony, and as a blessing, and is considered an honourable gift.

His native name is Hummingbird. He is from the wolf clan, and music resonates and flows from his very being. He plays and sings with his eyes shut, and as he does, he seems to be transported into another state of being. He shared with us how drumming is ceremony and that normally he would smudge first to cleanse himself and the room in which he was playing to centre himself and allow reflection on his life, parents, children, history, and journey. Through his shared knowledge, we understood that drumming was not just making music, it was connecting to ancient traditions. Music was a musical medicine that allowed us to reflect on our lives and to share and heal our past. "Drums are alive to me," he told us, "they are like my children."

It was a powerful and moving workshop, and the result was that more and more classes wanted him to present, so we added another day and a half for him to come in and work with the students and staff. The impact of Jacob's workshop was tremendous and wonderful to see. The students were deeply engaged in his words and music and when drumming with him, intent on what they were doing while very respectful of his music and leadership. Like Suzie Miller, Jacob shared the importance of women in Ojibwa culture. In that

Figure 18.2 Students Creating Indigenous Art as informed by Todd Jamieson, from Oneida of the Thames

culture too, they chose the chief and decided when to go hunting. As he put it, "They feel the heartbeat of the community."

Elder Todd Jamieson

Todd Jamieson, a visual artist and an Elder from the Oneida Nation of the Thames, came to the project through the recommendation of the York Catholic School Board. Todd had a significant impact on this project through several workshop sessions in the visual arts, music, and English classes. Those sessions inspired the creation of Birth Animal Totems, and he also helped guide students through the process of creating watercolour landscapes. If you look closely at the canoe you will see a turtle representing Turtle Island, as well as Trees of Peace and Mother Earth holding humanity in her arms. The canoe's concept and design were inspired by several conversations during which the design team sat in a circle around the canoe and shared ideas. This included many discussions about how the canoe could inspire or open dialogue about Truth and Reconciliation.

Todd opened each performance with an inspiring talk about the project's significance; he also shared a blessing, and smudged each First Nations performer and the production stage and space. He later told us that he smudged

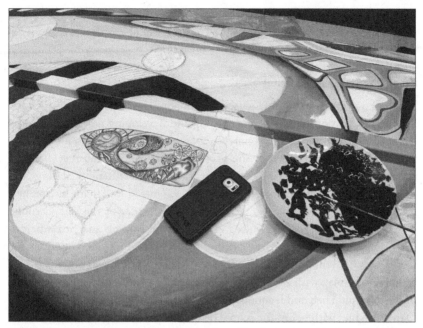

Figure 18.3 The Canoe was a collaborative art piece with a design created by art teacher, Julie Colucci and students from her classes.

the canoe every day when he came in. We feel strongly that Todd's work with the canoe, and his traditional teachings and ceremonial blessings, have inspired the amazing artwork on the canoe and given it a spiritual presence.

Student Voice

One of the most important aspects of the Sacred Canoe was ensuring that the students' voices would resonate throughout the production and the gallery show. The project's authenticity was guided by the cross-cultural learning and exchanges between the students and our First Nations facilitators. We began with a seminar overview of First Nations Culture, and onto these we layered workshops from our First Nations partners, prior to the creation of art, spoken word, and songs. It was fascinating to see and hear the level of understanding of and immersion in the historical components of our cultural study, as well as the depth of feeling that students developed over the course of the project. In their interactions with our guests, their questions were thoughtful and their manner was engaging. Perhaps the most significant outcome was the passion many students developed for the project and their strong concern for the history of First Nations people. The students were deeply concerned that our history was inaccurate, and they soon began emotionally connected to the struggles and challenges of growing up as First Nations people. Their belief in their individual contributions and in the project overall was resolute, and their passion came through in their work.

Consultation before Consent

Much of our initial planning focused on developing relationships with established First Nations partners and forging and developing new relationships based on personal and professional recommendations. Our search for partners was strategic only in terms of the project's clear needs. I had met our first contact, Jacob Charles, years before in a workshop, and remembered his gentle manner and passion for culture. Suzie Miller was introduced to me by Stephen Rensink, a flute maker. Todd Jamieson was recommended by the York Catholic District School Board. I consulted extensively with Jacob and Suzie before beginning the project regarding cultural protocols and recommendations for workshops with the students; we also reviewed our pre-project notes and narration for the play, with editing provided by Suzie when it came to knowledge of the Wampum belt and Iroquois culture. Todd Jamieson spoke at length with Dawn and met with her at the school before the project began; he also visited the school several times to consult on and guide the student art projects. The consultation prior to consent was valuable, for it helped us develop strong partnerships that reflected great respect to First Nations cultural practices and beliefs. Our relationships influenced and inspired our students to learn about First Nations culture. All of this created a mutual and synergistic learning framework throughout the project. We were greatly inspired by the our students, who offered thoughtful discourse and asked many good questions about the workshop facilitator's cultural history and present ideology. All of us fully embraced our model of equal partnership in answering the report's calls to action. The Canoe was symbolic of that partnership in that Todd's teachings guided the student's interpretation of Native art and of Canada's national story. This knowledge-sharing came full circle when they created a painting that told the story of creation utilizing the four elements. Fire, represented by the sun, was depicted at the very top of the canoe.

The Wampum belt curls around the circular objects that represent human spirits embraced by the arms of nature. It really is a spectacular creation. It was inspired by the authentic voice of Elder Todd Jamieson, the inspirational music and teachings of Jacob Charles and historical knowledge of the Haudenosaunee People and the Wampum belt as shared by Suzie Miller.

The Heart, Body, and Mind of the Sacred Canoe

The Sacred Canoe, like our history, reflects the many people who have come together to form its shell and give it strength. Each participant in this production can be considered part of the ribbing that gives the canoe its inner strength. Without their participation and their willingness to share their innermost thoughts and feelings, the production would not have developed with such deep emotions and connections to our history. In opening ourselves to our feelings about our history and our cultural past, the project allowed us to go deeper into our artistic experiences and to create beyond what we thought we were capable of. The canoe itself was a revelation; for all of us, it represented everything about the production and the history of First Nations People. It offered us a coming together in spirit with open hearts and minds working toward a common purpose. We were able to send our message to Canada and the world, that we can work together in an equal and respectful way.

Conclusion

Community music takes a broad view of creativity, one that can border on chaos. It allows a high level of innovation within the conventional boundaries of contemporary music and art, and at its best it kicks down the doors of convention by defying limitations. The driving force of community music is found within the name itself. It is created and developed within *communities*, and it creates new horizons within those borders, which is where its beauty and power reside and flourish, uninhibited by convention and traditional form.

Community music has been defined as boundary walking. I believe it is that and more. As community musicians we walk on boundaries, through them, around them, and within them, because our all-encompassing vision has no walls. We can merge all of the arts and create partnerships among artists, disciplines, presenters, community organizations, schools, corporations, and municipalities, to build an entirely new architecture whose purpose is defined only by the limits of the partnership's vision. It often takes on a life of its own and becomes something much different from and greater than the original vision. So it was with our project, which resembled a shapeshifter, that is, an organism growing and developing through constant flux. What started as a vision of creating a message of hope and a spiritual journey in a partnership with First Nations has become much more than originally imagined. The storylines have changed; stage plots, vision, and direction and content have all grown and shifted inside of the boundaries; but perhaps more than that is the collective spirit that has grown and enriched every facet of this production. On every level, there was a sense of pride, and of purpose, and there were moments of great elation as the project started to take on a beautiful, resilient artistic form. Herein lies the challenge for a community musician. You must maintain an incredibly broad vision to account for all your partners' goals, hopes, and aspirations, and you must maintain the relationships and investment in your project through these crucial relationships, which are continually growing and changing. Trouble can arise if you focus too intently on the targeted outcome and not enough on the core engine of your community project, the relationships. Without proper acknowledgment and homage to these established and developed relationships, art inevitably suffers. If perfection of the project's vision becomes too strong a focal point, the vision's scope will diminish, resulting in a loss of connection among the participants. An essential lesson we have learned through this project is relationships first, project details second, and in that realization, evident displays of gratitude are of the utmost importance, particularly because for me and my co-producer, Dawn Ellis-Mobbs, many of the relationships were newly formed within the pressure chamber of the project.

This project has been the culmination of a lifetime of work with First Nations Youth and communities. I started in Georgina, working with students in the First Nations language program. Through my work with the charity organization DARE Arts, I have travelled ten times to Webequie First Nations, twice to Marten Falls, and once to Attawapiskat. This journey has been one of uncovering cultural truths as well as knowledge of our nation's history. It is about growing as an artist and as a person through my work with isolated communities that have been greatly affected by residential school trauma and centuries of colonial oppression. Our history, quite simply, has it wrong. We have not heard the truth of our past, and it has left Canada with a poor foundation. Ultimately the strength of our nation and its continued status as a beacon of multiculturalism will depend on our acknowledgment of the past and our understanding of what truth and reconciliation are and how together these can work to heal the wounds of the past so that we as a united nation can move forward in strength and unity with our First Nations community. The Sacred Canoe may be an important vessel on this journey forward.

PART IV

COMMUNITY MUSIC

Walking the Boundaries of Health and Wellness

COMMUNITY MUSIC AND MUSIC THERAPY have found common ground in the foundational principle that participatory music-making can be therapeutic and provide pathways for living fully and wholly, even for those who are dealing with various types of suffering. Ahonen explores music's power to heal in post-traumatic settings. Elizabeth Mitchell describes her work in a camp where university students provide opportunities for children with disabilities to make music together. Foster describes her work in music care for the aging at a foundation that provides caregivers with musical resources. Pearson outlines pedagogical resources for training caregivers, and Judelson offers a case study of how people with dementia, their partner caregivers, and high-school-age volunteers find community and health through singing.

CHAPTER 19

Processing Refugee Journey and Promoting Self-Healing with Music and Art

Heidi Ahonen

Year 2016. For several years ISIS has attacked and controlled numerous cities in the Middle East. The world of hundreds of thousands of individuals has been shattered yet life still goes on in the refugee camps and temporary shelters ... Women cook, clean, take care of their children. Babies are born. Despite the trauma and loss, hoping for a better future helps keep people going. Somewhere in the Middle East, close to one of the big refugee camps, a group of Iraqi women are sitting in a circle. Each holds a copy of a map of the Middle East, coloured markers, and stickers. They are encouraged to draw their refugee route from their home city in Iraq to the refugee camp in a chronological order, and to write down the date they started their journey and the date they arrived in the camp. They are also encouraged to reminisce on details such as how they travelled, with whom, what they brought with them, where they first stayed when they arrived, and where after that. The activity ends with them writing down their future plans and hopes, what they want to do and where they want to move. In the end there is sharing and some musical improvisation. Their emotions are expressed. The meaning of trauma is explored. Revelations and new insight are gained. The details of events are being validated and witnessed.

Refugee Trauma Experience

The term trauma is derived from the Greek word for injury or wound. It was first used by neurologists and medical doctors to describe severe neurological or bodily injuries; later on, psychiatrists posited that extremely stressful events could also be viewed as traumatic. Perhaps, in this context, we could say that a trauma is a wound of the soul caused by horrific experiences. If so, it is natural that a traumatized person would try hard to avoid any reminders of those experiences and to suppress the feelings related to them. This is analogous to

someone who has had a physical injury and avoids further pain by not moving
or touching the injured part of the body.

Trauma has three elements: devastating physical and/or emotional pain,
a horrific experience of total helplessness, and a lack of empathy (Winnicott,
1986; Sanford, 1990; Harwood & Pines, 1998). After a traumatic event, suddenly we are no longer in control of what is happening around us. The world
as we know it is no longer safe and secure and we can no longer make sense of
it. Life once had meaning; suddenly it does not. Life is no longer fair and just
(Janoff-Bulman, 1992). In the midst of a trauma we feel disbelief, bewilder-
ment, and a paralyzing helplessness: "Why me? How can something like this
happen to me?" Although people from different cultures may have different
priorities, we all value justice and seek a secure, fair, and rational life. Chaos
and violence usually happen outside of our expectations. When they strike,
they throw us into a state of shock, confusion, and powerlessness. The world
we know has collapsed.

According to Van der Veer (1998, 4–5, 8–9) many refugees experience
both traumatization and uprooting, or *triple traumatization*. Before being forced
to flee their home country, many were subjected to extended traumatization or
to several different traumatizing events. They also experienced trauma during
their escape, for example a dangerous and unpredictable journey. At the refugee
camps they may experience harsh living conditions, lack of control, loss of social
status, and discrimination. Finally, in the new country, in an unfamiliar location,
they may be retraumatized by language and cultural differences, marginalization, ongoing distrust, and helplessness. Typically, refugee experiences can have
a traumatic impact regardless of whether the person was directly affected or
whether they only witnessed something horrible happening to someone else.
Many refugees have "missing" relatives who were arrested and have possibly
been killed. Furthermore, the refugees have to come face to face with a breach
of humanity – it was other human beings who intentionally caused their suffering. In many cases, the crimes against refugees are justified by those same
authorities who in normal circumstances would have protected them (i.e.,
police, army, or clergy). Refugee children often suffer pedagogical neglect with
schooling and education, as well as attachment issues because of the trauma
their parents experienced (Van der Veer, 1998; Mollica, 2006 a and b, 2011;
Schauer, Neuner & Elbert, 2011; Wilson & Drozdek, 2004).

According to Mollica (2006), terrorism, mass violence, and torture are not
random acts of brutality. They are deliberate acts whose intent is to exterminate
entire societies or drastically transform an entire culture. Humiliation and cultural annihilation are often the very goals and instruments of the perpetrators
(thus, rape and sexual violence have always been the principal methods for

torturing women and carrying out ethnic cleansing). Humiliation is closely linked to how people think the world sees them. "Humiliation takes away a person's power. Its goal is to turn you into a powerless person who cannot perform, who cannot work or take care of his family and friends" (Mollica, 2006, p. 8). Many refugees have experienced cultural erasure – that is, the destruction of historical statues, manuscripts, and legal documents, as if the person and their culture never existed (Mollica, 2006; Van der Veer, 1998).

Refugee Trauma Symptoms

Though their experiences are much the same, not all refugees suffer trauma. Factors affecting how refugees react to traumatic events include age as well as the empathy they encounter. There are also differences in vulnerability. For example, a past trauma makes us more vulnerable to a future trauma. Another factor is the level of violence (i.e., torture) and how responsible or guilty we feel for these events. Other factors are the amount of time refugees have to prepare for flight. Typically, refugees who have "missing" relatives face a more difficult trauma recovery process (Van der Veer, 1998).

Refugee trauma can have many consequences. By the time they arrive in a new country, most refugees suffer from post-traumatic stress disorder (PTSD), rather than acute stress disorder (ASD). Many refugees suffer major depression, sometimes for several years after arriving a new country, where they may suddenly start feeling terrible pain (Van der Veer, 1998).

PTSD symptoms are many. Among them are *avoidance symptoms*. When we have a physical injury, we naturally avoid aggravating it further. Similarly, after a psychologically traumatic event, we may try to avoid any reminders of that event. We may not want to talk about or think about the trauma. We may avoid people or places that remind us of the event. Sometimes the avoidance runs so deep that we cannot even remember details or important aspects of the event. We may also feel emotionally numb. *Hyper-arousal symptoms* include insomnia, anxiety, irritability and jumpiness, anger outbursts, and poor concentration. We may act guarded with excessive watchfulness – that is, always scanning our environment for threats. Related to this, we may find ourselves easily startled by noises or unexpected changes in our environment. Refugees often feel a continuous mortal fear. *Negative alterations in cognition and mood* mean the refugees may find it hard to recall key features of the traumatic event. They may also harbour profoundly negative beliefs and expectations about themselves or the world. They often experience emotional distress. They may have lost interest in activities they used to enjoy prior to the traumatic event (i.e. cooking, gardening, dancing, singing, playing an instrument, hobbies, etc.). They may have no interest in planning for the future and may feel isolated from others. They often find it hard to experience positive emotions like love and affection. Many refugees feel guilty, blaming themselves for causing the traumatic event or for not being able to help the loved ones they left behind. Some may have been tortured into giving up information. Others feel guilty simply for having survived when others did not. According to Van der Veer (1998), self-blame is sometimes a defence, that is, an attempt to restore a sense of control over the trauma that took place. It protects against overwhelming helplessness or rage by maintaining the illusion that the repetition of traumatic events can be prevented. *Intrusion or re-experiencing symptoms* refer to refugees having upsetting thoughts, images or memories, nightmares, flashbacks, and strong responses to reminders of the traumatic event (American Psychiatric Association, 2013).

According to research, in 80 percent of PTSD cases, one or more other psychiatric disorders are diagnosed as well (Schauer, Neuner, & Elbert, 2011, 15), such as depression, anxiety, and panic disorders. PTSD increases smoking, drug and alcohol abuse, family violence, and various physical illnesses (e.g., heart disease, stroke, diabetes). Trauma also impacts hormones (cortisol, stress hormones), the immune system, and bodily functions (i.e. increased heart rate, blood pressure, muscle tone, metabolism, and digestion) (Mollica, 2006, 2011).

Refugee children often experience problems in school due to PTSD, anxiety, and depression. They may have difficulty concentrating and focusing. Also common in children with PTSD are an inability to remember and to act spontaneously, both arising from their need to suppress reminders of their trauma. Emotional detachment is typical. They may have fantasies of rescue or of being a hero, or outbursts of aggression. They may avoid conflict, have a fascination with danger, and exhibit psychosomatic complaints: headaches, stomachaches, and death anxiety. Social and behavioural problems include poor impulse control, withdrawal from play or social activities, restlessness, and clinging behaviour. Typical adolescent trauma reactions include acting out, the resort to self-destructive behaviours to avoid sadness, premature adult behaviour and self-sufficiency, identity confusion, and feeling of guilt, shame, and pessimism. According to Van der Veer (1998), refugees who suffered a traumatic loss during adolescence feel that they lack control over their fate. Feelings of being deceived are also typical.

Why Refugees May Not Seek Help for Their Trauma Symptoms

Finding truth as well as regaining one's dignity are both important to healing (Mollica, 2006). According to Herman (1992), trauma survivors often tell their stories in a highly emotional, contradictory, and fragmented manner. Unfortunately, this undermines their credibility. Furthermore, trauma survivors cannot begin their recovery before the truth has been acknowledged. According to Van der Veer (1998) and Mollica (2006), many refugees never share their trauma experiences, nor do they seek help for their trauma symptoms. This may be because they do not know how, or there may be a language barrier or lack of trust in the therapists or translators available. Many refugees also feel too humiliated to speak about what happened. Deep inside, many victims want to scream and shout to the world about the horrible things that happened to them, but speechlessness is the typical, paralyzing emotion they feel instead.

All people know that violence is profoundly injurious and socially humiliating, but their responses to it differ from culture to culture. Trauma stories provide unique insights, both good and bad, within the narrator's cultural framework (Mollica, 2006). Many refugees feel it is inappropriate to express their emotions, so they only seek help for their somatic issues. They may deny their trauma symptoms for fear of being stigmatized as mentally ill within their community. Some may think that all mental illness is caused by evil spirits. In many cultures, mental illness is simply unknown and their language may lack the concepts to describe its symptoms (Van der Veer, 1998, 8). Interestingly, in some cultures, the victims may blame themselves for their trauma. For example, mental illness may be thought to be the consequence of karma, an experience of retribution for bad actions in a prior life, in which case the person feels responsible for his or her suffering (Mollica, 2006). In those cases, even a victim of torture may feel it is their own responsibility. Moreover, many torture victims feel deeply humiliated and shamed because they had been unable to rescue themselves.

It is crucial that we understand the meaning that trauma victims give to their experiences. For example, in some societies rape survivors are offered compassion while in others they are blamed and punished. Victims of sexual violence may feel a tremendous, silencing shame and decide to keep the whole episode a secret (Mollica, 2006, 21). In some cultures, it is inappropriate to talk about personal matters with outsiders. Furthermore, some refugees cannot share their trauma experiences with people of their own culture because they are afraid of generating gossip. Sometimes trust among refugees from the same country is strained because of the characteristics of different sub-groups as well as political differences. Naturally, mistrust is a major emotional experience among refugees. According to some studies (i.e., Schauer, Neuner, & Elbert, 2011; Van der Veer, 1998), if refugee who were unable to say goodbye to their friends before their flight may now be deeply reserved when it comes to establishing new contacts.

Notwithstanding the many cultural differences in understanding and dealing with trauma, there are also similarities. Broken hearts, wounded souls, and broken minds are part of being human. There are studies of PTSD from all continents (Schauer, Neuner, & Elbert, 2011, 19). According to Mollica (2006) traumatized refugees do not find it hard to accept that there may be a relationship between their symptoms and their trauma experiences.

Trauma Memory

The brain stores different types of memory in various regions of the brain, and normally we can recall any memory whenever we want. But this is not always the case with traumatic memories, which are stored differently and may be severely fragmented. Trauma memory is stored not as factual memory but as *emotional* memory or as a sensation, which explains why trauma survivors cannot always control the what, where, and when of traumatic memories – those memories surface too sporadically.

There are two types of memory that store our personal events. *Declarative* memory (also called *explicit autobiographical, chronological,* or *cool* memory) stores facts such as knowledge of the world, history, locations, and significant life events (i.e., one's wedding day). These memories can be purposefully retrieved. *Non-declarative* memory (also called *implicit, emotional, sensational,* or *hot* memory) stores skills, habits, emotional associations, and automatic or conditioned responses that do not require conscious recollection. Interestingly, a single event can be stored as two different types of memory. For example, even though I still remember the time when I was taking flute lessons, currently, in order to play the flute, I do not have to consciously remind myself about each and every step such as fingering. Because playing the flute is coded as a non-declarative memory in my brain, playing has become a skill that I can simply activate without any purposeful recall. Trauma memories can also be stored as two types of memories. The declarative memory system stores some details of the traumatic event as facts (i.e., date, time, place, people involved), but the intense emotions associated with the event are stored as sensations (non-declarative, fragmented, hot, emotional memories). This means that similar sensations that someone experienced during the original trauma event can trigger these emotional trauma memories. Any external cue such as a smell or a sound can trigger those memories, and the trauma survivor may not have conscious control over his or her reactions (Schauer, Neuner, & Elbert, 2011; Mollica, 2006).

There are also episodic and semantic memories. *Episodic* memories are stored as episodes that took place in particular places and times. They contain information about what, where, and when. Episodic memory allows us to recollect and to consciously re-experience previous events and to activate our sensory-perceptual experiences. *Semantic* memory is simply our knowledge base and is not necessarily related to experience. Memories of traumatic events are also twofold. A person may have very intense recollections of the event, including many sensory details (e.g., the smell of blood, loud sounds, pictures of soldiers in uniforms, the kinaesthetic sensation of feeling cold, etc.). At the same time, if asked to discuss their experiences, they may find it impossible to verbalize the details consistently and in chronological order. This is why victims of trauma may plainly be out of touch with their here-and-now and their feelings. The traumatic experience often feels timeless, without beginning or end. When trying to report their experiences to outsiders (e.g., immigrant officials), the lack of consistency and structure may make it sound as if the victims are lying, or are hiding certain events (Schauer, Neuner, & Elbert, 2011, 22).

Schauer, Neuner, and Elbert (2011) introduce the importance of *autobiographical* memories. Those are the ones that are retrieved immediately after a person retrieves a memory about their past (they can also be called *cold* memory or *verbally accessible* memory). Refugees who suffer PTSD have a substantial distortion in their autobiographical memory (chronological order of life events, general events, beginnings/endings). Furthermore, the traumatic event is not clearly represented as a general event, nor is it positioned in a particular period in one's life. Their memories and the sensory-perceptual representations of traumatic events are extremely strong, but there is no autobiographical structure to which the memory can belong. This may be one reason why refugees are often unable to narrate their traumatic experiences. Trauma memory is fragmented, and this disturbs the *cortical inhibitory control* of the fear response, with the result that the trauma victim cannot differentiate between past and present threats. Physically and mentally, the victim feels as if the trauma event is still going on. Interestingly, the person may see, feel, or hear the various sensory elements of their traumatic experience but be unable to speak about it. Not sharing the trauma memories is a poor solution, for it only leads to social isolation, numbness, flashbacks, and nightmares (Schauer, Neuner, & Elbert, 2011, 22–25, 31).

PTSD is essentially a problem with memories. Although memories themselves are not dangerous, they may sometimes *feel* dangerous. Allowing the feared memories to be triggered during a psychotherapeutic process with a therapist also allows the patient to experience and integrate the fact that "I am safe even though I may not feel safe." It is sometimes a challenge to reconstruct the trauma as well as autobiographical knowledge about the traumatizing event because these are connected to our basic beliefs about ourselves and the world. Anger, shame, and guilt are difficult to process, so it is natural to avoid them. Typically, because even thinking about the traumatic event causes painful emotions, many people naturally want to avoid this process and try to remove intrusive memories as soon as possible (Schauer, Neuner, & Elbert, 2011; Mollica, 2006.)

Flashbacks, Nightmares, and Triggers

Flashbacks in PTSD mean that a person involuntarily relives and experiences the traumatic event. Something in the environment (e.g., a certain smell, visual, sound, or sensation) triggers the traumatic memory that has been stored as a sensation. Because trauma memories are stored as emotional memory and as sensations, anything can trigger them and disturb our peace. When confronted with trauma reminders, our body goes into the same emergency response mode it went into during the original trauma (i.e., freeze, flight, fight, fright, flag, or faint). As a result of this we feel the same feelings that we experienced during the original event (e.g., fear, helplessness, horror). We also have same physical symptoms that we experienced then (i.e., flood of endorphins or adrenaline, increased heart rate and blood pressure, shallow and rapid breathing, tensed muscles, increased visual and auditory acuity, sweating, trembling, and hot or cold flashes). Because our body and brain both process danger similarly to the ways they did during the original, dangerous situation, it feels as if we are reliving and re-experiencing the same traumatic event again. A sensation in our environment triggered the trauma memory that had been stored in our brain as a sensation, and as a result, the entire body and mind are now alerted. How we reacted during the original trauma is the way we will react during the flashback. In a way, a flashback makes us feel we are in danger even though we are perfectly safe. The body and mind has been turned on like a light switch. Flashbacks are experienced in different ways. Some traumatized refugees recognize that flashbacks are just memories and feel safe in the here and now, in the new country. But with many refugees, their trauma memories dominate their life, and they see danger everywhere. As a result, they have difficulty concentrating on studying, working, or daily life. Interestingly, when we try constantly to avoid and suppress our unwanted thoughts and memories, they soon return even stronger than before (Schauer, Neuner, & Elbert, 2011; Mollica, 2006).

Nightmares are like delayed flashbacks and can be triggered by sensory perception, either while the person is asleep (dreaming) or during the previous day. For example, a nightmare can combine elements from a movie, TV news, and a person's own trauma experiences. Refugees often have traumatic nightmares that wake them up in a panic. Often the same dream repeats, reprocessing the trauma story (Mollica, 2006). In therapy I use different guided imagery techniques supporting the person to master their nightmares or tack on positive endings to them. I ask them to write down, draw, or improvise (make music of) their nightmare, and change the content – for example, by adding healing elements, rescue, heroes, whatever may be needed. I also encourage them to reflect on their nightmares, to find the meaning or message of their dreams.

PTSD and Brain Changes

The human body and brain are always ready to respond to any threat to survival. During a stressful situation, the brain releases stress hormones, such as adrenaline and cortisol, which trigger the body to flee from danger. Some traumatic events are so disturbing that the stress response never shuts off – the amygdala, the fear-response and emotion-processing centre in the limbic system, keeps on replaying the emotional memories like a broken record. With people who have PTSD, the amygdala is overresponsive and overloaded. Its size has actually increased, and it cannot properly regulate the fears, nor can it process the emotions any longer (Karlsson, 2011; Kolassa & Elbert, 2007; Gilbertson et al., 2002; Yehuda, 2001; Pitman, 2001; Gurvits et al., 1996; Bremner et al., 1995; Bremner, 2001; Sapolsky, Uno, Rebert, & Finch, 1990). By activating the body's adrenaline faster than the blink of an eye, the amygdala can also activate the emergency response so that we either freeze, flee, fight, fright, flag, or faint. This, when a traumatized refugee sees a soldier in a uniform or hears a loud noise, her automatic emergency response may activate. With PTSD, the amygdala does not wait around for the cortex and conscious mind to wonder whether a threat is real – it simply reacts (Schauer, Neuner, & Elbert, 2011.)

Too high a level of stress hormones in our body can cause numerous issues. One problem is that the anterior cingulate cortex, which is involved in rational decision-making, will decrease in size. This is why people with PTSD often have problems concentrating and focusing. Very high doses of stress hormones may also cause a decrease in size of the hippocampus, a part of the midbrain that stores our memories. This explains why PTSD victims suffer memory loss, have difficulty recalling certain parts of their traumatic event, or have vivid memories that are always present (e.g., Kolassa & Elbert, 2007; Gilbertson et al., 2002; Bremner, 2001; Yehuda, 2001; Pitman, 2001; Gurvits et al., 1996; Bremner et al., 1995; Sapolsky, Uno, Rebert, & Finch, 1990). It is encouraging that therapeutic interventions can shrink the hippocampus and the amygdala back to normal size. For example, Karlsson's (2011) study found that any change in our psychological processes also changes the functions or structures of the brain. PET and fMRI scans indicate that even our very subjective experiences affect the brain. Knowing that psychotherapy changes the brain, how much more can we do using music as a tool for psychotherapy?

Neurological Rationale for Using Music as a Tool for Telling Trauma-Stories

Oliver Sacks (1973, 2007) contended that music happens everywhere in our brain and that as a multisensory stimulus it can simultaneously stimulate many of the brain's sensory receptors. When my refugee group participants listen to or play music, their brain responses involve various regions outside the auditory cortex, including those commonly associated with other activities such as physical activity and thinking (Frühholz, Trost, & Grandjean, 2014). Music also activates the left and right hemispheres of the brain simultaneously (Peretz & Coltheart, 2003; Peretz & Zatorre, 2005; Liégeois-Chauvel, Peretz, Babaï, Laguitton, & Liégeois-Chauvel, 1998). Memories and emotions stored in the limbic system – the site that tags events as important and that "colours" them with emotions – can be triggered by listening to or improvising music (Jäncke, 2008; Koelsch, Fritz, Cramon, Müller, & Koelsch, 2010; Brown, 2004; Juslin & Västfjäll, 2008). According to Frühholz, Trost, and Grandjean (2014), it is the amygdala specifically that is involved in the initial decoding of music's emotional value, while the hippocampus processes more complex vocal and musical emotions, providing memory-based and contextual associations. Clearly, then, music can be a very useful tool when working with traumatized refugees. Because trauma memories are stored as sensations, similar sensations can trigger those memories. A good rationale for using music in trauma psychotherapy is that body memories include the nervous system, which communicates the somatic trauma memories between the brain and all other parts of the body. It is possible to experience an implicit (body) memory of trauma without the explicit (cognitive) memory that is often needed to make sense of it (Rothschild, 2000). Music can access implicit memories more easily than words.

There is also the thalamus, which regulates the hormones through the hypothalamus, in the limbic system. Which hormonal effect is attached to music has direct implications for the music therapy interventions I choose to use with therapeutic refugee groups. According to Chand and Levitin's (2013) review of music-as-medicine studies, music has documented effects on brain chemistry as well as health benefits in four areas: mood management, stress reduction, strengthened immunity, and social bonding.

As I noted earlier, people suffering with PTSD live with elevated amounts of the stress hormone cortisol, and this can cause measurable changes in their brain structures (i.e., the size of the amygdala and hippocampus). The fact that music decreases the amount of cortisol in one's body is an excellent reason for using it as a therapeutic tool with PTSD patients. Dozens of studies have concluded that cortisol levels drop after people listen to relaxing music (e.g., Möckel et al., 1995; Kuhn, 2002; Schwartz, 1997; Wiesenthal & Hennessy, 2000; Miluk-Kolasa et al.,1994; Fukui & Yamashita, 2003; Beck, Cesario,

Yousefi, & Enamoto, 2000; Evers & Suhr, 2000; Khalfa et al., 2003; Kreutz et al., 2004; Spintge & Droh, 1987; Fukui & Yamashita, 2003; Bradt & Dileo, 2009; Modesti, Parati, & Taler, 2008; Teng, Shatin, Wong, Zhang, 2007; Spintge & Roth, 1987).

In my therapy groups for refugees, I have found that it is important to use music that the participants like and feel is uplifting. This is because, according to research, uplifting music that we enjoy activates areas in the limbic system that release endorphins, which naturally increase our body's threshold for pain, mitigate depression, strengthen our overall immune system, and affect our emotions (Gangrade, 2012; Blood, Zatorre, Bermudez & Evans, 1999; Blood & Zatorre, 2001; Roth & Smith, 2008; Husain, Thompson, & Schellenberg, 2002; Salimpoor et al., 2009; Salimpoor & Zatorre, 2013; Salimpoor et al., 2011).

Another reason to use music with traumatized refugees is that it releases serotonin and in doing so counteracts depression (Evers & Suhr, 2000). Erkkila and colleagues' (2011) RCT study found that improvisational music therapy together with standard care is more effective than standard care only. At three-month follow-ups, the subjects in the intervention group were less depressed and less anxious than the subjects in the control group. Additionally, the subjects in the intervention group had better general functioning at the three-month measure point (see also Maratos & Gold, 2005; Maratos & Crawford, 2011). Brandes and colleagues' study (2010) of music listening and depression found that listening to music significantly decreased depression among hospitalized patients. Another reason I use music with my refugee groups is that it has been shown to increase levels of melatonin, and at the same time decrease insomnia, a typical symptom with PTSD (Kumar, Tims, & Cruess 1999).

As a therapist, I may play a sad chord after my group participant has played a sad chord or after there has been a discussion of a sad event. David Huron found (2001, 2008, 2010) that sad music feels warm and comforting, allowing us to "have a good cry." Music has the capacity to put our brain into a grief-like stage. The thalamus helps the body by releasing prolaktin, the same soothing hormone that is released when mothers are nursing their infants. On a cognitive level there may also be a soothing effect because of empathy. That is, when a client listens to sad, pre-composed music, he may realize that someone else has gone through a sad experience too. When they listen to the therapist playing a sad tune, it is a moment of validation: "My feelings have been heard. I have been understood!" Naturally, this can be a corrective and compensating experience. Prolaktin plays an important role in music psychotherapy with traumatized individuals. It explains why music plays so powerful a role during grief processes.

Oxytocin and dopamine are considered to be the "love transmitter" hormones, and both are needed for bonding, which may help explain why music has always played such a prominent role in rituals and emotional events in cultures around the world. When people listen to music and sing and play it together, the body releases oxytocin, which helps us feel a sense of belonging, connectivity, and trust in one another (Chand & Levitin, 2013; Kramer, 2003; Insel, 2010; Landgraf & Neumann, 2004; Seltzer, Ziegler, & Pollak, 2010; Nilsson, 2009; Insel, 2010; Landgraf & Neumann, 2004). I have often found that playing together heightens the sense of togetherness in music therapy groups. Many studies have also found that music releases dopamine into the brain, just like other pleasurable stimuli (Sutoo & Akiyama, 2004; Salimpoor, Benovoy, Larcher, Dagher, & Zatorre, 2011; Salimpoor, Benovor, Longo, Cooperstock & Zatorre, 2009; Levitin, 2009; Berridge, 2007; Schultz, 2010; Blood, Zatorre, Bermudez, & Evans,1999; Sutoo & Akiyama, 2004). Salimpoor and colleagues (2011) found during his MRI research that the mere anticipation of a favourite type of music stimulates the release of dopamine. The dopamine explains the spurts of pleasant memories we experience when listening to music we enjoy. It also explains the pleasure we feel during an anticipated chord resolution and the "peaks" we often experience during music. It certainly explains some of the cathartic feelings people often experience during improvisation.

Refugee Grief Process

Refugees have lost their home country, their home, everything they had in their home, their sense of safety. Many have also lost family members and friends, their social status, their profession, even their hobbies. Most have lost all their future hopes and have to start all over again. The grief process is always individual. There are overlaps between the various phases, which are seldom distinct. Sometimes grief starts in one phase and then spirals back into an earlier phase. Difficult emotions tend to come back like a roller coaster. Next, I will introduce the typical phases combined from Kubler-Ross (1969), Parkes and Weiss (1983), Bowlby (1980), Sanders (1999), and Worden (2002).

Shock Phase

Shock is the first response refugees experience. It includes a feeling of numbness or "unrealness" that protects us from the harsh reality of the pain we are going to experience. With refugees this phase may last days or weeks. The trauma survivor may also learn to be numb or to dissociate from reality.

I just remember that we walked and walked. We walked for weeks, or at least that's how it felt. We walked through a desert, through a forest, avoiding the roads because we were scared of the ISIS soldiers. It all felt unreal, like a nightmare, although I was awake and it was really happening. Even thinking back it is very foggy. I remember being very thirsty and so scared it felt numb. I almost lost my baby on that walk, you know, I almost lost her. I simply walked and walked, and we were all scared, but were walking like in a nightmare. (a refugee woman, describing her escape from Mosul to Jordan during the "My refugee journey" activity)

Outcry Phase

The outcry phase of the grief process includes a painful awareness of loss. For many refugees this reality sinks in at the refugee camp and includes extreme emotions, anger, guilt, anxiety, and sorrow. These feelings escalate and recede, rising to the surface and then sinking back. It is also typical that refugees deny the permanence of the loss. During this phase, it is important to begin to realize that the horror one encountered, the violence, was all wrong and that "there are no reasons or excuses that can justify these actions" (Mollica, 2006, 87). The refugees were victims, and none of what happened to them was their fault. They were "not in any way responsible for the violence that has occurred to them" (Mollica, 2006, 87). The first goal during this phase is to process and accept the reality of the loss, to allow oneself to begin to work through the pain, and to identify the feelings of humiliation. With refugee groups in Canada, I often ask the participants to list all the things they miss from their home country and to then share their emotions through musical improvisation. Using music from their youth usually supports their efforts at self-healing.

What do I want to teach others about my refugee experience? ... so many things. Mainly that it is horrible. It is something I don't even have words to really describe. It is hard to comprehend that [other] human beings purposefully wanted me and my family to suffer. That they would force us to leave, that they would do all those horrible things [to] us. It is wrong! Yes, that's what I want to tell them. That they should not believe everything the news tell[s] them, that it is wrong to harm others! We should all live in peace with our neighbours, mind our own business, and help each other. We should not hate and revenge. That's also what I would like to teach ... Hate and revenge ... they only make things worse. It is very painful. It is so painful that I never thought I could cry this much. But I keep crying. Every day. And I hope that one morning I wake up and see the sun shining and hear the birds singing and feel the pain has been cleansed away ... I think that's why I cry, to cleanse the pain away."

(a refugee woman during "What would I want to teach others about my refugee experience" activity)

Remembrance and Mourning Phase

It is important to understand that the first very stage of recovery is always stabilization and the restoration of safety. This concerns both practical issues such as food, shelter, sleep, a safe place to live, medical help, and protection, as well as psychosocial well-being such as having something meaningful to do. The remembrance and mourning phase will not start before the immediate danger has faded. The person needs to be able to distinguish between outside danger and inside danger, between "I am safe" and "I feel safe" concepts. Remembrance and mourning means that the emotional roller coaster continues. Most refugees feel tremendously worried and helpless as they constantly hear disturbing news from their home country. In the new country, they often experience continuous stress, confusion, retraumatizing situations, and culture shock. According to Van der Veer (1998), culture shock may be characterized by the word "loss," for example, loss of the familiar social environment, previous obligations, meaning of life, respect, and social status. For these people, sharing experiences with others and finding support is very important. In therapy situations, this means both confronting and accepting the horrible past experiences through the telling of the trauma-story (Schauer, Neuner, & Elbert, 2011).

> In my heart I have stored the following memories: Me playing with my dog at the backyard, the flowers of our garden, the big, delicious tomatoes, the date tree, the taste of the dates, my father sitting on the front porch with the neighbours, drinking tea and debating. My mother cooking in the kitchen, the aunt visiting and them complaining about the men. Such a normal afternoon it was ... Me planning my wedding with my cousin, trying out different outfits we had purchased at the local mall. ... Us having dinner [in] our living room, the feel of the heavy wooden furniture made by my grandpa, the colourful rug that had been in the family for generations, the tablecloth my grandmom had made ... I don't have my village anymore, I don't have my home, my backyard, garden, dog, date tree. I don't have my father, no neighbours, not my mother, not my aunt, not my cousin, not my grandpa, not my grandmom, not my living room, not my furniture, none of this I have anymore. But nobody can take away my memories. As they are stored in the bottom of my heart. (a young refugee woman after "Memories stored in my heart" activity)

Processing and Renewal Phase

The processing phase includes reflecting on the trauma and finding new meanings in it. This phase is also called a renewal phase because it is when the trauma survivors often begin to form a new identity as a survivor rather than a victim. The pain never goes away, and can the trauma experience can never be erased, but little by little the person learns to cope. Often, they will even find new meaning in the middle of a terrible loss. The proverbial silver lining.

> A group of refugee women, somewhere in the Middle East, sit in a circle. Each of them holds a copy of a river of life that has many curves. They are asked to write down or draw their life events using colours or stickers. They are to remember the good times and the bad times, the significant events, the turning points. The room is suddenly very silent while everyone concentrates on their lives. Sharing begins to take place, and the women begin to show their pictures to each other. Then we improvise different parts of their lives, different emotions, happiness and joy, sadness and despair. Music sounds as our feelings feel.

Reconnecting and Adjusting Phase

The reconnecting and adjusting phase often means starting all over again. At this stage, refugees come to terms with their past and no longer feel defined by it or trapped in it. Usually there is a new level of engagement, investment, and trust in the world, leading to new relationships and a return to life projects and plans. However, adjusting to the new country after resettlement is not easy. For example, difficulties finding a job can trigger feelings of helplessness.

> If I were a tree, this is how it would be. A very strong trunk, deeply rooted ... Some wounds on the trunk, as you can see, because of so many cut branches, a horrific storm that almost killed the tree, as it did many of them growing in the same forest ... but the tree is now healing ... the roots were not damaged, after all. There are some new leaves now, and there are birds who have nests there in my tree. See, I have my grandchildren even though I lost my sons. There are no leaves everywhere because there is still some wounds, but they are growing, they are growing and they are very green. See, there are also flowers growing in my tree. Perhaps it is a fruit tree. (a middle-aged refugee woman during "Me as a tree" activity)

Elements of Good Trauma Storytelling

None of us can fully avoid traumatic life experiences. That is why, as human beings, we can understand one another's experiences and feel compassion. According to research (Schauer, Neuner, & Elbert, 2011), trauma victims with weak social support are at an increased risk for developing PTSD. This may be because they were unable to talk about the event. "The refugee trauma story is their personal narrative told in their own words about the traumatic life events they have experienced and the impact of these events on their social, physical, and emotional well being" (Mollica, 2006, 21).

A chronological telling of the trauma story is the most powerful way to overcome the impacts of trauma and fear. Telling the story again, step by step, in every detail, in chronological order, while at the same time processing the related emotions, allows the brain to organize the fragmented memory and store it properly in the correct area of the brain. It allows the reconstruction of the *chronological/explicit/declarative/autobiographical* representation of the episode. It also allows the brain to regulate the original fear activation and gain control of the fear reactions (i.e., disturbing images). It allows us to learn that sensory and emotional memory can be activated without fear. Little by little we begin to distinguish between past and current dangers (Schauer, Neuner, & Elbert, 2011, 31). Harvard University researchers found that refugees are often relieved to share their stories, though they may not share everything right away. According to Mollica (2006), "perpetrators intentionally try to get the tellers of the trauma story to doubt their own sanity. Because of this, survivors in turn doubt a listener's ability to believe in the truthfulness of their experience" (pp. 70–71).

Many refugees seem to try to heal themselves by narrating their experiences. It is crucial to acknowledge that a refugee trauma story told in a therapeutic situation is always also a survivor's story. According to Mollica (2006), "all trauma stories are personal and historic accounts by ordinary people who want to heal themselves while also teaching others about survival and healing" (p. 48).

In *Healing Invisible Wounds* (2006b), Mollica introduces the four elements and basic principles that should always be present in a good telling of a trauma story: (1) a factual accounting of the events; (2) the cultural meaning of trauma; (3) revelations: looking behind the curtain; and (4) the storyteller–listener relationship. The factual accounting of the events is a natural element of any trauma story, and very early in the therapeutic process I encourage the person to include details such as what actually happened to him. I usually ask my group participants to draw their refugee journeys on a map. Often, they remember the exact date and time when the horrible things started to happen. I also try to help them reflect on their identities – that is, who were they the before the event, and who are they now? Sometimes trauma story should be told in brief segments. At the Harvard University clinic, they have a saying: "a little bit, a lot over a long period of time" (Mollica, 2006b, 124).

Refugees are extremely resilient people who have survived horrible events. "At the core of the psychological dimension of self-healing is the will to survive and recover" (Mollica, 2011, p. 94). Finding the personal and cultural meaning of trauma is an important part of a healing trauma-story telling. According to Mollica (2006), "self-healing occurs at the psychological level when the mind is able to construct a new meaning out of violence" (p. 97). Sometimes the new meaning is to help others who have experienced similar trauma. During my music and art groups I try not to focus solely on hearing only the facts and details of trauma stories; I also encourage the participants to look behind the curtain for fresh revelations. When trauma survivors are able to do this, while reflecting upon her experiences, they find themselves no longer stuck with the trauma but able to achieve deep insights and healthier perspectives. In every therapy process, I ask the following self-healing questions introduced by Mollica (2006): "What traumatic events have happened to you? How are your body and mind repairing the injuries sustained from these events? What have you done in your daily life to help yourself recover? What justice do you require from society to support your personal healing?" The aim of these questions is to help the trauma survivor modulate the intense emotions associated with their traumatic experiences and how they are expressed. It is crucial to contain the strong emotions so that they do not dominate the entire story" (p. 123).

Importantly, every trauma story needs witnessing in order to be therapeutic. The storyteller–listener relationship is vital to any compassionate, sensitive, patient, and empathetic therapeutic relationship. "Under ideal conditions, the storyteller is the teacher and the listener is the student" (Mollica, 2006, 47). In my music and art groups I always address this before any psychoeducational discussion.

> I remember a particular time with Iraqi refugee women in Jordan. The topic of that day's psychoeducational section was resilience and I had been showing some photos of trees growing in impossible places, flowers blooming in a dry desert, an entire forests of trees being twisted but still growing. The ladies then created a piece of artwork about a tree that represented themselves. I was surprised how all the women decided to stand up in front of the group, one by one, and share their trees with a great sense of pride, cheering each other on, and finding healing elements in each others' trees. (author)

Psychological Rationale for Using Music and Art as a Tool of Therapeutic Storytelling

It is easy to feel a sense of belonging and receive positive feedback while making music and art with others. Music-making and art-making enhance learning and improve self-image, self-confidence, and self-worth. Given the neurological impact of music, when working with traumatized refugees it is important to choose music they like. This is often music from their own cultural background.

One of the main psychological reasons why I use music and art in my refugee groups is that they can be viewed both as a transitional object and as a self-object (Winnicott, 1986; Kohut, 1977; Lehtonen, 1986). The role of music and art during the trauma therapy is to create a safety zone, a safe *symbolic distance* in which the trauma-story telling is possible without too much anxiety. Working with musical images and metaphors allows for the parallel processing of manifest and latent meanings.

Drawing, painting, and clay-sculpting after improvisation or during music listening creates a double symbolic distance and enhances insight into the metaphors. In therapeutic interventions I use postcards with different emotions, landscapes, atmospheres, and music listening activities that enhance imagination, fantasy, and problem-solving. During a guided imagination during music, I may guide the group through a forest or mountains to allow them to observe a new landscape and new possibilities. In one activity, I guide them to explore different doors or paths, from which they can choose. Sometimes I ask the group to imagine they are holding a crystal ball that shows their future. Symbolic distance allows us to imagine and fantasize with music. With traumatized refugees it is therapeutic to experience that everything is possible. They can fly, fight, or win a battle during music. I often ask the participants to bring in their favourite music, or particularly relaxing, comforting, energizing music, or music that makes them feel safe and strong or brings happy memories.

Music also reveals memories. As discussed before, the brain's limbic system contains all memories and all feelings associated with them. Different musical elements can activate the working-through process. Sometimes I ask group participants to remember their hometowns while music-listening and then to draw the lives they had to leave behind – their home, family, pets, garden, and so on. After the listening activities, the emotions are expressed with improvisations. Sometimes we improvise about a photo that represents something from their home country, or we write a song about it. Typically, the improvisations are recorded and then played back, at which time the participants process their feelings and images with other forms of art (i.e. paint, clay, writing).

It is natural to label and express emotions during music listening and after improvisation. Learning to recognize emotions helps us gain control over them. It is also therapeutic to experience that it is possible to be understood by others. Learning to recognize emotions during music helps us recognize typical flashback triggers and the bodily sensations often associated with them. This itself helps a person gain empowerment. Emotions experienced during music also teach that emotions come and go and are not dangerous. At a safe symbolic distance, it is possible to experience "This music sounds sad" and "I am sad ..." or "This music is loud and scary" and "I am scared or angry ..." processes. It also allows traumatized people to feel control over their emotions, for example, during improvisation: "Now I make chaotic sounds ..." "Now I make peaceful sounds ..." As a therapeutic intervention, I may ask group participants to improvise a the feeling of an emotion card, photo, or story, or to write a sad song, an angry song, or a future song, to play hopeful music, or confusing music, and so on. One intervention that I often do includes both clay and music. I ask participants to make two clay objects that represent two different feelings they have now or used to have, or I ask them to make one object that represents their healing process and personal growth. After the clay objects are ready, they will be discussed and the feelings will be improvised together.

Music allows both *externalization* and *internalization* processes. For instance, in the moment when group participants first listen to recorded music, it is heard as something "external" in relation to them. During the process, external abstract music turns into something concrete and personalized and touches emotions on a deeper level. There may also be some level of cathartic emotional release. When clients begin to play an instrument, they may not have any notion of what is going to happen. But when they play, their inner feelings take an audible form and become *externalized*. As an outcome of this process, trauma survivors may learn about themselves and find new perspectives, attitudes, or problem-solving strategies. They may be able to externalize their pain, despair, and confusion, or to internalize hope. The group participants may experience, for example, the following: "This [external] music sounds the way my [inner] feelings feel ...," "This [external] music sounds like me [inside] ...," "This song tells my story/journey ...," "This is how my anxiety sounds." Music may also activate the transference level (Ahonen, 2007), for example: "This is the atmosphere of my flashback or nightmare ...," "This music tells about my past/home country/my mother/my pet ..." Music can serve as a therapeutic self-representation allowing the participant to reflect different parts of themselves and their experiences, for example, "This music represents me/my family/my past/my feelings/my future fears or fantasies/my dreams ..."

As a therapist, my role is to help the participants engage in a therapeutic dialogue with their images, such as, "Why this image today? What does it tell about me, my strengths, and my healing process?" A typical therapeutic activity with refugee groups includes drawing a river of life that includes the time before *and* after the trauma episodes. After art work there is usually sharing and improvisation of emotions felt during different life events.

Living under horrifying trauma experiences is like being in a very dark room without windows or doors. Beginning to share the trauma experiences with others is like switching on the light. The trauma experience itself will not be erased, but because it is now fully visible, it will no longer control everything we are and everything we do. We will not feel so trapped anymore. We begin to gain empowerment and find new ways to cope. Core to the use of music and art as a therapeutic tool is to be able to communicate with it, to be able to work through the trauma story, to have it witnessed and validated, to work through sadness, loss, anger, guilt, and despair, to find the survivor's voice and the survival-story, to gain new meanings and healthier perspectives, and to instil hope. Music enhances the normal trauma and grief processing phases.

Therapeutic Music and Art Groups with Refugees

The structure for the therapeutic music and art groups I conduct with refugees typically includes the following: (1) relaxation/breathing exercise, (2) psychoeducational content and discussion, (3) break, (4) relaxation/breathing/grounding exercise, depending on the group's needs, (5) music and art activity that reflects the psychoeducational topic, (6) sharing/therapeutic discussion, and (7) relaxing and grounding (closing) exercise. A typical session lasts 2 hours and 15 minutes, including a break in the middle. The chairs and tables are in a circle. The participants all have their own art tools – markers, crayons, stickers, glue, colourful paper, and sometimes clay. The instruments available include various drums, rain sticks, chimes, singing bowls, flutes, and instruments from the participants' own culture. Each participant receives a hand-out including material of the session's psychoeducational topic.

Relaxation, Breathing, and Grounding Exercises. Relaxation, breathing, and grounding exercises are crucial to any trauma therapy group (Baranowsky, Gentry, & Schultz, 2011); they are also extremely important when working with traumatized refugees, who may not have received any prior psychological support. It is crucial to start both psychoeducational and music/art activity sessions with relaxation or grounding, depending on the group's needs. A variety of breathing and body relaxation techniques, including deep belly breathing and progressive relaxation, can be used during music listening. I will explain that the participants can consciously regulate their breathing when they become upset, thereby gaining control over disturbing images and flashbacks.

Choosing the right type of music is important. It must enhance body relaxation. The tempo should be steady and slow, with a repetitive melody that has no "hooks." The harmonic structure should be familiar to the participants. Breathing and body relaxation exercises can also be administered by me playing the flute or the singing bowls, or by all of us singing or humming together. Sometimes we play drums and rain sticks together while concentrating on breathing and body relaxation. In some groups we do relaxation by standing with our eyes closed and then moving body parts slowly.

Grounding exercises can include drumming or playing together, singing a particular theme song the group has adopted or written themselves, rhythmic body movements to music, or a grounding image during music listening. I teach participants how to use music to prevent and overcome their flashbacks and triggers. For example, what song or melody could they sing or hum when triggered by a disturbing memory? What song or melody reminds them they are safe? What song or melody makes them feel grounded or strong? I often incorporate different physical grounding exercises with music – for example, a *solo-tutti orchestra* is a good grounding exercise. It not only enhances auditive sensations but also gives a sense of empowerment. The idea of any physical grounding activities is to teach the participants to make conscious choices.

The aim of sensation exercises is to help the participants become aware of their real sensations in the here-and-now. Musical sound discrimination activities work great at helping connect with the here-and-now. The most popular activity is guided imagination with music listening, during which I invite the participants to experience their favourite place and then have them concentrate on their breathing and different body parts. When using it the first time, during rhythmically and melodically steady music, I will ask the participants to imagine their safe/nice/relaxing/favourite place or thing. This can be anything – something lovely from their past or an imaginary place, a place in nature, a favourite food, or a memory of doing something they really enjoy (perhaps cooking, gardening, or dancing). I will ask the participants to describe it to themselves in detail, write it down, or draw a picture of it. What is there? What colours? What sounds? What smells? What tastes? What do you do? How do you feel? During the intrusive thought or image, I encourage them to remember it.

The closing exercise often incorporates the grounding or relaxation exercises described earlier. Sometimes I have some well-selected objects in the middle of the circle that I ask participants to choose, reflect on, and take home with them. For example, stones that have words such as peace, love, trust, hope, written on them, postcards that have an encouraging message, colourful fall leaves with a motivational word or concept, brief poems, or verses of wisdom. A closing song or a particular drumming exercise may become a particular ritual with some groups. Whatever the activity, the aim is to make sure every participant leaves the room fully grounded and aware of their surroundings.

The Psychoeducational Section. The psychoeducational section usually takes thirty minutes at the beginning of each session. The chosen topics aim to help the participants begin to understand their trauma symptoms as normal reactions to abnormal situations, and to help them gain more understanding of their own and their loved ones' typical experiences. Different sessions have different topics, which may vary depending on the participant's' particular needs – for example, on whether they have already resettled in a new country. At the beginning of every session I explain that its aim is to show what the researchers have found from other refugees' experiences, encourage participants to reflect on their experiences, and highlight the fact that *they* are the experts who can teach *me* about refugee experiences and recovery. Every session also acknowledges resilience and self-healing, and that all the participants are indeed authors of a survivor's story.

The Sharing/Therapeutic Discussion. The group's therapeutic goals include these: to reduce shame and isolation; facilitate the sharing, validation, and witnessing of difficult experiences; provide unconditional acceptance, emotional support, and empathy; enhance self-healing and post-traumatic personal growth; and instil trust and hope. The therapeutic discussions after music and art activities follow the principles of the group analytic approach (Ahonen-Eerikainen, 2007). Every group member's voice is important, and their experiences are validated within the group. However, silence is also respected. I state clearly at the beginning of each session that it is totally up to the participants how much they feel comfortable sharing. The group members never share in any particular order; rather, they take their turns during a free-flowing discussion.

Table 19.1 Session 1

Relaxation/breathing/ grounding	Choosing of a soothing/grounding song, drumming circle.
Psychoeducational	Refugee trauma experience. Understanding the neurology of PTSD and typical symptoms. Children's trauma symptoms.

cont'd

Table 19.1 (cont'd from p. 310)   Session 1

Music and art activity	"My refugee Journey"-activity. The group participants are given a copy of a map of the Middle East, colourful markers, and stickers. They are encouraged to draw their refugee route from their home city in Iraq to the refugee camp in chronological order and to reminisce about any details. Then they draw/write their future plans and hopes, sharing and improvising.
Closing	Writing or drawing a postcard-sized cartoon: What makes their life meaningful? What advice would they like to give, or what would they want to teach others?

Table 19.2   Session 2

Relaxation/breathing/ grounding	Practising belly breathing (count three when inhaling, count six when exhaling). Practising how to feel grounded physically during music.
Psychoeducational	Flashbacks and triggers – preventing, coping, and overcoming. What to do before the trigger situation to avoid a flashback. What to do during a flashback. How to rescue yourself from a flashback. What to do after a flashback, how to reflect on it and learn from it.
Music and art	Safe- and nice-place visualization. Choosing a soothing and empowering proverb, wise saying, or poem and making a postcard of it. Creating something (e.g., a bracelet) to touch and feel during disturbing images.
Closing	A power song, musical rhythm, or dance step. Group participants choose their own and teach it to others. During a flashback trigger they are encouraged to use it

Table 19.3   Session 3

Relaxation/breathing/ grounding	Belly breathing with singing or music. A power song/rhythm/step from the previous session.
Psychoeducational	Surviving nightmares.
Music and art	Drawing and writing about one's nightmares. Imagining a positive ending or healing aspects. Sharing and improvising.
Closing	Small stones that have an encouraging word written on them. Group improvisation with drums, rain sticks, and chimes.

Table 19.4   Session 4

Relaxation/breathing/ grounding	Belly breathing with singing or music. A power song/rhythm/step from the previous sessions.
Psychoeducational	Life as a river that has different phases and episodes.
Music and art	"My river of life" activity. The participants think about their life from the birth until today and then make plans for their future. They mark down the sun and shadow experiences they had in their life, dark valleys and green pastures, dry deserts and refreshing waters, gates and turning points (drawing, writing, stickers). Sharing and improvisation.
Closing	"My good memories stored in my heart" activity. Participants are given a picture of a heart and explore the good memories they have stored in their heart.

Table 19.5   Session 5

Relaxation/breathing/ grounding	The rooted tree image and progressive muscle relaxation during music listening. Power song/drumming.
Psychoeducational	Self-healing and resilience.
Music and art	"Me as a tree" activity. Choosing a picture of a tree to represent them. Thinking or writing or drawing around the tree: What are my inner strengths, gifts and talents, where does the tree get its "nutrition," how does it take care of itself, etc.? Sharing and improvisation
Closing exercise	Improvising about the grounded and beautiful trees presented in the group.

Table 19.6   Session 6

Relaxation/breathing/ grounding	The rooted tree image during progressive muscle relaxation during music listening. Power song/drumming.
Psychoeducational	Grief and trauma recovery phases. Resettling adjustment phases.
Music and art	"Reflecting my survivor story: What do I want the world to know?" Writing a song about the wisdom the refugees want to share with the world about their experiences and recovery. Sharing and singing the song.
Closing	During guided imagination with music the participants are encouraged to imagine their future with all their dreams and hopes in a crystal ball.

Example of Typical Six Sessions with Refugee Women

Closing Words

Life sometimes takes us to places we did not plan to go. There are dark valleys that feel like caves, and we may not see light for the longest time because it is so dark out there ... Then there are the shadows, reminders of the past trauma that seem like they won't let go. Sometimes we only see the shadows. During my refugee trauma training, Richard Mollica, a professor at Harvard University, put it beautifully: "There is no shadow without a sun somewhere. It is important to know that the shadows are not the only reality ... There is also sun somewhere ... But we must look deeper. Sometimes, when we go through an extremely difficult time in our lives, it is as if these bad events take up the entire sky of our life. It is as if looking directly into a blinding sun, we cannot see anything else ... If you think about your entire life, you realize that your entire life is much more than this experience you are having now" (Mollica, 2014). Yes, our life contains all – sun and shadows and storms. Dark valleys and green pastures. Dry deserts and refreshing rivers. It may feel that the traumatic event destroyed our good memories too. However, nobody can take them away because they are stored in our hearts.

Even the darkest valley always has a beginning and the end. A valley is not a cave. And, sometimes, just when we feel it is too dark, we begin to see the stars guiding our way. My group participants may be living in refugee camps today, or perhaps they already have refugee status in a new country. But whatever the case, in reality, they are much more than refugees. Each of them has a unique life story, memories from better times, strengths, gifts, talents. Being a refugee is not the only thing that defines who anybody is.

The group experience itself is therapeutic, for it allows witnessing, validation, compassion, intimacy, empathy, corrective and compensating experiences. As therapists, we must be willing to truly *listen* at a deep level, to show authentic respect and kindness. We must try to "normalize" the symptoms, to acknowledge the group participants' own forces of self-healing, to reinforce the therapeutic optimism in survivors, and to encourage them to help one another.

When working with traumatized refugees, it is crucial that we be aware that the trauma stories we listen to may transform *us*. When we improvise with our clients, we empathetically attune to their disconnection, helplessness, disempowerment, and loneliness. When we bear witness to their experiences, write their songs, music takes us into their dark and insecure world. When our music sounds the way their feelings feel, it contains their grief, sorrow, anger, horror, vulnerability, anxiety, and helplessness. It is not always easy to contain the pain and suffering the storyteller transfers to us. We need to acknowledge the possibility of our own traumatization, which can easily happen when we, empathetic and open and therefore vulnerable, respond to their stories, while having to control our responses, our horror, rage, and sense of injustice (Izzo & Carpel Miller, 2011; McCann & Pearlman, 1990a; Pearlman, 1994; Pearlman & Saakvitne, 1995b).

How is one to sit with a suffering person? How is one to carry another person's burden without oneself becoming traumatized? How can we protect ourselves as we continue to listen? How are we to take care of ourselves, and how are we to empty our "containers" afterwards? I often explore these questions in the vicarious trauma workshops I conduct and when reflecting on my own emotions after working with refugees. There are no easy answers, no easy solutions. But I believe that self-care is crucial. As helpers, we must help ourselves first. If we do not, our containers will overflow from carrying other people's burdens. To keep the people we serve safe, *we* ourselves must remain safe. The first step in this is to learn to appreciate and recognize our own emotions, needs, and boundaries. It starts with a healthy balance between work and rest. We need a true connection with others, ourselves, and our personal power sources. We must regain our sense of interdependence, meaning of life, and hope.

CHAPTER 20

Musical Identities, Personal Identities
Performance for Children with Disabilities

Elizabeth Mitchell

Introduction

Each spring semester, around fifteen university students register for "Inclusive Arts for Children," a course offered by the Faculty of Music at Wilfrid Laurier University in Waterloo, Ontario. Course content is based in theory and practice from the creative arts therapies, community music, special education, and early childhood education. Enrolled students participate in experiential learning in music, drama, dance, and art while developing leadership skills and adaptation techniques for working with children with disabilities.

After completing twelve course modules, students become leaders at Arts Express, a week-long inclusive creative arts day camp. Forty children, ages six to fourteen, attend camp each year, where they engage in arts-based programming facilitated by these student leaders. Most of the children who attend Arts Express have been diagnosed with a physical, developmental, or neurodevelopmental disorder. Other campers have no diagnosed disabilities and attend camp because they have a friend or sibling who does. Camp culminates with a performance at the university's recital hall, where friends, family, community members, and faculty witness and celebrate the children dancing, acting, singing, and playing instruments.

Arts Express is an example of community music/arts practice. It has always been coordinated by a music therapist. From 2008 to 2017 I had the honour of serving as the program coordinator and music instructor. The program was initiated in 1993 by Dr. Rosemary Fischer and Dr. Leslie O'Dell of Wilfrid Laurier University, Dr. Ruth Priddle of the University of Waterloo, and Lana-Lee Hardacre of Conestoga College. Since the program's outset it has benefited from the support of these institutions, particularly the Faculty of Music at Wilfrid Laurier University, which funds the yearly course. Arts Express also relies on collaboration with a local child development centre – KidsAbility – which donates a beautiful and accessible space for the camp. KidsAbility also provides the invaluable support of a recreation therapist, who coordinates camp volunteers, instructs one night of the course, and provides behavioural support for children during camp. My involvement with this program and my relationships with campers and their families have sparked a fierce commitment on my part to provide participatory arts experiences, including performance opportunities, for children with disabilities. It has also made me curious as to the impact that participation has on them. The next section details my rationale for conducting this research.

Research Rationale

Humans are born with the capacity to develop musically (Hargreaves, Macdonald, & Miell, 2012; Lamont, 2002; Welch, 2001). Yet Western society's false notions about talent (Small, 1998) and narrow definitions of "musician" exclude many individuals from participation. Moreover, many children develop self-identities that do not include recognition of their musical capacities (Lamont, 2002); this includes children whose disabilities render "success" difficult within music education's traditional settings (Goodley, 2014). As a consequence, many children disengage from active music-making, becoming spectators and consumers but not "musicians" in their own or society's eyes. This issue has social justice implications. Given the role that musical and artistic involvement and expression has played in human societies for millennia, and the personal and communal benefits that involvement offers, access to participation in the arts must be construed as a human right (UN Office, 1989).

Musical identities "mediate" musical development (Hargreaves, MacDonald, & Miell, 2012); that is, the way children see and describe themselves musically impacts their ability to develop musical skills (Lamont, 2002). The research presented here sought to extend this established connection between musical skills and musical identity to the realm of personal identity by investigating the following questions: How does the way we view ourselves musically – and more broadly, artistically – interact with and inform our self-perceptions? In addition, how does participating in a musical performance impact personal identity? Arts Express provides a unique setting in which to explore these questions, given that for many of its participants the program provides their first, or only, opportunity to perform.

Based on the narratives shared by five young people and their parents, this chapter explores children's identity development through participation in and performance at the Arts Express camp. Participants described the program's cumulative performance as significant in that it afforded each child the opportunity to publicly experience themselves as capable and contributing: to perform *themselves* in these ways. Children's self-perceptions were indelibly linked to their audience's perceptions of them; as such, identity formation is framed as a narrative and relational phenomenon. As participants negotiated musical and personal aspects of their self-identities, they acknowledged the place of disability within this negotiation. Arts Express's commitment to inclusion, experienced by participants as an absence of pressure to meet ableist norms and as freedom to be themselves, was thus vital.

In the following section I summarize the relationship between community music and community music therapy; I then provide an overview of narrative, relational, and disability studies perspectives on identity.

Literature Review

Many of community music's foundational principles (Higgins & Willingham, 2017) deeply resonate with those of Arts Express. For example, the program's commitment to inclusivity and social justice is enacted through its provision of accessible and participatory artistic experiences to children who often would not have access these elsewhere (Mitchell, 2016). Arts Express's promotion and celebration of the wholeness and well-being of each participant reflects another principle of community music and an area of overlap with community music therapy (Higgins & Willingham, 2017; Mitchell, 2016). So there are many points of connection with community music therapy. However, the camp programming is implemented largely by university students who are *not* training to become music therapists, and it does not entail formalized processes of assessment, goal-setting, and evaluation, so Arts Express is framed as a setting of community music/arts practice rather than one of music therapy.

O'Grady and McFerran (2007) suggest that one difference between community music and community music therapy is that "the music therapist considers aesthetic value only if it serves the music participant's sense of ownership or self-expression, whereas the community musician sometimes prioritizes aesthetic value for its own sake or for the sake of social change" (p. 21). In this regard, Arts Express gravitates toward community music therapy's position along the "health-care continuum" (p. 19), for it focuses primarily on the developmental and social benefits of engagement in artistic *process* regardless of the "quality" of the final product. This is not a clear-cut distinction, however, given that many community music practitioners affirm that their work prioritizes participants' well-being (Higgins, 2012; Higgins & Willingham, 2017; Veblen, 2013). Music-centred theory in music therapy recognizes that many personal and social affordances emerge from "deep involvement in the music" (Aigen, 2014, p. 67), and thus "in some contexts there are strong continuities between clinical and nonclinical musicing that greatly outweigh their differences" (p. 87). Arts Express, like many community music programs, offers a clear illustration of the strong continuities between these fields.

Just as music-making presents affordances for individuals *and* communities, processes of identity development are both individual *and* social. Music education scholar O'Neill (2012) states that "personhood" is something we grant ourselves and others. Similarly, our musical self-perceptions are influenced not only by our own narratives but also by the narratives of significant others and society. Here, I frame identity as a narrative and relational phenomenon.

Identity: A Narrative and Relational Construct

High-modern/postmodern society is also "'post' any fixed or essentialist conception of identity – something that, since the Enlightenment, has been taken to define the very core or essence of our being (Hall, 1992, p. 275). As the "frameworks which gave individuals stable anchorage" (p. 274) no longer exist, self-identity has become an active and "reflexive project" (Giddens, 1991, p. 32), one for which narrative is a tool we can use to shape our external worlds and give form to ourselves (Bruner, 2004; Frith, 1996; McAdams, 1997; McAdams, Josselson, & Lieblich, 2006). As Giddens (1991) states: "A person's identity is not to be found in behaviour, nor ... in the reactions of others, but in the capacity *to keep a particular narrative going*" (p. 54, italics original). Narrative identities "function to organize and make more or less coherent a whole life, a life that otherwise might feel fragmented and diffuse" (McAdams, Josselson, & Lieblich, 2006, p. 5). Music can act as an invaluable resource for this task (Bowman, 2006; Ruud, 1997). For example, DeNora (2000) describes music as a "building material for self-identity" that is crucial within "the reflexive process of remembering/constructing who one is" (pp. 62–63).

In this reflexive process, our personal narratives intersect with the narratives of others and with society's grand narratives (McAdams, Josselson, & Lieblich, 2006). However, as society does not privilege all narratives equally, individuals do not have access to the same narratives (Hall, 1992; McAdams, Josselson, & Lieblich, 2006). For example, Western society's grand narratives concerning talent and musicality, already discussed, influence people's ability to integrate a musical identity within their personal identity narratives. Identity formation then is not only a narrative project but also a socio-cultural phenomenon – it is embedded in context, culture, and relationship (Hall, 1992).

Gergen (2009) posits that we are not individual selves who form relationships; rather it is through relationships that we develop as selves. "Within any relationship, we also *become somebody*. That is, we come to play a certain part or adopt a certain identity" (p. 136, italics in original). The concepts of self and identity and their ascribed value are culturally bound (Bochner, 1994), and Gergen's perspective contrasts the typical valorization of individualism within Western society. Gergen's scholarship also counters the patriarchal "ideal of psychological separation," which from a feminist perspective is "illusory and defeating because the human condition is one of inevitable interdependence" (Jordan, 2010, p. 3). Recognition of the relational nature of identity is fitting in a discussion of music, given that many ethnomusicologists, community musicians, and music therapists argue that music is a fundamentally social phenomenon (Cross, 2014; Higgins & Willingham, 2017; Stige & Aarø, 2012; Small, 1998). This frame opens space for examining interactions among performers and between performers and audience members, which in turn impact performers' identity-narratives.

Identity and Disability

Community musicians have historically resisted categorization, definition, and institutionalization (Higgins, 2012; Veblen, 2013); by contrast, music therapists have sought recognition as health professionals and scholars in medical and academic settings (Aigen, 2012). As a result, music therapists have long been complicit in the medical model's assumption "that disabled people need intervention and treatment from experts who can rehabilitate their impairments" (Rickson, 2014, "Four Models," para. 1). Music therapists, and perhaps community musicians too, could stand to learn from a social model of disability wherein "disability is not a problem of the individual ... it is created at structural levels, with environments/societies that are not flexibly adapted to allow for variability of humanness" (Rolvsjord, 2014, "Lessons from Disability Studies," para. 3). Community music therapy is one approach to music therapy, one that "builds on a more flexible ecological understanding of ... music, people, health, illness and well-being" (Rickson, 2014, "Music Therapy Theory," para. 2) than has traditional, individualized medical approaches.

The social model turns "disability-as-impairment (a classic medicalizing strategy) into disability-as-oppression" (Goodley, 2014, p. 7), which beneficially "shift[s] attention away from individuals and their ... deficits to the ways in which society includes or excludes them" (Shakespeare, 2014, p. 12). This also affords the possibility of viewing disability as "an identity that might be celebrated as it disrupts norms" (Goodley, 2014, p. 7). However, Shakespeare (2014) asserts that the social model just as extreme as the medical model, and warns that within both perspectives, "the agency of disabled people is denied" (p. 104). He proposes a critical-realist approach wherein "disability is always an interaction between individual and structural factors" (p. 74). This nuanced and holistic approach, drawn from Shakespeare's own lived experience of disability, resonates with the narratives of this study's participants.

Noting my own able-bodiedness, I strive to stay grounded in the words and experiences of my participants. All families told distinct stories of disability's impact on and intersection with their identities: narratives that fall in different places between the polarities of the medical and social models. I acknowledge my decision to use person-first language in this chapter, that is, to say "people with disabilities" rather than "disabled people." I do so while understanding the debate that exists surrounding this topic and recognizing that many activists for and adherents to the social model of disability will disagree with my choice (Goodley, 2014; Shakespeare, 2014; Sinclair, 1999). Language undoubtedly matters. Rigid admonitions to "separate the person from the disability" often stem from and/or unintentionally promote ableist perspectives in which "disability is something you should *want* to have separated from you" (Liebowitz, 2015, para. 4). For example, Goodley (2014) critiques the "neoliberal-ablism" implicit in person-first language, asserting that the signifier "person" in this context evokes neoliberalist ideals such as autonomy and independence that many people with disabilities will never meet (pp. 31–32). Weighing the importance of this academic and activist discourse, I choose to use "person-first" language because that was, for the most part, the choice of my participants. Rickson's (2014) call to monitor the "activist stance in the context of individual experience" (Abstract, para. 1) is relevant as I move to discussion of the research and its participants.

Methodology

Narrative inquiry recognizes the relational nature of all lived experience, including the act of researching itself (Clandinin & Rosiek, 2007; Polkinghorne, 1995). Alvesson and Sköldberg (2009) describe reflexive and "data-driven" studies as ones in which "'data' are regarded not as 'raw' but as a construction" and "reflection in relationship to the interpreted nature of all empirical material" (p. 283) is vital. As a researcher, my interpretations and chosen theoretical structure play a significant role in driving the story.

This study was approved by the Research Ethics Boards at Western University and Wilfrid Laurier University. Data were collected through in-depth and semi-structured interviews with five campers and their parents/guardians. As a portion of each interview, the child, parent, and I watched video footage of the child performing at a past Arts Express recital. Interviews were audio- and video-recorded. As the children varied in their capacity for verbal discussion and reflection, observation of body language and facial expressions, and support from parents, were vital. Interviews were transcribed and coded using first- and second-cycle techniques (Saldaña, 2013), whereby the researcher identifies all present themes and then, looking for relationships among them, collapses those themes into a smaller number of categories. Qualitative coding provided accountability through its systematized process as well as assistance in detecting commonalities and differences among participants. Recognizing that meaning can be lost when stories are fragmented (Riessman, 2008), each transcription was regarded as a complete narrative. Intact narratives allow for full recognition of individuals within their contexts and make "audible the voices and stories of people marginalized or silenced in more conventional modes of inquiry" (Bowman, 2006, p. 14).

My pre-existing relationships with the study's participants held potential benefits and constraints within the research process. It is possible that our rapport helped the participants – particularly the children – feel more comfortable within the unfamiliar setting of a research interview. It is equally possible that the participants felt hesitant to share their criticisms, given their knowledge of my involvement in the Arts Express program. I am confident that my "prolonged engagement" with the study's context (Lincoln & Guba, 1985, p. 304), as well as my "persistent observation" through in-depth and recursive data analysis (p. 304), highlight the study's credibility as well as my commitment to both reflexivity and the primacy of my participants' perspectives.

All participants wanted their real first names to be used in the presentation of this research. Though certain research contexts demand the protection of participants' identities, inflexible rules in this regard are part of a grand narrative stemming from positivistic research (Clandinin & Connelly, 2000). These individuals are proud of their involvement in Arts Express and happy to be identified. Recognizing the importance that research with marginalized populations not "add to their powerlessness" (Cohen, Manion & Morrison, 2011, p. 175), I present below narratives that have been vetted by these individuals. Here are their voices.

Narratives: Research Participants

Andrea. Andrea is not one to hide her effervescent personality, whether in conversation or on stage. She speaks with conviction, clarity, and a delightful sense of humour. Thirteen years old at the time of her interview, Andrea had attended Arts Express seven times. After listing her many community artistic involvements, she said, laughing, "So yeah, I really like the arts, just kind of." Her mom, Charmaine, added, "It allows her to, in a sense, be outside of herself and be unintimidated ... To bring a part her soul ... alive ... And not made to feel like she needs to fit into somebody else's box." I asked Andrea if her mom's words felt true, and she responded, "Yeah ... I don't really feel like I have to fit into, like, people's boxes, because some of the boxes people are in are really lame!"

When asked about the experience of performing, she replied, "It's quite fun when I'm on stage ... I learned to not get nervous ... because I have performed many times." Andrea brought up the theme of "taking risks" and explained that this means "doing something that you've never really done before." She felt this is important "because it allows [children] to, like, get outside of themselves ... stop worrying about what might happen and just do it, because that's pretty much what you need to do in life." She noted that performing and improvising had helped her confidence in other areas. Charmaine remembered a time when Andrea "could speak but couldn't communicate" and reflected that now, "she can advocate for herself, and she's deciding what courses she wants for high school ... Definitely the acting and the music and the whole program with Arts Express is really helpful with that." Andrea agreed. "Arts Express ... has helped me ... learning to communicate ... Since I have autism I, like, can't process social situations most of the time ... Arts Express has given me the social environment that's really inviting."

Andrea sees the arts as "a way to express yourself" and believes that the arts are a good way for children with disabilities "to find themselves, and not be labelled." She perceives herself as "lucky" in that she "got past [her disability]," but recognizes that other children might have fewer "opportunities to express themselves." She thought that the performance might "move" the audience "because you're seeing all these children who get rejected by society, like, thrive in this performance." Charmaine added that "it makes [the children's] lives bigger and richer ... And it makes the world bigger for other people observing it. 'Cause they realize that there's potential in ways that they may not have thought of." Andrea's commitment to the program led her to become a volunteer this past summer, working one-to-one with a young boy with autism.

Michael and Mackenzie. Brother and sister Michael and Mackenzie were ages fifteen and fourteen at the time of their interviews, and both had attended Arts Express seven times. Mackenzie would attend as a camper for one subsequent year before becoming a volunteer. Their mom, Lois, emphasized that Arts Express had acted as a "great introduction" to the arts "especially for people with autism ... It's the best environment ... if you want your children to be exposed to [the arts] ... It was a great way to find ... something that they can find fulfilment and enjoyment in and find their thing."

Mackenzie noted that her passion for the arts had started at Arts Express: "The more that I was doing it, I liked it and it made me grow more interest in it." Lois pointed out that singing provides her daughter with a medium for self-expression, and Mackenzie reiterated the importance of the arts to her identity and in helping her feel "better about myself." For example, during a recent challenge with friends, her participation in the arts had helped "because those are things that I like doing. So even though I was upset ... I could go back to doing those things." Mackenzie thought that Arts Express had helped her feel confident performing in other contexts "because I already know what it feels like," and Lois extended this to her daughter's overall confidence in many areas.

Mackenzie thought that performance is important to the camp because "it's a good feeling. Also ... it's not something you do every day!" One of Mackenzie's favourite memories from camp was performing a dance that featured her and a peer. She laughed, self-conscious, when her mom described, "she likes an audience," but then concurred and explained that this had been the "first time I got to do anything like that." Mackenzie exuded pride and a sense of accomplishment associated with performing at camp. "It's not just like, one of those kiddie shows from school ... It's like a big thing ... You work on it to make it good." Mackenzie's internalized sense of the audience's enjoyment was integral to her own pride: "I know that people are there because they wanna see it."

Michael joined us as we watched portions of the performances from 2009 and 2015. A few minutes into the older video, Michael put his head down and said, "I don't want to see flashbacks." Lois explained that Michael dislikes watching footage of himself from childhood, and Mackenzie piped in, "I like evidence that I was little." Michael comfortably watched portions from his most recent performance, alternating with focusing on the family's dog. Lois, Mackenzie, and I all enthusiastically pointed out a part in the video where Michael had played an important role in advancing the plot by holding a leaf in the air. Both siblings were featured during their group's dance, Mackenzie in a choreographed duet with a friend and Michael through jumping with a peer. Afterwards, I asked Michael, "What was it like watching the video of yourself?" He responded, "It felt pretty good actually!" and noted that he had liked "the leaf and dancing." I noted that he had had a bigger role in this performance than ever before, and I asked him if he felt proud of that. He replied, "Yes! I felt proud."

When asked whether he participates in the arts at school, Michael responded, "I perform instruments at school," and listed the marimba, ukulele, and trumpet. Lois explained that she and her husband would not have known about Michael's strong interest in musical instruments were it not for Arts Express. "It exposed him to many different things in such a great environment ... It was the perfect way to see what he likes." She also noted that Arts Express is "the only camp we have sent Michael to ... It's the only one we trust to leave him."

I provided Michael with a list of emotions to choose from regarding his experience of performing, and Michael exclaimed loudly, "Happy!" He also said that he liked "everything" about performing and feels "happy" when he is dancing as well. He hugged his mom as he said this, and I asked how he thinks his parents feel when they're watching him. He immediately said, "They feel happy," and Lois affirmed, "Yeah, we do!" Michael stated that Arts Express "helped me do sorts of stuff." With help from his mom, they identified that camp has helped him to have the confidence to play his marimba at school in front of other people. Regarding watching both of her children perform, Lois recalled:

> You have a good feeling ... Mackenzie's had a couple more experiences being on stage but for Michael, that's it ... We watched him from ... being that child who would stand in the middle of the stage looking for us ... to ... participating more ... We've seen him evolve. We like to watch [Mackenzie] shine on stage ... And, for [Michael]... I think he enjoys it.

Zhade. When I asked about the impact attending Arts Express has had on her, Zhade responded: "I didn't know who I am and it changed when I went to Arts Express ... I tell myself ... this is who I really am ... I learned that I can sing ... I can dance ... I love performing." Zhade was twenty years old at the time of her interview and had attended camp five times until she reached age fourteen. Along with her adoptive mom Lana, she had attended several recent performances as an audience member. Zhade alternated between using spoken speech and an augmentative communication device during her interview, and the speed at which she could program her device, piping in with articulate responses, insightful questions, or jokes, was striking. Lana named cerebral palsy as Zhade's "starter diagnosis," and then turned to Zhade and joked, "You got a whole bunch of add-ons just to be cool." One "add-on" is epilepsy, and Lana noted that Zhade had been having fewer seizures recently. "They give me grey hairs and I already have enough." Zhade grabbed Lana's hair and then quickly programmed her device, "I love you, grey hairs."

Lana recounted that in elementary school Zhade had been "systematically excluded from all of the arts performances," sharing several devastating examples while Zhade kept her eyes on me, nodding. These experiences sparked Lana's resolve that "this was not going to happen" in high school. Lana noted that inclusion in schools is usually "grudging" unless it's an "exceptionally committed school." That Lana's tireless advocacy has been worthwhile was evident in Zhade's smile and pride as she explained her recent roles in school plays and musicals. Lana and Zhade also enjoy attending live theatre. and Lana described the attitudinal barriers in live theatre settings: ushers see medical equipment on Zhade's wheelchair and assume that she will disrupt and that she is "unlikely to get anything out of it." "People think that her brain and her spirit work as well as her body does, and that's not the case." You need only speak with Zhade or watch her dance on stage to know this.

The importance of the arts in Zhade's life echoed throughout the interview. When asked how she feels while performing, Zhade said clearly, "I love performing," and added, "I feel like I'm having fun and I am with people I know." She noted that she feels "capable" in singing, playing instruments, and dancing. Lana described the arts as crucial to Zhade's identity because "it was about what she *could* do," and there was potential for "embracing [Zhade's] wholeness as a person." Lana reflected that "a lot of other systems are built on a very rigid foundation," whereas "the space, the openness and the possibility" within the arts is a way for "kids with disabilities ... to embrace life and for life to embrace them back."

Lana hopes that audience members without lived experiences of disability will see the Arts Express recital as "worth watching as something other than a sideshow ... The kids know the music ... they're having fun, they're participating, they're part of a group, they're part of something that matters. That's a powerful message." Lana noted that for many of the children on stage, camp is the only opportunity to perform without being relegated to the edges and for their families to see them "having successes like that." With pride, Zhade said she thought that audience members would be thinking, "Wow, I didn't know that they could do that!"

Max. When I asked Max if he would watch the video from last summer's performance, he replied, "No thanks. I'll just close my eyes and think about my adventure." Max enacted the adventures of Buzz Lightyear, the Hulk, and Mr. Incredible throughout our interview. His Mom, Mary, explained that in a sense, "Max is always performing." Mary insisted that Max watch the video, and as soon as Max saw himself on screen he sat down, turned his chair, and stared intently. He clapped enthusiastically each time the audience onscreen did, and at one point he raised his hands to perform a song's actions with his fellow campers. While watching Max create a movement onstage as a part of his group's dance, Mary exclaimed, "I like your little hopping!" Mom and son watched the video closely for a few more moments before Max stated matter-of-factly, "I did very well in there."

During our interview, Max often paced, gazed out the window, or recited lines from movies. He also often spontaneously gave his mom a hug or kiss or leaned against her. In these moments, Max would happily participate in conversation for a brief time. Through closed-ended questions, Max expressed that he prefers dancing over singing but likes singing too. Though answering questions about feelings was difficult, when asked if he would like to attend camp and perform again, Max smiled and said "yes" without hesitation. Mary noted that in the months following camp, Max's participation at school had improved and he was smiling more often. She wondered if these changes were partly related to having attended Arts Express.

Mary explained that the camp's artistic focus and performance opportunity had attracted her because "he's not going to have that at school." Prior to attending Arts Express, Max had never participated in a performance. After recounting an experience wherein Max was excluded from his kindergarten class's Christmas performance, Mary noted, "I think he likes the stage ... but he likes to control what he's performing." Like many children, Max engaged with the group at times and at other times was more independent. The structure of the Arts Express performance is designed for this, allowing Max to be an individual while also experiencing belonging to a group. Mary valued that Max could "express himself" and that camp programming aimed not simply to have children follow instructions "but to actually do something with the instructions."

That Max would have the opportunity to perform was important for Mary personally and for their relationship. "I thought, 'He's going to be on a stage!' Just to have him show me something ... Usually he's ... being interrogated or being told what to do." For Mary, watching her son perform "erased eight years of pain."

> It felt like everything lifted from me ... It was the first time ... I've been able to be proud. 'Cause I've never seen him do anything. I'm always trying to fix him ... Or somebody's trying to fix him ... Or tolerating ... or enjoying it but in a private way. This wasn't private. It was on stage!

She noted that at the performance "you see them for what they are ... The more they were themselves, the more the audience loved it." When I asked Max how his mom might have been feeling while watching, Mary chimed in, "Did I have a frown on my face? Or was I smiling?" Max quickly said, "Smiling!" and smiled himself.

Mary's reflections speak to the way in which our identity narratives develop relationally. Her pride in her son after witnessing his performance had no doubt impacted his own sense of accomplishment, evidenced by his statement, "I did very well in there." Performance affords opportunity for development and expansion in self-identity, both artistically and personally, due to its public setting and the relationships enacted therein. This will be discussed below.

Results and Discussion

Performance and Identity: Narrative and Relational. The narrative and relational features of identity formation are intertwined, as interactions with others, situated in specific contexts, are integral to the formation of our internal identity narratives. The intersections between individuals and their contexts are highlighted within musical performances, as performers' experiences are witnessed by and filtered through the social and relational features of the medium and setting. In the following section, I present the most prominent themes from data analysis pertaining to participants' self-identities. As evident in the narratives presented above, through the experience of publicly performing and sharing music, drama, and dance with their audiences, these children internalized feelings of personal accomplishment and the knowledge that they had contributed to their community. Children and families also described participation in the arts as enriching to their lives in somewhat ineffable ways, contributing to their overall sense of fulfillment and of feeling whole. Within each theme, the interdependency of its personal and social elements is evident.

I Am Capable. For each child, there was a sense of accomplishment and pride linked to performing. Mackenzie described this: "It's not just like, one of those kiddie shows from school ... It's like a big thing ... You work on it to make it good." Mackenzie took tremendous pride in the overall performance and her contributions to it. She also affirmed her brother's role in the performance, and when I asked Michael how it felt watching himself perform on video, he replied, "It felt pretty good actually!"

Andrea highlighted that performing had helped her self-confidence in other domains. She associated performing with "risk-taking" and noted that performing had "really gotten me, like, prepared for, like, class presentations and stuff like that." Charmaine described Andrea's involvement in the arts as allowing her to be "unintimidated by anything else that's around." Michael felt more confident playing the marimba at school because of his experiences at camp, and Lois noted that Mackenzie's involvement in the arts has boosted her overall confidence. Speaking directly to her daughter, Lois said, "You have to work really hard just to get by in some things. But this is something that you're naturally good at and enjoy ... You know this is your thing." Similarly, Lana noted, "It's not like math and sciences where there is only one right answer ... For kids with disabilities ... the space, the openness, and the possibility that the arts have is so different." Of her involvement with Arts Express, Zhade said with certainty, "I learned that I could sing, and that I could dance," and Lana piped in, "And you could do that in a group."

The sense of accomplishment, pride, and confidence in performing is particularly significant for the children who attend camp who would not otherwise access a performance opportunity. This was the case for Michael and Max. Mary's experiencing of public pride for her son at Arts Express had been significant for her personally, and in turn, it was significant for Max. Though not able to reflect in-depth, Max's statement "I did very well in there" appeared to indicate that he understood the significance of his accomplishment at his first performance. The impact of Max's performance on his mother also speaks to the positive contribution that children on stage make to the community of audience members.

I Can Contribute. Arts Express's performance embodies a subversion of norms surrounding the recital hall, sending a powerful message to its audience (Mitchell, 2016). Children with disabilities – who are typically excluded from the recital hall stage – are viewed as artists and creators, performing before an audience of caregivers, teachers, and policy-makers. As Lana described, the recital is "worth watching as something other than a sideshow." That the performance is anything but a "sideshow" arose as a theme in each interview. As audience members are moved to laughter, tears, cheers, and resounding applause, these young artists experience witnessing and affirmation and in turn internalize the notion that they can make a valuable contribution. Lana noted that the arts are important for Zhade not only because of the fulfillment they bring to her but also because of *how they allow her to be seen*; the arts are "her connect point with life and interaction ... and being seen as competent and ... participating and having a valuable opinion."

Mackenzie had internalized a sense of the audience's enjoyment of the performance that was integral to her own sense of pride: "I know that people are there because they wanna see it." Zhade thought many audience members would be thinking, "Wow, I didn't know that they could do that!" Andrea understood that attending Arts Express performances changes the perceptions of audience members. She noted that children with disabilities "don't fit into what society thinks a normal person is" and she thought that performance "brings a good way for [children] to find themselves and not be labelled ... just to be themselves." Andrea recognized that as children are afforded the opportunity to "find themselves," the audience simultaneously can witness them as more than a "label." Her insightful comment affirms the interconnection between the formation of one's own identity narrative and the perspectives of others.

Gergen (2009) states that "the removal of affirmation is the end of identity" (p. 168), thus validating the interdependence of self-narratives and the perspectives of those around us. As Mary reflected, at the Arts Express recital, "You see them for what they are." In turn, the children experience being *seen*. This experience of being seen, accepted, and celebrated by the audience no doubt in turn impacted the identity-narratives of individual participants. The Arts Express performance facilitates new perspectives, interactions, and identities for its participants. Through performing and being witnessed, participants experienced a somewhat ineffable sense of wholeness and fulfillment, which will be briefly explored below.

Wholeness. Participants spoke of artistic involvement as enriching their lives. With regard to identity particularly, viewing themselves as artistically capable broadened children's perceptions of themselves and contributed to a greater sense of wholeness. Lana described the arts as "where [Zhade] self-identifies ... where she shines." The arts "embrace her wholeness as a person" and are "integral to her concept of ... life being worth living." Zhade reflected emphatically, "I didn't know who I am and it changed when I went to Arts Express. I tell myself, this is who I really am." At various points in the interview, Charmaine described artistic performance as allowing children to be both "outside themselves" and "fully themselves." Though this language appears paradoxical, her message is the same: that the arts allow Andrea and her peers to be uninhibited by barriers and to experience freedom.

Lois told Mackenzie that she "shines" and "radiates" when she's performing and reflected that involvement with Arts Express has brought her children "fulfillment and enjoyment" and a way to "find their thing." Lois described the significance of singing as an expressive medium for Mackenzie, and Mary too felt that "Max was able to express himself" through the experiences at camp. She valued the program's focus upon creativity, describing that children have the opportunity to "actually do something with the instructions" rather than just follow them, and noting that this was different from many of her son's experiences at school.

The significance of Arts Express's performance component within each participant's narrative is worth revisiting here in the context of an acknowledgment of performance's place within community music and music therapy discourse and practice. Though performance has always played a significant and uncontested role in community music, its role within music therapy has been tenuous. Historically, as music therapy gained recognition in health care and academic settings, performance was viewed as antithetical to psychotherapeutic or medical approaches to practice, in that it posed risks to clients and the profession's credibility (Aigen, 2012). More recently, as community music therapy has gained recognition as a valid approach to practice, many music therapists are again recognizing the musical and personal significance of performance and suggesting that it represents a resource rather than a risk (Ansdell, 2005) and is one of many "natural modes of relating to music" (Aigen, 2012, "Origins and Foundations," para. 9). Music therapists can continue to learn from community music endeavours, such as Arts Express, which celebrate the benefits that performance affords for performers and audience members alike, affordances not necessarily available within the walls of a closed therapy space.

"Community engagement, while dependent upon an individual act of participation, connects the musician to something larger, fulfilling that need to belong to something greater than one's self" (Higgins & Willingham, 2017, p. 101). Certainly, this is one of the resources offered by performance: the opportunity to make an individual contribution while belonging to something bigger. Our identities are not developed in a vacuum. While settings such as music therapy sessions, private lessons, classrooms, and camp sessions undoubtedly play a role in personal growth and skill development and offer their own affordances, for these five children, the public nature of the performance at Arts Express was crucial. Performing offered them the opportunity to narrate their own identities in new ways, based on their own lived experiences as well as the perceptions and witnessing of audience members.

Performance and Disability Identity. During interviews, though I posed general questions about participants' experiences of inclusion and barriers within the arts, I did not otherwise inquire about their lived experiences of disability. All participants voluntarily shared in this area however, reflecting upon the intersections between disability, identity, and participation in the arts. Because of common threads weaving through each interview along with notable differences between participants, I mention this briefly here. The diversity in these participants' perspectives emphatically reinforced the diversity within individuals' lived experiences of disability.

Andrea and Charmaine appreciated that the majority of children who attend Arts Express have diagnosed disabilities. Charmaine felt that within this environment, Andrea did not need to worry about being "one out of 35 that doesn't quite fit the norm ... There was no norm there. And so, everybody just came ... as they were. And they learned how to communicate and accept each other's challenges and exceptionalities and it was beautiful." In an environment as notably diverse, there was no one to be but herself, and Charmaine felt that this had helped her daughter's social functioning.

Similarly, Lois described her and her husband's reluctance to enrol Mackenzie or Michael in most community programs. "It would be more them feeling left out ... It didn't make sense to try to put them in something mainstream if it wasn't geared toward people with special needs." Mackenzie explained, "I normally don't tell people about my disability because I don't want people to treat me differently." She described feeling more comfortable at programs like Arts Express, where it is known that many children attending have disabilities: "Everybody already knows so it's not like there's that secret ... you can be more open ... You can have fun and it's not looming ... like, should I or should I not [tell]." These families' statements can be read as arguments for the importance of programming geared toward individuals with disabilities. Alternatively, they can be interpreted as reflections of the amount of work we have left to do as a society to ensure that our schools and communities are truly inclusive and accepting places. Either way, their valuing of programming geared toward individuals with disabilities is important to hear and respond to.

Lana explained that Zhade "doesn't identify just as a person with a disability ... She doesn't necessarily walk into a room and see the people sitting in wheelchairs ... and go join them. She would tend more to find somebody in the ambulatory neurotypical group ... that she knows." Lana views the arts as "an ongoing way to belong in a community, to matter in a community, rather than just going to the segregated workshops and ... the special needs dances." Zhade nodded and noted that she would rather go to a performance where there are "all sorts of people" rather than attend an event for people with disabilities. At Arts Express, Zhade learned that she enjoyed and was capable of singing, playing instruments, dancing, and performing. From there, she became involved in mainstream productions at her high school with the help of Lana's tireless advocacy. Because identity as a disabled person is not primary for Zhade, participation in mainstream experiences reinforces the parts of her identity that are primary, such as the arts.

As noted earlier, Mary described the experience of watching her son on stage for the first time as "erasing eight years of pain." I did not ask Mary to expand upon what she meant by "pain," but based on other parts of our dialogue, I can only assume that she was referencing both societal barriers, for example Max's exclusion from his kindergarten class's performance, along with impairments connected to Max's diagnosis such as, for example, his social struggles. The strength of Mary's words is striking, and Shakespeare's (2014) critique of a purely social model of autism resonates here: "Minimizing the extent to which autism is an impairment – seeing it simply as 'an alternative way of being' – could be a denial of the pervasive and sometimes devastating impact of autism on both the child and the family" (p. 96). Also offering a perspective that challenges a purely social model of autism, Andrea describes herself as "lucky" because she "got past her disability," and Charmaine reflected that she finds attending the performance "difficult" because she is "reminded of how different life could be." Along with feeling pride in her daughter, she asks herself "unanswerable questions" such as, "Why is Andrea so lucky that she's been able to overcome a lot of the challenges and other kids haven't?"

Mary hopes that many people attend the Arts Express performances who "don't have ... access to children with disabilities." Laughing at her use of the word "access," she continued, "They don't know enough ... I think it would actually change their lives." Her use of the word "access" here is noteworthy; that it is not only children with disabilities who need access to the arts, but also general community members who need to and could be enriched by "access" to children with disabilities. Mary recounted being approached by one university camp leader at the end of the performance. "I'm like, 'Oh god,' because I know [Max] can be a handful. [The student] goes, 'I just want to tell you that I think I've decided my major ... because of Max.'" Mary reflected, "I'm not used to Max having an impact!" Goodley (2014) notes that sidelining disability experience is "tragic" for a variety of reasons, including cultural ones: "While the disabled Other is made ever more a rejected entity, the centre-staging of the neoliberal-able self is, let us be clear, woefully, dull and inadequate" (p. 34). As Lana stated, this performance is far more than "a sideshow." Participation here, as performer or audience member, is light-years away from "dull and inadequate"; it has an impact, and it changes lives.

Conclusion

At the 2016 conference of the Canadian Association for Music Therapists, music therapist and disability studies scholar Dr. Cynthia Bruce gave a keynote address in which she spoke candidly of her lived experiences as a blind woman. She challenged common discourse in music therapy that conceptualizes music as allowing clients to "transcend" disabilities, for this reinforces ableist perspectives of disability as something to be rid of (Bruce, 2016). I left her talk with a renewed understanding that it is never my role to decide that the individuals with whom I work need the experience of "transcending" their disabilities, and with a humbling realization of the many ways in which my discipline has, both subtly and not so subtly, historically promoted a largely ableist agenda.

The stories of these participants resonate with Bruce's (2016) profound words. Arts Express provides opportunity for children with disabilities to experience artistic creation and performance, experiences from which they are often barred. There is transcendence in the sense of rising above false limits placed upon them by societal barriers. On the Arts Express stage, diversity is celebrated and there are no ableist norms to fit into. Andrea said this most effectively: "I don't really feel like I have to fit into like people's boxes!" As Mary recalled, the children "were free to be up there ... The more they were themselves the more the audience loved it." As the children on stage receive public witnessing and support from their audience, they in turn adopt narratives that include their ability to contribute, just as they are.

Acknowledgments

I wish to extend my deepest gratitude to the following individuals:

- To Dr. Kari Veblen and Dr. Cathy Benedict – thank you for your guidance during the process of conducting research and preparing this manuscript.

- To the families who shared their stories here – thank you for your generosity, resiliency, and heart.

CHAPTER 21

Music Care and the Aging Population

The Room 217 Story

Bev Foster

Music in Liminal Spaces

I will never forget the call that came on that cold, crisp January afternoon. My Dad was dying. The hospital was calling the family to come to Room 217 and say our farewells.

I was close to my Dad, and one thing that drew us together was our love for music. As a child, a favourite Sunday afternoon pastime was playing hymns with him. He would be at the organ and I would be at the piano. When Dad had his first and second quadruple bypasses, it was no wonder that music played a role in his recovery. The tunes that lived in Dad's spirit energized him and gave him hope for recovery. The diagnosis of late-stage cancer was as unexpected as a snowfall in July.

My dad was a successful businessman. I watched his bottom line change from profit and loss, pro quotas, and board meetings to blood tests, CAT scans, antibiotic pics, and a maze of health care infrastructure. A man who had been on the front lines became sidelined. That summer, everything that could go wrong did.

I remember one August morning like it was yesterday. I was home for a visit. Dad sat battle-worn in the rocking chair. I sat on his organ bench experiencing waves of grief that seemed to strike as surreptitiously as a tsunami. Intuitively, we knew that our talk would be around those hymns we had played for years. Our tears sang the words that day.

The notion of death and dying wasn't something I had been afraid to talk about. I believe death is a transition, not a destination. I had always thought that sudden death is preferable. But now I was seeing first-hand that terminal illness offered tremendous opportunity for relationship, as well as precious moments for connecting, caring, and closing.

Those last hours at the hospital with Dad are still etched on my heart. Lady Morphine was doing her job while my five siblings, our mom, and I were around his bedside singing the hymns he loved. Dad tried singing along. The sound he uttered was unlike any sound I had ever heard. It was neither guttural nor diaphragmatic. It came from a different place. I think it was a place deep in his soul. I saw with my eyes and experienced with my heart how music supported Dad and helped us, his family, both contain and give voice to our feelings. The music became our collective expression. We mostly hummed. It seemed to match what was happening with the pacing of Dad's breath, and the sacredness of the space.

I wondered, what did other families do during those suspended moments when a loved one is imminently dying? Why had Dad not been offered music … ever … live or recorded … in the 100 nights he was in a large Toronto hospital? Could my experience with music around his bedside in Room 217 be helpful to others? Could my professional experience as a performing musician and music educator contribute to others' care? As I walked through the parking lot having just said goodbye to Dad for the last time, I committed myself to pursue answers to these questions, and to do something about it. Several hours later, I got the call he was gone.

By the fall of 2004, I had developed the idea and design for a palliative care music collection. I would call it Room 217, in honour of Dad. We went into the studio and completed an eight-song demo that would be used in focus groups to help inform performance and production practices for Room 217 music.

Little did I realize that I would immediately see the effects of Room 217 music. The day after I picked up the demo CD, the long-term care home called to say my grandma was dying. Nan had vascular dementia caused by a series of mini-strokes, each one taking her farther away from the person we recognized. For more than five years, she had sat in a chair, somewhat catatonic, head drooped, and non-verbal. On this night, our tiny treasure lay in her long-term care bed looking as comfortable as I had seen her in years with her head slightly turned to listen to the music, the Room 217 demo.

Familiar songs like *You'll Never Walk Alone*, the second movement of the *New World Symphony, Somewhere Over the Rainbow,* and *On Eagle's Wing* seemed like a solace that blanketed her. We knew this by her breathing. Songs were performed gently at 60 beats per minute in order to entrain with resting heart rate. Phrase endings were relaxed and seemed to breathe with her. Instrumentation was gentle: piano, oboe/English horn, and some vocals. There was ebb and flow with no startling moments. The music was a peaceful presence for all of us.

Room 217 music became a bridge between the living and the dying. It expressed words that were hard to find and difficult to say. I watched Mom gently rub and squeeze Nan's hand as the lyrics, "Did you ever know that you're my hero" were sung. There was a tacit understanding among my sisters and I that Mom was letting her go. Room 217 music accompanied Nan's final moments. She took her last breath on the last beat of the last measure of the last song – *All Through the Night*. Evidently, this song was a lullaby in Nan's generation. In every sense, the music rocked her to sleep.

In less than two years, I had lost two important people in my life. Their trajectories were very different, one a courageous eighteen-month battle with cancer, the other marked by a slow, debilitating brain condition. Yet there were similarities. Music was significant in their palliation and end-of-life experience. Their receptivity to music when they were imminently dying never wavered. It was as though music was the thread between life and death, that liminal in-between space, sustaining them when body systems were shutting down. And the music helped me in closing both relationships. My lived experience would be the basis for what would follow.

Identifying the Gaps

During the next several years, I read and learned more for myself about why music works in care. I travelled across Canada to hospice palliative care conferences, teaching caregivers about the healing capacity of music and sharing with them my personal story. I was also growing the palliative music collection as well as other Room 217 resources.

Several things became clear to me. I sensed a hunger among caregivers – professionals, volunteers, and loved ones – for more of the science behind why music works as a healing agent. They wanted and needed education. They wanted and needed targeted resources designed for persons who were palliative and dying. I became aware of a number of clinical music practices that existed in Canada. Music therapy was a growing scope of practice: harp therapists and certified music practitioners had specialized training; some provinces used professional musicians in care settings; and groups like the Health Arts Society were expanding. Community musicians were emerging in care settings. Intergenerational programs between local schools and long-term care homes were springing up across the country.

Based on the sheer number of these music practices, it was clear that another clinical group wasn't needed. Room 217 would provide support in between places, in the gaps. Several gaps existed. Access to music clinicians is uneven in Canada, especially in rural and remote areas. Creating music care resources that could be available to all would bridge the accessibility gap for purposefully designed music in care. Not every care setting can afford music clinicians. Creating reusable products (e.g., palliative music albums, dementia-friendly videos, engaging music conversation cards) would make music programming affordable and cost-effective when funding was an issue. Most importantly, music clinicians aren't always available. For example, music therapists might provide one session per week for their clients. Health Arts Society concerts might happen once a month. What about the other hours of the day and night when music could be used for supportive care? Cognitive stimulation? Social engagement? Imminent end-of-life? We identified the need to support professional, volunteer, and family caregivers with tools they could use regardless of their musical ability at any time of the day or night. Hands-on musical resources for caregivers would be designed and targeted for specific clinical outcomes (e.g., engagement, comfort, behaviour mitigation). Music education and training that could be baseline and integrated into regular care practice by all caregivers would be a focus. Applied research and knowledge translation would be important for evidence to mount and be understood and accepted.

A colleague I had met along the way, Michael Aherne, founding director of Pallium Canada, suggested that my project was more than a series of CDs. The vision could be the basis for a social enterprise. So was born the Room 217 Foundation, an organization that seeks to enrich the care experience with music. In April 2019 we incorporated as a not-for-profit registered Canadian charity, a model that fit the scope of the work. Getting music into care, making it truly accessible right across Canada at nursing stations, in recreational, psychosocial, and spiritual care programs, and in the community as an adjunct approach to care, was a big vision. This work was bigger than me and could outlive me. The vehicle needed to be a public foundation that could allow for partnerships, build bridges among other music and health groups, and combine efforts to make our collective impact stronger.

Starting an organization from scratch was exciting but also daunting. The first task was to form a board of directors. This needed to be a group of people who could help shape the vision and mission of Room 217 strategically, who could help develop the enterprising aspect of Room 217, and who could help me refine and articulate my rather large vision. We had a staff of three who all worked part-time. Each staff member was a music-lover with a caregiving story to tell and a specific business skill set. We kept overhead low. In the early years, we were building resources and a community of learning. We were making relationships and establishing a database. Practical resources for specific populations with specific targeted outcomes were being produced and delivered.

The Unfolding Mission

Our mission was fourfold: produce and deliver music care resources, offer music care education and training, deliver resources philanthropically to groups with financial barriers, and promote collaborative research in music and care. Our funding model consisted of sales of resources and services, donations, and grants. We would need to build the work one step at a time yet concurrently within the four streams.

In 2010 we held our first Music Care Conference (MCC). It was strategically held at Wilfrid Laurier University in Waterloo, Ontario. Dr. Lee Willingham and Dr. Amy Clements-Cortes, both founding directors of the Room 217 board, helped lay foundations for Room 217 to work alongside music therapy and community music practices. The day was inspirational and informational; over its course we identified and integrated common themes and issues highlighting the social and medical effects of music in care. The presenters were experts in their field either through academic training or through clinical or lived experience. All kinds of people came – it was a nexus for academics, health care practitioners, volunteers, musicians, educators, family caregivers, and others.

The impact of MCC continues. The music care learning community has since grown to more than 3,000 people. In 2018, Room 217's model was the basis for the first United Kingdom "Power of Music" conference, hosted by the University of Nottingham. MCC has provided an opportunity to bring together a variety of music and health initiatives, projects, agencies, and practices in Canada and beyond. It has been an opportunity for dialogue and learning.

In 2011, we began a music care blog and published a *Music Care Resource Guide* as an orientation tool for caregivers who wanted to learn more about music and care. This has proven helpful to caregivers by providing a framework within which to understand music and care. Exploring basic sound and music principles such as entrainment, associations, preference, and breath, and how these practically impact a care situation, helps caregivers begin to think about new care approaches and solutions.

In 2012, the second collection of palliative music was completed, making a total of 12 one-hour albums. Recollections videos for reminiscence were produced. We were ready to offer our first donor-driven program. Our business model allowed us to create philanthropic programs where cost was a barrier. We recognized that hospice palliative care resources were slim, so we developed a delivery program called Room to Room (R2R). In 2013 and 2014, Room 217 partnered with the GlaxoSmithKline Foundation to deliver music care resources to eighty-four hospice palliative sites across Canada. In return, each site collected qualitative data on the effects that Room 217 music was having. R2R reporting showed five positive outcomes:

1. *Improved quality of life* by promoting sleep, reducing agitation and restlessness, and making eating enjoyable.

2. *Assisted in relationship completion* through release and closure, promoting presence even when no one was there, providing intimate space between caregiver and loved one/client.

3. *Decreased feelings of isolation and fear* by destressing caregivers, reducing anxiety, and mitigating resistance.

4. *Helped meet psychosocial and spiritual needs* by providing comfort, enhancing communication through reminiscence, providing a backdrop for expressing grief and/or mutual support, and supporting reflection and meditation.

5. *Provided distraction from pain* through soothing relaxation and by providing an alternative (e.g., to TV).

Around this time, I began an MA focusing on music and health at the University of Toronto Faculty of Music, which had just begun the Music and Health Research Collaboratory. Dr. Lee Bartel, my supervisor, insisted that learning be as applicable to Room 217 as we could make it. My major research paper was about perceptions and attitudes of leadership towards music care in fifty-five long-term care homes across Canada (Foster & Bartel, 2016.) I wanted to understand how music was understood and delivered in this health care setting. A key output of the research was a tool called *10 Domains of Music Care Delivery* (Foster, Pearson, & Berends, 2016), which helps long-term care leaders clarify, navigate, and optimize music delivery. The resulting scientific poster earned first prize in the Masters' Category at the Canadian Association of Gerontology conference in 2014. This was significant, because it amounted to an acknowledgment that music was a legitimate care modality in the aging population and an important piece of its future landscape. Things were shifting. Music and the arts were becoming more accepted in Canada.

The feedback we were getting from MCC evaluations during the early years was that attendees wanted more education. So we began to create a Music Care Training (MCT) program that would be used as continuing education for caregivers. Our vision was to help caregivers integrate music into their regular scopes of practice effectively and responsibly. In this course, we defined music care and the music care approach. Music care is the intentional use of music by anyone to improve health and well-being. The music care approach is a paradigm within which music is understood as part of life and as integral to all aspects of caregiving and care settings. Music care is intended to be relational and to improve quality of life and care, thus contributing to overall culture change in health care. The goal of music care is to integrate and assimilate music into the care environment as a primary approach to whole-person care. In the spring of 2014, we piloted the first level of MCT. By the fall of 2017 we had trained more than 700 caregivers in Level 1, around 115 in Level 2, and 36 in Level 3.

That same year we collaborated and consulted on a research project at Bridgepoint Health Centre, a new 400-bed rehabilitation and continuing care hospital in Toronto. This state-of-the-art facility wanted to develop a framework for optimizing music in their patients' daily lives. It was during this study that the *10 Domains of Music Care* tool was refined and tested.

Concurrently, the *Pathways Singing Program* for dementia care was being designed and produced. Pathways was not just a resource – it was a ready-to-use program that could be used over and over again by professional, volunteer, and family caregivers in various care settings. We had conducted pilot and beta tests of the program. There were five key results:

1. *Improved musical responsiveness* indicated by singing, humming, whistling, and clapping.

2. *Increased socialization* through alertness, interest in surroundings, and participation.

3. *Reduced responsive behaviours* – specifically agitation, apathy, and wandering.

4. *Changes in behaviour*, including prolonged eye contact, facial expressions, and verbal communication.

5. Increased pleasure and happiness.

Pathways was launched in the fall of 2015. It is being used today in hundreds of care settings.

By this time, our staff had doubled in size. We had added program development and support staff. In 2016, we developed and produced Music Care Conversation Cards, a tool used in one-to-one visits with older adults. The cards are a collection of pictures and questions that catalyze memories and conversations about music in our lives. It is used by volunteers and staff in a variety of settings to begin dialogue and musical exchanges.

Looking back over the first decade, we had accomplished a lot. Room 217 had created a music care approach that everyone can use; developed a brand of music care resources and educational services to support caregivers; and collected evidence about how music makes meaningful changes in care. Inadvertently, we had become leaders in an emerging field.

Music Care Leadership

From my perspective, leadership is a process of social influence involving visioning, motivating, communicating, risk-taking, team building, creating, serving, being empathetic, managing, and improving. Room 217 contends that music care leadership involves at least two more things: personal insight about music, and contextual understanding about issues of care (Foster & Pearson, 2016). Personal insight can be developed through lived experience and academic learning. In either case, insight comes through reflecting on how we relate to music and how it relates to us. The Room 217 story exemplifies that. Every member of our staff has a story to tell about music in personal and professional caregiving situations and is keenly aware of its effects. Additionally, some of us have pursued more knowledge and credentials in the area of music and health. Insight is a valuable platform from which to lead.

Music care leadership also involves understanding the context in which it is being delivered. Being connected to the issues, people, and facts brings relevancy and opportunity. Several converging realities exist in Canada that provide the context for Room 217's work.

Relational care (Wyer, Alves, Post, & Quinlan, 2014; Downie & Llewellyn, 2008), also known as "person-centred care" (Kitwood, 1997, 1992; Carlstrom & Ekman, 2012), "patient-centred care" (Squire et al., 2006; Epstein & Street, 2011; Armstrong, 2011; Feo & Kitson, 2016), and "whole person care" (Hutchinson, 2011; Hansen, Walters, & Howes, 2016; Donadio, 2005; Freeman, 2015), are increasingly being accepted as standards of care in Canada. For example, Canada's 2012 Mental Health Commission's national strategy for mental health is titled "Changing Lives, Changing Directions," and calls on Canadians to promote mental health in everyday settings and to reduce stigma by recognizing how much we all have in common. The Alzheimer Society of Canada released a 2012 brief calling for new language to be used when discussing persons with dementia that would help validate personhood rather than victimhood. In 2009, HealthCareCAN called on the government to address the larger issue of quality of care, specifically in long-term care, and to de-emphasize the sole focus on tasks of physical care and prioritize emotional, cognitive, social, and spiritual care. Since 2015, medically assisted death has been legal in Canada and provides an option for persons meeting specific eligibility requirements. The social model of person-centred care focuses on relationships and quality of life. The intention is that a person be honoured and empowered, and not lost in the daily tasks of care.

Canada's population is aging, and the Canadian health care system is coming under incredible stress on two fronts: volume, and increased longevity. In 2016, for the first time, more Canadians were over sixty-five than were under fourteen. There is a shortage of resources, beds, and staff within the system to handle this tsunami of older people. Canadians are living longer. According to a World Health Statistics 2014 report, the average life expectancy in Canada for males born in 2012 is 80, and for females 84. Compare this to males born in 1990 (74) and females (81). HealthCareCAN recognizes that baby boomers will have a dramatic impact on the Canadian health care system by doubling in number over the next twenty years. It is projected that more than one quarter of Canadians will be over sixty-five by 2036.

Because of this pressure on the health care system, care is shifting to the community. Community programs and supports for mental health, hospice palliative care, outpatient clinics, and so on are helping meet the demand. More older adults are aging in place with home support. Those who are still being placed in long-term continuing care often have complex medical conditions. Most residents of Canadian long-term care homes have some form of dementia. The possibility of comorbidities – that is, the simultaneous presence of two chronic diseases or conditions (e.g., dementia + Parkinson's Disease, or dementia + neuropathy) – has increased, which makes care provision more complex. This juxtaposition of complex medical care and a changing relational social framework provides both challenges and opportunities.

The turn toward non-pharmacological solutions, particularly in long-term care, is driving organizations such as the Canadian Foundation for Healthcare Improvement to launch pan-Canadian research and initiatives aimed at reducing the use of anti-psychotics in dementia care. It is encouraging that efforts are being made to integrate efforts and form partnerships where there is duplication of services. Research into innovative technological solutions to health care delivery, rehabilitation, programming, and so forth, is being funded by organizations such as the Canadian Centre for Aging and Brain Health Innovation and the Holland Bloorview Kids Rehabilitation Hospital.

Music-specific realities in care delivery are varied. That care could look like services provided by music therapists, who are accredited and self-regulated. Community musicians and music care specialists such as harp therapists and certified music practitioners may provide bedside care. A variety of sound/music-based interventions are being used by a variety of professional practitioners – for example, speech pathologists are using melodic intonation therapy for speech rehabilitation. Room 217 has developed a Music Care Delivery framework that describes 10 Domains of Music Care Delivery in Canada. (Foster, Pearson, & Berends, 2016).

In light of these converging realities in Canadian care culture, Room 217 seeks to answer a number of questions. How does music fit into person-centred care? Do personal support workers, nurses, and other care providers have the confidence, training, and resources to integrate music into their caring practices? How can caregivers integrating music care into their daily practice ensure that music is used safely and ethically? If music is to be part of the changing culture of care in Canada, where are the measures indicating that music is making a difference to quality of life across the care spectrum and across the lifespan? If the impact of music care is not measured, then how can it be improved or sustained? Do administrators and key stakeholders recognize the value of music delivery? Where is the common music care understanding that applies to all music-based interventions? How does music become a more primary approach to health care?

The implications of these converging realities and the scope and magnitude of the subsequent questions they generate pave created a leadership agenda in which Room 217's future chapters will unfold.

Challenges and Opportunities

Executive educator James Kouzes says it well: "Change is the province of leaders. It is the work of leaders to inspire people to do things differently, to struggle against uncertain odds, and to persevere toward a misty image of a better future" (p. 1). Room 217's work comes with both challenges and opportunities.

Health care in Canada is administered provincially, not nationally. While there may be national strategies from federal associations and groups, it is the provinces that deliver the nuts and bolts of care with their own standards of practice, regulations, and funding models. Caring practices may be called different things in different provinces (i.e., long-term care may be known as nursing homes; personal support workers may be known as health care aides). For Room 217, the challenge is to learn these variations in the language of care and to keep on top of provincial priorities. We have developed some internal tools to help us track language and have established significant relationships in many of the provinces and territories.

The impact of what we do can be measured using traditional business and research models, but measuring social impact, or "social return on investment" (SROI), is challenging. SROI is the measure for social enterprise – a relatively new design (Martin & Osberg, 2007). Learning SROI's protocols for impact measurement is a challenge. We are finding tools and support networks to help us measure and report using best practices.

Each week, new opportunities present themselves that can be stimulating and overwhelming at the same time. Learning to stay focused and true to our direction, being able to know who we are and who we are not, is essential. We have a three-year strategic planning process that keeps us focused and have developed internal tracking tools that will keep us moving forward while allowing for the unexpected. We are beginning to look at scaling our model into other countries, and he we have encountered some initial interest in Britain and the United States.

Room 217 represents neither a scope of practice nor a context of care. We are an organization that moves *in between* scopes of practice and contexts of care. We bridge these gaps. The challenge is that our voice represents an approach to care, not a specific practice or specific location of care. We do our best to leverage this position as a strength and as an opportunity to be non-partisan and inclusive in our outlook on music in care.

For example, Music Care Partners is a program we are developing to help long-term care communities make music a more primary approach and solution to the challenges residents face. In a pilot study at three long-term care homes in Ontario, Room 217 was able to leverage music care as a specific solution to reducing residents' isolation and loneliness. Using an adapted participatory action research model (Baum, MacDougall, & Smith, 2006), and building on the music care framework and models of music care delivery, we designed and implemented an operational music care process. This process, which is managed by a site team, makes it possible to integrate music initiatives and interventions into daily life and make meaningful changes.

We are able to collaborate with a variety of local partners such as academic research institutes, organizations for the aging, music therapy businesses, Alzheimer's organizations, and cultural music centres to present Music Care Conferences across Canada. We speak to and write for a variety of stakeholder groups ranging from professional practice groups, to outreach and education groups, to service clubs and other community organizations, to academic institutions and journals, on a wide range of topics surrounding music and care.

The notion of learning through the arts in Canada has been developed over the past several decades to include settings beyond school classrooms. For example, in 2003, the Royal Conservatory of Music developed a program called Living through the Arts that provided opportunities for challenged individuals (i.e., those living with chronic illness, brain injury, substance abuse, or trauma) to communicate more effectively through various art forms, thus promoting a sense of personal capacity. Community music education and the development of community musicians has helped blur the boundaries. Sasha Judelson, a Masters in Community Music student, created a community choir that placed people living with dementia, their care partners, and high school student volunteers together in a choir as her capstone project. Borders that once siloed music education from health care have become blurred and provide an opportunity for enriched, multidisciplinary arts learning. Situating music care learning centres in care homes, hospices, and cultural centres as well as online is creating a new kind of applied music care education that may serve as a model for other health arts modalities to employ.

We recognize we can't be all things to all people. That said, our greatest opportunity may be to provide a voice for music in care that is grounded in lived personal and professional experience, expanded through research literature, and responsive to changing health care priorities and realities. As we have opportunity to speak, we continue to listen and learn.

Key Learnings and Contributions

A key learning for Room 217 has been this: we must not assume that gatekeepers in health care understand or perceive how powerful and therapeutic music can be. While the term "complementary" has largely been dropped from its association with music in care, we still have a long way to go in educating gatekeepers, pursestring holders, and the public at large about the healing capacity of music. One contribution Room 217 has made is to articulate in everyday language what the music care approach is, clarify its language, define its terms, debunk myths about it, and strengthen perceptions about music as a primary approach to care.

One thing we learned early on was that having everyone "at the table" makes for a stronger learning environment. We learned this from our friends in hospice palliative care. All stakeholders come to their conference table: physicians, nurses, personal support workers, family caregivers and loved ones, hospice volunteers, media, musicians, cannabis suppliers, community agencies, death with dignity advocates, social workers, and so on. We bring our specialized understanding, lived experiences, and questions about death and dying into a larger collective. In this way, we gain a more comprehensive and possibly authentic perspective on death and dying. Room 217 has adopted this cross-disciplinary, inclusive view of education. All stakeholders around music and care are welcome to come together at our conference table. Many stakeholders aren't musicians, nor do they have music training. But they bear witness to music's impact on care. Other stakeholders are clinicians. We feel that our collective sharing with one another creates a more authentic and relevant learning experience that continues to shift care cultures from within.

Change takes time and does not come steadily. Global leaders in music and care present their latest research and interventions at our conferences, and as they do, our thinking evolves. Post-MCC evaluations have shown us that the greatest takeaway for MCC participants is that they learn that music is more than entertainment – it has a powerful therapeutic capacity. This shift in thinking, undeniable once it is experienced, opens the door for expanding music care in any context. We have learned it always starts here. Patience, then, becomes an important virtue.

The same is true for building relationships. As a pioneering social enterprise in Canada, we work with customers, donors, and various stakeholder groups; all of that requires relationship-building. We have learned that relationships take time to develop. Trust is built on being able to deliver over time. Taking calculated risks that involve people with their own strengths and limitations is part of being courageous. Staying open to conversations and possibilities enables us to build bridges leading to partnerships and affiliations that may first have seemed unattainable. We've seen this time and again. As we share our experiences with other health arts groups, we emphasize the importance of relationship-building.

Knowing who we are and who we are not has been a key learning. I recall that in the development phases of the Room 217 Foundation, board members wondered how our pieces fit together. We stayed true to some core principles. We determined that Room 217 would not be clinical; rather, we would partner with and support clinicians. We are committed to music in care; while the broader vision of health arts is scintillating, our contribution is about music. We support care partners, those who are and who are not musicians. We are knowledge translators and consultants. We collaborate in research, which is then applied. We have learned to stay true to that vision, and the pieces fit. Differentiating ourselves from clinical practices and other programs is an important means to strengthen our identity and to clarify others' misunderstandings or misperceptions. For example, music *care* is an approach that anyone can use, whereas music *therapy* is a clinical practice conducted by accredited professionals.

Our regard for measuring what we do has increased. We have learned that having specific outcomes to measure and evaluating them is important. Impact needs to be substantiated. Every Room 217 initiative has been put through a measuring process. As we grow in our understanding of social impact, we anticipate this being an area of continuing development.

I'm often asked what Room 217's greatest contribution has been. It could be that we have been leaders and risk takers around music and care in Canada. It could be that we have created a learning community, a hub for Canadians from all kinds of contexts to come together around music and care. It might also be that we have defined the music care approach and have begun to operationalize it with processes, tools, and resources. For me, the answer goes back to the original Room 217 at the hospital with my dying Dad. Our greatest contribution is that we have changed the experience for people living in life-limiting and complex care circumstances and for their caregivers.

Here is a sample of some of our greatest contributions, shared by caregivers from across Canada:

I read an article about your music recently, looked you up on the web and knew your music was something I have been searching for. My Mom and Dad were killed in a car accident last summer and we are really just beginning to grieve their loss. As the anaesthetic of shock and disbelief wear[s] off, I have found your music so soothing and comforting. There are times when I just want to be alone with my grief and I find listening to your music helps me to be still and experience and sort through what I am feeling. What a great gift to give someone who is experiencing a recent loss. – *Kate*

The special man for whom I bought Country Road was having a particularly restless morning. He is young – just turned 61 – and has been with us for 3 years already. No nursing home will take him. He has a very advanced frontal lobe dementia which, at present, leaves him with little speech except for the occasional "no!!" or a simple yell. He paces constantly. From morning to night, if he isn't pacing, he is sitting only momentarily at the edge of his bed. I brought the CD player to his doorway, turned it on and was quite frankly stunned to see his reaction. He stopped pacing, stood perfectly still, started to simply walk himself around in a small circle (something brand-new) and when he did start to pace again, it was much more slowly, much more calmly and every once in a while, he would turn again in a circle. I had brought in a glider rocker to his room, before the music began and after 4 songs, was able to guide him to sit. And he did, for 3 more songs! And tap his toes to the beat. Incredible! He had not sat still for more than 4-5 seconds in months. It brought me to tears. – *Theresa, hospital nurse*

My husband is in late stage Alzheimer's-related dementia. He enjoys the pictures and music and occasionally makes accompanying sounds (his version of singing). I have noticed when I play Recollections at meal time, when I am feeding him, it is easier for him to eat. I think it's because he has lost control of his tongue. When he eats, his tongue gets in the way and frustrates him. The music and pictures take his mind off his anxiety and he is better able to eat and enjoy his meals. – *Sandra, family caregiver*

I have, in the 2 days since the workshop, found an opportunity to use the [music care] training several times. One resident in particular had just come out of a showering experience that had put her into a state of sobbing, shivering, rocking, crying and moaning shock. I was able to use the call and response, the humming, the singing and the breathing to calm her and lull her to sleep. Without your training I may have been at a loss as I have never seen this resident so upset. Thank you so much for giving me the knowledge and confidence to use music care. – *Theresa, volunteer and program coordinator, long-term care*

My dad is really enjoying the Room 217 albums. The song that he recognized after just a few notes was "Old Man River." He then began to give a commentary about the "slave trade" in the deep south. Very fascinating. The nurses also told me that one night he was restless and not sleeping. So they turned on the Room 217 music in the CD player and he fell fast asleep almost immediately. – *Anne, family caregiver*

I just wanted to let you know that we have a music therapy intern doing his preceptorship here at Bobby's Hospice. What a difference he is making to our patients and families! We had a patient dying yesterday on his birthday. The family asked our music therapist to come into the room and sing Happy Birthday and some other favourite tunes. The patient died immediately after and the family was so thankful for the peaceful, music-filled death. We have already started to plan to keep him on staff for at least 8 hours per week once his preceptorship is complete. Thank you so much for all your leadership in this field and for supporting us and working with us over all these years. We are so pleased to finally be in a position to have a music therapist. – *Sandy, executive director, hospice*

We use *Pathways* as an interactive tool and watch the clients transform before our very eyes. One client, who is unable to converse, can sing. She sings word for word. Songs are so deeply embedded in this woman's neural pathways that even disease can't take them away. In another instance, a man who is visually impaired and usually quiet, sings at the top of his lungs, and is totally engaged in the music session. – *Audrey, program manager, adult day program*

Conclusion

Since the foundation began, there have been moments when I wish my Dad was sitting here in my office. I would ask him business advice. I would share my vision with him, and he would feed it back to me with penetrating questions and considerations that would open new perspectives, thinking, and approaches to music and care. That's just the way it was with him: vision, insight, and pragmatism, like three strands braided into a lovely work of art. And of course, I would ask him more directly about what it was like with all of us singing around his bedside as he was dying.

In some transcendental way, Dad is here with me in this work. His memory is revived each time I share this story. He is the face I see when I think about our end users of music care resources, representing the complexities of suffering and the desire to live. His story does inspire me.

It is my core belief and lived experience in the power of music as a healing agent that continues to motivate me. Music has a profound reach into every human domain and into the liminal spaces, touching and healing places that are sick, tired, broken, atrophying, dysregulated, hidden, throbbing, arrhythmic, and disconnected. Music has the capacity to meet us where we're at and be truly transformative, improving gait, enhancing mood, lowering blood pressure, providing an opportunity for social engagement and participation, triggering memory, offering peace and comfort and a host of other good things.

I'm certain that neither Dad nor I could have possibly imagined what would be resurrected from his death in Room 217.

CHAPTER 22

Finding Our Music, Strengthening Care
A Case for Baseline Music Care Training

Sarah Pearson

Introduction

AS A CERTIFIED MUSIC therapist, practising musician, and psychotherapist, one of my core beliefs is in the power of music to transform spaces and connect people to the best of themselves. Client after client I encounter share stories of being told they couldn't carry a tune, of being slapped on the wrist by piano teachers, or of being instructed to mouth the words in their school choirs. I also encounter clients who, as professional musicians, feel disconnected from the spontaneous joy they once drew from their instrument and burdened by the high musical standards they've come to expect of themselves.

My own relationship to music has been coloured by physical and emotional challenges – the pain of losing a solo, the fierce desire to compete with my peers, the heartbreak of vocal injury, the terror of revealing original songs. It is, in fact, this complex relationship with music that led me to become a music therapist in the first place. In spite of the roller coaster my musical path has taken me on, there was always something transcendent about music I have found worth fighting for. A therapist's job is to help clients understand the blocks in their lives that are keeping them from their true selves, in order to move through them and let their true selves come out. As a music therapist, I consider it my job to understand and move through the blocks keeping people from their true music, and let that true music – and ultimately, their true selves – come out.

My primary site of music therapy practice is a hospital, and while my official role is to provide excellent clinical music therapy sessions to patients and families, it is, by default, also to represent music in health at large. Like many hospital-based music therapists, I am known by many as the "music person."

I've embraced this role over the years by becoming, also often by default, the point person for wider music initiatives in the hospital. When the local symphony wants to send musicians to perform for patients, they are directed to me. When musicians contact Volunteer Services to arrange playing in some of the open clinical spaces, they are sent to me to be interviewed and supervised. When Christmas rolls around, I coordinate the caroling. Not everyone I work with understands the distinction between music therapy and other forms of health musicking. I focus on being a bridge-builder between different approaches to music in care, while trying to demonstrate my clinical skills by example rather than words. Being the "music person" alongside being a clinical music therapist means I must consciously lean in to the grey area between different forms of health musicking, bridge the gaps between them by clearly identifying roles, and, ultimately, take a leadership position as the music expert.

I would like to think that my master's degree and the thousand-hour internship I completed to become a music therapist gives me an expert edge on how music impacts health and wellness. I am also aware that music can have adverse effects on people as much as it can have positive ones (Isenberg, 2012; Swayne, 2014), and that health-musicking experiences can range from surface-level to profound. So when I'm intersecting and collaborating with community musicians, volunteers, and other health-musicking initiatives, I have these questions in my mind:

1. What is our shared baseline understanding of how music impacts well-being?

2. How can we ensure the quality of the music being used?

3. How can we mitigate against the negative effects that music can have?

These questions point to the increasing complexity of having a growing body of unregulated musicians in health care settings. Ultimately, I am interested in exploring the potential beneficial outcomes embedded in this phenomenon: the potential of creating a shared language, a shared community of practice, and a shared vision of music being used in care in a plurality of ways, which all inevitably result in more music for more people. With so many opportunities for music in care, so many people doing it, and so little standardization of music in care, a framework for locating practices seems to be a needed tool (Loewy & Aldridge, 2014).

It is with these questions in mind that, alongside my music therapy career, I have created a training program for care providers and musicians of all backgrounds to develop a basic understanding of music in care, called Music Care Training (MCT). It is this program – its content, context, and function, and the ripples it has caused –that will be the focus of this chapter.

Music Care Training: An Overview

Music Care Training (MCT) is a three-level, fifty-two-hour continuing education program that I developed as a project with a social enterprise dedicated to promoting the wider presence of music in health care. The training is meant to be complementary to other scopes of practice, particularly those of allied health providers, and seeks to provide these caregivers with music-based tools and a theoretical basis to enrich their care practice. The course is grounded in the emerging theoretical framework of "music care." The music care approach (Foster, Pearson, & Berends, 2016, p. 199) is a theory-of-care practice that supports care providers of all backgrounds as they integrate the healing properties of music into their care, in a way that fits with their role and their scope of practice.

The course was piloted in 2014 to two cohorts of Level 1 students in Toronto, Ontario; forty-five people were trained in those first two courses. Level 2 of the course was launched several months later, as were the first out-of-province course offerings, and in 2015, Level 3 was piloted for the first time. At the time of writing, just over three years after the first Level 1 pilot, almost 750 students have completed Level 1, 160 have completed Level 2, and 36 have completed Level 3. Courses have been offered in two countries.

The course is marketed to allied health providers and family caregivers across communities, and registration is managed by the social enterprise's administrative team. Tuition is kept low to make it as accessible as possible to volunteer and family caregivers as well as professionals, and courses are offered across the country in diverse regional hubs, in order to reach caregivers where they live and work.

The Curriculum

The objective of MCT is to support caregivers in integrating music into regular care practice by:

+ developing an understanding of the music care approach, musical elements, and an evidence base for using music in care;

+ providing tools and strategies to use music more freely and intention-ally in professional and personal life; and
+ creating an individualized music care initiative for the care context.

Level 1 is a two-day, in-person course that aims to prepare students to (1) understand the basic principles of music in care, (2) gain confidence using specific music care techniques, and (3) begin developing a Music Care Initiative (MCI) – an action plan for how to use music in care.

Level 2 is also a two-day in-person course. Building upon Level 1, it surveys in more depth the research and evidence of how music is used in care. The aims are (1) to build music care strategies that are unique to the student's role and care setting, (2) increase knowledge of research about music in care, and (3) develop an awareness of the role that music can play in the circle of person-centered care.

Level 3 is an eight-week course that mostly happens online, with regular individual mentoring between students and instructors, and culminates with one in-person retreat day, where students present on their work. The course prepares students to become music care advocates by (1) developing practical skills to optimize their ability to use music in their care context, (2) developing a deeper awareness of how music can address issues in their care context, and (3) deepening their personal relationship to music.

None of these courses require prior knowledge or skill in music. We take the stance that a person can become a music care advocate in ways that extend beyond having explicit clinical or musical skill. For example, a person can advocate for music care by taking a leadership role to leverage funds to hire experts; a front-line care provider can significantly change her approach to care by starting to sing with their care receivers while performing tasks; and, a seasoned clinician can develop a self-care plan using music that significantly mitigates his risk of burnout. At the heart of the course is a belief that music belongs to all people and that we all have music within us, and that with some skilful nudging, this music can be used to make others' lives better.

Participants, Instructors, and Delivery

To date, the course has been taught in twenty different communities across Canada and Britain, with registration open to the whole community and with a cap of twenty-four participants per group in Levels 1 and 2, and ten participants in Level 3. The course has also been taught as exclusive in-house training for care settings and groups of staff. Participants have included volunteers with older adults, physiotherapists, massage therapists, recreation therapists, chaplains, health care aids, therapy assistants, music therapists, program managers in a long-term care (LTC), social workers, day program managers, hospital volunteers, hospice staff, nurses, radiation therapists, administrative assistants, food services managers at a LTC, community musicians, and students.

Seven instructors have been trained to teach the course and meet the demand for regional courses throughout the year. The instructors all have advanced degrees and experience in music and health and are experienced adult educators. Roughly half the instructors are music therapists, and all have significant caregiving experience.

Giving Students Frameworks: Strategies, Effects, Tools, Fundamentals. As a baseline training, the curriculum offers students sets of tools, techniques, and concepts that are meant to be transferable to their unique contexts. These frameworks consist of the following:

- *Ten Domains of Music Care.* Based on a study by Foster and colleagues (2016), the Ten Domains of Music Care Delivery offer ten general dimensions that a music care approach can fall under. These include community music, music medicine, music therapy, music programming, environmental sound, music technology, musicking, training, research, and specialties. When this framework is emphasized at each level of the course, students grow from being able to vaguely describe the ways they use music in care, to becoming adept at identifying what they do specifically and how it may differ from or be similar to other scopes of practice or approaches to music care.

- *Ten Strategies.* During Level 1, after learning some fundamentals of music care and music theory, participants are offered ten simple strategies for applying music in care. These include singing simple songs, humming, creating a self-care plan using music, and listening to music intentionally together, as well as developing a strategic plan. The simplicity of each strategy is deliberate – it is meant to generate new ideas for caregivers, provide them with easily transferable music tools for a plurality of care settings, and boost their confidence that they too can deepen their care practice with music in ways they may not have expected.

- *Six Fundamentals of Music.* Throughout Levels 1 and 2, six fundamentals of music theory are explored. This gives everyone a shared language regarding how music works. It also questions students' personal assumptions they are "unmusical" and enhances their confidence. These fundamentals include rhythm, timbre, melody, harmony, dynamics, and form. The teaching approaches for these sections are experiential and strongly music-centred and focus on how the different musical elements can impact people and relationships, particularly in care contexts.

+ *Ten Effects.* In Level 2, students are introduced to more of the research base supporting music's impact on care. To reflect the diverse ways that music has been shown to impact the whole person, ten effects of music are explored, each with its own module and bibliography of evidence. Diverse teaching methodologies are used, ranging from experiential to didactic. These ten effects, which have been chosen as the most relevant for the students, include rehabilitation, pain management, community narratives, socialization, mood, grief management, memory, attention, meaning-making, and creativity. The literature cited draws on diverse populations and issues, such as mental illness, memory care, hospice care, hospitals, youth settings, and religious communities.

+ *Ten Tools.* In Level 3, ten tools for music care advocacy are offered to students. These tools are meant to help develop the four main components of music care advocacy as found in the curriculum: personal insight into music and care approaches, awareness of the care community in which we work, communication skills, and ability to effect operational change. The tools include but are not limited to these: care community profile (an assessment of community needs); a template for creating an elevator pitch; tools for creating a personal creative music project, such as an original song; templates for grant applications; and evaluation metrics.

+ *The Music Care Initiative.* The music care initiative (MCI) follows the student through all three levels. This course is built on the belief that intentionally integrated music can transform care culture. We want to ensure that students leave the training with a changed approach to care. In Level 1, students are introduced to the MCI: they name a new initiative they would like to undertake and are given a template planning tool to begin filling out, which helps track and evaluate the initiative. Some class time is dedicated to sharing and receiving feedback on ideas as a group. In Level 2, students are required to complete the template and submit it for feedback. In Level 3, students are expected to complete an initiative in their community during the duration of the course and present on the results. They receive regular individual mentorship as they do this.

The music care initiative does not need to be a specialized program. In fact, the beauty of the music care approach is that no initiative is too small. The broader goal of the training is not to implement specific music programs but to contribute to culture change in health care. Here are some past music care initiatives: a chaplain creating a simple sound environment plan in a nursing home, so as to reduce the ambient noise that comes from radios at nursing stations and from TVs left on at random times and stations; a recreation therapist learning the skills to run a simple bell choir with clients in an adult day program; a mental health worker facilitating a coffeehouse with a community mental health agency; and a program director at a LTC home hiring a music therapist. One student took on the project of writing "wake up" songs for each of his kids, to help support the often rocky morning routine in their household.

Personal Insight. An essential component of a person-centered care culture is that it treats the caregiver as a whole person just as much as it does the care receiver (Morgan & Yoder, 2012). So it was essential for us to build into this curriculum some element of self-awareness through music. A core competency of Level 3 is demonstrating a personal insight into music. This competency requires students to move beyond any assumptions about what "good" music is as well as any learned beliefs about their ability or lack of ability as musicians. The music care approach purports that anyone can connect with music regardless of ability, and MCT students are no exception.

One requirement of Level 1 is to create a music self-care plan. Experiential components in Level 2 enable students to forge new connections among music theory, science, and their own lived experience. In Level 3, each student is required to facilitate a live group musicking experience. Whether they grow more vulnerable with themselves about the impact of recorded music on them or their care partners, learn to play an instrument, challenge themselves to sing in public for the first time, or write a song despite swearing that they "don't have a creative bone" in their body, all students are expected to push their personal comfort zones and grow in their awareness of how they personally relate to music.

Instructors. At the time of writing there are seven active instructors for this course. Instructors must meet certain criteria, which include musical, caregiving, and teaching experience. They must have formal music training at a professional level; an ability to freely improvise; degrees in disciplines or music education related to health musicking; two years' experience in the caregiving sector; experience using music in care settings; a basic knowledge of research in music and health; and two years of adult education experience. Finally, they must be flexible when it comes to using creative teaching methodologies. Instructors first train by shadowing a course. Ongoing training retreats are held annually.

MCT is a set, standardized program with specific delivery criteria. Each MCT course has a student manual as well as an instructor's guide that offers pedagogical approaches and timing suggestions as well as a list of the materials needed. An instructor's handbook outlines roles, expectations, and operational tasks that Room 217 expects of its instructors. Each instructor is invited to deliver the curriculum using his or her own unique delivery style and is encouraged to use comfortable teaching approaches. Instructor retreats focus predominantly on mutual sharing of different teaching strategies.

Locating Ourselves

Each level of MCT begins with an exercise called "Locating Ourselves." We are invited to identify the roles we bring to the music care training. These roles include "parent," "nurse," "teacher," "musician," and so on. We then write this role into a blank space in a sentence in the textbook:

I am a _____ and I use the music care approach.

This exercise reinforces that the music care approach is not a unique set of skills or techniques. It is a philosophy of care, and it is up to the students to know their professional or volunteer roles and to strengthen those roles with music. Students who take these baseline courses are introduced to some of the broad reaches of music and health research and experience the impact of music on themselves. This provides them with the insight and context to use music within their skill sets and with more intention and responsibility.

Locating ourselves helps reinforce the need for a music care framework. At present, there is little regulation of music in care, and in health care communities and among the broader public, any act of health musicking is often referred to as "music therapy." This points to a serious misunderstanding of health musicking and of the multiple roles that community musicians, clinically informed musicians, and other music medicine interventions can play.

Locating ourselves is a critical component of the Music Care Training: (1) it helps reinforce the importance of clear nomenclature around music and health roles; (2) it highlights the multiplicity of roles that music health can encompass; (3) it trains students to educate the wider public about the breadth of music and care roles; and (4) it helps students clarify how they use music in their practice and how to develop this further within their professional parameters.

Students at Level 3 are expected to achieve the competencies of an advocate. The advocacy competencies for students are as follows: insight into their personal relationship with music, an awareness of the impact of music on their care community, an understanding of communication tools, and an ability to effect operational change. This does not presume that they have all the skills of a practitioner, but it does presume an awareness that they understand the scope of music care approaches, that they understand how music can impact their own care community, and that they can advocate for music care to be optimized and for experts to deliver the highest calibre of practices.

The Need for a Baseline Training

The rationale for a baseline training approach is that music is already used pervasively in care. With mounting evidence that music can have both positive and adverse effects on well-being, some basic training standard should be the norm for care providers. This is demonstrated in the following example. I often ask Level 1 students this question in Day 1 of the training, during the module on Environmental Sound:

> "How many of you have TV or radio playing in you care space (often a nursing home or hospital)?" Almost all hands go up.
>
> "How many of you have guidelines about what channel the TV or radio is set to?" No hands go up.
>
> "Guidelines about volume?" Crickets. "Duration of time the TV is on?" I go on. "Many health care centres now have scent-free policies. Can you envision having a sound environment policy? What if there were some *very simple* guidelines about when the TV goes on and who is responsible for turning it off? What if there was a designated quiet time? Some conversation about radio channels or volume control? What if there was someone deemed responsible to implement this? Do you see this as doable?" Inevitably, heads start nodding and ideas start churning. What I'm proposing isn't terribly complex; students recognize the impact it could have on their community.

Examples like this one prove a point – that music is widely incorporated into the daily fabric of most care cultures, but without intention, deliberation, or leadership. A recent study of music in long-term care in Canada found that *all* LTC homes use music, but *none* provided training for caregivers who use music (Bartel & Foster, 2016). It is hard to imagine any other intervention used that widely with a vulnerable sector that *doesn't* have a baseline training requirement.

It is the nature of music that many of us want to use it for well-being. I encounter people both within and outside my care community who offer various unregulated services such as "singing therapy," "music healing," and "resonance therapy." Because the term "therapy" is unprotected in Canada, there is nothing stopping people from offering these services, and it is up to the public to make informed choices when accessing them. Regulating any form of health musicking would be akin to regulating music itself. Yet with so many practitioners and services, it seems timely and necessary that there be some general education about the scope of music in care, as well as a research-informed base of more established practices.

The curriculum itself could serve as a standard for understanding different approaches to health musicking. The curriculum is not a regulatory tool, but it does offer a language for understanding the multitude of ways music can be used for health and well-being. One of the most significant outcomes of this training is that it has provided students with the tools to define their roles more clearly.

Embedded in the MCT curriculum is the message that it is a baseline training, not a specialized training. It is made clear in both the course materials and the instructor's teachings that the training does not offer a certification or licence in a particular technique or practice. This means that, as a baseline training, it can offer students the following:

1. an awareness of the scope of music's role in well-being and care;

2. a tool to help locate and define their unique approach;

3. a rudimentary sensitivity to basic music principles and how they impact care relationships; and

4. simple techniques, tools, and methods that can be applied to unique roles or scopes of practice.

In Canada, the Canadian Hospice Palliative Care Association offers an affordable baseline training in the palliative approach called "Fundamentals of Palliative Care." Offered in communities across the country, this course has no prerequisite – it is open to volunteers, nurses, chaplains, physicians, and anyone else interested in learning the baseline philosophy of palliative care. I took this course when I first started working in a palliative setting, and when I began to design MCT, I reviewed my materials from this course for inspiration. Like music care, palliative care is an approach to practice that can be used by anyone, from volunteers to family members to physicians. Not everything in the palliative care course I took was relevant to my particular role (music therapy), but it exposed me to the wider world of palliative care and gave me a sense of how much I *didn't* know. It helped me locate where some of my strengths lay.

For example, while I wouldn't be able to do much in the way of prescribing the right narcotics, I could do much in the way of supporting healthy grieving.

The MCT curriculum has been designed to fit the need for baseline training. MCT addresses that need in the following ways:

1. *Understanding Context.* Any individual who hopes to make the best use of music in a caring role must know both the environment they are working in and their role within it. By surveying music- and health-related research, students gain a clearer context for their own approach to using music in care; they also enrich the landscape in which they will be situating themselves. MCT helps define boundaries. Community musicians, for example, may learn about music psychotherapy, helping them understand where the breadth of what they do with music begins and ends. A harp therapist taking the course may learn about neurologic music therapy, opening their eyes for the first time to the notion of combining scientific uses of music with their interventions. This course does not train them in these approaches. It informs them about those approaches, thus helping them locate themselves and define their scope of practice.

2. *Music as a Tool for Culture Change.* The music care approach is meant to contribute to a changing culture of care, from the medical model to person-centred, relational-care models. This is supported by the core belief that music can enhance the well-being of *all* people in the circle of care.

3. *Understanding the Scope of Music in Care.* The rationale for baseline training is also rooted in the current climate of health and social care, where the presence of music is only increasing (Raglio, 2011, 2015). With this has come a growing body of formal and informal approaches and subsequent trainings, with varying degrees of regulation. These include continuing education to practise neurologic music therapy (four days), and trainings to become a sound healer (100 hours), a certified health care musician (two semesters), or a certified clinical musician (six to twelve months), as well as apprenticeships to become musicians in health care (varying training requirements). Music therapy certification in North America requires a minimum of four years of post-secondary education and a 1,000-hour internship. Awareness of the diversity of music care delivery models is crucial to making informed leadership decisions about incorporating music effectively into care plans.

Bridging the Gaps: Embracing a Dual Role as a Music Therapist and Curriculum Developer

For me, wearing both hats as a music therapist and a curriculum developer has been critical to the MCT program's development. It is only because I am confident that my advanced music therapy training has positioned me as an expert that I have been able to co-develop the baseline curriculum with my colleague, whose expertise in music education, music health research, family caregiving, and leadership has also been critical to the curriculum.

The response from my fellow Canadian music therapy colleagues to MCT's roll-out and to its subsequent growth across the country has been mixed. The concerns expressed have been basically two:

1. The program poses a risk to the music therapy profession, for a training program in music care sends mixed messages to potential employers and perhaps threatens music therapy jobs.

2. The program poses a risk to the general public and to potential care receivers. The use of music in care requires a skill level that is at least equivalent to a bachelor's in music therapy.

The positive feedback from music therapy colleagues in Canada has made the following points:

1. Supporting more people to use music authentically and effectively falls under our vocation as music therapists.

2. With so many people using music in care, it is important to set a baseline understanding that can serve as a standard.

3. The training provides an exemplar for how music therapists can take a leadership role as both clinicians and expert trainers of people interested in health musicking, particularly as music therapists are among those instructing the course.

The concerns raised about MCT by music therapists point to wider issues within the music therapy profession. The issue of protecting jobs is synonymous with music therapy's readiness to define its scope of practice. Currently in Canada, music therapy does not have a defined scope of practice, and this makes it a challenge to promote music therapy while critiquing the use of music in health care by other practitioners. Music therapists often facilitate programs and groups that could, theoretically, be practised ethically by non-clinical musicians (e.g., bell choirs, sing-along groups). What makes music therapy unique is (1) the primacy of the therapeutic relationship, which requires extensive training and supervision for those who wish to qualify as practitioners, and (2) the focus on clinical goals. Not every health care setting will see the value of these factors or be willing to pay for them, and their interest may be in boosting music programming rather than boosting the clinical team. In such cases, if other capable musicians are available, it is unreasonable to claim that these positions pose a threat to music therapists' jobs.

Some MCT participants have signed up on the expectation that they will receive training in music therapy, only to learn quickly that music therapy is something far more specific than they had assumed. Occasionally someone will claim that they are "already doing music therapy" because, for example, they are leading a hymn-sing with residents at a nursing home, and leave the course understanding how more accurately to locate their work within a framework of music care.

Music therapists continue to advocate for what they do, but they are also aware of the grey areas that separate health musicking practitioners. Our roles are challenging to define, yet identifying them is critical if music is to be used and integrated effectively, and if as many qualified stakeholders as possible are to be involved in music. Community musicians, music therapists, music care advocates, music educators, and other invested people work together best when they know one another's roles and when each feels that his or her own role is supported in the circle of care and among communities of invested health musickers.

Bridging the Gaps – Testing the International Waters with MCT in England

Because MCT is a baseline curriculum, it is crucial that it be transferable to a plurality of contexts. In the fall of 2017, around three years after launching MCT in Canada, the University of Nottingham invited us to come teach this course, through a combined effort with their continuing education department and their Arts and Dementia research group. The university's rationale for bringing this curriculum all the way from Canada was twofold. First, the organizers claimed that no similar training was available in England. Second, with so much interest in arts and health in their country, and no formal thread linking those interests together, a baseline training seemed a significant step toward starting a formal conversation about effective music delivery.

The UK is a particularly interesting place for MCT to be taught. More so than in Canada, music and arts practices in health and social settings are both abundant and diverse. Because of the multitude of practices and practitioners for integrating music into care (Raglio, 2011, 2015; Loewy & Aldridge, 2014), from health care musicians and music practitioners to music therapists and community musicians, the need for a framework may be more timely in the UK than in Canada. One of the students who attended MCT in England addressed this issue with me.

"There's a whole group of us in England that don't know where we fit," she said, in reference to the Ten Domains of Music Care Framework I had just presented. "We are music practitioners. We aren't therapists or formally defined specialists, and no one knows where to put us."

This student is one of the large community of musicians in the UK who have significant experience bringing the arts into care settings but who do not enjoy a formal title or scope of practice. Her struggle to express both the place and the significance of her work points to the need for some shared framework. As the course instructor, I found it fascinating how the curriculum unfolded just as naturally with a group of British students as it did in the country where it had been created. It is the job of MCT instructors to adapt the core aspects of the curriculum to a multiplicity of care settings, and this worked effectively in another country.

Outcomes – Moving from a Community of Learning toward a Community of Practice

Because this is a baseline training, students who participate end up applying these tools and frameworks to a diverse range of care settings. Each student's journey with MCI is unique; they combine MCT frameworks with their real-life scenarios in multiple ways.

At the time of writing, there are close to forty graduates of Level 3 across Canada, and dozens of unique and effective music care initiatives are being launched. These initiatives seem to fall into three categories: new programs, new practices, and new models.

For example, two participants from Level 3 teamed up to create a new program for a nursing home. This program brought volunteers from the community into the home for formally tracked music visits and small group interactions with residents. A training program for the volunteers was developed, and the program was piloted in a nursing home with an evaluation system in place. The combination of music and advocacy skills learned in MCT enriched this program and made it sustainable and replicable.

Another student was able to define her practice, which, like that of so many music practitioners, was both effective and challenging to locate. A professional musician by trade, this student had been working for years with children and adults with various special needs, facilitating musicking experiences with them in her music studio. Their activities together ranged from song writing to playing instruments and from singing to recording music together. Through her experience as a professional bass player, she had built skills and honed her intuition for working with clients. She had developed this approach on her own without formal training. She does not identify as a clinician, for she has no formal clinical training. Through MCT, she found more language for defining what she does, was able to develop clearer marketing targets and funding possibilities for her work, and was able to connect with a learning community of people passionate about music and well-being. "Finally, I'm not alone," was one of the strongest statements I recall her sharing.

Another student has been developing an entire model for music care at her workplace, a children's hospice. She has been exploring ways she can make music a more active part of all levels of care culture, using the Ten Domains as an inventory tool. From harnessing funds to incorporate more music therapy, to facilitating weekly "flash mob" music moments in the hospice, to creating a music room full of instruments, to incorporating music into her own programming, to recruiting volunteer community musicians, she is systematically advocating for music care to become a core value at the hospice. While not an expert herself in music and well-being, the three levels of training have given her tools to be the point-person to advocate for the optimization of music.

As more students graduate from the training, and as music care initiatives are consequently fostered in different communities, a new phenomenon is emerging: a community of practice. This is a diverse group of people with varying professional and informal roles, all of whom engage with music in intentional yet *very different* ways and with different musical and caregiving strengths. They all have something in common: a shared language. The curriculum has provided a forum for people to work diversely while still under the umbrella of a music care framework. They understand their roles and their care settings and the impact of music on both.

Supporting people to connect with and know better their personal relationship to music is a central goal for me both vocationally and personally. What I see growing from the MCT is more widespread encounters between people and their communities and the music within themselves. In Canada and around the world, I hope this training will become be part of a wider movement to create new meeting grounds for health-musickers. I hope that people who already use music in care come out of the course with more awareness of what they do, as well as clearer language that will enable them to replicate and report on it. I hope that the people who have been told for years that they shouldn't sing come out of the course having found their voice and experienced the spark of the joy that comes from musicking together in safe spaces. I hope that the course can bring out the music in people and places that is waiting to be heard.

CHAPTER 23

The Circle of Music Intergenerational Choir
Bridging Generations While Extending Boundaries of Understanding, Supporting and Mentoring

Sasha Judelson

Introduction

LIKE MANY PARTS of the world, Kitchener-Waterloo in Ontario has an aging population, and it needs to find ways to weave everyday activities into the lives of those living with dementia. Continuing to allow those living with dementia and their partners in care to perform social activities not only fosters a wider understanding of their needs and what contributes to their well-being, but also helps us realize what these people can contribute to society.

There are a number of choirs in the KW region, and there are musical activities for those living with dementia in long-term care, but to date there has been no intergenerational choir. Music-making in the region is often geared toward public performance, which obviously entails a striving for perfection. There are also many music festivals in the region where one can participate as an observer; but when the event is over, the connection to music-making fades.

The benefits derived from an intergenerational choir purposefully set up to take place within a local community differ from those that arise from a choir in a long-term or day care centre. For this study, we founded an intergenerational choir with two questions in mind. First, in an intergenerational choir, how does its members' empowerment and sense of purpose grow as the choir becomes established? And second, how does such a choir help the community achieve a greater understanding of dementia? This chapter sets out a possible methodology for an intergenerational choir to discover what aspects of this model can provide its participants with a sense of purpose. This research project is in its beginning stages, so it has not yet yielded answers. Qualitative research does not necessarily give answers. As the researcher, creator of The Circle of Music, and author of this chapter, I hope to inspire curiosity rather than present neatly wrapped results.

The Circle of Music (CofM) is an intergenerational choir for those living with dementia, their partners in care, and volunteer high school students. At its heart, CofM is about fostering understanding, empathy, and support and about bringing people together to embody the meaning of the word "community," whose root is *communitas*, Latin for "a sense of belonging." It aims to foster social change by creating a community of people who might not otherwise interact with one another; by providing the opportunity for exposure, it is possible to effect social change. This in turn provides the window for, in the case of CofM, participants to want to implement social justice, which does not necessarily manifest itself or unfold in the same way for all (Mantie 2009). Levinas's idea that humans are open to understanding the vulnerability and suffering of others (Levinas, 1988) is central to how CofM's weekly sessions build empathy, sociability, encouragement, and mentoring between generations. The choir sessions are carefully designed to balance ritual, familiarity, and challenge so as to ensure a sense of welcoming and inclusivity to all participants – those living with dementia, their partners in care, and the students. The participants also enjoy a sense of purposeful challenge (Hanser, Butterfield-Whitcomb, Kawata & Collins, 2011; Gordon, 1984).

Literature Review

Previous studies have noted the benefits of singing for those living with dementia. Little has been published on group recreational music activities, so the potential benefits of this are relatively unknown. Even less is known about the benefits of music-making in an intergenerational setting.

Mood, Understanding of Dementia, and Community. Lee (2002) suggested that music is so personal that the choice of music matters a great deal. Lee also found that singing has a definite impact on happiness – quite possibly a stronger impact than other activities such as art, writing, and dance.

Clements-Cortes (2015) found that for dementia patients, music improved mood, fostered a sense of belonging and community, and strengthened bonds with between the person living with dementia and their partner in care; indeed, the caregivers enjoyed it too. Hanser and colleagues (2011) found that partners in care seemed calmer and less anxious after spending time making music with the person living with dementia. However, they have difficulty sometimes undertaking the practicalities of music without an expert to lead.

Baker, Grocke, and Pachana (2012) found that music has a stronger social impact when it is shared, as measured through reflective personal journals. Ridder, Stige, Qvale, and Gold (2014) and Sacks (2008) suggested that music scaffolds a connection for people with dementia to others and brings them into the present. Coffman (2008) found that active music-making offered emotional, cognitive, and social benefits to older adults. In a study by Lee, Davidson, and Krause (2016), the participants emphasized how good they felt for some time after leaving the choir and that they were keen not to miss any sessions because of the positive impact that the socialization and singing had on them.

The Alzheimer Society Waterloo Wellington and the Murray Alzheimer Research and Education Program at the University of Waterloo shows that educating the community in how dementia affects people, besides demonstrating best practices, can be used to support and involve those living with dementia (Alzheimer Society of Ontario, 2012).

Choice of Location. Delaney's (2015) study emphasized the importance of continuity, including a familiar location. Hanser and colleagues (2001), who sought ways to improve the mood of those living with dementia, reported that their work was possibly less effective when conducted in a long-term care environment, because caregivers did not feel empowered to continue choral activity without guidance.

Intergenerationality. A 2016 study by the Stanford Center for Longevity found that social engagements for retirees have a positive health impact that can significantly reduce the public health costs of both physical and mental care. This study also suggested that the support intergenerational activities offer adolescents can improve their life skills, such as connecting with others and accepting others' differences, besides promoting strategies for school success. The study identified the importance of the emotional stability and life experience that the older adults can provide. As Parker (2014) stated, "support during the teenage years encourages teenagers to meld with adults and helps to alleviate the feeling of hopelessness that can afflict those teenagers who are not supported at this time of their development." Parker added that teenagers within a group tend to be guided by the behaviour of the group – in particular, singing helps break down the self-consciousness that is so often associated with this age group. Furthermore, young participants in community choirs have reported feeling good about their involvement and that being part of a group offered social support and a feeling of acceptance (Davidson & Bailey, 2005).

Conway and Hodgman (2008) emphasized the need to be aware of how generations work together. They noted that by the end of their project, no one thought age was a barrier. In fact, the energy of the youth had been transferred to the retirees, and the maturity of the older members and the energy of the younger members provided a good balance. Conway and Hodgman's study culminated in a performance during which all members declared that the concert was better than if it had been just one group, and that the brightness of the young voices combined well with the boldness of the older voices. This study suggested that music or singing deepened intergenerational interactions and experiences.

Impact. Creating a sense of purpose in each session is especially important for the participants in CofM and takes on further emphasis with a non-performance-oriented group. They are there for the social connections (i.e., to support and mentor others) as much as for the music. Social connection and purpose are central to human nature. Delaney (2015) found that stimulation of the brain and regulation of emotion supported this sense of purpose.

Mentoring and Supporting. The Stanford Center on Longevity (2016) emphasized the benefits of intergenerational activities on mentoring and the impact of support. It also developed recommendations for establishing successful projects. This included training for those working in intergenerational settings, which the study noted, leads to participants staying longer and demonstrating more commitment and investment.

Music and Dementia. According to Clair (2002), singing can produce responses in late dementia that other activities do not. Also, music produces more reaction from dementia sufferers than being read to or than silence. Harmony and layering engage more of the brain than one-line melodies, and familiar music uses the part of the brain responsible for semantic and episodic memory (Särkämö, Laitinen, Tervaniemi, Numminen, Kurki, & Rantanen, 2012). There is also evidence that many older adults use music to regulate mood and emotions so as to avoid feeling isolated (Särkämö et al., 2012). Observational data collected over numerous CofM sessions indicate that participation in music boosts the mood of those so engaged.

A 2012 report from the Alzheimer Society (2012) indicates that dementia is affecting more Canadians and that its impact is expected to grow. This same report notes that 10,100 people in Waterloo Region currently live with dementia. That figure is expected to rise. In 2004, the World Health Organization's *Global Burden of Disease* report predicted that the number of people worldwide with dementia would double every twenty years. The 2015 edition of the same report stated that 47.5 million people worldwide were living with dementia, with 7.7 million new cases each year. Delaney (2015) writes that a rise in dementia will require innovative approaches to care. According to Davidson and

Faulkner (2010) and Ridder, Stige, Qvale, and Gold (2013), music intervention constitutes an innovative approach to improving the quality of life for people living with dementia, including their verbal and non-verbal communication.

A study conducted in the Bronx by Hall and colleagues (2009) found that cognitive stimulation of the kind known to occur during participatory musical activities delays the accelerated memory loss associated with Alzheimer's disease and dementia. As Anita Collins of Canberra University states, "taking part in music is similar to lighting up your brain with fireworks" (Collins, 2014).

Impact of Singing on Communities. The positive social impact of singing has been well-documented (Davidson & Bailey, 2005; Camic, Williams, & Meeten, 2011; Creech, Hallam, McQueen, & Varvarigou, 2013; Hillman, 2002; Lehmberg & Fung, 2010; Livsey, Morrison, Clift, & Camic, 2012; Southcott & Joseph, 2010). Researchers have commonly noted that singing provides "emotional release" to those who participate. Cohen and colleagues (2006) reported that older adults who sang reported improved health and morale and that their sense of loneliness decreased. Social networks and group activities support emotional well-being and are the most effective factors in arresting cognitive decline, though this impact weakens with age (Bugos, 2014). Of strong resonance with the priorities of CofM is that that singing has fewer barriers to participation than playing a musical instrument (Dassa & Amir, 2014).

Methodology

The Circle of Music

The format for the weekly sessions is a circle. There is no hierarchy in CofM; the music chosen to be sung each week enables everyone to feel able to participate, and this both encourages and empowers social change. Every student participating in CofM undertook a dementia training session provided by the Alzheimer Society Waterloo Wellington. In this setting, an understanding of dementia and the inclusion of those living with it are empowering factors. The break from everyday life, achieved during the musical activity when the student volunteer takes the mantle of guiding the person living with dementia, is supportive of the well-being of both young and old (Davidson & Bailey, 2005). Attachments between the seniors and the students consistently assigned to them quickly developed into strong relationships; seniors would check in with concerns the students had expressed the previous week ("How is your math going?") and would ask after them when they were absent ("Will she be warm enough at camp?").

CofM sessions took place in a community setting, similar to the one for the London (Ontario) Alzheimer's Choir. The London choir has served as a template for creating a successful intergenerational choir for those living with dementia, their caregivers, and students and has been described in studies by Hutchison and Beynon (2014) and Beynon (2014, 2016, 2018). The consistent community location for CofM provided older adults with an opportunity to come to a neutral location that was not within their usual circuit of movement. Around halfway through the first eleven-week session, it became apparent that within the building, the nearby lounge was more appropriate for the number of people, besides having better acoustics. Also, the lounge was adjacent to the kitchen, facilitating an easy segue into the social time that followed the choir sessions. A piano was available for the accompanist in both locations. The talented pianist who attended each session injected levity with his flourishes and improvisations in the welcome and farewell portions of the sessions.

The choir met at the same time each week. Clements-Cortes (2015) emphasizes that for people living with dementia, dusk can be a sad and difficult time, associated as it is with the fading of daylight. With that in mind, CofM choir sessions were scheduled for mid-afternoon, always during daylight. Each session was bookended with the same hello and farewell song. The welcome was part of the hospitality; the personal greeting by name was meant to underscore that this was a place of equal opportunity and diversity. The welcome song allowed for a smooth transition; it also provided a recognizable custom for all and enabled them to greet one another through familiarity. Only after the welcome song would the choir members learn which songs were to be sung.

Partway through the initial sessions, the lounge was set up with nametags and the song lyric binders were placed on the chairs, ready for when people entered. We experimented with a variety of configurations of where each person living with dementia, their partner in care, and their assigned student should sit in relation to one another. It was critical that the partner in care be supported but feel less immediately inclined to intervene, and for the student to sit next to their partner with dementia, so that they could most easily guide this person where necessary, as well as to support the connection between them. Previously, it was noted that older adults often arrived before the students and tended to sit together; suggestions to move were not always greeted positively. Setting the places ahead of time seemed to alleviate any tension or confusion that arose when people were asked to move seats after they had sat down. The final determination, through student-to-facilitator feedback, was that seating the student between the person living with dementia and the partner in care was the least intrusive approach and the one that most strengthened the caring and supporting role. Placing the person living with dementia on the left of the student provided the greatest ease of guidance.

The arc of the sessions was important, albeit in a subtle way (Bannan & Montgomery-Smith, 2008). The songs were chosen by this researcher, as was the order in which they were to be sung, although suggestions and requests were incorporated on an ongoing basis. The flow of the sessions was informal though not casual. As Parker (2014) has suggested, music-making is socially integrative, and it is the leaders who create the unity. Parker further suggests that the amount of time together, group size, and intensity of rehearsals all impact the group's strength.

The "Welcome" song was followed by familiar songs. The choice of songs seemingly put all members at ease. The sessions were designed to include harmony through rounds and ostinato about a third and then two-thirds of the way through, acting as a means to refocus and also to create simple musical layering. Although this could be a challenge for some choir members, it was also more satisfying musically to the entire group, and it is noteworthy that the choir members enjoyed rising to the challenge. The musical layering that could be heard through rounds and ostinato was particularly interesting, because to hold the assigned melody, the participant had to use the same part of the brain engaged in multitasking, which is a more burdensome requirement for those living with dementia. Janata, Tomic, and Haberman (2012) and Patel (2003) have demonstrated that harmony and layering engage more of the brain. Dassa and Amir (2014) reported that participants were thrilled to remember lyrics and talked without prompting about the quality of singing. This suggests that the melodic shape and feel of the music influenced conversation and that the excitement of involvement may have led to spontaneous talking, (i.e., not prompted by the researcher). According to Dassa and Amir, certain songs had a greater impact in this regard.

A key part of each session was the social time at the end. CofM is not dissimilar to the New Horizons Bands for older adults across North America, except that youth are included. Sattler (2013) wrote of the importance of the social network that New Horizons brings, noting that an intergenerational project provides an opportunity for the community to absorb the "values and wisdom" of elders. The concept of "unconditional hospitality" (Higgins, 2012), integral to CofM, is also a feature for New Horizons.

The five elements of well-being identified by Seligman (2011), below, are relevant to the investigative study:

+ positive emotions
+ engagements
+ relationships

+ meaning – bigger than just oneself, and
+ accomplishment

These elements underscore the importance of a sense of purpose and the non-performance orientation of CofM.

CofM set out to create something ongoing, not a one-time event. It is intended to be a place where participants could feel they belonged. It is structured to impact a broad section of society so that the impetus for social change would remain strong (Mantie, 2015). This has the subtle but continuous effect of enlightening all to the need for awareness and understanding of how dementia affects those living with it, their families, and the community, as well as the need to advocate for those living with dementia and their caregivers (Mantie, 2009; Cresswell & Cresswell, 2018).

Data Collection and Analysis

The investigative study took place during two eleven-week sessions of CofM, held in 2016 and 2018. The study took a mixed-methods approach that combined survey data from all participants with interview data from individual participants, excluding the high school students, who were not part of the research questions in this study and had not been not included in the ethics review.

At the start and end of each of the eleven sessions, the participants were surveyed on their mood. They indicated their mood each time by a "show of hands" according to the emoji illustration being shown at the time (e.g., sad, neutral, or happy). CofM examined how welcome participants in CofM felt, the change in mood from the start of each session to the end, the longevity of the effects of the choir, the renewal of personality traits believed to have been lost in those living with dementia, and the mentoring and support achieved through the sessions. Observational data were gathered through qualitative methods during each session, and encompassed reactions to particular songs, interactions between participants, and perceived mood.

The main research questions emerging from the literature are:

+ To what extent do inclusion, hospitality, and non-performance-oriented intergenerational singing support the building and sustainability of social connections between choir members?
+ Can a non-performance-oriented intergenerational choir build a positive mood for participants?

The surveys in this study were designed to determine (a) what effect CofM had on mood, and (b) the effect of the songs on the social atmosphere.

The research study used a combination of quantitative and qualitative approaches. Participation, enthusiasm, comfort level, engagement, and atmosphere were qualitatively assessed each week, with caveats and limitations noted where applicable. Quantitative data, acquired through surveys and interviews, included recording the mood of participants at the beginning and end of each session. The results are shown in the graphs and charts in the appendices.

The questions asked of the older adult participants focused on the following:

1. How successfully the choir made participants feel welcomed, supported, and mentored by others present.

2. The mood of all participants at the start and end of each session.

3. Through observation and qualitative interviews, how deep or how long the impact of the singing and choir was on the person living with dementia.

These questions were asked of senior participants on three occasions, and results were recorded using the ten-point Likert scale, from strongly agree to strongly disagree. The questions were worded so as to give the researcher a chance to ask specifics about the potential effects of the choir and to encourage people to offer more detail in their comments.

The interviews were conducted three times over a four-month period. This provided an opportunity for the researchers to note substantive differences participants might perceive from their attendance at the choir over the duration. This study duration also afforded the possibility of collecting enough data to identify any significant trends.

Consent was sought from all older adult participants, and given. The survey questions related to mood were asked each week at the beginning and end of the sessions. The data gathered from the survey questions were assimilated for each session so as to track the difference in mood for participants as the weeks passed. Data from the interview questions were analyzed to reflect similarities and differences between respondents. Graphs (see appendices) were generated to reflect the analysis.

Results

Four questions were asked of the senior participants, both the person living with dementia and their partner in care. The responses were recorded on a ten-point Likert scale (results are shown in Appendix 2):

1. I have noticed a change in mood on choir day before the choir rehearsed.

2. After choir, the observed change in mood was significantly positive.

3. [To the partners in care only] There are indications that through participation in the choir your partner has displayed personality traits that had been thought to be lost due to the onset of dementia.

4. [To the partners in care only] I have met people in the choir with whom I feel able to both give and take support.

To the first question, there was strong agreement that participants noticed an improvement in mood once they remembered or realized that it was Thursday, the day they would be attending CofM choir. The choir was something they looked forward to.

Similarly, the second question elicited overwhelmingly strong agreement. Participants indicated that they continued singing that day and the next, even in their sleep!

The third question had the most inconsistent responses. The first time the question was asked, participants strongly agreed with the statement. The last time they were asked, they were less uniform, although still in agreement. This result could be due to the day-to-day variability of dementia.

The results for the fourth question were also strongly in agreement on most occasions. Participants enjoyed the interaction and support offered, not only by others in the same position as themselves, but by the students as well. Perhaps more significant was the perspective on the giving and receiving of support offered by many of the partners in care, who stated in conversation that their person living with dementia actively liked to come and looked forward to it, and that they enjoyed the sense of inclusivity regardless of singing prowess.

Also illuminating were the general comments that accompanied these answers: "It's like family." "He loves to sing and it's something we can do." "We love it, we love coming." "It's awesome." "We were disappointed when we couldn't come, we look forward to it."

Each week, all participants were surveyed on their mood at the start and end of each session; results were through a show of hands. The graphs in Appendix 3 illustrate the results of the mood surveys and the variation over the session. Most interesting from these results is that on each occasion all participants declared themselves to be happy at the end of the sessions; the one exception was an older adult who declared himself sad that the session was over (on 10 November 2016). One care partner spoke of the joy of being able to "forget all my other problems while I am here," while their partner living with dementia said, "[Coming here] works for me."

The second question in the survey concerned the effect of using the same "Hello" and "Farewell" songs to bookend each session. It asked: "Does the welcome and farewell activity help you to socialize with other choir participants?" This question was important because we were taking time to greet each member by name. The song used was simple, which allowed participants to look up and connect with one another right at the start and again at the end.

Giving everybody a sense of purpose was, and remains, critical to CofM. To this end, the leaders and facilitators took responsibility for the ebb and flow of each session. The sense of welcome and belonging was intended to enrich the lives of each participant and to help partners in care develop coping strategies, such as using music to enhance their mood and balance their lives while living with a partner with dementia. We were there to sing each week, but we were also there to connect to, mentor, and support one another, as well as to remind each member of the value of *all* participants' contributions both to the singing and to civil society. This was facilitated by empowering the participants: by taking their song requests; by providing an environment for them to express why they were happy, sad, or neutral, by reflecting with students, by explaining and encouraging the sharing of song origins, by providing opportunities for conversation to flow from that sharing, and by ensuring that visitors were included and provided with explanations for their roles.

Taking requests supported self-efficacy, which led to better emotional health (see Bugos, 2014). It was noteworthy how pleased the person who requested a song was when we sang their request. Some requests were more successful than others. Those songs that were less enjoyed we sang at just one session; others, such as "I'se the B'y" and "Let's Go Fly a Kite," were sung on numerous occasions, with people remembering and announcing who had originally requested the song.

Discussion

Community music has two basic goals. The first is to create a supportive and accepting community, "with a particular emphasis on the impact it has on those who participate" (Higgins, 2012). The second is to ensure that the positive change is absorbed into the community in such a way that it can spread to other contexts. According to Dr. Gagandeep Sakaria, lead geriatrician at both Grand River Hospital and St. Mary's Hospital in Kitchener, Ontario, medication can help with symptoms of dementia, but it is important to focus on including these people in the community, which can itself be rehabilitative (Särkämö et al., 2012).

By bringing together people living with dementia and their partners in care as well as high school students, CofM provides an opportunity to gather both quantitative and qualitative data on the benefits and potential progressions of music-making.

It was often possible during the sessions to notice where the positive mood created in the sessions was coming from – it could be from hearing familiar songs, making song requests, rising to the challenge of singing in parts or rounds, having social time, or forging a connection between students and older adults.

In Parker's study (2014), the participants most enjoyed singing *together* – a shared rather than individual success. They enjoyed being part of the choir and contributing to the social group. During some of our CofM sessions it was clear why a mood would be sad or neutral. It was owing to factors such as difficult traffic conditions ("Driving always makes me anxious"), lack of knowledge about what to expect, or nervous anticipation of exams ("Exams are next week"). The participants occasionally offered explanations for their moods. One was particularly negative at the start of a session because "I don't have my phone" on a day he needed it. During the choir session, the member forgot his need for the phone. (As a side note, the pianist noticed that he was rarely in a good or happy mood until the music started, but that it always helped to bring him into a more positive mood.) It quickly became apparent that people in the group were committed to making this choir a success for all. As one senior couple put it, "we were hesitant at first, now we're hooked and it's the highlight of our week."

The intentionally informal beginning of each session translated into an ease within the sessions that was passed back and forth from the leaders to the participants. These sessions are best described not as the participants learning about music *per se*, but as the music supporting the participants' – in particular, the student volunteers' – understanding of themselves, their role in society, and the effects of dementia. By freeing oneself from the idea of perfection, one facilitates the scaffolding of community-building, of developing caring relationships.

One component of the social time that followed each session involved alleviating isolation through conversation. Dassa and Amir (2014) suggest that intergenerational activities should be rewarding and meaningful for *all* generations involved. Making a contribution supports elders' sense of belonging to the community, and when the youth see that support they similarly want to give back and make those social connections. Anecdotal conversations and teacher feedback from this study very much support these assertions. Indeed, one student participant shared with the teacher that "being a part of CofM has helped me to realize who I want to be as a person."

The 2016 Stanford Centre on Longevity's (2016) study agrees strongly that older adults have a positive impact on youth. For the older adults, involvement gives a sense of being part of the community, with benefits to their general health. Coffman (2008) notes the emotional, cognitive, and social benefits of active music-making for older adults. The nature of community music-making by its nature helps maintain the brain's cognitive function, especially when tasks are constructed so as to be progressively more difficult. New tasks stimulate the brain. In sum, successfully setting up CofM projects within the community in a neutral space, with a purposeful arc in song choices, benefits the intergenerational participants.

There are certain limitations and caveats associated with this study. We decided not to ask what stage of dementia the participants were in, as this was not necessarily relevant to the research outcomes. A future study might account for this variable. Oostendorp and Montel (2014) suggest that the stage of dementia may make a difference regarding the ability to remember song words and that perhaps singing is more effective in mild Alzheimer's patients in terms of preventing memory loss. While lyrics were supplied, our observations suggested that a number of the participants living with dementia were nevertheless accessing the words through memory or rote. Oostendorp and Montel also suggested that for Alzheimer's patients, it may be easier to remember the words when singing as opposed to speaking.

In addition, the impact of dementia varies with the day and season, among other things. For that reason, answers to questions about mood and long-term impact could vary according to how the person living with dementia is doing on that particular day. In future studies, a longer data collection period would likely reduce the impact of this variable. This also means that facilitators, leaders, and researchers cannot have rigid expectations; week to week, our sessions are not an absolute firm state, as perhaps the philosopher Kant would advocate. Although no one dropped out of the study, not every member of the study was able to attend every week that CofM met.

Gordon (1997) and Gardner (1993) found that musical aptitude is as natural as walking and talking but that it is best supported at a very young age. Also, its development should continue until the foundation is solid, after which practice and participation will help maintain it. There is very strong evidence (consider the Dalcroze, Kodàly, Orff, and Suzuki music programs, which follow after early childhood music) that this musical foundation, once built, becomes deeply embedded in the brain – especially in the hippocampus, the area primarily associated with memory. As such, music can be the last piece of memory to be lost as dementia gradually erodes the memory (Finke, Esfahani, & Plonger, 2012; Beynon, 2018). In looking at the musical responsivity of the adult participants with dementia, we are reminded of the importance of early childhood music education. Building the foundation of musical aptitude at an early age, and helping older adults access these musical memories, can be done through cognitive supports such as the CofM choir and similar activities. The results of the present study strongly suggest that people living with dementia are more easily reached if they developed a musical foundation as children.

Conclusion

At its core, CofM is about using music as a vehicle to support and mentor intergenerational community groups and to bring about social change in terms of understanding and accepting dementia. The purposeful nature of our sessions aligns with what we see in the art works of Jackson Pollock, Joan Mitchell, Barnett Newman, and Mark Rothko – an ambiguous purpose that allows participants to take what they are ready to take from the buffet of creativity. CofM has changed our expectations of people living with dementia by enabling them to participate in relationships and contribute to the whole with meaning. The bonds formed within our group enable us to celebrate both individuals and the group as a whole. We have become a community in the most profound sense of *communitas*": a sense of belonging. Our circle has rejected hierarchies, even while each individual member has a unique level of responsibility. We are all equal facilitators of social change. The trust, respect, responsibility, and friendship developed during CoM support positive anticipation and afterthought in the individual as well as supporting our community.

There is also something intangible about our sessions. CofM is not just a "dream that is a passion though in fact impossible to achieve" (Higgins, 2012). There are many benefits to CofM: the high school students learn to understand others; all the members get used to not striving for perfection; the person living with dementia and their partner in care develops a close and caring relationship with the student; and everyone involved in the choir more deeply comprehends the impact of dementia. For the students in particular, this choir has helped them form who they want to be as people, informed them about the myriad possibilities and opportunities open to them after high school, and helped them come out of their shell and feel like there are other ways of doing things, and other people who would happily support and mentor them. This support and connection is at the core of what CofM does. The act of hospitality and inclusivity, of supporting and mentoring, that is at the heart of community music as it is generally defined, is also at the heart of CofM. The older participants – both those living with dementia and their partners in care – are aware of this as well. Being able to create an environment where participants anticipate happiness and continue that positive mood beyond the sessions is of increased value as our society attempts to find ways to include and support older adults. As our sessions continue, the results to date support further investigation of how we can support ongoing music-making outside of the sessions and how to deepen the mentoring and supporting aspects of the choir.

Appendix 1

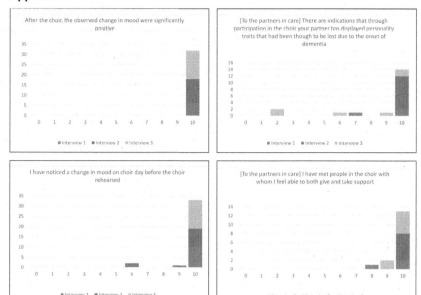

Figure 23.1 Results of the same four repeated questions asked on three occasions during the research study period.

Appendix 2

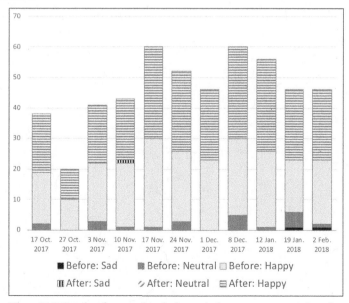

Figure 23.2 Results of surveys from before and after responses to emojis each week

PART V

COMMUNITY MUSIC
Walking the Boundaries of Prisons

IN CHAPTER 26, prison as community is defined as a closed universe in which the barriers that usually separate the individual spheres of life (residence, work, recreation) are removed under a common authority and in which the co-participants are the same. The four chapters in this section offer insights into how music can serve as a means of restorative justice within prison settings. Cohen, Kana, and Winemiller give the reader a glimpse of the power of music in healing and transformation, while Anderson sheds light on the work and impact of arts facilitators in Scottish prisons. Ines, Rodrigues, and Mota relate a research study in which women in a Portuguese facility are continuing their personal growth and development through study – in this case, piano. Finally, Jordan-Miller investigates "community" as a concept within the prison culture and describes a project in which music participation and music therapy enable community to be realized, with demonstrable results.

CHAPTER 24

Life within These Walls

Community Music-Making as a Bridge of Healing and Transformation in Prison Contexts

Mary Cohen, Johnathan Kana, and Richard Winemiller

Introduction

> I don't know what inspired Paul Simon to write this song, "Bridge Over
> Troubled Water," but one thing is for sure, it inspired me to look back
> to appreciate bridges in my life. I feel fortunate to say that I have always
> had a bridge in my path, and I have also been a bridge for other people.
> The bridge in my life is what I call Celito, which means a piece of heaven,
> which is my wife. We have been a bridge over troubled water for each
> other ... And even in the difficult times like the ones we are living, we are
> still a bridge for each other. (inside singer at Oakdale Concert, "Evolving
> Lives," May 2015)

THE MAN WHO wrote this introduction to the Oakdale Choir's performance of
"Bridge over Troubled Water" dearly loves his wife, who is separated from him
by prison walls. She sat in the audience for this concert inside the gymnasium
at Oakdale (officially, the Iowa Medical and Classification Center), listening
to her husband recite this introduction to an audience of more than 150. The
choir was comprised of both inside singers (incarcerated men) and outside
singers (women and men from the community who come into the prison to
join the inside singers) and was performing its fourteenth themed concert,
"Evolving Lives."

I (Mary Cohen) began the Oakdale Community Choir in February 2009
to provide choral singing experiences for men incarcerated in Oakdale and for

women and men in the community who want to learn more about the prison system. Together, we intend to build this community of caring through the messages in our concerts, the model of incarcerated singers sharing a communal voice with outside community members, and the creation of original songs through songwriting workshops. I seek to provide opportunities for all choir members to explore, affirm, and celebrate their sense of ideal relationships – a very difficult process when everyone in the choir has their own life experiences and reasons for singing in the group. Nevertheless, we create community among members each season and exchange reflective writing pieces between members. For our audience members who are unfamiliar with life inside prison walls, our concerts have the potential to transform and broaden their sense of ideal relationships, including relationships with people living inside prisons.

Through choral singing, performing, and sharing audio recordings with family and friends, at least three bridges have surfaced: (a) bridges among people in the Oakdale choir; (b) bridges between audience members and choristers; and (c) bridges within families – especially the inside singers' families. We describe these bridges next.

Bridges among People in the Oakdale Choir

When the choir began in February 2009, inside singers were concerned about how the outside singers would view them. Just three weeks into the initial season, one inside singer wrote, "I've learned through our practices and meeting people from the outside world that we are human and that is a very strong self-esteem builder" (Gromko & Cohen, 2011, p. 111). Through writing exchanges, original songs created and performed, performances for incarcerated and outside audiences, and regular choir rituals season after season, a profound sense of community has developed among the members of the choir. As of fall 2018, 132 outside singers have participated as well as 162 inside singers. Each season, returning members welcome new singers to develop renewed and deeper feelings of community within the choir. At our concerts, former inside singers return to provide motivation and support for current inside singers and inspiration for all.

Ubuntu: Bridges between Audience Members, Society, and Choristers

The Oakdale Choir's grounding framework is a South African concept, *ubuntu*. This concept means that a person is a person through other people. Christopher Small (1998), in his concept of *musicking*, defines music as a verb and maintains that musicking experiences allow us to explore, celebrate, and affirm our sense of ideal relationships, which are dependent on each individual's perception of "ideal." We sing original songs, bringing individual expressions into a communal voice, and create themes for concerts, such as "Community of Caring" (December 2015), that summarize key ideas expressed in our performance. The choir's goal is to create a community of caring inside and outside the prison walls. We've incrementally grown this goal. Community-building began within its membership and within the prison walls. New educational programs started inside the prison, including a writers' workshop, a parenting class, a job club, and a University of Iowa speaker series. In spring 2018, incarcerated students earned University of Iowa college credit for participating in activities like the Oakdale Choir, the songwriting workshop, the speaker series, and a yoga class. This program, the University of Iowa's Liberal Arts Beyond Bars, has continued to grow in course offerings and participation.

Christopher Small (1998) asserts that "our relationships specify us; they change as we change and we change as they change" (p. 142). In musical performances, relationships depend on the interactions between audience and performers; the experience is not complete unless it is shared with others. The Oakdale Choir performs two concerts each season: one primarily for an incarcerated audience, and the other for outside guests. After the choir began, for the first fourteen seasons about eighty-five audience members came into the prison per concert. When the prison administration changed in the fall of 2015, Warden Jim McKinney allowed larger audiences of 200 to 300 outside guests. Audience members include family and friends of the choir; faculty, staff, and students from the University of Iowa; local community members; state and local politicians; and, as often as possible, employers, prosecuting attorneys, property owners, and survivors of crimes. The choir also collaborates with the Iowa Department of Corrections Office of Restorative Justice and Victims Services to extend whatever forms of support we can offer for survivors of criminal behaviour. The social mission behind these activities and events is to create healing opportunities through song. For example, one survivor, Elma, shared an original poem titled "Inside a Mother's Heart," which the men in the summer 2010 songwriting workshop set to music. After Elma came to hear the men perform her song, she shared that being a lyricist and an audience member for the songwriting workshop's informal performance was one of the experiences that helped her see herself as "more than a victim" and to realize that we are more than the worst thing we have ever done.

With larger and larger concerts reaching more and more deeply into the surrounding community, the Oakdale community is expanding its altruistic works. For example, at the December 2017 concert, themed "May I See Beauty Too," audience members donated 103 pounds of peanut butter to two local food pantries and donated $635 to the Iowa Organization for Victim Assistance. Very often, the people in the audience have had no prior direct connection with people in prison. In these cases, the concerts often serve to shatter the "prisoner" stereotypes that audience members bring with them. It is the choir's hope that new ways of seeing prisoners may one day lead enfranchised citizens to speak and act in support of a justice system in which punishment is tempered by care.

Bridges within families. Some of the incarcerated members of this choir still have connections with their family members, while others have burned bridges and lost their family connections. For those who still have connections, the choir bridges the separation imposed by prison and strengthens these relationships through original songs, poems, and performances. Richard Winemiller's section of this chapter describes his experience of family relationships developed through musicking in the choir. The professional audio recordings from our live performances are shared with approved family or friends of the inside singers. The sounds of incarcerated loved ones speaking or singing have the potential to provide connections through voice, melody, and song.

Next, this chapter explores the processes of building a community of caring through the eyes of Richard Winemiller (inside singer) and Johnathan Kana (a formerly incarcerated composer from Texas who wrote a song the choir performed in May 2017 and who attended its premiere in this Iowa state prison), supplemented with my own reflections.

Bridging the Gaps of Outside and Inside through the Oakdale Community Choir

Richard Winemiller

I have had the opportunity to get to know many outside volunteers over the years. For example, I was a chapel worker at Anamosa State Penitentiary for nine years before coming to the Oakdale Prison. The fall of 2017 was the fourth season I participated with the Oakdale Community Choir, and it has been one of the most rewarding events of the past thirty-two years of my incarceration. The men and women I have come to know are friendships that will last a lifetime.

Inside, many men believe they will never have the chance to meet people such as the outside singers once they are released. They see through the lens of stereotypical understanding. Because of this limited view, they fail to recognize the dynamics at play between individuals and the group (choir), and the relationships that are being folded together. The walls are very difficult to tear down for some of us. Through participation in the choir, one begins to understand that the walls that much of our society believes we need to separate outsiders and insiders can be torn down in short order when the right people are involved. The outside singers of the Oakdale Choir are the right people. Getting to know one another is difficult in the choir, however, because there is rarely time to have extended conversations. The short time before, during, and after our practice sessions does not lend itself to this, and this is saddening as I believe communication is the only way we can continue to tear down those walls. And still, it does manage to happen.

[Interjection from Mary Cohen: As we developed this chapter, I reflected on Richard's comments as well as on weekly writing reflections from an undergraduate student in the choir who completed an independent study. As a result, I implemented a short time for structured conversations about the songs we were singing in choir. These conversations provided a chance for all members to think more deeply about the original songs and to build personal relationships with their fellow singers.]

Collaboration

The collaboration between Dr. Cohen and me for the song, "The Person I See," is my first attempt at writing for the purpose of composing a song. I wrote the lyrics, and Dr. Cohen set them to music. Each time we sang the song, I was moved to the point of tears and noticed a number of others, both insiders and outsiders, in the same state. It is very uplifting to think that I had a hand in bringing about such positive and peaceful emotions, using the power of the song to unite.

"The Person I See" by Richard Winemiller
Let me fade, let me fade
So that you may shine.
Let me fade, let me fade
So that I can climb.

Chorus:
The person I see inspires me to be
The person in you.
The person I see inspires me to be
The person in you.

Let me lose, let me lose
So that you may find.
Let me lose, let me lose
So that I am kind.

(Repeat chorus)

Let me kneel, let me kneel
So that you may rise.
Let me kneel, let me kneel
So that I'll be wise.

Let me be, let me be
The person I see in you,
Who inspires me to be
The person I see in you.
In you.

[Interjection from Mary Cohen: When I first read Richard's text, I was immediately struck by how it resonates closely with our choir's foundational framework, Ubuntu: a person is a person through other people. I was inspired to set this text to music because it expresses so well this vital message about what our choir represents.]

The inspiration for the song "The Person I See" came wholly from Melody Rockwell. I met Melody in early 2004 at the Anamosa State Penitentiary, when she served as a volunteer with "Education for Ministry," a four-year course in theology through the Episcopal Church. From the first day that I met Melody, I knew that she was someone I needed to pay attention to. Two years after we met, she invited me to participate in her discernment team when she was being considered for deacon's orders within the Episcopal Church. We became very good friends. In many of the outside singers of the Oakdale Choir, I find the same qualities that I found so important in Melody: a bare honesty that can cut quickly and directly to the root, a simple and pragmatic approach to life in general, a proclivity to always look for the good that is in everyone, and a willingness to look beyond one's past and to focus on the present.

After further reflection, I realized that the collaboration process to create this song involved more than Dr. Cohen and me. One outside singer, Mary Trachsel, a rhetoric professor at the University of Iowa and founder/volunteer of the Writers' Workshop at IMCC, provided weekly writing prompts for a reflective writing exchange among the choir members. These prompts consisted of four to five items asking our personal thoughts and life experiences relatable to one of the songs we were learning. Inside and outside singers exchange their responses in order to share brief written comments with one another. Dr. Cohen reads all the reflections and comments, and then they are returned to the original writer. The choir website has archives of past choir newsletters comprised of pieces from these writing exchanges. It has been a wonderful way for the singers to get to know one another on a higher level than only engaging in small talk during practices. For many, including me, it is easier to write about intimate experiences and thoughts than to express them verbally. The writing reflections offered another opportunity to create bridges among choir members as well as with our audiences.

Melody attended the concert during which we premiered "The Person I See." After hearing this original song based on the positive energy and influences she had on me, she told me how honoured she felt, as no one had ever spoken of her in this way. More than any words could communicate, the look upon her face after hearing "The Person I See" expressed volumes, and the hug afterwards was the exclamation mark.

Similar to the ideas expressed in the quotation earlier, where my peer introduces the song "Bridge over Troubled Water," for me, the Oakdale Choir has been a bridge to build my relationship with my mother, Wanda, and with my sister, Kat. It has opened our relationship in positive ways. Both no longer see me as their son/brother in prison, but as one that is engaged in positive activities. Both have known about other things I do and have accomplished since coming to prison, but I believe that it is their participation in the audience that has made a vast difference and brought us closer together. Their presence in the audience is like all of us working toward the common good of the concert. The audience's encouragement, singing along, and applause brings all the singers and other listeners together, creating a unified community. After all, without the audience, there could be no concert.

My mom and sister were in the audience at the first concert where I performed. We talked about the lyrics of all the songs and the messages they were meant to convey. We had spent a lifetime talking *at* each other while never really hearing what the other was trying to say. During the conversations regarding the lyrics, we began to talk *with* each other, listening and trying to understand one another, and as we became more comfortable with this (it did not happen overnight), we more regularly spoke about topics that were once taboo. For example, when I met with them to talk about my "Do Not Resuscitate" request, we were able to have a thoughtful, smooth conversation with no fighting, in which each of us really heard one another. When I speak with them on the telephone or during our visits, they always ask about Dr. Cohen, Mary Trachsel, and other outside singers they have met at the concerts.

I sometimes have to chuckle when I think of how long it took me to step forward and join the choir. I was afraid I would not "fit in." I worried that some people would make fun of me for my lack of experience, and then I would have another item on my list of life failures. This has not been the case, though, and my only regret is that I did not join earlier! The fact is, I have spent much of my life looking for the type of people found in both the outside and many of the inside singers. I just did not look in the right places.

Interlude

Reflections from Mary Cohen

After leading this choir for over eight years and reflecting on Mr. Winemiller's comments, it has become clear to me that the concerts provide a conduit for inside singers to connect in new ways with their family members. One inside singer had not had a visit for six years, and then two of his family members drove more than four hours to attend a choir performance. A mother of an inside singer drove more than ten hours to come and watch her son perform. The first time one inside singer's parents saw their son perform at a concert, he sang a solo to the Leslie Bricusse song, "Happiness," from the musical Scrooge, with the line: "Happiness is whatever you want it to be." As they walked out of the prison gym, his mother's eyes were red with tears. Once, a daughter, age seventeen at the time – under the minimum age to come to the concert – had not seen her father in four years. The warden granted special permission for her to come to the concert, and they reunited. The opportunities for family members to reconnect and see their loved ones in a positive activity are remarkable in a prison setting, particularly in the United States, where a punitive approach to imprisonment has long been the norm.

In addition to providing a context for family reunification, these concerts afford an opportunity for community members who have never been inside a prison or reflected much about the prison system to see inmates as people. Stereotypes are shattered, as in the case of filmmaker Daniel Kolen, who decided to create a documentary about the choir, The Inside Singers. Mr. Kolen had produced films about crime, and when he learned that his mom had joined a choir where she went inside a prison to sing with men who were incarcerated, he was concerned. She invited him to attend a concert, and in that seventy-five-minute experience, his view of prisoners was completely changed. He wanted a larger number of people to experience the same new awareness he had gained, so he sought and received permission to collect video footage of the spring 2015 choir season for a documentary film.

"Life within These Walls"

On 19 February 2016, I received an email from Johnathan Kana, a Texas musician, requesting permission to profile the Oakdale Choir and me for his blog and offering to compose an original song for the group to perform. Kana, himself a former inmate, had learned about the Oakdale Choir by way of an e-newsletter circulated by the Christian restorative justice ministry Prison Fellowship (Rempe, 2016) – which included a news feature in the Cedar Rapids Gazette published during the first choir season in 2009. A cordial email exchange followed during which I learned more about Kana's experiences and motivation to write for the ensemble, and I became intrigued by the possibility of the Oakdale Choir creating new bridges by collaborating with a returning citizen from an entirely different part of the country. Several months later, Kana presented a first draft of his score for a complex choral piece:

"Life within These Walls" by Johnathan Kana

Life within these walls:
Secret, dangerous game
Death by institution

Life within these walls:
Love, hope, compassion
So far away, just a faint
Luminous memory

Stranger's unseen grace:
Where the prisoner languishes
Dawns a new freedom

Community mends broken hearts
Souls move forward,
Dignity restored

Stranger's unseen grace:
Life within these walls

The composition I received from Johnathan was completely different from other selections the Oakdale Choir had performed. The harmonies were more dissonant, most of the setting had more than four vocal parts, and the rhythmic flow was quite free. I knew it would be a musical challenge for this group. The context of the composition was remarkable and provided an opportunity to develop our choir's goal of building a community of caring in fresh, new ways. This collaboration allowed our group to build a new bridge through choral singing and original composition with someone we had never met.

Kana collaborated with Paul Soderdahl, our accompanist, to simplify the arrangement for our singers. Soderdahl offered feedback throughout the rehearsal process as we negotiated its challenges. Working on this difficult composition would prove to be one of the OCC's most interesting and formative experiences to date. Through choir funds, we supported Kana's visit to Iowa to meet the choir and attend the premiere. As the choir learned the piece and choir members explored its meaning through the writing exchange, the outside singers developed new insights about the difficulties of prison and how volunteers' presence can influence inmates. Inside singers resonated with the ideas in Kana's song:

> Everyone inside prison carries his own secret, dangerous experiences ... It doesn't matter how different our experiences are. They all have a common denominator: fear. Fear for the future, and the absence of love, hope, and compassion. Death by institution is a daring thing to say, but it is true. To me it means [a] disoriented and confused institution that struggles to find a remedy for the recovery of sons, fathers, grandfathers, and husbands from their society. Death is everywhere in these walls, filled with questions and expectations for a tomorrow that may not come for a prisoner. Will I have a fresh start? Will I be embraced or ignored when I enter society? Will I have a chance to build a future? But piercing darkness is also the unseen grace of strangers by the community we're nurturing here with our choir. It's proof of beginning a new freedom. Love and compassion restores dignity to lost souls trying to heal where institution fails.

In a personal letter Kana wrote to the choir prior to its first reading of his piece, he expressed that, even though he had never met any of the singers in person, he already felt like he was "part of your group – or at least a part of what your group is out to achieve together." In the next section, he reflects on the experiences that inspired him to write this particular musical composition.

Community Mends Broken Hearts

Johnathan Kana

I don't have many fond memories from my relatively brief stint in prison. It was a miserable, dehumanizing existence, during which time itself functioned as a bludgeon of terror. Nevertheless, I'm grateful for certain things I could only have experienced in that particular context – like the peculiar challenges (and unexpected rewards) of making music behind bars.

I entered prison as a classically trained vocalist and keyboard musician, but I had no outlet for those skills until the unit chaplain invited me to audition for the chapel worship band. I was delighted to join the group because it seemed like a relatively easy gig that, if nothing else, would provide a welcome reprieve from the incessant clamour and routine stresses of jailhouse life. But as it turned out, the assignment was neither easy nor comfortable for me. Instead, it was one of the most deeply formative experiences of my life – musically and otherwise.

I soon found that I would have to work exceptionally hard just to keep pace with my peers in this place. My formal training put me ahead of the crowd in the free world, but it was grossly out of step with the other prisoners' musical backgrounds. Unlike me, the majority of them sang and played "by ear" and had never learned to read music notation – including our leaders, who could easily "pick up" a new song on the fly and start teaching it to the rest of us but couldn't notate anything for me to read at the piano. So, while I was the only one in the group with a four-year music degree, I was also the only one who had no idea what to play when one of the others would say something like, "Okay guys, let's do a blues progression in A." While the others played along as though they were rehashing a familiar tune they'd known all their lives, I'd be over there fumbling around at the keyboard, trying desperately to interpret the chords our lead guitarist called out for my sake. By the time I knew what notes to play, they had already mastered their parts.

This role adjustment was difficult for me. I was accustomed to being a leader among my peers, not the one holding others back. Back in college, I had shared the stage with major symphony orchestras, conducted volunteer and semi-professional ensembles, and even co-founded a student new music organization. I had studied under celebrated performers and prize-winning composers, graduating at the top of my class. I was a modestly successful career musician at the time of my arrest but playing with these guys somehow made me feel like a rank amateur. Indeed, had it not been for the surprisingly charitable attitude of my peers, I might have quit the group in disgrace after only a few months.

It was their kindness and persistent encouragement that made me want to swallow my wounded pride and rise to the occasion as a fully contributing team player. I admired the humility those men exhibited, despite their considerable skills, and I could tell they genuinely respected mine, even if I was the least experienced pop musician in the group. I also quickly learned that these men weren't simply gifted musicians; they were dedicated artists who recognized their musical limitations and wanted to grow past them. Several of them sought my help learning to read and write traditional notation, for instance, and in exchange they taught me a number of improvisational techniques that are traditionally not taught in college. Though I still consider myself a novice session player, I actually left prison a better-rounded musician than I was when I first got locked up. And it wasn't lost on me that, in the free world, such a group might have kicked me out and found a better player; but in prison, where having nothing makes you treasure everything, those men gladly took me in and made me one of their own.

It wasn't always sunshine for us, of course. Our donated instruments left much to be desired, and security protocols constantly jeopardized our rehearsals. Our songbooks consisted of handwritten lyric sheets, meticulously copied down on commissary-issue recycled paper and loosely bound together with small pieces of plastic "yarn" fashioned from used food packages. Once, these songbooks were inappropriately confiscated as "contraband publications" by overly zealous correctional officers during a unit shakedown, and they were destroyed before the chaplain could intervene. That set us back for several weeks as we scrambled to fashion new ones from memory. Meanwhile, our obsolete sound equipment malfunctioned more often than not, and we were thoroughly strip-searched before and after each rehearsal just to make sure none of it left the supply closet. Several officers openly resented our chaplaincy privileges and even went out of their way to make things difficult for us – particularly one kitchen sergeant, who hated having to listen to us rehearse what he called "jailhouse religion songs" while his crew prepared dinner in the cafeteria.

Nevertheless, we treasured our time together and came to think of ourselves as something of a surrogate family for one another. We cared less about what individual members had done in the past than about what we could accomplish together in the future. As we played games and studied the Bible together in the dorms, we cultivated genuine friendships that helped temper the loneliness of prison life. We shared the intimacy of mutual confession and prayer out on the recreation yard, leaning into the healing power of community and allowing ourselves to be vulnerable to one another in a place where such things can be extremely dangerous. Along the way, we held each other accountable for following institutional rules, lest someone's behaviour compromise our ability to stay together as an ensemble. We jealously guarded our privileged little community because we knew that we had built something special for ourselves. We were more than just musicians. We were a beacon of hope and encouragement in a dark place, and that lent a distinct sense of purpose to our otherwise miserable existence.

Stranger's Unseen Grace

There was a particular local pastor, Benny, who led worship services for the prisoners every Thursday night in the unit cafeteria. Most of the time, he brought his sister with him, and the two sang rousing country gospel songs before Benny delivered an equally rousing message. They were among the most beloved volunteers at that particular institution, not merely because we enjoyed hearing their music, but because they were easily the most faithful and unabashedly tender people we encountered in that place. While most chaplaincy volunteers visited no more than once or twice a month, Benny was there very nearly every single week, no matter what – and that kind of constancy isn't lost on people who may have gone a long time without a letter or visit from loved ones at home. Unlike the staff at the prison, Benny and his sister came to know many of us by name and treated us, not like the beneficiaries of a charitable "side ministry," but like *bona fide* members of their home congregation.

For one precious hour each week, therefore, we were something other than mere "offenders." We were brothers and sisters, worshipping together and experiencing the kind of inner freedom that only such restored dignity can bring. No matter how discouraged we might have felt going into the service, we always left with a renewed sense of hope, and that helped us endure the indignity of our punishment during the next week with just a little more grace.

Benny and his sister had sung together for so many years that they could have easily performed *a cappella*, but they preferred for us to back them up. As they began singing, our lead guitarist would cautiously strum along until he had picked up on their key and rhythm. Then, one by one, the rest of us would join in, and others in the congregation would slowly begin clapping along. We never formally rehearsed any of these things – they were all improvised on the spot. But after several months of these impromptu singing sessions, Benny began referring to us as their official "backup band," insisting that we share the applause.

That was surreal enough – being on the receiving end of something other than people's scorn – and I'll never forget one particular night when Benny decided to forgo singing one of his own favourites in order to have us reprise our band's rendition of the popular Christian song, "I Can Only Imagine." He prefaced the request by telling us about how he had recently heard the song performed live at a concert headlined by the artist MercyMe (whose front man, Bart Millard, wrote the song in 1999). Members of his church group were excitedly talking about the song afterward, and Benny decided to brag to them about *our* gospel-soul variation on the MercyMe favourite, and it made him eager to hear us play it again.

Never before had we been asked to perform for the pleasure of a free-world outsider. It was an unprecedented honour, and we were all too happy to oblige. To our delight, Benny and his sister joined our lead vocalists in perfect harmony just as we reached the first chorus, accompanied by a number of our peers in the congregation. By the time we finished, all were on their feet in a massive standing ovation. Even some of the correctional officers applauded!

The moment wasn't lost on Benny, who used it to drive home a keen spiritual observation. "Gentlemen," he said, "I want you to know that this is what heaven is going to be like someday. Just a bunch of redeemed sinners, all singing our hearts out because it's all we know how to do."

Dignity Restored

When I first learned about the Oakdale Community Choir, memories like that came flooding back to me, energized by the indelible vision of prisoners and free-world citizens joyfully uniting their voices as one ensemble. I didn't have to wonder what it might feel like for a prisoner to participate in such a group because I already knew the exhilaration of sharing the applause with Benny and his sister – of receiving life-giving affirmation in a place engineered to take it away. I already knew from working with the chapel band the kinds of fraternal relationships that emerge when musicians of diverse backgrounds get together each week to hammer out the details of music and lyrics for an upcoming performance. I also had a deeply personal appreciation for the transformative impact that such an ensemble might have, not only on its own participants, but also on both the outside and inside communities to which its individual members belong.

One of the most insidiously traumatic aspects of doing time is the way it radically warps one's concept of human relationships. Prison culture largely deconstructs the pro-social skills people bring with them into the penitentiary, supplanting them with a new set of skills designed to help them survive in a profoundly miserable environment where all vestiges of individuality have been stripped away and even the slightest hint of weakness opens the door for predatory exploitation. In such a place, it can be extremely difficult to discern who is truly interested in your welfare and who is simply manipulating you for personal gain, so relationships become a liability rather than a coping resource. Instead of building bridges and risking vulnerability, prisoners do their best to look tough and stay aloof. They keep their friendships superficial and carefully guard their emotions, lest their secrets be used against them. It's an effective strategy, but one that tends to perpetuate the cruellest irony of a prisoner's existence – namely, that even though he or she might be surrounded by hundreds of other people at any given time, a prisoner often feels as though he or she were hopelessly stranded on a desert island. And the longer a human being remains on that island, the more he or she forgets what it means to be human.

Bold, visionary initiatives like the Oakdale Community Choir are a desperately needed remedy for this cultural blight. Participating in a musical ensemble immerses prisoners in the give-and-take of authentic relationships that, unlike the ones that prevail behind bars, are neither forced nor conditioned by the circumstances of incarceration itself. The relationships between musicians are based upon truly reciprocal expectations and mutual contributions to something larger than themselves, and this prepares prisoners to reclaim many of the interpersonal skills they'll need if they hope to be successful post-release. Representing the truest sense of what we mean by the word "ensemble" – a community of like-minded individuals working together toward a common goal – groups like this are uniquely poised to channel the potentially destructive influences of long-term incarceration into a more rehabilitative paradigm that would celebrate rather than denigrate prisoners' ability to be restored to a meaningful place within the communities they have wronged. After all, people who have been stripped of all the things that once made them "somebody" are peculiarly sensitive to the vanity of the things we use to define ourselves in the free world. Intelligence, education, achievements, income level – these and other status symbols mean nothing when you're wearing the same drab uniform as everyone else. And once you submit to the force of that reality, you begin to realize something else: for all their diversity, people actually have much more in common with each other than they might prefer to believe. If the human potential for evil knows no racial, ethnic, or socio-economic barriers, then neither does the human potential for greatness and magnanimity. Properly handled, an individual's past stumbling blocks can become stepping stones on the path to new life. When Dr. Cohen extended to me the invitation to compose something original for the choir to perform, my thoughts immediately drifted back to the tiny community of caring I had known during my own incarceration. The chapel band provided a sanctuary in space and time where my peers and I explored the kind of vulnerability that would allow us to go deeper in our relationships, affirming one another – even in our spiritual infirmity – as human beings with basic worth that couldn't be taken away from us just because we had committed a crime in the past. It helped us appreciate that we still had both the privilege and the responsibility of defining our own identities and that we were the ones ultimately in control of whether and how we would realize that inner potential. We were still miserable – as well we should have been – but being part of the ensemble meant having a creative outlet for exploring and expressing the best in us. And that meant smiling more often, resting more comfortably at night, and sowing more seeds of optimism back into the prison culture around us.

When you truly begin to believe that your life still matters to others – even in prison – then you also come to realize that who you are (or who you'll someday become) is far more important than what you've done in the past. And that kernel of redemptive insight is what ultimately empowers you to overcome your past rather than be defined by it.

[Interjection from Mary Cohen (origami theme in "Life within These Walls"): One of Johnathan's themes was related to the art of origami. The artist envisions a three-dimensional design like a rose or a grasshopper, and creates it from folding two-dimensional paper. More intricate origami pieces require two or three sheets of paper to create one delicate work of art. Each inside singer has on file a piece of paper upon which he places his thumbprint after sentencing. Kana expressed a vision of that piece of paper being folded into a beautiful work of art as a result of gracious initiatives like the Oakdale Choir. Metaphorically, he evoked the power of inside singers connecting with a group of outside volunteers and uniting their voices in one communal, embodied expression of newfound beauty, together creating a musical performance for and with (given our tradition of sing-alongs) an audience.]

Leaning into the Dissonance

The piece I wrote for the choir, "Life within These Walls," is a difficult composition to perform, particularly for an ensemble comprised of individuals with such diverse levels of vocal experience. But one of my favourite things about it is the way it refuses to let individual singers "play it safe" by retreating into their tonal "comfort zones." A successful performance of this piece requires singers to lean into the dissonance of its unresolved phrase endings and to patiently – one might say courageously – endure the uncomfortable clash of notes that don't necessarily seem to belong together in order to form more complex chords that make for a far richer and more interesting listening experience for the audience.

It's a not so subtle metaphor for the counterintuitive wisdom of restorative justice, generally. In the aftermath of crime, particularly violent crime that rends communities and leaves a trail of human suffering in its wake, our instinct is to unleash a torrent of retribution upon those responsible for the damage before summarily banishing them into a lifetime of exile – or at least a lifetime of second-class citizenship. But such a response isn't really "tough on crime." It's tough on our communities. Like it or not, if we truly aim to break the cycle of offence and recidivism fuelling the growth of our massive prison system, we must someday address the complex social issues that precipitate criminal deviance and cultivate meaningful rehabilitative programs that define justice in terms of making amends and successfully reintegrating offenders rather than simply punishing them.

As I composed the opening bars of "Life within These Walls," I thought about Benny and his sister, faithfully venturing week after week into that east Texas prison facility, never knowing for sure that they'd safely walk back out. I tried to imagine the kind of courage it would take for them to lean into the dissonance of that commitment, when no one in the world would have condemned them for choosing a safer, more conventional path of ministry. And then I thought about the thirty-something "outside singers" of the Oakdale Community Choir, who must exhibit a similarly quiet heroism each week to stand in the gap alongside men that many in society have already given up on, looking past their faults long enough to see the human beings within them.

To write anything less dissonant would have been untrue to the spirit of the work that the choir represents. I knew I was taking a risk writing something so challenging, but somehow I sensed that my peers in Iowa – both those inside and outside the prison walls – would "get" the piece in a way that others might not. I decided it was worth the risk.

On the night of the premiere, I had the privilege of finally meeting the men and women who helped bring my composition to life. Interestingly, the most memorable thing about that night for me wasn't the actual experience of hearing my piece sung by real people for the first time. What sticks with me most vividly is the comfortable sense of belonging I felt in the presence of those people – even behind the walls of an unfamiliar penal institution in a faraway place. Meeting them felt less like being introduced to strangers than being welcomed home by old friends.

That's when I knew that there truly was life within the walls of that institution. And because of that, there was hope – for the prisoners, for the Iowa communities to which they would someday return, for the families and friends of the inside singers, and for anyone fortunate enough to catch the choir's vision of a stronger community that dares to lean into the dissonance of restorative justice.

Choral Singing as a Conduit for Exploring, Affirming, and Celebrating Relationships Behind and Beyond Prison Walls

Christopher Small's (1998) concept of musicking is much deeper than the basic actions of music-making and listening. In his 2009 essay "Pelicans," Small (2016) articulates the point, based on Gregory Bateson, that "concepts of beauty ... are most fruitfully approached by thinking about our concepts of relationships, especially those relationships we believe we ought to have" (p. 229). Small argues that the experience, perception, or "sensation of beauty" comes from one's appreciation of ideal or desired relationships. Musicking, Small contends, allows us to explore, affirm, and celebrate our sense of ideal relationships.

In my dissertation (Cohen, 2007), I explore the nuances, details, and applications of Small's concept of musicking for prison choirs. I propose a theory of interactional choral singing pedagogy that includes three levels (p. 296) that interrelate with one another dynamically. The first level is the basic actions of singing and socializing in choir. The second level is the awareness of word and somatic factors within rehearsals and performances, and the third level is the transfer of choral experiences to life. An example of the third level is when a chorister perceives the choir as "family" and acts in ways that demonstrate care, respect, and support for one another. These actions include attending consistently, practising outside of choir rehearsals, and implementing the choir's goals, namely building a community of caring inside and outside prison walls. The seeds for this goal were planted early on, and the actual phrase "community of caring" was clarified in our seventh year through the writing exchange component of the choir. In this sense, the choir as a collective unit has developed the third level of interactional choral singing pedagogy, while individuals within the choir experience different levels of interactional choral singing pedagogy depending on their length of time in the group and their attitudes toward learning and singing.

Throughout 2018, the choir reached new plateaux of each level. Through an audio-recording session of a two-minute excerpt from the final portion of Beethoven's "Prisoners' Chorus" from his only opera, *Fidelio*, our attention to detail with respect to singing and performing was enhanced tremendously. This recording and some videos of the choir were used in Heartbeat Opera's New York production of *Fidelio*. Thirty-three inside singers with a high school diploma earned two semester hours of college credit through the University of Iowa Liberal Arts Beyond Bars program in the spring 2018 season. Students read research on community music, and on choral singing in prisons, and explored musical elements of rhythm, melody, and harmony. Consistent attendance, written reflections on course content, and performing with the choir were required to earn credit. With this added college credit incentive, deeper levels of engagement occurred individually and collectively. Connections beyond prison walls happened in numerous ways. In January, we welcomed six international visitors who were learning how to develop social justice through the arts. One of the twelve original songs premiered at the Summer 2018 Song writing Workshop performance included "Backwoods Brotherhood," which led to a reunification between the songwriter and his two brothers, who hadn't seen one another in more than three years. On 12 November, we hosted a learning exchange with the Soweto Gospel Choir, singer/songwriters Maggie Wheeler and Sara Thomsen, and more than 200 people from the region. At the end of November, we welcomed a survivor of childhood sexual abuse to speak with the choir in efforts to build awareness and care for people dealing with criminal trauma. The choir sang at a "Negative to Positive" graduation ceremony, and we were featured in an Iowa Public Television short documentary film.

In my theory, I suggest that with appropriate pedagogy, choir members can grow in measurable ways. What I had not anticipated was the potential for social growth beyond the confines of chorister participation. The three levels of interactional choral singing pedagogy are clearly interrelated and allow for deep transfers of the goals of the choir – creating communities of caring – into life outside of weekly rehearsals. Through the multiple opportunities for people to come into the Oakdale Prison to participate in learning and musical events, and the outcomes of people viewing the film "Greetings from Iowa" from Iowa Public Television, this sense of caring flows far beyond the confines of prison walls. Ripple effects of community music-making can grow in unimagined directions.

As described above, when Mr. Kana commented on "Life within These Walls" at our spring 2017 concert, he introduced the parallel symbolism of the art of origami and the weaving of inside and outside voices in the Oakdale Choir to create new levels of beauty. Mr. Winemiller has observed that inside singers who become friends through their choir experiences tend to form connections that would traditionally be quite rare in prison contexts – namely, friendships with inmates who have committed sexual crimes. He noted that the power of singing together allowed them to look beyond labels. He described how these new views have expanded beyond choir members. According to Mr. Winemiller, one man used to denigrate some of the homosexual inmates when he was with his buddies but was later seen playing cribbage with one of the same fellows he used to ridicule.

In this collective case study, Mr. Winemiller described his experiences with his song "The Person I See." He illustrated how participation in the Oakdale Choir's performances served to create more positive relationships with his family. Mr. Kana's reflections on his music-making while incarcerated highlighted the extreme contrast between his previous formal musical training and what he learned from band members inside a Texas prison. Kana's creation of "Life within These Walls" and the bridges built between him and the Oakdale Choir, and between the choir and the audience, suggest that choral singing can be a conduit for interactions among incarcerated people, prison volunteers, and audience members from outside prison walls. Furthermore, the fact that Kana discovered the Oakdale Choir through a blog post written by someone not connected with the choir is evidence that the Oakdale Choir is building bridges it never set out to build by virtue of creating something so unprecedented. Community music-making, anchored with mindful intentions such as creating a deep sense of care among all participants, has the potential to build, create, and sustain relationships.

CHAPTER 25

Creative Conversations with Justice and Arts Scotland

Kirstin Anderson

Introduction

JUSTICE AND ARTS SCOTLAND[1] (JAS) was created by a group of artists and arts practitioners who decided to develop a network for arts practitioners working in Scottish prisons after attending the conference "Arts in Prisons: Their Impact and Potential" in Edinburgh, Scotland, in 2010. The conference was part of a year-long pilot called Inspiring Change, which involved a program of arts interventions that ran in five Scottish prisons in 2010. Inspiring Change was the first joint partnership of its kind and scale in Scotland (Anderson, 2015) and involved New College Lanarkshire (formally Motherwell College), the Scottish Prison Service, and seven national arts organizations: Scottish Opera, the Scottish Chamber Orchestra, National Youth Choir of Scotland, Scottish Ensemble, Citizens Theatre, the Traverse Theatre, and the National Galleries of Scotland.

One finding in the final report on Inspiring Change (see Anderson et al., 2011, for a full summary) found that the quality of artistic engagement is important. Participants valued working with professional musicians and artists, often recounting that these people treated them like "musicians" or "artists" and not "prisoners"; "the personal qualities, commitment and positive attitude of the artists also seemed important to the participants" (p. 42). The qualities and skills of arts practitioners working in the criminal justice sector need to

---

1 Justice and Arts Scotland was known as the Scottish Prison Arts Network (SPAN) until the organization changed its name in January 2019 due to the development of work outside of prisons in the justice and arts communities in Scotland.

be developed and cultivated throughout a practitioner's career, just as with any profession.

Creative Conversations Workshops in 2017

Creative Conversations was designed in 2017 as JAS's new platform to innovate and support the ongoing development of an active and strategic network for all individuals and organizations that work across a range of art forms with people in custody and in the community (often supporting individuals once released from custody). The concept was to develop a program of workshops to address topics of current interest and concern in the field, and to bring together arts and non-arts practitioners to discuss ways of bridging gaps across the many professional sectors that work with people in criminal justice settings and in the community. It is not uncharacteristic in Scotland for artists and arts practitioners to work in partnership with other professionals in different fields; however, it was felt that specifically designed events to highlight opportunities for collaboration were needed for arts practitioners working in the criminal justice sector.

The workshops were announced on JAS's website[2] and on social media platforms. Participants were asked to register online; however, there was no fee to participate in the workshops. Feedback forms were shared with participants after each workshop, and asked three questions: (1) What did you think of today's workshop?, (2) Would you come to another Creative Conversations event? Why or why not?, and (3) What topic would you like the Creative Conversations series to address? Feedback from participants will be shared throughout this chapter.

Creative Conversation One: Meet, Contribute, and Develop

The first workshop was designed to jumpstart JAS's series of Creative Conversations; it consisted of an after-work event that was short, engaging, and meaningful. The main aim of the first Creative Conversation: Meet, Contribute and Develop, was to build a time capsule of current arts practice in Scottish prisons and community groups.[3] Participants included freelance practitioners; individuals who teach music and arts in a number of Scottish prisons ;and individuals who work in a variety of arts-based groups (including arts charities and companies). Participants contributed materials to the time capsule (e.g., photographs, a report, a piece of artwork, a recording); each contributor was

---

2 http://www.justiceandartsscotland.org.

3 Justice and Arts Scotland keeps hold of the time capsule for safekeeping.

Table 25.1. Event information for Creative Conversation workshops in 2017

Creative Conversations 2017			
Event	Date	Location	Participants[1]
CC1: Meet, Contribute and Develop	26 April 2017	Citizens Theatre, Glasgow	24
CC2: Families, Relationships and the Arts	27 June 2017	HM YOI Polmont, Polmont	44
CC3: Arts, Older People and the Criminal Justice System	24 October 2017	Perth Theatre, Perth	18

1 An effort has been made to indicate the participants' varied professional roles, however, individuals are not always named in the description of participants. It should also be noted that there were new participants at every event who had never participated in a JAS event previously and/or were new to the sector.

invited to share the item with the group and describe how it represented the current practice taking place within arts in criminal justice in Scotland. Participants also used this time to ask questions about other people's practice and experiences working in the sector. The types of questions varied from practical aspects of delivering projects in prisons and community spaces (project design, funding, access, etc.) to how people engaged with the arts projects and the outcomes for participants.

The second part of the workshop asked participants to form small discussion groups in order to discuss the question, "The Future of JAS: What do you want?" Many groups reported that they would like JAS to focus on promoting what work is taking place throughout Scotland, to be more clear on the JAS website how members can send information to JAS that can be shared on the website, to support Knowledge Exchange opportunities among members, to showcase guest speakers, to profile artists, to build a body of evidence of work based in Scotland, and to develop a database of individuals and organizations that work across the arts and criminal justice field in Scotland.

Feedback showed that participants found the workshop to be "excellent," "interesting," "informative," "refreshing," and "energizing." Participants wrote that they "really enjoyed the atmosphere" of the event, and thought there were "great conversations" and they "discovered lots of new projects" taking place in Scotland. Some participants noted that it was "great to meet people from different organizations" and "to hear new perspectives," and that they "felt the contributions [given by other participants] were constructive and positive."

Creative Conversations Two: Families, Relationships, and the Arts

The focus of the second Creative Conversation: "Families, Relationships and the Arts," was an exploration on how the arts can support relationships, and the development of relationships, for individuals in the criminal justice sector and their families.

The event was held in the Performing Arts Space at HM YOI[4] Polmont. Participants represented a number of arts and non-arts organizations, including Edinburgh Youth Music Forum, the Scottish Prison Arts Network, the Garthamlock Community Group, the Citizens Theatre, Artlink Central, Fèis Rois, Families Outside, Vox Liminis, Creative Scotland, HMP Kilmarnock (a private prison in Scotland), Faith in Throughcare, Edinburgh University, Early Years Scotland, the Royal Conservatoire of Scotland, the Centre for Youth and Criminal Justice, Northumbria University, Inverclyde Council, Barnardo's, the Scottish Prison Service, freelance practitioners, and young men and women in custody at HM YOI Polmont.

A series of three small presentations and conversations were presented by organizations that work with people in custody and their families. These included the following: (1) an excerpt from the play "A Family Sentence," created by the Garthamlock Community Group and the Citizens Theatre. There was also a small presentation given on the development of the piece with members of the Garthamlock community and men in HMP Barlinnie; and (2) a group discussion led by KIN, an arts collective of young people, ages 16 to 25, who have been affected by a family member being in prison, organized by Vox Liminis. The group works together to create art informed and inspired by their experiences. The group showed a short film they had made, *First Words*, and discussed their experiences being in the group and creating art together. Finally, the Arts Officer at HM YOI Polmont and a youth worker with Barnardo's, the UK's largest children's charity, made a short presentation on their collaborative work in the Performing Arts Space at HM YOI Polmont. This was followed by a performance of the Polmont Band, which was made up of four young men who participate in music-making in the young offenders' institution, performing on guitar, bass, and drums, with one young man responsible for the soundboard. The performances were followed by a panel discussion with Professor Nancy Loucks, chief executive of Families Outside, a national charity that supports the families of people involved in the criminal justice system, and representatives from the Garthomlock Community Group, KIN, and the Polmont Band.

---

4 For clarification, HM YOI is an acronym for "Her Majesty's Young Offender Institution" and HMP is an acronym for "Her Majesty's Prison."

Participants found the workshop to be "excellent," "eye-opening," "helpful," "interesting," and "inclusive." Participants also found the workshop to be a good opportunity to meet other artists, teachers, and practitioners working in prisons. One participant wrote that they found the event "really inviting, welcoming and inclusive" and that it was "so encouraging to hear common themes and opening up conversations of stigma and arts as a connector." As described above, four young men currently in HM YOI Polmont participated in the event and gave feedback. One young man suggested that, "as an inmate, it shows people outside in the community really do care," and another young participant wrote that it "was a great experience. I will take a lot of stuff I didn't know away with me." One participant in the event, who has participated in JAS event for many years, wrote, "I have been attending [JAS] for years and today's event has been the single most important [one] for me. I have been working in the prison system for years but needed a reminder of how families also are affected."

Creative Conversations Three: Arts, Older People, and the Criminal Justice System

SPAN collaborated with Luminate, Scotland's creative aging festival, and Horsecross Arts for the third workshop in the Creative Conversations series, "Arts, Older People and the Criminal Justice System." The Mental Health Foundation (2011), through a review of thirty-one studies, found that more and more research is showing how the arts, specifically participation in creating art, can improve health, well-being, and quality of life for people over sixty-five. Aging in general can bring physical and mental challenges, challenges that can be magnified in a prison environment. Older prisoners are more likely to have social care needs and to need support with daily living activities (e.g., eating meals, using the toilet, washing, dressing). The crossover of these two areas, aging and criminal justice, is what led to the collaboration of SPAN and Luminate in developing the event.

The workshop was the smallest in the series ($n = 18$) and invited a range of participants across the health, arts, and criminal justice systems, including the Travelling Gallery, Horsecross Arts, Arts Beat, Fife College, Luminate, Citizens Theatre, Artlink Central, Scottish Care, Musicians in Healthcare, HM Inspectorate of Prisons, Dance Base, Tricky Hat Productions, Age Scotland, and the Scottish Prison Service.

The program consisted of three sets of reflections representing different experiences in the field of arts, older people, and criminal justice. First, there was a presentation by an experienced arts practitioner on leading music workshops with older people experiencing dementia, who gave a practical demonstration (with *boomwhackers*) of a musical exercise she uses with groups. Second, there was a slide show prepared by an artist who had experienced custody about his personal reflections on creating art in custody and the importance of art in maintaining his mental and social health while in prison. Finally, an officer from the Scottish Prison Service shared his experiences in managing a hall for older prisoners. He gave a presentation, with visuals of the hall and artwork, that reviewed the daily life of an older person navigating prison life. The presentations were followed by an hour-long session of group discussions during which feedback was shared on what they thought were the challenges and opportunities in working with older people in custody.

Participant feedback showed that participants found the workshop to be "hugely informative," "eye-opening," and "proactive." Feedback also showed that participants found there to be a "helpful mix of practitioners and disciplines," that it was "useful to hear other people's views," and that the workshop was "a great opportunity to start learning about a really important emerging area of concern."

Participants noted in the feedback that they were especially interested in developing further events that would focus on the role of the arts to support older people in custody, especially those older people with learning disabilities, autism, and mental health needs.

Discussion

Justice and Arts Scotland developed the Creative Conversations platform with the intention of bringing together artists, practitioners, and professionals who work across the many sectors that play a role in Scottish criminal justice settings and in the community so that they could learn from one another, collaborate, and develop a professional support network. More and more organizational reports and academic articles are being produced related to arts programs in prisons and the experiences of people in custody, but there is a significant lack of work that addresses professional development for individuals working in the field of arts and criminal justice. This is especially important for freelance practitioners or arts teachers working as part of an education team, for their work can be isolating, as well as lacking in opportunities for professional development and networking.

When participants were asked if they would attend another Creative Conversations event, they were overwhelmingly affirmative in their replies. Their specific reasons for wanting to attend another event varied from wanting to "learn and network" to wanting to learn more about arts and justice in Scotland. They offered many suggestions for topics the Creative Conversations series could address in later workshops, including "advice on funding" and "getting the press on board." They also suggested "more time to talk informally, without structure, with others working in the field." The participants made it clear that they valued the presence of an organization for artists and practitioners, and they had suggestions for JAS – for example, that it focus on promoting work being done throughout Scotland, support knowledge exchange opportunities among members, showcase guest speakers, profile artists, and build a body of evidence related to arts practice in Scottish criminal justice settings.

The Creative Conversations series had been designed to focus on the development of artists and practitioners. The second and third workshops, however, set out to include the voices of individuals with lived experience of imprisonment or individuals with a family member in prison. The participants commented that these sessions were "inclusive," "inspiring," and "eye-opening." Arts practitioners who work in criminal justice settings often find themselves collaborating with people in custody; less often do they have time to reflect with those people on their experiences of the practice itself. Participants found that including people in custody in the Creative Conversations workshops was extremely valuable, and called for more opportunities of this kind.

Conclusion

The Creative Conversations platform provided arts practitioners in Scotland with the opportunity to meet one another and contribute to one another's understanding of the role of the arts in criminal justice settings. The workshops also gave Justice and Arts Scotland the opportunity to work with non-arts-based organizations, largely from the fields of health and criminal Justice. The participant feedback indicates that more opportunities are needed for professionals across these fields to come together to learn from one another when developing programs and opportunities for people in custody and in the community. It is a positive development that the sector is seeing an increase in research and evaluation that highlights the value of the arts in custody. That said, the literature lacks studies that describe and discuss how arts practitioners in the criminal justice field develop and sustain their practice.

CHAPTER 26

Exploring the Boundaries of Community Music
Tales of a Piano Journey inside a Female Prison

Ines Lamela, Paulo Rodrigues, and Graça Mota

Introduction

AFTER MANY YEARS of increasingly sophisticated discourse – and too often a broadening gap between active practitioners and passive appreciators – art today is being recognized not only for its intrinsic aesthetic dimension but also as a powerful tool for social intervention. This is especially relevant when the process of creating and making art becomes available to individuals who has not had access to artistic experiences. The exponential growth in community music (CM) research, development, and practice can be viewed as a direct result of this paradigm shift.

Within the kaleidoscope of CM, the practice of music with prisoners is emerging as a special field of research. In a prison, a "closed universe where the barriers that usually separate the individual spheres of life (residence, work, recreational) are removed under a common authority, and where the co-partic-ipants are the same" (Cunha, 1994, p.2), each musical project is unique.

Forty years ago, Michel Foucault (1995) described the prison as an insti-tution possessing mechanisms to mould, to discipline, and to control the con-demned individual, transforming him or her into a "good" citizen. Since the 1990s, with the rise of the New Penology, little interest has been shown in understanding the cultural narrative of delinquency: for the public, the only thing that matters is to keep crime distant from their lives (Cunha, 2008). Musi-cal projects inside prisons are opportunities to develop the prisoners' ability to express themselves and to (re)construct their sense of community (Cohen, 2010). To those ends, various projects have been developed inside prisons all over the world. The following sections describe the project "On the Wings of a Piano ... I Learn to Fly," developed in a Portuguese prison in 2013 and 2014.

The Research Scenario

The Estabelecimento Prisional Especial de Santa Cruz do Bispo (EPESCB) opened in January 2005. It has a special management regime, unique in Portugal, involving the Santa Casa da Misericórdia do Porto (SCMP) and the Direção-Geral de Reinserção e Serviços Prisionais (DGRSP). This new intervention model is described in the Cooperation Protocol between the SCMP and the DGRSP: SCMP manages the canteen and the health services, supports the penitentiary management, provides day care, maintains the facilities and equipment, and offers religious and spiritual counselling, as well as education and training; DGRSP deals with security, surveillance, and coordination with the courts (Santa Casa da Misericórdia do Porto, 2015). The EPESCB facilities include a fully equipped day care centre for the children of the women in custody; it is staffed by educators and assistants specifically hired for this purpose (one of the assistants is an inmate). Also, larger individual cells are equipped for the cohabitation of mother and children/infants; each has a crib, a bathtub, and a space for preparing small meals).

While in the EPESCB, the women in custody can continue their studies if they choose, or they can take a prison job such as cleaner, laundress, cook, or beautician. Or they can work in prison workshops making textiles, footwear, handicrafts, or automotive parts.

EPESCB has developed a variety of artistic projects through collaborations with cultural institutions in music (in close collaboration with the Educational Service of Casa da Música), theatre, or dance.

EPESCB is very different from most Portuguese prisons, many of which are run-down and dehumanizing. Also, the vicissitudes of female imprisonment and the essence of imprisonment as a regulator of behaviour cannot be forgotten. From the prisoners we constantly heard anguished complaints about the realities of prison life. Indeed, the paradox of imprisonment is revealed at every moment. As noted by Pat Carlen,

> although the programmers' promises seek to legitimize imprisonment based on the idea that it is possible to reduce recidivism by matching the appropriate program to the prisoner's criminal needs, the essential logic of imprisonment, that the prisoners must be closed, means that when this postmodern ideology of multiple, individualized programming is actuated in contemporary prisons, it is not implemented in a therapeutic environment but rather side by side with all the old modernist

disciplinary principles of confinement and spatial triage, normalization and hourly regulation, and in background of even more pre-modern controls. (Carlen, 2007, p. 1017)

Participants

On 31 December 2013, the year we began our project, the EPESCB held 311 women (the total capacity of the institution is 354). The EPESCB board, in coordination with the social workers and educators who supervised the women's rehabilitation program, chose our project's participants: four con- victed women of Portuguese nationality, aged forty-three to fifty-two. Three of the them – Marta, Maria João, and Helena – were enrolled in the Regime Aberto para o Interior, a flexible regime that allows prisoners to circulate and perform some activities inside the prison without permanent supervision. It also extends them the privilege of spending some days outside the prison two or three times a year. Note that although three of the participants came under this special regime, the four of them had the same authorizations and could participate with no restrictions in all of the project's activities, be they inside and outside the prison.

Regarding schooling level, one participant had completed grade nine (Hel- ena), two held a secondary diploma (Marta and Clara), and one held a higher education diploma (Maria João). In other words, they were better educated that most female Portuguese prisoners (on 31 December 2013, 12.3 percent of the 853 women detained in Portugal had no education at all; of the 707 with education, 34.5 percent had only primary education).

Regarding their routines inside the EPESCB, Marta worked in the library, Clara in the handicraft workshops, and Helena in the laundry. Maria João had no full-time job in the prison, but she was often involved in activities such as cleaning the church room, editing the prison's internal newspaper, and leading workshops for the general prison population.

The four women had already participated in other arts projects inside the prison – music, theatre, and dance. Also, Maria João and Clara had taken basic music lessons (through the continuing education programs mentioned earlier) prior to the project, and they continued to attend those lessons after the project ended.

Methods and Research Considerations

Since CM is characterized by the democratization of the musical experience, with an emphasis on the participants, the research carried out in this field should grow from those participants (including the leader). Furthermore, the researcher-as-practitioner is highly relevant for the development of research in this field, given that there are "issues that cannot be adequately addressed without practical work experience" (Higgins, 2010, p. 10).

In the work presented here, these principles led to a research study that focused on the four participants. As a qualitative research study, the analysis is highly influenced by the people who undertook this project, and it is data from their personal experiences that will be interpreted. The aim is not to present general findings that can be applied in other prisons and produce similar results. We are aware that this study addressed specific conditions – four unique women and unique external variables (e.g., the prison leaders, educators, guards, ongoing activities in the prison). We do hope that, as Denzin and Lincoln (2011) noted, this study will serve as an instrument from which others can draw their own conclusions and generalizations and, having interpreted them in the light of their previous knowledge, generate new ideas about the universe of music made in prison.

As a case study, the analysis is based on two different sets of parameters: (1) the concrete experience of working in the EPESCB, that is, in the musical project developed in the specific space of that prison (here we mean the notion of space in a global way that goes beyond the physical space, also involving the people who inhabit the space and the rules that guide it); and (2) the individual work developed with each woman. These two "bundles" are not mutually exclusive – they intersect throughout the analysis. Thus, greater emphasis is given to the musical work that has been done, but it is always analyzed in light of the significance of the events for the various actors involved (both the participants and the facilitator).

Working inside a prison involves a permanent confrontation with issues regarding the privacy and anonymity of the people in custody. Despite that, from day one our approach to this research was based on people and on what being able to play music meant to them. This allowed us not only to tell a story about four women but also to tell it with names, with faces, with people who, for eight months, lived the experience of discovering themselves through music. Each of the stories has a name – Marta, Maria João, Helena, Clara. To safeguard their anonymity, those names are fictitious, but they were not chosen at random: Marta, Maria João, Helena, and Clara evoke four women who marked (or still mark) the history of the piano – Marta Argerich, the Portuguese pianists Maria João Pires and Helena Sá e Costa, and Clara Schumann. The choice of these fictitious names is our simple tribute to the four participants in this project.

Data Collection

For this research, data were collected in various forms: video recordings of all sessions; field notes compiled in thirty two logbooks, written chronologically; two interviews with each of the four participants; and written testimonies from the participants.

Video Recordings

In the individual sessions, the camera was always placed laterally to the piano, on the right side, in a tight frame that included the woman and the piano so that it was possible to observe in detail both technical and musical aspects of the performance, as well as to identify emotions and behaviours. In the group sessions and concerts, the camera was placed so as to capture a more open span of the space. Although it was difficult to have a detailed perception of the piano performance and of the intimate interactions among the participants due to their distance from the camera, this video recording allowed the correct identification of the sequence of activities, as well as perception of the group dynamics.

Field Notes and Logbooks

Each musical session was described in field notes, "the written account of what the researcher hears, sees, experiences and thinks" (Bogdan and Biklen, 1994, p. 150). The logbooks included mostly reflective notes: impressions, ideas for the following weeks, logistical constraints, and comments on the evolution of each of the participants and on their reactions to the musical work proposed and accomplished. The descriptive dimension of the field notes was, however, constant, with regular mentions of small episodes occurring at times that were not recorded (during breaks or before each session began).

Interviews

Eight interviews (two with each participant) were conducted in two scheduled periods during the project, always individually (1) on the first day of individual sessions – 16 November 2013 – prior to the beginning of the musical work itself, in the space where the sessions would take place; and (2) about three months after the end of the project.

The first interview was conducted as a spontaneous and informal conversation, across various issues that would be crucial later on when analyzing the project and each participant's individual path: (1) the relationship with music and the importance of music in their lives; (2) previous musical experience; (3) musical tastes; and (4) expectations regarding participation in this project, special wishes and requests; (5) motivations; and (6) availability/predisposition for public presentations.

The final interviews followed a semi-structured model. The questions were framed beforehand but were flexible so that the participants could let fly in other directions as they chose. At this point, the project having been completed, it was pertinent to obtain information on (1) the relationship between the initial expectations and the actual results of the project; (2) the individual experience; (3) the impact of the various public performances; and (4) the participant's future, inside and outside the prison. All of the interviews were audio-recorded and later transcribed.

Written Testimonies

The individual written testimonies date from the final phase of the project. They were requested as a complement to the preparations for the last concert (the use of these texts will be described later in this work). Some general guidelines were given to the women (their life in prison, their relationship with music, their experiences during the project), with no restrictions as to length. The texts vary greatly in content and style, and though the writing was inevitably conditioned by the closed relationship with Lamela (the facilitator) throughout the project, they turned out to be rich reports of the experiences of each participant.

Besides these written testimonies, there is also a short text spontaneously written by one of the women after the second individual session, that offered her impressions about her first contact with the piano.

The Project "On the Wings of a Piano ... I Learn to Fly"

The project was developed over thirty-four days of work between 16 November 2013 and 12 July 2014. Within those thirty-four days, there were ninety-one individual sessions, thirteen group sessions, and three public presentations. The thirteen group sessions were primarily aimed at preparing the three concerts. The only exception to this was the first group session, on 20 December 2013.

The sessions were held weekly for both individuals and groups, with hiatuses for Christmas, New Year, and Easter (these interruptions were already planned in advance). Also, there was a one-week interruption after the first two public concerts.

The sessions were set for Fridays between 2 and 5:30 p.m., more or less. According to the activities of each of the participants and the operating routines of the EPESCB (opening of the cells after lunch and dinner time), a schedule was made for each individual session.

The sessions were planned individually. Thereafter, planning was constantly adapted to ensure a balance between the duration of the session (the logistics of taking each woman into and out of the room were always changing, depending on the prison guards on duty), the time needed to complete a certain task (such as mastering a difficult part of a piece), the tasks that most pleased each woman, and the answering of musical and technical questions that arose in the moment (such as an explanation of the piano's mechanisms, in the first session, at the request of Maria João, or a brief explanation of harmony and chords, to Marta's question "How can you play so many notes at the same time?" in the fourth session).

No less important was the willingness to give space, in each session, for the development of a progressively more intimate relationship with each of the women. During the eight months of the project, there were many times when, for various reasons, each of the women wanted to share her feelings, emotions, concerns, or life story. These moments of sharing were undoubtedly important in the development of this project, fostering a greater will and motivation to work.

The Individual Sessions: Working on Three Dimensions

There were three dimensions to the musical/pianistic work developed during the project: technical work, creative work (including improvisation and composition), and the development of musical literacy (understood here as the development of reading/writing skills, and as the knowledge gained through the repertoire work, such as learning specific musical concepts, technical vocabulary, and basic harmony or music history). The sessions combined these different dimensions at three different levels: (1) free improvisation, (2) structured creation, and (3) learning music by others.

Technical Work

The acquisition of basic technical skills is fundamental to learning a musical instrument. When questioned about the main characteristics of effective teaching, all teachers mentioned that attention to technical development was fundamental (Mills, 2007).

Because of the unique context of the EPESCB project, its purposes (i.e., music as a medium rather than music as an end), and the fact that it was developed for adults without previous pianistic training, the approach taken to technical work during the individual sessions was very different from the one usually taken for children or young people. In the EPESCB project, the main goal was to enable each woman to feel that the music she played was her own, as a tool for personal development. So they needed to feel that they had mastered basic piano technique. Hence, the development of technical skills applied to a specific task was much more frequent. Technical work isolated from any musical task, with warm-up exercises for fingering articulation, was used in the earlier sessions to introduce the basics of piano technique. *Staccato, legato,* and *non legato* techniques were also developed with specific exercises, especially in a later stage of the project, when the women learned some piano-specific repertoire.

Creativity

For Lee Higgins (2012), a musical workshop should be a space of hospitality where all participants feel welcome. It should be a place of "safety without safety" (Higgins, 2012, p. 150). All participants should feel safe to discover and to create, in a dynamic that embraces risk and uncertainty but the results of which are unknown.

During the project, creativity was developed through improvisation and composition. According to Lehmann, Sloboda, and Woody (2007), improvising and composing allow a deeper understanding of musical structure.

In the EPESCB project, it was improvisation – from the very first session – that opened the door to initial contact with the piano. None of the participants had had previous training on this instrument, and all showed some fear when they were told, simply, "Let's play." It was the project's first act of hospitality (Higgins, 2012), one that offered freedom to explore the instrument without any goals except to make music that sounded good. It was also a way to welcome the women to the physical, emotional, and psychological space of the session, and a very effective means to foster concentration, focus, and relaxation – it let the women "fly away" from the stress of prison life.

During all sessions, the improvisation was played in four hands. The accompaniment patterns varied in each session, with different base material (white keys, in Doric mode or C major; black keys in F♯ major or in a pentatonic scale), tempo (from slow to very fast), metrics, and style (from *bossa nova* to a more pop/rock sound). There were no indications about the characteristics of the music they were going to play, and they were always asked to listen to the accompaniment for a few seconds before starting to play.

Analyzing the data, we can conclude that improvisation brought five important dimensions to the project:

1. Personal satisfaction from being able, from the first day, to make music that was aurally pleasant. This was often evident in their reactions: "It's wonderful ... wonderful! I have to learn more! ..." (Helena, 3rd session); "So beautiful ... " (Clara, 3rd session).

2. Concentration. Maria João was sometimes less attentive to the musical product. Otherwise, during the improvisation moments the women were very focused on the sound of what they were playing. This was evident in how they reacted to more or less subtle changes in the

dynamics or *tempo* of the accompaniment, or in their search for con-
sonances at key moments, such as at the end of a passage.

3. The opportunity to address other issues, be they technical, musical,
    or theoretical.

4. The development of a critical musical sense and structured musical
    thinking.

5. The exploitation of technical and musical skills.

Regarding composition, Barrett (2006) points out the benefits of including it as part of the music learning: it promotes musical knowledge, it deepens
understanding of musical theory and practice, it provides practical experience
for beginner composers, it leads to a greater sensitivity and understanding of
contemporary music, and it opens the way for exploration of creative experiences. References to knowledge, understanding, and creative experience are
especially important for the universe of the project presented here.

During the initial interviews (November 2013), when the women spoke
about their expectations and hopes for the project, Marta said: "I'd like to play
something original ... Mine, really mine, because ... to play other people's music ...
do you know what I mean?" (Marta, initial interview, 16 November 2013).
Marta was the only participant who volunteered a desire to create her own
music. However, all them were very enthusiastic about doing so when it was
suggested to them in the second session.

The composition process was developed mainly during the first stage of
the project (from November to December 2013). It started from free improvisation on white or black keys at the beginning of the individual sessions. The
construction of each piece followed a cyclical model: (1) improvisation, (2)
identification, (3) memorization.

The women first chose the kind of music they wanted to create (fast, slow,
sad, or joyful; white or black keys). The creative process was then launched,
starting with the discovery/creation of brief musical phrases occurring within
the musical material generated during the improvisation. This could be a set of
four notes, as was the case with the first motif in Maria João's composition, or a
complete phrase of four bars, as with Marta's composition. These starting ideas
were then isolated and shaped and strengthened. Once one motif was memo-
rized, the search for more material started again, beginning with the playing of
the parts previously defined. In this way, each composition was developed over
a very clear overall structure. Overlapping the various parts enabled the women
to stretch their capacity to memorize progressively longer parts.

Figure 26.1 "Esperança" ("Hope"), by Maria João

This process was carried out in the course of a permanent dialogue with the women, with their active and effective participation. Each of them gave her musical piece a name, and Lamela wrote conventional musical scores. Here are the titles and a brief description of each musical piece:

- "Esperança" ("Hope"), by Maria João – a slow piece in Dorian mode, in double meter and slow tempo, in a rondo structure with *coda* (A-B-A-C-A-*coda*). The section B of the rondo was improvised, using both hands alternately.

- "Ousadia" ("Daring"), by Helena – a powerful, energetic piece in G flat major, in double meter and fast tempo. The rhythmic cell dotted quaver-semiquaver characterized the entire piece, written in an A-B-A-coda structure. Helena used only black keys.

Figure 26.2 "Ousadia" ("Daring"), by Helena

Figure 26.3 "Anjos d'Amor" ("Angels of Love"), by Marta

+ "Anjos d'Amor" ("Angels of Love"), by Marta – a C major piece in a *bossa nova* mood. The structure was A-B-C-A-coda, with many syncopated rhythms. As part of the musical piece, Marta wrote a poem to be read along with the music.

+ "Sero" (a game of letters with Lamela's and the participant's first names), by Clara. This was a medium-fast piece in G flat major, with an A-B-A-coda structure and double meter. Clara used only black keys.

Figure 26.4 excerpt from "Sero"

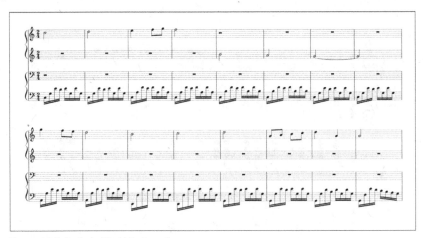

Figure 26.5 Prelude (Bach) by Lamela

In May 2014, Clara expressed a strong desire to compose another piece. Following the same creative process, she developed "SaBach" (again a game of letters, this time with the participant's name and Bach, the musical inspiration to this piece) over an accompaniment based on the Prelude of J.S. Bach's Cello Suite no. 1. In this piece Lamela offered greater input by mixing musical phrases created by Clara with some musical quotations from Bach's works that Lamela had taught her (the well-known Musette in D major, and the Minuet in G major, both from the *Notenbüchlein für Anna Magdalena Bach*).

All of these pieces were later performed in public, with different arrangements.

Literacy

Music literacy (understood here comprehensively, as including repertoire work, reading skills, and building a "bank" of specific musical concepts and vocabulary) brought to the project a dimension that in many ways carried it closer to music education, notwithstanding the gap between the universe of CM and formal music education (i.e. Mullen, 2002; Coffman, 2006; Koopman, 2007; Schippers and Bartleet, 2013).

There were no decisions beforehand as to what repertoire would be worked in the individual sessions. Which pieces were introduced depended on several factors: Lamela's judgment as to which pieces were best suited for each woman, their music personal tastes, and their special requests. Here is a list of repertoire:

Table 26.1 Repertoire worked with each participant

Marta	"My Heart Will Go On" (Horner/Keveren)
	"Dr. Faust's Jux mit schwarzen Tasten" (Fritz Emonts)
	Gymnopédies #1 (Satie)
	"On a Field Trip" (Czerny)
	Pièce no. 1, op. 149 (Diabelli)
Maria João	"My Heart Will Go On" (Horner/Keveren)
	"Ode to Joy" (Beethoven/Keveren)
	"Dr. Faust's Jux mit schwarzen Tasten" (Fritz Emonts)
	"Beauty and the Beast" (Menken/Alexander)
	"Watercolors" (Keveren)
	"Wading in the Water" (Gurlitt)
	Pièce no. 1, op. 149 (Diabelli)
Helena	"Ode to Joy" (Beethoven/Keveren)
	"Dr. Faust's Jux mit schwarzen Tasten" (Fritz Emonts)
	"Feiticeira" (Represas)
	"Corrente" (Mário Neves)
	Pièce no. 1, op. 149 (Diabelli)
Clara	"My Heart Will Go On" (Horner/Keveren)
	"Dr. Faust's Jux mit schwarzen Tasten" (Fritz Emonts)
	Gymnopédies #1 (Satie)
	Pièce no. 1, op. 149 (Diabelli)
	"The Pipers Are Coming" (Thompson/Lamela)

The learning process for "Dr. Faust's Jux mit schwarzen Tasten," and for some of the songs presented in the first concert (more details about this concert will be given later) involved imitation and memorization, without any written support.

Regarding all of the other music pieces mentioned in Table 26.1, and some of the women's, both conventional and non-conventional scores were used during the learning process. Early in the project, written support mostly took the form of non-conventional graphic scores specially created for our purposes. In these scores the information was presented through the fingering (numbers) and the names of the notes, or, for pieces that used only black keys, through fingerings and a demonstration of the position of the fingers through drawings of the keyboard. Here are two examples (the upper notes are for the right hand, the down notes for the left hand):

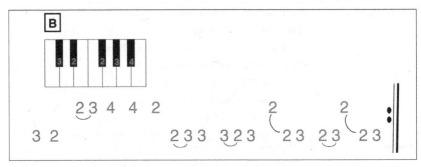

Figure 26.6 Fingering Scores

Though not as accurate as conventional scores (concerning rhythm, for instance), these jury-rigged scores were very important as a means to accelerate learning and memorization. Some traditional musical signs were used in these special scores, such as the repeat bars, dynamics indications, and the names of the various section parts.

An Important Achievement: Individual Time for Practice

"In order to acquire skills in any domain of expertise, everybody has to practice" (Lehmann, Sloboda, & Woody, 2007, p. 62). We were well aware of this, and throughout the project we often discussed the importance of practice time with the EPESCB's board. But because of the logistics that implied (i.e., the constant presence of a prison guard), our pleas were not accepted during the first three months of the project.

As the weeks passed, the women realized they were having difficulty recalling the work that they had done over the previous weeks and preparing a solid musical piece without practising more than the forty-five-minute-a-week sessions. They were provided with some strategies for overcoming these problems (such as tabletop fingering exercises over a paper-drawn keyboard with the exact dimensions of the piano keys, or singing their pieces while they moved their fingers on this paper keyboard). However, this type of work was not motivating, and except for Clara (who claimed that she practised daily on the paper keyboard), none of the other participants followed these suggestions.

We were finally able to convince the prison administration that the women needed individual practice time. In mid-February 2014, three weeks before the first public performance, they were finally allowed to practice during the weekdays.

The individual practice routine was maintained until the end of the project, from Tuesday to Thursday, for about sixty minutes per session (sometimes on Mondays as well, when the room was available). A schedule was crafted so as to coordinate with other activities in the same room and with the women's occupations inside the prison. The women were almost always left alone during their practice sessions.

The results of the individual practice sessions transcended mere (although very important) musical issues. The authorization for them had originally been linked solely to the quality of the pianistic performance, but it soon became clear that the women valued, above all, the opportunity to be by themselves, alone with the piano. It was a very special moment of their lives, when they could choose what to do with their time. These sessions served as a refuge, both mental and physical, from the prison routines. Marta: "That hour ... silence ... just me and the piano and the music ... I could really relax when I went to that room to practice" (final interview). Maria João: "The name of our project 'On the Wings of a Piano ... I Learn to Fly ...' defines all that I feel when I sit at the piano and start to play" (written testimony, p. 1).

Clara highlighted the importance of being left alone during her practice time: "[It] for us is very important. In here, we value little things like that" (final interview). Helena, the woman who took less advantage of the authorization to practice, confessed: "My life experience tells me that if I had been that student like Maria João, if I had been there daily, practising for an hour or a half an hour, I would have played a little better!" (final interview).

These testimonies are further evidence of the holistic dimension of the musical experience: human development seems to go hand in hand with music learning. In a context of the depersonalization encountered in prisons (let us remember, for example, that people in custody are called by their numbers, not by their names), it seems particularly important to point this out.

Public Presentations

The three public presentations were not scheduled in advance: they arose from an alignment between the opportunity to perform and the readiness to perform. This lack of definition or plan in turn aligned with the parameters of CM within which the project was conceived: there was no program, and no curriculum, nor were there previously defined objectives. Rather, there were guiding principles that were explored over time and in a different way with each participant (such as improvisation, composition, aural work, arrangements of well-known themes, and the learning of some specific repertoire for piano). Here is a brief description of each public performance.

Stories of a Piano That Taught How to Fly

This first public presentation, on 7 March 2014, was dedicated to the babies and children living inside the prison with their mothers (in Portugal, women in custody can have their children with them until they are five years old). The performance was conceived with a strong scenic/theatrical component, and the children were often invited to participate during the performance with singing, gestures, and circle dances.

From the repertoire that had by then been worked in the individual sessions, the following pieces were chosen for this concert:

1. The pieces composed by each of the participants.

2. "Dr. Faust's Jux mit schwarzen Tasten" from the *Europäische Klavierschule* by Fritz Emonts, originally written for four-hand piano, but on this occasion presented in an arrangement for two pianos and 10 hands, with all the participants involved, together with Lamela.

3. "My Heart Will Go On" (James Horner), from the soundtrack of the movie *Titanic*, based on the four-hand arrangement by Phillip Keveren that, for this occasion, was turned into an arrangement for two four-handed pianos.

There was also material selected and worked for this specific concert, chosen to boost the participation of the infants and children. For this, three songs were chosen: "Vamos lá saindo" ("Let's go out"), a Portuguese popular song from Alentejo; (2) "Olá Bebé" ("Hello Baby"), by Paulo Maria Rodrigues); and (3) "Plic Ploc" ("Rain Drops") by Paulo Maria Rodrigues.

The project, which had until then focused on the four women, gained an extra dimension by creating an opportunity for the babies and children living in EPESCB to have a positive musical experience. Sharing their achievements, making music for others, and contributing to the well-being of other people placed the women in a position that was new to them. The women found themselves facilitating positive musical experiences, as the channels through which each of the infants and children could experience hospitality.

The metaphor of travel and freedom was present in small details during the concert and transformed simple scenic and musical ideas into moments of great poetic beauty. With very few resources (an upright piano, a digital piano, eight wooden boxes, paper folds, blankets, and cushions) it was possible to construct an appealing scenario for babies and children: airplanes and newsprint boats around and glued to the pianos invoked the children's imaginations and, at the same time, symbolized the journey that each of the participants had made on board a piano. Seated on the blankets and cushions at the foot of the piano, the children were invited to enter this voyage, without barriers.

The women were proud to have been able to play the piano in public for the first time, and especially proud to provide a positive experience for the babies and children. The little ones were able to escape from the stressful prison conditions and relax and share emotions and energy through music, confirming that "musical experiences can somehow compensate for the social and learning deprivation of these children in prison" (Rodrigues et al., 2010, p. 86).

Project X

This project brought together on the same stage the four women of the EPESCB, six male inmates from the Estabelecimento Prisional Regional de Aveiro (EPRA), and fifteen students from the Masters of Music Education program at the University of Aveiro (UA). The performance was based on a modular triangular structure (EPESCB, EPRA, UA): music was prepared by each of the three groups, which allowed the development of three distinct human and musical identities, but the goal was to arrive at a coherent final presentation. The exchange and collaborative work between the three different groups included a group session in the female prison where male inmates were allowed to participate, as well as the reverse, always with the participation of the ensemble of students from UA.

The repertoire chosen for "Project X" included the work done with the four women in the EPESCB and a strong vocal and literary component provided by six men from the EPRA. Students from UA contributed instrumentals. The result was a solid and aesthetically consistent final presentation.

The final presentation of "Project X" was held on 10 June 2014, in the main auditorium of UA's Department of Communication and Art. The energy and the emotion felt at this moment are almost impossible to describe. In the last item presented, "Muda" (a poem about freedom, human dignity, and forgiveness, recited over an arrangement by UA students of Clara's piano piece "SaBach"), we sensed that each of the participants was living word by word what was being said. The spontaneous applause from all the participants and from the public was one of the strongest moments of the entire project. The strength of these moments is impossible to describe accurately, especially in the context of academic research on musical experience as a vehicle for human expression and development. But if we ignored the emotional intensity of this concert, we would be leaving out much that is too important to ignore.

Fugue for 4 Voices

This last presentation was a solo introspective, an intimate moment where the participants could truly make the music speak for them. After performances *for* others (babies and children) and *with* others ("Project X"), it was necessary to close the project, returning it to its original conception, which was to use the piano as an instrument of self-expression, to find in the music an inner space beyond the prison walls, and to use the piano as a vehicle of communication and sharing.

A traditional music recital in which each student plays one or several pieces in a sequence of small presentations can be rather impersonal. We wanted to find a way to transform this last presentation into an opportunity to hear not only the women's "musical voices" (the material they had worked on the piano) but also their "human voices," which are so important in a project developed in a prison. To achieve that, each of the women was asked to write a text about their connection with music and their life inside the prison. Between the performances of the several pieces presented, an invited professional actor staged parts of the women's written testimonies, along with some excerpts from Lamela's logbook.

"Fugue" served as a double metaphor for this last moment of the project. On the one hand, it signified an escape, through music, from the condition of being imprisoned (in Portuguese, the words for "escape" and "fugue" are the same). On the other, a baroque "fugue" has several voices, and these would be heard in a counterpoint of four unique human and musical identities. Lamela chose to leave her own "voice" out of the concert title, although it would be heard in some of the actor's interventions. Since she had to be on stage (several pieces were for four hands), the actor chose also some quotations from Lamela's logbooks.

For this particular performance, a grand piano was brought to the prison. Recordings of the participants' voices were made as they talked about the meaning of music and their emotions, expectations, and feelings when playing the piano. These recordings were arranged in a digital composition and played through three small vibration loudspeakers placed inside the piano, using the piano soundboard to amplify the sound. In this way, the voices mixed with the natural reverberation provided by the piano strings. This audio file served to introduce this final presentation and was used several times during the musical performance – as if "memories and voices" had been inscribed in the actual body of the instrument – in counterpoint with the reading of texts by the actor. This added a new dimension to the concept of using the piano as the vehicle of communication and sharing.

"Fugue for 4 voices" was presented in the EPESCB on 12 July 2014. It was the last day of the project.

The importance of public performances for music projects developed inside prisons has been well documented (i.e. Cohen, 2010; Henley, Caulfield, Wilson, & Wilkinson, 2012; Mendonça, 2010; Mota, 2012; Warfield, 2010). During our project, we found strong evidence that public presentations were important milestones for the participants to work toward. They nourished the participants' will to perform and increased their self-esteem and well-being. "The concerts fed our ego!" (Maria João, final interview); "It's great to show to the others what we had learned" (Clara, final interview); "The magic of work on something to present to the others, to show to people we don't know what we are able to do, brings will and adrenaline to continue working" (Helena, final interview). The public presentations also confirmed the women's musical growth. "One thing is you [Lamela] telling us that we are playing well. Another thing is to watch a person, or a bunch of people, applauding and telling me I played well" (Maria João, final interview).

Conclusion

The project presented here was based on individual music sessions with each participant, which culminated in three performances. The CM principles of "decentralization, accessibility, equal opportunity, and active participation in music-making" (McKay & Higham, 2011, p. 5) were the foundations that sustained a strong triangular relationship between the women, the piano/music, and the facilitator. The closed universe of the individual lessons later acquired a new dimension in the three public performances, during which all the participants working together.

Higgins (2012) locates the foundation of CM activities in cultural democracy, as opposed to the faulty idea of the democratization of culture (which overvalues one particular type of art to the detriment of others). True cultural democracy is not about access to art galleries, concert halls, or opera houses – it is about active participation, "making art," and "being an artist." Our project can be viewed an example of cultural democracy in two different dimensions. First, it allowed the four women to make music (their own and others') through the piano. Second, those women made music that respected their culture, their tastes, and their experience while also enabling them to connect with music distant from their daily lives.

We realize that the four women were not typical prisoners and that with another group of participants, the project would have turned out differently. But this is simply more evidence connecting our work with the CM universe: the participants' flexibility and adaptability – two essential aspects of the CM philosophy – grounded these eight months of intense work. A close look at the four narratives that can be told through this project tells us that four different paths were forged. Each narrative had its own story, its own scenario, and its own outcome. Other participants (and other scenarios) would have generated other stories.

The core of the sessions was the creativity tasks (especially during the first stage, up until the first public presentation). However, learning music from classical composers was an important way to open new possibilities for the creative tasks in the later sessions, because it allowed the women to discover new tools and a new musical vocabulary. Also, it was important to offer the participants contact with a musical language that was almost absent from their lives, to play it and to understand it.

During their initial interviews, all of the women said that music was present in their routines: "Always music! When I wake up, music!" (Maria). However, they were referring mainly to passive listening and to mainstream music on radio and television. Therefore, the balance between different languages and musical styles during the project was one of its bigger virtues: there was time to improvise or compose over a rock or *bossa nova* pattern, time for learning Satie's "Gymnopédies #1," time to play some pop music from *Titanic*, and time to learn a popular Portuguese song, sometimes all of these in one session.

Music projects inside prisons tend to be based in approaches involving voices or instruments associated mainly with collective practice (choirs, gamelan, percussion, rock bands). As far as the authors know, the project described here was rare, if not unique, in that it was piano-based. A piano is not a community instrument. In fact, learning the piano entails often intimidating individual work of the kind that is very hard to do in a prison. Yet in this project the "elitist" piano became part of the lives of four women from what is often seen as one of the lowest strata of society – prisoners. Ways were found to use the piano to promote group work and sharing. CM is usually seen as "an intentional intervention, involving skilled music leaders, who facilitate group music-making experiences in environments that do not have set curricula" (Higgins, 2012, p. 4). New paths and boundaries were explored in this project to engage with the piano as a communal activity. This was possible because music points to "something in common" to every man and women – the belief that "we *are* musical" (Welch, 2005, p. 117).

"It may be that music is the most important thing that we humans ever did" (Cross, 1999, p. 14). "Without music, it could be that we would never have become human" (Cross, 2001, p. 101). On the wings of a piano, through composition, improvisation, performance, discovery, and experience, it was possible to tune the singular existence of four women to this essence.

CHAPTER 27

"The Song Bird House"

Clinical Applications of Music Therapy as a Central Source
Of "Community" in a Women's Federal Prison

Rebekah Jordan-Miller

Initial Impressions

MY FIRST GROUP SESSION at a women's federal prison brought me three women who had come directly from a methadone clinic to a 9 a.m. music therapy session. I will call this group "The Trio." Our session was in the "spirituality centre," a space shared by the various religious groups at the facility. The room was round, surrounded by windows, and had an electronic keyboard, a small portable sound system, and two closets crammed with yoga mats, hymnals, and a random selection of percussion instruments, many of which were in poor repair or non-functional.

In preparation for my first "session," I had prepared a detailed session agenda with potential therapeutic goals and objectives. I set up the space ahead of time and diligently prepared several different music therapy interventions. I felt I was prepared for anything. I was wrong. Around 9 a.m., the doors of the spirituality centre flung open and in flew three young women, all of whom were speaking loudly and at the same time. One woman yelled, "Hi!" and told me her name as she walked to the electronic keyboard and started playing random notes while still talking to her two friends. Another grabbed one of the percussion instruments and started beating it violently and laughing. The other was moving around to the different stations I had set up, taking several pieces of tape and taping them to her arm as well as taking a few markers and putting them in her sweater pockets. I stood there in amazement at this human tornado that had entered the room, realizing that my session agenda was obsolete at this point. One of the women noticed my binder of music and started flipping through it. The rest of the session was spent with the three of them spread out on the floor, lying on yoga mats, singing along to songs they requested from my music binder. As I sat there analyzing what had just happened and trying to figure out my next steps, I realized that this group of three was already a community and that I was the outside observer, except for my assigned role as music DJ. I started asking the question, "Is it enough for me to simply provide an enjoyable music experience for this community, or is there another purpose for this group that I should be striving to fulfill?" As weekly sessions with The Trio continued, it was clear that a structured, traditional therapeutic format was not feasible, nor would it serve the specific needs of this community.

Introduction

Assumptions. Like many individuals when they first start work in a correctional facility, I brought with me a number of assumptions and expectations. I expected bars, dismal surroundings, and security everywhere, and I anticipated a palpable aura of anger and resentment. As a Caucasian woman, privileged with years of classical music training and multiple graduate degrees, I wondered whether the inmates and staff I encountered would ever accept or trust me. I assumed that I would have to work hard for a long time to "earn" their trust, acceptance, and respect. But within a week, I realized that many of my assumptions had been naive and ignorant, and that my own life would be changed during my time there.

Communities. "Community" is a highly valued concept in treatment and therapy in secure forensic settings. It is generally assumed that effective therapy requires something more structured than an informal social group. An informal social group "may be thought of as a number of persons possessing established patterns of social interaction, similar social attitudes, social values, and group loyalties, mutual interests, and the faculty of cooperation in the performance of a natural function" (Caldwell, 1956, p. 649). Informal groups include any group that aids in the achievement of a specific group goal – for example, horticulture groups, photography groups, culture-specific groups, religious groups, and music therapy groups. By contrast, Gittler (1952) describes formal groups in a prison setting as groups that follow "explicit rules set down in constitutions, established precedents, charters of incorporation, and directives ... Interpersonal relationships of members are impersonal, formal, deliberate, rational, and planned" (p. 57). Examples of formal groups in the prison community include:

1. *The student community* – inmates who attend regular classes to obtain high school and university degrees and skilled labour certificates.

2. *The inmate senate* – inmates who are voted into specific roles – such as president, vice-president, and secretary – and who bring inmate concerns and requests to prison staff.

3. *The working community* – inmates who perform assignments at the prison (e.g., groundskeepers, house representatives, etc.) and who receive "credits" that function as a form of currency to buy groceries, personal items, and so on.

When I entered this correctional facility for the first time, I observed both formal and informal communities. The hallways were filled with invitations to join cultural communities, religious communities, musical communities, life sentence communities, and fitness communities – an overt attempt to provide opportunities for activity and engagement. The informal communities were less obvious but present nonetheless. These communities gathered in small corners or unpopulated hallways, on the front porches of living pods, and along walking paths in between buildings. These communities were private, segregated from staff, and restricted to like-minded inmates, and membership was by invitation only. These communities seemed less inhibited than the formally structured communities; within them, the women communicated with one another without censorship, with broad smiles and laughter, and, occasionally, through flat-out confrontation. From these initial observations, I learned that formal groups in a prison setting are like formal groups everywhere. They rarely function with the same authenticity as informal groups.

How could my music therapy – clearly a structured and formal undertaking – provide a venue for healthy engagement and interpersonal skills development? This challenge seemed particularly difficult in a place where individuals are reminded every day of the mistakes they have made, where they have lost their right to privacy, and where every action and word is monitored and authenticity is feared instead of valued. Why would anyone participate in a structured group activity whose stated purpose makes it sound like just another program and where the participants must follow a set of rules and guidelines that were created by an outsider? This is where my challenge began.

Foundations

When I began conducting music therapy sessions, my on-site support staff recommended that I only conduct group sessions with the general population to help them learn how to "get along." Practically, this meant attempting to conduct a group session using music – a new medium for most – with a group of women from very different walks of life, with very different personal goals, interests, and abilities, and – perhaps most importantly – with different musical preferences. I discovered quite quickly that I could attempt to start as many groups as my schedule would allow, and individuals might come once because they were curious, but longevity and trust in a music therapy group required careful attention to group dynamics, clearly stated goals, and a strong sense of community, often building on relationships established outside the music therapy space. The experience described at the beginning of this chapter, as chaotic as it may have appeared, provided a very successful beginning to a music therapy group because of the strong sense of community already present within The Trio. In a traditional music therapy group, I might have started by conducting individual assessments of the group members to ensure compatibility, the potential for strong group dynamics, and similar goal areas. However, The Trio grew to include eight members and became a musical community due to the trust and relationships established outside of the music therapy group sessions. The *Group of Eight* will be discussed later in this chapter.

There is a significant body of research that supports group psychotherapy for adults with psychiatric disorders. Research indicates that group psychotherapy is an effective form of therapy for incarcerated individuals specifically with regard to the development of anger management strategies, the reduction of anxiety and depression, institutional adjustment, consistent improvement in interpersonal relations, and the development of increased self-esteem (Morgan & Flora, 2002). In the field of music therapy, clinical outcomes for adults diagnosed with psychiatric disorders include increased self-expression, improved social communication, increased cognitive functioning, improvement with organization strategies, deeper insight and awareness, and modification of emotions (Baker & Wigram, 2005).

It should be mentioned that group psychotherapy does not consistently result in positive change. Some research suggests there is potential for *negative therapeutic change* in group psychotherapy. Negative therapeutic change can be defined as a worsening of a patient's functioning or symptoms as a result of treatment (Dies & Teleska, 1985). Factors contributing to negative therapeutic change are the "therapist's leadership style, selection errors, and personality factors (adjustment, countertransference)" (Roback, 2000). Leadership style contributed to negative therapeutic change when a therapist was overly charismatic, pressuring clients for personal self-disclosure, or when a therapist was negligent about providing group members with adequate structure. Selection errors occur when a therapist and client are mismatched – for example, when the severity of a client's pre-existing psychopathology mismatched a therapist's therapeutic modality. Also, a therapist's negative countertransference can have harmful consequences for group members in group psychotherapy. Being mindful of these potential therapeutic pitfalls is especially important when working with a vulnerable client population. In a correctional facility, therapy is often considered a "dirty word," even when the issues highlighted by Roback are avoided. Many individuals are reluctant to enter into any form of therapy, hesitant as they are to lower the defensive barriers that protect them from being assessed or judged. In my music therapy work in a women's correctional facility, I observed that defensive barriers are considered necessary for personal survival and for projecting strength. "Defenses are a normal and necessary part of psychic development because they help to contain some of the overwhelming anxiety that would otherwise be caused by the awareness of threatening feelings, thoughts, impulses, and memories" (Hadley, 2003, p. 13).

An "us/them" paradigm among the women was another major hurdle to building trust and joining the women in their community. When I was introduced to the community as a staff member, it was an immediate challenge to directly relate to the women or their experiences, which immediately placed me on the side of "the other."

Finally, a significant challenge I faced in developing a supportive musical community was my own ignorance of the "community rules." These rules were distinct from the official facility rules, which had been presented to me in depth during my orientation (don't leave any object I bring on-site unattended, do not meet with anyone in an isolated location, do not take any object given to you by group members off-site, etc.). It took time and experience to learn the community rules, and as it turned out, they would have a direct bearing on therapeutic goals and techniques. For example, pre-existing issues between group members were not raised in the group setting because "we don't rat on one another." Individuals who had committed a crime against a child were "not allowed" in the group because "certain crimes are unforgivable." No other individuals would attend if such an person attempted to join the group. I witnessed what appeared to be unbreakable bonds of friendship shattered in an instant due to broken trust agreements because "trust broken is trust lost." These rules influenced the course of therapy and needed to be acknowledged. However, regular reflection through journaling and debriefing with my supervisor helped ensure that my own personal judgment and professional duty remained independent of these rules.

Another *West Side Story*

Since I had been trained as a music therapist, the prison staff expected me to work primarily with the inmates who had the most significant psychological needs and emotional and behavioural deficits. So I began my work in the psychiatric pod. The pod's structure had two sides – *East* and *West*. Each side housed a similar number of women, typically between five and ten. Living in the pod had its perks. The temperature was evenly regulated, and there were twenty-four-hour support staff in the pod at all times. The women were expected to be "working on their tools," which included tools acquired in dialectical and cognitive behaviour therapy sessions. The last thing the women wanted to see walk through the doors was yet another *therapist*. Notoriously, the women on the east side did not get along with the women on the west side, and to minimize conflict potential, staff were encouraged to keep them separate unless they were in group therapy together.

It was my first day back in the facility after a brief hiatus between contracts, and I did not know any of the women in the psychiatric pod. Until the staff could evaluate my ability to manage group dynamics, I was encouraged to keep the two sides separate while conducting therapy, for there were some challenging interpersonal issues between certain inmates. With my new contract, I was only permitted to be in the facility two days a week, which limited my available therapy time. As it turned out, I was only available for one hour with the east side and one hour with the west side. During my second week, there was a heated argument about which side should go first. During week three, one of the women who was new to the east pod suggested that the two sides meet together and that we extend the session to two hours. To my surprise, all of the women agreed that this was an acceptable solution. At the time, I suspected the joint session was viewed as an acceptable solution because one of the individuals who was at the centre of much of the internal conflict had been moved to a different institution. This suspicion was never confirmed by any of the group members. Our meeting space was arranged with long tables in the shape of a square. The women naturally divided themselves into the east and west groupings with an empty seat separating the two groups.

We began our first large group session by discussing musical preferences. In the introductory section of this chapter, I noted that an *informal community* consists of "a number of persons possessing established patterns of social interaction, similar social attitudes, social values, mutual interests." Well, this group ranged in age from under twenty-five to over sixty. There were women who had children and women who could never have children because of years of physical abuse. There were women who loved lesser-known artists from the underground hip hop scene around Toronto and women who adored well-known country artists like George Strait and Willie Nelson. Initially, it appeared there was very little common ground within this small group of women. However, the women established a broad goal for the group – to share part of their personal journey through the songs they requested. Tia DeNora, in her ethnographic studies, suggests that "music is used as an ongoing resource for identity work and emotional work ... Music can be a resource you may use to configure your identity, which is particularly interesting when considering how people inside or newly released from prison can rediscover themselves through music by reconnecting with other parts of their identities related to being human rather than being a prisoner" (DeNora, 1999, p. 51).

Each week the women provided me with a list of music they wanted to listen to the following week. I compiled their requests into a new playlist each week and the women would introduce their musical selections to the group, singing (and occasionally dancing) along. Once again, I felt like a glorified DJ.

Then, during week four, I noticed something subtle and yet perhaps significant. I noticed that the women were no longer sitting in their east/west seating arrangement. They were scattered about the room, and our shape was more circular, rather than a segregated square. I also noticed the women assigning themselves specific roles. One called herself "the DJ" since she kept the CDs in order and found the tracks the women were requesting. Another functioned as the peacemaker. When tempers flared, she reminded everyone of how important it was for them to support one another and how their disagreements were not worth disrupting the group. I gained a greater understanding of the importance of these roles one day when an informal discussion arose regarding the responsibilities of the "house manager" position identified by the facility. There was a mixture of both respect and disdain toward the woman who held the title because it gave that individual "authority" over the other women in the house. The house manager was responsible for collecting the grocery orders as well as distributing the orders to the other members living in the unit. Group members expressed suspicion that the house managers were selling certain grocery items to other house managers. In our music therapy group, there was no externally imposed hierarchy, and roles were agreed upon by all group members. The presence of "roles," however, was extremely important for the success of the group. In an atmosphere where it can be challenging to find personal purpose, this group provided members with a unique role that connected directly with their own personal strengths. No role was deemed more important than another, and I believe that was one reason the east and west sides were able to coexist successfully during music therapy sessions.

There was one soft-spoken young woman who was perhaps the most diligent group member – always the first to arrive and a strong support to other group members. For the purpose of this narrative, I will call her "Janice." Janice was always the first to arrive and the last to leave. She rarely made any song requests, and several staff told me she refused to speak to any of the on-site psychologists. During our first meeting, Janice asked if I would teach her how to write songs. She explained how she often journaled and that it might be "fun" to learn how to put her words to music. I provided a few ideas and gave her a couple of sheets of paper with sections divided into chorus/verse/bridge. As I spoke with another member of the group, I glanced at Janice and saw that she had already filled two pages with lyrics for a song. She asked if I would put them to music. After getting some ideas about the chord sequences Janice liked best, I began playing and singing her song. As I played and sang, Janice looked down at the floor and started to weep. The lyrics detailed a heartbreaking story of betrayal, abuse, and loss. The following week she came back with two more songs, and the next week two more. In eight weeks of group meetings, Janice wrote ten different songs. While the other group members requested songs that were personally meaningful to them, Janice asked that her lyrics be set to music and played for the whole group. So, Janice and I began singing her songs to the group every week, and this became a regular part of the group format. Eventually, a few of the women learned Janice's songs so well that they began singing with her during our time of music sharing. In an analysis of community structures, Philip Alperson (2002) describes community in the absolute broadest sense as a state of being held in common. At first glance, this community had very little "in common," but they operated in a state of common engagement with an activity (music) that bridged their personal issues, differences, and expectations and strengthened their behavioural and psychological "tools." Our weekly music-sharing was a safe vehicle by which they could all express themselves freely and voice their own musical identity within the group. Janice described feeling a sense of "release" in sharing her story through song, and she indicated that the consistent support of the group had helped validate the pain she felt when expressing her emotions in the lyrics. That support was observed by several staff members, who witnessed the personal growth in Janice and the increased sense of *community* that lingered across the east and west sides of the psychiatric pod.

Windows

Every space in which I worked at the correctional facility was surrounded by windows. Windows are important for the safety of both the incarcerated women and the staff. Ironically, the windows also proved to be barriers to establishing trust and community because those present in the music group were keenly aware that others outside the space could observe their participation. Frequently, staff would stop and look through the windows for a few minutes. They were not purposefully trying to disrupt the group, but their presence usually had an adverse effect on the dynamics of the group. Prison culture is often "marked by mistrust, fear, high levels of verbal and physical victimization, physical and emotional deprivation, boredom, overcrowding and an intense lack of privacy ... [which] presents particular obstacles to cohesive social relations" (Phillips, 2007, p. 79).

During the second week of my first music therapy internship, as I was preparing for a group music therapy session, I met a woman I will call "Julia" in the heavily windowed music therapy space. She first peered through a window then opened the door and asked, "Are you a preacher?" while propping the door open with her foot. The room I used for music therapy was regarded by many as a sacred space and was typically reserved for events connected with the chaplaincy department. I told her I was a music therapy intern and explained that I would be working in the facility for the rest of the summer. She entered the room quickly and announced, "I love music!" I will never forget the electricity and vitality in her eyes. The tentative uncertainty with which she had first opened the door disappeared, and she asked me if I could teach her piano. She said that she had always wanted to learn but that she never had the money for lessons.

At this stage in my own development as a student music therapist, I was unsure of my own therapeutic approach. I was also unsure if or how *music lessons* could function as *music therapy*. However, I could not resist this "electric" human being whose appetite for acquiring a new skill was irresistible. I told her we would work on her piano skills during our individual sessions. At the time I first met Julia, the facility had a policy that any individual who was meeting individually with a therapist also had to be enrolled in group therapy, again to work on interpersonal skill development. Given her interpersonal challenges, group sessions were often difficult for Julia. She became easily frustrated when she felt that her musical preferences and personal needs were not being addressed. Turn-taking was a challenge for Julia, and she often tried to take control of group sessions to ensure her "voice" was being heard and her needs met. After her tenth group session, I met with my on-site supervisor to discuss these challenges and request permission to only meet one-on-one with Julia. The request was granted, and Julia's musical journey entered a new phase.

When we began our weekly individual sessions, Julia asked to work on John Legend's "All of Me." Her desire to learn was insatiable. Julia would be practising piano when I arrived at the facility every week at 8:15 a.m. She remained in the space until I started my first group session at 9 a.m. At the end of our first individual session I asked Julia what she liked about the song, "All of Me." I think she could sense that I was "fishing" – seeking to enter into a deeper therapeutic relationship and learn more about her. She told me that she only wanted to learn music and had no desire to "talk about feelings." This initial stage with Julia was some of the most frustrating work in music therapy that I have experienced so far. The piano lesson format I was using with Julia did not resemble the traditional approaches to music therapy I had learned during graduate school, and meanwhile, Julia resisted moving into the type of therapy I thought she "needed." During the first six individual meetings, Julia requested popular songs to learn, and I would bring the music and teach her these songs during a sixty-minute session. During session eight, I decided to bring in a new song that Julia had not requested but that I thought she would connect with both musically and emotionally. The song was "Rise Up" by an artist named Andra Day. Julia sat quietly as she listened to me play and sing the song. As I finished, she responded without hesitation, "I have to learn that song!" Without me asking why she appreciated the song, Julia indicated that it provided her with a sense of "hope." During the next session, Julia played and sang the entire chorus from memory. The chorus is a bold declaration that replaces feelings of self-doubt and defeat with resilience and determination for the singer and for those they love. Up to this point, Julia had avoided disclosing any personal information. During session eight, Julia indicated that she thought of her daughter when she sang and played this song by Andra Day. This was Julia's second prison sentence. She had been diagnosed with borderline personality disorder (BPD) and had previously struggled with opioid dependence. Prior to her arrest, Julia had given birth to a daughter at twenty-two weeks.

In total, Julia attended twenty-three individual sessions. As she selected various songs to learn on the piano, it became clear that these songs formed her own *musical autobiography*. They were windows through which she could see where she had come from. She was telling her own story through the songs she was singing – songs about lost love, songs about regret, songs about pain, songs about anger. She connected with each song personally.

Dorit Amir (1992) describes "meaningful moments" as moments within the therapeutic process that are transformative and that can facilitate a shift in the client's perception of themselves or others. Ansdell and colleagues (2010) describe these moments as "windows for relational and therapeutic change" (p. 22). One of Julia's meaningful moments happened in session eighteen, when she asked to learn a song titled "A Broken Wing" by Martina McBride. As I read the lyrics, it became clear the song was telling part of Julia's story. It expressed the pain that Julia felt upon realizing she would never be able to return to a relationship with the father of her child until he had his own realization of the need for change and personal growth. After playing through the song, Julia opened up about the emotional pain and disappointment she was feeling after a discussion she had with her mother, following a recent letter from her ex-boyfriend.

Julia was frustrated that her mother expected her "to fail" after her release from prison, assuming Julia would go back to her ex-boyfriend. This discussion was significant because Julia acknowledged being frustrated with herself. She described feeling frustrated that her past decisions were now causing an undermining of her mother's trust. Julia expressed a determination to show her mother, by her actions, that she had changed and matured. If the songs in her musical autobiography were windows into her past, this song was a window that framed her future and inspired her dreams. Julia knew she wasn't perfect, and though she may have a "broken wing," she would keep flying and continue her personal journey toward becoming the kind of mother she wanted to be for her daughter.

Open Doors

Among the many meaningful moments and individual stories, there was one central narrative that unfolded within the music therapy community in a women's prison. In the "Foundations" section, I described the human tornado, or The Trio as I liked to call them. This group of three women soon grew to eight. This "Group of Eight" consistently attended the "music group" at 9:00 a.m. for ten weeks. Five of the women in this group also met with me for thirty-minute individual meetings every week. In its early days, the group saw me functioning as a DJ of sorts, not part of the community but serving a purpose nonetheless. This began to change as my own identity developed within the facility. One day I was walking across the prison grounds with a staff member. Several of the women yelled my name from a pod porch or waved to me from a window as we made our way across the facility. "My ... you are quite *connected*," the staff member said. It dawned on me. At first, I was so afraid to make a mistake, say the *wrong* thing to one of the women, do the *wrong* thing at a security checkpoint, or look at someone the *wrong* way. One of my primary goals was to help create bridges through music, establishing a space for community and support. As I worked toward these goals, I was so preoccupied with what *I* was doing and whether *I* was facilitating groups to the best of my ability, that I failed to see what *the music* was doing within the group. I will explain what I observed in the remainder of this chapter.

Within The Trio, which expanded to the Group of Eight, there was one woman, whom I will call "Sarah." Sarah was a beautiful person with a beautiful singing voice and an ability to write haunting musical melodies. Sarah was also introspective. After the rest of the group left, she would often linger in the room to reflect on life, science, art, and the question of how she arrived in this institution and what she was going to do when she got out. Sarah was a leader. Sarah was also a very gifted songwriter and social activist. The first time I encountered Sarah, she was standing outside with a garbage bag over herself because it was pouring rain and she was yelling supportive encouragement to the women who were on the other side of a locked door in solitary confinement. She was a significant force and not a favourite inmate to many because she didn't follow the "inmate code" of keeping her head down and doing her time. Sarah was in everybody's business and was a loud voice for change and women's rights.

One day Sarah approached me about an "exchange." She knew that I taught piano to several of the women and that I did not play guitar, but that I wanted to learn. Sarah said that she would give me guitar lessons if I would give her piano lessons. I taught her how to play her favourite Stevie Nicks song, and she taught me how to play "the important" chords on the guitar, complete with a hand-drawn chord diagram. Sarah's advocacy for the rights of every woman in the facility was evident in the songs that she wrote.

> In rehabilitation settings, the songwriting process has empowered individuals to tell their story. Within rehabilitation settings [clients] are often disempowered as a result of illness or injury [or imprisonment]. The resulting lack of control can negatively affect the course of rehabilitation. (Vander Kooij, 2009, p. 40)

As Sarah witnessed how women were gaining confidence, new supportive friendships, joy, and a sense of empowerment through the Group of Eight, she decided she was going to start a music group. With the help of a supportive staff member who was a very skilled musician, she started weekly guitar and songwriting workshops. Twelve or more women regularly attended these workshops even though there were only six guitars, many missing a string or two. Higgins (2012) describes an element of community music as community musicians working "to provoke discourse, stimulate active participation, and enable a sense of 'voice,' both for individuals and those complicit groups or communities of which they are part" (Higgins, 2012, p. 134). The realization that I came to was that I was now a community musician in *this* community and that many others were leading without any direct input from me.

The next step the Group of Eight wanted to achieve was to host their own "coffee house" performance. They wanted it to be by invitation only to ensure that attendees would be supportive voices (i.e., not mocking). They wanted a sound system, rehearsal time, sound checks, and a printed program. Because we had the support of a lead staff person who had helped conduct the guitar workshops, the administration approved the event. But logistics were not my main concern. The music group was supportive of one another, but this would be a first-time performance for many individuals. In music therapy literature, many authors have focused on the ways that a public performance may compromise or conflict with the therapeutic values of privacy and containment (Maratos, 2004; Turry, 2005). Less attention is given to the potentially detrimental effects that performance anxiety can have on the body. Ansdell (2010) perhaps provides the most integrated view by arguing that performance in music therapy has potential for both pressure and epiphany. He suggests that individuals may feel pressure, self-judgment, peer judgment, and a sense of expectation on one hand, but on the other hand, many experience the "natural highs," a significant sense of accomplishment, identity work, and a sense of belonging in a particular music community. Despite the potential risks, the coffee house doors were opened, and the event had a profound impact on all participants, performers and observers alike.

Julia, who primarily met with me one-on-one because of her behavioural challenges in a group setting, also participated in the coffee house performance. She accompanied another woman who sang a solo. They arranged rehearsal times and colour-coordinated their outfits. She also sang while another woman accompanied her on the piano. In the final phase of therapy with Julia, the importance of completion through performance became a vital part of her personal process. Baker (2013) writes: "When clients' life experiences resonate with those of their audiences, they experience a sense of self-worth that is coupled to the ability to convey their emotional reality in a way that has a clear impact and meaning for the audience" (p. 24). For Julia, it was important to share the final phase of her music therapy journey with a group of women who could understand the deep emotions connected with oppression and incarceration.

Reflections

I am profoundly grateful for the significant impact that each woman I encountered had on my own personal journey. I came to work in a correctional facility because of my own desire to "help oppressed women." After a mere ten months' work with these women, I discovered my own voice as a woman and as a music psychotherapist. For many of these women, their voices had been silenced. Because of their crime, they were told that their voices didn't matter any longer. Some had relinquished their voices, sick of fighting. Others, like Sarah, fought and fought to hang on to their voices. Others, like Julia and Janice, found a safe space to grow by hearing their own voices and telling their stories.

The coffee house doors are still open: these experiences became a regular event in the facility. Many of the women from the music groups moved into the same living pod so they could share musical ideas outside of the designated scheduled music groups. Julia has left the correctional facility. She will have regular supervised visits with her daughter. Before she left, Julia requested that her halfway house have a piano. Her request was granted.

In her writings about her own work with women in a prison setting, Shoshana Pollack (2007) provides a quote from St. Augustine that resonates with my work in a correctional facility: "Hope has two beautiful daughters. Their names are anger and courage; anger at the way things are, and courage to see that they do not remain the way they are" (p. 105). I have experienced both anger and courage working with incarcerated women and others in the prison system. These women had the courage to reach out to a stranger. As a result, they created their own musical autobiographies, found their musical voices, and helped a young music therapist find her own voice in the process.

Zharinova-Sanderson (2005) referred to the music therapist as a "campaigner for music as a force for change in the community" (p. 245). As I struggled to find my "role" in this community, it became clear that I was to be a *campaigner for music*. Many more stories could be told of how music changed this community and gave renewed hope to those who participated and those who witnessed the process. Maya Angelou (1983) has given us a profound poem about a caged bird who found freedom through its song. Imprisoned with clipped wings and tied feet, the bird opens its throat to sing clearly and wistfully of things longed for:

> ... *for the caged bird*
> *sings of freedom.*

PART VI

COMMUNITY MUSIC
Walking the Boundaries of Cultural Identity

MUSIC-MAKING IS a practice embedded in and influenced by various cultural and historical traditions. Sirek examines the identity of those engaged in music activities through the Grenada (West Indies) carnival. In contrast, Leis focuses on the traditional worship practices of Mennonite churches in southern Ontario (Canada) in the interest of reclaiming worship through a fresh approach to singing. Southcott and de Bruin describe music-making in Australia by Italian immigrants and descendants, while Heesun, Veblen, and Potter recount the joy that music brings by presenting narratives evoking memories of experiences within Korean cultural communities. Yun summarizes this final section by addressing ethical and cultural concerns in intercultural music-making and by providing models of intercultural sharing.

CHAPTER 28

At the Panyard, in the Calypso Tent, on the Soca Stage

Exploring "Ideal" Identity through
Community Music Activities during Carnival
in Grenada, West Indies

Danielle Sirek

GRENADA'S CARNIVAL, CALLED SPICEMAS, is the largest cultural festival in
Grenada, West Indies. Community music activities that take place over the
course of the Carnival season foster conceptualizations of "ideal" (Small, 1998)
Grenadian identity across generations. However, notions of this ideal identity
often differ between older and younger people in Grenada. Many older Grenadians cling to folk cultural practices during Carnival, such as steel pan and
calypso, in order to combat cultural and social fragmentation. They embrace
community music activities, often viewing them as interventions designed to
"rescue" a traditional Grenadian identity, which they see as rapidly disappearing
(Sirek, 2013, 2018a). Older Grenadians hope to find a sense of "authentic"
Grenadianness in a Grenada that has undergone constant political upheaval
in recent decades: authoritarianism, oppression, revolution, and invasion. Just
as robustly, younger Grenadians embrace musicking of popular genres such as
soca music during Carnival, as a way of expressing modern, globalized notions
of Grenadianness. Although some Grenadians participate in musicking that
contrasts with the group to which they "belong," it is useful to make these distinctions here, for this chapter concerns older and younger people in Grenada
and the perceived fracture between generations.

Grenada has a history of political revolution and foreign invasion. After a
nearly thirty-year dictatorship under Eric Matthew Gairy, a Marxist-Leninist

445

revolution broke out in 1979, led by Maurice Bishop. Soon after, however, there developed an ideological schism in the revolutionary government, and in 1983 a coup was launched during which Bishop and several other high-ranking officials were killed. The island was placed under a twenty-four-hour curfew; those who broke it risked being shot on sight. Six days after the coup, the United States invaded Grenada – an island with barely more than 100,000 people. A generational divide in Grenada has grown in part from this tumultuous political history: the older generation lived through revolution and the American invasion, the younger did not (Shemer, 2012; Sirek, 2013). This generational divide is often made visible in acts of musicking (Sirek, 2018b).

Methodology and Methods

This research focused on two questions, which grew out of a larger study on the relationship between musicking and identity in Grenada (Sirek, 2013, p. 1). (1) What are some community music activities that take place during the Carnival season? And (2) how does community musicking during the Carnival season contribute to conceptualizations of "ideal" (Small, 1998) Grenadian identity across generations in Grenada? After ethics approval was received, data were collected via field notes (i.e., participant- and non-participant observation); photographs and audio and video recordings; and interview transcriptions over a period of eleven months (2010–11). An online study followed over a period of six years (2011–17). This online component was informed by and expanded on the ethnographic data collected in the field and included investigation of Grenadian news sources, blogs, social media, and YouTube videos.

During data collection, I sought to facilitate dialogical spaces with my informants and to use co-constructive methods of research, offering my own voice and experiences alongside those of the participants. This was mainly to acknowledge my positionality as an outsider researcher and to recognize that positionality as contributory to my research. Data were collated and analyzed for themes such as "identity," "culture," "older/younger generation," "Carnival," "Spicemas," "steel pan," "calypso," and "soca"; these were examined using a constructivist approach. Though I viewed myself as working alongside my informants, I acknowledge that negotiations of power, positionality, and representation are inherent in this chapter, for ultimately, I as researcher am the one giving voice to this study. All names used in this chapter are pseudonyms. Local grammar and syntax have been preserved.

Historical Context: Carnival

Carnival likely started as a Roman Catholic appropriation of the Roman Feast of Saturnalia. It was originally a festival of eating, drinking, and merry-making, held the Monday and Tuesday before the commencement of Lent (the solemn six weeks before Easter, which in the Christian tradition celebrates the resurrection of Jesus Christ). European settlers introduced the festival to enslaved persons in the Caribbean in the late 1700s. The region's enslaved blacks began holding their own celebrations after Emancipation, fusing African rituals with French traditions (in the case of Grenada and other French possessions). These celebrations involved emulating characters from West African folklore, reciting folktales, dressing up and mocking plantation owners, and stick-fighting. Over time, Carnival became dissociated from the French upper class and became largely a celebration of the formerly enslaved population, who appropriated it as their own, as a means to resist European culture and to protect their own traditions (Liverpool, 1993).

The modern-day Carnival in Grenada, called Spicemas, encompasses a number of music events, such as Dimanche Gras (calypso), Panorama (steel pan), J'Ouvert Morning (jab jab soca), and Soca Monarch (soca). Music is omnipresent as Grenadians and tourists "play mas" during Carnival: dressing up in ornate, colourful costumes and headdresses decorated with beading, sequins, feathers, and sparkles for Pageant Mas or as various folkloric characters such as the Shortknee and Moko Jumbie for Traditional Mas. At one time, Grenada's Carnival was held in February; it now takes place in August so as to not conflict with Grenada's Independence celebrations and to encourage more tourists to visit the island.

The Way *We* Do It: "Ideal" Identity and Musicking during Carnival

Community musicking during the Carnival season contributes to the representation and construction of ideal Grenadian identity for both older and younger people, albeit in different ways. I take the words "musicking" and "ideal" from Christopher Small (1998), who coined the term "musicking" to reconceptualize music as an action instead of a "thing." Fundamental to his writings about musicking is a focus on *how* people "explore, affirm, and celebrate" desired (what he calls "ideal") relationships through music (Small, 1998), and *why* they do so. The word "ideal" here does not imply that those relationships are inherently good or virtuous; rather, it reflects our views of what are "right relationships" for *us*. Since identity is constantly in flux and based on relational encounters, musicking that reflects and constructs ideal relationships also reflects and constructs dynamic ideal identities. Yet what is ideal for some may not be for others – this is precisely the case in Grenada – and can change moment-to-moment and over time. The notion of "ideal" is contextual and ever changing.

Multiple informants told me that musicking during Spicemas is a way for Grenadians to showcase their authentic Grenadianness, sharing that perhaps if one does not know Grenadian Carnival, one does not really know Grenada or Grenadian people. This was verbalized by even some of my youngest interviewees, such as Shanna, a ten-year-old: "Carnival tells us that Grenada is very special and unique. And its people like to show their true colours. And make themselves proud and show the world what they really are and how wonderful Grenada is."

Many articulated that they did not consider Grenadian music to be distinctive from that of other Caribbean countries. Rather, it is the unique way Grenadians *do* music – the unquantifiable Grenadianness of musicking – that makes it so intimately linked with Grenadian identity. Antoine framed this as a uniquely Grenadian expression of culture: "One of the things indigenous to us, I think, is [our] expression. In any shape, form, or fashion."

Gabriel, a younger gospel singer, put it to me as simply, "the way *we* do it": "See, we won't sing folk songs like St. Lucians sing folk songs. It is just the way *we* do it. We would do it a different way. This is *our* way of doing it. Even if it's the same folk songs, it's different."

"The way we do things" was viewed as more important than the musical materials themselves. Truly music-as-identity – the way *we* do things; the way *we* sing this song; the way *we* play this tune; the way *we* listen to, dance to, and experience music. Within this "*we*-ness" is the feeling of belongingness and of collective identity through which one has the sense of "I am": the sense of self, of culture, and of nation; the sense of past, of present, and of future; and also the sense of what I am *not* or we are *not*. Anything, according to Gabriel, *can* be Grenadian, both signifying and adding to the collective Grenadian identity, and it is the doing of it that is the most important.

Bernadette, a historian and supporter of the arts, said that this Grenadian "way of doing things" must be taught to younger generations: "You start with [the folk songs] first, the dances, the steelband, and things like the music that accompanies Carnival, now we need to say calypsos and so but there is a lot of kinds of music that accompanies the traditional masquerade ... The children must know how to do this *properly*."

Teaching "our" music "our" way is regarded as a method of educating children about Grenadian values and ideals. And according to Bernadette, it is not simply the musical materials that are involved in this teaching, but also knowing how to do this musicking in a "properly" Grenadian way.

Although both older and younger Grenadian informants emphasized the importance of teaching Grenadian musical and cultural practices in a specifically Grenadian way, ideas of what those musics and cultural practices are, and what "that Grenadian way" is, often differ across generations. This leads to Grenadian identity being perceived by some as fractured and in need of rescue or reinvention (Sirek, 2018a). I am now going to take you to three different Community musicking activities associated with Carnival to illustrate some of these generational tensions: the panyard, the calypso tent, and the soca stage.

At the Panyard

> It is a week before Carnival, about 10:00 p.m., and I am standing in a panyard. People mill around on this warm summer night talking and laughing, some playing little motifs on their pans, as they get ready for one of the last practices before Panorama. "Good night everybody! Let's get started!," shouts Aubrey. A drum kit gives four beats, and at once the chatter and laughter is replaced with running melismas played at breakneck speed – a virtuosic introduction played by Aubrey and the other tenor pannists that echoes across the field. The rest of the steelband joins in, and the sound is incredible. At break, around 11:30 p.m., we sit and eat chicken, rice, and peas together. The practice finishes shortly after 2:00 a.m., and I am incredulous to see that as I leave, more people are just arriving to help make costumes in the band house.

Steel pan and other drumming have strong resonances in Grenadian society. Pan grew out of tamboo bamboo, a rhythmic stomping of pitched bamboo sticks utilized in the late nineteenth century as a response to European suppression of drumming (Thomas, 1992). Steel pan is strongly intertwined with conceptualizations of identity in Grenada, and with "authentic" Caribbean culture. There are several steelband groups on mainland Grenada, including Angel Harps (Tanteen, St. George's), Commancheros (St. Paul's Community Center, St. Paul's), Rainbow City All Stars (The Quarry, Chapel Road, Grenville), New Dimensions (Melville Street, St. George's), Florida All Stars (Florida, St. John's), Pan Wizards (River Road, St. George's), Pan Lovers (Grand Anse Valley, St. George), Corinthians (Corinth, St. David), Pan Angels (Grand Roy, St. John), West Side Symphony (Florida, St. John), and Pan Ossia (Back Street, Gouyave).

In Grenada and other Caribbean countries, steelbands usually rehearse in panyards: flat, vacant spaces that are big enough to accommodate large numbers of pannists and their instruments as well as a band house, which is a building or overhang that provides a sheltered area. Historically, panyards were places frequented by poor men with reputations for thievery and drunkenness. Today, however, pan is regarded as a national art form, and adults and youth of all backgrounds play in community and school ensembles. Often, rehearsals begin with a few players early in the evening, but by the end of the night (or the wee hours of the morning), the panyard is in full swing. It is not uncommon for young people and adults to play in the same group, and sharing food and drink is often part of the evening. Much or all of the learning is done by rote.

Steelbands perform at various events throughout the year. The most important event is Panorama, which is the biggest steelband competition in Grenada. Pan groups from across the island spend significant amounts of time in the panyard working on new tunes by pan arrangers and rehearsing choreography in preparation for the competition, which takes place annually during Carnival at the National Stadium. At Panorama, the bands take the stage with their instruments one by one and play their selections. Points are given for performance and for the arrangements they have created. The winning band receives a trophy, accolades, and prize money.

Despite the number of Grenadians who play pan, Panorama concert attendance has been steadily declining. It is now the least popular event during Carnival: audiences are small and mostly comprised of older Grenadians and tourists. Also, Panorama is being sidelined in favour of private events that generate much larger sums of money. In 2016 a music event called Xtreme White was scheduled at the same venue (the National Stadium) the same evening as Panorama. This resulted in the winners of Panorama 2016 being barred from coming onstage to collect their trophy, and the annual post-Panorama celebration of pan music was effectively prohibited. Many pannists attributed this incident to the ongoing commercialization of Carnival.

Spicemas has, over the years, become increasingly commercialized, transitioning from a traditional festival in which every village played mas to a national festival held in the main city of St. George's. Shaynee, an older female calypsonian, who grew up in rural Grenada, gave me an especially poignant description of the effects of commercialization on Carnival:

> But what you see happen now, is they commercialize it. Since they commercialized the Carnival, they lost the original traditional mas. With the commercialization of Carnival, and everything culture and everything, you find these things are different. We lost, we're sort of a lost, losing. Instead of we holding on to ours, we let the others take over within.

This commercialization has fostered an atmosphere in which many older Grenadians feel increasingly compelled to "save" certain aspects of Spicemas, including Panorama. In a CC6 News Night interview detailing the "unprecedented and gross disrespect" experienced by pan players at Panorama 2016, the manager of the steelband Angel Harps, Brian Sylvester, lamented:

> Nobody seems to be interested. We are digging a hole of people without a sense of their past ... You know, it's a dangerous road. And I'm begging the government to get involved, intervene. Because like I said, we are disrespecting our culture, we are not showing our kids the right direction. And then we get on and off when they do something wrong, something bad. We chastise them. What are we showing them, what are we telling them? (11 August 2016)

The association here between perceived disrespect for culture and the "wrong" road or "wrong" direction of young people in Grenada suggests that to not learn, create, and perform pan music is to not pass on cultural knowledge. But it is more than that: it is dangerous, it is digging a hole – a burial. Here, pan is seen as powerful, even being held up as responsible for children's moral decision-making.

While many young Grenadians play in steelbands, they often participate only at school or at certain times of year, such as Carnival or Independence Day – the "time of year" to play pan. Perhaps this is why pan initiatives with a distinct focus on young people are widespread. As I have written elsewhere, such initiatives are sometimes viewed by an older generation of Grenadians as efforts to "rescue" a dying "authentic" Grenadian identity (Sirek, 2013, 2018a). This is also evident in the rhetoric in Grenadian news interviews and on the Grenada Steel Pan Events Facebook page, where phrases such as, "Doing our part to keep pan alive," "Working with young people to keep the thing moving," and "Save our dying artform" are often encountered.

After the events of Panorama 2016, the Grenada Steelband Association launched an initiative in which steel pan events were hosted by each Grenadian steelband in turn. Some events were held in the panyards, others at performance venues such as the Spice Basket Theatre. One such event was the Steel Pan Jam and Rhythm Section Competition, hosted by the Pan Wizards on 2 October 2016. According to CC6 News Night, the jam was created "with the hopes of building interest and attraction to pan in Grenada" and to "build a following [for pan] through the events." Mykal Blaize Robertson, a member of the Grenada Steelband Association and leader of the Pan Wizards, said in an interview with CC6 News Night: "We need to constantly keep pan in people's mind, their ears, their eyes; let them see that the steelband movement is alive, it's vibrant" (15 September 2016).

In the same interview, Robertson discussed the recruitment campaigns of the various steelband groups – both community and school based. He stressed that the Grenada Steelband Association and Grenadian government are focusing on involving more youth in pan. Most steelbands have junior learners' programs for young people; many groups, like the Angel Harps and the Commancheros, boast large numbers of Grenadian youth in their ranks (*The New Today*, 4 October 2016). Many of these young pannists participate in Junior Panorama, the biggest steel band competition for youth in Grenada, which began in 1992. Various steel bands also work with schools on mainland Grenada, and since 2009, a pan program for both primary and secondary schools has existed in Grenada and in Carriacou (a dependency island of Grenada). Several pan groups, like the Pan Wizards, invest significant time in community engagement, educating Grenadian youth about drugs and alcohol.

Despite the efforts of the bands and the Grenada Steelband Association, Panorama 2017 did not go on as scheduled: with the stage incomplete (or, in the words of Brian Sylvester, "stolen – matter of fact, I shouldn't say stolen: but has been sold" (Sylvester, 2017), the pannists refused to go onstage. The incomplete stage was unexpected: the night of the show, all eight of the bands – and their truckloads of instruments – were waiting outside the National Stadium, while several hundred patrons waited inside.

The Grenada government has since launched an investigation into the cancellation of Panorama, which Prime Minister Keith Mitchell called a "national embarrassment" (Caribupdate Channel, 16 August 2017). The government said in an official statement: "The Government is extremely concerned about the fact that Panorama did not take place as planned and pan lovers as well as pan players, including the large numbers of young people, were deprived of an opportunity to participate in this rich annual cultural tradition" (16 August 2017).

In this statement, the Grenadian government was identifying Panorama specifically and pan playing in general as a "rich cultural tradition" and articulating the importance of not "depriving" young people of the "opportunity" of pan music. Sandra Ferguson, a writer for NOW Grenada who called this conflict "a capture of public spaces by private actors" (Ferguson, 2017, par. 5) expressed similar thoughts:

> Panorama is the premier pan event of the country, and everyone knows
> of the dedication, the effort, and the hours put in by all involved. It is

one of those events that display the best of Grenada. It also bridges the inter-generational gap and is a significant youth development investment since most bands are dominated by young people, most of whom are school students. What does this decision signal about the respect and value that the "authorities" place on the investment and contribution of those in the pan movement? (2017, par. 7)

Again, we see pan as intimately linked with Grenadian identity and as an important art form that can "rescue" Grenadian youth. Although framed as a bridge-builder, that bridge is perhaps only one-way: pan is regarded as an opportunity to be bestowed upon young people; it is seen as an investment by the older generation in the younger's development. This perpetuates the idea that pan musicking endorses the older generation as having the best and most authentic Grenadian identity, and that this must be imparted to the younger generation, who may or may not, however, be keen to receive it. And even the most devoted older-generation pan enthusiasts may push pan to the sidelines if there is a possibility for financial gain, as was the case for Panorama 2016.

In the Calypso Tent

The crowd gathers in the calypso tent, waiting to hear the two rivalling contenders, Teacher and Mighty Sam. The dance band blares out tunes percussively with syncopated rhythms, and each calypsonian in turn ruminates on political and social issues of the day dramatically, analyzing governmental policies, moral decisions, or perceived wrongdoings through word play and double entendre. The calypsonians invite the audience to participate: to move, to dance, to sing. Mighty Sam, the calypso king, emerges victorious.

Like steel pan, calypso music in Grenada is associated with African heritage and the history of enslavement. Although the exact origins of calypso are unknown, extensive histories of the art form have been developed based on legend and oral history. It is believed that enslaved blacks brought with them from West Africa a tradition of expressing social commentary through music (Liverpool, 1993). This custom of storytelling through song likely originated with West African *griots* or praise singers, whose responsibility it was to sing the history and social expectations of their communities (Gallaugher, 1991; Liverpool, 1993). African-based praise songs, songs of derision and protest, and work songs evolved into early calypso, which melded with French, English, and Spanish song forms. These songs were sung by workers on plantations, and in communities during daily events as well as rituals and ceremonies, as a means to rebel against the oppressive colonial powers (Liverpool, 1993). Calypsos to this day are generally political or satirical. Clearly, then, the calypso song form is closely linked to the collective memory of Africa and slavery, so that it carries within it delineated meanings of African ancestry and nationhood, as well as of resistance and power.

Contemporary calypsos have a verse-chorus song form and follow clear conventions as to melody, harmony, rhythm, tempo, and timbre. The Grenadian musicker knows these conventions well (Green, 2008), having imbibed them from childhood. The lyrics are almost always social or political, with calypsonians interrogating political concerns or problems in the community. Calypso is viewed as both *representative* of Grenadian identity (as a reflection of society) and *constructive* of identity (with calypsonians singing in support of or against political candidates, governmental decisions, or moral issues). Simone explained to me that Grenadian calypso is a mirror of Grenadian society: "So the calypso is a mirror of the society. In the calypso, you get all the social issues, the political issues, and the economic issues." Isaac affirmed the important role of the calypsonian in Grenadian politics: "Calypsonians, normally, are the transformers in the way people think about the government."

Calypso generates feelings of belonging by inviting the audience to participate through call-and-response interactions, verbal extemporizations, and collective movements, all of this mixed with insider language and information. Regis explored the affect displayed by Caribbean audiences in response to Caribbean music, noting that the call and response style "cultivates an atmosphere of harmonious interaction" between the calypsonian and the audience, for the audience feels compelled to sing along with the response (Regis, 1998, p. 210). The participatory element of calypso means it is inclusive by nature (or at least, invites the possibility of inclusion), and within this inclusiveness, older Grenadians feel belongingness, fulfilment, and a sense of self. Small posits that it is in such experiences of belongingness that we often have personally meaningful musicking experiences in which we feel more wholly ourselves: "When we have been present at a good and satisfying musical performance we feel more fully ourselves, more fully realized, and more in tune with ourselves and with our fellows. We feel we have been afforded a glimpse of how the world really is" (Small, 1990, p. 1).

During calypso competitions, calypsonians sing the calypsos they have written about social or political issues of the day and are evaluated by a panel of calypso judges on lyrical content (expression, wordsmithing, satire, double entendre, flow), music (melody, arrangement with band and backup singers), and performance (interpretation of the song, execution, stage presence, dress, props). Although the genre was once dominated by men, there are now many female calypsonians, and anyone is welcome to compete.

Traditionally, calypso competitions took place in calypso tents (a stage area covered by cloth material). At contemporary calypso tents, there is usually a permanent covered stage as well as seating for the audience. In Grenada, most calypso tents are in schools or similar buildings. The tents are community-oriented – patrons attend not just to hear good music or to support their favourite calypsonian, but also to socialize and learn about political and social issues in their communities. Several calypso tents currently exist in Grenada, including Kaiso Bards (Deluxe Cinema, Grenville, St. Andrew), Calypso Cave (Ft. Matthew, Richmond Hill, St. George), Majestic Band (Marigot, St. John), All Star @ Natural Works (La Sagesse, St. David), Images House of Soca (Hermitage Govt. School, St. Patrick), The Kingdom (Pomme Rose RC School), and Kingman Calypso Tent (La Sagesse).

Support for the tents has been dwindling in Grenada as calypso audiences have shrunk and calypso has become more commercialized. According to my informants, most of the time, calypso holds little interest for younger Grenadians. Younger informants likewise often expressed to me that they did not feel a sense of connection to Grenadian calypso music despite usually perceiving it as integral to their cultural heritage and identity. Samson, a young gospel singer, said, "Our own music, we're not hearing it ... If you put it on, they will say like, 'that's boring man, I would rather to listen to hip hop!'"

The younger generation's rejection of calypso is acutely felt by many older-generation Grenadians. One informant, Renelle, lamented that when she tries to teach her students calypso, they have no desire to learn about calypso music or what it stands for. This is conceivably both meant and understood as applying also to calypso's associated values, ideals, and identities. Older Grenadians, who generally consider calypso to be an authentic representation of Grenadian identity, see the younger generation's rejection of calypso as a rejection of Grenadianness and simultaneously a rejection of an older generation of Grenadians. While calypso represents and constructs ideal Grenadian identity for some, it evidently does not for others.

In recent years there has been a push to revitalize the tents, which were historically a prominent feature of Carnival, despite decreased funding and an ongoing rift between the Grenada Professional Association of Calypsonians and Tents (GPACT) and the Grenada Progressive Calypso Association (GPCA). Commenting on the importance of the revitalization in a 2014 interview, calypsonian Ajamu said in an interview with NOW Grenada: "The tent ... has been dying for many years ... This is the culture of our people. I often ask, 'What are we leaving for our children and grandchildren?'"

Another calypsonian, Black Wizard, said in a 2016 interview: "[As long as] you have people willing to sing on the issues, kaiso (calypso) *can't* die" (Grenada Broadcasting Network, 2 June 2016).

There is an acute sense that if social and political calypsos are not performed, and if the historically accurate way of calypso musicking is not revived, then older Grenadians will have nothing to leave their children in terms of authentic Grenadian identity. Once again, we see an older generation of Grenadians exploring, affirming, and celebrating ideal – for *them*, Grenadian – identity through a specific type of musicking. Calypso tells *their* history, helps to form *their* decisions and world views, and represents *their* sense of self. It is intrinsically tied to their conceptualization of Grenadian identity, but this is not so for many or most younger Grenadians.

On the Soca Stage

> The stadium floor is so packed that it seems as though the entire island has come out to see who will be crowned the next Soca Monarch, and we move up a level to escape the crowd. The air is ripe with excitement and sweat: a sense of corporeal abandonment and visceral enjoyment as people jammed against one another "jump up," fete, dance, and wine to the music, waving their flags and their rags, and responding with cheers and shouts every time the artistes rev up the crowd by singing, "Anybody from Trinidad? Anybody from St. Vincent? Anybody from ... GRENADA?" The energy is infectious and I find myself totally caught up in the "jump and wave" of it all, singing along to choruses I don't know, pumping my rag to the beat, and cheering loudly when the artistes call out to people from St. George's, where my home is. In that moment, it feels like it doesn't matter that I'm white, an outsider, different: here, it feels like I am nobody. A body, with other bodies, moving to the beat, being and thinking of nothing except the music.

Soca is the music of the younger generation in Grenada. The message of soca exists in the body, with lyrics emphasizing pleasures of partying, sex, and alcohol. Soca artistes invite the feting and abandonment that is so important to the art form by jumping and dancing energetically onstage, enticing listeners to wine (a dance move in which one winds the hips, sometimes seen as overtly sexual in nature), and encouraging audience participation, for instance in the form of waving flags and rags. In so doing they engage the audience in participatory musicking – dancing and vocalizing along with, or in response to, the artiste.

Soca music is a verse-chorus song form characterized by up-tempo melodies in 4/4 time on top of sparsely textured, pre-recorded digital riddims (rhythms) that are fast and driving. Dudley, writing in 1996, noted that the soca singer functions "more as another instrument" than as a voice in creating a groove for partying and dancing (Dudley, 1996, p. 294). This groove (more commonly known as the song's rhythm or beat), with its digital and highly repetitive nature, lends itself to almost hypnotic movement and dancing. Producer and musician Shawn Mitchell (Mr. Roots) articulated in an interview with *LargeUp* that soca, and the jab jab rhythm unique to Grenada's Carnival specifically, is

> Supposed to embolden you, make you feel like nothing can touch you ... It also makes you forget whatever troubles you might have. Somehow, it awakens some form of your spiritual connection to your ancestors. That is the deep part of it. Sometimes you hear a piece of music and it sounds familiar to you although you've never heard it before. That is because it is a part of you. That's what makes Jab Jab so captivating. (*LargeUp*, 2016, para. 10)

Soca is the most popular musical genre on the island. Since it generates huge sums of money every year, it is unsurprising that there is an emphasis on soca music performance during the Carnival season. Carnival City, for example, is launched in June and includes weekly events at which artistes have the opportunity to perform their socas. The purpose of this initiative is to popularize the developing soca artistes and their songs and to prepare for the Soca Monarch competition, the biggest music event on the island. Other soca events during the 2017 season included Jab Jab Fest (4 August), 10 to 10 Soca Fete (5 August), Fete Nation Monday (7 August), Pree Day (9 August), Xtreme White (12 August), and Pure White @ Moonlight City (12 August) – an impressive number of soca concerts in a little over a week for an island with fewer than 110,000 people.

Some older Grenadians see the younger generation's love of soca music and its associated values as a rejection of authentic Grenadianness. Annie, for example, said that Grenadian youth are only interested in listening to modern music, which stifles not only traditional Grenadian music but also Grenadians themselves: "They're not hearing the local ... Everybody's working in the same so-called big world culture. But – it's a big world now ... so we're kind of stifled out. You know? And so, our music is going to be sort of stifled out."

Raya commented that the "stupidness" of soca infringes not only on her musical preferences but also on her ability to be informed about social and political issues:

These days you don't even hear those, like what you call social commentary. You don't even hear those calypsos being played ... They play all the stupidness for the Soca Monarch, and the Groovy [Monarch], and the songs that are supposed to be sung for the Calypso Monarch for the night, you don't know them because you hardly hearing them. Because those are like, lyrical songs that talk about things that are happening, issues that are happening, social issues and so, in the community and with the government, and you know, you could come down and tell the government, "this is what's going on." But you hardly hear that!

Those who do not enjoy or relate to soca often describe soca-loving younger Grenadians as apathetic about social and political matters, obsessed with sex, unconcerned about religious interests and authorities, and influenced by alcohol and/or drugs – and as therefore unreliable, dangerous, and indifferent to their responsibilities. These characterizations are widespread, as I learned through discussions with informants, in watching Grenadian news, and in reading literature on soca. For example, one document on engaging youth at risk in Trinidad and Tobago – prepared by scholars at the University of the West Indies and found on the Trinidad and Tobago Parliament website – identifies soca music as very likely linked to youth crime:

> While it is impossible to draw a definitive correlation between the violence or explicitness of lyrics and the level of criminality of youth, the lyrics of popular Soca hits in 2012 do tend to support the idea of a contemporary youth culture that is very consistent with the rebellious behaviour of previous generations of youth ... We need to examine the relationship between the current musical culture of youth and its relationship to violence and criminality and its potential for cooptation by the seedier elements of society that draw young impressionable minds. (Ryan et al., 2013, pp. 47–48)

An online commentary by Kent State University Professor Emeritus Kwame Nantambu (2008) blames soca music for the "moral decadence" in Trinidad and Tobago:

> As quiet as it is kept, Trinbagonians seem to be in long-term denial that there is a direct correlation between Soca [sic] music and moral decadence in TnT. As of this writing, the evidence is very clear and convincing that immorality and public sexual vulgarity have surpassed the nadir of their bottomless pit. (Nantambu, 2008, par. 1)

However, soca musicking is a prominent means for young people to construct identities that distinguish them from older Grenadians. Soca, whatever its associated identities of immorality, apathy, promiscuity, and irresponsibility, is important to young people. They perceive it as connecting them to their past and enabling a connection to their ancestors – as explained by soca artiste Shawn Mitchell above – and also as representing and constructing corporeal and intellectual freedom. Jeremiah said that soca promotes globalization, integration, and Grenada's development:

> We believe in globalization and integration and this and that ... That shows us that we are one step closer to becoming in a sense, one market. One step closer to becoming further developed, because if we weren't developed, then we wouldn't have heard this music, because there was no way to get this music. So, in a sense hearing this music tells us that we are, in a sense, becoming more and more developed.

For young people, embracing soca means embracing modernity, globalization, and technology, and that Grenada has moved beyond its status as a developing country. In coming together to create, learn, and perform soca music, young Grenadians are acting out ideal identity – for them. But this is not without contention, since many older Grenadians regard soca music as being an inappropriate or even dangerous representation of Grenadian culture, and in fact as eroding authentic Grenadian culture and identity.

Conclusion

In this chapter, I have argued that community musicking during Carnival affirms ideal identity across generations in Grenada. Grenadians "explore, affirm, and celebrate" relationships that are *right for them* (Small, 1998) by musicking in a way that is perceived as uniquely Grenadian, and by engaging in participatory musicking that promotes feelings of belongingness and an acknowledgment of collective history. These relationships in turn inform ideas of Grenadian identity and authentic Grenadianness in an acute way, since conceptualizations of identity are intimately linked to our interactions with others.

While both older and younger Grenadians engage in community musicking during Carnival to celebrate Grenadian cultural identity, different generations tend to do this in different ways. Older Grenadians take part in community musicking activities that express and construct traditional Grenadian identities, such as steel pan and calypso. Both of these art forms take their histories and community-based practices in slavery and resistance and represent authentic Grenadian identity for an older generation of Grenadians.

These art forms are also viewed as having the capacity to "save" Grenadian youth and bridge the perceived gap between generations in Grenada. These narratives become more complicated when there is perceived financial gain or loss, however, as seen with the events of Panorama 2016 (the National Stadium being double-booked for a more profitable soca concert), Panorama 2017 (the unfinished stage), and decreased funding for the calypso tents.

Despite a widespread acknowledgment by both older and younger people that steelpan and calypso are integral to Grenadian identity, these art forms are in decline. Since these forms are interconnected to traditional identity and sense of self, the younger generation's rejection of this musicking also feels like a rejection of self to many of my older informants. It is also portrayed this way in the media. Younger Grenadians prefer soca and other popular musics to express Grenadian identity and prefer engaging in affiliated participatory musicking that promotes associated globalized identities and world views. Grenadian youth express that soca music connects Grenada to the world. They also express that soca links them to their cultural history in a way that is more relatable and engaging than musics associated with traditional notions of Grenadian culture. While soca is presently the most popular music on the island, it is bound up with conceptualizations of irresponsibility, apathy, sex, and alcohol consumption. Many older Grenadians therefore may feel distanced from soca music and are reluctant to see soca representing Grenadian identity. This research illustrates the ways in which community musicking during cultural festivals can construct and articulate representations of identity, and how these experiences and representations may differ across generations.

CHAPTER 29

Reclaiming Worship
Community Music Practices and Their Application to the Music-Making in the Anabaptist Mennonite Church

Brandon Leis

Introduction

"We do not think ourselves into new ways of living, we live ourselves into new ways of thinking."
– *Richard Rohr*

IN THIS CHAPTER I will show the transformational effects of applying a community music approach to musical "equipping" in two faith-based settings. I will briefly discuss points of intersection between community music and the Anabaptist Mennonite faith tradition and then describe the study that brought out the transformational effects of such an application. While this study was limited to music-making in the Anabaptist, Mennonite tradition, it is easy to infer the benefit that the approaches undertaken in this study would have if applied to other Christian and non-Christian faith-based contexts, particularly those that engage in a regular worship practice with adherents to the faith. I hope that you, as a reader, will resonate with these striking similarities and modify the study's elements for application in your own context.

The non-formal "interactive workshop" approach this study took was important for a number of reasons. First, it engaged the members of the congregation in ways that allowed them to "play" with the different elements of worship music outside of a worship setting and reflect on that praxis. Second, it removed the materials of worship from the act of worship in such a way as to remain respectful to worship as sacred ritual. Third, since the workshops were held within the congregations' home church building and included both musical leaders and regular attendees, the conversations, interventions, and experimentation were always contextually applicable and organic to the environment. This stands in stark contrast to common models, where a few leaders from disparate congregations gather for a retreat with an external resource person, for the application of explored material diminishes greatly when applied back in one's home congregation. Finally, as an engaged facilitator in the workshop environment, I was able to companion the process as topics were being discussed. I could encourage and enable gifts, assess flow, ensure that all voices (not just those of leaders) were heard, identify emerging themes, and affirm insights and observations as they were made – all fairly standard ways of operating for community music facilitators.

The format and progression of the workshops are outlined in moderate detail in order that the reader may draw clearer connections from the process to the outcomes. Results are shared regularly throughout the chapter, relying heavily on the specific words of the participants. Please feel free to modify and use this format as you wish, to apply it in your own context.

Intersections between Community Music and the Anabaptist, Mennonite Tradition

I feel it prudent to briefly identify some points of intersection between community music and the Anabaptist-Mennonite faith tradition, if only to inform the reader about the latter (not so much the former). While the connections between community music theories and practices and church ethics seem quite natural to this researcher, who grew up in Canada as a Mennonite, the idea of community music practices mirroring church music practices has seemed less clear to those familiar with other faith traditions, especially in the international community.

What chiefly defines community music and distinguishes it from other forms of music-making is its mode of facilitation and the process of its practice. Focusing strongly on community music as an "act of hospitality," facilitation as a strategy for musical leadership, democratization of knowledge and insight, reduction or removal of hierarchical structure, and unknowable or undetermined "products" of practice, Lee Higgins sought to positively define community music as a discrete music-making practice in his book *Community Music: In Theory and Practice* (Higgins, 2012).

A large number of qualities that Higgins points to as distinguishing community music from other forms of music-making are the same as or, in the least, strikingly similar to those practices that are believed to be central to the Ethics of the Anabaptist faith tradition, particularly those emphasized by authors and theologians writing in the current "post-Christendom" paradigm (Ministerial Leadership Services, 1996; Krabill, 2011; Murray, 2010; Yoder, Kropf, & Slough, 2006).

The following is a comparative list of some of those points of commonality. The reader should note that this list has been simplified in order to present

Table 29.1 Intersections between Community Music and the Anabaptist, Mennonite tradition

Community Music	Anabaptist Mennonite
Affirmation of the rhizomic nature of the unknown and openness to uncertainty	Affirmation of the unpredictable and active work of the Holy Spirit within the church
Importance of and focus on community	Importance of faithfulness to God as lived out in community with others
Non-hierarchical structures of leadership	Priesthood of all believers – neutralizing human authority, creating non-hierarchical structures of leadership
Abundance (Athenian) mindset	Belief that gifts have been given to all
Focus on participation and engagement	Faith through works (action) and focus on active social justice and peacemaking
Context-driven music-making	Individual churches encouraged to act and discern independently based on context
Focus on hospitality and being open	Focus on hospitality and welcome
Focus on inclusivity	Multi-voiced discernment and participation, and inclusion of those otherwise marginalized by society

a brief illustration; it is not meant to form or defend an argument that these significant points of connection and complexity deserve.

There are many differences, both subtle and profound, between faith traditions and the developing field of community music. The above list provides an ample context and opportunity to begin bridge-building between those two discrete domains. In particular, the non-formal educational models that are germane to community music practitioners should be seen as highly applicable to congregational church settings. In a conversation with Lee Higgins in November 2013, I was surprised to hear that very little investigation had been done as to the intersections between community music and music-making in the churches, Anabaptist or otherwise. That conversation encouraged this study.

Some Definitions

Gifts/giftedness. One's God-given abilities. The biblical/cultural belief that gifts and abilities have been given to all.

Lay-leader. An official member or attendee of a church who serves in a leadership role (as worship leader, committee/ministry chairperson, song leader, etc.).

Song leader. The person who leads singing by singing and/or conducting the congregation and any instrumentalists during worship.

Congregant/member/participant. Used synonymously in this chapter in reference to a non-paid attendee of the church.

Case Study

The congregations involved. This study was conducted in two Mennonite churches in southwestern Ontario, Canada: Bethel Mennonite Church (Bethel), and Cassel Mennonite Church (Cassel). Both churches are relatively small (fifty to seventy attendees on a Sunday morning). Both are rural, and both had undergone a pastoral leadership change in the previous eighteen to twenty-four months. Both felt they were experiencing a depletion or deficit of musical gifts within their congregations, and both were open to new ways of approaching music and worship. Both churches have one paid full-time pastor and rely heavily on volunteer lay-leaders to carry out their work and ministry. Much of the worship is based on "local tradition," and leadership roles are typically learned by observing others fulfilling those roles. Note that music and the quality of the music-making are very important to these specific churches, and to Mennonites in general, and are closely linked to the Mennonite identity.

This study was conducted in two different congregations but, because the processes and the results were so similar between the two, they will be treated as one, unless specified otherwise.

Primary Goals. This study set out to apply community music facilitation strategies in a congregational setting in order to:

+ develop a stronger sense of empathy within the congregation between those who regularly plan/implement worship and those who do not, and between "camps" of stylistic preference (as identified by one of the congregations);

+ enable the congregations to identify their musical gifts and how best to express those in worship, thus enabling them to transition from a mindset of "deficit" to one of "abundance" through conversation and application;

+ equip the leaders and congregation with some of the praxial experience and skills to move into new and emerging forms of music-making with confidence and a sense of unity;

+ provide an experiential place of "encounter" for the congregation;

+ make playing as a congregation "fun"; and

+ gain deeper insight into the human elements of music-making in the congregational context and the relatability of community music facilitation skills in such a church setting.

Data Collection

Data were collected before the workshops began, during the workshop sessions, between the workshops, and after the final session.

There were pre- and post-study questionnaires designed for the lay-leadership of each congregation, as well as for regular members. The researcher kept private notes during the sessions, and there were times when ideas and responses to group conversations were documented on large pieces of poster paper. The researcher also kept a journal after each session.

Research Design

This study included two initial meetings with church leaders and four tailored workshop sessions at both Bethel and Cassel. The workshops ran over a period of three or four months. The spacing out of the workshops allowed the leaders some time to develop new skills and to implement new ideas within worship while being companioned throughout the process. We could establish and modify goals over this time period that reflected the changing inclinations of the congregations. The timing of the process also encouraged the leaders to adopt reflective practices. Involving the congregational members in these workshops was also integral, for it allowed all voices to be heard throughout.

Initial Meetings

An initial meeting was held with the pastor from each congregation (individually) to propose the process and ascertain whether that person was open to it and what they saw as the strengths and weaknesses in their congregation's current worship and music practice. This gave me insight into the existing dynamics within each congregation. From this initial meeting, I was able to develop a document listing some potential workshop topics and the proposed format for the workshops, which I would present to the Worship and Music committees from each church.

A subsequent meeting was then held with the Worship and Music committees from each church. Each committee was comprised of four to seven volunteers from the congregation, who, along with the pastor, provided leadership to all elements of worship. These leaders had been set apart by their congregations to discern the overall direction for worship planning and implementation.

These groups identified which workshop topics they felt would best resonate with their congregations; we should focus on these in our subsequent workshops. Seeking direction from these committees was critical as it allowed them to "own" the process before the workshops began.

Workshops/Sessions and Some Initial Feedback

Workshop #1 (Full Congregation – 1 Hour). This workshop immediately followed a regular worship service. It was held in the basement of each church, and we sat in a circle. Note: In both churches, since I had been present for the service, I was invited to play instruments along with worship – whenever I wanted! At Bethel I played some Djembe, trumpet, and guitar, and at Cassel I was welcomed to play guitar and trumpet. I was struck by this openness, trust, and hospitality.

During this workshop we sang new and easy songs (taught by rote), rearranged one or two of the hymns the congregation had already sung in worship that morning (by modifying the tempo, or by exchanging the text with a different hymn), played some musical games (playing with pitch/rhythm/involving the body) – all of this intermingled with group discussion. Some of the responses to the intentional questions are provided below, to give the reader a sense of the congregation's "starting point."

1. What role does music play in worship?

   Identified by both churches:

   - Connects us to and allows us to express our emotions.
   - Invites us to participate and allows us to share our gifts and overcome fears.
   - Binds us together and allows us to feel the spirit – even internationally – and makes us feel like part of the community, singing with others.
   - Creates, or helps us create, focus in the service; it can integrate with other elements.
   - Joyful noise unto the Lord.

   Some other responses (not represented in both churches):

   - Helps us to pray.
   - Aids in bringing us closer to God.
   - Expands the lungs, opens your sinuses.
   - "It calms me."

2. Why do we sing?

   Identified by both churches:

   - Brings unity, is something we can do together without too much segregation, and is a way of including others.
   - Invites.
   - Eases tension and takes away fear and brings comfort/peace.
   - Avenue of worship and praise.
   - We have to – the song leader tells us to! [There was plenty of humour in these sessions!]
   - Conveys a message and helps us learn.

   Some other responses (not represented in both churches):

   - Brings happiness and allows us to express emotions.
   - Because we can.
   - Meaningful inspiration
   - How can we not? We must!

+ Music does something that words alone do not
+ We enjoy it.
+ Because it's powerful.

Two further questions were "What do we sing?" and "How do we sing?" Both questions offered lively dialogue and debate.

At Bethel I was also able to get to this question: "What would the music of your ideal worship service be like with unlimited resources?" This prompted varying responses, from "Grand Orchestras with every instrument and language" to "What we currently have." One comment, however, shifted the conversation and was the concluding thought for the morning; "But is [the music of our worship] for us, or is it for God?" In a church where there had been significant conflict over the "style" of music within their worship, this was a *profoundly* helpful way to frame the discussion.

If the study had finished after the first session, there would have already been benefits for each congregation. Open group dialogue is something these congregations were already used to, but not necessarily around music or about specific questions that get to the heart of music as ritual practice. The lively dialogue and debate was framed safely around music but spoke to themes that ran much deeper within each congregation. One participant remarked at the end: "[The workshops were a] chance for us to voice our 'likes and dislikes' and to ask questions." Since style and preference are divisive, this discussion allowed the congregation members to move toward a greater understanding of and empathy for one another. It was also quite clear from this discussion that while there were differing preferences, there was also acceptance and room for disagreement.

Workshop #2 (Worship and Music Leaders Only – 90 Minutes). This was an evening session and focused on specific practical skills related to leading music in the worship context. The topics were chosen mainly from the Worship and Music ministry meeting and the first "Leader" questionnaire. Some were drawn from the conversation during the first workshop session. Topics in this session included the following:

+ *The worship space.* How the physical building and the arrangement of the participants/leaders within that space together effect the music-making.
+ *Teaching a new song.* How and when to teach new music.
+ *Hymnal "tour."* Exploring the various indices in the congregation's worship hymnal so to be better prepared to select and modify/manipulate hymns – that is, the scriptural index, which pairs scripture with

hymns based on the text; and the metrical index, which allows one to pair a text with a different tune that supports the same metrical footing.

- *Playing with hymns*. What is possible? Retexting tunes, changing meter, changing mode, what to play (from the piano) as accompaniment, adding instruments, pairing one hymn with another (such as the alternation of verses, which could serve to form a conversation between two different "voices" – that is, God and the congregation).
- *Song leading.* Who leads and how to lead a song.
- *Inclusion.* How to include children and those with varying degrees of musical gifts.

While this session focused on equipping the leaders with new strategies and skills, there was a conscious effort to open the participants to the possibilities that existed within the music of their worship for which they were already equipped (shifting deeper into the "abundance" mindset and further from the feeling of "deficit"). Much of the discussion was led in a Socratic manner, which involved responding to questions with questions in order to stimulate critical thinking and to generate context-specific ideas. Again, the non-formal, non-threatening format of this session was critical, for it allowed the educational components to be tailored to the participants' abilities and interests.

Workshop #3 (Full Congregation – 90 Minutes). Note: both congregations insisted that this session follow a noon meal together ... Who was I to argue?!

This Sunday afternoon session was held in the church sanctuary with both congregation members and music leadership present. This session was designed to provide an opportunity for the leaders to try some of their new ideas and approaches to leading music in an open, non-worship, non-"performative" congregational environment. The primary focus of this session was on the leadership, but it also gave the congregation a chance to become more fully aware of the various elements that go into selecting, leading, and creating the music of worship, and it allowed the congregation to engage in further dialogue while having fun "playing" together!

Workshop #4 (Full Congregation – 2.5 hours). Worship service, with musical focus followed by "wrap-up" session. This final workshop was where "the rubber met the road" and where the ideas that had been generated by the music and worship leaders were applied during worship. There was a new corporate mindfulness to the music's intention that was both expressed by the leaders and engaged with by the congregants.

A final session followed worship, during which was discussed some of the themes that had arisen in the course of the broader process. We also sang and engaged in exercises that highlighted the value of individuals' differing perspectives in a community context.

Results and Emerging Themes

The following themes emerged from the final questionnaire, which was issued to the congregation members and their leaders. This section relies heavily on the words of the leaders and the congregational members, to allow them, not me, to share the impact of the workshops.

1. Confidence and Encouragement

> This little light of mine, I'm gonna let it shine! (verse 2) Hide it under a
> bushel? NO! I'm gonna let it shine!
> – Lyrics from a popular camp song

As a music minister and educator, I have found that the level of confidence people have in their own abilities is a significant factor in their willingness to share and/or develop their gifts. Factors like self-doubt, comparisons to others who are "better," more "talented," or more "creative," and the low perceived value of what one has to offer can often hinder growth and the expression of gifts.

These workshops proved to be transformative for some leaders' confidence and, at the very least, encouraging and confidence-boosting for the rest.

Confidence by the Numbers (Before). At the beginning of the study, all of those who identified as having a leadership role in some aspect of worship were asked to rank their "level of confidence as it related to their giftedness in 16 musical traits/abilities that could be used in preparing and leading the music of worship (on a scale of 1-5)."

Patterns emerged from the data that grouped traits together in terms of higher, moderate, or lower levels of confidence.

Two of the traits that ranked *higher* in confidence on this initial survey, for all leaders from both congregations, were "Singing" and "Your ability to improvise." Two further traits that ranked higher in the musical leaders from both congregations were "General musical abilities" and "Selecting appropriate music for service" (see Figure 29.1).

Two traits that trended toward *moderate* from both congregations were "Song leading" and "Actively incorporating others into the music-making process." One additional trait from Cassel that also ranked as *moderate* was "Teaching new songs" (see Figure 29.2).

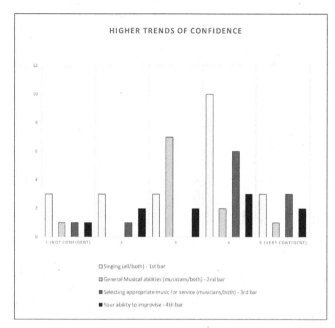

Figure 29.1 Higher trends of confidence.

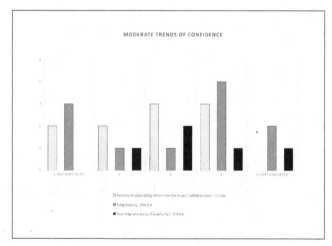

Figure 29.2 Moderate trends of confidence.

Three traits that trended toward *lower* for the music leaders of both congregations were "Arranging music for singers/instrumentalist," "Composing song/hymn texts," and "Composing song/hymn music." One trait that trended

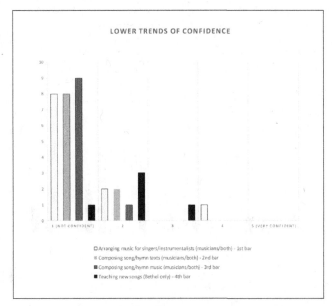

Figure 29.3 Lower trends of confidence.

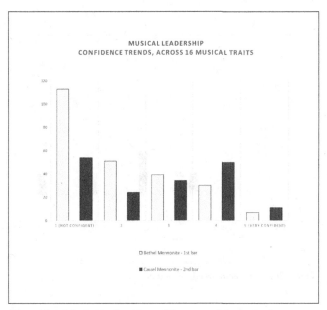

Figure 29.4 Musical leadership confidence trends between the two churches.

lower for the music leaders at Bethel was "Teaching new songs" (see Figure 29.3).

The results of the overall ranking, in all sixteen elements, identified the musical leadership from Bethel as slightly less confident than for the leaders at Cassel. Most responses for both churches fell under the category of "1 – not very confident" (see Figure 29.4).

Confidence by the Numbers (After). The final questionnaire asked all of the worship and music leaders to look at the same traits and rank their own perceived level of confidence as *higher, lower,* or *unchanged.* None of the respondents ranked any trait as *lower* (which was reassuring for the researcher!), and multiple leaders from both churches ranked their level of confidence as *higher* in fourteen of the sixteen categories. Among those who ranked their confidence as HIGHER, there were some specific trends of note:

Table 29.2

Trait	Those who ranked a *higher* confidence
Teaching new songs	All song leaders plus 2 non-song leaders!
General musical abilities	All who had initially rated as 1, 2, or 3 (low-medium)
Playing an instrument	All accompanists plus 2 non-instrumentalists!
Composing song/hymn texts	Many, although this subject was not specifically explored in either workshop.
Selecting appropriate music for a service	All who have such a role (except one who was already a 5).
Your general creative abilities	Good mix of musicians and non-musicians.
Actively incorporating others into the music-making	All who had previously ranked 1 or 2 at Bethel.
Song leading	All song leaders plus some non-song leaders.
Accompanying	All accompanists.

One leader added the category of "Willingness to take more risks" to the final questionnaire, to which they happily rated their confidence as *higher*!

Confidence and Encouragement, in Their Own Words

Since confidence and encouragement typically go hand in hand, I thought it important to combine the two. Without my asking for specific comments on confidence and/or encouragement, both leaders and congregational members made comments that spoke to this theme of confidence in their own gifts, musical and otherwise.

One leader "[felt] more confident at the front of the church while leading singing." Another mentioned that while leading singing, he "[makes] more eye contact with congregation, [tries] to smile so others see the enjoyment singing brings." One leader shared: "I continue to try to stretch my creativity and to own a new sense of confidence as I share my gifts. I strive to be as expressive as possible; expanding the limitations of the 'norm' or 'comfort zones' of the music." One leader mentioned that he now had "better leading skills," and another remarked, "I feel like taking more risks with the congregation."

Some leaders began feeling more comfortable with their own abilities and were able to be more vulnerable. On the workshops, one leader commented that they were "all very helpful sessions to make us comfortable with musical expression and our abilities." Another felt that the researcher/facilitator "modelled for us not to be afraid of trying something different or of making mistakes or of showing emotion." Another leader mentioned that "[the workshops had] a sense of worship and encouragement to give ourselves wholeheartedly in voice to God."

In moving forward in their own practice, one leader mentioned that they now had "a better sense of what questions [he] might ask or what advice [he] would seek from other music leaders." Another leader "felt encouraged to continue to try some new music or use more instrumentation (percussion) with some of the music." Another leader, in recognizing the impact of his own leadership/facilitation inclinations, mentioned: "I'm trying to encourage others to take leadership and by stepping back hope that it will create space for others, especially younger people to get more involved in making music."

Congregation members shared what they had observed in their leaders. One noted that they had "new confidence in trying new music." Others mentioned that the leaders "seem more confident" and "more comfortable teaching new songs," and that they seemed to have "more willingness to step out and try something new and step out of their comfort zones," which speaks to a greater sense of confidence. One member reflected that "[the sessions] encouraged them," and another congregant felt that the workshops gave their leaders a "boost of energy and boost to their belief of their abilities."

For their own part, one congregation member noted: "Not important HOW we sing but that we DO sing – for those of us inclined to be 'shy' about our voices," which speaks to a new confidence within the congregation during *their* singing within worship.

These workshops led both the leaders and the congregation to feel more confident in their abilities, which helped them move toward a posture of "abundance" from one of "deficit."

Strengthening of Empathy

Through open, facilitated dialogue and the open process of exploring the development and execution of leadership strategies within worship, both the leaders and the congregational members of each church developed a stronger sense of empathy. This was evident throughout the sessions and was reflected in the written feedback. Sometimes in congregations – indeed, in relationships generally – operational patterns develop and walls or barriers are put up between people or ideals in order to maintain functionality. These community music workshops allowed the voicing of disparate ideas with a spirit of inclusivity in order to address these barriers and reconcile polarizing views.

Through the sessions, leaders became more aware of the thoughts and opinions of the congregants. One leader remarked, "I tried to listen for the worship desires of people and will advocate/participate in helping some of those be realized." Another leader spoke to underlying disagreement and to the unifying nature of music by mentioning that "singing is an act of worship that gives us the opportunity to use our combined voices to create unity, if only for the space of the song." This sentiment was expressed in both churches.

The congregants also became more aware of the processes behind the various elements of music-making in a worship context and the role their leaders played. One member, who was beginning to understand these elements, felt that the workshops "emphasized [the] VERY important role of music and paying attention in the choosing and expression of music as an instrument of praise to God." Another realized that "a lot of hard work must happen behind the scenes." As a result of this process, one member felt "more appreciation of [the] musicians and leaders" and "fortunate to have good leaders." Yet another congregant had a "greater understanding of what goes into choosing/leading songs as part of worship."

Due to the leaders' willingness to be vulnerable and open during the process, one congregational member now "ha[d] a better understanding of the comfort level of some of our musicians/leaders." This might neutralize critical judgment in the future.

There was also greater understanding among the congregation. One congregant developed a "new appreciation for various styles of music and how they speak to different people." One congregant mentioned "being [more] aware of those worshipping around you." One member had "gained a broader perspective of what worship with music can span – a variety of styles and abilities," and another felt that "we have a better understanding and willingness to learn" following the workshops.

One long-time member remarked on the transformational change. This person could now "see an evolution of heart after 'music wars'" within the congregation – truly a sign of hope!

Renewed Focus on Inclusivity and Participation

Each congregation hoped to be inclusive and to call up the gifts within itself. However, each church also felt challenged to put these principles into practice when it came to the music of their worship. Both the leaders and the congregants held certain expectations around the "quality" of their music, often relying largely on an "objective" aural aesthetic. This is becoming a typical point of contention for congregations in a broader societal context that focuses on the "stars" of shows like *American Idol* and in church contexts where worship is "produced" as more of a concert or performance event.

Within both congregations in the study, the perceived "quality" of music had declined due to a loss of trained or more proficient musicians. Language comparing the congregation to "what we used to be" or to "the other congregation down the road" was leading to a diminished sense of value within each congregation.

So a concerted effort was made to focus on the musical gifts that *were* present and to find ways to utilize those gifts to maximize both the aural aesthetic and, more importantly, congregational participation and inclusion. This necessitated conversation and mutual understanding. The congregations needed to give their leaders permission to risk the current "quality" of their congregational sound, in favour of a different metric for identifying quality.

This process succeeded in both churches. The leaders became better equipped to align their *practices* of inclusion with their *beliefs* about inclusion. Many acknowledged this would be an ongoing process in their work.

One leader hoped to "include others and encourage more musical instruments." Another leader had "considered broader use of persons from congregation for Easter Service" beyond the "usual" participants. Another leader felt that the workshops had "been a good experience for all with the 'fun ways of inclusion.'"

The congregation too felt this shift toward more inclusion. One member noted that the congregation now "understood how important their involvement and participation is/was." Another congregant "realized we all have gifts – if we can't sing, we can still make a joyful noise," which sounds like it signified a change in metric for that individual.

One member sensed the value of this shift, remarking that "it was good timing for our congregation as we are still regrouping after becoming a smaller, more elderly group. The encouragement to value and nurture the musical gifts of the young children was important."

Another member summed up the value of inclusive music-making in the congregational context by remarking that "music is expressed in many different ways and we need all of us to make it right for us!"

Openness to What Is New and/or Possible

The real voyage of discovery consists not in seeking new landscapes, but in having new eyes.
– Marcel Proust

To transition from a posture of "deficit" to one of "abundance," each church needed to open itself to new ways of making music and to new standards for music-making. This posture of openness, which I feel was already present in other aspects of their community life, was re-enforced and strengthened through the workshop process. By reframing the current musical abilities as "sufficient for worship" and breaking down the hymns, the music, and other materials of their current worship practice, both the congregation and the leaders were able to realize new possibilities from their existing worship repertoire and to develop more openness to learning new repertoire.

"I liked looking for themes or songs that can be paired together and the experience of doing this enriched my own appreciation of those hymns" remarked one leader. Another "found it helpful to look for ways to interchange words and music, expanding our hymn 'vocabulary,' especially when a song is new and we'd like to use the words but haven't learned it yet." One leader felt that during the workshops, "we learned new hymns and sometimes new ways of singing old familiar hymns"; another "got some new insights into how songs can be used."

Many leaders expressed openness to changing their leadership styles. In reflecting on what had changed since the beginning of the workshops, one leader remarked, "I strive to be as expressive as possible; expanding the limitations of the 'norm' or 'comfort zones' of the music." Another leader was now "incorporating music into prayer time," and another mentioned "look[ing] forward to 'playing' around more with tempo and the 'feel' of different songs." Another leader had begun "making notes about what went well and how we could have done things differently."

During Workshop #2 at Cassel, after hearing a remark that there were too few percussion instruments in the church, I gathered a bunch of durable containers and implements from the church kitchen. This caused one leader to reflect, "He made us think 'outside the box.' – Don't have instruments? 'Here's a dishpan full of perfectly good instruments' (from the kitchen)!" Another congregant gaining from that experience realized that "you can use many items to worship and make music." That was a fun session!

One congregant noted that the leaders had developed an awareness about how to integrate music with the other elements of worship. This entailed "evolving to plan a theme, which helps with the 'flow' of worship, instead of 'whatever.'"

One member remarked, "Now I look forward to learning new hymns." Another felt that the workshops "created openness in [their] congregation." Another person felt that the congregation was now "more comfortable singing something new." A forward-looking congregant stated that "participating in workshops, together, gives us a sense of untapped potential."

Renewed and Enriched Worship

Sing unto the Lord a new song!
– Psalm 33:3

For some, the "proof is in the pudding," so I thought it important to inquire about potential changes in the worship experience following the workshops. All but one respondent to the questionnaire felt that the experience of worship had changed noticeably since the workshops. The one who responded that it had not added, "*not yet,* but [I] feel there is a collective openness for leaders to lead in new ways – outside the 'box' – and in different ways that go beyond our traditional script."

Since a number of congregants used "outside the box" imagery in their responses and in our sessions, I present below some words congregants used to express how their experience of worship *had* changed since the workshops began:

Table 29.3 Participants' outside-the-box statements

"More enthusiasm toward group singing"	"Music takes over"	"We try to follow the leader"
"I look forward instead of down"	"Movement has been encouraged"	"Now I look forward to learning new hymns"
"The singing has improved!"	"Songs are very meaningful"	"There are more suggestions"
"I pay more attention to songs, including the words and rhythm"		"Made more aware of words in songs"
"Re-enforced importance of music in worship"	"Singing improved!"	"Learning new songs"
"More opportunities to sing"	"Additional variety"	"New styles"
"Freer"	"Brought more life to worship"	"More upbeat"
"Everyone joins in"	"More meaningful"	"More vibrant"

Final Thoughts

If not here, then where? It is a question that I continually ask myself in my role as a minister of music and community musician. It is a question that I ask myself when someone who cannot sing in tune asks to join the choir or someone asks me to help them harmonize and write out a hymn that came to them in the night – but they cannot read music. It is a question I ask myself when there is someone just learning to play an instrument who offers to play for worship or when someone will not sing a solo because they do not feel confident enough to share their gifts – even though they have had many years of lessons and possess a beautiful voice. Yet for some reason they claim they simply "cannot sing."

Too often, church music – a potential vehicle *for* worship – becomes an object *of* worship, thus changing its role in the life of a congregation. The metrics we use to discern quality are often conflated with the ones we use when talking about music produced for commercial means. This leaves us conflicted with the resulting activity of worship. Paid professionals, better-quality materials, higher production values, and stylistic tribalism are some approaches we take to bridge the divides between what the congregation wants out of worship and what the church is able to provide. Unfortunately, this leads to a heightening of mode and style over inclusion and participation, and, ultimately, to alienation from the capacity to worship.

This study has shown that when community music practices are applied to a church context, the results are transformational. This should not be surprising, given that church congregations are actively seeking weekly meetings out of a social desire to be in communion with one another and with God. Practically speaking, these workshops were permission-giving and gave validation to many ideas and gifts that were already present within these congregations. The results were an increase in the level of confidence of the leaders and congregants, an increased sense of empathy within the congregation, a renewed focus on inclusivity and participation, a renewed openness to what is new and/or possible, and a renewal and enrichment of the worship experience.

It is incumbent on music directors and leaders within the church to look at our "traditional" and habitual ways of operating and to readdress questions of "congregational suitability" to the music of our worship as our congregations grow and change. Investing more time, energy, and money in modes and styles of worship music that no longer fit the expressive voice of the congregation takes a toll on the vitality and energy on worshipping communities. This is not to say that our worship music should be capricious; rather, we should remain vigilant in ensuring that our practice of worship remains accessible, hospitable, and meaningful for each congregational member.

As community music practices continue to germinate and evolve, I believe they easily have the capacity to strongly influence existing communities that are already brimming with well-intentioned, caring people, from disparate socio-economic circumstances, who are striving to live well with one another and in relationship with the communities in which they abide. The church is such a place.

Further Questions for Investigation/Consideration

+ What will the worship look, sound, and feel like in one, five, or ten years in these congregations? Are the effects of this study lasting or temporary? Does this process bring about a "cultural" shift in the "being" of a congregation that will play itself out in ways beyond worship?
+ What would it look like to apply these types of workshops in other Christian denominational settings, or in other faith traditions? What of this process is transferrable?

+ Would individuals be less inclined to improve on an instrument or as a vocalist if their level of talent is already deemed acceptable for application, as is? Is a competitive, proficiency-based model more likely to motivate growth and development?

+ Would the same workshop be as effective in a church that has many musically gifted and confident musicians? How would one modify a community music approach to address the challenges faced by such congregations?

+ What skill set is required by the paid pastoral leadership to maintain and companion this process once the workshops are finished?

CHAPTER 30

"If you don't change you get left behind"

Playing in the Banda Italiana Musicale Vincenzo Bellini
in Melbourne, Australia

Jane Southcott and Leon de Bruin

Italians in Melbourne

ITALIANS ARE ONE of the world's most migratory peoples, and they carry with them their culture, including their music (Barwick & Keller, 2012). In the mid-nineteenth century, many Italians came to Victoria, Australia, initially drawn by the gold rushes, but many remained to establish farming communities in rural districts. The Italian migrant presence in Australia became significant in the decades immediately following the Second World War (Mecca & Tence, 2008). The choice of Australia as a destination was largely due to a weak Italian postwar economy and North American immigration restrictions. Initially, Australia was reluctant to accept Italian immigrants, given the existing White Australia policy and trade unions' fears of competition from cheap labour. It is said that the British and US governments, as well as the Vatican, influenced the Immigration Agreement of 1951, which facilitated the mass migration of Italians to Australia (Bosworth, 1988).

Migration from Italy to Australia has continued, and most postwar immigrants have been from southern Italy. In 1947, 8,305 Italians immigrated; by 1961, that number had increased to 91,075 (Museum Victoria, 2013). Italian immigration peaked in 1971, and Italian in-migrants settled in urban and regional enclaves across Victoria. They established clubs and associations that attempted to replicate village life and the community networks they had left behind (Mecca & Tence, 2008). The 2011 census recorded 76,906 people born in Italy (Museum Victoria, 2013). Italians are now the fifth-largest immigrant community in Victoria, and most of them live in Melbourne. They are also the largest group for whom English is not their first language (Cavallaro, 2010). *Il Globo* (first published in the 1920s) was the most widely read Italian-language newspaper in Victoria. In 2001, 42 percent of Italian speakers in Australia were older than fifty-five (Clyne & Kipps, 2006). In 2010, "Italian-born immigrants represent[ed] the largest group of older Australians from a culturally and linguistically diverse background, and nearly 40 percent of Italian-born immigrants are aged 70 years and over" (Stanaway et al., 2010, p. 158).

The Banda Tradition

The formation of Italian community concert bands in Australia was an outgrowth of mass postwar migration. Many of the original Bellini Banda musicians had played in their hometown *bandas* before immigrating, and Melbourne was their principle destination. Italian immigrants, including those who founded the *bandas*, carried memories of their homeland bands, which for many were closely tied to their memories of village and town life in Italy as well as to their religious traditions. The sponsorship system maintained by the Italian and Australian immigration authorities in many ways fostered immigrant identities and connections to the homeland (Baldassar, 2011). All of this was strengthened by a "village out" pattern of migration that resulted in migration flows comprising entire families and groups from the same town.

The Banda movement has its roots in rural southern Italy, the source of most Italian immigrants to Australia. The Bellini Banda is named after the Sicilian musician Vincenzo Bellini (1801–1835), reinforcing its connection with homeland. By the mid-nineteenth century, Italy was home to a multitude of wind bands, which bridged regional and class distinctions. As of 1888, there were 6,000 civilian bands. They played an eclectic repertoire of marches, opera excerpts, and popular pieces by Verdi, Rossini, Puccini, and others. These ensembles had evolved from military bands in instrumentation and style (Simonett, 2017). Across Italy, the *banda* provided music for community events and brought Italian operatic works to poor, remote villages. The *bandas* also performed at ceremonies celebrating the patron saints of Italian towns. At these *feste*, the music played by the *banda* celebrated Italian culture – in particular, they celebrated southern Italian village life and community identity. *Feste* asserted regional individuality, including dialect, as well as memories of the many "'Italie' and their preindustrial loyalties to family and village rather than to nation State" (Bosworth & Melia, 1991, p. 78). The overtly social experience of regional Italian Catholicism was far different from prevailing "Irish" Roman Catholic proceedings in Australia (Lewins, 1978; Dimattina, 1979).

Bringing a sonic palette that is now traditional for Melbourne *feste* activities, the Banda Bellini has performed at Italian national day celebrations, music festivals, and gala nights, as well as at its own concerts and fundraising events. It has officially welcomed Pope John Paul 11 and two Italian Presidents. The Banda has become a pan-Italian symbol that is especially meaningful to older generations of the Australian-Italian community. In many ways, it has been the glue joining the sacred and secular aspects of Italian immigrant life in Australia. Word of its enterprise and energy has spread throughout willing communities, which are eager to employ such bands. The Italian-Australian community newspaper *Il Globo* regularly reports on *feste* activities, and annual *feste* celebrations are held in Melbourne and in environs that celebrate the patron saints of particular towns and regions in Italy (around forty-five of them) (Scott-Maxwell, 2007).

A vibrant account of a performance of the Banda in 2005 for the *festa di Santissima Trinità* describes the band as wearing service uniforms and caps and as gathering near the church entrance. When the mass ended, the priests, helpers, and congregation emerged carrying a statue of the feted saint on a wooden platform, at which point the band struck up the spritely march "Borgosesia" as the followers ambled to a nearby park. There they played several more marches and hymns, with many in the crowd singing along, before returning to conclude the church service. Returning to the park, the band performed a concert that included selections from *Il Trovatore* by Verdi, *Carmen* by Bizet, and *Aïda* by Verdi. All the while, food and drink, a spaghetti-eating contest, and a tarantella contest were enjoyed as part of the day's entertainment, which culminated in a fireworks display (Scott-Maxwell, 2007). The musical celebrations of Italian culture were interwoven with social connections encompassing family, friends, compatriots, supporters, and the wider community.

However, with the passing of time, social expectations have changed, and the Banda members are now faced with significant issues. The Banda started in 1971 as a young man's band, but its members have grown old, and some have left, while others have passed on.

The Banda is not unique. Its music selections and performance styles are the same as those of many Italian town bands, which still exist in Italy and which diasporic Italians have carried with them around the globe. In Australia, the Banda tradition is very different from the Anglo-Australian tradition of wind bands, and the ensemble is isolated musically from other Australian band movements. Both repertoire and musical culture separate the ensemble. Rehearsals – so we have observed – are conducted in both Italian and English so as to accommodate older players whose first language is Italian, second-generation Italians, and non-European players. The music-making and social participation of the original members of the Banda Bellini act within the bands as a transplanted and localized tradition. This study sought to answer these questions: What are the musical and social practices of the members of the Banda? And how is their music-making linked to their ethnicity and identity?

This qualitative case study explored the understandings and meanings of band membership held by the members of the Bellini Banda. In case studies, researchers collect deep data from a small and carefully selected group of participants (Merriam, 1998; Yin, 2009). Data collection was undertaken through a series of semi-structured interviews in English with individuals or pairs of participants, according to their preference. English was chosen because the members all speak English, in addition to a range of other languages. Both authors are practising musicians who are familiar with ensemble playing in amateur and professional groups. This permitted the rapid development of rapport, for we were able to talk easily about music and musical instruments. This insider perspective fostered trustworthiness; it also positioned us well to interpret the data.

The Participants

All members of the Bellini Banda were invited to participate. Explanatory statements were distributed in English and Italian, and all who volunteered to participate were interviewed. The participants ranged in age from forty-nine to eighty-five, reflecting the aging profile of the ensemble. The older players included founder members, all of whom were men, reflecting older Banda practices in Italy and Australia. Some of the older band members were declined to take part. Other participants had joined more recently, but only two were born in Australia (see Table 30.1).

Participant Vignettes

Before discussing the themes, we offer a series of vignettes that introduce the voices and personal histories of the participants.

Larry. I was thirteen and my dad asked if I wanted to join the local brass band. I played cornet there in Shepparton for five years but got married and came to Melbourne. I played in dance band for fifteen years and when that finished, I got asked to join the Banda Bellini. I think my stimulation from this Banda music comes from when I was a little boy in Italy, they had lots of festivals and bands coming to town, and my father used to play in them too. I didn't know at first, but they convinced me and I've been here ever since as secretary and treasurer. I found that when I'm on the stage I forget everything, I'm in a different world, everything else becomes oblivious, you enjoy the moment.

Table 30.1 Interview participants

Participant	Place of birth	Age	Instruments played	Years in Banda
Larry	Calabria	70	Trumpet	30
Quinto	Sicily	75	Clarinet, trombone, saxophone, euphonium	10
Michael	Greece	85	Clarinet, horn	30
Stefan	Italy	70	Clarinet	11
Renato	Trieste	68	Clarinet, tuba (E♭ then B♭)	15
Ann	Anglo-Celtic Australian	49	Clarinet, bass clarinet	6
Elaine	Malta	53	Clarinet	11
Frank	Vizzini	72	President (non-playing)	29
Carmelo	Australian-Italian (Sicily)	51	Conductor (*maestro*)	3

Quinto. I started to play at twenty-two. I played guitar and tried a band but didn't get along. I gave up, had a family and kids. Then ten years ago I met the conductor of the Banda. He said try the clarinet. I said I didn't have one, so he gave me one to start. Soon I bought my own, and I did pretty good, but my fingers hurt, so I got the trombone. After three years my shoulder didn't allow me – I didn't want to stop, so I got the baritone, and when I get sick of that I play the saxophone at home.

Michael. I was eleven when I started, trying to learn the theory – major and minors. I started on horn, but moved to Rome, and then Australia. I got a clarinet and a friend who taught me at his home. Then the past *maestro* showed me things, music, and after two years, he called me and said, you are ready to go to the band now. We did lots of jobs for ten years, but now not so much. Some of our friends are gone or don't play anymore, we did big concerts, with symphonic and operatic works, but now we play music I don't like, and there's a big decline.

Stefan. I started at ten, in the village I was born in. We had a small band, but I moved towns and studied, lost time for music. But I came to Australia in 1974, and I decided to buy a clarinet. It came easy but playing solo, something was missing, no sharing with others. So, eleven years ago, my neighbour who played trombone asked if I wanted to join the Banda. I have a happy positive experience in this band. But, I'm worried, maybe we can be an inspiration for younger musicians to participate and secure its existence.

Renato. There was a conductor at that time that was from Trieste and so I went to him and he said oh join the Banda Bellini because I went to him for lessons, but I lived in Heidelberg and he lived in St Albans and I found it difficult, but he said come along to the Banda Bellini, and I didn't know how to play the clarinet at that time, so he found me another teacher in Donvale, closer to where I worked, and then I came to the Banda Bellini. But I don't know whether it was an Italian band, but when I got here there was a lot of uncles, you know, people who I felt comfortable with and I stayed here ever since.

Ann. I've been playing with my community orchestra since I was fifteen, and I met a percussionist walking across a railway line with my instrument in my hand – we chatted, and he said why didn't I join them, and I thought okay, no harm done! Playing Italian master operas was a real cultural experience for me. I looked on YouTube to get the feel of the music – it's wonderful. There's such a diversity of people, wonderful personalities, and those with minimal formal training, and it's got a real community feel about it.

Elaine. I was nine years old, and the local band taught music free and loaned instruments. My brothers joined, there weren't many girls, but I convinced my mum to let me go learn. I got a clarinet, with lessons once a week, and at twelve I started playing in the actual band. I got my very own clarinet, and we came to Australia at seventeen. I joined a Maltese band and did gigs – it was such an outlet – most girls in my culture rarely came out from the home environment. I got married at twenty-two and gave it up. But fifteen years later, my brothers urged me about the Bellini. The music was beautiful, what my grandmother used to hum [and] I wanted to embrace it. I returned to playing with this band, and I've been playing ever since. I like to come here on a Friday – it's the night off for me, when I don't do the housework or the cooking. My husband doesn't play, but he comes and sits next to me and he's made friends in the percussion section. Friday is band night. Everyone's got a story; they all have their idiosyncrasies – some will have their grappa during the break, there's another one who's always cracking jokes. The older ones have a certain charm.

Frank. I've been the President for twenty-nine years. I work as the manager, finding the money, door-knocking sponsors, paying the bills, the rental, writing grant applications to multicultural organizations and councils. The band was about to fold in 1988 and they said Frank, could you please come for two or three months, organize our funds? I never played an instrument, but to get a feeling of being a part, I learnt some theory, and I bought lots of CDs of baroque and classical music, so I got to know what it was the band was playing so I could understand it better, and explain it as a master of ceremonies at functions. I've organized more than 130 concerts all over the state, the metropolitan area, every town hall. It's been a continual learning process – my friends are here now, and we are getting on, but if four or five of us stop, the band will disappear and just collapse because no one else is prepared to do it.

Themes

The data revealed a complex community with generational layers of understandings of music, culture, and community. Added to this are the concerns of an aging group of Italian-Australians who recognize but resist the accretions of time. The themes are presented under three broad headings: Erosions, Resistances, and the Future.

Erosions. Erosions are diminishing or gradual destructions over time. At their weekly rehearsals, the Banda see their selves and their ensemble eroding, while the community they celebrate is changing. Our participants spoke of advancing age and pointed out that most of the players are over seventy. Stefan succinctly named the crisis facing the Banda: "We are getting old and we need new musicians you know because when we die, if we don't have new musicians then the band doesn't exist." Larry agreed that the "members are getting older, and unfortunately not enough people are replacing them." Members have stopped coming due to infirmity, and past players have died. They are getting old and have less energy than before. We heard stories of hip and knee replacements and other ailments. This impacts their performances in that they can no longer walk or march for long periods of time; also, some find it difficult to sustain playing and have little patience waiting for the masses to finish so they can play. Renato, a retired doctor in general practice, laughingly observed that there were a few that should stay home, but they won't.

To counterbalance this and to explain the players' fierce determination to continue, Stefan insisted that we record that for him, "this is a happy, very positive experience. I've been able to further develop my interest and improve my skills playing with my fellow musicians." Larry described the group as "like a second family." He described the pleasure of performing with this group: "When you're on stage you forget everything, you know you're in a different world of your own. You know what you're doing and everything else becomes oblivious, and you enjoy the moment." Larry recounted the words of his first bandmaster in Italy, who told him,

Larry, when you get older and you move from town to town, if you go to the local band you'll find twenty-five new friends just like that. And I never forgot that and it's true isn't it? I mean here we are and we've got about forty if everyone's well and they turn up, but of course we've at least got twenty, twenty-five our band, and we all come every Friday night.

This solidarity and affection outweighs the tribulations of aging until members are faced with a complete inability to take part. A number of members have died or retired from the Banda, and the health of the remaining members makes impossible some of the performance practices that are central to the band's ethos. Failing limbs have made marches and parades almost impossible for the Banda.

The Banda today faces a significant erosion of demand for its performances, with the result that Banda finances have become a critical issue. They need funds for rent of the rehearsal venue, for the players, and for incidentals. Playing at *feste* was the mainstay of the ensemble. Larry explained that "our main jobs would have been the Italian religious festivals, and they're slowly dying because the elderly people that ran them are elderly and they can't carry on and the young people aren't interested ... I suppose it's evolution and things are happening." *Feste* performances now attract a dwindling, segment of the Italian population. Elvira offered her explanation: the Church was celebrating fewer *feste*, possibly because "the people they're not going to church; no tradition to go to church, have a procession, maybe a little concert. Too many people do not go anymore to church." With only several *feste* held throughout the year attended by about 2,000 people, these events are no longer a reliable income stream for either the organization or the players. Larry recalled the festivals of his childhood in Italy when the big bands came to town. He enjoyed listening to them. This tradition had been transplanted to Australia when the Banda began performing in the 1970s. Renato explained what occurred. The central element of the *feste* was the mass, usually to celebrate a saint's day. The Banda would play for about half an hour before the mass. During the mass, it would wait, and then at its conclusion the congregation would come out and the statue of the saint would be paraded in procession as the Banda played. The event took about two and a half hours, and the Banda would be paid about $1,100. If the Banda only played after the mass, the fee was about half. Currently, about twenty-five players turn up, and each is paid about $25 for their time. Renato added that for the older members, being paid is very important. Larry recalled his father playing mandolin in a community band during the war in Italy. It used to play serenades "because things were a bit difficult, and they actually used to get fed, which was a bonus [laugh] back then." The current *maestro*, Carmelo, explained the current situation:

> There's just less demand for it. It's very time consuming to play a procession, wait outside the church before and during mass, which goes extra-long because the priest talks a lot. So, ninety minutes later the band gets into formation, they march around for half an hour. It might be three hours of waiting, which is an equation that does not add up.

The Banda members proudly attend weekly rehearsals with relentless regularity, a regimen sweetened somewhat by the lure of small payments for their engagements. Their determined president drives up the band's fees but finds himself regularly undercut by another band that will play a procession for a fraction of the price. Carmelo elaborates: "They used to do thirty-five appointments where they got $25 dollars, but now they are lucky to do ten and they are pricing themselves out of the market." But for the older players, the money is non-negotiable.

Resistances. The Banda's older members are unwilling to change. Their musical identity is as a member of an Italian Banda that plays for and marches in *feste*. They play the occasional concert, but these are not their core musical practice. Their playing style is intended for outdoor, mobile performances, so it is relentlessly loud and fast. The players have considerable technical prowess, but this is untempered by nuances of expression. To change to a concert band, the Banda would need to change its musical practices, and that is not something the older players are prepared to do. They are unwilling to evolve. Elaine described it as "brio," an Italian term for vivacious. Ann explained:

> This is the way we played it forty years ago, they just blast away, not try things or accept suggestions from the conductor ... The older ones are thinking, this is the way we do it and the conductor can scream his head off saying softly softly, but you can hear the blare in your ear – no changes there as each player is enjoying himself and he's not going to change.

Ann continued:

> They can have a tiff over the timpani or the trumpets being too loud ... They will stand there, and they will scream, and then bang their hands, clap, and then they will sit down and it's blown over – that seems to be the way they want to operate.

The older players see the current *maestro*, Carmelo, as the embodiment of unwanted change. They recall with affection their previous *maestri*, who embodied their memories of their early music learning in Italy. Larry described *maestro* Guido Benzi as "a great composer of music, he did all the arrangements by hand, we have files full of them, original transcriptions of the operas. He wrote the pieces for each member of the band. For each instrument, which was incredible." Michael and Stefan pointed out that Carmelo was born in Australia of Italian parents, and Michael explained that "he's not bad, he brought some new music, but I told him four or five times that Stefan and I don't like this music, that's not our music, no, send it back." Carmelo challenges the older band members. He is a teacher, Australian-born, and he tries to get them to play new music in a more expressive and nuanced way. The old guard are having none of it. They speak with reverence of their previous Italian-born conductors who maintained the same cultural understandings as them. A young player from Italy who has joined the band is given more respect because of his place of birth.

Carmelo is aware of this attitude. He explained that he had played with the Banda briefly in his youth and that when he saw an advertisement for the position of *maestro*, he applied, because "I felt sorry for them, because they were not progressing. I found their attitudes set in stone and they react to being challenged by any stylistic understanding, and finesse, and ability to execute that in performance." He added that he "quickly understood the difference between *musicante* a musician, and *sonatore* an instrumentalist – an amateur." Carmelo believes that the older Italian players were "schooldropouts who were told by their teachers that they weren't any good, you can't do maths, you're no good at writing, how about we give you an instrument and you go visit the *maestro* down the road, see what he can do, you be a *sonatore*."

For Carmelo, the local town band was in some ways the dropout centre for students who were weak academically. Understandably, these boys did not like teachers *per se*, for it was teachers who had rejected them. Carmelo recognized that he is "a teacher by profession, a conductor, I am the embodiment of the thing that these guys hate. And in rehearsals, they say, well this guy is not really good, let's get someone better." Several of the older interviewees commented that they were not used to paying the *maestro* a fee per rehearsal, but others commented that this had occurred in the past. Overall, the older players mistrust and disrespect the current *maestro*, resisting him in every way.

Carmelo recognized that the old guard do not want to change and accept that "when they die, the ensemble dies with them." He considered them to be "arrogant in their uncaring for the ensemble, their unwillingness to change, and their attitude to accommodating an audience." He observed that "they are happy being loud and out of tune, and new musicians come and hear that and think they don't want to give up their Friday nights for that." The resistance of the older players to change has meant that the performance program is hamstrung. The committee has already talked with older Italian groups in Melbourne that would welcome concerts by the Banda, but the players will not consider the changes to their repertoire, practices, and pocket money that would be involved. As times passes, the Banda is losing touch with the community organizations that cater to older Italian-Australians. Despite the best efforts of the president and the committee, change is unlikely with the ensemble's present membership.

Future. The members of the Banda realize that without new and younger members, the ensemble is finished. They want to be role models for future players. Stefan said that "I want to be an inspiration for younger musicians to participate in the band in order to secure its existence." But recruiting and keeping younger players is difficult. Renato explained that they had tried in the past. They had advertised via social media and their webpage, but this only brought in five new members. He realizes that this is not enough. *Maestro* Carmelo had brought along some of the students of his school, but they were not interested in committing to the ensemble – every Friday night is a lot to ask of a teenager, especially when everyone else is their grandparents' age, the repertoire is dated, and the playing is without variation. A large part of the problem is the older players, who, according to Larry, are "strict in their ways and they won't bend. There's an old saying – if you don't change you get left behind."

Both the participants and the *maestro* pointed out that the band had great potential. The Banda plays music that is highly significant to members of the Australian-Italian diaspora. It also has a rich and extensive library of transcribed treasures of the Italian musical world and thus has an excellent opportunity to place a unique stamp on the musical landscape. The members value their past repertoire both culturally and personally. For example, Elaine referred to the "classical operas" as the songs her grandmother used to play. Carmelo contemplated that

> this band could offer a rare opportunity to play orchestral transcriptions and master works in a community setting, that could attract fine players and cater for a wider Italian and Australian market that is interested in this repertoire performed excellently. Th[ese] operatic, orchestral, popular Italian, symphonic works could be a real signature point for a really unique group.

The players realize that the band is shrivelling away as the players grow older, and they dream of finding younger players to replenish their ranks. This is unlikely without change. Carmelo is well aware that the Banda is on the brink of extinction. For him, it may be that this has to happen:

> Maybe it is the case of pulling the pin on this band in its current state. Rebuilding the band with capable musicians, making a workable performance and rehearsal platform, expanding the repertoire without hindrances, and actually using the vast library as a source of concert themes. Really presenting everything Italian musical culture has to offer can expand the audience base and incentivise the musicians willing to work to a quality product.

Carmelo muses that it may be that the Banda has to die to be reborn: "It's a fascinating social experiment beyond being the conductor. How long will I stay? I'm having fun pushing their buttons, but let's see what happens."

The band members are mainly Italian-Australian but include in their ranks people from other immigrant populations. The older players hold firm to their identity as Italian *banda* players. The word *banda* means more than a music ensemble. In Italian it also connotes a gang, a crew, with the overtones of comradeship and protection for the group. The older players close ranks when faced with change that threatens their understanding of the ensemble – something they learned to do as youths in Italy.

Discussion

Music and migration are universal phenomena, and "migratory peoples tend to take their music along with them, especially if there are sufficient numbers of them to sustain its practice in a social context" (Keller & Barwick, 2012, p. 225). Both phenomena cross borders, and music may help migrants find a balance between their old and new cultures. Cultural borders are underpinned by ethnic identities, and in multicultural societies there are opportunities for people to cross boundaries. Migrant experiences have been depicted "as a kind of package of attributes carried across from the homeland" (Bottomley, 1992, p. 4). Ethnic identity is anchored to shared cultural, linguistic, and religious core values (Smolicz, Hudson, & Secombe, 1998). For the individual, the maintenance of cultural identity is paramount, with original national identity worth remembering, but for the older members of the Banda, their tenacity makes border-crossing impossible. Being a member of the Banda has contributed to the health and well-being of the players, but with the passing of time, challenges have arisen that place the survival of the ensemble in jeopardy. Unfortunately, the perspectives and horizons of the older *sonatore* are circumscribed by their history and sense of self.

For many immigrants, notions of culture, tradition, and identity encompass complex and overlapping social worlds. Immigrant communities develop complicated webs of social interaction that draw upon and create fluid and multiple identities grounded both in their old homeland and in their new one. Acknowledging the complex perspectives on immigration allows us to see it not simply as a finite act of relocation but as a continuous cultural process, one in which the "importance [of] connections, place, homelands," even if only imagined, "are of central importance to migrants' lives" (Gupta & Ferguson 1992, p. 11). Ethnic groups do not melt and blend, but rather re-form and transform their original sources of identity (Glazer & Moynihan, 1963). Immigrants have often faced a different language, different expectations, and a new set of limitations that can feel like "a labyrinth in which [the migrant] has lost all sense of his bearings" (Schutz, 1964, p. 105). Immigrants, therefore, not only "consciously reconstruct practices and beliefs carried across with them, but also literally embody certain predispositions" (Bottomley, 1992, p. 138). The members of the Banda have in some ways frozen in a kind of "time warp" of motherland tenets and behaviours and remain enmeshed in the culture of their place of origin and the era of their departure. Admittedly, this was not true for all interviewees. As one participant stated, "most of those guys have got an Italian passport, and they still feel Italian. I don't feel Italian. I'm an Australian but I've got Italian culture."

Immigrants do continue to perform, or "carry," practices from their country of origin to their new host country. Although usually framed in terms of maintenance of identity (Graham & Connell, 2006), from a social practices perspective, "personal histories of practice are never entirely personal" (Shove & Pantzar, 2007, p. 157). Practices, like memories, are entrenched in the social that emerges from the collective. Early adolescent practices by immigrants coalesce into "imprints" or "preserved traces" that codify behaviours and feelings (Pantzar & Shove, 2010). These preserved iconic memories strengthen the links between the practice as performed in the past and the practice as performed in the present. Practices travel between countries as immigrants mediate processes of carriage, integration/disintegration, and transferral (Maller & Strengers, 2013). These practices are embodied by performers through the mental resurrection of memories associated with their performance; in this way, they retain the remembered feel of certain places (Bourdieu, 1990).

Understanding the meanings of hometown attachment is crucial to understanding the actions, meanings, culture, and traditions the participants celebrate and derive from their membership in the Banda. Important values, orientations, and symbols that immigrants brought to their new homes were rooted in the context of their previous village life. Immigrants formed communities, reproducing traditions and culture via various organizations and activities (Panagakos, 2003). Observing the Banda as a shared national and ethnic expression offers a significant insight into the way the group has operated as a unifying force in how its members have organized cultural and social activities. They have in effect formalized the conflation of two contemporary cultural processes – the reiteration of a national tradition, and the formation of this as a popular tradition – in a new, multicultural landscape. An important factor attributable to this reification of homeland, traditional practices, and the process of legitimizing such rituals is the implicit or overt evocation of historical traditions as a source of apparent continuity with the past (Hobsbawm & Ranger, 1983). Tradition, for these participants, is a "function not of origin but of continuance of a culture kept alive and hermetically sealed" through iterative reperformance (Boyes, 1993, p. 12). In Victoria, the Banda afforded immigrant Italian musicians effect and function, linking community music-making, traditions, customs, and historical enactments, which together solidified the Banda, its music, the social behaviours of its members, and the moral obligation to performers and audiences (Boyes, 1993). The participants in this study represent a complex array of traditions, beliefs, and incentives that either maintain a cultural "difference" associated with their homeland or allow for assimilation into a more widespread Anglo-Celtic way of life. Levitt (1998) describes the ideas, behaviours, identities, and social capital that flow from homeland to new home as social remittances. These social and cultural resources play a significant role in the transitioning and establishing of new immigrant communities and social organizations, besides fostering political integration and entrepreneurship.

In their efforts to understand migrant movements and actions, scholars have described the re-forming nature of immigrant populations in new lands in terms of "transnational communities" (Portes, 1996; Smith, 1997; Goldring, 1992) or "binational societies" (Guarnizo, 1994). It is important to retain a transnational perspective when considering the flow of Italian immigrants to Australia and their ongoing connections to families and communities in Italy (Barwick & Keller, 2012). These lenses of understanding allow exploration of the ways in which choices and affordances to motherland routines and norms effect, curtail, facilitate, and shape new immigrants' behaviours, views, and functions regarding how things were done "at home." There are blending scenarios of new immigrant behaviours (Derby, 1994), with new social relations and cultural patterns created by an intermingling of arrived-nation and migrant beliefs and actions (Foner, 1994). Some migrant cultures weaken and wane while others flourish unchallenged owing to minimal interaction with other cultures (Portes & Zhou, 1993).

Investigating immigrants' experiences of social and community organization through membership in the Banda Bellini provides insights into the extent
to which this musical community is an imagined village experience for some
of the members. The immigrant experiences of displacement and travel to an
entirely new country are tempered by their arrival with kinfolk of similar age,
from the same region, who speak and understand the same dialect and culture.
These people feel a sense of duty not only to salvage but indeed to enshrine cultural tenets and ideology as well as the socio-cultural milieu they experienced
as young *sonatore* in their village Bandas. Their past defines their self-identity,
their localized roots as *paese*, or peasantry, and the Italian identity thrust upon
them by others. Creating a Banda in an Australian landscape represents for
all intents and purposes a relocation of Banda ethos and identity from their
homeland village. The change-averse protocols within the Banda extend beyond
simple social isolation. The band's social and musical aims have been subjugated to more simplistic ones: to imagine what once *was*, back when they were
adolescent learners. In defining this dialectical relationship between structured
circumstances and people's actions, perceptions, and embodiment of history,
Anderson posits an "imagined community" distinguished, not by falsity or gen-
uineness, but rather by the style in which it is imagined (Anderson, 1983). In
these men's Italian homes, the church was geographically and culturally central.
Baldassar (2011) describes a community sense of *campanilismo*, meaning a
localism or parochialism among Italian immigrant populations in Australia.
Derived from the word *campanile* (bell tower), it captures the notion "that historically the bell tower of the local church was the focal point of every town
and therefore a symbolic expression of the inhabitants' community identity"
(p. 24). In Australia, playing music for the Church and the *festes* became the
central expression of the Banda. Their identity was enacted repeatedly through
village-style re-enactments and performances. The church supported the Banda
financially, and the community celebrated the transplantation of traditions. In
their heyday, the frequent *festes* offered the players remuneration and confirma-
tion of identity, but with the dwindling of community demand, opportunities
for the older players to enact their traditional roles have waned. With the attrition caused by aging, and with the changing expectations and understandings
of the contemporary Italian-Australian community in Melbourne, the days
of the band in its current form are numbered. The older players will not or
cannot entertain change. The Banda may have to die before it can be remade
into a concert band that provides performances celebrating Italian music and
culture in the Australian community. Many of their prospective audiences are
themselves aging, so concerts of nineteenth-century Italian music will continue

to evoke imagined cultures of the past. When the Banda arises phoenix-like from the ashes, the first challenge will be to recruit new members, and the second will be to identify new audiences. The Banda might then become the premier Italian concert band in Victoria and thereby contribute to the cultural life of Italian-Australian community.

Acknowledgments

We thank all of the study participants who generously gave their time and so openly shared their stories with us.

CHAPTER 31

Remembering a Hard Life with Joy

Music-Making among Korean Elders

Elisha Jo Heesun, Kari K. Veblen, and Patrick J. Potter

THE WORLD HEALTH ORGANIZATION (WHO) estimates that the number of people aged sixty or older is expected to more than triple between 2000 and 2050, from approximately 605 million to 2 billion, representing 22 percent of the world's population (WHO, 2014). WHO has called upon stakeholders to enact policies and programs to promote active aging. Defined as "the process of optimizing opportunities for health, participation and security in order to enhance quality of life" (WHO, 2002), the term *active aging* is more inclusive than *healthy aging* because it acknowledges other dynamics in addition to health care. Recognizing that seniors can make meaningful contributions, the WHO chooses to use the term "active" because it entails continuous involvement in social, economic, cultural, spiritual, and civic affairs. In this context, opportunities for social engagement through lifelong learning, volunteering, and leisure activities become more important, given that older adults are less likely to continue in the workforce.

This research expands on an ongoing ethnographical case study of an ethnocultural community program for Korean immigrant seniors (Jo, Veblen, & Potter, 2015). Previous work found that shared musical knowledge plays a vital role in this program structurally and through fostering group membership. Our current study goes deeper into individual experiences to explore narratives of active aging through music.

Literature Review

Researchers suggest that a major deterrent to active aging is social isolation, which is a widespread health concern among older adults living in the community (Nicholson, 2012; Statistics Canada, 2006). Social isolation is associated with an array of negative health consequences, such as risk of cognitive decline (Beland et al., 2005) and physical risks such as an increased number of falls (Faulkner et al., 2003). Community programs for older adults, and community music programs in particular, have been found to promote active aging through multiple domains of health by generating opportunities for social engagement.

Group music-making – for example, New Horizons Bands in North America – makes a positive contribution to the overall health and well-being of seniors who participate (Carucci, 2012; Coffman, 2002; Jutras, 2011). Such events are also socially, culturally, and/or musically meaningful to the participants (Dabback, 2007; Creech et al., 2014; Kruse, 2007; Lally, 2009; Phinney, Moody, & Small, 2014) since they actively engage participants in their own interests and knowledge. In a comparative study, Cohen and colleagues (2006) found positive health outcomes for seniors who participated in a choir: fewer doctor visits, lower medication use, fewer falls, and less loneliness, as well as higher morale and activity involvement than among those who did not participate. Research focusing on musical engagement has demonstrated the positive influence of music on seniors' emotional, cognitive, physical, and social health and well-being (Clift et al., 2010; Creech, Hallam, McQueen, & Varvarigou, 2013; Hays & Minichiello, 2005a; 2005b; Solé, Mercadal-Brotons, Gallego, & Riera, 2010; Sun, Buys, & Merrick, 2013).

Venues for social engagement are especially valuable for immigrant seniors from ethnic minority communities, who face a higher risk of isolation, for they often lack social support from others (Kim, 1999a, 1999b, 2013; Lee, 2007). Older Asian immigrant adults often suffer from psychological distress, resulting in poorer physical and psychological health than among their native-born counterparts (Choi, 2001; Kim et al., 2010; Tendulkar et al., 2012; Wong, Yoo, & Stewart, 2007). Many community music programs offer benefits to seniors living in the community; however, immigrant seniors from backgrounds markedly different ethnically and linguistically from mainstream culture may face barriers to participation if the program or service is only offered in the dominant language, such as English (Emami, Torres, Lipson, & Ekman, 2000; Kim et al., 2011; Mui, Kang, Kang, & Domanski, 2007; Stewart et al., 2011). This necessitates culturally sensitive programs such as CESC, designed for Korean immigrant seniors.

Method

Our research examines (1) individual perceptions of music-making within a community program, and (2) that program's influences on participants' health and well-being. The study employs a mixed method design, but at its core, it is a qualitative inquiry consisting of narrative case studies within a larger ethnography, augmented with quantitative data.

Narrative approach. This phase of the research relies most heavily on a narrative approach that follows Clandinin and Connelly (2000) – "telling a life story, retelling a life story and reliving a life story" (p. 418) – to best understand how music may reveal identity construction through various stages of life. As a dialogic and collaborative practice, a narrative approach takes a sensitive approach to culture through listening, telling, and sharing (Bochner, 2001; Bochner & Ellis, 2003). Older adults' needs may vary, from training to continued or voluntary employment, to health and wellness, to digital literacy, to caregiving, to leisure and travel, to personal development (Merriam & Kee, 2014). However, the most significant learning needs in this stage of life may be the ones that focus on seeking the meaning and value of one's life, for a person's purpose in life is no longer delineated by his or her employment (Fisher & Wolf, 2000), nor as that person's identity.

We interviewed five participants for their life stories and musical experiences. These narratives serve as the heart of our data (Polkinghorne, 1995). The individuals who shared their stories were among the more than 150 participants in the Enoch College program; circumstances, natural affinity with the interviewer, and willingness to be part of the project were the determining factors in their initial selection.

Semi-structured interviews, with open-ended questions, were conducted in an informal manner. Participants chose the location of the interview – for example, a favourite coffee shop or park. Each interview lasted more than two hours, with follow-up conversations over the phone, via email, and in person during school hours at Enoch College. Interviews were recorded, transcribed into Korean, and then translated into English.

The actual interviews followed improvisatory routes as prompted by open-ended questions; later, though, the information was organized chronologically for analysis (Creswell, 2007; Josselson, 2010). Each narrative was fit into a narrative sequence, using a beginning, middle, and end, a process referred to as restorying (Creswell, 2007). Through reflective and repetitive reading of the texts, the key elements were determined (Green & Thorogood, 2009). More detailed sub-themes were drawn from field notes and additional sources such as publications and choral compositions.

Continuing ethnographic framework. Since CESC is integral to our contributors' worlds, we continued participant observation of the program at the Presbyterian Church in Mississauga. The principal researcher's proficiency in the Korean language and cultural understanding from a shared musical knowledge aided data collection. Findings were cross-checked for validity and possible bias from an emic perspective. Other sources included field notes, document analysis, observation of classes, informal conversations, and self-reflection (Denzin & Lincoln, 2005), with video recording to supplement data collection (Bogdan & Biklen, 2003; Goldman-Segall, 1998).

Five Narratives

1. Song's story: "Wind from a mountain and wind from a river." Song was born in 1942, and his father died soon after that, leaving his mother as sole breadwinner. When the Korean War (1950–53) and Communist regime inflicted further hardship, the family fled Seoul, clinging to the rooftop of the train, as they could not afford to ride inside. They reached safety in Busan, at the southern tip of the country, but poverty continued to haunt them: "I think my childhood was greatly affected by the war, psychologically and emotionally."

Song remembers singing at his primary school for refugee children. It was not much of school, for it consisted of a marquee set up for children and teacher to gather around in the open air. Nevertheless, he recalls his singing with pride, for he had a good voice with "a clear and loud tone ... My teacher must have picked up my voice while we were singing as a class, because she selected me out of all classmates to sing for the class." Standing tall in front of his class, Song belted out his favourite song, "The wind from a mountain, and the wind from a river." This song expresses gratitude to the wind that blows and comforts hard-working laborers, refreshing their souls.

Another early memory is of the keyboard instruments at school: "I just loved the sound of the small organ and piano. Even though I didn't know how to play the piano, I would imitate and play the few notes and remember being so thrilled to hear the sound of it."

Song recalls early successes, such as being elected vice-president at his new school. This was a notable triumph, since only students with high marks were eligible to run for presidency and were then elected by popular vote. Despite these triumphs, some barriers were insurmountable – lack of funds meant that he never had formal music lessons, couldn't go on class field trips, and, worst of all, was rejected for class registration due to unpaid fees.

However, Song studied music on his own, and when he was eleven he found his outlet through choral singing in the Sunday school choir. This experience nurtured a love of music that led to him conducting his Sunday school choir only a decade later. His memories of this choir are so vivid that he can still recall each child's name: "When children sang a song in the open air near the coastline, people could not help but listen intently, peeking their heads out to search for the angelic voices echoing through the railway."

Under Song's direction, the children's choir won numerous competitions. He notes: "As a conductor, there's always part of me that longs for more, to make the best kind of music with my choir." His thirst for learning motivated him to become a very good musician himself. For example, although he had no professional training, he wrote a manual for his choristers. Consisting of thirty-six pages of handwritten comprehensive instruction, this handbook includes vocal anatomy, pedagogy, basic theory, musical terms, history, and a philosophy of singing.

In 1993, after a life as a successful businessman who travelled to more than twenty countries, Song immigrated to Canada, where he again faced challenges in a foreign land. Here, too, music eased his mind. "I was having a quiet moment, deep in thought, standing by the window in my high-rise condo." he recalled. "I wrote lyrics, something like a poem. It was about asking why are you so anxious when God takes care of you? He will lead the way and so you should not worry." There, he confronted his fears, doubts, and worries and found comfort in God and expressed it through a song: "With this lyrics, I composed a simple melody and harmony for choral singing."

Today, at seventy-two, Song still feels a longing for the creative process. However, his physical condition prevents him from more active music-making. Six years ago, a triple bypass surgery forced him to retire from conducting, although he occasionally helps out. He is increasingly subject to exhaustion. Song comments: "I have unfulfilled aspirations as a conductor, and wish to make great music, and at the same time, I am also aware that I am aging."

Although physical infirmities slow him down, Song continues to make music. Most recently, he directed a small ensemble for the semester-end recital, with a short song with rhythmic clapping that he had composed. Song has recognized the need for programs like Enoch College for what he calls "Young Seniors," as he is acutely aware of the diminishing role for seniors, particularly immigrant seniors, in society. In fact, one reasons why he registered at Enoch was to observe the program for possible implementation in his own church.

2. Yong's story: Harmonica and "Heidenröslein." Yong was born in 1932 to a doctor's family in rural Korea. His father declined a secure position in the Severance Hospital in Seoul to care for the underprivileged farmers in a rural area reachable only by miles of gravelled pathways. Yong remembers the country in turmoil, the Japanese annexation (1910–45), and the Korean War, when hundreds of thousands of South Koreans fled south after the North Korean army invaded.

Yong's early musical memories are of singing in the Sunday school choir until one day, he found a mysterious object in a desk drawer. When he blew air into the holes, he realized that it was a musical instrument, and thus began his a lifelong absorption with music-making, experimenting with the sounds and playing his harmonica alone. Such an outlet was doubly welcomed since daily life was incredibly difficult at this time. Social and religious activities were restricted, for the Japanese occupiers were seeking to eradicate Korean culture and language.

Yong also remembers music in schools, such as his first day of high school German class. The new teacher had just returned from Germany with pedagogical ideas: "He told us that 'the best way to learn German, a foreign language, is to learn the song first,' and to illustrate, he began singing 'Heidenröslein' to the class." This Romantic *lied* from a poem by Goethe tells of unrequited love. Yong immediately fell in love with the song's sad beauty and learned it by heart. Since then, the song has resonated with Yong through his life, and he sings it now at Enoch College.

At age eighteen, Yong was forcefully recruited as a soldier into the Korean War, which cut short his dreams of becoming a medical doctor like his father. After the war, he continued in the army, working as an electronics technician. This brought opportunities to study in the United States for a year. Opportunities also came through Yong's wife Kay, whose profession as a nurse allowed her to go to Winnipeg, Canada, in 1966. After a few months, Yong followed her with their two young children. The family moved to Toronto in 1974 when Yong found a job there as an aviation technician for Air Canada.

After retiring, the couple began attending Enoch College and taking an active role in a harmonica ensemble, where he facilitates music learning and making. He continues to learn various musical instruments such as guitar, accordion, and clarinet, most of which he picked up after retiring, to play alone, in a duet, or in a group.

3. Kay's story: Joy of singing, thirst for learning. Kay was born in 1932, the only child of a landowning family in the northern part of Korea. Her earliest memory of music is singing at school. There was one coveted musical instrument: "As kids, we would sneak into the classroom to play the piano. At times, the class would line up and take turn[s] to have the chance to play the piano."

Kay's most influential musical experiences started when she was at freshman at Yonsei University's College of Nursing. Daily chapel services were part of this university, established by Christian missionaries. Kay became a Christian, joined a choir, and began what she calls her lifetime "joy of singing." In 1950, Kay's life changed forever when Communist troops invaded, separating her from her parents and kidnapping her classmates. Only eight of forty students in her freshman class survived to graduate. Worse still, she never saw her parents again.

Although only a student, Kay worked as a nurse, since there was a shortage of medical professionals during the war. She experienced trauma and brutality first-hand in hospitals and at UN prison camps. When the Korean War ended in 1953, she returned to her school, now relocated to a remote island in southern Korea. The reunited student choir began singing again as they had in the chapel. But now, as war survivors, the choir found new meanings of hope, strength, and resilience in the old songs.

Kay graduated into a responsible nursing career, teaching at the university. She also fell in love with and married Yong, who shared her passion for choral singing. When an opportunity arose for Kay to immigrate to Canada as a nurse at a hospital in Winnipeg, she took the job. Canada was still in the early years of accepting immigrants from Asian nations, having begun to ease national origin criteria in 1960s, and the young couple was among the first wave of Korean immigrants in Canada (Kim, Noh, & Noh, 2012; Yoo, 2002). Since there was no social or family support system in place, they shared responsibilities for their two young children. Kay took permanent evening shifts in the hospital, while Yong worked during the day. Although in Yong's words: "Leisure did not even occur to us," Kay and Yong joined the church choir and sang on Sundays when they could.

Now retired from nursing, Kay has time to pursue her many musical and artistic interests. She took a certification course for interior design from a local college, is a member of the Etobicoke Quilters' Guild, and is planning her first quilt show. Although very active, Kay is increasingly aware of the work required for her to participate in music at age eighty-two. She notes:

> Last Christmas, I joined the choir for the fundraising benefit concert for North Korea. In addition to added choir rehearsals, I rewrote the words in large letters in thick black ink for easy reading. I marked difficult sections in the score and listened to the recordings constantly as the music for this event was a challenging Christmas Cantata sung in Latin. It required exceptional attention to detail both in the music and unfamiliar language.

Kay's strong work ethic and high level of professionalism are evident not only in her personal endeavours but in other areas as well. As a member of the

Korean Canadian Women's Association since its inception in 1985, when the organization faced challenges that jeopardized its existence, she even switched her full-time position to part-time in order to take on additional responsibilities to provide support for the organization. This year, the KCWA will be celebrating its thirtieth year of supporting the lives of Korean Canadian women in Ontario. This is only a glimpse of Kay's achievements. She continues to share and take a leading role in music-making with her husband Yong, be it in choral or small ensemble settings. She continues to relish opportunities for learning. This year, Kay took up the saxophone, noting: "Not that I always wanted to play the saxophone ... I've been meaning to learn to play a new musical instrument, with no particular preference." In a recently published collection of Canadian immigrant experiences, Kay reflects: "I have only tried to live honestly and with diligence."

4. Kim's story: Music in a life for others. Born in 1940 in Busan, Korea, Kim comes from a poor but devout Christian family that was dominated by a very strict father. Kim was a shy and quiet child; his earliest musical memories are of singing hymns in church. By age fourteen he was already teaching at Sunday School: "There was always a shortage of Sunday School teachers, so I started to help out at a young age. As I become more involved, I felt a pressing need to teach children singing." To this end, he began looking for ways to strengthen his teaching: "There was a small organ in the church that no one played, so I decided that I will somehow figure out how to play."

Since no one in his family or church played an instrument, and Kim had no idea how to begin, he prayed to God for wisdom. Building on scant notation reading skills taught at school, he slowly worked himself toward playing note by note. He explained:

> At first, God gave me the wisdom to begin with an easy hymn without sharps or flats. I picked "I Gave My Life for Thee," and it turned out to be a very good piece for me since the refrain also had the same melody/repeats. I first began with my right hand only. Then I practised with left hand, and eventually added both hands together ... From then on, I began expanding my hymn repertoire from practising hymn with one flat, then moving on to two flats and so on. After about a year of diligent practice of building repertoire like that, I became good enough to manage to play the songs for the children.

Leading others in worshipful song filled Kim with joy, but economic necessity dictated that he work to maintain the family. Kim and his older brother established a business selling watches from a small booth at a dangerous intersection in Busan. Shocked by the sight of frequent horrific car accidents, he remembers wondering: "If I was the one who died today, what would have been the meaning of my life?" It occurred to Kim, now in his early twenties, that he should not waste his life, as today is only given once.

As if in direct response to his internal questioning, a friend working with hospital ministry invited Kim to join him. "I said, 'Good! I want to devote my life for doing a meaningful and valuable work for others!'" Straight away, he left the business to his older brother and went to Seoul. Resources were limited, and the hospital ministry provided only a meagre living, but it did not matter, for Kim was increasingly determined to live for a higher purpose.

While working in the hospital ministry, God called Kim to become a pastor. From then on, he answered his call without concern for language, national, or cultural barriers. Kim followed his inner compass to Germany, France, and eventually, Canada, responding to requests from small churches.

Music for Kim has been a calling, not his only calling but one of many to which he has cheerfully answered, "Yes!'" This man is unassuming, quiet, and reserved, but his entire being becomes illuminated when he sings and plays his accordion, joining in the choir, leading small musical ensembles, and – as he has for most of his life – leading choirs. Kim is not always paid for his ministry and supports himself by working as a janitor at a local church. For this upcoming Sunday, he will be leading the choir in singing "There is a peace that the world never gave." As he meditates on the words, Kim adds, "I hope that God will bless me to serve Him through music for as long as I live."

5. Min's story: Grief opens the heart. Born in 1944, Min has no childhood musical memories since, until recently, music has had "no relevance whatsoever" to her life. While she worked as a secretary for the major Korean affiliate of Gulf Oil Corporation in Seoul, she was exposed to Western culture via the American Gulf employees. She believes that this influenced her decision to immigrate to Canada as an independent immigrant in 1973. She settled in Toronto, where she worked for the University of Toronto Alumni Association. In 1975, Min met her future husband at a neighbour's dinner party. Lightning struck, but the timing was off, since he was returning to Korea. The couple wrote to each other until he returned to marry her.

Min recalls the time when the newlywed couple took a dancing class together:

> You know if one partner can lead, then the other will follow, but I got more confused because of him. We failed so miserably and were so embarrassed that after few try-outs we gave up. Since then, in all our life together, we sat through all the parties. We never got to enjoy dancing together.

Min also struggled at singing, particularly in a choir. "I will just sing which-ever part one sitting beside me sings. And it wouldn't matter whether the per-son is singing soprano, alto or tenor," she says.

Min's life revolved around her family, their small businesses, and her beloved husband until his sudden death four years ago. Soon after his passing, she looked into a mirror and could not recognize herself in the very old lady looking back (she had lost 14 pounds after his death). Her family was so con-cerned that her son moved in to be with her.

It was a year after her loss that music found her. She remembers the day vividly:

> One morning my son had gone to work and I was taking a shower ... as bright sunlight shone through the window. Suddenly, a hymn, came into my heart, just like the ray of sunshine ... Following my heart, I closed my eyes and began singing the song, then soon a wonderful peace overflowed in me like never before.

Since then, Min says that a song comes into her heart while walking along a park trail.

> I've been singing meditatively like praying in my walks ever since. Every time I sing ... I am reminded that Jesus is with me, that I am not alone ... Sometimes I sing for hours, but not a complete song. Two verses from here, and two verses from other songs ... weaves into a whole when I sing alone.

A year later, Min found Enoch College and began to participate in singer's competitions, although her intention is to share joy rather than to compete. She explains:

> Even though I am not good at singing at all, ... if the Holy Spirit enables me, then I will answer, "Yes, Lord" and sing. So, I overcame my fear of singing ... When you sing songs of praise, peace comes into your heart, and all your worries that seemed as enormous as the mountains turn to small pebbles – that's what I wanted to share.

In the process of claiming her musical self, Min has begun to memorize songs and now can sing two from memory for the first time in her life. She explains:

I write down the words in big letters on a piece of paper so that I can see it without my glasses and carry it with me during my walks ... Memorization is a challenge for me ... [but] this is indeed my struggle and my story. What I told you might not be significant to others, but this is the story of my life.

As Min shares her life, there are many memories of over thirty years with her husband, but now these memories bring joy instead of grief. Her story is one of finding freedom and peace through music.

Discussion

Each of these narratives tells of challenges and hardships through upheaval, wars, and immigration. Each person now experiences old age, a time of life frequently associated with fear and with loss of control, and each endures a measure of personal problems, such as physical or emotional/mental health concerns, economic limitations, and lack of social position due to immigration.

Nonetheless, these seniors celebrate their lives through music. They enjoy an "encore life," one of revitalized sense of self and group. Song's early love for music continues to shape his life. Yong's lifelong involvement with music began with the solace of a harmonica in his adolescence and now emerges as he leads the harmonica ensemble. Yong also expands his musical endeavours through learning new instruments. Kay has begun studying the saxophone while planning her first quilt show at age eighty-two. In seeking to help children to sing, Kim began his musical journey and found his calling in God. He combines these passions as he devotes his life to a music ministry. Min found a source of hope through music in the depths of grief and now shares comfort and peace with others through singing hymns.

An obvious and uniting thread through these narratives is the role that CESC has played in bringing people together. Although this community program sponsors a wide range of courses including literature, history, and arts, even classes that are not focused on musical performance encourage daily music-making. The day begins and ends with prayer and songs. Students prefer to sing familiar Korean songs that resonate with a personal and collective past; school and children's songs are an essential component. In this way, students remember their lives and come to terms with the present (Moody, 1986).

While some students continue musical endeavours solely at home, others actively further their skills through supplemental singing or instrumental lessons elsewhere. Many seniors take advantage of CESC's opportunities to showcase their music learning. A regular performer, Kyung, shared her story, "It is from Enoch College I've found my love for singing because until then, I didn't know much about singing. I've been taking singing classes to learn new Korean songs and I practise them to sing it by heart so that I can sing them for my Enoch friends."

While musical engagement promotes active aging, there are seniors who cannot or do not participate. Age-related health issues, such as declining mobility, vision, or hearing, may limit social interaction (Mikkola et al., 2015; Public Health Agency of Canada, 2006; Sloan-Seale & Kops, 2008). Specific to this study, research indicates that older Koreans were found to have the highest psychological stress among other older Asian-American subgroups (Kim et al., 2010; Kim, Kang, & Kim, 2018). This may relate to Koreans having a shorter immigrant history in North America than other Asian cultures (Mui, Nguyen, Kang, & Domanski, 2006). Seniors who come to Canada through sponsorship by family members often lack social resources and can experience social isolation even while living with family (Koehn, Jarvis, Sandhra, Bains, & Addison, 2014; Sadavoy, Meier, & Ong, 2004). They are also less likely to participate in ethnospecific programs like CESC due to time constraints or responsibilities to provide care for grandchildren (Choi, Kushner, Mill, & Lai, 2014). Furthermore, transportation issues or a poor location may present further barriers to participation (Moody & Phinney, 2012; Sloane-Seale & Kops, 2008).

These barriers to participation seem to apply for some of Enoch College's students. Hyo, a quiet lady who loves Korean traditional music and has been known to write beautiful poems, said, "Although I knew about the CESC since its inception in 2003, it's been only few years since I could participate because I was helping out with grandchildren." Sook, another participant who immigrated to Canada with her husband to care for their grandchildren, shared her reluctance to participate in the next term, as her daughter had been driving them to the CESC. Enoch College is accessible by public bus, but many participants carpool together instead. Some participants, like Sue, rely on their grown-up children for rides. The use of public transit can be difficult, especially when a transfer is required or the weather is unfavourable. Indeed, a significant drop in attendance is observed on colder days.

There are many ways in which CESC addresses the usual barriers to participation. Concerns such as straitened finances (Koehn, 2009; Narushima, 2008) and cultural and linguistic barriers (Emami, Torres, Lipson, & Ekman, 2000; Stewart et al., 2011) are ameliorated through this all-volunteer church-sponsored community program. Enoch College is free for all and provides home-cooked hot Korean specialties at lunch. The entire program is offered through the Korean language with Korean content.

A final and subtle barrier to participation is psychological. Korean elders at Enoch College, like older people everywhere, work to accept their age and the perceived limitations of aging. For example, Joon, who has been a member of CESC for four consecutive terms with his wife, shared his reluctance to participate in the beginning:

> At first, I did not like to be surrounded by only old people. On your right, on your left, and even when you turn around, all you see is grey hair! Of course, I know that I am no different than they are. But we forget our age because our heart is still young as if no time has passed ... I have asked some friends to come with me to the CESC, they refused because they believe they are not old-aged enough to belong to a senior group.

This distancing (not wanting to be seen as old), but at the same time valuing programs that involve a similar age group, has been observed in other studies (Sharon, Hennessy, Brandon, & Boyette, 1997; Stead, Wimbush, Eadie, & Teer, 1997; Yardley et al., 2006). While internalized negative age stereotypes may restrict behaviours (Chung & Yung, 2014; Kim, Jang, & Chiriboga, 2012; Yeom, 2014), it is possible to challenge and change participant perceptions (Fernández-Ballesteros et al., 2013). In this regard, the CESC program actively promotes affirmative views about aging. For example, if, instead of referring to participants as seniors, they are referred to as students, participants are empowered to adopt a positive attitude toward learning, for education spans one's lifetime and has no age limitations. Through a wide range of course offerings and opportunities for self-expression, students are encouraged to live life to the fullest. As Joon articulated, "Here at Enoch, there are joy, sharing, and feelings of gratitude with hope!"

Conclusion

This research presents a portrait of five seniors who find a renewed sense of self through music. Music has been woven into their lives in their moments of joy, as a friend and faithful companion, and as an answer to prayers or an affirmation of faith. The indispensability of music is not limited to these five elders only; it extends to all at Enoch College, for their days are filled with music-making. Although varying degrees of music accompany each individual's life, the sharing of music in this community setting bridges differences of age, gender, and the past to make the present meaningful.

CHAPTER 32

Music as Gift

Ethical Exchange through Intercultural Improvisation

Gerard Yun

MUSIC PLAYS A KEY role in the holding of social, economic, political, and cultural space (Revill, 2000). Although music is often claimed to be a universal language, cultural music practices and systems are distinct and highly differentiated (Cohen, 2015). Cultural identities and authenticities are not constants, as their stereotypes are often perceived; rather, they are "a dynamic and never-ending set of attitudes, determined through the familiar in confrontation with the unfamiliar" (Baumann, 2001).

Intercultural improvisation offers community music practitioners an opportunity to negotiate the borders of differentiated cultural practices and values in a meaningful and transformative way, free of the risks of appropriation and exoticism. This chapter presents theoretical and practical strategies for exploring and implementing intercultural improvisation between two or more divergent cultures, which can often differ sharply in terms of identity, traditions, world views, and other ways of knowing.

This chapter is offered in the spirit of support and encouragement for community music scholars and practitioners seeking ways to work with peoples of varied and diverse cultures. It represents several decades of experience working with large numbers of groups from diverse backgrounds and is informed by my own experience as a person of visible racial and cultural difference, an immigrant, and a classically trained musician who has dared to explore outside the classical canon.

Facing One Another, Singing Together (Why Practice Intercultural Music?)

We face one another across a circle in a Mennonite Chapel: a university choir, a Chinese classical orchestra (Chinese traditional music), a choir of diaspora Chinese (Western music), and a professional contemporary vocal/instrumental improvisation ensemble. What will we play? What will we sing? What will we do together?

We face one another across a room: a Persian choir made up of diaspora peoples from Iran who sing for culture, for belonging, for identity; and a university choir exploring the sharing of songs across cultures. How shall we share this music of the other? What will we sing together? Can we just buy this music and read it?

We face one another across a small space: a group of Protestant church musicians, a community choir from a variety of cultural backgrounds, a healing circle of song drummers from First Nations, a group of contemporary Jewish singers, and a professional singer of contemporary Islamic *nasheed*. We gather around the issue of missing and murdered Indigenous women in Canada – not a few, but hundreds of them – madness. Many of us turn to music in times of madness, times of sadness, times of great social fatigue. How do we sing as one into the mourning, hopelessness, and anger with which we all resonate?

In each case, we have gathered to interact and to share. We have gathered to model a sense of hope across problematic differences in our contemporary world and to use our music for the common good. All of us bring our most meaningful musics – the musics we most wish to share – but what music exists that we can we sing together? Our cultural practices are in no way universal. Our musics are constructed from conflicting systems, differing in modes, scales, tunings, pitches, vocal and instrumental techniques – completely different sound systems. We need to share, to offer what is good. We need to receive what others bring. We need to make music together.

In meeting the needs of diverse communities, community music practitioners need to work authentically with peoples from a variety of cultures. Due to combined factors of technology, immigration, and unprecedented levels of forced migration and refugees today (Runde et al., 2018; UNHCR, 2017), community music practitioners must often negotiate cultural boundaries with the intent of fostering cultural relations, understanding, and common good. The intent of doing social good is important in this context, for creating music together is a powerful step toward creating relationships across differences. There are myriad situations in which community music facilitators may find themselves ill-equipped and perhaps uninformed. What do we do? What music do we play or sing?

Why Is This So Difficult?

Community music espouses openness and the creating of bridges across social boundaries, while walking along the boundaries of these differences. As a collection of dedicated scholars and practitioners, the field of community music successfully focuses on bridging differences in age, health, and socio-economic class. But racial power dynamics may be overlooked, perhaps perceived as too fraught with painful colonial histories, cultural appropriation, cultural theft, and disturbingly visible trends in global racism. Intercultural understanding, conversation, and negotiation are difficult. Intercultural and cross-cultural artistic interactions are often accompanied by misunderstandings, concerns about cultural appropriation, and anxieties over behaviours that could be construed as disrespectful, ignorant, or racist.

Since the sequencing of the human genome in the early 2000s, researchers have argued that there is no relevant or accurate genetic basis for the phenomenon we call race (Roberts, 2011; Serre & Pääbo, 2004). More recently, an article was published in *Science* calling for the elimination of race-related differentiation in biological research (Yudell, Roberts, DeSalle, & Tishkof, 2016). Race does not exist as a differentiating human quality at the genetic level, yet in our social world, issues of race are more contentious today than ever (Roberts, 2011).

Experience within Western classical music and along its many boundaries has taught me that working with different musical systems, instruments, and cultural practices is entangled in situations deeply resembling classical racism – that is, bias along perceived racial lines. This bias can be emotionally charged, deeply entrenched, and confusing in terms of power relationships. Given such a situation, it may be more comfortable altogether to declare one form of music universal, perhaps using that term as a cover for the word "better" or "superior." Practitioners have turned to children's songs, secular festival works, and myriad other musics to avoid the pitfalls of working across cultures in the tinderbox of race.

For North American churches and schools, engaging with musical traditions outside of the established Western classical canon is fraught. From a pessimistic perspective, these engagements can be motivated by a fascination with the exotic and by a search for differentiation in a musical landscape of homogeneity (Locke, 2011). The accessing of commercial sheet music is often tainted by cultural appropriation implicit in the processes of commercial music dissemination. While performing "the music of others" can be a powerful social act of solidarity, it is inevitably enmeshed in complex issues of conflicting identities and authenticities, cultural appropriation, and outright theft or mimicry.

Currently, there are limited ways in which to approach music-making free of the pitfalls described above. But community music practitioners seek cultural-musical interactions beyond the avoidance of cultural pitfalls. As we work toward meaningful intercultural music engagement, we aspire for musical interaction that is authentic, honest, and ethical. The space and process of our music-making is equally crucial and should support an equitable balance of power and the intention to work toward the social good. In my experience with a variety of methods, techniques, systems, and solutions, intercultural improvisation within the ethical space wherein music is intended and understood as "gift" is just such a way forward.

Three Models of Intercultural Sharing

At the opening of the chapter, three different transcultural musical situations were introduced, each posing questions about what music to perform together and how to go about doing it. Each of these cases represents a different attempt at intercultural sharing with the intent of not only creating a viable collaborative musical experience, but also helping to form real, ongoing relationships among the participants. The approaches used in each case were different and met with various levels of success. The following sections describe how the stage was set in each scenario.

Improvisational Performance Ensemble with Guest Musicians

The East-West concert series was co-sponsored by Renison University College and Conrad Grebel University College and ran for four years. A resident improvisational ensemble made up primarily of Western-trained, though globally minded, professional musicians hosted other musicians for each concert. These guest performers would perform sets on their own and then offer works in combination with the resident ensemble. Combined works were rehearsed together and often required precomposed elements.

While relationships within the resident performance ensemble blossomed, there was no lasting musical or social discourse between the members of the resident ensemble and any of the guest ensembles, even Western music-oriented ones. Musical results were always intriguing and popular, with sold-out concerts the norm, yet from a perspective of ongoing relationships, this approach failed.

Choral Song Sharing

The University of Waterloo Concert Choir engaged in a song-sharing study across several seasons, in which cultural groups or representatives would share songs with the ensemble with the intent of creating collaborative performances. The sharing project also involved members of the choir sharing songs with their peers, especially if these works were from lesser-known or otherwise compelling cultural backgrounds.

In one term, a group of singers from the local Persian choir joined the ensemble and attempted to share/teach a number of songs with the intent of performing them together in concert. Despite numerous attempts, these songs were never well-integrated and never performed. Only a few choir members continue social relationships with members of the Persian choir today. Song-sharing indicated a clear need for a stronger, more viable ethical framework in which to conduct authentic cultural musical exchange and create new music.

Intercultural Improvisation Events

Sing Fires of Justice is an annual festival of word and song held in the Kitchener-Waterloo region each fall. Each iteration of the event centres around a different issue of social justice: homelessness, education justice, environment, refugees, and so on. In 2013, Sing Fires took on the then little-acknowledged issue of missing and murdered Indigenous women in Canada in "Sing Fires of Justice for Stolen Sisters." According to Royal Canadian Mounted Police (RCMP) statistics, between 1980 and 2014, 1,017 Indigenous women were murdered and 164 were reported missing. By 2012, Indigenous women constituted 23 percent of female homicide victims in Canada. The problem hit the national news prominently in 2014 when the RCMP and Statistics Canada officially identified 250 additional victims (Roach, 2014).

Sing Fires for Stolen Sisters was the first attempt at First Nations inclusion in the event, which had largely been an interdenominational, interfaith event combined with university ensembles in a massed choir. Previous events had brought together practicing Jewish music groups and Islamic practitioners. These cultural groups gladly returned for this event, which featured them at points in a larger space: a space that we came to recognize as an ethical space of engagement through our First Nations scholars and practitioners.

Through this space we encountered one another as equals. My own role of facilitator was as an equal participant, a Buddhist musician playing the *shakuhachi*. The result was inspiringly successful. Since then, using the awareness of ethical space, numerous intercultural events have been carried out successfully with the explicit intent of fostering and encouraging relationships. The most recent intercultural improvisational circle was held as part of a musical event called "Uncommon Grounds," designed to bring Indigenous teachings and ways of knowing to settler church ministers and musicians. It was an overwhelming success that nurtured ongoing relationships and formed new ones that remain in place at the time of writing.

Why were these events more successful in creating lasting relationships between cultural groups and peoples? In each case, musical interactions were gladly participated in and performances praised. But the efficacy of Sing Fires of Justice, Uncommon Grounds, and other such events featured the intentional creation of a space of musical negotiation named and modelled after the ethical space of engagement. These events also mirror theories of gift exchange and reciprocity as a model of social cohesion.

Dimensions of Ethical Intercultural Musical Interaction

Crossing cultural boundaries can mean crossing into unfamiliar territory where norms of hospitality are confusing. While "music as hospitality" is the agreed upon textbook definition of Community Music, even the framework of hospitality implies an unequal power relationship (Higgins, 2012). For those working to create bridges of understanding across different systems of belief, power, or social norms, the ethical dimensions of intercultural music practices need to be addressed in order to remove trepidation in the practitioner and to foster practices and spaces of trust, meaningful interactivity, and effective, viable engagement.

The sections that follow introduce elements of an ethical framework and present intercultural improvisation as a model and vehicle for the formation of real relationships across the boundaries of living cultures through the sharing and exchange of music. The process of intercultural improvisation places participants on equal footing, allowing them to act and interact as free as possible from the negatives created by cultural appropriation, exoticism, commercialism, and tokenism.

This process requires the creation and holding of an ethical space of engagement. Ethical space is a powerful framework for authentic dialogue across cultures with starkly different world views. Within the ethical space, the sharing and co-creation of music is understood as a social act of gift exchange. The entire process is activated by a communal act of deep listening described as listening presence.

Interculturalism: Sharing across the Boundaries of Living Cultures

In order to work across cultural boundaries where power imbalances, racism, and issues of appropriation, theft, or exoticism are concerns, it is important to adopt a framework of cooperation that focuses on relationship and sharing among cultural groups on an equal footing. There are many terms used to describe the silos of cultural categorization in music. It is worthwhile to pause here to elucidate several commonly used terms and the social relationships they imply and to explain why I have adopted the term "intercultural."

The most widely used term for music outside the Western canon (i.e., European classical music) and European/North American popular culture is "world music." Originally created by the music retail industry to sell non-Western musics to largely Western classical and popular music consumers in the 1980s, it was adopted by academics and journalists shortly thereafter (Frith, 2000). By the early twenty-first century, this term and the closely related term "ethnic music" were considered limiting, offensive, and outdated, for they implied that artists from America and Europe were culturally superior, besides segregating music from "exotic" parts of the world (Birrell, 2012). Ethiopian producer and musician Endeguena Mulu (2015) explains:

> Not only are these labels confusing, they are offensive and unnecessary, and they do more harm than good. They perpetuate the idea that music that influences everything else around it should be treated with respect and all seriousness. On the other hand the music that comes from the other places, from the "colonised places" can all be put in one category, one basket, because it is something you play at a dinner party to impress your very important guests.

The notion of world music positions various musics in an inferior relationship to more dominant (read "economically successful" or "mainstream") forms. These world musics become "others" less powerful and simultaneously exotic in relation to what is "normal," that is, the Western mainstream. This relationship of one dominant culture to others that are considered lesser is implied in the term "cross-cultural." The cross-cultural approach to music is illustrated by various "outreach" and "crossover" projects, in which others' musics are acknowledged and often featured as centrepieces. But this is not a sharing of equals, and the potential for cultural appropriation and exploitation is high.

The dominant versus less dominant cultural perspective stands in contrast to another common idea: "multiculturalism." This philosophy supports the presence of distinct but equal cultures within a society, each maintaining its cultural diversity, but there is no definable relationship among them. This is the view that gave rise to the cultural policy of multicultural recognition in Canada, which was adopted to replace a policy of biculturalism (French and English) in 1971. It implies the acknowledgment of multiple cultures existing equally and in parallel, yet Canada's efforts to build its cultural policy on multiculturalism have not resulted in much sharing across perceived cultural boundaries. The result has been siloed cultures existing in a carefully legislated balance (Kunz & Sykes, 2007).

To create the foundations for lasting relationships among cultures, we need language that emphasizes interaction and sharing. "Interculturalism" focuses on the relationships between cultural groups and how they go about working toward social equilibrium. These relationships are not of dominant or main-stream to others, nor of equals in parallel existence, but rather of cultures sharing across their respective boundaries. The intercultural perspective allows for sharing, mixing, and co-creating new cultures (Cantle, 2016). Within the framework of interculturalism, the formation of living culture is acknowledged and affirmed.

Equality and Inclusivity through Improvisation

If, in attempting to create truly inclusive music, we use conventional paths, first we might search for a prearranged work to purchase. We might engage an arranger or composer. But what would that person arrange or compose?

The mindful arranger inevitably asks what these musical cultures have in common. This is transcultural inquiry – an important step. But within musi-cal systems crossing cultures and faiths, we are confronted with a plethora of diverse systems such as functional tertial harmony, European Renaissance modes and proportional rhythms, Chinese pentatonicism, Indonesian micro-tonality, Arabic modes, South Indian Carnatic ragas, First Nations drumming and singing, and a variety of systems that at various junctures have been labelled "non-music," including the *honkyoku* of the Japanese Zen *shakuhachi* and the call to prayer in Islamic traditions.

Note too, that each of these musical systems is far more than a collection of pitches and rhythms. Each proceeds according to its own contextual cultural norms. For example, certain ragas are used only for certain occasions or certain parts of the day. Zen *honkyoku* is used to support meditation requiring consid-erable "space" or "*ma*" as part of the musical structure built into incredibly long single notes and precise differentiations in timbre and microtones. Whatever the ubiquitous claims throughout history, there is no single universal music.

An arranger or composer faced with this impossible situation will inevitably resort to his or her training and zone of familiarity, privileging some system or tradition over others, or simplifying others' systems until they are barely recognizable. In most cross-cultural crossover attempts by Western composers, Western procedures (i.e., functional harmony) and pitches (i.e. twelve-note chromaticism or diatonicism) are privileged. Surprisingly often, non-Western or "colonized" musical systems are identified as "tribal" or "world music," and the composer completely fabricates languages, notes, and so on. These are extreme examples, which I can only assume are attempts to avoid obvious cultural appropriation. Yet this sort of mimicry of musical/cultural stereotypes sends up ethical red flags. Although these works are most prevalent in school music – programs and festivals – their pedagogical agenda is highly suspect.

Song-sharing is another strategy for intercultural music-making, in which a representative group shares and teaches a song to others. This is a common approach and one that I personally had great faith in, but in terms of creating intercultural dialogue and real relationships within the community, my experience was ultimately unsuccessful.

Over the course of the choral song-sharing project described earlier, the university choir shared with one another, learning songs from various cultural traditions via fellow choir members, guest ensembles, and artists, many of whom joined the ensemble for at least one academic term if not longer: Estonian, Persian, Chinese, South African, Senegalese, French, and more. These were worthwhile projects in themselves, but while the experiences were generally positive, none resulted in ongoing relationships with the contributing artists, all of whom reside locally.

Two observations are significant regarding this failure. First, given that it was an institutional choir reaching out to others, an unequal power relationship was built in. In such a relationship, sharing is constrained. In my position as ensemble leader, I often assumed the role of cultural translator and was repeatedly peppered with the question from guests and choir members: "What do you want?" Second, especially within the choir itself, we had significant difficulty sharing songs with one another. Members would habitually stop, refer to their computers or phones, or give up entirely and play a commercial recording for the group. This was akin to learning camp songs badly outside of the camp context. It was more mimicry than cultural sharing, and ultimately we abandoned this practice altogether.

Given the levels of disappointment in results with both song-sharing and prearranged/composed works, turning to improvisation was probably inevitable. While it had been used extensively as a cross-cultural (outreach and integration) technique in the East/West concert series and even by the choir in conjunction with a First Nations ensemble, those early attempts suffered from unequal power between parties, constrained sharing, and ultimately, reliance on professionals to create or significantly edit the musical result.

Adaptation of ethical space as a space of intercultural musical engagement was the key, and eventually, intercultural improvisation within the ethical space of engagement became a practice. This type of improvisation allows participants a relatively equal level of power; it also allows them to bring whatever music they choose as "gift" with the intent of creating something new, in the moment, together with other musicians. Because the musical works offered by various groups are part of their own cultural practices, they are accepted by others as unquestionably authentic. Likewise, the contributions they bring to the co-creation stage of the improvisations are accepted as sincere and are beyond judgment as long as the listening presence is held.

The Ethical Space of Engagement

The term and concept "ethical space" was coined by philosopher Roger Poole in his seminal work *Towards Deep Subjectivity* (1972). In that book is a photograph showing three soldiers seated on a park bench. Seated at a right angle to the soldiers are a young couple. The soldiers are gazing straight ahead; the couple are looking directly at the soldiers as if to say, "You do not belong here." The park is in Prague, in the former Czechoslovakia, in the wake of the occupation of that country by Russian forces. The soldiers are from the occupying Russian military. The photograph captures a palpable tension between occupier and occupied – two different ways of seeing their world, two very different realities in one space. Poole calls the space between these parties the ethical space.

The notion of ethical space was taken up by Indigenous scholar Willie Ermine as a way of describing the necessary space of negotiation between First Nations and the Government of Canada – two parties often deeply at odds. He proposes ethical space as a framework for engagement between groups with different identities, different world views, and therefore different ways of knowing: "The 'ethical space' is formed when two societies, with disparate worldviews, are poised to engage each other. It is the thought about diverse societies and the space in between them that contributes to the development of a framework for dialogue between human communities" (Ermine, 2007, p. 193).

Ermine calls this "the ethical space of engagement," a space where parties can work together in dialogue toward their best interests. The creation and holding of ethical space is essential to intercultural musical dialogue generally and to intercultural improvisation specifically. Without a framework of ethical space, it is extremely difficult to balance the various power relationships that are built into our socio-musical processes.

Although ethical space sets up whenever differences are present, our ability to use it as a space of negotiation across differences requires intention as well as an understanding of its nature. In particular, there are some aspects of ethical space that are essential to its efficacy. For our purposes as musicians, those aspects especially include the presence of considerable or magnified moral and ethical meaning. That is, any action undertaken in the ethical space has a sort of ethical weight – it means more than it would in a casual context: "There can be no flaccid action, no action which is not immediately imbued with an ethical ballast, filled in from our point of view in the world of perspectives ... Acts in space are embodied intentions" (Poole, 1975, p. 6). For cultural musicians engaging one another in ethical space, this means that a glance, a sounded pitch, or even the closing of eyes, is immediately processed and interpreted in an atmosphere of hyper-awareness.

In practice, this means that approaching the ethical space between cultural groups is a tenuous exercise. There is a palpable sense of uncertainty, and many participants indicate that the first few moments are scary. In these initial moments, participants share a common sense of vulnerability and uncertainty. This discomfort is crucial. It serves to humanize and equalize power imbalances by creating the common experience of not knowing. Within the ethical space and throughout the improvisational process, the sense of equal "not knowing" is negotiated between participants. Within a short time, this gives way to a new, communal way of knowing.

While the holding of the ethical space is essential, it does not in itself provide a framework for musical exchange. For this, we turn to Marcel Mauss's notion of the gift, which describes the acts of giving, receiving, and reciprocating as essential to social cohesion.

The Gift in Ethical Space: Giving, Receiving, and Reciprocating

The neoclassical model of economics teaches that most of our contemporary social and economic interactions are determined by self-interest and the direct exchange of money for goods and services. Anthropologist Marshall Sahlins refutes the assumption that economies are comprised of independent economically rationally acting individuals working to amass material wealth through self-interest. Sahlins argues instead that our understanding of economic and social life must start from cultural principles and that so-called primitive societies were closer to true affluence – meeting of wants – as a result of social cohesion (Sahlins, 2017).

For our purposes, the sharing of music, followed by the resultant formation of relationships through the creative process, is what makes us collectively vital as opposed to presenting our musics as products to be assessed, assigned a value, and collected, exchanged, or preserved. Intercultural improvisation supports a type of exchange that goes beyond sonic elements such as pitches and rhythms, enabling a communicative, collaborative working process that builds cooperative skills while privileging social interactive process over sonic end-product. Consistent with Sahlins's theory that processes of social cohesion fulfill human wants (as opposed to wants determining the processes), it is the cooperative process of creative music-making that becomes the performance.

To enable intercultural musical dialogue within ethical space, a model of exchange is needed that facilitates power equalization and musical sharing. The musical exchange that takes place during intercultural improvisation is best understood using the framework of gift exchange as elucidated by Émile Durkheim, Marcel Mauss, and Lewis Hyde.

Marcel Mauss was a nephew and pupil of Émile Durkheim, one of the founders of sociology. Durkheim's work centred on communities – how they socialize, and how they create meaning. He was especially interested in "the shared experiences, perspectives, values, beliefs, and behaviors that allow people to feel that they are a part of a group and that working together to maintain the group is in their common interest" (Cole, 2018).

Because his focus was on the collective rather than on individual motivations and desires, Durkheim's work is especially relevant to community music and its concern with social connections. While Durkheim wrote primarily about how societies sustain themselves or maintain equilibrium, his student Mauss developed a theory of exchange *within* societies, characterizing exchange in terms of various practices of gift-giving. Mauss saw gift exchange as important to creating and reinforcing social connections – the glue that holds societies together.

Although Mauss was observing the exchange of material gifts, it is not a huge stretch to construe music in a parallel light. Musical interaction, particularly the way we make music together, is often considered a corollary of social interaction: "Musicians in an ensemble communicate with each other, and these interactional patterns replicate the essential interactional processes found in all human communication" (Sawyer, 2005, p.47).

What is clear both in Mauss's work and in our observation of everyday music-making is that more is exchanged than the material or medium in question. An audience at a symphony concert receives much more than notes and rhythms. The coffee shop singer exchanges more than a few sounds for a few dollars. There's more going on: the dialogue of emotions between player and receiver, the sense of personal narrative, emotional exchange, expression, receiver resonance, and more. This is why the experience of music itself is so difficult to package and monetize, even with today's advanced technologies of recording and distribution.

But how does gift apply to intercultural improvisation? Intercultural improvisation was born out of a need for a music that was truly inclusive, intercultural, authentic, and free from the perils of cultural appropriation and commercial processes. Over the past several years of development at community events, it has become an established art practice whereby music is gifted and shared by authentic cultural practitioners within a negotiated musical ethical space (Yun, 2016).

Mauss examined several types of exchange systems and noted that across various systems there are three parts to the gift: an obligation to give, an obligation to receive, and an obligation to reciprocate (Mauss, 1990). I will illustrate each of these parts of the gift in the context of an intercultural improvisation by describing a scenario drawn from the Sing Fires of Justice event described earlier.

There are multiple performers/groups, each working in a different cultural tradition, and a facilitator who also participates as a musician: for example, a massed choir, First Nations drummers/singers, an Islamic *nasheed* singer, and a facilitator playing the *shakuhachi*. Each group is positioned around a common space facing one another. Each performer acknowledges the others. The facilitator sounds a single note and silently invites others to sound.

This simple opening is the first example of giving and receiving. In an intercultural improvisation, giving is akin to initial soundings. It needn't be anything more complex than one note or one strike on the drum. In my experience, giving can be non-sonic as well, with simple gestures, facial expressions, and often a silent greeting, followed by laughter.

Receiving means acknowledging the gift being given, the note offered. In receiving the offering through the state of listening presence and sounding as acknowledgment of receiving, a unique musical act occurs: the acts of giving and receiving, happening simultaneously and continuously between multiple individuals, become the same act. In most cases this sounded note is joined at octave or unison by the others and forms the basis of a musical support structure. It also serves to sonically inscribe the ethical space itself.

At this point one group or performer brings their own song fragment, chant, or other offering to the circle. The others take on the role of support, either in silence or with simple supportive long-tones. In some cases, rhythmic support is offered as well. These supporting actions also function as indications of receiving. The group's musical offering concludes by rejoining the support drone, and another group is signalled for their turn to offer. This continues until all groups have brought their music to the circle.

Next, the facilitator signals for the groups to interact. Usually, a group will begin to sound their offering again, and almost immediately others will improvise around it. The unstated goal is to make the various and multiple musics work together somehow. The process of improvisation allows this solution to be worked, and the working out itself creates unexpected interactions and relationships across the groups.

In every case the unfolding of these improvisations is experienced by participants as fascinating and deeply moving if not aesthetically beautiful. The music is allowed to rise and fall on its own, with multiple participants negotiating the use of musical fragments, rhythms, and harmonies across converging and often conflicting sonic cultural systems.

There is one more aspect of the gift that we have yet to mention with regard to the above example: the obligation to reciprocate. I posit that the entire improvisatory process that occurs after the initial musical offerings embodies reciprocation. The offering and receiving of gifts is followed by an obligation to participate in creating something new, to continue to offer musical feedback, encouragement, affirmation, and materials that will help "make things work out." This is the seeking of equilibrium across the various forces – the solving of musical challenges by equals.

This type of music-making is representative of social modelling; furthermore, its performative aspect is altered from what we think of as "normal performance music," where the ending performance is the product (the sonic result). Instead, intercultural improvisation privileges process over product. That is, the interaction between the musicians is the performance – the most poignant and important part of the music (Nachmanovitch, 1990).

To participate in such an improvisation is to be part of creating the "glue that holds society together." In this improvisatory act, the separate groups take on the role of a unified musical ensemble, but with each group maintaining its individualized cultural identity. Together, they create a new communal identity. They also create new music through personal and cultural resources negotiated in the ethical space of engagement.

Engaging the Ethical Space: The Listening Presence

In intercultural improvisation, the first step is not sounding but listening. Mauss doesn't mention the act of listening in his work on the gift, perhaps because he isn't contemplating art, and specifically music, in this way. Composer Pauline Oliveros doesn't conceptualize music as gift, but her work in deep listening is particularly apt for this discussion of intercultural engagement and especially intercultural improvisation:

> People's experiences are all different, and you don't know what the person experienced. They know, but you don't, so I think it's important to listen carefully to what a person has to say. And not to force them into any direction at all but simply to model what you've experienced, model it and also be what I call a *Listening Presence*. If you're really listening, then some of the barriers can dissolve or change. (Andrews & Maloney, 2015)

Oliveros is suggesting an idealized type of musical/social listening, which she describes in her seminal work *Deep Listening* (2005). She emphasizes the need to consider perspectives of personal experience and to establish a frame of mind she calls "listening presence." This way of listening through boundaries transcends our tendency to judge, evaluate, analyze, and criticize.

The importance of a non-judgmental approach to interaction is also emphasized in engaged Buddhism through the concepts of right speech and right listening (Nhat Hanh, 2018) as well as in the inclusive type of listening outlined by Lewis Hyde in his classic work *The Gift: Creativity and the Artist in the Modern World*. Hyde extends Mauss's original discussions on gift by applying it to art. In addressing the relationship between performers and audiences, he describes an open and inclusive state of mind: "We participate in the esemplastic power of the gift by way of a particular kind of unconsciousness; then: unanalytic, undialectical consciousness ... [We] must enter that illusion that [we] and the audience are one and the same thing"(Hyde, 2007, pp. 196–97)

"Esemplastic" means becoming or forming into one. This is an undivided state of consciousness where it is not us and the other, but rather all of us together as one. The Buddhist term for this state of knowing is "non-duality," an expanded awareness that encompasses differences. It is also embodied in the South African concept of Ubuntu – I am who I am because of who we are (together) (Battle, 2009).

I believe that Oliveros and Hyde are describing the same state of mind that suspends judgment, manipulation, and myopic analysis while privileging openness and support. The listening presence is essential to activating ethical space in intercultural improvisation. It is this way of approaching one another that transforms the natural feeling of tension and confrontation into one of relative safety and engagement. The listening presence becomes a way of being for both the individual and the group – a way to behave in a new microculture being formed in the space between cultures. While the ethical space itself sets up an excellent framework for intercultural dialogue, without the listening presence the sense of safety and non-judgment, so important to the unfolding of the co-creation process, can be difficult to maintain.

Conclusion

Intercultural improvisation within the ethical space of engagement offers socially engaged music practitioners a way to work across boundaries that are chronically fraught with imbalances of power. There are other ways of engaging musically across cultural divides, such as song-sharing and the mediation of professionally composed and arranged works. But intercultural improvisation offers a way forward by muting the effects of appropriation, theft, and mimicry through direct engagement of real people in living cultural practices. In our current global political and social atmosphere, the cultural pitfalls so easily stumbled into can easily trigger thoughts of and reactions to racism – a situation that would likely render any attempt at musical and social dialogue a failure.

This chapter has been written with the intent to help people facilitate and form genuine relationships across cultural divides of divergent identities and differing world views through a workable, flexible, and powerful musical practice. I hope this offering and others like it will serve to remove at least a modicum of the fear that many of us have in engaging in this type of Community Music.

By its very nature, intercultural improvisation does not dwell in the past. Nor does it lend itself to the classical model of the lone artist labouring to produce a great work of art. Instead it involves a diverse group of music practitioners negotiating their collective skills, and their own ways of knowing and being, to co-create. It is a practice that involves real people – living, practicing musicians – as they are in the moment and works to move them together to create something new in the spirit of hope. What is this something if not new relationships, new ways of practising, new ways of knowing? Activist-facilitator Debbie Lou Ludolph says it best: "We sing our hope in the midst of the current realities, which help us imagine our way forward" (personal communication, 12 November 2017).

Intercultural improvisation offers community music practitioners the opportunity to negotiate the borders of differentiated cultural practices and values in a meaningful and transformative way. By modelling this musical practice on gift exchange, we can articulate a medium of social and spiritual exchange that moves community music well beyond the limitations of monetary systems. We focus on where we are now and where we wish to go or what we wish to create together. Intercultural improvisation is a musical act of hope, something much needed in the Community Musician's repertoire of materials and sorely needed as one of many types of communal music practices.

POSTSCRIPT

Lee Higgins

AS I BEGAN TO THINK about what I might say as a postscript to this volume, I initially reflected on the extensive array of ideas, concepts, and illustrations that are currently being understood under the auspices of community music. As Brydie-Leigh Bartleet and I wrote in our Introduction to *The Oxford Handbook of Community Music*, "The growing internationalization of the field has brought with it insights from cultural contexts that have both expanded and challenged accepted approaches, priorities and ideas regarding what is labelled 'community music.'" By engaging in *Community Music at the Boundaries*, you have experienced a continuation of this sentiment. New ideas, concepts, contexts, and approaches both reaffirm the practice of community music and, importantly, challenge previous perspectives.

As I have previously articulated, a trio of scholarly works published in 2012–13 solidified community music as a field of scholarship. Alongside the *International Journal of Community Music*, this was a time when those invested in the work could speak of solid grounds for claiming the emergence of community music as a field. In this sense, the notion of a "field" recognized its longstanding practical activities, well-established in some parts of the world, and, importantly, acknowledged its growing research agenda. This combination – let's name it theory and practice – enabled doors to be opened that perhaps either had been previously shut or were just not visible. We see evidence of this in an increased dialogue between community music and other music domains, for example, music therapy, ethnomusicology, and music education. We can also see a marked increase in engagement within the academy, a wider array of courses, programs, residencies, and interdisciplinary inquiry reflecting an interest in community music as a practice, in and of itself, but also as a critical lens through which to consider ideas beyond what might be considered as its borders. It is also rewarding to witness community music texts being written in local languages alongside translations of existing texts; a sign that the ideas are migrating beyond a bounded context.

   Community Music at the Boundaries is part of this history. Its trajectory is partly set, adding to a growing body of scholarship that offers ideas and approaches to musical doing that challenge the status quo and at the same time validate practices that have decades of tradition behind them. As an invested onlooker, partner, and occasional contributor to the community music developments at Wilfrid Laurier University in Waterloo, Ontario, I am proud to have been asked to write this postscript. As Roger Mantie points out in his foreword, the notion of boundary walker has been an important trope in my work. So it is very exciting to engage in this collection of essays, celebrating its diversity and commitment to issues pertaining to music, people, participation, context, and inclusivity. Diving deep into these pages reveals that musicking has a knack for seeping through borders, boundaries, and walls. This collection edges us toward new thresholds, each one providing an opening through which to encourage further explorations in this growing world often described as community music.

BIBLIOGRAPHY

Abbott, S. & Freeth, D. (2008). Social capital and health: Starting to make sense of the role of generalized trust and reciprocity. *Journal of Health Psychology, 13*(7), 874–883.

Aboriginal Affairs and Northern Development Canada. (2008, 11 June). *Statement of Apology.* http://www.aadnc-aandc.gc.ca/eng/1100100015644/1100100015649

Abreu Anselmi, J. A. (2006). Failoni, H. *L'altra voce della musica.* Il Saggiatore.

Abril, C. R., & Gault, B. M. (2016). *Teaching general music: Approaches, issues, and viewpoints.* Oxford University Press.

Absolon, K. E. (2011). *Kaandossiwin: How we come to know.* Fernwood.

Absolon, K. E. (2016). Wholistic and ethical: Social inclusion with Indigenous peoples. *Social Inclusion, 4*(1), 44–56. doi:10.17645/si.v4i1.444

Ahonen, H., & Mongillo Desideri, A. (2014). Heroines' journey – emerging story by refugee women during group analytic music therapy. *Voices.* March.

Ahonen-Eerikainen, H. (2007). *Group analytic music therapy.* Barcelona.

Aigen, K. S. (2012). Community music therapy. In G. E. McPherson & G. F. Welch (Eds.), *The Oxford handbook of music education* (Vol. 2). Oxford University Press. http://doi.org/10.1093/oxfordhb/9780199928019.013.0010

Aigen, K. S. (2014). *The study of music therapy: Current issues and concepts.* Routledge.

Aira, C. (2008). *Ghosts.* Translated by Chris Andrews. New Directions.

Alfano, C. (2008). Intergenerational learning in a high school environment. *International Journal of Community Music, 1*(2), 253–66.

Alfred, T. (2014, 23 May). *The failure of reconciliation: Taiaiake Alfred* [Web cast]. http://taiaiake.net/2014/05/14/the-failure-of-reconciliation

Allan, J. (2010). Arts and the ininclusive imagination: Socially engaged arts practices and Sistema Scotland. *Journal of Social Inclusion, 1*(2), 111–22.

Allred, K. D., Byers, J. F., & Sole, M. L. (2010). The effect of music on postoperative pain and anxiety. *Pain Management Nursing, 11*(1), 15–25.

Allsup, R. E. (2016). *Remixing the classroom: Toward an open philosophy of music education.* Indiana University Press.

Alperson, P. (2002). *Diversity and community: An interdisciplinary reader.* Blackwell.

Alvesson, M., Ashcraft, K., & Thomas, R. (2008). Identity matters: reflections on the construction of identity scholarship in organization studies. *Organization*, 15(1), 5–28.

Alvesson, M., & Skoldberg, K. (1999) *Reflexive methodology: New vistas for qualitative research.* Sage.

Alvesson, M., & Sköldberg, K. (2009). *Reflexive methodology: New vistas for qualitative research* (2nd ed.). Sage.

Alzheimer Society of Canada. (2012). Person-centered language. http://www.alzheimer .ca/~/media/Files/national/Culture-change/culture_person_centred_language _2012_e.pdf

Alzheimer Society of Ontario (2012, July). Dementia Evidence Brief. Waterloo Wellington Local Health Integration Network.

Amagoalik, J. (2012). Reconciliation or conciliation? An Inuit perspective. In S. Rogers, M. DeGagné, J. Dewar, & G. Lowry (Eds.), *Speaking my truth: Reflections on reconciliation and residential school.* Aboriginal Healing Foundation.

American Psychiatric Association. (2013). *Diagnostic and statistical manual of mental disorders* [DSM-V] (5th ed.) (2013). Author.

Amir, D. (1993). *Awakening and expanding the self: Meaningful moments in the music therapy process as experienced and described by music therapists and music therapy clients* (Doctoral dissertation, New York University). Retrieved from ProQuest on 25 March 2016. (9237730).

Amnesty International Canada. (2009). *No more stolen sisters: The need for a comprehensive response to discrimination and violence against Indigenous women in Canada.* https://www.amnesty.ca/news/no-more-stolen-sisters-need-comprehensive -response-discrimination-and-violence-against

Anderson, B. (1983). *Imagined communities: Reflections on the origin and spread of nationalism.* Verso.

Anderson, C. (2009). *The longer long tail: How endless choice is creating unlimited demand.* Random House Business.

Anderson, K. (2015). Documenting arts practitioners' practice in prisons: "What do you do in there?" *Howard Journal of Criminal Justice*, 54(4), 371–383.

Anderson, K., Colvin, S., McNeill, F., Nellis, M., Overy, K., Sparks, R., and Tett, L. (2011). Inspiring change: Final project report of the evaluation team. www.motherwell.co.uk/inspiringchange/research.aspx

Andrews, B., & Maloney, P. (2015, 26 January). Interview with Pauline Oliveros. https:// www.artpractical.com/column/bad-at-sports-interview-with-pauline-oliveros

Anfam, D., Davidson, S., & Lewison, J. (2016). *Abstract expressionism.* Royal Academy Books.

Angelou, M. (1983). *Shaker, why don't you sing?* Random House.

Ansdell, G. (2005). Being who you aren't; doing what you can't: Community music therapy and the paradoxes of performance. *Voices: A World Forum for Music Therapy*, 5(3). doi:http://dx.doi.org/10.15845/voices.v5i3.229

Ansdell, G. (2010). Where performing helps: Processes and affordances of performance in community music therapy. In B. Stige, G. Ansdell, C. Elefant, &

M. Pavlicevic (Eds.), *Where music helps: Community music therapy in action and reflection* (pp. 161–188). Aldershot: Ashgate.

Ansdell, G., Davidson, J., Magee, W. L., Meehan, J., & Procter, S. (2010). From "this f***ing life" to "that's better" … in four minutes: An interdisciplinary study of music therapy's "present moments" and their potential for affect modulation. *Nordic Journal of Music Therapy, 19*(1), 3–28.

Appiah, K. A. (2016, 11 May). Mistaken identities: Colour. *Reith Lectures.* http://www.bbc.co.uk/programmes/b080t63w

Apsler, R. (2009). After-school programs for adolescents: A review of evaluation research. *Adolescence, 44,* 1–19.

Armstrong, D. (2011). The invention of patient-centred medicine. *Social Theory and Health Suppl. Special Issue: ESHMS Ghent Congress, 9*(4), 410–418.

Aróstegui J. L. (2016). Exploring the global decline of music education. *Arts Education Policy Review.* Taylor and Francis.

Arvelo, A. (2005). *Tocar y luchar* [film]. Fundación Musical Simón Bolívar. http://www.youtube.com/watch?v=L9p7_Jnk9_Q

Ashley, L., & Lines, D. (Eds.). (2016). *Intersecting cultures in music and dance education: An oceanic perspective* (Vol. 19). Springer.

Atkinson, J. (2002). *Trauma trails, recreating song lines: The transgenerational effects of trauma in Indigenous Australia.* Spinifex Press.

Australian Government (2008). Apology to Australia's Indigenous Peoples. Author. http://www.australia.gov.au/about-australia/our-country/our-people/apology-to-australias-indigenous-peoples

Australian Human Rights Commission (AHRC). (2007). Social Justice Report 2007 – Chapter 3: The Northern Territory "Emergency Response" Intervention. https://www.humanrights.gov.au/publications/social-justice-report-2007-chapter-3-northern-territory-emergency-response-intervention#fn1

Bajekal, N. (2014, 24 December). Silent night: The story of the World War 1 Christmas Truce of 1914. *Time Magazine.* http://time.com/3643889/christmas-truce-1914

Baker, F., & Wigram, T. (Eds.). (2005). *Songwriting: Methods, techniques, and clinical application for music therapy clinicians, educators, and students.* Jessica Kingsley.

Baker, F. A. (2013). Front and center stage: Participants performing songs created during music therapy. *The Arts in Psychotherapy, 40,* 20–28.

Baker, F. A., Grocke, D, & Pachana, N. A. (2012.) Connecting through music: A study of a spousal caregiver-directed music intervention designed to prolong fulfilling relationships in couples where one person has dementia. *The Australian Journal of Music Therapy, 23,* 4–19.

Baker, G. (2015). *El sistema: Orchestrating Venezuela's youth.* Oxford University Press.

Bakhtin, M. M. (1984). *Problems of Dostoevsky's Poetics.* (C. Emerson, Ed.). University of Minnesota Press.

Balandina, A. (2010). Music and conflict transformation in the post-Yugoslav era: empowering youth to develop harmonic inter-ethnic relationships in Kumanovo, Macedonia. *International Journal of Community Music, 3*(2), 229–244. https://doi.org/10.1386/ijcm.3.2.229_1

Baldassar, L. (2011). Italian migrants in Australia and their relationship to Italy: Return visits, transnational caregiving, and the second generation. *Journal of Mediterranean Studies, 20*(2), 1–28.

Balkwill, L. L., & Thompson, W. F. (1999). A cross-cultural investigation of the perception of emotion in music: Psychophysical and cultural cues. *Music Perception, 17*(1), 43–64.

Balkwill, L. L., Thompson, W. F., & Matsunaga, R. (2004). Recognition of emotion in Japanese, Western, and Hindustani music by Japanese listeners. *Japanese Psychological Research, 46*(4), 337–349.

Balough, T. (1982). Grainger as author: A philosophical expression. In F. Callaway (Ed.)., *Percy Aldridge Grainger – Symposium* (pp. 90–100). Reprint of *Studies in Music* No. 16 (1997). Callaway International Resource Centre for Music Education, The University of Western Australia.

Balsnes, A. H. (2016). Hospitality in multicultural choral singing. *International Journal of Community Music, 9*(2), 171–189. https://doi.org/10.1386/ijcm.9.2.171_1

Bamberger, J. (1999). *Developing musical intuitions: A project based introduction to making and understanding music.* Oxford University Press.

Bamberger, J., & Hernandez, A. (Producer). (1999–2000). Impromptu. http://www.tuneblocks.com

Banks, J. A., Au, K. H., Ball, A. F., Bell, P., Gordon, E. W., Gutierrez, K., and Zhou, M. (2007). Learning in and out of school in diverse environments: Life-long, life-wide, life-deep. UW Center for Multicultural Education & The LIFE Center.

Banks, J. A. (2012). *Encyclopedia of diversity in education,* Vol. 1. Sage Reference. https://sk.sagepub.com/reference/diversityineducation

Bannan, N., & Montgomery-Smith, D. (2008). "Singing for the brain": Reflections on the human capacity for music arising from a pilot study of group singing with Alzheimer's patients. *The Journal for the Royal Society for the Promotion Health, 128*(2), 73–78.

Baranowsky, A., Gentry, E., & Schultz, F. (2011). Trauma practice: Tools for stabilization and recovery. Hogrefe.

Barker, A. (2010). From adversaries to allies: Forging respectful alliances between Indigenous and settler peoples. In L. Davies (Ed.), *Alliances: Re/envisioning Indigenous-non-Indigenous relationships* (pp. 316–333). University of Toronto Press.

Barnes, G. V. (2013). The University of South Carolina String Project: Teaching and learning within a community music program. *International Journal of Community Music, 6*(1), 23–31. https://doi.org/10.1386/ijcm.6.1.23_1

Barney, K., & Mackinlay, E. (2010). "Singing trauma trails": Songs of the stolen generations in Indigenous Australia. *Music and Politics, 4*(2). https://quod.lib.umich.edu/m/mp/9460447.0004.202?view=text;rgn=main.

Barnhart, P., Hogin, S., & House, J. (1997). A broken wing [Song recorded by Martina McBride]. On *Evolution* [CD]. RCA Nashville.

Barrera, M. E., Rykov, M. H., & Doyle, S. L. (2002). The effects of interactive music therapy on hospitalized children with cancer: A pilot study. *Psycho-Oncology, 11*(5), 379–388.

Barrett, F. S., Grimm, K. J., Robins, R. W., Wildschut, T., Sedikides, C., & Janata, P. (2010). Music-evoked nostalgia: Affect, memory, and personality. *Emotion*, *10*(3), 390–403.

Barrett, M. (2006)."Creative collaboration": An "eminence" study of teaching and learning in music composition. *Psychology of Music*, *34*(2), 195–218.

Barrett, M. S., & Westerlund, H. (1917). *Practices of music education and learning across the lifespan: An exploration of values and purposes* (pp. 75–89). The Palgrave Handbook of Global Arts Education. Palgrave Macmillan.

Bartel, L., & Cameron, L. (2004). From dilemmas to experience: Shaping the conditions of learning. In L. Bartel (Ed.), *Questioning the music education paradigm*. Volume II of the series "Research to practice: A biennial series." Canadian Music Educators Association, 39–61.

Bartel, L., and Foster, B. (2016). Understanding music care in Canadian facility-based long term care. *Music and Medicine*, *8*(1), 29–34.

Bartleet, B.-L. (2009). Sound links: Exploring the social, cultural, and educational dynamics of musical communities in Australia. *International Journal of Community Music*, *1*(3), 335–356. https://doi.org/10.1386/ijcm.1.3.335_1

Bartleet, B.-L. (2012, 15 July). *Bridging universities and Indigenous communities through service learning projects in music.* Paper presented at the annual meeting of the ISME World Conference and Commission Seminars, Thessaloniki Concert Hall, Thessaloniki, Greece. http://www98.griffith.edu.au/dspace/bitstream/handle/10072/52342/84778_1.pdf?sequence=1

Bartleet, B.-L. (2016). *Can music change the world?* YouTube. Lecture presented at Queensland Conservatorium Research Centre, Griffith University. https://www.youtube.com/watch?v=WNH-1W2V_wc

Bartleet, B.-L. (2017). Die wachsende Interkulturalisierung und Internationalisierung von Community Music Einblicke aus dem asiatisch-pazifischen Raum [Translation: The growing interculturalisation and internationalisation of community music: Insights from the Asia Pacific Region]. In B. Hill & A. Banffy (Eds.), *Community music: In Theorie und Praxis* (pp. 63–72). Waxmann.

Bartleet, B.-L., Bennett, D., Marsh, K., Power, A., & Sunderland, N. (2014). Reconciliation and transformation through mutual learning: Outlining a framework for arts based service learning with Indigenous communities in Australia. *International Journal of Education and the Arts*, *15*(8). http://www.ijea.org

Bartleet, B. L., Bennett, D., Marsh, K., Power, A. & Sunderland, N. (2014). Working and learning with First Peoples of Australia in the creative arts: A framework to support respectful and mutually beneficial service learning partnership in the creative arts. *Griffith Experts*, Griffith University, https://experts.griffith.edu.au/publication/ne29103216a701bb940828ce8445ba561

Bartleet, B.-L., Bennett, D., Power, A., & Sunderland, N. (2016). Arts-based service learning with Australian First Peoples: Concepts and considerations. In B. L. Bartleet, D. Bennett, A. Power, & N. Sunderland (Eds.) *Engaging First Peoples in arts-based service learning* (pp. 3-14). Springer.

Bartleet, B.-L., Carfoot, G., & Murn, A. (2016). Exploring university-community partnerships in arts-based service learning with Australian First Peoples and arts organizations. In B. L. Bartleet, D. Bennett, A. Power, & N. Sunderland (Eds.), *Engaging First Peoples in arts-based service learning: Towards respectful and mutually beneficial educational practices* (pp. 31-49). Springer International.

Bartleet, B.-L., & Higgins, L. (2017). An overview of community music in the 21st century. In B. L. Bartleet & L. Higgins (Eds.), *The Oxford handbook of community music*. Oxford University Press.

Bartleet, B.-L., & Higgins, L. (2018). *Oxford Handbook of Community Music*. New York: Oxford University Press.

Bartleet, B.-L., Sunderland, N., & Carfoot, G. (2016). Enhancing intercultural engagement through service learning and music making with Indigenous communities in Australia. *Research Studies in Music Education, 38*(2), 173–191.

Barwick, L., & Keller, M. S. (2012). Transnational perspectives on Italy in Australia's musical landscape. In L. Barwick & M. S. Keller (Eds.), *Italy in Australia's musical landscape* (pp. 3–14). Lyrebird Press.

Bassuk, E. L., DeCandia, C. J., Beach, C. A., & Berman, F. (2014). *America's youngest outcasts: State report card on child homelessness*. National Center on Family Homelessness. https://www.air.org/sites/default/files/downloads/report/Americas -Youngest-Outcasts-Child-Homelessness-Nov2014.pdf

Bassuk, E., Konnath, K., and Volk, K. (2006). Understanding traumatic stress in children. The National Center on Family Homelessness.

Bassuk, E. L., & Friedman, S. M. (2005). Facts on trauma and homeless children. National Child Traumatic Stress Network Homelessness and Extreme Poverty Working Group.

Bassuk, E. L., Richard, M. K., & Tsertsvadze, A. (2015). The prevalence of mental illness in homeless children: A systematic review and meta-analysis. *Journal of the American Academy of Child and Adolescent Psychiatry, 54*(2), 86–96.

Bates, V. C. (2014). Rethinking cosmopolitanism in music education. *Action, Criticism & Theory for Music Education, 13*(1), 310–327.

Battell Lowman, E., & Barker, A. (2015). *Settler: Identity and colonialism in 21st century Canada*. Fernwood.

Battle, M. J. (2009). *Ubuntu: I in you and you in me*. Seabury Books.

Bauer, W., & Dammers, R. (2016). Anxiety technology in music teacher education: A national survey. *Research Perspectives in Music Education, 18*(1), 2–15.

Baum, F., MacDougall, C., & Smith, D. (2006). Participatory action research. *Journal of Epidemiology and Community Health, 60*(10), 854–857.

Baumann, M.P. (2001). Festivals, musical actors, and mental constructs in the process of globalization. *The World of Music, 43*(2), 9–29.

Beck, C. K., Vogelpohl, T. S., Rasin, J. H., Uriri, J. T., O'Sullivan, P., Walls, R., Phillips, R., & Baldwin, B. (2002). Effects of behavioral interventions on disruptive behavior and affect in demented nursing home residents. *Nursing Research 51*(4), 219–228.

Beck, R. J., Cesario, T. C., Yousefi, A., & Enamoto, H. (2000) Choral singing, performance perception, and immune system changes in salivary immunoglobulin A and cortisol. *Music Perception: An Interdisciplinary Journal, 18*(1), 87–106.

Bee, H. L. (1996). *Journey of adulthood* (3rd ed.). Prentice Hall.

Beland, F., Zunzunegui, M. V., Alvarado, B., Otero, A., & Del Ser, T. (2005). Trajectories of cognitive decline and social relations. *The Journals of Gerontology. Series B, Psychological Sciences and Social Sciences, 60*, 320–330.

Bélanger, P. (2015). *Self-construction and social transformation: Lifelong, lifewide, and life-deep learning.* UNESCO Institute for Lifelong Learning.

Belanger, Y. (2014). *Ways of knowing: An introduction to Native studies in Canada.* Nelson Education.

Bell, J. L. (2008). God welcomes all. [The Themba Amen]. Traditional South African transcription. In *Kanata Centre for Worship and Global Song* (p. 40). Waterloo Lutheran Seminary. M&T.

Bennett, D. (2012). *Life in the real world: How to make music graduates employable.* Common Ground.

Bennett, D., & Burnard, P. (2016). Human capital career creativities for creative industries work: Lessons underpinned by Bourdieu's tools for thinking. In R. Comunian and A. Gilmore, *Higher education and the creative economy: Beyond the campus* (pp. 123–142). Routledge.

Bergh, A., & Sloboda, J. (2010). Music and art in conflict transformation: A review. *Music and Arts in Action, 2*(2), 2–17.

Berlach, R. G., & Chambers, D. J. (2011). Interpreting inclusivity: An endeavour of great proportions. *International Journal of Inclusive Education, 15*(5), 529–539. https://doi.org/10.1080/13603110903159300

Berridge, K. C. (2007) The debate over dopamine's role in reward: The case for incentive salience. *Psychopharm, 191*, 391–431.

Beynon, C., & Lang, J. (2018). The more we get together, the more we learn: Focus on intergenerational and collaborative learning through singing. *Journal of Intergenerational Relationships, 16*(1–2), 45-63. doi: 10.1080/1530770.2018.1404405

Beynon, C., Little, B., McNaughton, K., Beynon, J.G., Lang Hutchison, J. M. J., & O'Regan, N. (2016). Singing my way back to you: Learnings from the intergenerational choir project for singers with Alzheimer's disease, their caregivers, music educators, and students. *The Journal of the Alzheimer's Association, 12* (supp. 799). doi:10.1016/j.jalz/2016.06.1613

Bick, M. (2013). The role of hubs in reaching the "hard to reach" groups: Experiences and reflections from Gloucestershire. In C. Harrison & P. Mullen (Eds.), *Reaching out* (pp. 53–61). Music Mark.

Biesta, G. J. J. (2006). *Beyond learning: Democratic education for a human future* (1st Ed.). Paradigm.

Bird, F. (2017). Singing out: The function and benefits of an LGBTQI community choir in New Zealand in the 2010s. *International Journal of Community Music, 10*(2), 193–206. https://doi.org/10.1386/ijcm.10.2.193_1

Birrell, I. (2012, March 22). The term "world music" is outdated and offensive. https://www.theguardian.com/music/musicblog/2012/mar/22/world-music-outdated-offensive

Bithell, C. (2014). *A different voice, a different song: Reclaiming community through the natural voice and world song.* Oxford University Press.

Blackstock, C. (2016, 14 October). Keynote address. *Integrating Knowledges Summit.* University of Waterloo.

Blair, Nerida. (2016). Australian Aboriginal knowledges and service learning. In B.-L. Bartleet, D. Bennett, A. Power, & N. Sunderland (Eds.), *Engaging First Peoples in arts-based service learning: Towards respectful and mutually beneficial educational practices* (pp. 99-117). London: Springer International Switzerland.

Block, P. (2009). *Community: The structure of belonging.* Berrett-Koehler.

Blood, A. J., & Zatorre, R. J. (2001). Intensely pleasurable responses to music correlate with activity in brain regions implicated in reward and emotion. *Proceedings of the National Academy of Science of the United States of America, 98*(20), 11818–11823.

Blood, A. J., Zatorre, R. J., Bermudez, P., & Evans, A. C. (1999). Emotional responses to pleasant and unpleasant music correlate with activity in paralimbic brain regions. *Nature Neuroscience, 2*(4), 382–387.

Blum, J., Estabrook, H., Litvak, M., & Lancaster, D. (Producers) & Chazelle, D. (Director). (2014). *Whiplash* [Motion Picture]. Bold Films, Blumhouse Productions, & Right of Way Films.

Bochner, A. P. (2001). Narrative's virtue. *Qualitative Inquiry, 7*(2), 135–157.

Bochner, A. P., & Ellis, C. (2003). An introduction to the arts and narrative research: Art as inquiry. *Qualitative Inquiry, 9*(4), 506–514.

Bochner, S. (1994). Cross-cultural differences in the self-concept. *Journal of Cross-Cultural Psychology, 25*(2), 273–283.

Boeskov, K. (2017). The community music practice as cultural performance: Foundations for a community music theory of social transformation. *International Journal of Community Music, 10*(1), 85–99. https://doi.org/10.1386/ijcm.10.1.85_1

Bogdan, R. C., & Biklen, S. K. (1994). *Investigação Qualitativa em Educação.* Porto Editora.

Bogdan, R. C., & Biklen, S. K. (2003). *Qualitative research for education: An introduction to theories and methods* (4th Ed.). Allyn and Bacon.

Bolkan, C., Hooker, K., & Coehlo, D. (2015). Possible selves and depressive symptoms in later life. *Research on Aging, 37*(1), 41–62. doi: 10.1177/0164027513520557

Bond, J. (2008). Reconciliation: A non-Indigenous Australian perspective. In M. Brant Castellano, Linda Archibald; Mike DeGagneì, *From truth to reconciliation: transforming the legacy of residential schools.* Aboriginal Healing Foundation, 259–80.

Bonde, L. O. (2010). Health musicing: Music therapy or music and health? A model, empirical examples, and personal reflections. *Music and Arts in Action, 3*(2), 120–140.

Bonny, H. (2002). Guided imagery and music (GIM): Mirror of consciousness. In L. Summer (Ed.), *Music consciousness: The evolution of guided imagery and music* (pp. 93–102). Barcelona Publishers.

Boon, E. T. (2015). Everybody is a musician, everybody is an orchestra: Musical and bodily dialogues with physically disabled children in Turkey. *International Journal of Community Music, 8*(2), 149–161. https://doi.org/10.1386/ijcm.8.2.149_1

Booth, E. (2011). El Sistema's open secrets. *Teaching Artist Journal, 9*(1), 16–25.

Bosworth, R. (1988). Australia and assisted immigration from Britain, 1945–1954. *Australian Journal of Politics and History, 34*(2), 187–200.

Bosworth, R., & Melia, M. (1991). The Italian 'feste' of Western Australia and the myth of the Universal Church. In R. Bosworth & M. Melia (Eds.), *Studies in Western Australian History: Aspects of Ethnicity in Western Australia*, (12), 71–84.

Bottomley, G. (1992). *From another place: Migration and the politics of culture.* Cambridge University Press.

Bourdieu, P. (1977). *Outline of a theory of practice* (J. Goody, Ed., R. Nice, Trans.). Cambridge University Press.

Bourdieu, P. (1979). *Distinction* (1st Ed.). Routledge.

Bourdieu, P. (1984). *Distinction: A social critique of the judgement of taste.* Routledge & Kegan Paul.

Bourdieu, P. (1990). *The logic of practice.* Polity Press.

Bourdieu, P. (1993). *The field of cultural production: Essays on art and literature.* Polity Press.

Bourdieu, P. (1996). *The rules of art: Genesis and structure of the literary field by Pierre Bourdieu.* Polity Press.

Bourdieu, P., Chamboredon, J.-C., & Passeron, J.-C. (1991). *The craft of sociology: Epistemological preliminaries.* De Gruyter.

Bowers, J. (1998). Effects of an intergenerational choir for community-based seniors and college students on age-related attitudes. *Journal of Music Therapy, 35*(1), 2–18.

Bowlby, J. (1961). Process of mourning. *International Journal of Psycho-Analysis, 42,* 217–340.

Bowlby, J. (1969). *Attachment and loss* (Vol. 1), *Attachment* (2nd Ed.). Basic Books.

Bowman, W. (2006). Why narrative? Why now? *Research Studies in Education, 27*(1), 5–20.

Boyce, B. (Ed.). (2011). *The mindfulness revolution: Leading psychologists, scientists, artists, and meditation teachers on the power of mindfulness in daily life.* Shambhala.

Boyes, G. (1993). *The imagined village: Culture, ideology, and the English folk revival.* Manchester University Press.

Bradt, J., & Dileo, C. (2009). Music for stress and anxiety reduction in coronary heart disease patients. *Cochrane Database Systematic Reviews 2,* CD006577.

Brandes, V. M., Terris, D., Fischer, C., Loerbroks, A., Jarczok, M. N., Ottowitz, G., Titscher, G., Fischer, J. E., & Thayer, J. F. (2010). Receptive music therapy for the treatment of depression: A proof-of-concept study and prospective controlled trial of efficacy. *Psychotherapy and Psychosomatics, 79,* 321–322.

Brant Castellano, M. (2015). Presentation. "Aboriginal Research Ethics Symposium: Responsible and Compliant Best Practices," Wilfrid Laurier University. Waterloo.

Bremner, J. D. (2001). Hypotheses and controversies related to effects of stress on the hippocampus: An argument for stress-induced damage to the hippocampus in patients with post-traumatic stress disorder. *Hippocampus, 11,* 75–81.

Bremner, J. D., et al. (1995). MRI-based measurements of hippocampal volume in combat-related post-traumatic stress disorder. *American Journal of Psychiatry, 152,* 973–978.

Brennan, K., Monrroy-Hernandez, A., & Resnick, M. (2010). Making projects, making friends: Online community as catalyst for interactive media creation. *New Directions for Youth Development, 128,* 75-83.

A brief history of America's first established youth orchestra (2018). In *Portland Youth Philharmonic.* https://portlandyouthphil.org/about/history

Bronfenbrenner, U. (1979). *The ecology of human development: Experiments by nature and design.* Harvard University Press.

Bronfenbrenner, U. (2005). *Making human beings human: Bioecological perspectives on human development.* Sage.

Brown, S. (2004), Passive music listening spontaneously engages limbic and paralimbic systems. *NeuroReport* 15, 2033–2037

Brown, S., & Volgsten, U. (Eds.). (2005). *Music and manipulation: On the social uses and social control of music.* Berghahn Books.

Bruce, C. (2016, May). *Performing "normal": Restless reflections on music's dis/abling potential.* Keynote address at the conference of the Canadian Association of Music Therapists, Kitchener, ON.

Bruner, J. (2004). Life as narrative. *Social Research, 71*(3), 691–710.

Bruner, J. S. (2009). *La cultura dell'educazione. Nuovi orizzonti per la scuola.* Feltrinelli.

Bruser, M. (2011). Making music. In Boyce, B. (Ed.), *The Mindfulness Revolution* (p. 111). Shambhala.

Brussat, F., & Brussat, M. A. (n.d.). *Spirituality and Practice.* https://www.spirituality andpractice.com/films/reviews/view/4664

Bryce, A. J. (2014). *Proposing new media narratives to create an ethical space of engagement between Indigenous and non-Indigenous people in Canada.* (Unpublished master's thesis). https://dspace.royalroads.ca/docs/bitstream/handle/10170/735/bryce_andrew.pdf?sequence=1

Buckner, J. C., Bassuk, E. L., Weinreb, L. F. (2001). Predictors of academic achievement among homeless and low-income housed children. *Journal of School Psychology, 39*(1), 45–69.

Bugos, J. A. (2014). Community music as a cognitive training program for successful aging. *International Journal of Community Music, 7*(3), 319–331. doi: 10.1386/ijcm7.3.319_1

Burke, M. (1997). Effects of physioacoustic intervention on pain management of post-operative gynecological patients. In T. Wigram & C. Dileo (Eds.), *Music vibration and health.* Jeffrey Books.

Burns, S., & Bewick, P. (2012). In Harmony Liverpool: Interim report year three. In Harmony Liverpool.

Burridge, E. (2006). *Bridge between worlds.* http://www.emilyburridge.com/WHWMCD03_bridge.php

Bushouse, B. K. (2005). Community nonprofit organizations and service learning: Resource constraints to building parternships with universities. *Michigan Journal of Community Service Learning, 12*(1), 32–40.

Caldwell, B., and Vaughan, T. (2012) *Transforming education through the arts.* Routledge.

Caldwell, M. (1956). Group dynamics in the prison community. *Journal of Criminal Law and Criminology, 46*(5), 648–657.

Calhoun, C., & Bauman, Z. (2013). *Community: Seeking safety in an insecure world.* Polity Press.

Camic, P., Williams, C. M., & Meeten, F. (2011). Does a "singing together group" improve the quality of life of people with a dementia and their carers? A pilot evaluation study. *Dementia, 12*(2), 157–176.

Camlin, D. A. (2015a). This is my truth, tell me yours: Emphasising dialogue within participatory music. *International Journal of Community Music, 8*(3), 233–57.

Camlin, D. A. (2015b). Whose quality is it anyway? Inhabiting the creative tension between presentational and participatory music. *Journal of Arts and Communities,* 6(2), Artworks Special Edition, 99–118.

Camlin, D. A. (2016a). Libraries gave us power. Presented at the ICCM Student Research Conference, International Centre for Community Music, York St. John University.

Camlin, D. A. (2016b). *Music in three dimensions.* (Doctoral thesis). University of Sunderland.

Camlin, D. A. (2016c). Music in three dimensions. In *International Society for Music Education conference.* ISME.

Camlin, D. A. (2016d). Whatever you say I am, that's what I'm not. In *Community Music Activity commission.* ISME. https://www.isme.org/other-publications/cma-proceedings-2016

Camlin, D. A. (2017). Singing the rights we do not possess. In A. Banffy-Hall & B. Hill (Eds.), *Community music: Beitrage zur theorie und praxis aus internationaler und Deutscher perspektive* (pp. 137–148). Waxmann.

Camlin, D. A., & Zeserson, K. (2018). Becoming a community musician: A situated approach to curriculum, content, and assessment. In B.-L. Bartleet & L. Higgins (Eds.), *Oxford Handbook of Community Music* (pp. 711–733). Oxford University Press.

Campbell, P. S. (1997). Music, the universal language: Fact or fallacy? *International Journal of Music Education,* (1), 32–39.

Campbell, P. S. (1998). *Songs in their heads: Music and its meaning in children's lives,* Oxford University Press.

Campbell, P. S., & Scott-Kassner, C. (2013). *Music in childhood: From preschool through the elementary grades.* Nelson Education.

Canada Council for the Arts. (2016). {Re} Conciliation: A groundbreaking initiative which aims to promote artistic collaborations that look to the past and future for new dialogues between Aboriginal and non-Aboriginal peoples in Canada. http://canadacouncil.ca/aboriginal-arts-office/reconciliation

Canadian Foundation for Healthcare Improvement. http://www.cfhi-fcass.ca/WhatWeDo/reducing-antipsychotic-medication-use-collaborative

Canadian Healthcare Association (2009). New directions for facility-based long-term care. http://www.healthcarecan.ca/wp-content/uploads/2012/11/CHA_LTC_9-22-09_eng.pdf

Canadian Mental Health Strategy (2012). Changing lives, changing directions. http://strategy.mentalhealthcommission.ca/pdf/strategy-images-en.pdf

Cantle, T. (2016). The case for interculturalism, plural identities and cohesion. In
    N. Meer, T. Modood, & R. Zapata-Barrero (Eds.), *Multiculturalism and intercul-
    turalism – debating the dividing lines* (pp. 133–157). Edinburgh University Press.

Cao, L. (2014). Aboriginal people and confidence in police. *Canadian Journal of Crim-
    inology and Criminal Justice, 56*(5), 499–525. doi: 10.3138/cjccj.2013.E05

Carfoot, G. (2016). Musical discovery, colonialism, and the possibilities of intercultural
    communication through music. *Popular Communication, 14*(3), 178–86.

Caribupdate Channel. (1917, 16 August). Grenada PM speaks on Panorama and Car-
    nival. https://www.youtube.com/watch?v=l42dIKL14ho

Canadian Paediatric Society. (2016). Caring for ids Nenw to Canada: A guide for
    health professionals working with immigrant and refugee children and youth.
    www.kidsnewtocanada.ca/mental-health/ptsd

Carlen, P. (2007). A reclusão de mulheres e a indústria de reintegração. *Análise Social,
    42*(185), 1005–19.

Carlstrom, E., & Ekman, I. (2012). Organizational culture and change: Implement-
    ing person-centred care. *Journal of Health Organization and Management, 26*(2),
    175–91.

Carpenter, S. (2015). A philosophical and practical approach to an inclusive commu-
    nity chorus. *International Journal of Community Music, 8*(2), 197–210. https://doi
    .org/10.1386/ijcm.8.2.197_1

Carr, C., D'Ardenne, P., Sloboda, A., Scott, C., Wang, D., & Priebe, S. (2012). Group
    music therapy for patients with persistent post-traumatic stress disorder – an
    exploratory randomized controlled trial with mixed methods evaluation. *Psychol-
    ogy and Psychotherapy: Theory, Research and Practice, 85*(2), 179–202.

Carruthers, G. (2005). Articulating diverse music-learner populations. In D. Forrest
    (Ed.), *A celebration of voices* (pp. 48–54). Proceedings of the Australian Society
    for Music Education XV National Conference, Parkville.

Carruthers, G. (2012). Conservatories and universities: Emergent new roles. In
    J. Weller (Ed.), *Educating Professional Musicians in a Global Context* (pp. 32–36).
    Proceedings of the 19th International Seminar of the Commission on the Edu-
    cation of the Professional Musician, International Society for Music Education,
    Philippos Nakas Conservatory, Athens.

Carruthers, G. (2016). Marshall McLuhan and higher music education. *Intersections,
    36*(2), 3–11.

Carruthers, G. (2018). Percy Grainger, Community music, and higher music edu-
    cation. In *Proceedings of ISME 2018*, (pp. 48–58). https://www.isme.org/sites/
    default/files/documents/2018_isme_conference_proceedings.pdf.

Carucci, C. (2012). An investigation of social support in adult recreational music
    ensembles. *International Journal of Community Music, 5*(3), 237–252.

Casellas, J. P., & Ibarra, J. D. (2012). Changing political landscapes for Latinos in
    America. *Journal of Hispanic Higher Education, 11*(3), 234–258.

Cavallaro, F. (2010). From trilingualism to monolingualism? Sicilian-Italians in Aus-
    tralia. *International Journal of the Sociology of Language, 206*, 109–154.

Cavanaugh, J. C. (1997). *Adult development and aging* (3rd Ed.). Brooks/Cole.

CC6 News Night. (2016, 11 August). Gross disrespect to 2016 Grenada Panorama. https://www.youtube.com/watch?v=3X23SQ5jB4s

CC6 News Night. (2016, 15 September). The steel pan jam and rhythm section competition. https://www.facebook.com/CC6FlowGrenada/videos/666402203523641

Cepeda, M. S., Carr, D B., Lau, J., & Alvarez, H. (2006). Music for pain relief. *Cochrane Database Systematic Review*, 2, CD004843.

Chadwick, S. (2011). Lift every voice and sing: Constructing community through culturally relevant pedagogy in the University of Illinois Black Chorus. *International Journal of Community Music*, 4(2), 147–162. https://doi.org/10.1386/ijcm.4.2.147_1

Chambers, H. (2013). Music and looked after children. In C. Harrison & P. Mullen (Eds.), *Reaching out* (pp. 67–79). Music Mark.

Chan, W., & Chunn, D. (2014). *Racialization, crime, and criminal justice in Canada*, xiii–xix, 10–24, 27–31. University of Toronto Press.

Chand, M. L., & Levitin, D. J. (2013). The neurochemistry of music. *Trends in Cognitive Sciences*, 17(4), 179–193. doi:10.1016/j.tics.2013.02.007

Charuvastra, A., & Cloitre, M. (2008). Social bonds and posttraumatic stress disorder. *Annual Review of Psychology*, 59, 301–328.

Chase, S. E. (2011). Narrative inquiry: Still a field in the making. In N. K. Denzin & Y. S. Lincoln (Eds.), *The Sage handbook of qualitative research*, (4th Ed.) (pp. 421–432). Sage.

Chevalier, J. M., & Buckles, D. J. (2013). *Participatory action research: Theory and methods for engaged inquiry*. Routledge.

Choi, J., Kushner, K. E., Mill, J., & Lai, D. W. L. (2014). The experience of Korean immigrant women adjusting to Canadian society. *Journal of Cross-Cultural Gerontology*, 29(3), 277–297.

Choi, N. (2001). Diversity within diversity: Research and social work practice issues with Asian American elders. *Journal of Human Behavior in the Social Environment*, 3(3–4), 301–319.

Christmas, R. (2012). The people are the police: Building trust with Aboriginal communities in contemporary Canadian society. *Canadian Public Administration*, 55(3), 451–470.

Chung, S., & Yung, Y. (2014). Age norms for older adults among Koreans: Perceptions and influencing factors. *Ageing and Society*, 34(8), 1335–1355.

Clair, A.A. (1996). Alert responses to singing stimuli in institutionalized persons with late stage dementia. *Journal of Music Therapy* 33, 234–47.

Clandinin, D. J., & Connelly, F. M. (2000). *Narrative inquiry: Experience and story in qualitative research*. Jossey-Bass.

Clandinin, D. J., & Rosiek, J. (2007). Mapping a landscape of narrative inquiry: Borderland spaces and tensions. In D. J. Clandinin (Ed.), *Handbook of narrative inquiry: Mapping a methodology* (pp. 35–75). Sage.

Clements-Cortes, A. (2015). Singing for health connection and care. *Music and Medicine*, 7(4), 13–23.

Clift, S., Hancox, G., Morrison, I., Hess, B., Kreutz, G., & Stewart, D. (2010). Choral singing and psychological wellbeing: Quantitative and qualitative findings from

English choirs in a cross-national survey. *Journal of Applied Arts and Health, 1*(1), 19–34.

Cline, D. E. (2012). Community music education partnerships for social change: Six unique adaptations of *El Sistema* in the United States of America. Unpublished MMus. thesis, University of Cincinnati.

Clyne, M., & Kipps, S. (2006). Australia's community languages. *International Journal of the Sociology of Language, 180*, 7–21.

Coates, R. (2012). Accommodating band students with visual impairments. *Music Educators Journal, 99*, 60–66.

Cocklin, C., & Alston, M. (2003). *Community Sustainability in Rural Australia: A Question of Capital.* Wagga Wagga, Australia: Centre for Rural Social Research, Charles Sturt University.

Coffman, D. (2002). Music and quality of life in older adults. *Psychomusicology, 18*(1–2), 76–88.

Coffman, D. (2006). Community musicians and music educators: Minding the gap. In *Creating partnerships, making links, and promoting change: Proceedings from the 2006 seminar of the Commission for Community Music Activity*, 44–52.

Coffman, D. D. (2008). Survey of New Horizons International Music Association musicians. *International Journal of Community Music, 1*(3), 375–390. doi:10.1386/ijcm.1.3.375_1

Coffman, D. D. (2009). Learning from our elders: Survey of new horizons international music association band and orchestra directors. *International Journal of Community Music, 2*(2–3), 227–240.

Coffman, D. D. (2013). Community music ensembles. In C. H. Garrett (Ed.) *The Grove Dictionary of American music,* Vol. 2 (2nd Ed.) (pp. 366–367). Oxford University Press.

Coffman, D. D., & Adamek, M. (1999). The contributions of wind band participation to quality of life of senior adults. *Music Therapy Perspectives, 17*(1), 27–31. doi:10.1093/mtp/17.1.27

Coffman, D. D., & Higgins, L. (2012). Community music ensembles. In G. E. McPherson & G. E. Welch (Eds.), *The Oxford handbook of music education* (pp. 844–859). Oxford University Press. doi:10.1093/oxfordhb/9780199730810.013.0051

Coffman, D. D., & Levy, K. M. (1997). Senior adult bands: Music's new horizon. *Music Educators Journal, 84*(3), 17–22. http://www.jstor.org/stable/3399051

Coffman, D. D., & Schilf, P. (1998). Band instrument gender associations by senior citizen musicians. *Southeastern Journal of Music Education, 10*, 212–221.

Cohen, C. (2015). Music: A universal language? In O. Urbain (Ed.), *Music and conflict transformation: Harmonies and dissonance in geopolitics* [2008] (pp. 26–39). I.B. Tauris.

Cohen, G. D. (2000). *The creative age: Awakening the human potential in the second half of life.* HarperCollins.

Cohen, G. D., Perlstein, S., Chapline, J., Kelly, J., Firth, K. M., & Simmens, S. (2006). The impact of professionally conducted cultural programs on the physical health, mental health, and social functioning of older adults. *The Gerontologist, 46*(6), 726–734.

Cohen, L., Manion, L., & Morrison, K. (2011). *Research methods in education* (7th ed.). Routledge.

Cohen, M. (2007). *Christopher Small's concept of musicking: Toward a theory of choral singing pedagogy for prison contexts.* (Doctoral dissertation). ProQuest 3277678

Cohen, M. L. (2010). Select musical programs and restorative practices in prisons across the US and the UK. In Coffman, D. D. (Ed.), *Proceedings from the International Society for Music Education 2010 Seminar of the Commission for Community Music Activity* (81–86).

Cole, N. L. (2018, 22 June). How Émile Durkheim made his mark on sociology. https://www.thoughtco.com/emile-durkheim-relevance-to-sociology-today-3026482

Collins, Anita. "The Benefits of Music Education." https://www.ted.com/talks/anita_collins_the_benefits_of_music_education?language=en

Collins Online English Dictionary. (2019). s.v. "Social Capital." https://www.collins dictionary.com/dictionary/english

Comack, E. (2012). *Racialized policing: Aboriginal people's encounters with the police.* Fernwood.

Conway, C., & Hodgman, T. M. (2008). College and community choir member experiences in a collaborative intergenerational performance project. *Journal of Research in Music Education, 56*(1), 220–237.

Coppi, A. (2016). Music education, legality, and social inclusion in Italy. International Conference on Arts and Humanities: Educating for change. Conference Selected Proceedings, 35-55.

Coppi, A. (2017). *Community music: nuovi orientamenti pedagogici.* FrancoAngeli.

Cort, R. W., Field, T., Nolin, M., Sheane-Duncan, P. (Producers) & Herek, S. (Director). (1995). *Mr. Holland's Opus* [Motion Picture]. United States: Hollywood Pictures, Interscope Communications, & PolyGram Filmed Entertainwment.

Cox, F. (May 2013). Trauma. *British Journal of Pain, 7*(2), 65.

Cranton, P. (2002). Teaching for transformation. *New directions for adult and continuing education, 2002, 93,* 63–72.

Cranton, P. (2016). Understanding and promoting transformative learning (3rd ed.). Stylus.

Creating partnerships, making links, and promoting change. Proceedings from 2006 seminar of the Commission for Community Music Activity. Singapore: National Institute of Education. (44-54)

Creech, A., González-Moreno, P., Lorenzino, L., & Waitman, G. (2016). *El Sistema and Sistema-Inspired programmes: A literature review of research, evaluation, and critical debates.* 2nd ed. Sistema Global.

Creech, A., Hallam, S., McQueen, H., & Varvarigou, M. (2013). The power of music in the lives of older adults. *Research Studies in Music Education, 35*(1), 87–102.

Creech, A., Hallam, S., Varvarigou, M., Gaunt, H., McQueen, H. & Pincas, A. (2014). The role of musical possible selves in supporting subjective well-being in later life. *Music Education Research, 16*(1), 32–49.

Creech, A., & Long, M. (2012). Self-directed and interdependent learning in musical contexts. Paper presented at the Proceedings of the Twenty-fourth International Seminar on Research in Music Education, Thessaloniki, Greece, 8–13 July.

Creswell, J. W. (2007). *Qualitative inquiry and research design*. Sage.

Cresswell, J., & Cresswell, J. D. (2018). *Research design: Qualitative, quantitative, and mixed methods approaches*. Sage.

Croom, A. M. (2015). Music practice and participation for psychological well-being: A review of how music influences positive emotion, engagement, relationships, meaning, and accomplishment. *Musicae Scientiae*, 19(1), 44–64.

Cross, I. (1999). Is music the most important thing we ever did? Music, development, and evolution. In Yi, S. W. (Ed.), *Music, Mind, and Science*. http://www-personal .mus.cam.ac.uk/~ic108/PDF/IRMCMMS98.pdf

Cross, I. (2001). Music, mind, and evolution. *Psychology of Music*, 29(1), 95–102.

Cross, I. (2014). Music and communication in music psychology. *Psychology of Music*, 42(6), 809–819. http://doi.org/10.1177/0305735614543968

Crossick, G., & Kaszynska, P. (2016). *Understanding the value of arts and culture: The AHRC cultural value report*. Arts and Humanities Research Council. http://www .ahrc.ac.uk/documents/publications/cultural-value-project-final-report

Crozier, W. R. (1997). Music and social influence. In D. J. Hargreaves & A. North (Eds.), *The social psychology of music*. Oxford University Press.

Csikszentmihalyi, M. (1990). *FLOW: The psychology of optimal experience*. Harper and Row.

Csikszentmihalyi, M., & Larson, R. (1984). *Being adolescent: Conflict and growth in the teenage years*. Basic Books.

Cullinan, N. (2008). Double exposure: Robert Rauschenberg's and Cy Twombly's Roman Holiday. *Burlington Magazine*, 460–470.

Cunha, M. I. (1994). *Malhas que a reclusão tece. Questões de identidade numa prisão feminina*. Gabinete de Estudos Jurido-Sociais. http://repositorium.sdum.uminho .pt/handle/1822/5237.

Cunha, M. I. (2008). Disciplina, controlo, segurança. No rasto contemporâneo de Foucault. In Catarina Frois (Ed.), *A sociedade vigilante. Ensaios sobre privacidade, identificação e vigilância* (pp. 67–81). Imprensa de Ciências Sociais.

Custodero, L. A. (2002). The musical lives of young children: Inviting, seeking, initiating. *Journal of Zero-to-Three*, 23(1), 4–9.

Custodero, L. A. (2006, February). *"If you listen .."*: Flow experience and educative engagement. Invited address, Cerebral Palsy Greece International Symposium, Athens.

D'Alexander, C. M. (2015). Voices from within: Perceptions of community youth orchestras and music identity from the child musician. Proquest UMI#3704228

Dabback, W. M. (2006). Toward a model of adult music learning as a socially-embedded phenomenon (Order No. 3249214). ProQuest 304917902

Dabback, W. (2007). *Toward a model of adult music learning as a socially-embedded phenomenon* (Unpublished doctoral dissertation). ProQuest 304917902

Dabback, W. M. (2008a). Identity formation through participation in the Rochester New Horizons Band Program. *International Journal of Community Music*, 1(2), 267–286, doi:10.1386/ijcm.1.2.267_1

Dabback, W. M. (2008b). The sociological foundations of identity and learning in the Rochester New Horizons Band. *Sociological Explorations: Proceedings of the*

5th International Symposium on the Sociology of Music Education, ed. B. A. Roberts (pp. 97–110). The Binder's Press.

Dabback, W. M. (2009). Exploring social networks, reciprocity, and trust in a senior adult band. CMA XI: Projects, Perspectives, and Conversations. *Proceedings from the International Society for Music Education (ISME) 2008 seminar of the Commission for Community Music Activity*, ed. D. D. Coffman (pp. 102-111). Printing courtesy of Levinsky College, School of Music Education.

Dale, A., & Onyx, J. (Eds). (2005). *A dynamic balance: Social capital and sustainable community development*. UBC Press.

Daria, J. (2018). Community music on campus: Collaborative research, activist methods, and critical pedagogy in a fandango-based participatory music programme. *International Journal of Community Music, 11*(1), 91–108. https://doi.org/10.1386/ijcm.11.1.91_1

Dark-Freudeman, A., and West, R. L. (2016). Possible selves and self-regulatory beliefs. *International Journal of Aging and Human Development, 82*(2/3), 139–165. doi: 10.1177/0091415015627666

Darrow, A. (2003). Dealing with diversity: The inclusion of students with disabilities in music. *Research Studies in Music Education, 21*(1), 45–57.

Dassa, A., & Amir, D. (2014). The role of singing familiar songs in encouraging conversation among people with middle to late stage Alzheimer's disease. *Journal of Music Therapy, 51*(2), 131–153. doi:10.1093/jmt/thu007

Davidson, J.W., & Faulkner, R. (2010). Meeting in music: The role of singing to harmonise carer and cared for. *Arts & Health, 2*(2), 164–70. https://doi.org/10.1080/17533010903488608

Davidson, J. W., & Bailey, B. A. (2005). Effects of group singing and performance for marginalized and middle-class singers. *Psychology of Music, 33*(3), 269–303.

Davies, A. (2011). Local leadership and rural renewal through Festival Fun: The case of Snowfest. In C. Gibson & J. Connell (Eds.), *Festival places: Revitalising rural Australia* (pp. 61–73). Channel View.

Davis, L., & Shpuniarsky, H. Y. (2010). The spirit of relationships: What we have learned about Indigenous/Non-Indigenous alliances and coalitions. In L. Davis (Ed.), *Alliances: Re/Envisioning Indigenous-non-Indigenous relationships* (pp. 334–348). University of Toronto Press.

Day, A. (2015). Rise up. On *Cheers to the fall* [CD]. Warner Bros./Buskin.

De Michele, M. (2015). Improv and ink: Increasing individual writing fluency with collaborative improv. *International Journal of Education and the Arts, 16*(10). http://www.ijea.org/v16n10

Deane, K., & Mullen, P. (2018). Strategic working with children and young people in challenging circumstances. in B.-L. Bartleet & L. Higgins (Eds.), *The Oxford handbook of community music* (pp. 177–194). Oxford University Press.

Deane, K., Holford, A., Hunter, R,. & Mullen, P. (2015). *The power of equality 2: Final evaluation of Youth Music's musical inclusion programme 2013–2015.* Sound Sense and Youth Music.

Deane, K., Holford, A., Hunter, R., & Mullen, P. (2014). *The power of equality: Interim evaluation of musical inclusion.* Sound Sense and Youth Music.

Deane, K., Hunter, R., & Mullen, P. (2011). *Move on up: An evaluation of youth music mentors.* http://network.youthmusic.org.uk/sites/default/files/research/MoveOn Up_v02.pdf

Deci, E. L., & Ryan, R. M. (1985). *Intrinsic motivation and self-determination in human behavior.* Plenum.

Deci, E., & Ryan, R. (2000a). Self-determination theory and the facilitation of intrinsic motivation, social development, and wellbeing. *American psychologist, 55*(1), 68–78. https://selfdeterminationtheory.org/SDT/documents/2000_RyanDeci _SDT.pdf

Deci, E., & Ryan, R. (2000b). Intrinsic and extrinsic motivations: Classic definitions and new directions. *Contemporary Educational Psychology, 25,* 54–67. doi:10.1006/ ceps.1999.1020

Deci, E. L., & Ryan, R. M. (2000c). The "what" and "why" of goal pursuits: Human needs and the self-determination of behavior. *Psychological Inquiry, 11*(4), 227–268. https://selfdeterminationtheory.org/SDT/documents/2000_DeciRyan _PIWhatWhy.pdf

Decter, L., & Isaac, J. (2015). Reflections on unsettling narratives of denial. In *The land we are: Artists and writers unsettle the politics of reconciliation* (pp. 96–129). Arbeiter Ring.

Deguara, J. (2019). Young children's drawings: A methodological tool for data analysis. *Journal of Early Childhood Research, 17*(2), 157–174.

Delaney, A. (2015). The intimate simplicity of group singing: A reflection of practice. *The Australian Journal of Music Therapy, 26,* 71–83.

DeNora, T. (1999). Music as a technology of the self. *Poetics, 27,* 31–56.

DeNora, T. (2000). *Music in everyday life.* Cambridge University Press.

Denzin, N. K., & Lincoln, Y. S. (2005). *The Sage handbook of qualitative research* (3rd Ed.). Sage.

Derby, L. (1994). Between state and nation: The Dominican Republic and the U.S. world order. Paper presented at the Latin American Studies Association, 10-12March, Atlanta.

Department for Digital, Culture, Media & Sport. (2016). *The Culture White Paper.* https://www.gov.uk/government/publications/culture-white-paper

Derrida, J. (2000). *Of hospitality: Cultural memory in the present.* (R. Bowlby, Trans.). Stanford University Press.

Devlin, M. (2006). *Inequality and the stereotyping of young people.* The Equality Authority.

Devroop, K. (2012). The social-emotional impact of instrumental music performance on economically disadvantaged South African students. *Music Education Research, 14*(4), 407–416.

Dewey, J. (2008). *Democracy and education: An introduction to the philosophy of education.* Macmillan.

DfE (Department for Education). (2011). *The Importance of Music: A national plan for music education.* DfE. https://www.gov.uk/government/publications/ the-importance-of-music-a-national-plan-for-music-education

Diamond, B. (2016). Resisting containment: The long reach of song at the Truth and Reconciliation Commission on Indian Residential Schools. In D. Robinson & K. Martin (Eds.), *Arts of engagement: Taking aesthetic action in and beyond the Truth and Reconciliation Commission of Canada* (pp. 239–266). Wilfrid Laurier University Press.

Dickason, O., & McNab, D. (2009). *Canada's First Nations: A history of founding peoples from earliest times.* Oxford University Press.

Dickeson, R. (2010). *Prioritizing academic programs and services: Reallocating resources to achieve strategic balance.* Jossey-Bass.

Dies, R., & Teleska, P. (1985). Negative outcomes in psychotherapy. In D. Mays & C. Franks (Eds.), *Negative outcomes in psychotherapy and what to do about it* (pp. 118–142). Springer.

Diggins, G. (2016). *Tuning the eardrums: Listening as a mindful practice.* Friesen Press.

Dillon, L. (2010). *Looked after children and music making: An evidence review.* Youth Music.

Dillon, S., Bartleet, B.-L., & Leong, S. (Eds.). (2012). *International Journal of Community Music. Special Issue: Music in the Asia Pacific Region,* 5(1).

Dimattina, S. (1979). Some priest-sociologist's reflections on the situations of Italians and the Church. *The Australasian Catholic Record,* 56, 22–29.

Dissanayake, E. (2005). Ritual and ritualization: Musical means of conveying and shaping emotion in humans and other animals. In S. Brown & U. Volgsten (Eds.), *Music and manipulation: On the social uses and social control of music* (pp. 31–56). Berghahn Books.

Dissanayake, E. (2008). The arts after Darwin: Does art have an origin and adaptive function? In W. Van Damme and K. Zijilmans (Eds.), *World art studies: Exploring concepts and approaches* (pp. 41–263.) Valiz.

Donadio, G. (2005). Improving health care delivery with the transformational whole person care model. *Holistic Nursing Practice,* 19(2), 74–77.

Donald, E., Stathopoulos, T., & Lorenzino, L. (2012). Adopt or adapt? *El Sistema* as an inspiration for music education in Canada. Paper presented at the 30th International Society for Music Education World Conference, Thessaloniki.

Dorfman, J., & Dammers, R. (2015). Predictors of successful integration of technology into music teaching. *Journal of Technology in Music Learning,* 5(2), 46–59.

Douglas, K. A. (2011). A descriptive analysis of the psychological needs of adults participating in music ensembles: A survey of the new horizon international music association ensemble participants ProQuest 895096383

Downie, J., & Llewellyn, J. (2008) Relational theory and health law and policy. *Health Law Journal, Special Edition,* 193–210.

Dozza, L. (2007). Il Laboratorio come contesto di co-costruzione di specifiche intelligenze. F., Fabbroni, G., La Face (2007). *Educazione Musicale e Formazione.* FrancoAngeli.

Dudley, S. (1996). Judging "By the Beat": Calypso versus Soca. *Ethnomusicology,* 40(2), 269–98. DOI:10.2307/852062.

Dudt, S. (2012). From Seoul to Bonn: A journey through international and European music education policies. In C. Harrison, & S. Hennessy (Eds.), *Listen out: International perspectives on music education* (126–37). NAME.

Duffy, M., & Waitt, G. (2011). Rural festivals and processes of belonging. In C. Gibson & J. Connell (Eds.), *Festival places: Revitalising rural Australia* (pp. 44–60). Channel View.

Dunphy, K. (2009). *Developing and Revitalizing Rural Communities Through Arts and Creativity: Melbourne, Australia.* Creative City Network of Canada. http://www .culturaldevelopment.net.au/downloads/RuralCommunities_KimDunphy.pdf

Dupuis, J. K., & Ferguson, K. (2016). Fostering remembrance and reconciliation through an arts-based response. *In education, 22*(1), 127–147. http://www .ineducation.ca

Edwards, P. (2001). *One dead Indian: The premier, the police, and the Ipperwash Crisis.* Stoddart.

El Sistema programs worldwide (2018). In *Sistema Global.* from http://sistemaglobal .org/el-sistema-global-program-directory

Elliott, D. (2008). Music for citizenship: A commentary on Paul Woodford's *Democracy and Music Education: Liberalism, Ethics, and the Politics of Practice. Action, Criticism, and Theory for Music Education, 7*(1), 45–73.

Elliott, D., Higgins, L., & Veblen, K. (Eds.). (2008). *International Journal of Community Music, 1*(1), 3–4.

Elliott, D., Silverman, M., & Bowman, W. (2016). *Artistic citizenship: Artistry, social responsibility, and ethical praxis* (1st Ed.). Oxford University Press.

Elliott, D. J. (1995). *Music matters: A new philosophy of music education.* Oxford University Press.

Elliott, D. J. (1998). *Community music and postmodernity.* Unpublished conference presentation at the International Society for Music Education's Community Music Activities Commission Seminar, Durban.

Elliott, D. J., and Veblen, K. (2000). Community music: Foundations and practices. In *Seminar Reader, Lived Music. Shared Music Making: Community Music in the New Millennium.* CCMA, 104–13.

Elliott, J. (2005). *Using narrative in social research: Qualitative and quantitative approaches.* Sage.

Emami, A., Torres, S., Lipson, J. G., & Ekman, S. D. L. (2000). An ethnographic study of a day care center for Iranian immigrant seniors. *Western Journal of Nursing Research, 22*(2), 169–188.

Empathy. (2017). In Merriam-Webster.com. https://www.merriam-webster.com/ dictionary/empathy

Epstein, R., & Street, R. (2011). The values and value of patient-centred care. *Annals of Family Medicine, 9*, 100-103. doi:10.1370/afm.1239

Erkkilä, J., Punkanen, M., Fachner, J., Ala-Ruona, E., Pöntiö, I., Tervaniemi, M., et al. (2011). Individual music therapy for depression: Randomised controlled trial. *British Journal of Psychiatry, 199*, 132–139.

Ermine, W. (2007). The ethical space of engagement. *Indigenous Law Journal, 6*(1), 193–203.

Ernst, R. E., & Emmons, S. (1992). New Horizons for Senior Adults: Roy E. Ernst and Scott Emmons recount the creation and first year of the New Horizons Band, made up of senior adults with little or no instrument experience. *Music Educators Journal, 79*(4), 30–34. doi:10.2307/3398527

Erstad, O., & Sefton-Green, J. (Eds.). (2013). *Identity, community, and learning lives in the digital age.* Cambridge University Press.

Etherington, K. (2004) *Becoming a reflexive researcher: Using our selves in research.* Jessica Kingsley.

European Institute for Gender Equality. (n.d.). *Gender Roles.* https://eige.europa.eu/rdc/thesaurus/terms/1209

European Music Council. (2012). *The Bonn declaration for music education in Europe.* European Music Council. https://www.emc-imc.org/cultural-policy/declaration-on-music-education/bonn-declaration

Evans, W. R., & Carson, C. M. (2005). A social capital explanation of the relationship between functional diversity and group performance. *Team Performance Management, 11*(7–8), 302–315.

Everitt, A. (1997). *Joining in: An investigation into participatory music.* Calouste Gulbenkian Foundation.

Evers, S., & Suhr, B. (2000). Changes of the neurotransmitter serotonin but not of hormones during short time music perception. *European Archives of Psychiatry and Clinical Neuroscience, 250*(3), 144–147.

Faed, P., Murphy, S., & Nolledo, R. (2017, November). Child homelessness and trauma: The connections and a call to action. https://www.first5la.org/files/ChildHomelessnessTrauma.pdf

Farokhi, M., & Hashemi, M. (2011). The analysis of children's drawings: Social, emotional, physical, and psychological aspects. *Procedia – Social and Behavioral Sciences, 30*, 2219–2224.

Faulkner, K. A., Cauley, J. A., Zmuda, J. M., Griffin, J. M., & Nevitt, M. C. (2003). Is social integration associated with the risk of falling in older community-dwelling women? *The Journals of Gerontology. Series A, Biological Sciences and Medical Sciences, 58*, M954–M959.

Fautley, M., & Whittaker, A. (2017). *Key data on music education hubs 2016.* Faculty of Health, Education and Life Sciences, Birmingham City University. http://www.artscouncil.org.uk/sites/default/files/download-file/key_data_music_report.pdf 3/11/2017

Feo, R., & Kitson, A. (2016). Promoting patient-centred fundamental care in acute healthcare systems. *International Journal of Nursing Studies, 57* (May), 1–11.

Ferguson, S. (2017, 15 August). Keeping an eye on the people's business: Panorama 2017 and the "capture of public spaces." *NOW Grenada.* http://www.nowgrenada.com/2017/08/keeping-an-eye-on-the-peoples-business-panorama-2017-and-the-capture-of-public-spaces

Fernández-Ballesteros, R., Caprara, M., Schettini, R., Bustillos, A., Mendoza-Nunez, V., Orosa, T., and Zamarrón, M. D. (2013). Effects of university programs for older adults: Changes in cultural and group stereotype, self-perception of aging, and emotional balance. *Educational Gerontology, 39*(2), 119–131.

Finke, C., Esfahani, N. E., & Plonger, C. J. (2012). Preservation of musical memory in an amnesic professional cellist. *Current Biology, 22*(15), 591–592.

First Peoples of Australia in the creative arts: A framework to support respectful and mutually beneficial service learning partnership in the creative arts. *Griffith Experts*, Griffith University. https://experts.griffith.edu.au/publication/ne29103216a701bb940828ce8445ba561

Fischer, T., & Kugemann, W. (2008). Intergenerational learning in Europe – policies, programmes and practical guidance. FIM-NewLearning, University of Erlangen-Nurenberg, Germany, EAGLE Consortium.

Fisher, J. C., & Wolf, M. A. (2000). Older adult learning. In A. L. Wilson & E. R. Hayes (Eds.), *The handbook of adult and continuing education* (pp. 480–492). Jossey-Bass.

Fitzgerald, P. (1995). *The blue flower*. Mariner Books.

Flynn, P., & Johnston, T. (2016). *Possible selves in music: Summary of a research partnership between music generation and St Patrick's College, Drumcondra*. http://www.musicgeneration.ie/content/files/Possible_Selves_in_Music_summary_report_2016.pdf

Foner, Eric (1994). "The Meaning of Freedom in the Age of Emancipation." Presidential Address, 1994. *Journal of American History, 81*(2), p435–60.

Forlin, C. (2004). Promoting inclusivity in Western Australian schools. *International Journal of Inclusive Education, 8*(2), 185–202. https://doi.org/10.1080/1360311032000158042

Foster, B., & Bartel, L. (2016). Understanding music care in Canadian facility-based long-term care. *Music Med, 8*(1), 29–35.

Foster, B., & Pearson, S. (2016). Becoming music care advocates. *Music Care Training, Level 3*. Room 217 Foundation.

Foster, B., Pearson, S., & Berends, A. (2016). Ten domains of music care: A framework for delivering music in Canadian healthcare settings. *Music and Medicine, 8*(4), 199–206.

Foucault, M. (1995). *Discipline and Punish: The Birth of the Prison*. Vintage Books.

Fratianne, R., Prensner, J., Huston, M., Super, D., Yowler, C., & Standley, J. (2001). The effect of music-based imagery and musical alternate engagement on the burn debridement process. *Journal of Burn Care and Rehabilitation, 22*(1), 47–53.

Frazier, L., Johnson, P., Gonzalez, G., & Kafka, C. (2002). Psychosocial influences on possible selves: A comparison of three cohorts of older adults. *International Journal of Behavioral Development, 26*(4), 308–317. doi: 10.1080/01650250143000184

Freeman, J. (2015). Providing whole-person care: Integrating behaviour health into primary care. *North Carolina Medical Journal, 76*(1), 24–25.

Freer, P. K., & Bennett, D. (2012). Developing musical and educational identities in university music students. *Music Education Research, 14*(3), 265–284. doi:10.1080/14613808.2012.712507

Freire, P. (1998). *Pedagogy of Freedom: Ethics, Democracy, and Civic Courage*. Rowman and Littlefield.

Frideres, J. S. (2011). *First Nations in the Twenty-First Century*. Oxford University Press.

Frith, S. (1996). Music and identity. In S. Hall & P. du Gay (Eds.), *Questions of cultural identity* (pp. 108–127). Sage.

Frith, S. (2000). The discourse of world music. In G. Born & D. Hesmondhalgh (Eds.), *Western music and its others: Difference, representation, and appropriation in music* (pp. 305–322). University of California Press.

Frühholz, S., Trost, W., and Grandjean, D. (2014). The role of the medial temporal limbic system in processing emotions in voice and music. *Progress in Neurobiology*, *123*, 1–17.

Fukui, H., & Yamashita, M. (2003) The effects of music and visual stress on testosterone and cortisol in men and women. *Neuroendocrinology Letters*, *24*(3–4), 173–180.

Gall, M. (2013). Trainee teachers' perceptions: Factors that constrain the use of music technology in teaching placements. *Journal of Music, Technology, and Education*, *6*(1), 5–27.

Gallaugher, A. (1991). *From Trinidad to Toronto: Calypso as a Way of Life*. (MA thesis), University of Toronto.

Gangrade, A. (2012). The effect of music on the production of neurotransmitters, hormones, cytokines, and peptides: A review. *Music and Medicine*, *4*(1), 40–43.

Gardner, H. (1993). *Multiple Intelligences: The Theory in Practice*. Basic Books.

Garofolo, R. (2011). Not your parents' marching bands: The history of HONK!, pedagogy, and music education. *International Journal of Community Music*, *4*(3), 221–236. https://doi.org/10.1386/ijcm.4.3.221_1

Garrett, S. (2010). The role of community music in helping disadvantaged young people in South Wales to confront social exclusion. *International Journal of Community Music*, *3*(3), 371–377. https://doi.org/10.1386/ijcm.3.3.371_1

Garrido, S., & Davidson, J. (2013). Music and mood regulation: A historical enquiry into individual differences and musical prescriptions through the ages. *Australian Journal of Music Therapy*, *24*, 89.

Gergen, K. J. (2009). *Relational being*. Oxford University Press.

Ghanbari, S. (2015). Learning across disciplines: A collective case study of two university programs that integrate the arts with STEM. *International Journal of Education and the Arts*, *16*(7). www.ijea.org/v16n7.

Gibson, C., & Stewart, A. (2009). *Reinventing rural places: The extent and impact of festivals in rural and regional Australia*. University of Wollongong.

Giddens, A. (1991). *Modernity and self-identity*. Stanford University Press.

Gilbertson, M. W., Shenton, M. E., Ciszewski, A., Kasai, K., Lasko, N. B., Orr, S. P., & Pitman, R. K. (2002). Smaller hippocampal volume predicts pathologic vulnerability to psychological trauma. *Nature Neuroscience*, *5*, 1242–1247.

Gillard, J. (2011). Gillard laments treatment of "forgotten" veterans. (2011, 25 April). ABC News. http://www.abc.net.au/news/2011-04-24/gillard-laments-treatment-of-forgotten-veterans/2604692

Gillard, J. (2011, 19 August). PM notes "shameful" treatment of Viet vets. *The Weekend Australian*. http://www.theaustralian.com.au/national-affairs/pm-notes-shameful-treatment-of-viet-vets/news-story/46ece16972e3861c8b99b8160967b435?sv=16bf84105101275a332e4d9867c2b2c6

Gittler, J. (1952). *Social dynamics.* McGraw-Hill.

Glazer, N., & Moynihan, D. P. (1963). *Beyond the melting pot: The Negroes, Puerto Ricans, Jews, Italians, and Irish of New York City.* Harvard University Press.

Goldman-Segall, R. (1998). *Points of viewing children's thinking: A digital ethnographer's journey.* Lawrence Erlbaum.

Goldring, L. (1992). Diversity and community in transnational migration: A comparative study of two Mexico–U.S. migrant communities. Doctoral dissertation, Cornell University, Ithaca.

Goleman, D. (1998). *Working with Emotional Intelligence.* Bloomsbury.

Good, M., Anderson, G. C., Stanton-Hicks, M., Grass, J. A., & Makii, M. (2002). Relaxation and music reduce pain after gynecologic surgery. *Pain Management Nursing, 3*(2), 61–70.

Good, M., Stanton-Hicks, M., Grass, J., Anderson, G., Lai, H., Roykulcharoen, V., & Adler, P. (2001). Relaxation and music to reduce postsurgical pain. *Journal of Advanced Nursing, 33*(2), 208–15.

Goodley, D. (2014). *Dis/ability studies: Theorising disablism and ableism.* Routledge.

Goodman, D. J. (2011). *Promoting diversity and social justice: Educating people from privileged groups.* Routledge.

Goodrich, A. (2013). Health musicing in a community orchestra. *International Journal of Community Music, 6*(1), 45–63. https://doi.org/10.1386/ijcm.6.1.45_1

Gordon, E. E. (1984). *Learning sequences in music: Skill, content, and patterns.* GIA.

Gordon, Edwin E. (1997). *A music learning theory for newborn and young children.* GIA.

Govias, J. (2010). Inside *El Sistema. Strad,* 121(1445), 50–54.

Govias, J. (2012). In (partial) defense of a *Sistema* hater [Blog post]. http://jonathan govias.com/2012/07/19/in-partial-defense-of-a-sistema-hater

Govias, J. (2013). Hard to reach, harder to let go: A practice of social action through music inspired by Venezuela's *El Sistema.* In C. Harrison & P. Mullen (Eds.), *Reading out: Music education with hard to reach children and young people* (pp. 32–40). Music Mark.

Govias, J. (2014). The challenges of Sistema. *Canadian Music Educator,* 56(1), 27.

Grafton Jacaranda Festival. (2017). History. 2017 from https://jacarandafestival.com/history

Graham, S., & Connell, J. (2006). Nurturing relationships: The gardens of Greek and Vietnamese migrants in Marrickville, Sydney. *Australian Geographer,* 37(3), 375–393.

Grainger, P. (1930). Community music. *Playground,* 24, 235–236.

Green, J., & Thorogood, N. (2009). *Qualitative methods for health research* (2nd Ed.). Sage.

Green, L. (1997). *Music, gender, education.* Cambridge University Press.

Green, L. (2002). *How popular musicians learn: A way ahead for music education.* Ashgate.

Greene, M. (2000) *Releasing the imagination: Essays on education, the arts, and social change.* Jossey-Bass.

Green, L. (2008). *Music on deaf ears: Musical meaning, ideology, and education* [1998]. Manchester University Press.

Greher, G. R. (2017). Technology in music teacher education and the enigma of invisibility. In S. A. Ruthmann & R. Mantie (Eds.), *The Oxford handbook of technology and music education, Vol. 1* (pp. 539–544). Oxford University Press.

Greher, G. R., Hillier, A., Dougherty, M., & Poto, N. (2010). SoundScape: An interdisciplinary music intervention for adolescents and young adults on the autism spectrum. *International Journal of Education and the Arts, 11*(9).

Grenada Broadcasting Network. (2016, 2 June). Calypso Tent Open 01.06.16. https://www.youtube.com/watch?v=XUQHk5-hLtI

Grenfell, M. J. (Ed.). (2012). *Pierre Bourdieu: Key concepts* (2nd Ed.). Routledge.

Griffith, M. J. (2006). Personality traits and musical interests of adult learners in an instrumental music program. ProQuest 305299594

Griffiths, M. (2014). Music education must move beyond classical and become more inclusive. *The Guardian.* https://www. theguardian.com/culture-professionals -network/culture-professionals-blog/2014/aug/11/music-education-inclusive -funding-hubs 1/11/2017

Gromko, J. E., & Cohen, M. L. (2011). Choir in prison: The relationship of psychological needs to perceptions of meaning in music. In P. Madura (Ed.), *Advances in social psychology and music education research* (pp. 107–114). SEMPRE: Society for Education, Music, and Psychology Research.

Gruzelier, J. (2007). Moshpit menace and masculine mayhem. In F. Jarman-Ivens (Ed.). *Oh boy! Masculinities and popular music* (pp. 59–75). Routledge.

Guarnizo, L. E. (1994). Los Dominicanyorks: The making of a binational society. *The Annals of the American Academy of Political and Social Science, 533*(1), 70–86.

A Guide to working with young people who are refugees. (2000). Victorian Foundation for Survivors of Torture.

Gullette, M. M. (1997). *Declining to decline: Cultural combat and the politics of the midlife.* University of Virginia Press.

Gullette, M. M. (2011). *Agewise: Fighting the new ageism in America.* University of Chicago Press.

Gupta, A., & Ferguson, J. (1992). Beyond "culture": Space, identity, and the politics of difference. *Cultural Anthropology, 7*(1), 6–23.

Gurvits, T. V., et al. (1996). Magnetic resonance imaging study of hippocampal volume in chronic, combat-related post-traumatic stress disorder. *Biological Psychiatry, 40,* 1091–1099.

Hadley, S. (2003). *Psychodynamic music therapy: Case studies.* Barcelona.

Hall, C. B., Lipton, R. B., Sliwinski, M., Katz, M. J., Derby, C. A., & Verghese, J. (2009). Cognitive activities delay onset of memory decline in persons who develop dementia. *Neurology, 73*(5), 356–361. doi:10.1212/WNL.0b013e3181b04ae3

Hall, H. (2012). Movement and music as elements in overcoming trauma: Leisure as a therapeutic coping strategy. *PsycEXTRA Dataset.*

Hall, S. (1992). The question of cultural identity. In S. Hall, D. Held, & T. McGrew (Eds.), *Modernity and its futures* (pp. 274–316). The Open University.

Hallam, S. (2010). The power of music: Its impact on the intellectual, social and personal development of children and young people. *International Journal of Music Education, 28*(3), 269–289.

Hallam, S. (2015). *The power of music: A research synthesis of the impact of actively making music on the intellectual, social and personal development of children and young people.* International Music Education Research Centre.

Hallam, S., Creech, A., Varvarigou, M., McQueen, H., & Gaunt, H. (2014). Does active engagement in community music support the well-being of older people? *Arts and Health, 6*(2), 101–116.

Hammel, A. M. (2001). Preparation for teaching special learners: Twenty years of practice. *Journal of Music Teacher Education, 11*(1), 5–11.

Hammerstein, O. (Lyricist), & Rodgers, R. (Composer). (1945). *You'll never walk alone.* For *Carousel* [Broadway Musical]. http://www.songfacts.com/detail .php?lyrics=7300

Hansen, E., Walters, J., & Howes, F. (2016). Whole person care, patient-centred care, and clinical practice guidelines in general practice. *Health Sociology Review, 25*(2), 157–170.

Hanser, S. B., Butterfield-Whitcomb, J., Kawata, M., & Collins, B. E. (2011). Home-based music strategies with individuals who have dementia and their family caregivers. *Journal of Music Therapy, 48*(1), 2–27.

Hardy, C. (2008a). Hysteresis. In M. J. Grenfell, *Pierre Bourdieu: Key concepts* (2nd Ed.) (pp. 126–144). Routledge.

Hardy, C. (2008b). Social space. In M. Grenfell, *Pierre Bourdieu; Key concepts* (pp. 229–249). Routledge.

Hargreaves, D. J., MacDonald, R., & Miell, D. (2012). Musical identities mediate musical development. In G. E. McPherson & G. F. Welch (Eds.), *The Oxford handbook of music education,* Vol. 1. doi:10.1093/oxfordhb/9780199730810.013.0008

Harkins, D. (2014). *Beyond the campus: Building a sustainable university community partnership.* Information Age Publishing.

Harrison, C., & and Mullen, P. (Eds.). (2013). *Reaching out: Music education with "hard to reach" children and young people.* Music Mark.

Harvard Program for Refugee Trauma. (2013). Global mental health: Trauma and recovery.

Harwood, I., & Pines, M. (1998). Self-experiences in group: Intersubjective and self-psychological pathways to human understanding. International Library of Group Analysis, No. 4. Jessica Kingsley.

Hase, S., & Kenyon, C. (2001). Moving from andragogy to heutagogy: Implications for VET. http://pandora.nla.gov.au/nph-wb/20010220130000/http://ultibase .rmit.edu.au/Articles/dec00/hase2.htm

Hase, S., & Kenyon, C. (2007). Heutagogy: A child of complexity theory. *Complicity: An International Journal of Complexity and Education, 4*(1), 111–118. https:// journals.library.ualberta.ca complicity/ index.php/ complicity/ article/ view/ 8766/7086

Hassan, N. (2017). Re-voicing: Community choir participation as a medium for identity formation amongst people with learning disabilities. *International Journal of Community Music, 10*(2), 207–225. https://doi.org/10.1386/ijcm.10.2.207_1

Hawkins, S. (2007). [Un]Justified: Gestures of straight-talk in Justin Timberlake's songs. In F. Jarman Ivens (Ed.), *Oh boy! Masculinities and popular music* (pp. 197–212). Routledge.

Hayes, E. M. (2010). *Songs in black and lavender; Race, sexual politics, and women's music*. University of Illinois Press.

Hays, T., & Minichiello, V. (2005a). The contribution of music to quality of life in older people: An Australian qualitative study. *Ageing and Society, 25*(2), 261–278.

Hays, T., & Minichiello, V. (2005b). The meaning of music in the lives of older people: A qualitative study. *Psychology of music, 33*(4), 437–451.

Heines, J. M., Walzer, D. A., Crawford, R. R. M., & Al-Rekabi, F. (2018). Teaching a computer to sing: Integrating computing and music in a middle school, after-school program. *Journal of Computing Sciences in Colleges, 33*(6), 63–75.

Helguera, P. (2011). *Education for socially engaged art: A materials and techniques gand-book*. Jorge Pinto Books.

Helin, C. (2006). *Dances with dependency*. Orca Spirit.

Henley, J., Caulfield, L., Wilson, D., & Wilkinson, D. J. (2012). Good vibrations: Positive change through social music-making. *Music Education Research, 14*(4), 499–520.

Herman, J. (1992) *Trauma and recovery*. Basic Books.

Hess, J. (2014). Radical musicking: Towards a pedagogy of social change. *Music Education Research, 16*(3), 229–250.

Higgins, L. (2007a). Acts of hospitality: The community in community music. *Music Education Research, 9*(2), 281–292.

Higgins, L. (2007b). The impossible future. *Action, Criticism, and Theory for Music Education, 6*(3), 74–96. http://act.maydaygroup.org/articles/Higgins6_3.pdf 30/12/2018

Higgins, L. (2010). Representação de prática: música na comunidade e pesquisa base-ada nas artes. *Revista da ABEM, 23*, 7–14.

Higgins, L. (2002). Towards community music conceptualizations. *Proceedings of the 2002 ISME Commission on Community Music Activity*, http://www.cdime-network .com

Higgins, L. (2012). The community within community music. In G. E. McPherson & G. F. Welch (Eds.), *The Oxford handbook of music education*, Vol. 2 (pp. 104–119). Oxford University Press.

Higgins, L. (2012). *Community music: In theory and in practice*. Oxford University Press.

Higgins, L. (2016). The call, the welcome, and the "yes": Community music and music education. Keynote address to the Centre of Excellence in Music Pedagogy, Laval University, Quebec City. http://yorksj-test.eprints-hosting.org/id/eprint/1390/

Higgins, L. (2020). Rethinking community in community music: The call, the wel-come, and the 'yes.' In B. Jansen (Ed.), *Rethinking community through transdisci-plinary research*. Palgrave Macmillan.

Higgins, L. D. (2006). Boundary-walkers: Contexts and concepts of community music, PhD Dissertation, University of Limerick.

Higgins, L., & Campbell, P. S. (2010) *Free to be musical: Group improvisation in music*. Rowman and Littlefield.

Higgins, L., & Bartleet, B.-L. (2012). The community music facilitator and school music education. In G. E. McPherson & G. F. Welch (Eds.), *The Oxford handbook of music education*, Vol. (pp. 495–511). Oxford University Press.

Higgins, L., & Bartleet, B.-L. (Eds.). (2017). *The Oxford handbook of community music*. Oxford University Press.

Higgins, L. and Willingham, L. (2017), *Engaging in community music: An introduction*. Routledge.

Higham, B. (2014). Community music questioned. *Sounding Board 2014*, (2), 9–11.

Higham, B., & McKay, G. (2011). *Community music: History and current practice, its constructions of 'community', digital turns, and future soundings: An Arts and Humanities Research Council research review*. http://www.ahrc.ac.uk/Funding-Opportunities/Research-funding/Connected-Communities/Scoping-studies-and-reviews/Documents/Community%20Music%20-%20History%20and%20Current%20Practice.pdf 28/8/2014

Hill, B. (2016). Sociocultural work and community music in Germany. *International Journal of Community Music*, 9(1), 7–21. https://doi.org/10.1386/ijcm.9.1.7_1

Hillier, A., Greher, G. R., Poto, N., & Dougherty, M. (2012). Positive outcomes following participation in a music intervention for adolescents and young adults on the autism spectrum. *Psychology of Music*, 40(2). 201–215.

Hillier, A., Greher, G. R., Queenan, A., Marshall, S. H., & Kopec, J. (2015). Music, technology and adolescents with autism spectrum disorders: The effectiveness of the touch screen interface. *Music Education Research,18*(3), 269–82.

Hillman, S. (2002). Participatory singing for older people: A perception of benefit. *Health Education*, 102(4), 163–171. doi.org/10.1108/09654280210434237

History in the Making: 90 Years at the Saraton (2016, 21 October). https://www.dailyexaminer.com.au/news/history-in-the-making-90-years-at-the-saraton/3103192

Hobsbawm, E. J., & Ranger, T. O. (Eds.). (1983). *The invention of tradition*. Cambridge University Press.

Hodges, D. A. (2000). *Why are we musical? Support for an evolutionary theory of human musicality*. ICMPC Proceedings.

Hoffer, C. (2017). *Introduction to music education*. Waveland Press.

Hoffman, C. (2013). *Making music cooperatively: Using cooperative learning in your active music-making classroom*. GIA.

Hoppmann, C. A., Gerstorf, D., Smith, J., & Klumb, P. L. (2007). Linking possible selves and behavior: Do domain-specific hopes and fears translate into daily activities in very old age? *The Journals of Gerontology Series B: Psychological Sciences and Social Sciences*, 62(2), 104–111.

Horne-Thompson, A., & Grocke, D. (2008). The effect of music therapy on anxiety in patients who are terminally ill. *Journal of Palliative Medicine*, 11(4), 582–590.

Hourigan, R. M. (2009). Preservice music teachers' perceptions of fieldwork experiences in a special needs classroom. *Journal of Research in Music Education*, 57(2), 152–168.

Howell, G. (2013). Finding my place: Examining concepts of community music as a visiting artist in rural East Timor. *International Journal of Community Music*, 6(1), 65–78. https://doi.org/10.1386/ijcm.6.1.65_1

Howell, G., Higgins, L., & Bartleet, B.-L. (2017). *Community music practice: Intervention through facilitation* (pp. 601–618). York St. John University.

Hsu, Y. T., Lu, F. H., & Lin, L. L. (2014). Physical self-concept, possible selves, and well-being among older adults in Taiwan. *Educational Gerontology, 40*(9), 666–675. doi:10.1080/03601277.2013.871868.

Hungerford-Kresser, H., & Amaro-Jiménez, C. (2012). Urban-schooled Latina/os, academic literacies, and identities: (Re)conceptualizing college readiness. *PennGSE. Perspectives on Urban Education, (9)*2. http://www.urbanedjournal.org/archive/volume-9-issue-2-fall-2012/urban-schooled-latinos-academic-literacies-and-identities-reconc

Hunter, J., Micklem, D., & 64 Million Artists. (2016). *Everyday Creativity.* 64 Million Artists. http://64millionartists.com/everyday-creativity-2

Huron, D. (2001). Is music an evolutionary adaptation? *Annals of the New York Academy of Sciences, 930*(1), 43–61.

Huron, D. (2008). *Science & music: lost in music. Nature, 453*(7194), 456–457.

Huron, D., & Margulis, E. H. (2010). *Musical expectancy and thrills.* In P. N. Juslin & J. A. Sloboda (eds.), *Series in affective science. Handbook of music and emotion: Theory, research, applications.* Oxford University Press, 575–604.

Husain, G., Thompson, W. F., & Schellenberg, E. G. (2002). Effects of musical tempo and mode on arousal, mood, and spatial abilities: Re-examination of the "Mozart effect." *Music Perception, 20*(2), 151–171.

Hutchinson, T. (Ed). (2011). *Whole person care: A new paradigm for the 21st century.* Springer Science and Business Media.

Hutchison, J., & Beynon, C. (2014). "It's all about confidence and how you perceive yourself": Musical perceptions of older adults involved in an intergenerational singing program. *Literacy Information and Computer Education Journal, 5*(2), 1556–1565.

Huxley, A. (2009). *The Devils of Loudun* [1952]. New York: Harper Perennial Modern Classics.

Hyde, L. (2007). *The gift: Creativity and the artist in the modern world* [1979]. Random House.

Hyde, L. (2012). *The gift: How the creative spirit transforms the world.* (Main-Canons Imprint Reissue Ed.). Canongate Canons.

Hyyppä, M. T. & Mäki, J. (2003). Social participation and health in a community rich in stock of social capital. *Health Education Research Theory and Practice, 18*(6), 770–779.

Ibarra, H. (1999). Provisional selves: Experimenting with image and identity in professional adaptation. *Administrative Science Quarterly, 44,* 764–792.

Ilari, B. S., Keller, P., Damasio, H., & Habibi, A. (2016). The development of musical skills of underprivileged children over the course of 1 year: A study in the context of an *El Sistema*-inspired program. *Frontiers in Psychology, 7*(62), 1–13.

Indigenous Australian Studies Performance Classroom. In B.-L. Bartleet, D. Bennett, A. Power, & N. Sunderland (Eds.), *Engaging First Peoples in arts-based service learning: Towards respectful and mutually beneficial educational practices* (pp. 213–226). London: Springer International.

Indigenous women. *CBC News: Politics.* http://www.cbc.ca/news/politics/mmiw-4000-hajdu-1.3450237

Insel, T. R. (2010) The challenge of translation in social neuroscience: A review of oxytocin, vasopressin, and affiliative behavior. *Neuron, 65*, 768–779.

Isenberg, C. (2012). Prinum nil nocere (above all do no harm): A direction for the development of music therapy. *Canadian Journal of Music Therapy, 18*(1), 62–78.

Izzo, E., & Carpel Miller, V. (2011). *Second-hand shock: Surviving and overcoming vicarious trauma.* High Conflict Institute Press.

Janata, P. (2009). The neural architecture of music-evoked autobiographical memories. *Cerebral Cortex, 19*(11), 2579–2594.

Janata, P. (2012). Effects of widespread and frequent personalized music programming on agitation and depression in assisted living facility residents with Alzheimer-type dementia. *Music and Medicine, 4*(1), 8–15.

Janata, P., Tomic, S. T., & Haberman, J. M. (2012). Sensorimotor coupling in music and the psychology of the groove. *Journal of Exploratory Psychology, 141*, 54–75. doi:10.1037/a0024208

Jäncke, L. (2009). Music drives brain plasticity. *Biology Reports, 1*, 78.

Janoff-Bulman, R. (1992). *Shattered assumptions: Towards a new psychology of trauma.* Free Press.

Janoff-Bulman, R. (2004). Posttraumatic growth: Three explanatory models. *Psychological Inquiry, 15*, 30–34.

Janoff-Bulman, R., & Frantz, C. (1997). The impact of trauma on meaning: From meaningless world to meaningful life. In M. Power & C. Brewin (Eds.), *The transformation of meaning in psychological therapies* (pp. 91-106). John Wiley.

Jeffreys, B. (2018, January 30). Creative subjects squeezed, say schools. *BBC News.* http://www.bbc.co.uk/news/education-42862996

Jeynes, W. H. (2003). A meta-analysis: The effects of parental involvement on minority children's academic achievement. *Education and Urban Society, 35*(2), 202–218.

Jhally, S., & Kilbourne, J. (2010). *Killing us softly 4: Advertising's image of women.* Media Education Foundation.

Jo, H. E., Veblen, K. K., & Potter, P. J. (2015). Korean immigrant seniors' music making in an ethno-cultural community program in Canada. *Proceedings from the 2014 ISME Community Music Activity Commission Seminar,* Salvador, Brazil.

Jo, H. E., Veblen, K. K., & Potter, P. J. (2018). The effect of a community program on older adults' quality of life and well-being: Canada Enoch Senior's College (CESC) for Korean immigrant seniors. *Canadian Journal on Aging / La Revue Canadienne du Vieillissement, 37*(3), 346–359. doi:10.1017/So714980818000211

Johnson, H. (2012). Drumming in the transcultural imagination: Taiko, Japan, and community music making in Aotearoa/New Zealand. *International Journal of Community Music, 5*(1), 11–26. https://doi.org/10.1386/ijcm.5.1.11_1

Jordan, J. V. (2010). *Relational-cultural therapy.* American Psychological Association.

Jorgensen, E. R. (2008). *The art of teaching music.* Indiana University Press.

Joseph, D. (2014). Community music-making in regional Australia: Creating, improvising, and performing at a festival. *International Journal of Community Music, 7*(3), 379–395. https://doi.org/10.1386/ijcm.7.3.379_1

Josselson, R. (2010). Narrative research. In N. J. Salkind (Ed.), *Encyclopedia of research design* (pp. 869-875). Sage.

Judith, A. (2004). *Eastern body, western mind: Psychology and the chakra system as a path to the self*. Random House Digital.

Juslin, P. N., and Västfjall, D. (2008). Emotional responses to music: The need to consider underlying mechanisms. *Behavioral and Brain Sciences, 31*, 559–621. https://doi:10.1017/S0140525X08005293

Jutras, P. J. (2011). The benefits of New Horizons Band participation as self-reported by selected New Horizons Band members. *Bulletin of the Council for Research in Music Education, 187*, 65–84.

Kabat-Zinn, J. (1995). *Mindfulness meditation*. Nightingale-Conant.

Kabat-Zinn, J. (2011). Why mindfulness matters. In B. Boyce (Ed.), *The mindfulness revolution* (p. 61). Shambhala.

Kakoliris, G. (2015). Jacques Derrida on the ethics of hospitality. In *The ethics of subjectivity* (pp. 144–156). Palgrave Macmillan. doi.org/10.1057/9781137472427_9

Kapyrka, J., & Dockstator, M. (2012). Indigenous knowledges and Western knowledges in environmental education: Acknowledging the tensions for the benefits of a "two-worlds" approach. *Canadian Journal of Environmental Education, 17*, 97–112.

Karlsson H. (2011). How psychotherapy changes the brain – understanding the mechanisms. *Psychiatric Times, 28*(8), 1–5. art nro: 10168/1926705

Karr, A., & Wood, M. (2011). Mindfulness, photography, and living an artistic life. In B. Boyce, (Ed.), *The mindfulness revolution* (p. 15). Shambhala.

Kawaja, J., Sereny, J., & Tierney, K. (Producers), & Southam, T. (Director). (2006). *One dead Indian* [Motion Picture]. Canada: Sienna Films.

Kawase, S., & Ogawa, J. (2020). Group music lessons for children aged 1–3 improve accompanying parents' moods. *Psychology of Music, 48*(3), 410–20.

Keller, M. S., & Barwick, L. (2012). Thoughts on music and migration. In L. Barwick & M. S. Keller (Eds.), *Italy in Australia's musical landscape* (pp. 225–251). Lyrebird Press.

Kelly-McHale, J., & Abril, C. R. (2015). The space between worlds. In C. Benedict, P. Schmidt, G. Spruce, & P. Woodford (Eds.), *The Oxford handbook of social justice in music education* (pp. 156–172). Oxford University Press.

Kelm, M. (1998). *Colonizing bodies: Aboriginal health and healing in British Columbia 1900–50*. UBC Press.

Kennedy, M. C. (2009). The Gettin' Higher Choir: Exploring culture, teaching, and learning in a community chorus. *International Journal of Community Music, 2*(2), 183–200. https://doi.org/10.1386/ijcm.2.2-3.183_1

Kertz-Welzel, A. (2016). Daring to question: A philosophical critique of community music. *Philosophy of Music Education Review, 24*(2), 113-130. Doi:https://doi.org/10.2979/philmusieducrevi.24.2.01

Kester, G. (2005). *Conversation pieces: Community and communication in modern art* (Rev. Ed.). University of California Press.

Khalfa, S., Bella, S. D., Roy, M., Peretz, I., & Lupien, S. J. (2003). Effects of relaxing music on salivary cortisol level after psychological stress. *Annals of the New York Academy of Sciences, 999*, 374–376.

Kim, A. H., Noh, M. S., & Noh, S. (2012). Introduction: Historical context and contemporary research. In S. Noh, A. H. Kim, & M. S. Noh (Eds.), *Korean immigrants* in Canada: Perspectives on migration, integration, and the family (pp. 3–18). University of Toronto Press.

Kim, G., Aguado Loi, C. X., Chiriboga, D. A., Jang, Y., Parmelee, P., & Allen, R. S. (2011). Limited English proficiency as a barrier to mental health service use: A study of Latino and Asian immigrants with psychiatric disorders. *Journal of Psychiatric Research, 45*(1), 104–110.

Kim, G., Chiriboga, D. A., Jang, Y., Lee, S., Huang, C., & Parmelee, P. (2010). Health status of older Asian Americans in California. *Journal of the American Geriatrics Society, 58*, 2003–2008.

Kim, G., Jang, Y., & Chiriboga, D. (2012). Personal views about aging among Korean American older adults: The role of physical health, social network, and acculturation. *Journal of Cross-Cultural Gerontology, 27*(2), 139–148.

Kim, G., Lai, C.Q., Arnett, D.K., Parnell, L.D., Ordovas, J.M., Kim, Y., & Kim, J. (2017). Detection of gene–environment interactions in a family-based population using SCAD. *Statistics in Medicine,* 36(22), 3547–59. https://doi.org/10.1002/sim.7382

Kim, I., Kang, S.Y., & Kim, W. (2018). The Effects of Religious Participation and Familial Assistance on Mental Health among Older Chinese and Korean Immigrants: Multiple Mediator Analyses. *Journal of Cross-Cultural Gerontology 33*, 411–25. https://doi.org/10.1007/s10823-018-9355-7

Kim, J. (2014). The trauma of parting: Endings of music therapy with children with autism spectrum disorders. *Nordic Journal Of Music Therapy, 23*(3), 263–281.

Kim, O. (1999a). Predictors of loneliness in elderly Korean immigrant women living in the United States of America. *Journal of Advanced Nursing, 29*(5), 1082–1088.

Kim, O. (1999b). Mediation effect of social support between ethnic attachment and loneliness in older Korean immigrants. *Research in Nursing and Health, 22*, 169–175.

Kim, Y. S. (2013). Ethnic senior schools, religion, and psychological well-being among older Korean immigrants in the United States: A qualitative study. *Educational Gerontology, 39*, 342–354.

Kim, Y., Bender, K., Ferguson, K. M., Begun, S., & DiNitto, D. M. (2018). Trauma and posttraumatic stress disorder among homeless young adults: The importance of victimization experiences in childhood and once homeless. *Journal of Emotional and Behavioral Disorders, 26*(3), 131–142.

King, H. Kersh, N. Potter, J. & Pitts, S. (2015) Learner-led and boundary free: Learning across contexts. In Hohenstein & H. King (Eds.), *Learning beyond the classroom. British Journal of Educational Psychology.* Monograph Series: Psychological Aspects of Education, No. 11, 39–50.

King, K. L. (2014). *Grade 6-12 string performers' perceived meaning of school and community youth orchestra experience.* Doctoral dissertation. http://holocron.lib.auburn.edu/bitstream/handle/10415/4318/final%20draft%20dissertation%207-25.pdf?sequence=2

King, L., & Hicks, J. (2007). Lost and found possible selves: Goals, development and well-being. *New Directions for Adult and Continuing Education 2007*, 114, 27–37. doi:10.1002/ace.254

King, T. (2013). *The inconvenient Indian: A curious account of Native people in North America*. Anchor Canada.

Kirmayer, L., Simpson, C. & Cargo, M. (2003). Healing traditions: Culture, community, and mental health promotion with Canadian Aboriginal populations. *Australian Psychiatry, 11*(1), 15–23.

Kitwood, T. (1997). *Dementia reconsidered: The person comes first*. Open University Press.

Kitwood, T., & Bredin, K. (1992). Towards a theory of dementia care: Personhood and well-being. *Ageing and Society, 12,* 269–287.

Knight, W. J., & Rickard, N. S. (2001). Relaxing music prevents stress-induced increases in subjective anxiety, systolic blood pressure, and heart rate in healthy males and females. *Journal Of Music Therapy, 38*(4), 254–272.

Knowles, M. S., Holton, E. F., & Swanson, R. A. (2012). *The adult learner: The definitive classic in adult education and human resource development* (7th ed.). Routledge.

Ko, H., Mejía, S., & Hooker, K. (2014). Social possible selves, self-regulation, and social goal progress in older adulthood. *International Journal of Behavioral Development, 38*(3), 219–227. doi:10.1177/0165025413512063

Kochhar, C. A., & Heishman, A. (2010). *Effective collaboration for educating the whole child*. Sage.

Koehn, S. (2009). Negotiating candidacy: Ethnic minority seniors' access to care. *Ageing and Society, 29*(4), 585–808.

Koehn, S. D., Jarvis, P., Sandhra, S., Bains, S., & Addison, M. (2014). Promoting mental health of immigrant seniors in community. *Ethnicity and Inequalities in Health and Social Care, 7*(3), 146–156.

Koelsch, S. (2010) Towards a neural basis of music-evoked emotions. *Trends in Cognitive Sciences, 14,* 131–137.

Koelsch, S., Fritz, T., von Cramon, D. Y., Müller, K., & Friederici, A.D. (2006). Investigating emotion with music: an fMRI study. *Human Brain Mapping, 27*(3), 239–250.

Kohut, H. (1977). *The restoration of the self*. University of Chicago Press.

Koka, B. R., & Prescott, J. E. (2002). Strategic alliances as social capital: A multidimensional view. *Strategic Management Journal, 23,* 795–816.

Kolassa, I. T., & Elbert, T. (2007). Structural and functional neuroplasticity in relation to traumatic stress. *Current Directions in Psychological Science, 16,* 321–325.

Kolawole, H. (1995). Sisters take the rap ... but talk back. In S. Cooper (Ed.), *Girls! Girls! Girls! Essays on women and music* (pp. 8–21). Cassell.

Koopman, C. (2007). Community music as music education: On the educational potential of community music. *International Journal of Music Education, 25*(2), 151–163.

Kouzes, J., & Posner, B. (2017). *Leadership Challenge* (6th ed.). John Wiley and Sons.

Kowal, E. (2015). *Trapped in the gap: Doing good in Indigenous Australia*. Berghahn.

Krabill, J. R. (Ed.). (2011). *Forming Christian habits in post-Christendom: The legacy of Alan and Eleanor Kreider*. Institute of Mennonite Studies.

Kramer, K. M., Cushing, B. S., & Carter, S. (2003). Developmental effects of oxutocin on stress response: Single versus repeated exposure. *Physiology & Behavior, 79*(4–5), 775–782.

Kratus, J. (2007). Music education at the tipping point. *Music Educators Journal, 94*(2), 42–48.

Kraus, N., Slater, J., Thompson, E. C. Hornickel, J., Strait, D. L., Nicol, T., & White-Schwoch, T. (2014). Music enrichment programs improve the neural encoding of speech in at-risk children. *Journal of Neuroscience, 34*(36), 11913–11918. https://doi.org/10.1523/JNEUROSCI.1881-14.2014

Kreutz, G. (2008). Music students' health problems and health-promoting behaviours. *Medical Problems of Performing Artists, 23*(1), 3–11.

Kreutz, G., Bongard, S., Rohrmann, S., Hodapp, V., & Grebe, D. (2004). Effects of choir singing or listening on secretory immunoglobulin A, cortisol, and emotional state. *Journal of Behavioral Medicine, 27*(6), 623–635.

Kreutz, G., Ott, U., Teichmann, D., Osawa, P., & Vaitl, D. (2008). Using music to induce emotions: Influences of musical preference and absorption. *Psychology of music, 36*(1), 101–126.

Krout, R. E. (2007). Music listening to facilitate relaxation and promote wellness: Integrated aspects of our neurophysiological responses to music. *The Arts in Psychotherapy, 34*(2), 134–141.

Krumhansl, C. (1990) *Cognitive foundations of musical pitch.* Oxford University Press.

Kruse, N. B. (2007). *Andragogy and music: Canadian and American models of music learning among adults.* Unpublished doctoral dissertation. ProQuest 304843147

Kruse, N. B. (2009)."An elusive bird": Perceptions of music learning among Canadian and American adults. *International Journal of Community Music, 2*(2–3), 215–225. doi:10.1386/ijcm.2.2-3.215_1

Kubler-Ross, E. (1969). On death and dying. Macmillan.

Kuhn, D. J. (2002). The effect of active and passive participation in musical activity on the immune system as measured by salivary immun9oglobulin A (sigA). *Journal of Music Therapy, 39*(1), 30–39.

Kumar, A. M., Tims, F., Cruess, D. G., Mintzer, M. J., Ironson, G., Loewenstein, D., Cattan, R., Fernandez, J. B., Eisdorfer, C., & Kumar, M. (1999). Music therapy increases serum melatonin levels in patients with Alzheimer's disease. Alternative Therapies in Health and Medicine, 5(6), 49–57. PMID: 10550905

Kunz, J. L. & Sykes, S. (2007). *From mosaic to harmony: Multicultural Canada in the 21st century.* Policy Research Initiative.

La Face, G. (2017). Pedagogical-didactic implications in the writings of Fedele d'Amico. *Musica Docta, 7*(1), 65–79.

Laes, T. (2017). The (im)possibility of inclusion: Reimagining the potentials of democratic inclusion in and through activist music education. *Sibelius Academy of the University of the Arts Helsinki Studia Musica 72.*

Lally, E. (2009). The power to heal us with a smile and a song: Senior well-being, music-based participatory arts, and the value of qualitative evidence. *Journal of Arts and Communities, 1*(1), 25–44.

Lamela, I., and Rodrigues, P. M. (2016). Understanding leadership in community music-making projects behind bars: Three experiences in Portuguese prisons. *International Journal of Community Music, 9*(3), 257–271.

Lamont, A. (2002). Musical identities and the school environment. In R. Macdonald, D. Hargreaves, & D. Miell (Eds.), *Musical identities* (pp. 41–59). Oxford University Press.

Landgraf, R., & Neumann, I. D. (2004). Vasopressin and oxytocin release within the brain: A dynamic concept of multiple and variable modes of neuropeptide communication. *Frontiers in Neuroendocrinology, 25*(3–4), 150–176.

Lane, C. (2016). Growth spurt. *Symphony,* (Spring), 36–41.

Langer, S. (1953). *Feeling and form.* Routledge and Kegan Paul.

LargeUp. (n.d.). Grenada's oil-soaked jab mas is the Caribbean's ultimate celebration of freedom. http://www.largeup.com/2017/08/11/playing-jab-oil-mud-grenada-carnival

Lave, J., & Wenger, E. (1991). *Situated learning: Legitimate peripheral participation.* Cambridge University Press.

Lave, J., & Wenger, E. (1998). Communities of practice. *Iberian Journal of Information Systems and Technologies,* E1, 105–118.

Lawthom R., & Whelan, P. (2012). Understanding communities. In A. Azzopardi & S. Grech (Eds.), *Inclusive communities: Studies in inclusive education,* Vol. 16. SensePublishers. https://doi.org/10.1007/978-94-6091-849-0_2

Lebrecht, N. (1991). *The maestro myth: Great conductors in pursuit of power.* Carol Publishing Group.

Lee, H-J. (2002). *The effect of music and reminiscence on the mood of elderly persons with dementia.* MA thesis, Texas Women's University.

Lee, J., Davidson, J. W., & Krause, A. (2016). Older people's motivations for participating in community singing in Australia. *International Journal of Community Music, 9*(2), 191–206. doi:10.1386/ijcm9.2.191_1

Lee, O. K., Chung, Y. F., Chan, M. F., & Chan, W. M. (2005). Music and its effect on the physiological responses and anxiety levels of patients receiving mechanical ventilation: A pilot study. *Journal of Clinical Nursing, 14*(5), 609–620.

Lee, Y. (2007). The immigration experience among elderly Korean immigrants. *Journal of Psychiatric and Mental Health Nursing, 14*(4), 403–410.

Leglar, M. A., & Smith, D. S. (2010). Community music in the United States: An overview of origins and evolution. *International Journal of Community Music, 3*(3), 343–353.

Lehmann, A. C., Sloboda, J. A., & Woody, R. H. (2007). *Psychology for Musicians.* Oxford University Press.

Lehmberg, L. J., & Fung, C. V. (2010). Benefits of music participation for senior citizens: A review of the literature. *Music Education Research International,* 4, 19–30.

Lehtonen, K. (1986). Musiikki Terveyden Edistajana. WSOY.

Leonard, M. (2007). *Gender in the music industry: Rock, discourse, and girl power.* Ashgate.

Levinas, E. (1988). *Useless suffering.* In R. Bernasconi & D. Wood (Eds.), *The provocation of Levinas: Rethinking the other* (pp. 156–167). Routledge.

Levitin, D. J. (2007). *This is your brain on music: The science of a human obsession.* Penguin.

Levitin, D. J. (2009a). The neural correlates of temporal structure in music. *Music and Medicine, 1*(1), 9–13.

Levitin, D. J. (2009b). The world in six songs: How the musical brain created human nature. Plume.

Levitt, P. (1998). Social remittances: Migration driven local-level forms of cultural diffusion. *International Migration Review, 32*(4), 926–948.

Lewins, F. W. (1978). *The myth of the universal church: Catholic migrants in Australia.* Faculty of Arts, Australian National University.

Lewis, A. (2016, 16 June). Reconciliation with First Nations requires action. *Toronto Star.* https://www.thestar.com/opinion/commentary/2016/06/16/reconciliation-with-first-nations-requires-action.html

Lewis, D., & Greene, J. (1983). *Your Child's Drawings ... their hidden meaning.* Hutchinson.

Li, S., & Southcott, J. (2012). A place for singing: Active music engagement by older Chinese Australians. *International Journal of Community Music, 5*(1), 59–78. https://doi.org/10.1386/ijcm.5.1.59_1

Lieb, K. J. (2013). *Gender, branding, and the modern music industry.* Routledge.

Liebowitz, C. (2015). I am disabled: On identity-first versus people-first language. https://thebodyisnotanapology.com

Liegeois-Chauvel, C., Peretz, I., Babai, M., & Laguitton, V. (1998). Contribution of different cortical areas in the temporal lobes to music processing. *Brain, 121*(10), 1853–1867.

Lin, N. (2001). *Social capital: A theory of social structure and action.* Cambridge University Press.

Lincoln, Y.S., & Guba, E. G. (1985). *Naturalistic Inquiry.* Newbury Park, CA: Sage Publications.

Lindgren, M., Bergman, Å., & Sæther, E. (2016). The construction of social inclusion through music education: Two Swedish ethnographic studies of the *El Sistema* programme. *Nordic Research in Music Education Yearbook, 17,* 65–81.

Lindley, A. M. (2013). Developing inclusive instrumental musicking through a primary school orchestra. In C. Harrison & P. Mullen (Eds.), *Reading out: Music education with hard to reach children and young people* (pp. 135–140). Music Mark.

Lines, D. (2018). The ethics of community music. In B.-L. Bartleet & L. Higgins (Eds.), *The Oxford handbook of community music* (pp. 385–402). Oxford University Press.

Lingis, A. (1994). *The community of those who have nothing in common.* Indiana University Press.

Liverpool, H. U. (1993). *Rituals of power and rebellion: The Carnival tradition in Trinidad and Tobago, 1783–1962.* Doctoral dissertation, University of Michigan, Ann Arbor.

Livsey, L., Morrison, I., Clift, S., & Camic, P. (2012). Benefits of choral singing for social and mental wellbeing: Qualitative findings from a cross-national survey of choir members. *Journal of Public Mental Health, 11*(1), 10–26. doi.org/10.1108/17465721211207275

Locke, R. P. (2011). *Musical exoticism: Images and reflections* [2009]. Cambridge: Cambridge University Press.

Loewy, J., & Aldridge, D. (2014). Prelude to music and medicine. *Music and Medicine, 1*(1), 5–8.

Loewy, J. V., & Spintge, R. (2011). Prelude to the special issue in music and medicine: Music therapy and supportive cancer care. *Music and Medicine, 3*(1), 5–6.

Longboat, C. (2008). Ethical space in the intellectual terrain: A cultural perspective. *Canadian Journal of Native Education, 31*(1), 72–83.

Longboat, C. (2011). *Designing ethical space: A story of success.* Circle of Light Conference. http://www.edu.gov.on.ca/eng/aboriginal/6GDesigningEthicalSpace.pdf

Lonie, D. (2010). *Attuned to engagement: The effects of a music mentoring programme on the agency and musical ability of children and young people.* Youth Music.

Lonie, D. (2011). *Attuned to engagement: The effects of a music mentoring programme on the agency and musical ability of children and young people. Paper 2.* Youth Music.

Lonie, D. (2013). Why music? A research rationale for making music with children and young people experiencing additional challenges. In C. Harrison & P. Mullen (Eds.), *Reaching out: Music education with "hard to reach" children and young people* (pp. 3–11). Music Mark.

MacDonald, R. A. (2013). Music, health, and well-being: A review. *International Journal of Qualitative Studies on Health and Well-Being, 8*(1), art. no. 20635.

Macdonald, R., Mitchell, L., Dillon, T., Serpell, M. G., Davies, J. B., & Ashley, E. A. (2003). An empirical investigation of the anxiolytic and pain reducing effects of music. *Psychology of Music, 31*(2), 187–203.

Mackinlay, E. (2008). Making space as white music educators for Indigenous Australian holders of song, dance, and performance knowledge: The centrality of relationship as pedagogy. *Australian Journal of Music Education, 1*, 2–6.

Mackinlay, E. (2016). A diffractive narrative about dancing towards decoloniality in an Indigenous Australian Studies performance classroom. In B. L. Bartleet, D. Bennett, A. Power, & N. Sunderland (Eds.). *Engaging first peoples in arts-based service learning: towards respectful and mutually beneficial educational practices.* Springer. 213–26.

Mackinlay, E., & Barney, K. (2014). Unknown and unknowing possibilities: Transformative learning, social justice, and decolonising pedagogy in Indigenous Australian studies. *Journal of Transformative Education, 12*(1), 54–73.

Magill, L., & Berenson, S. (2008). The conjoint use of music therapy and reflexology with hospitalized advanced stage cancer patients and their families. *Palliative and Supportive Care, 6*(3), 289–296.

Majno, M. (2012). From the model of *El Sistema* in Venezuela to current applications: Learning and integration through collective music education. *Annals of the New York Academy of Sciences, 1252*(1), 56–64.

Majno, M., & Fabris, D. (2012). Il Sistema italiano delle orchestre giovanili. *Musica salva vita, serie bianca,* 147–152.

Mäkelä, M., Nithikul, N., & Heikkinen, T. (2014). Drawing as a research tool: Making and understanding in art and design practice. *Studies in Material Thinking, 10,* 1–12.

Makine, A. (1999). *once upon the river love*. (Trans. Geoffrey Strachan). (Originally published in 1994 as *Au temps du fleuve Amour*). Penguin.

Maller, C., & Strengers, Y. (2013). The global migration of everyday life: Investigating the practice memories of Australian migrants. *Geoforum, 44*, 243–252.

Manegold, C. S. (1994). At home with: Yeou-Cheng Ma: The Hidden Melody [*New York Times* interview]. https://www.nytimes.com/1994/03/10/garden/at-home-with-yeou-cheng-ma-the-hidden-melody.html

Mann, J. (n.d.). *The importance of performing*. http://blog.studiohelper.com/performance/the-importance-of-performing

Mantie, R. (2008). Getting unstuck: the One World Youth Arts Project. *Music Education Research, 10*(4), 473–483. doi:10.1080/14613800802547706

Mantie, R. (2009). Take two aspirins and don't call me in the morning: Why easy prescriptions won't work for social justice. In E. Gould, J. Countryman, C. Morton, & L. S. Rose (Eds.), *Exploring social justice: How music education might matter* (pp. 90–104). Canadian Music Educators' Association.

Mantie, R. (2014). Liminal or lifelong, leisure, recreation and the future of music education. In C. Randles (Ed.), *Music education: navigating the future* (pp. 181–196). Routledge.

Mantie, R., & Smith, G. D. (Eds.). (2016). *The Oxford handbook of music making and leisure*. Oxford University Press.

Manuel, A., & Derrickson, R. M. (2015). *Unsettlling Canada: A national wake-up call*. Between the Lines.

Maratos, A. (2004). Whatever next? Community music therapy for the institution! In M. Pavlicevic & G. Ansdell (Eds.), *Community music therapy*. Jessica Kingsley.

Maratos, A., Crawford, M. J., & Procter, S. (2011). Music therapy for depression: It seems to work, but how? *The British Journal of Psychiatry, 199*, 92–93.

Maratos, A. S., Gold, C., Wang, X., & Crawford, M. J. (2008). Music therapy for depression. *Cochrane Database Systems Review, 1*.

Marcia, J. E. (1993). *Ego identity: A Handbook for psychosocial research*. Springer.

Markus, H., & Nurius, P. (1986). Possible selves. *American Psychologist, 41*(9), 954–969.

Martin, K., & Mirraboopa, B. (2003). Ways of knowing, being, and doing: A theoretical framework and methods for indigenous and indigenist research. *Journal of Australian Studies, 27*(76), 203–214.

Martin, R. L., & Osberg, S. (2007). Social entrepreneurship: The case for definition. *Stanford Social Innovation Review, 5*(2), 28–39.

Marturano, J. (2014). *Finding the space to lead: A practical guide to mindful leadership*. Bloomsbury.

Maslow, A. H. (1943). A theory of human motivation. *Psychological Review, 50*, 370–396.

Mason, P. (2016). *PostCapitalism: A guide to our future*. Penguin.

Mastnak, W., & Neuwirthová, A. (2017). Children with Williams syndrome make music: A community-based care model in the Czech Republic. *International Journal of Community Music, 10*(3), 341–356. https://doi.org/10.1386/ijcm.10.3.341_1

Matarasso, F. (1997). *Use or ornament? The social impact of participation in the arts.* Comedia.

Matarasso, F. (2010). Rethinking cultural policy. In *Culture Watch Europe Conference 2010.* Council of Europe. http://www.coe.int/t/dg4/cultureheritage/cwe/Rethink_EN.pdf

Mathis, E. (n.d.). Cross cultural psychology [Blog post]. https://blogs.longwood.edu/emilymathis/cross-cultural-psychology

Mauss, M. (1990). *The gift: The form and reason for exchange in archaic societies* [1925]. (Trans. W. D. Halls). Routledge.

McAdams, D. P. (1997). The case for unity in the (post)modern self: A modest proposal. In R. D. Ashmore & L. Jussim (Eds.), *Self and identity: Fundamental issues* (pp. 46–78). Oxford University Press.

McAdams, D. P., Josselson, R., & Lieblich, A. (2006). Introduction. In D. P. McAdams, R. Josselson, & A. Lieblich (Eds.), *Identity and story: Creating self in narrative* (pp. 3–11). American Psychological Association.

McCaffrey, R., & Freeman, E. (2003). Effect of music on chronic osteoarthritis pain in older people. *Journal of Advanced Nursing, 44*(5), 517–524.

McCann, I. L., & Pearlman, L. A. (1990a). Vicarious traumatization: A framework for understanding the psychological effects of working with victims. *Journal of Traumatic Stress, 3,* 131–149.

McCann, L., & Pearlman L. A. (1990b). *Psychological trauma and the adult survivor: Theory, therapy, and transformation.* Brunner and Mazel.

McCarroll, J. E., Ursano, R. J., Wright, K. M., et al. (1993). Handling bodies after violent death: Strategies for coping. *American Journal of Orthopsychiatry, 63,* 209–214.

McClusky, H. Y. (1974). Education for aging: The scope of the field and perspectives for the future. In S. Grabowski, & W. D. Mason (Eds.), *Learning for aging.* Adult Education Association of the U.S.A.

McCoy-Roth, M., Mackintosh, B., & Murphey, D. (2012). When the bough breaks: The effects of homelessness on young children. *Child Trends.* http://www.childtrends.org/wp-content/uploads/2012/02/2012-08EffectHomelessnessChildren.pdf

McFerran, K. S., & Rickson, D. (2014). Community music therapy in schools: Realigning with the needs of contemporary students, staff, and systems. *International Journal of Community Music, 7*(1), 75–92. https://doi.org/10.1386/ijcm.7.1.75_1

McHenry, J. A. (2009). A place for the arts in rural revitalisation and the social wellbeing of Australian rural communities. *Rural Society, 19*(1), 60–70.

McIntosh, P. (2004). White privilege: Unpacking the invisible knapsack. *Race, class, and gender in the United States, 6,* 188–192.

McKay, G. A., & Higham, B. (2011). Community music: History and current practice, its constructions of "community," digital turns, and future soundings. University of Salford, http://usir.salford.ac.uk/18930/

McKay, G. A., & Moser, P. (2005). *Community music: A handbook* (p. 16). Russell House.

McKinney, C. H., Tims, F. C., Kumar, A. M. & Kumar, M. (1997). The effect of selected classical music and spontaneous imagery on plasma ß-endorphin. *Journal of Behavioral Medicine, 20*(1), 85–99.

McLean, B. (1981–82). Symbolic extension and its corruption of music. *Perspectives of New Music 20*(1/2), 331–356.

McLeod, S. A. (2017). Maslow's hierarchy of needs. www.simplypsychology.org/maslow.html

McLuhan, M. (1962). *The Gutenberg galaxy: The making of typographic man.* University of Toronto Press.

McLuhan, M. (1970). *Culture is our business.* Ballantine Books.

McLuhan, M., & Fiore, Q. (1967). *The medium is the massage: An inventory of effects.* Coordinated by Jerome Agel. Bantam Books.

McNiff, J. (2013). *Action research: Principles and practice* (3rd Ed.). Routledge.

Mecca, L., & Tence, M. (2008). Italians. In *eMelbourne – the city past and present.* School of Historical Studies, Department of History, University of Melbourne. http://www.emelbourne.net.au/biogs/EM00767b.htm

Mendonça, M. (2010). Gamelan in prisons in England and Scotland: Narratives of transformation and the "good vibrations" of educational rhetoric. *Ethnomusicology, 54*(3), 369–394.

Menon, V., & Levitin, D. J. (2005) The rewards of music listening: Response and physiological connectivity of the mesolimbic system. *Neuroimage, 28*(1), 175–184.

Mental Health Foundation. (2011). An evidence review of the impact of participatory arts on older people. https://www.mentalhealth.org.uk/sites/default/files/evidence-review-participatory-arts.pdf

Merriam, S. (1998). *Qualitative research and case study applications.* Jossey-Bass.

Merriam, S., & Kee, Y. (2014). Promoting community wellbeing: The case for lifelong learning for older adults. *Adult Education Quarterly, 64*(2), 128–144.

Michel, D., & Chesky, K. (1996). Music and music vibration in pain relief: Standards in research. In R. Spintge & R. Dron (Eds.), *Music medicine, Vol. 2* (pp. 218–226). MMB Music.

Miina Sillianpaa Foundation, Helsinki, https://www.miinasillanpaa.fi

Mikkola, T. M., Porteigs, E., Rantakokko, M., Gagne, J., Rantanen, T., & Viljanen, A. (2015). Association of self-reported hearing difficulty of objective and perceived participation outside the home in older community-dwelling adults. *Journal of Aging and Health, 27*(1), 103–122.

Milloy, J. (1999). *A national crime: The Canadian government and the residential school system, 1879-1986.* University of Manitoba Press.

Mills, D., & Brown, P. (2004) *Art and wellbeing: a guide to the connections between community cultural development and health, ecologically sustainable development, public housing and place, rural revitalisation, community strengthening, active citizenship, social inclusion and cultural diversity.* National Library of Australia. https://trove.nla.gov.au/work/33524092

Mills, J. (2007). *Instrumental teaching.* Oxford University Press.

Miluk-Kolasa, B., Obminski, X., Styobucjum, R., & Golec, L. (1994). Effects of music treatment on salivary cortisol in patients exposed to pre-surgical stress. *Experimental and Clinical Endocrinology*, 1029, 118–120.

Mindfulness. (2017). In *Merriam-Webster.com.* https://www.merriam-webster.com/dictionary/mindfulness

Ministerial Leadership Services (Eds.). (1996). A Mennonite polity for ministerial leadership. In *Joint Committee on Ministerial Leadership, Mennonite Board of Congregational Ministries and General Conference Mennonite Church.* Faith and Life Press.

Minshall, P. (1999). To Play Mas'. *Caribbean Quarterly*, 45(2–3), 30–35.

Mitchell, E. (2016). Arts Express: Performance, community, and creativity for children with exceptionalities. *TOPICS for Music Education Praxis, 2.*

Möckel, M., Röcker, L., Störk, T., Vollert, J., Danne, O., Elchstädt, H., and Hochrein, H. (1994). Immediate physiological responses of healthy volunteers to different types of music: Cardiovascular, hormonal, and mental changes. *European Journal of Applied Physiology*, 68(6), 451–459.

Möckel, M., Stork, T., Vollert, J., Röcker, L., Danne, O., Hochrein, H., & Frei, U. (1995). Stress reduction through listening to music: Effects on stress hormones, hemodynamics, and mental state in patients with arterial hypertension and in healthy persons. *Deutsche medizinische Wochenschrift*, 120(21), 745–752.

Modesti, P. A., Parati, G., & Taler, S. J. (2008). Daily sessions of music can reduce 24-hour ambulatory blood pressure in mild hypertension. American Society of Hypertension Meeting. Abstract, p. 230.

Mollica, R. (2006a). Trauma story assessment and therapy. *Therapists' Journal for Field and Clinic.* Harvard Programme for Refugee Trauma.

Mollica, R. F. (2006b). *Healing invisible wounds: Paths to hope and recovery in a violent world.* Vanderbilt University Press.

Mollica, R. F.(2011). *Global mental health: Trauma and recovery: A companion guide for field and clinical care of traumatized people worldwide.* Harvard Program in Refugee Trauma.

Mollica, R. F. (2014). Lecture during Global Trauma Recovery Certificate Course in Orvieto, Italy, November 2014.

Monchalin, L. (2016). The colonial problem: An Indigenous perspective on crime and injustice in Canada. University of Toronto Press.

Moody, E., & Phinney, A. (2012). A community-engaged art program for older people: Fostering social inclusion. *Canadian Journal on Aging / La Revue Canadienne Du Vieillissement*, 31(1), 55–64.

Moody, H. R. (1986). Late life learning in the information society. In D. A. Peterson, J. E. Thornton, & J. E. Birren (Eds.), *Education and aging* (pp. 122–148). Prentice-Hall.

Moore, F. (2016). Flexible identities and cross-border knowledge networking. *Critical Perspectives on International Business*, 12(4), 318–330.

Morewitz, S. J. (2016). *Runaway and homeless youth: New research and clinical perspectives.* Springer.

Morgan, R. D., & Flora, D. B. (2002). Group psychotherapy with incarcerated offenders: A research synthesis. *Group Dynamics: Theory, Research, and Practice, 6*(3), 203–218.

Morgan, S., & Yoder, L. H. (2012). A concept analysis of person-centered care. *Journal of Holistic Nursing, 30*(1), 6–15.

Mota, G. (2012). A music workshop in a women's prison: Crossing memories, attributing meanings. In *Proceedings of the XXIV International Seminar on Research in Music Education* (pp. 160–66). Thessaloniki.

Mui, A. C., Kang, S., Kang, D., & Domanski, M. D. (2007). English language proficiency and health-related quality of life among Chinese and Korean immigrant elders. *Health and Social Work, 32*(2), 119–127.

Mui, A. C., Nguyen, D. D., Kang, D. Y., & Domanski, M. D. (2006). Demographic profiles of Asian immigrant elderly residing in metropolitan ethnic enclave communities. *Journal of Ethnic and Cultural Diversity in Social Work, 15*(1–2), 193–214.

Mullen, P. (2002). We don't teach, we explore: Aspects of community music delivery. *International Society for Music Education Community Music Activity commission conference.* Rotterdam, Holland, July. http://www.worldmusiccentre.com/uploads/cma/mullenteachexplore.PDF.

Mullen, P. (2008). Issues in leadership for community music workers. In *CMA XI: Projects, perspectives, and conversations* (pp. 253–262). ISME.

Mullen, P. (2011). *Working with children in challenging circumstances.* Unpublished conference presentation at Leading Music Education Conference, London, Ontario.

Mulu, E. (2015, 29 September). Why the term "world music" is bullshit. https://trueafrica.co/article/endeguena-mulu-aka-ethiopian-records-on-world-music

Murray, S. (2010). *The naked Anabaptist: The bare essentials of a radical faith.* Herald Press.

Murray, S. S. (2017). Basic psychological needs and the New Horizons musician: A cross-case analysis of six older adults participating in a New England New Horizons music ensemble. ProQuest 1878241267

Museum Victoria. (2013). History of immigration from Italy. http://museumvictoria.com.au/origins/history.aspx?pid=32

Music Manifesto (2005). *Music Manifesto Report No. 1* http://webarchive.national archives.gov.uk/20130401151715/http://education.gov.uk/publications/eorderingdownload/1-84478-533-5%20pdf1.pdf

Myerhof, B., & Ruby, J. (1982). Introduction. In J. Ruby (Ed.), *A crack in the mirror: Reflexive perspectives in anthropology* (pp. 1–35). University of Pennsylvania.

Nachmanovitch, S. (1990). *Free play: Improvisation in life and art.* Tarcher/Putnam.

Nakata, M. (2002). Indigenous knowledge and the cultural interface: Underlying issues at the intersection of knowledge and information systems. *IFLA Journal, 28*(5–6), 218–221.

Nakata, M. (2007). *Disciplining the savages: Savaging the disciplines.* Aboriginal Studies Press.

Nantambu, K. (2008). Soca music and moral decadence. http://www.trinicenter.com/kwame/2008/2503.htm

Narushima, M. (2008). More than nickels and dimes: The health benefits of a community-based lifelong learning programme for older adults. *International Journal of Lifelong Education, 27*(6), 673–692.

National Center on Family Homelessness at American Institutes for Research. (2014). *America's youngest outcasts: A report card on child homelessness.* The National Center on Family Homelessness.

Native Women's Association of Canada. (2017). *Sisters in Spirit vigils.* https://nwac.ca

Neelands, J., Belfiore, E., Firth, C., Hart, N., Perrin, L., Brock, S., Holdaway, D., & Woddis, J. (2015). *Enriching Britain: Culture, creativity, and growth.* University of Warwick. Retrieved from https://warwick.ac.uk/research/warwickcommission/futureculture/finalreport/warwick_commission_report_2015.pdf

Neville, H. J., Stevens, C., Pakulak, E., Bell., T, Fanning, J., Klein, S., & Isbell, E. (2013). Family-based training program improves brain function, cognition, and behavior in lower socioeconomic status preschoolers. *Proceedings of the National Academy of Sciences of the United States of America, 110.*

The New Today. (2015, 18 June). Scholar and wizard out of 2015 competition. http://thenewtoday.gd/local-news/2015/06/18/scholar-and-wizard-out-of-2015-competition/- gsc.tab=0

The New Today. (2016, 4 October). "Blaize" – the steel band movement is alive. http://thenewtoday.gd/local-news/2016/10/04/blaize-the-steel-band-movement-is-alive/-gsc.tab=0

Nhat Hanh, T. (2018, 19 March). Listening deeply for peace. https://www.lionsroar.com/listening-deeply-for-peace

Nicholson, N. R. (2012). A review of social isolation. *The Journal of Primary Prevention, 33*(2–3), 137–152.

Niland, A. (2017). Singing and playing together: A community music group in an early intervention setting. *International Journal of Community Music, 10*(3), 273–288. https://doi.org/10.1386/ijcm.10.3.273_1

Nilsson, U. (2008). The anxiety- and pain-reducing effects of music interventions: A systematic review. *AORN Journal, 87,* 780–807.

Nilsson, U. (2009) Soothing music can increase oxytocin levels during bed rest after open-heart surgery: A randomised control trial. *Journal of Clinical Nursing, 18,* 2153–2161.

North, A. C., & Hargreaves, D. J. (1999). Music and adolescent identity. *Music Education Research, 1*(1), 75–91.

NOW Grenada. (2014, 22 July). Calypso tent revival sponsored by Netherlands Insurance. http://www.nowgrenada.com/2014/07/netherlands-sponsors-calypso-tent-revival

Nussbaum, M. C. (2001). *Women and human development: The capabilities approach,* Vol. 3. Cambridge University Press.

Obomsawin, A., & Koenig, W. (Producers), & Obomsawin, A. (Director). (1993). *Kanehsatake: 270 years of resistance* [Motion Picture]. National Film Board of Canada.

OECD. (n.d.). Policy challenges for the next 50 years. http://public.tableau.com/shared/78NYMDX97?:embed=y&:showVizHome=no&:host_url=https%3A%2F%2Fpublic.tableausoftware.com%2F&:toolbar=yes&:animate_transition=yes&:display_static_image=no&:display_spinner=no&:display_overlay=yes&:display_count=yes&:showVizHome=no&:load OrderID=1

OECD insights: Human capital: How what you know shapes your life. (2007). https://www.oecd.org/insights/37966934.pdf.

Oehrle, E. (2010). Values infusing UKUSA: A developmental community arts programme in South Africa. International Journal of Community Music, 3(3), 379–386. https://doi.org/10.1386/ijcm.3.3.379_1

O'Grady, L. (2008, July). The role of performance in music-making: An interview with Jon Hawkes. In Voices: A world forum for music therapy, 8(2)

O'Grady, L., & McFerran, K. (2007). Community music therapy and its relationship to community music: where does it end? Nordic Journal of Music Therapy, 16(1), 14–26. http://doi.org/10.1080/08098130709478170

Oliveros, P. (2005). Deep listening: A composer's sound practice. iUniverse.

O'Neill, S. (2012). Personhood and music learning: Connecting Perspectives and narratives. CMEA.

O'Neill, S. A. (2012). Introduction: Perspectives and narratives on personhood and music learning. In S. A. O'Neill (Ed.), Personhood and music learning: Connecting perspectives and narratives (pp. 1–14). CMEA.

Ontario Universities Application Centre. (2012–2015). Secondary school [OUAC 101] application statistics, full time, first year (September). https://www.ouac.on.ca/docs/stats/uapp [Statistics are not archived on the OUAC website.]

Oostendorp, J. C., & Montel, S. R. (2014). Singing can enhance episodic memory functioning in elderly people with Alzheimer's disease. Journal of the American Geriatrics Society, 62(5), 982–983.

Orman, E. K. (2002). Comparison of the national standards for music education and elementary music specialists' use of class time. Journal of Research in Music Education, 50(2), 155–164.

Osborne, N. (2009). Music for children in zones of conflict and post-conflict: A psychobiological approach. In S. Malloch & C. Trevarthen (Eds.), Communicative musicality: Exploring the basis of human companionship (pp. 331–356). Oxford University Press.

O'Sullivan, S. (2016). Translating Indigenous reciprocity into university-led arts practice and assessment. In B.-L. Bartleet, D. Bennett, A. Power, & N. Sunderland (Eds.), Engaging First Peoples in arts-based service learning (pp. 15–29). Springer.

Otto, D., Clair, A. A., & Johnson, G. (2001). The effect of instrumental and vocal music on adherence to a physical rehabilitation exercise program with persons who are elderly. Journal of Music Therapy, 38(2), 82–96.

Paldam, M. (2000). Social capital: One or many? Definition and measurement. Journal of Economic Surveys, 14(5), 629–653.

Panagakos, A. N. (2003). Downloading new identities: Ethnicity, technology, and media in the global Greek village. *Identities: Global Studies in Culture and Power*, 10, 201–219.

Pantzar, M., & Shove, E. (2010). Temporal rhythms as outcomes of social practices. *Enthnologia Europaea*, 40(1), 19–29.

Parker, E. C. (2014). The process of social identity development in adolescent high school choral singers: A grounded theory. *Journal of Research in Music Education*, 62(1), 18–32. doi:10.1177/0022429413520009

Parkes, C. M., & Weiss, R. (1983). *Recovery from bereavement*. Basic Books.

Patel, A. D. (2003). Language, music, syntax, and the brain. *Nature Neuroscience*, 6, 674–681.

Pavlicivic, M. (2012). Between beats: Group music therapy transforming people and places. In R. MacDonald, G. Kreutz, & L. Mitchell (Eds.), *Music, health, and wellbeing* (pp. 196–212). Oxford United.

Pear, L. (2016). The magic of music. *Canadian Music Educator*, 3, 15–18.

Pearlman, L. A., & Mac Ian, P. S. (1995). Vicarious traumatization: An empirical study of the effects of trauma work on trauma therapists. *Professional Psychology: Research and Practice*, 26, 558–565.

Pearlman, L. A., & Saakvitne, K. W. (1995a). Treating therapists with vicarious traumatization and secondary traumatic stress disorders. In C. R. Figley (Ed.), *Compassion fatigue: Coping with secondary traumatic stress isorder in those who treat the traumatized*. Brunner/Mazel.

Pearlman, L. A. & Saakvitne, K. W. (1995b). *Trauma and the therapist: Countertransference and vicarious traumatization in psychotherapy with incest survivors*. Norton.

Pele (n.d.). *PELE Presentation*. https://www.apele.org/a-pele-en

Peppler, K. (2017). Equity and access in out-of-school music making. In S. A. Ruthmann & R. Mantie (Eds.), *The Oxford handbook of technology and music education*. Oxford University Press.

Peretz, I., & Coltheart, M. (2003). Modularity of music processing. *Nature Neuroscience*, 6(7), 688–691.

Peretz, I., Belleville, S., and Fontaine, S. (1997). Dissociations between music and language functions after cerebral resection: A new case of amusia without aphasia. *Canadian Journal of Experimental Psychology*, 51(4), 354–68.

Peretz, I., & Zatorre, R. J. (2005). Brain organization for music processing. *Annual Review of Psychology*, 56, 89–114. doi:10.1146/annurev.psych.56.091103.070225

Perras, M., Strachan, S. M., & Fortier, M. S. (2015). Back to the future: Associations between possible selves, identity, and physical activity among new retirees. *Activities, adaptation, and Aging*, 39(4), 318–335. doi:10.1080/01924788.2015.1090279

Perras, M., Strachan, S. M., & Fortier, M. S. (2016). Possible selves and physical activity in retirees. *Research on Aging*, 38(8), 819–841. doi:10.1177/0164027515606191

Phelan, H. (2008). Practice, ritual, and community music: Doing as identity. *International Journal of Community Music*, 1(2), 143–158. https://doi.org/10.1386/ijcm.1.2.143_1

Phillips, C. (2007). Ethnicity, identity, and community cohesion in prison. In M. Wetherell, M. Lafleche, & R. Berkeley (Eds.), *Identity, ethnic diversity, and community cohesion* (pp. 75–86). Sage.

Phinney, A., Moody, E. M., & Small, J. A. (2014). The effect of a community-engaged arts program on older adults' well-being. *Canadian Journal on Aging / La Revue Canadienne du Vieillissement, 33*(3), 336–345.

Picard, D., & Gauthier, C. (2012). The development of expressive drawing abilities during childhood and into adolescence. *Child Development Research, 2012,* art. no. 925063.

Pitman, R. K. (2001). Hippocampal diminution in PTSD: More (or less?) than meets the eye. *Hippocampus, 11,* 73–74.

Plowright, D. (2010). *Using mixed methods: Frameworks for an integrated methodology.* Sage.

Pluck, G., Kwang-Hyuk Lee, David, R., Macleod, D. C., Spence, S. A., & Parks, R. W. (2011). Neurobehavioural and cognitive function is linked to childhood trauma in homeless adults. *British Journal of Clinical Psychology, 50*(1), 33–45.

Polkinghorne, D. E. (1995). Narrative configuration in qualitative analysis. In J. A. Hatch & R. Wisniewski (Eds.), *Life history and narrative* (pp. 5–23). Falmer Press.

Pollack, S. (2007). Hope has two daughters: Critical practice within a women's prison. In D. Mandell (Ed.), *Revisiting the use of self: Questioning professional identities* (pp. 105-120). Canadian Scholars' Press.

Poole, R. (1972). *Towards deep subjectivity.* Northumberland.

The pornography of everyday life. (2007). Produced by S. Rosenkranz & J. Caputi. Jane Caputi LLC. Berkeley Media. 35 mins.

Portes, A. (1996). Transnational communities: Their emergence and significance in the contemporary world-system. *Contributions in Economics and Economic History, 181,* 151–168.

Portes, A., & Zhou, M. (1993). The new second generation: Segmented assimilation and its variants. *The Annals of the American Academy of Political and Social Science, 530*(1), 74–96.

Pratt, C. (1952). Music as the language of emotion. Lecture delivered in the Whittall Pavilion of the Library of Congress, 21 December 1950. US Government Printing Office.

Price, D. (2013). *Open: How we'll work, live, and learn in the future.* Crux.

Probst, B., & Berenson, L. (2014). The double arrow: How qualitative social work researchers use reflexivity. *Qualitative Social Work, 13*(16), 813–827.

Pruitt, L. J. (2014). *Youth peacebuilding: Music, gender, and change.* SUNY Press.

Public Health Agency of Canada (PHAC). (2006). *Healthy aging in Canada: A new vision, a vital investment from evidence to action- a discussion brief.* http://www.phac-aspc.gc.ca/seniors-aines/publications/public/healthy-sante/vision/vision-bref/index-eng.php

Putnam, R. D. (1993). *Making democracy work: Civic tradition in modern Italy.* Princeton University Press.

Putnam, R.D. (2000). *Bowling alone: The collapse and revival of American community.* Simon and Schuster.

Quintela, P. (2011). Estratégias de mediação cultural: Inovação e experimentação no Serviço Educativo da Casa da Música. *Revista Crítica de Ciências Sociais*, 94, 63–85.

Raglio, A. (2011). When music becomes music therapy. *Psychiatry and Clinical Neurosciences*, 65: 682–683.

Raglio, A., & Oasi, O. (2015). Music and health: What interventions for what results? *Frontiers in Psychology*, 6, 230.

Rakena, T. (2018). Community music in the South Pacific. In B.-L. Bartleet & L. Higgins, (Eds.) *The Oxford handbook of community music*. Oxford University Press.

Rauscher, F. H., et al. (1997). Music training causes long-term enhancement of preschool children's spatial-temporal reasoning. *Neurological Research*, 19, 2–8.

Reed, K., Beeds, N., Elijah, M. J., Lickers, K., & McLeod, N. (2011). *Aboriginal peoples in Canada*. Pearson Canada.

Regan, P. (2010). *Unsettling the settler within: Indian residential schools, truth telling, and reconciliation in Canada* (pp. 1–18). UBC Press.

Regelski, T. A., & Gates, J. T. (Eds.). (2009). *Music education for changing times: Guiding visions for practice*, Vol. 7. Springer Science and Business Media.

Regis, H. (1998). Empirical approaches to etermining Afafect displayed by Caribbean people for the works of Caribbean musicians. *Western Journal of Black Studies*, 22(4), 209-217.

Reilly, M. (1997). Music distraction in burn patients: Influencing post procedure recall. *Perioperative Nursing*, 6(4), 242–245.

Rempe, S. (2016, 18 February). Singing a new song [Web log post]. https://www.prisonfellowship.org/2016/02/singing-a-new-song

Renshaw, P. (2013). *Being – in Tune*. Guildhall School of Music and Drama and Barbican Centre. http://www.gsmd.ac.uk/fileadmin/user_upload/files/Research/Being_In-tune_report_2013.pdf

Resnick, M. (2017). *Lifelong kindergarten: Cultivating creativity through projects, passion, peers, and play*. MIT Press.

Resnick, M., & Rosenbaum, E. (2013). Designing for tinkerability. In M. Honey & D. Kanter (Eds.), *Design, make, play: Growing the next generation fof STEM innovators* (pp. 163–181). Routledge. http://www.lifewideeducation.uk/lifewide-learning.html

Revill, G. (2000). Music and the politics of sound: Nationalism, citizenship, and auditory space. *Environment and Planning D: Society and Space*, 18(5), 597–613.

Revington, S. (n.d.). *Defining authentic learning*. http://authenticlearning.weebly.com

Rickard, N. S., Appelman, P., James, R., Murphy, F., Gill, A., & Bambrick, C. (2013). Orchestrating life skills: The effect of increased school-based music classes on children's social competence and self-esteem. *International Journal of Music Education*, 31(3), 292–309.

Rickson, D. (2014). The relevance of disability perspectives in music therapy practice with children and young people who have intellectual disability. *Voices: A world forum for music therapy*, 14(3).

Ridder, H. M., Stige, B., Qvale, L. G., & Gold, C. (2013). Individual music therapy for agitation in dementia: An exploratory randomized control trial. *Aging and Mental Health*, 17, 667–678. doi:10.1080/13607863.2013.790926

Riessman, C. K. (2008). *Narrative methods for the human sciences.* Sage.

Rifkin, J. (2015). *Zero marginal cost society* (Reprint Ed.). Griffin.

Rinde, F. B., & Schei, T. B. (2017). Towards an understanding of community music in Norway. *International Journal of Community Music, 10*(1), 19–31. https://doi .org/10.1386/ijcm.10.1.19_1

Roach, K. (2014). Missing and murdered Aboriginal women [Editorial]. *Criminal Law Quarterly, 61*(1), 1–4.

Roback, H. (2000). Adverse outcomes in group psychotherapy: Risk factors, prevention, and research directions. *The Journal of Psychotherapy Practice and Research, 9*(3), 113–122.

Roberts, D. (2011). *Fatal invention: How science, politics, and big business re-create race in the twenty-first century.* New Press.

Robeyns, I. (2005). The capability approach: A theoretical survey. *Journal of Human Development, 6*(1), 93–117.

Roche, J. (2006). Socially engaged art, critics, and discontents: An interview with Claire Bishop. American Community Arts Network. doublesession.net/index hibitv070e/files/bishopinterview.doc

Rodrigues, H., Leite, A., Faria, C., Monteiro, I., & Rodrigues, P. M. (2010). Music for mothers and babies living in a prison: A report on a special production of "BebéBabá." *International Journal of Community Music, 3*(1), 77–90.

Rodriguez, C. X. (2012). Popular music ensembles. In G. E. McPherson & G. F. Welch (Eds.), *The Oxford handbook of music education,* Vol. (pp. 878–889). Oxford University Press.

Rogers, C., & Koch, S. (1959). *A theory of therapy, personality, and interpersonal relationships.* McGraw-Hill.

Rohwer, D. (2009). Adult musicians' perceived and measured pulmonary function. Medical Problems of Performing Artists, 24(1), 10–14. https://search.proquest .com/docview/1402800

Rohwer, D. (2012). Going to the source: Pedagogical ideas from adult band members. *Journal of Band Research, 48*(1), 45–57. https://search.proquest.com/ docview/1266691714

Rohwer, D. (2013). Making music as an adult: What do the spouses think? *Texas Music Education Research,* 40–46. https://www.tmea.org/assets/pdf/research/ TexasMusicEducationResearch_2013.pdf.

Rohwer, D., & Coffman, D. D. (2006). Relationships between wind band membership, activity level, spirituality, and quality of life in older adults. *Research Perspectives in Music Education, 10,* 22–27. http://www.ingentaconnect.com/contentone/fmea/ rpme/2006/00000010/00000001/art00008

Rolvsjord, R. (2014). The competent client and the complexity of dis-ability. *Voices: A World Forum for Music Therapy, 14*(3).

Romer, C. (n.d.). Music A-level "in danger of disappearing from state schools." https:// www.artsprofessional.co.uk/news/music-level-danger-disappearing-state-schools

Rønningen, A. (2017). The Norwegian municipal music and art schools in the light of community music. *International Journal of Community Music, 10*(1), 33–43. https://doi.org/10.1386/ijcm.10.1.33_1

Rosenbaum, E. (2015). *Explorations in musical tinkering.* Media Arts & Sciences. MIT School of Architecture and Planning. https://static1.squarespace.com/static/561c2019e4b0ee65a89cee14/t/580e408cbe6594278d2616d6/1477329067597/rosenbaum-musical-tinkering-dissertation.pdf

Rossiter, M. (2007). Possible selves: An adult education perspective. *New Directions for Adult and Continuing Education*, 29 June, 5-15. doi:10.1002/ace.252

Roth, E., & Smith, K. (2008). The Mozart Effect: Evidence for the arousal hypothesis. *Perceptual and Motor Skills*, 107, 396–402.

Rothschild, B. (2000). *The body remembers: The psychophysiology of trauma and trauma treatment.* Norton.

Rowan, B. (2017). Talk, listen, and understand: The impact of a jazz improvisation experience on an amateur adult musician's mind, body, and spirit. *LEARNing Landscapes*, 10(2), 257–269. http://www.learninglandscapes.ca/index.php/learnland/article/view/814

Royal Commission on Aboriginal Peoples (1996). *Gathering strength: Health and healing. The report of the Royal Commission on Aboriginal peoples*, Vol. 3(3). Queen's Printer.

Royal College of Music. (2019). Community music network. *Royal College of Music London.* https://www.rcm.ac.uk/research/projects/communitymusicnetwork

Runde, D. F., Yayboke, E., Milner, A. N., Ridge, T., & Smith, G. (2018) *Confronting the global forced migration crisis.* CSIS/Rowman and Littlefield.

Rusk, N., Resnick, M., & Cooke, S. (2009). Origins and guiding principles of the computer clubhouse. In Y. B. Kafai, K. Peppler, & R. N. Chapman (Eds.), *The computer clubhouse: Constructionism and creativity in youth communities* (p. 192). Teachers College Press.

Ruud, E. (1997). Music and identity. *Nordisk Tidsskrift for Musikkterapi*, 6(1), 3-13. doi:10.1080/08098139709477889

Ryan, R. M., & Deci, E. L. (2008). A self-determination theory approach to psychotherapy: The motivational basis for effective change. *Canadian Psychology*, 49(3), 186–193. doi:10.1037/a0012753

Ryan, S., Rampersad, I., Bernard, L., Mohammed, P., & Thorpe, M. (2013). The influence of popular music culture on crime. In *No Time to Quit: Engaging Youth at Risk. Executive Report of the Committee on Young Males and Crime in Trinidad and Tobago.* University of the West Indies.

Saarikallio, S. (2011). Music as emotional self-regulation throughout adulthood. *Psychology of Music*, 39, 307–327.

Saarikallio, S., & Erkkilä, J. (2007). The role of music in adolescents' mood regulation. *Psychology of Music*, 35, 88–109.

Sacks, O. (1973). *Awakenings.* Duckworth.

Sacks O. (2007). *Musicophilia: Tales of music and the brain.* Picador.

Sadavoy, J., Meier, R., & Ong, A. Y. M. (2004). Barriers to access to mental health services for ethnic seniors: The Toronto study. *Canadian Journal of Psychiatry / Revue Canadienne De Psychiatrie*, 49(3), 192.

Sage Gateshead. (n.d.). Sage Gateshead. http://www.sagegateshead.com

Sahlins, M. (2017). *Stone age economics* [1972]. Routledge.

Saldaña, J. (2013). *The coding manual for qualitative researchers*. Sage.

Salimpoor, V. N., Benovoy, M., Larcher, K., Dagher, A., & Zatorre, R. J. (2011). Anatomically distinct dopamine release during anticipation and experience of peak emotion to music. *Nature Neuroscience, 14*(2), 257–262. https://doi.org/10.1038/nn.2726

Salimpoor, V. N., & Zatorre, R. J. (2013). Neural interactions that give rise to musical pleasure. *Psychology of Aesthetics, Creativity, and the Arts, 7*(1), 62–75.

Salimpoor, V. N., Benovoy, M., Longo, G., Cooperstock, J. R., & Zatorre, R. J. (2009). The rewarding aspects of music listening are related to degree of emotional arousal. *PLoS ONE, 4*(10): e7487. doi:10.1371/journal.pone.0007487

Sanders, C. (1989). *Grief: The mourning after*. John Wiley.

Sandler, I. (1987). *Mark Rothko 1903–1970* (pp. 9–20). Tate Publications.

Sanford, L. T. (1990). *Strong at the broken places*. New York: Random House.

Santa Casa da Misericórdia do Porto (2015). *Dez nos de Afairmação de um projeto penitenciário moderno e humanista*. Santa Casa da Misericórdia do Porto.

Sapolsky, R. M., Uno, H., Rebert, C. S., & Finch, C. E. (1990). Hippocampal damage associated with prolonged glucocorticoid exposure in primates. *Journal of Neuroscience, 10*, 2897–2902.

Särkämö, T., Laitinen, S., Tervaniemi, M., Numminen, A., Kurki, M., & Rantanen, P. (2012). Music, emotion, and dementia: Insight from neuroscientific and clinical research. *Music and Medicine, 4*(3), 153–162. doi 10.1177/1943862112445323

Sattler, G. (2013). Playing outside the generational square: The intergenerational impact of adult group music learning activities on the broader community. *International Journal of Community Music, 6*(3), 311–320. https://doi.org/10.1386/ijcm.6.3.311_1

Saunders, J., & Welch, G. (2012). *Communities of Music Education*. Youth Music/iMerc, Institute of Education.

Sawyer, R. K. (2005). Music and conversation. In D. Miell, R. MacDonald, & D. J. Hargreaves (Eds.), *Musical communication* (pp. 45–60). Oxford University Press.

Schafer, R. M. (1975). *The rhinoceros in the classroom*. Universal Edition Canada.

Schaie, K. W. (1996). Intellectual functioning in adulthood. In B. E. Birren & K. W. Schaie (Eds.), *Handbook of the psychology of aging* (4th Ed.) (pp. 266-286). Academic Press.

Schauer, M., Neuner, F., & Elbert, T. (2011). Narrative exposure therapy: A short-term treatment for traumatic stress disorder. *In International Encyclopedia of the Social & Behavioral Sciences, 2nd edition, Volume 16*. Elsevier, 198–203.

Schellenberg, E. G. (2004). Music lessons enhance IQ. *Psychological Science, 15*, 511–514.

Schellenberg, E. G. (2006). Long-term positive associations between music lessons and IQ. *Journal of Educational Psychology, 98*, 457–468.

Scherber, R. V. (2014). Perceptions of participation in a youth community ensemble. *Research Perspectives in Music Education, 16*(1), 23–31.

Schippers, H. (2010). *Facing the music: Shaping music education from a global perspective*. Oxford University Press.

Schippers, H. (2018). Community music context, dynamics, and sustainability. In B.-L. Bartleet & L. Higgins, (Eds.), *The Oxford handbook of community music.* New York: Oxford University Press.

Schippers, H., & Bartleet, B.-L. (2013). The nine domains of community music: Exploring the crossroads of formal and informal music education. *International Journal of Music Education, 31*(4), 454–471.

Schmidt, P. (2005). Music education as transformative practice: Creating new frameworks for learning music through a Freirian perspective. *Visions of Research in Music education, 6*(1), 1–14.

Schultz, W. (2010). Dopamine signals for reward value and risk: Basic and recent data. *Behavioral and Brain Functions, 6,* 24.

Schutz, A. (1964). *Collected papers, Vol. 2, Studies in social theory.* Nijhoff.

Schwartz, F. J. (1997). Perinatal stress reduction, music, and medical cost savings. *Journal of Prenatal and Perinatal Psychology and Health, 12*(1), 19.

Scott, S. (2006). A constructivist view of music education: Perspectives for deep learning. *General Music Today, 19*(2), 17–21.

Scott-Maxwell, A. (2007). Melbourne's Banda Bellini: Localisation of a transplanted Italian tradition. *Victorian Historical Journal, 78*(2), 251–271.

Scripp, L. (2015). The need to testify: A Venezuelan musician's critique of *El Sistema* and his call for reform. [Unpublished report]. http://www.researchgate.net/publication/285598399

Selby, J. (2004). Working divides between Indigenous and non-Indigenous: Disruptions of identity. *International Journal of Qualitative Studies in Education, 17*(1), 143–156.

Seligman, M. E. P. (2011). *Flourish: A visionary new understanding of happiness and well-being.* Free Press.

Seltzer, L. J., Ziegler, T. E., & Pollak, S. D. (2010). Social vocalizations can release oxytocin in humans. *Proceedings of the Royal Society of London, B: Biological Sciences, 277*(1694), 2661–2666.

Serre, D., and Pääbo, S. (2004). Evidence for gradients of human genetic diversity within and among continents. *Genome Research, 14,* 1679–1685.

Shakespeare, T. (2014). *Disability rights and wrongs revisited* (2nd Ed.). Routledge.

Shansky, C. (2010). Adult motivations in community orchestra participation: A pilot case study of the Bergen Philharmonic Orchestra. *Research and Issues in Music Education, 8*(1). http://www.stthomas.edu/rimeonline/vol8/shanksy/htm

Sharon, B. H., Hennessy, C. H., Brandon, J., & Boyette, L. (1997). Older adults' experiences of a strength-training program. *Journal of Nutrition, Health, and Aging, 1*(2), 103–108.

Shemer, N. (2012). *Public ideologies and personal meaning-making in postcolonial Grenada.* UC San Diego. ProQuest ID: Shemer_ucsd_0033D_12225. Merritt ID: ark:/20775/bb7032061b. https://escholarship.org/uc/item/0ms4z8vb.

Shieh, E. (2015). Relationship, rescue, and culture: How *El Sistema* might work. *The Oxford handbook of social justice and music education* (pp. 568–581). Oxford.

Shove, E., & Pantzar, M. (2007). Recruitment and reproduction: The careers of and carriers of digital photography and floorball. *Human Affairs, 17,* 154–167.

Silverman, M. D. (2005). Community music? Reflections on the concept. *International Journal of Community Music*, 3, 1–19.

Simonett, H. (2017). Banda. *Grove Music Online*. http://www.oxfordmusiconline .com.ezproxy.lib.monash.edu.au/subscriber/article/grove/music/A2092842

Simpson, L. (2011). *Dancing on our turtle's back: Stories of Nishnaabeg re-creation, resurgence, and a new emergence*. Arbeiter Ring.

Sinclair, J. (1999). Why I dislike "person first" language. *Autism mythbusters*. http:// autismmythbusters.com

Sinclair, M. (2016, 13 September). *Conversations with leaders*. Sanderson Centre.

Singapore Ministry of Education, Student Development Curriculum Division (2016). *Teaching and learning syllabus music*. Singapore. https://www.moe.gov. sg/docs/default-source/document/education/syllabuses/artseducation/files/ 2015_Music_Teaching_and_Learning_Syllabus_%28Primary_and_Lower_ Secondary%29.pdf

Sirek, D. (2013). *Musicking and identity in Grenada: Stories of transmission, remembering, and loss*. Doctoral dissertation, Royal Northern College of Music, Manchester.

Sirek, D. (2018a). Our culture is who we are! "Rescuing" Grenadian identity through musicking and music education. *International Journal of Music Education*, 36(1), 47–57.

Sirek, D. (2018b). "Until I die, I will sing my calypso song": Calypso, soca, and music education across a generational divide in Grenada, West Indies. *Action, Criticism, and Theory for Music Education*, 17(3), 12–29.

Slevin, M., & Slevin, P. (2013). Psychoanalysis and *El Sistema*: Human development through music. *International Journal of Applied Psychoanalytic Studies*, 10(2), 132–140.

Sloane-Seale, A., & Kops, B. (2008). Older adults in lifelong learning: Participation and successful aging. *Canadian Journal of University Continuing Education*, 34(1), 37–62.

Sloboda, J. A., Lamont, A., Greasley, A. E. (2009). Choosing to hear music: Motivation, process, and effect. In S. Hallam, I. Cross, I., and M. Thaut (Eds.), *The Oxford handbook of music psychology* (pp. 431–440). Oxford University Press.

Small, C. (1990, 28 March). Whose music do we teach, anyway? Music Educators National Conference, Washington. http://www.musekids.org/musicking.html

Small, C. (1996). *Music, society, education*. Wesleyan University Press.

Small, C. (1998). *Musicking: The meanings of performing and listening*. Wesleyan University Press.

Small, C. (2011). *Music, society, education*. Wesleyan University Press.

Small, C. (2016). Pelicans. In R. Walser (Ed.), *The Christopher Small Reader* (pp. 227–229). Wesleyan University Press.

Smalley, S., & Winston, D. (2011). Is mindfulness for you? In B. Boyce (Ed.), *The mindfulness revolution* (p. 15). Shambhala.

Smith, C. J. (2013). Holding the lotus to the rock: Creating dance community in red-state America. *International Journal of Community Music*, 6(1), 113–123. https:// doi.org/10.1386/ijcm.6.1.113_1

Smith, G., & Gruenewald, D. (2007). Place-based education in the global age: Local diversity. Routledge.

Smith, J., & Freund, A. (2002). The dynamics of possible selves in old age. *The Journals of Gerontology, Series B: Psychological Sciences and Social Sciences, 57*(6), 492–500. doi:10.1093/geronb/57.6.P492

Smith, M. K. (2003). Communities of practice. http://www.infed.org/biblio/communities_of_practice.htm

Smith, M. K., Lave, J., & Wenger, E. (2005). *Communities of practice: The encyclopedia of informal education.* http://www.infed.org/biblio/communities_of_pratice.html

Smith, M., Casey, L., Johnson, D., Gwede, C., & Riggin, O. Z. (2001). Music as a therapeutic intervention for anxiety in patients receiving radiation therapy. *Oncology Nursing Forum, 28*(5), 855–862.

Smith, R. C. (1997). Transnational migration, assimilation, and political community. In M. E. Crahan & A. Vourvoulias-Bush (Eds.), *The city and the world: New York's global future* (pp. 110–132). Council on Foreign Relations.

Smolicz, J. J., Hudson, D. M., & Secombe, M. J. (1998). Border crossing in "multicultural Australia": A study of cultural valence. *Journal of Multilingual and Multicultural Development, 19*(4), 318–336.

Snake-Beings, E. (2017). Community of difference: The liminal spaces of the Bingodisiac Orchestra. *International Journal of Community Music, 10*(2), 109–120. https://doi.org/10.1386/ijcm.10.2.109_1

Snell, D. (2014). "'The black sheep of the family": Bogans, borders, and New Zealand society. *International Journal of Community Music, 7*(2), 273–289. https://doi.org/10.1386/ijcm.7.2.273_1

Snow, M. (2013). Community music perspectives: Case studies from the United States. *International Journal of Community Music, 6*(1), 93–111. https://doi.org/10.1386/ijcm.6.1.93_1

Söderman, J., Burnard, P., & Hofvander-Trulsson, Y. (2015). Contextualising Bourdieu in the field of music and music education. In *Bourdieu and the Sociology of Music Education* (pp. 1–12). Routledge.

Solé, C., Mercadal-Brotons, M., Gallego, S., & Riera, M., (2010). Contributions of music to aging adults' quality of life. *Journal of Music Therapy, 47*(3), 264–281.

Soley, G., & Hannon, E. E. (2010). Infants prefer the musical meter of their own culture: A cross-cultural comparison. *Developmental Psychology, 46*, 286–292.

Somerville, P. (2013). Understanding homelessness. *Housing, Theory, and Society, 30*(4), 384–415.

Son, J. T., & Kim, S. H. (2006). The effects of self-selected music on anxiety and pain during burn dressing changes. *Taehan Kanho Hakhoe Chi, 36*(1), 159–168.

Sound Sense (2007). Music education code of practice for music practitioners, http://www.soundsense.org/metadot/index.pl?id=25842&isa=Category&op=show and http://www.musicleader.net/content.asp?CategoryID=1279 12/4/2011

Southcott, J. (2006). "Putting on a show": Engaging and authentic learning in experiential music education. *Proceedings of the AARE International Education Research Conference.* Australian Association for Research in Education.

Southcott, J., & Joseph, D. (2010). Sharing community through singing: The Bosnian Behar Choir in Victoria. *Australia e-journal of Studies in Music Education, 8*(2), 17–25.

Southcott, J., & Joseph, D. (2013). Community, commitment, and the Ten Commandments: Singing in the Coro Furlan. *International Journal of Community Music, 6*(1), 79–92.

Southcott, J., & Joseph, D. (2014). Singing in La Voce Della Luna Italian women's choir in Melbourne, Australia. *International Journal of Music Education: Practice, 33*(1), 91–102.

Sparkes, A. C. (2002) Autoethnography: Self-indulgence or something more? In A. Bochner & C. Ellis (Eds.), *Ethnographically speaking: Autoethnography, literature, and aesthetics* (pp. 209–232). AltaMira Press.

Spintge, R., & Droh, R. (1987). Effects of anxiolytic music on plasma levels of stress hormones in different medical specialties. In R. R. Pratt (Ed.), *The Fourth International Symposium on Music: Rehabilitation and Human Well-Being* (pp. 88–101). University Press of America.

Squire, S., Greco, M., O'Hagan, B., Dickinson, K., & Wall, D. (2006). Being patient-centred: Creating health care for our grandchildren. *Clinical Governance, 11*(1), 8–16.

St. John, P. A. (2010). The learner in community. In H. A. Abeles & L. A. Custodero (Eds.), *Critical issues in music education* (pp. 87–112). Oxford University Press.

Stanaway, F. F., Cumming, R. G., Naganathan, V., Blyth, F. M., Creasey, H. M., Waite, L. M., Handelsman, D. J., & Seibel, M. J. (2010). Depressive symptoms in older male Italian immigrants in Australia: The Concord Health and Ageing in Men Project. *Medical Journal of Australia, 192*(3), 158–162.

Standley, J. M. (1992). Clinical applications of music and chemotherapy: The effects on nausea and emesis. *Music Therapy Perspectives, 10*(1), 27–35.

Stanford Centre on Longevity. (2016). *Hidden in plain sight: How intergenerational relationships can transform our future* (Working paper). https://longevity.stanford.edu/wp-content/uploads/sites/24/2018/09/Intergenerational-relationships-SCL.pdf.

Statistics Canada. (2006). *A portrait of seniors in Canada.* http://www.statcan.gc.ca/pub/89-519-x/89-519-x2006001-eng.pdf

Statistics Canada (2016). Population by age and sex, 2016 census of population. http://www.statcan.gc.ca/pub/11-627-m/11-627-m2017016-eng.htm

Stead, M., Wimbush, E., Eadie, D., & Teer, P. (1997). A qualitative study of older people's perceptions of ageing and exercise: The implications for health promotion. *Health Education Journal, 56*(1), 3–16.

Steele, J. S. (2017). *El Sistema* fundamentals in practice: An examination of one public elementary school partnership in the US. *International Journal of Music Education, 35*(3), 357–368.

Steinman, E. (2011). "Making space": Lessons from collaborations with tribal nations. *Michigan Journal of Community Service Learning, 18*(1), 5–19.

Stevenson, D. J. (2004). Laughter and leadership. International Center for Studies in Creativity, Buffalo State College.

Stewart, M., Shizha, E., Makwarimba, E., Spitzer, D., Khalema, E. N., & Nsaliwa, C. D. (2011). Challenges and barriers to services for immigrant seniors in Canada: "You are among others but you feel alone." *International Journal of Migration, Health, and Social Care, 7*(1), 16–32.

Stige, B. (2012). Health musicking: A perspective on music and health as action and performance. In R. MacDonald, G. Kreutz, and L. Mitchell (Eds), *Music, health, and wellbeing.* Oxford University Press.

Stige, B., & Aarø, L. E. (2012). *Invitation to community music therapy.* Routledge.

Stolle, D. (1998). Bowling together, bowling alone: The development of generalized trust in voluntary associations. *Political Psychology, 19*, 497–525.

Stringham, D. A. (2016). Creating composition community in your classroom. *Music Educators Journal,* March, 46–52.

Styres, S., Zinga, D., Bennett, S., & Bomberry, M. (2010). Walking in two worlds: Engaging the space between Indigenous community and academia. *Canadian Journal of Education, 33*(3), 617–748.

Sun, J., Buys, N., & Merrick, J. (Eds.). (2013). *Health promotion: Community singing as a vehicle to promote health.* Nova Science.

Sussman, E. (2014). Perspective: The biggest challenges facing music ed. http://sbo magazine.com/commentary/4770-perspective-the-biggest-challenges-facing-music-ed.html

Sutherland, M., Maar, M., & Fréel, S. (2013). *Dignitas international feasibility study draft report: Improving access to quality and culturally safe health care for Aboriginal communities in Canada.* http://dignitasinternational.org/wp-content/uploads/2015/08/Dignitas_Aboriginal_Health_Feasibility_Study_Report_Feb_2014.pdf

Sutoo, D., & Akiyama, K. (2004). Music improves dopaminergic neurotransmission: demonstration based on the effect of music on blood pressure regulation. *Brain Research, 1016*(2), 255–262.

Swayne, Steve. (2014). "The Dangers of Overestimating Music Therapy." *The Atlantic.* July 15, 2014.

Sylvester, B. (2017, 12 August). No panorama (Gren Snaps Facebook Live). https://www.facebook.com/grensnaps/videos/1403399483100592/?hc_ref=ART4l zedbNPektIS_HgjJomenDUHhjX5mvers6pyS5TTAo3lGtYi5mFrJKw FIOcDmD

Tan, X., Yowler, C.J., Super, D.M., Fratianne, R.B. (2010). The efficacy of music therapy protocols for decreasing pain, anxiety, and muscle tension levels during burn dressing changes: a prospective randomized crossover trial. *Journal of Burn Care Research 31*(4): 590-597. PMID: 20498613.

Tarr, B., Launay, J., & Dunbar, R. (2014). Music and social bonding: "Self-other" merging and neurohormonal mechanisms. *Frontiers in Psychology, 5*(1096). https://doi.org/10.3389/fpsyg.2014.01096

Tasker, J. P. (2016). Confusion reigns over number of missing, murdered indigenous women. CBC News, 17 February 2016. https://www.cbc.ca/news/politics/mmiw-4000-hajdu-1.3450237

Taylor, C. (2012). *Improving alternative provision.* Dept. of Education. https://www.gov.uk/government/uploads/system/uploads/attachment_data/file/180581/DFE-00035-2012.pdf 20/10/2013

Tehanetorens. (1993). *Wampum belts*. Iroquois Reprints. Iroqrafts.

Tendulkar, S. A., Hamilton, R. C., Chu, C., Arsenault, L., Duffy, K., Huynh, V., and Friedman, E. (2012). Investigating the myth of the "model minority": A participatory community health assessment of Chinese and Vietnamese adults. *Journal of Immigrant Minority Health, 14*, 850–857.

Teng, X. F, Wong, M. Y. M. & Zhang, Y. T. (2007). Study on the responses of hypertensive patients to music. 4th ISSS-EMBS International Summer School and Symposium on Medical Devices and Bosensors.

Terracini, L. (2007). *Platform papers 11 – A regional state of ind: Making art outside metropolitan Australia*. Currency House.

Thomas, J. (1992). *Forty years of steel: An annotated discography of steel band and pan recordings, 1951–1991*. Greenwood.

Tiernan, J. (2009). Higher education in the community. *Sounding Board 2009, 5*, 9–12.

Tomlinson, G. (2015). *A million years of music: The emergence of human modernity*. MIT Press.

Toronyi-Lalic, I. (2012, 27 June). Simón Bolívar Symphony Orchestra, Dudamel, Royal Festival Hall: Politics aside, the Venezuelans deliver an electrifying night of music. *The Arts Desk*. http://www.theartsdesk.com/classical-music/simón-bol%C3%ADvar-symphony-orchestra-dudamel-royal-festival-hall

Trainor, L. J. (2010). The emotional origins of music. *Physics of Life Reviews, 7*, 44–45.

Truth and Reconciliation Commission of Canada. (2012). *They came for the children: Canada, Aboriginal peoples, and residential schools*. http://www.attendancemarketing.com/~attmk/TRC_jd/ResSchoolHistory_2012_02_24_Webposting.pdf

Truth and Reconciliation Commission of Canada (2015). *Final report of the Truth and Reconciliation Commission of Canada*, Vol. 1: *Honouring the truth, reconciling the future* (pp. 135–144). Lorimer.

Tsugawa, S. (2009). Senior adult music learning, motivation, and meaning construction in two new horizons ensembles. ProQuest 304828334

Tunstall, T. (2012). *Changing lives: Gustavo Dudamel, El Sistema, and the transformative power of music*. Norton.

Turino, T. (2008). *Music as social life: The politics of participation*. University of Chicago Press.

Turino, T. (2016). Music, social change, and alternative forms of citizenship. In D. Elliott, M. Silverman, & W. Bowman, *Artistic citizenship: Artistry, social responsibility, and ethical praxis*. Oxford University Press.

Turner, K. (2016) Regenerating community/regenerating self: Reflections of a community musician on working within a process of social regeneration. In B. Leigh-Bartlett, F. Candusso, M. L. Cohen, M. Kleber, P. Moser, and M. Shiobara (Eds.), *Innovation and change in community music: Proceedings of the XV International Seminar of the ISME Commission on Community Music Activity*, Edinburgh.

Turry, A. (2005). Music psychotherapy and community music therapy: Questions and considerations. *Voices: A World Forum for Music Therapy, 5*(1).

UNESCO (1994). *The Salamanca Statement and framework for action on special needs education*. Paris.

UNESCO (2010). *The Seoul agenda: Goals for the development of arts ducation.* www
.unesco.org/new/fileadmin/.../Seoul_Agenda_EN.pdf

Ungunmerr, M. R. (1988). Dadirri. *Compass Theology Review, 22,* 9–11.

UNHCR (2017). *Global trends: Forced displacement in 2017.* http://www.unhcr
.org/5b27be547.pdf

UNICEF (1989). *Convention on the Rights of the Child.* https://www.unicef.org/crc

United Nations (2008). *Committee on the rights of the child, forty-ninth session consideration of reports submitted by states parties under article 44 of the convention.* http://
www2.ohchr.org/english/bodies/crc/docs/AdvanceVersions/CRC.C.GBR
.CO.4.pdf 1/11/2017

United Nations (2015). *World population prospects* (No. 2015 revision). https://esa.
un.org/unpd/wpp/publications/files/key_findings_wpp_2015.pdf

UN Office of the High Commissioner of Human Rights (1989). *Convention on the
rights of the child.* http://www.ohchr.org

US Census Bureau (2013). *State and county quickfacts: Los Angeles County: CA.* http://
quickfacts.census.gov/qfd/states/06000.html

US Department of Education. (2004). FY 2003 Guidance for the education for homeless children and youth program. http://www2.ed.gov/programs/homeless/index
.html

US Department of Housing and Urban Development. (2018). *2018 continuum of care
homeless assistance programs omeless Poppulations and s ubpopulations* (pp. 1-2). doi:
https://files.hudexchange.info/reports/published/CoC_PopSub_NatlTerr
DC_2018.pdf

US Department of Housing and Urban Development. (2018). *Annual homeless assessment report to Congress* (2018). Part 1: Point-in-time Estimates of Homelessness.
https://www.hudexchange.info/resources/documents/2018-AHAR-Part-1.pdf

Van Dalen H. P., Henkens, K., & Schippers, J. (2009). Dealing with older workers
in Europe: A comparative survey of employers' attitudes and actions. *Journal of
European Social Policy, 19*(1), 47-60. doi:10.1177/0958928708098523

Van der Kolk, B. A. (2002). Posttraumatic therapy in the age of neuroscience. *Psychoanalytic Dialogues, 12*(3), 381–392.

van der Merwe, J. (2017). "We make a song": Moving beyond active music-making
in the Field Band Foundation. *International Journal of Community Music, 10*(2),
121–138. https://doi.org/10.1386/ijcm.10.2.121_1

Van der Veer, Guus (1998). Counselling and therapy with refugees and victims of
trauma. Psychological problems of victims of war, torture and repression, 2nd
Edition, Wiley.

Vander Kooij, C. (2009). Recovery themes in songs written by adults living with serious mental illnesses. *Canadian Journal of Music Therapy, 15*(1), 37–58.

VanderArk, S. D. & Ely, D. (1993). Cortisol, biochemical, and galvanic skin responses
to music stimuli of different preference values by college students in biology and
music. *Perceptual and Motor Skills, 77*(1), 227–234.

VanderArk, S. D. and Ely, D. (1992). Biochemical and galvanic skin responses to
music stimuli by college students in biology and music. *Perceptual Motor Skills,
74,* 1079–1090.

Vanderbeck, R., & Worth, N. (2015). *Intergenerational space*. Routledge.

Vaugeois, L. (2009). Music education as a practice of social justice. In E. Gould, J. Countryman, C. Morton, & L. Stewart Rose (Eds.), *Exploring social justice: How music education might matter* (pp. 2–22). Canadian Music Educators' Association.

Veblen, K. (2002). Apples and oranges, solar systems and galaxies: Comparing systems of community music. In *International Society for Music Education, Community Music Activity Commission Conference Proceedings* (pp. 115–126) ISME. http://issuu.com/official_isme/docs/2002_cma_proceedings/115

Veblen, K. (2010). *The many ways of community music: Chinese supplement of the International Journal of Community Music*, (pp. 51–66). ISME. https://www.intellect books.co.uk/MediaManager/File/IJCM(Chinese%20supp)finallayout.pdf

Veblen, K. (2013). The tapestry: Introducing community music. In K. Veblen, S. J. Messenger, M. Silverman, & D. J. Elliott (Eds.), *Community music today* (pp. 1–9). Rowman and Littlefield.

Veblen, K. K. (2007). The many ways of community music. *International Journal of Community Music, 1*(1), 5–21.

Veblen, K., & Elliott, D. J. (2000). *Community music: Foundations and practices*. Unpublished seminar reader, ISME CMA.

Veblen, K. K., Elliott, D. J., Messenger, S. J., & Silverman, M. (Eds.). (2013). *Community Music Today*. Rowman & Littlefield Education.

Veblen, K., & Olsson, B. (2002). Community music: Toward an international overview. In R. Colwell & C. Richardson (Eds.), *The new handbook of research on music teaching and learning* (pp. 730–744). Oxford University Press.

Veblen, K., Messenger, S. J., Silverman, M. & Elliott, D. J. (Eds.). (2013). *Community music today*. Rowman and Littlefield.

Ventres, W. B. (2016). Building power between polarities: On the space-in-between. *Qualitative Health Research, 26*(3), 345–350. doi:10.1177/1049732315609573

VicHealth. (2004). Arts for health. *VicHealth Letter*.

Vuoskoski, J., Thompson, W. F., McIlwain, D., & Eerola, T. (2011). Who enjoys listening to sad music and why?. *Music Perception, 29*(3), 311-318.

Wakin, D. J. (2012, February 17). Music meets Chávez politics, and critics frown. *The New York Times*. https://www.nytimes.com/2012/02/18/arts/music/venezuelans -criticize-hugo-chavezs-support-of-el-sistema.html

Walker, M., Hennessy, J., Ingraham, M., Lewis Hammond, S. (2014, 29 May). *What is the value of a Bachelor of Music degree?* Canadian University Music Society Annual Conference, Brock University.

Ward, E. (2012). *Music leading with challenging circumstances*. Sound Connections.

Ward, S., & van Vuuren, K. (2013). Belonging to the ainbow regions: Place, local media, and the construction of civil and moral identities strategic to climate change adaptability. *Environmental Communication Journal, 7*(1), 63–79.

Ware, J. E., Jr., & Gandek, B. (1998). Overview of the SF-36 Health Survey and the International Quality of Life Assessment (IQOLA) project. *Journal of Clinical Epidemiology, 51*, 903–912.

Ware, J. E., Jr., Kosinski, M., & Dewey, J. (2000). *How to score version 2 of the SF-36 health survey*. QualityMetric.

Ware, J. E., Jr., & Sherbourne, C. D. (1992). The MOS 36-item short-form health survey (SF-36®): I. Conceptual framework and item selection. *Medical Care, 30*(6), 473–483.

Weber, S., Nuessler, V., & Wilmanns, W. (1997) A pilot study on the influence of receptive music listening on cancer patients receiving chemotherapy. *International Journal of Critical Care, 8*(4), 220–230.

Weber-Pillwax, C., King, M., Reading, C., Denis, J., Bourassa, C., Castleden, H., Shea, B., Prentice, T., Peltier, D., Brascoupé, S., Blind, M., and Voyageur, E. (2012, February). National colloquium on racism, cultural safety, and Aboriginal peoples' health. Aboriginal Health Research Networks Secretariat, Victoria. http://ahrnets.ca/files/2013/02/AHRNetS-Racism-Cultural-Saftey-Colloquium-Report_Final1.pdf

Welch, G. (2001). *The misunderstanding of music.* University of London.

Wells, Thomas. 2013. Reasoning about development: Essays on Amartya Sen's Capability Approach. Doctoral thesis, Erasmus University Rotterdam. http://repub.eur.nl/pub/40509

Wenger, E. (1998). Communities of practice: Learning, meaning, and identity. Cambridge University Press.

Wenger, E. (1999). *Communities of practice: Learning, meaning, and identity.* Cambridge University Press.

Wetter, O. E., Koerner, F., & Schwaninger, A. (2009). Does musical training improve school performance? *Instructional Science: An International Journal of the Learning Sciences, 37*(4), 365–374.

WHO (World Health Organization). (2001). *The world health report 2001: Mental health: New understanding, new hope.* http://www.who.int/whr/2001/en

WHO (World Health Organization). (2002). *Active ageing: A policy framework.* http://whqlibdoc.who.int/hq/2002/who_nmh_nph_02.8.pdf

WHO (World Health Organization). (2008). *The global burden of disease: 2004 update.* World Health Organization. https://apps.who.int/iris/handle/10665/43942.

WHO (World Health Organization). (2014). *Ageing and life courses.* http://www.who.int/ageing/en/

WHO (World Health Organization). (2014). *World health statistics.* http://www.who.int/gho/publications/world_health_statistics/2014/en

Wiesenthal, D. L., & Hennessy, D. A. (2000). The influence of music on driver stress. *Journal of Applied Social Psychology, 30*(8), 1709–1719.

Wilks, L. (2011). Bridging and bonding: Social capital in the music festival experience. *Journal of Policy Research in Tourism, Leisure, and Events, 3*(3), 281–297.

Williams, D. A. (2015). The baby and the bathwater. *College Music Symposium, 55.*

Williams, D. B. (2011). The non-traditional music student in secondary schools of the United States: Engaging non-participant students in creative music activities through technology. *Journal of Music, Technology, and Education, 4*(3), 131–147.

Williams, K. P. (2013). *A case study of three African-American string players participating in a community orchestra.* (Doctoral dissertation). Proquest (3593177)

Williams, R. (2014). *Keywords: A vocabulary of culture and society* (revised Ed.). Oxford University Press.

Willingham L., and Carruthers, G. (2018) Community Music in Higher Education (pp 595-616) in B.-L. Bartleet & L. Higgins (Eds.), *The Oxford handbook of community music* (pp. 177–194). Oxford University Press.

Wilson, J., & Drozdek, B. (2004). Broken spirits: The treatment of traumatized asylum seekers, refugees, war and torture victims. *American Journal of Psychiatry 162(9)*: 1768–69.

Wilson, N., Gross, J., & Bull, A. (2017). *Towards cultural democracy: Promoting cultural capabilities for everyone.* King's College London.

Wilson, S. (2008). *Research is ceremony: Indigenous research methods.* Fernwood.

Winnicott, D. W. (1986). *Holding and interpretation: Fragment of an analysis.* Grove Press.

The Women's Circle. (2008) *Education and support group for Bhutanese women: A Manual for Facilitators.* The Center for Victims of Torture.

Wong, S. T., Yoo, G. J., & Stewart, A. L. (2007). An empirical evaluation of social support and psychological well-being in older Chinese and Korean immigrants. *Ethnicity and Health, 12(1)*, 43–67.

Woodford, P. (2005). *Democracy and music education: Liberalism, ethics, and the politics of practice.* Indiana University Press.

Worden, J. W. (2002) *Grief counseling and grief therapy: A handbook for the mental health practitioner* (3rd Ed.). Springer.

Wright, R. (2003). *Stolen continents: Conquest and resistance in the Americas.* Penguin Canada.

Wyer, P., Alves, S., Post, S., & Quinlan, P. (2014) Relationship-centred care: Antidote, guidepost or blind alley? The epistemology of 21st century health care. *Journal of Evaluation in Clinical Practice, 20(6)*, 881–889.

Yardley, L., Bishop, F. L., Beyer, N., Hauer, K., Kempen, G. I., Piot-Ziegler, C., Todd, T., and Holt, A. R. (2006). Older people's views on falls-prevention intervention in six European countries. *The Gerontologist, 46*, 650–660.

Yehuda, N. (2011). Music and stress. *Journal Of Adult Development, 18(2)*, 85–94.

Yehuda, R. (2001). Are glucocortoids responsible for putative hippocampal damage in PTSD? How and when to decide. *Hippocampus o 11*, 85–89.

Yeom, H. (2014). Association among ageing-related stereotypic beliefs, self-efficacy, and health-promoting behaviors in elderly Korean adults. *Journal of Clinical Nursing, 23(9–10)*, 1365–1373.

Yerichuk, D. (2014). "Socialized music": Historical formations of Community Music through Social Rationales, *13(1)*, 124–154.

Yerichuk, D. (2015). Grappling with inclusion: Ethnocultural diversity and socio-musical experiences in Common Thread Community Chorus of Toronto. *International Journal of Community Music, 8(3)*, 217–231. https://doi.org/10.1386/ijcm.8.3.217_1

Yerichuk, D., and Krar, J. (2019). From inclusion to inclusivity: A scoping review of community music scholarship. *International Journal of Community Music, 12(2)*, 165–84. doi:10.1386/ijcm.12.2.165_1

Yin, R. K. (2009). *Case study research: Design and methods.* Sage.

Yoder, J. A., Kropf, M., & Slough R. (Eds.). (2006). *Preparing Sunday dinner: A collaborative approach to worship and preaching*. Herald Press.

Yoo, Y. (2002). Canada and Korea: A shared history. In R. W. L. Guisso and Y. Yoo (Eds.), *Canada and Korea: Perspectives 2000* (pp. 9–43). University of Toronto Press.

Youth Music (2014). *Do, review, improve: A quality framework for music education*. Youth Music. http://network.youthmusic.org.uk/learning/resource-packs/do-review-improve-quality-framework-music-education

Youth Music (2016). *Making music, changing lives: Youth Music impact report 2015-6*. Youth Music.

Youth Music (2017). Youth Music quality framework. http://network.youthmusic.org.uk/sites/default/files/uploads/posts/Youth%20Music%20Quality%20Framework%202017%20edition-2.pdf 1/11/2017

Youth Music / Drake Music (2017). Do, review, improve ... A quality framework for use in music-making sessions working with young people in SEN/D settings. http://network.youthmusic.org.uk/resources/do-review-improve-quality-framework-music-education

Youth orchestra profile (2016). In League of American Orchestras. https://americanorchestras.org/knowledge-research-innovation/youth-education-and-community/youth-orchestra-profile.html

Yudell, M., Roberts, D., DeSalle, R., & Tishkof, S. (2016). Taking race out of human genetics. *Science*, 351(6273), 564–565.

Yun, G. (2016). Interfaith-cross-cultural improvisation: Music and meaning across boundaries of faith and culture. *Consensus*, 37(2), Article 2.

Zharinova-Sanderson, O. (2005). Promoting integration and socio-cultural change. In M. Pavlicevic and G. Ansdell (Eds), *Community music therapy* (pp. 233–248). Jessica Kingsley Press.

Zimmerman, L., Pozehl, B., Duncan, K., & Schmitz, R. (1989). Effects of music in patients who had chronic cancer pain. *Western Journal of Nursing Research*, 11(3), 298–309.

LIST OF CONTRIBUTORS

HEIDI AHONEN, PhD, RP, MTA, FAMI, is a Professor of music therapy at Wilfrid Laurier University and Director of the Manfred and Penny Conrad Institute for Music Therapy Research. Heidi's clinical work involves working with refugees in Canada and internationally. She also conducts vicarious trauma workshops for volunteers working with refugees.

KIRSTIN ANDERSON is a Lecturer in Criminal Justice at the University of the West of Scotland. She was also the Artist Producer for Justice and Arts Scotland in 2017 and was responsible for the design and delivery of the Creative Conversation Series.

BRYDIE-LEIGH BARTLEET is Director of the Queensland Conservatorium Research Centre, Griffith University, Australia. She is known worldwide for her research in community music and community engagement and has led many projects that explore the social impact of the arts. Her partnerships have led to new and interdisciplinary approaches to music research that intersect with health and well-being, corrections and criminology, Indigenous and cultural policy, social justice, regional arts development, and human rights.

DAVE CAMLIN is a musician from Cumbria, England whose musical practice spans performance, composition, teaching, and research, grounded in a passionate belief in the humanizing nature of music-making. He lectures in music and music education at Royal College of Music and Trinity-Laban conservatoires in London. He leads a number of community choirs in the Natural Voice Network (NVN) tradition, and was Musical Director of the award-winning Fellowship of Hill and Wind and Sunshine project in 2018.

GLEN CARRUTHERS was Dean of the Faculty of Music at Wilfrid Laurier University (Canada) from 2010 to 2020. His articles have appeared in such sources as *Arts and Humanities in Higher Education, International Journal of Musiac Education,* and *Journal of Musicology,* and he is a contributor to several books, including the *Oxford Handbook of Community Music.* He was named an honorary member of the Canadian University Music Society in 2016 and received the Canadian Association of Fine Arts Deans Academic Leadership Award in 2018.

Ed. Note: The Laurier University community and friends from around the world were deeply saddened by Glen's passing on December 23, 2020. He is greatly missed, and we are honoured to have one of his last publications as Chapter 5 of this book.

LINDSAY CASTELLANO is a Research Associate at the Center for Arts Education and Research, the Florence Geffen Fellow for Music Assessment, and an applied violin and viola instructor at Teachers College, Columbia University.

DON D. COFFMAN, M.M., PhD, chairs the Department of Music Education and Music Therapy in the Frost School of Music at the University of Miami. He is Associate Editor of the *International Journal of Community Music* and the Editor of *Research Perspectives in Music Education.*

MARY COHEN, PhD, is Associate Professor and Area Head of Music Education at the University of Iowa where she researches music-making and well-being. She founded the Oakdale Choir in 2009 and the Oakdale Songwriting Workshop in 2010. Some of the original songs and reflective writing are available at http://oakdalechoir.lib.uiowa.edu/.

ANTONELLA COPPI is Junior Professor in Music Pedagogy at the Faculty of Education, Free University of Bolzano, Italy. Her background includes degrees in piano performance, Vocal Composition and Choir Conducting, and Music Pedagogy in an interdisciplinary context. www.antonellacoppi.it

CHRISTINE D'ALEXANDER is Assistant Professor of Music Education at Northern Illinois University. She has been an active music educator in both California and Illinois. Her research focuses on the integration of community music programs for children within underserved neighbourhoods.

WILLIAM DABBACK, M.M., PhD, is Professor and Coordinator of music education in the James Madison University School of Music. Active as a scholar in adult music learning, community music, and instrumental music pedagogy, he is the founder of the Harrisonburg New Horizons Band for senior adults, formed in conjunction with the JMU Lifelong Learning Institute.

LEON R. DE BRUIN is an educator, performer and researcher. He works at the Conservatorium of Music, University of Melbourne. His research work spans instrumental music teaching pedagogies and practices, creativity in education, improvisation, cognitive processes, self-regulation, collaborative learning, creative pedagogies, as well as school leadership and ITE.

BEV FOSTER is the Founder and Executive Director of the Room 217 Foundation (https://www.room217.ca/), an organization dedicated to music and care. She is an experienced musician and teacher who speaks and writes extensively on the power of music, especially in life limiting situations. Her passion for music enhancing quality of life is contagious.

GENA R. GREHER is Professor of Music Education at University of Massachusetts Lowell and oversees the new Master of Music Education, Community Music Option. She is a contributor to the Herbie Hancock Institute of Jazz website, https://mathsciencemusic.org/, and co-authored *Computational Thinking in Sound: Teaching the Art and Science of Music and Technology*. The contributions of Christian Hernandez and Nicole Vasconcelos are acknowledged in this chapter.

ELISHA JO HEESUN is a PhD candidate in music education in the Don Wright Faculty of Music, Western Univeristy, with expertise in early childhood musical development, piano performance, and cultural perspectives. Her work explores identity, music's role within community, and Canadian ethnic diversity through the lens of music-making and music learning.

REBEKAH JORDAN-MILLER is a piano pedagogue, accredited music therapist, and accomplished pianist. Rebekah's area of research is music psychotherapy practice in a forensic setting, exploring the application of educational techniques within music psychotherapy. Rebekah maintains a private piano studio and music therapy practice at the Beckett School at Wilfrid Laurier University.

SASHA JUDELSON is a graduate from the Master of Arts in Community Music program at Wilfrid Laurier University, and the Director of Great Lakes Music Together, where she also teaches. She created The Circle of Music Intergenerational Choir as part of her Master's capstone, which has continued to operate and has received federal funding.

JOHNATHAN KANA, BMus, is a freelance writer who advocates for restorative justice from an evangelical Christian perspective. He is also a hobbyist composer and arranger with extensive experience directing and participating in church- and community-based ensembles. He lives with his family in central Texas.

JUSTIS KRAR is a musician studying in the Bachelor of Music Therapy program at Wilfrid Laurier University. Justis is focused on how music connects with well-being, community, and education.

INÊS LAMELA, INET-md, is a pianist and a piano teacher especially recognized for her work with young children. She finished her PhD on Community Music and on music in prisons at the University of Aveiro (Portugal) and continues to develop projects and research within this field.

KELLY LAURILA is of Settler Sáami Indigenous and Irish heritages and she has been given many Anishinaabe teachings. She is song-carrier of an Indigenous women and girls' community drum circle. The drum has helped Kelly reclaim her Indigenous identity and sense of belonging. Kelly holds these insights and teachings of the drum close to her and they have inspired her to help Indigenous and Settler peoples find balance and positive relationships with themselves and one another. Following a twenty-three-year career in counselling, Kelly felt a calling to contribute to the reconciliation process underway in Canada. She is now in her final year of doctoral research pertaining to a conflict transformed relationship between an Indigenous women and girls' drum circle and a male police chorus. Kelly has been teaching for eight years in courses that bring Indigenous epistemology and insights into curriculum in social work, reconciliation, public policy and community organization.

BRANDON LEIS is a music educator, church musician, conductor and performer. He is currently contract teaching faculty, teaching voice at Wilfrid Laurier University in Waterloo, music director at Stirling Avenue Mennonite Church in Kitchener and is artistic director of the Menno Singers.

GLENN MARAIS is a singer-songwriter with a Juno nomination and SOCAN Number One Award. Glenn uses his music to heal and help teaching character education through his company, Music in Mind, inspiring thousands of people, young and old, to get involved locally and globally with the universal motto, "give to live." As a graduate from Laurier's Master of Arts in Community Music, Glenn accepted the position of Programs Manager for ArtCan Circle and as Indigenous Programs Lead for DAREarts. http://www.glennmarais.ca/

RICHARD MARSELLA is the director of the Regent Park School of Music in Toronto, and a PhD candidate at the University of Toronto. Things are busy with Friendly Rich (his composer alter-ego) and The Pumpkin Pie Corporation (his own eclectic record label), but as Friendly says, "one can either produce, or become produce." http://rpmusic.org/

ANNIE MITCHELL, PhD, is an Associate Professor in Southern Cross University's Contemporary Music Program. Her research includes pedagogy, community music, adult education, edutourism, musical careers on cruise ships. Annie is double bassist in three orchestras and pianist in several big bands.

ELIZABETH MITCHELL, PhD, RP, MTA, is an Assistant Professor at Wilfrid Laurier University, where she currently coordinates the Bachelor of Music Therapy program. Prior to taking this role, Liz was Laurier's first Music Therapist -in-Residence, a position that encompassed teaching and supervising students at Laurier, conducting practice-based research, and working clinically at Homewood Health Centre, a mental health and addictions facility in Guelph, Ontario. Liz has extensive experience working in mental health settings with individuals of all ages. To fill up her musical soul, Liz loves playing and singing pop tunes at open mics and singing in the Canadian Chamber Choir.

PETE MOSER is a composer, performer, producer, and facilitator, and was the founder and Artistic Director of More Music, one of the foremost community music charities in the UK (www.moremusic.org.uk). He co-edited and wrote chapters in Community Music: A Handbook, a book that is aimed at inspiring and empowering music leaders. He is the Fastest One Man Band in the World: www.petemoser.com

GRAÇA MOTA, CIPEM/INET-md, is the Director of the CIPEM (Research Center in Psychology of Music and Music Education) branch of INET-md (Institute of Ethnomusicology – studies in music and dance) at the Porto Polytechnic. Her present research is mainly concerned with the social impact of making music and music in the community.

PHIL MULLEN, PhD, is one of the world's leading Community Music trainers. He has worked for over 30 years developing music with people suffering from social exclusion, including homeless people, offenders, through to seniors. Phil specializes in working with excluded children and young people. Phil has a PhD from Winchester University.

LIZ PARKER-COOK has been a secondary school music teacher since 2008. She earned a Master of Community Music and Bachelor of Music degrees from Wilfrid Laurier University, and a Bachelor of Education from the University of Toronto.

SARAH PEARSON, MMT, RP, MTA, is a certified music therapist, registered psychotherapist, and musician based in Kitchener, Ontario, Canada. She has co-developed the Music Care Training with the Room 217 Foundation, where she is the Program Development Lead. Sarah is a music therapist with Grand River Hospital's oncology, palliative care, and outpatient mental health programs, as well as a member of the hospital's team of Ethics Consultants, and holds a small music psychotherapy practice.

PATRICK J. POTTER is Professor Emeritus in the Department of Physical Medicine and Rehabilitation at Western University and Consultant at Parkwood Institute, St. Joseph's Health Care, London, Ontario. His widely published research involves spinal cord injury, musculoskeletal medicine, and musicians' injuries.

PAULO RODRIGUES, INET-md, is a composer, performing musician, and educator. He co-founded Companhia de Música Teatral, was the coordinator of the Education Service at Casa da Música from 2006 to 2010, and since 1999 is a Professor at the Department of Communication and Art of the University of Aveiro (Portugal).

BRENT ROWAN is a professional community musician. Brent is the founding director of the Guelph Youth Jazz Ensemble and the New Horizons Band for Guelph, teaches in the Community Music Program at Wilfrid Laurier University and at his private music studio. www.brentrowan.ca

DANIELLE SIREK teaches undergraduate and graduate courses at the University of Windsor, Canada. She received her PhD from the Royal Northern College of Music, UK. Her research focuses on sociology of music education; and intersections between music education, community music, and ethnomusicology.

JANE SOUTHCOTT is an Associate Professor in the Faculty of Education, Monash University, Australia. She is also a hermeneutic phenomenologist who researches community engagement with music, multicultural music education, and cultural identity with a particular focus on positive aging. She is the editor of the *International Journal of Music Education*, a member of the editorial boards of international and national refereed journals.

KATHLEEN TURNER is a singer, songwriter, community musician and researcher who lives and works in Limerick, Ireland. She is the Course Director of the MA Community Music at the Irish World Academy of Music and Dance, a centre of excellence for research and practice in the arts at the University of Limerick.

JOHANN VAN DER SANDT completed his studies at the University of Pretoria, and his choral conducting at the Institute of Choral Conducting in Gorinchem, Netherlands. His research interests revolve around multicultural perspectives in music education, aspects of collective and community singing, and attitudes and perspectives of children toward singing and choir participation. He is a Full Professor of Music Education, Faculty of Education, at the Free University of Bolzano.

KARI K. VEBLEN serves as Professor of Music Education at the University of Western Ontario where she teaches undergraduate and graduate courses. Research interests include community music networks, lifespan music learning, traditional transmission, and social media. Veblen's work on music learning in on and offline convergent music communities of practice is funded by the Social Science and Humanities Research Council of Canada.

LEE WILLINGHAM (editor) is a professor in Wilfrid Laurier University's Faculty of Music, Waterloo, Ontario, Canada. He coordinates the graduate community music program, directs the Laurier Centre for Music in the Community (research centre) as well as coordinating the music education and choral programs. He is co-chair of the 2020 Community Music Activities conference at ISME in Helsinki, and has recently co-authored *Engaging in Community Music, an Introduction*, published by Routledge.

RICHARD WINEMILLER is an incarcerated individual having spent 33 years in the Iowa correctional system. He has been a member of the Oakdale Community Choir for six seasons, participating both in the concert seasons, and in the Songwriters' Workshop. He also writes poetry, short stories, and social commentary.

DEANNA YERICHUK is currently leading research on music and racial justice in Waterloo high schools, funded by the Social Sciences and Humanities Research Council. As an Assistant Professor, she coordinates the Community Music program at Wilfrid Laurier University in Canada.

GERARD J. YUN, Assistant Professor, teaches courses in community music, music and meaning, and social justice in the Faculty of Music at Wilfrid Laurier

University and the program for Global Citizenship at Martin Luther University College. He trained concurrently in Western classical music and traditional cultural forms. His research interests include cross-cultural music ethics, cross-cultural improvisation, and global community music.

INDEX

64 Million Artists, 75, 86

abandonment, 98, 456

Abbado, Claudio, 209, 210

Aboriginal Affairs and Northern Development Canada, 261

aboriginal, 253, 261, 267; band corruption, 275; gift, 256; husband and wife. 267; Justice Murray Sinclair, 260; Northern Territory, 251; research collaborators, 255; Royal Commission on Aboriginal Peoples, 261

Abreu, José Antonio, 196, 209

Absolon, K. E., 261, 266

abuse, 70, 186, 187, 261, 274, 436; physical, 434

access, 8, 12, 14, 19, 23, 54, 74, 91, 92, 184, 196, 317, 318, 332, 404, 409, 427; a performance opportunity, 328; advocating greater, 28; broadening, 76, 90; changes in, 94; disparity in, 72; cultural, 76, 91–93, 95, 171, 173, 176, 177, 182–83; educational, 176, 179, 183, 195; equality of, 26, 28; gap in, 93; granting, 12; implicit memories, 298; in instrumental music, 158; inequality(ies), 73, 94, 95; lack of, 84, 173; -ing of commercial sheet music, 513; musical, 19, 153, 216, 336; opportunities, 26; political, 72; practices of worship remains accessible, 480; problem of, 66; restricting, 13; students, 195; these musical memories, 377; to appropriate musically inclusive programs, 113; to

children with disabilities, 332; to different learning types, 214; to music education, 111, 144, 196, 199, 215, 230; to participation in the art music be construed as a human right, 316; to participatory music is a university right, 203; to publicly funded arts and culture, 90; to the arts, 332, to training, 84

accessibility, 219, 237, 317, 427; and safety, 2, 159; cultural, 176; gap, 337

accomplishment, 36, 51, 207, 224, 327, 328, 372; sense of, 62, 158, 190, 192, 223, 323, 327–28, 441

accordion, 503, 506

achievement, 45, 68, 71, 109, 111, 114, 120, 164, 184, 196, 207, 209, 397, 424, 430, 505

acute stress disorder (ASD), 291

administration, 224, 225, 385, 423, 440

adult(s), 33, 34, 35, 38, 69, 110, 114, 141, 151, 217, 222, 363, 367, 415, 432, 450; beginners, 158; choirs, 200; day program, 348, 356; developing positive relationships with, 114; development, 156; education, 156, 163, 356; educators, 354; experienced homelessness, 70; facilitators, 216; homeless young, 49; immigrant, 499; learning, 162–63, 187; premature adult behaviour, 292; older, 107, 146, 340, 342, 353, 367–71, 373–74, 376–78, 498–500; self-worth in, 151; singers, 245; 155–70; workshop, 222; young, 153

321; populations, 1, 174, 179, 321, 463; socially, 90, 173; students, 218

mariachi, 149

marimba, 323, 324, 327

Marsella, Richard, 107, 229

Marten Falls, 286

Marturano, Janice, 186

Maslow's hierarchy, 51

Massachusetts Institute of Technology (MIT), 220, 221

Masters of Community Music, 127

Masters of Education, 127

Matarasso, François, 73–74, 246

McBride, Martina, 438

McHale, Grainne, 29

McIntosh, Peggy, 257, 258

McLean, Barton, 102

McLuhan, Marshall, 98, 101–3, 105

meaning-making, 55, 107, 169, 355

Melbourne, 482–83, 485; Italians in, 482–84, 492, 496

Mennonite churches, 443, 464; Anabaptist, 461; Indigenous-friendly, 270

mental health, 113, 166, 168, 237, 356; commission's, 341; concerns, 508; foundations, 406; global, 53; needs, 407; programs, 173; supports for, 342; technological change on, 173

Mental Health Commission (Canada, 2012), 341

mentoring, 82, 87, 114, 145, 147, 149, 151–54, 167, 183, 216, 226, 232, 237, 242, 353, 368, 373, 375, 378; music-mentoring, 114; social, 152; students and, 87; supporting and, 365–66, 368, 372

mentorship, 78, 355; tiered, 153

MercyMe, 395

Merriam-Webster, 185

microsystem, 54, 57, 58, 61

migrants, 493, 494, 495; backgrounds, 213; first-generation, 251; Italian, 482; populations, 144

Miller, Steve, 240

Miller, Suzie, 279–81, 284

mindfulness, 107, 469

Ministerial Leadership Services, 463

Ministry of Child and Youth Services (Ontario), 234

Mino Ode Kwewak N'gamowak (Good-Hearted Women Singers), 269

minorities, 226; cultures, 18; elite, 73, 74; ethnic minority communities, 499; non-identified, 18

misogyny, 134, 138

Mitchell, Adrian, 242

Mitchell, Annie, 107, 171

Mitchell, Elizabeth, 287, 315, 317, 328

Mitchell, Keith, 452

Mitchell, Shawn, 457, 459

Mohawk Institute Residential School (Brantford, Ontario), 271

Mollica, Richard, 313

monetization, 103, 104, 523

money, 83, 100, 104–5, 180, 231, 437, 457, 480, 487, 490, 492; bringing in, 87; exchange for goods and services, 521; less, 196; prize, 450; raise, 84; wastage of public money, 120; worth, 86

mood, 48, 65, 117, 291, 355, 366, 367, 372, 373–77; bad, 62; bossa nova, 419; enhancing, 349; family, 56; management of, 298; positive, 376, 378; regulation of, 368; uplifting, 149

Morecambe Streets, 243

Moser, Pete, 107, 189, 190–92, 240

Mota, Graça, 381, 409, 427

motivation, 65, 159, 160, 163–65, 169–70, 187, 206, 208, 226, 279, 310, 384, 391, 413, 415, 522; -al system, 169; intrinsic, 115, 163; stronger, 166; Theory of Human, 51

Mountain Ridge, 145–46; Orchestra, 146–51

Mozart, Wolfgang Amadeus, 241; *Requiem*, 183

Mullen, Pete, 27, 29, 107, 109–10, 112–19, 121, 189, 420

Mullen, Phil, 27, 29, 107, 109, 110, 112–19, 121, 189, 420

multiculturalism, 208, 213, 214 286, 517, 518; accents, 213; jewel, 274; landscape, 495; organizations, 487; recognition in Canada, 518; societies, 493